THE INTERNATIONAL SURVEY OF FAMILY LAW

2003 EDITION

PUBLISHED ON BEHALF OF
THE INTERNATIONAL SOCIETY OF FAMILY LAW

THE INTERNATIONAL SURVEY OF FAMILY LAW

2003 EDITION

General Editor

Andrew Bainham

Fellow of Christ's College, Cambridge
Reader in Family Law and Policy, University of Cambridge, UK

Associate Editor (Africa)
Bart Rwezaura
Associate Professor of Law
University of Hong Kong
Hong Kong

Family Law

Published by Family Law
a publishing imprint of
Jordan Publishing Limited
21 St Thomas Street
Bristol
BS1 6JS

British Library Cataloguing-in-Publication Data

A catalogue record for this book is available from the British Library.

ISBN 0 85308 866 7

Typeset by Jordan Publishing Ltd
Printed in Great Britain by MPG Books Ltd, Bodmin, Cornwall

THE INTERNATIONAL SURVEY OF FAMILY LAW

PUBLISHED ON BEHALF OF
THE INTERNATIONAL SOCIETY OF FAMILY LAW

A   THE HISTORY OF THE SOCIETY

On the initiative of Professor Zeev Falk, the Society was launched at the University of Birmingham, UK, in April 1973. The Society's first international conference was held in West Berlin in April 1975 on the theme *The Child and the Law*. There were over 200 participants, including representatives of governments and international organisations. The second international conference was held in Montreal in June 1977 on the subject *Violence in the Family*. There were over 300 participants from over 20 countries. A third world conference on the theme *Family Living in a Changing Society* was held in Uppsala, Sweden in June 1979. There were over 270 participants from 26 countries. The fourth world conference was held in June 1982 at Harvard Law School, USA. There were over 180 participants from 23 countries. The fifth world conference was held in July 1985 in Brussels, Belgium on the theme *The Family, The State and Individual Security*, under the patronage of Her Majesty Queen Fabiola of Belgium, the Director-General of UNESCO, the Secretary-General of the Council of Europe and the President of the Commission of the European Communities. The sixth world conference on *Issues of the Ageing in Modern Society* was held in 1988 in Tokyo, Japan, under the patronage of HIH Takahito Mikasa. There were over 450 participants. The seventh world conference was held in May 1991 in Croatia on the theme, *Parenthood: The Legal Significance of Motherhood and Fatherhood in a Changing Society*. There were 187 participants from 37 countries. The eighth world conference took place in Cardiff, Wales in June/July 1994 on the theme *Families Across Frontiers*. The ninth world conference of the Society was held in July 1997 in Durban, South Africa on the theme *Changing Family Forms: World Themes and African Issues*. The Society's tenth world conference was held in July 2000 in Queensland, Australia on the theme *Family Law: Processes, Practices and Pressures*. The eleventh world conference was held in August 2002 in Copenhagen and Oslo on the theme *Family Life and Human Rights*. The Society has also increasingly held regional conferences including those in Lyon, France (1995); Quebec City, Canada (1996); Seoul, South Korea (1996); Prague, Czech Republic (1998); Albuquerque, New Mexico, USA (June 1999); Oxford, UK (August 1999); and Kingston, Ontario (2001). In 2003, regional conferences will take place in Oregon, USA; Beijing, China; Tossa de Mar, Spain; and Lyon, France.

B   ITS NATURE AND OBJECTIVES

The following principles were adopted at the first Annual General Meeting of the Society held in the Kongresshalle of West Berlin on the afternoon of Saturday 12 April 1975.

(1) The Society's objectives are the study and discussion of problems of family law. To this end the Society sponsors and promotes:

   (a) International co-operation in research on family law subjects of world-wide interest.

   (b) Periodic international conferences on family law subjects of world-wide interest.

(c) Collection and dissemination of information in the field of family law by the publication of a survey concerning developments in family law throughout the world, and by publication of relevant materials in family law, including papers presented at conferences of the Society.

(d) Co-operation with other international, regional or national associations having the same or similar objectives.

(e) Interdisciplinary contact and research.

(f) The advancement of legal education in family law by all practical means including furtherance of exchanges of teachers, students, judges and practising lawyers.

(g) Other objectives in furtherance of or connected with the above objectives.

C MEMBERSHIP AND DUES

In 2003 the Society has approximately 560 members.

(a) Membership:
- Ordinary Membership, which is open to any member of the legal or a related profession. The Council may defer or decline any application for membership.
- Institutional Membership, which is open to interested organisations at the discretion of, and on terms approved by, the Council.
- Student Membership, which is open to interested students of law and related disciplines at the discretion of, and on terms approved by, the Council.
- Honorary Membership, which may be offered to distinguished persons by decision of the Executive Council.

(b) Each member shall pay such annual dues as may be established from time to time by the Council. At present, dues for ordinary membership are 41 USD (or equivalent) for one year, 100 USD (or equivalent) for three years and 155 USD (or equivalent) for five years, plus 7 USD (or equivalent) if cheque is in another currency.

D DIRECTORY OF MEMBERS

A Directory of Members of the Society is available to all members.

E BOOKS

The proceedings of the first world conference were published as *The Child and the Law* (F Bates, ed, Oceana, 1976); the proceedings of the second as *Family Violence* (J Eekelaar and S Katz, eds, Butterworths, Canada, 1978); the proceedings of the third as *Marriage and Cohabitation* (J Eekelaar and S Katz, eds, Butterworths, Canada, 1980); the fourth, *The Resolution of Family Conflict* (J Eekelaar and S Katz, eds, Butterworths, Canada, 1984); the fifth, *Family, State and Individual Economic Security (Vols I & II)* (MT Meulders-Klein and J Eekelaar, eds, Story Scientia and Kluwer, 1988); the sixth, *An Ageing World: Dilemmas and Challenges for Law and Social Policy* (J Eekelaar and D Pearl, eds,

Clarendon Press, 1989); the seventh *Parenthood in Modern Society* (J Eekelaar and P Sarcevic, eds, Martinus Nijhoff, 1993); the eighth *Families Across Frontiers* (N Lowe and G Douglas, eds, Martinus Nijhoff, 1996) and the ninth *The Changing Family: Family Forms and Family Law* (J Eekelaar and T Nhlapo, eds, Hart Publishing, 1998). The proceedings of the tenth world conference in Australia were published as *Family Law, Processes, Practices and Pressures* (SS Parker and J Dewar, eds, Hart Publishing, 2003). These proceedings are commercially marketed but are available to Society members at reduced prices.

F   THE SOCIETY'S PUBLICATIONS

The Society regularly publishes a newsletter, *The Family Letter*, which appears twice a year and which is circulated to the members of the Society and reports on its activities and other matters of interest. *The International Survey of Family Law* provides information on current developments in family law throughout the world and is received free of charge by members of the Society. The editor is currently Andrew Bainham, Christ's College, Cambridge, CB2 3BU, UK. The Survey is circulated to members or may be obtained on application to the Editor.

PREFACE

The 2003 edition of the *International Survey of Family Law* begins with an annual review of developments in international law affecting the family. This is followed by articles from 27 jurisdictions – 15 from Europe, four each from Africa and the Americas, three from Australasia and one from Asia. This geographical distribution clearly illustrates the problems of obtaining contributions from large areas of the world. It is especially difficult to make headway in Asia. In Africa, a great deal of progress has been made in extending the Survey's coverage. I would again like to offer my thanks to our Associate Editor, Bart Rwezaura, for his indispensable assistance with the commissioning in the African continent.

As in previous years, I have been fortunate in being able to rely on the expertise of Peter Schofield who, on this occasion, provided translations of the articles from Argentina, France and Spain and assisted with the translation of the Brazilian contribution. I have been fortunate too in having the secretarial support of Ed Carter who has, once again, grappled with my editorial scrawls without complaint and of Jo Morton who has turned the manuscript into proofs. Finally, as always, I am grateful to all those who have submitted articles for this volume and who make the Survey what it is.

ANDREW BAINHAM
Christ's College Cambridge
May 2003

INTERNATIONAL SOCIETY OF FAMILY LAW
SUBSCRIPTION FORM

☐ I prefer to communicate in ☐ English ☐ French

☐ Please charge my credit card ☐ **MASTERCARD or EUROCARD** ☐ **VISA or JCB**

☐ Subscription for 1 year $41/$37 USD

☐ Subscription for 3 years $100/$89 USD

☐ Subscription for 5 years $155/$138 USD

Name of Card Holder: _____

Card no. | | | | | | | | | | | | | | | | | | | |

CVC-code (three figures at the back of your card behind the 16 figures): | | | |

Expiry date: _____ / _____

Address of Card Holder: _____

_____

☐ I pay by *postgiro* to **63.18.019** $155[1] for 5 years, $100 for 3 years or $41 for one year, plus $7 if cheque in another currency (from)

The International Society of Family Law,
Den Hooiberg 17
4891 NM Rijsbergen
The Netherlands

(We have a bank account at the Postbank, Amsterdam, The Netherlands.)

☐ Payment enclosed *by cheque* to the amount of $155[1] for 5 years, $100 for 3 years or $41 for one year, plus $7 if cheque in another currency

Date: _____ Signature: _____

☐ *New member, or*

☐ *(Change of) name/address:* _____

_____

Tel: _____

Fax: _____

e-mail: _____

Comments: _____

_____

To be sent to the treasurer of the ISFL:
Prof. Paul Vlaardingerbroek
International Society of Family Law
Den Hooiberg 17
4891 NM Rijsbergen
THE NETHERLANDS (or by fax: +31-13-466 2323;
e-mail address P.Vlaardingerbroek@kub.nl)

[1] Or its *counter*value in US dollars.

ASSOCIATION INTERNATIONALE DE DROIT DE LA FAMILLE FORMULAIRE DE COTISATION

☐ Je désire de communiquer ☐ en français ☐ en anglais

☐ Je vous prie de charger ma carte de crédit: ☐ **MASTERCARD/EUROCARD** ☐ **VISA/JCB**

    ☐ Souscription pour une année $41/$37 USD

    ☐ Souscription pour trois années $100/$89 USD

    ☐ Souscription pour cinq années $155/$138 USD

Le nom du possesseur de la carte de crédit: _____

Carte no   ⌴⌴⌴⌴⌴   ⌴⌴⌴⌴⌴   ⌴⌴⌴⌴⌴   ⌴⌴⌴⌴

CVC-code (trois numéros sur l'arrière-coté de votre carte)   ⌴⌴⌴⌴

Date d'expiration: ——— / ———

L'adresse du possesseur de la carte de crédit: _____

_____

☐ Je payerai par postgiro à **63.18.019** $155[1] pour 5 ans ou $100 pour 3 ans ou $41 pour 1 an, *plus* $7 surcharge si paiement est un autre cours,

(du) International Society of Family Law
Den Hooiberg 17
4891 NM Rijsbergen
Les Pays-Bas
(Nous avons un crédit au Postbank, Amsterdam, les Pays-Bas)

☐ Paiement est inclus avec un chèque de $155[1] pour 5 ans ou $100 pour 3 ans ou $41 pour 1 an, *plus* $7 surcharge si paiement est un autre cours.

La date: _____ Souscription: _____

☐
☐ *Nouveau membre, ou*

(Changement de) nom/adresse: _____

_____

Tel: _____
Fax: _____
e-mail: _____

Remarques: _____

_____

Veuillez envoyer ce formulaire au trésorier de l'Association:
Prof. Paul Vlaardingerbroek
International Society of Family Law
Den Hooiberg 17
4891 NM Rijsbergen
LES PAYS BAS (ou par fax: +31-13-466 2323; e-mail address
P.Vlaardingerbroek@kub.nl)

[1] Ou la contrevaleur en francs français ou US dollars.

CONTENTS

ANNUAL REVIEW OF INTERNATIONAL FAMILY LAW

Gillian Douglas and Nigel Lowe[*]

We begin this necessarily selective survey by reviewing some major developments under the Hague Convention on the Civil Aspects of International Child Abduction 1980 ('the 1980 Hague Abduction Convention'). We then discuss the proposed reform of the so-called 'Brussels II Regulation' and conclude with a review of human rights and family law focusing primarily on the activities of the United Nations Committee on the Rights of the Child and the European Court of Human Rights.

I   THE 1980 HAGUE ABDUCTION CONVENTION

In terms of ratifications and accessions,[1] the 1980 Hague Abduction Convention continues to go from strength to strength with Slovakia's ratification coming into force and El Salvador, Estonia, Nicaragua, Peru and Sri Lanka each acceding during 2001. As of 31 December 2001 there were 69 Contracting States.[2] This compares with 42 Contracting States to the Hague Convention on Intercountry Adoption 1993[3] and two Contracting States to the Hague Convention on the Protection of Children 1996.[4]

The key event in 2001, so far as the 1980 Convention was concerned, was the holding in March of the Fourth Special Commission to review its practical operation. This meeting, which was held at The Hague, attracted a record number of 200 participants from 54 States and 14 international organisations.[5] As with the previous Special Commissions, the focus of the first part was an examination of the co-operation among Central Authorities but the novelty was that the second half centred on the role of the courts and their international co-operation (Member States were encouraged to include judges in their delegations). As usual, considerable work had been undertaken by the Permanent Bureau in preparation

---

[*]   Professors of Law at Cardiff Law School.

[1]   Under Art 37 only States which were Members of the Hague Conference on Private International Law at the time of its 14th Session can ratify but any other State can accede. The difference between ratifications and accessions is that all Contracting States must accept a ratification but (see Art 38) they can choose whether to accept an accession. At the time of the 14th Session there were 29 Member States, but during 2001 membership expanded to 55 States following the admission of Belarus, Bosnia-Herzegovina, Brazil, Georgia, Jordan, Peru and Sri Lanka.

[2]   As of 31 December 2002, there were 73 Contracting States with Guatemala, Latvia, Lithuania and Thailand acceding in 2002.

[3]   As of 1 January 2003 there were 62 Contracting States.

[4]   But, as mentioned in last year's *Survey*, the Convention finally came into force on 1 January 2002 when Slovakia's ratification took effect. As of December 2002, four States have ratified (Monaco, Czech Republic, Slovakia and Morocco). Estonia's accession is due to come into force on 1 June 2003, and Ecuador formally notified its accession on 5 November 2002.

[5]   Including the ISFL, which was represented by Professors Carol Bruch and Nigel Lowe.

for the Commission, including the circulation of a detailed questionnaire into the working of the Convention,[6] the answers to which provided the basis for the key document 'Checklist of issues raised and recommendations made in response to the Questionnaire concerning the practical operation of the Hague Convention of 25 October 1980 on the Civil Aspects of International Child Abduction'.[7] William Duncan, the Deputy Secretary General, had also drawn up a Preliminary Report on Transfrontier Access/Contact.[8] Finally, to inform and assist the Special Commission, a statistical analysis of applications made in 1999 under the Convention had been prepared for the Bureau by Cardiff Law School.[9]

(a)   The statistical survey

This latter work, which has since been updated and is available on the Hague Conference website,[10] analysed all applications made under the 1980 Hague Abduction Convention in 1999. Information was collected on the gender and nationality of abductors,[11] the number, age and gender of the children, outcomes up to 30 June 2001, the speed of outcomes and whether the application was concluded after an appeal. The survey calculated that there was a maximum of 1280 applications (it had information on 1268)[12] comprising 1060 return applications (83%) and 220 access applications (17%) involving an estimated total of 2030 children (it had information on 2015). Over a fifth (22%) of all applications were made to the USA, with England and Wales receiving the second greatest number of applications (14%).

The report is in two parts comprising a global survey and a detailed analysis by country. Concentrating on the former, so far as return applications were concerned, 69% of abductors were found to be female, virtually all of whom were likely to be mothers, and over half (52%) had the same nationality as the Requested State so can be presumed to have been going home.[13] Sixty-three per cent of return applications involved a single child and 30% two children. One application involved a sibling group of six children. Thirty-eight per cent of the children were under the age of five, 42% aged between five and nine, and 21% aged between 10 and 16. Half of all applications ended either in a voluntary return (18%) or a judicial order for return (32%) but 11% of applications were rejected either because of location difficulties or because they fell outside the Convention criteria and a further 14% were withdrawn.[14] Nine per cent of applications were

---

6   Preliminary Document No 1 of March 2001 for the attention of the Special Commission of March 2001.

7   Preliminary Document No 5.

8   Preliminary Document No 4.

9   Preliminary Document No 3, drawn up by Lowe, Armstrong and Mathias. The project had been generously funded by the Nuffield Foundation.

10   At *http://www.hcch.net/e/conventions/reports28e.html.*

11   Referred to in the report as the 'taking person'.

12   The information is based on detailed responses by the Central Authorities of 34 Contracting States and on numbers provided by four other States.

13   But note the interesting regional differences.

14   A small study of applications made to and from England and Wales found a variety of reasons for withdrawing, including the cessation of communication between the applicant and the lawyer or

still pending by 30 June 2001.[15] Of those applications resulting in the child's return, 64% were the result of judicial orders and 36% of voluntary agreements. Of the cases that went to court, 74% ended in a judicial return order and 26% in a refusal (judicial refusals accounted for 11% of all applications). The report includes a detailed analysis of the basis of all refusals. The most frequently relied upon reason was Art 13(b). (21% of all refusals were based on a sole ground.) The second most popular reason was the child's objections. No refusal was found to be based on Art 20. So far as speed of outcome is concerned it was found that voluntary returns took on average 84 days, judicial returns, 107 days, and judicial refusals, 147 days, but these findings mask enormous variations and both median, minimum and maximum figures are also included in the report. So far as appeals were concerned, 14% of all applications made to court were found to have been appealed and of these 72% were found to have upheld the first instance decision with an overall 56% resulting in a return and 44% in a refusal.

A similarly detailed analysis was made of the access applications. There were some interesting differences from return applications. For example, 86% of respondents were female (compared with 69% in return applications). Only 40% (as against 52%) were of the same nationality as the Requested State. Applications were slightly more likely to concern single children – 69% as against 63% of return applications. Overall, 43% of applications concluded with the applicant gaining access either as a result of a voluntary agreement or court order. This compares with 50% of return applications ending with a voluntary or judicial return. Coincidentally, of the applications that reached court, exactly the same proportion of access applications as return applications, 74%, were granted. A higher proportion of access applications, 13% were still pending as of 30 June 2001 as against 9% of return applications, and considerably more applications were withdrawn – 26% as against 14%. On the other hand, rather less access applications were rejected, 5% as against 9% of return applications, principally because it seems less difficulty was experienced in locating the child. Access applications were found to be much slower in reaching a conclusion than return applications with barely 5% being judicially resolved within six weeks (compared with 26% of return applications) and 71% taking over six months (compared with 19% of return applications). Voluntary settlements were also slower with 18% being reached within six weeks (compared with 50% of return settlements) and 42% taking longer than six months (compared with 14% of return settlements).

(b) The Conclusions and Recommendations of the Special Commission

The Special Commission adopted 58 Conclusions and Recommendations.[16] Part I concerns the role and functions of Central Authorities. It deals, inter alia, with '*Structural issues*' entreating States to give Central Authorities 'a mandate which is sufficiently broad, and the qualified personnel and the resources, including modern means of communication, necessary to act dynamically and carry out their

---

Central Authority, legal aid problems, private agreements between the parties and because an application for access was made instead.

[15] A significant proportion (33%) of these applications was to Mexico.

[16] See Annex III to the Special Commission (April 2001) drawn up by the Permanent Bureau.

functions effectively';[17] '*Communication and co-operation in respect of individual cases*' stressing the need for immediate communication and responses between Central Authorities; '*Exchange of information*' calling upon Central Authorities to publish 'on its website, if possible and/or by other means, such as a brochure or flyer' a range of information to enable potential users to see what services are available and how to use them; '*Locating the child*' stating that Central Authorities should be able to obtain information from other governmental agencies and authorities; '*Securing the voluntary return of the child*' recommending Contracting States to 'encourage voluntary return where possible' and '*Securing the safe return of the child*' stating that:

> 'To the extent permitted by the powers of their Central Authority and by the legal and social welfare systems of their country, Contracting States accept that Central Authorities have an obligation under Art 7(h) to ensure appropriate child protection bodies are alerted so that they may act to protect the welfare of children upon return in certain cases where their safety is at issue until the jurisdiction of the appropriate court has been effectively invoked.'

The final Recommendation in this Part on '*Promoting good practices*' was only agreed upon after lengthy discussion and debate. In the end the following wording was adopted, namely:[18]

> 'Contracting States to the Convention should co-operate with each other and with the Permanent Bureau to develop a good practice guide which expands on Art 7 of the Convention. This guide would be a practical, "how-to" guide, to implement the Convention. It would concentrate on operational issues and be targeted particularly at new Contracting States. It would not be binding nor infringe upon the independence of the judiciary. The methodology should be left to the Permanent Bureau.'

The major concerns about this proposal, largely accommodated by the penultimate sentence, were as to its status and application. In particular there were concerns about any purported guide dictating to judges what they should do. Despite these anxieties and reservations, as will be discussed in next year's *Survey*, the subsequent guide produced by the Permanent Bureau did not prove at all controversial.[19]

Part II of the Recommendations deals with 'Securing State Compliance with Convention Obligations' and contains a standard questionnaire for newly acceding States (an idea mooted but never adopted at previous Special Commissions). The idea of this questionnaire, as Recommendation 2.2 expressly states, is both to assist newly acceding States to implement the Convention effectively, and to provide relevant information to existing Contracting States in considering whether to accept accessions.

Part III deals with 'Judicial Proceedings, Including Appeals and Enforcement Issues, and Questions of Interpretation'. In a notable change from the previous Special Commission, it begins by calling upon Contracting States 'to bear in mind the considerable advantages to be gained by a concentration of jurisdiction to deal with Hague Convention cases within a limited number of courts'. It emphasises

---

[17] See Recommendation 1.1.

[18] See Recommendation 1.16.

[19] It was adopted at the Special Commission held at The Hague in September 2002.

the need for States to process return applications expeditiously and calls upon trial *and appellate courts* 'to set and adhere to timetables that ensure the speedy determination of return applications'.

Part IV deals with 'Interpretation of Key Concepts'. It emphasises the continuing importance when interpreting the Convention of the Explanatory Report by Elisa Pérez-Vera. It notes that the Art 13(b) 'grave risk' defence has generally been narrowly construed[20] which is in keeping with the objectives of the Convention. It also recommends that efforts to achieve an amicable resolution should not be construed as giving rise to acquiescence or consent.

Part V deals with 'Issues Surrounding the Safe and Prompt Return of the Child' (and the Custodial Parent Where Relevant)'. It calls upon Contracting States:

> '[to] consider the provision of procedures for obtaining, in the jurisdiction to which the child is to be returned, any necessary provisional protective measures prior to the return of the child.'

It also calls upon States to take measures 'to ensure that parents who participate in custody proceedings after a child's return are given adequate access to a country's legal system to adequately present their case'.[21]

This Part also contains a number of Recommendations on '*Direct judicial communications*', including nominating an international liaison judge who is able to facilitate at the international level communication between judges; encouraging international judicial co-operation inter alia through attendance at judicial conferences and noting the following 'commonly accepted safeguards' in States in which direct judicial communications in individual cases are practised, namely, that they:

> '... be limited to logistical issues and the exchange of information; parties to be notified in advance of the nature of proposed communication; records to be kept of communication; confirmation of any agreement reached in writing; parties or their representatives to be present in certain cases, for example, via conference call facilities.'

Part VI deals with Cross-Frontier Access/Contact, in which the Special Commission recognised the Convention's deficiencies in achieving the objective of securing protection for rights of access in transfrontier situations. However, notwithstanding that Contracting States regarded it as a 'serious problem requiring urgent attention', it made no concrete recommendations, other than to recommend that the Permanent Bureau carry out further consultations on the basis of the Preliminary Report.[22]

The final Parts deal with 'Matters of General Nature' recommending inter alia ratification or accession to the Hague Convention on the Protection of

---

[20] But see *DP v Commonwealth Central Authority* (2001) 180 ALR 402, discussed below.

[21] In this respect States are reminded of the Hague Convention on International Access to Justice 1980, which inter alia generalises the principles of Art 25 of the 1980 Hague Abduction Convention.

[22] Viz Preliminary Document No 4 of 2001.

Children 1996; welcoming 'with enthusiasm' the establishment of Incadat;[23] recognising the value of research and supporting the publication and circulation of *The Judge's Newsletter.*

As can readily be seen from even this short summary, the Fourth Special Commission was especially productive; the idea of including a judicial focus was clearly successful and is likely to be a continuing feature of future Special Commissions.

(c)   Judicial developments

One of the most significant decisions in 2001 was that of the Australian High Court in *DP v Community Central Authority; JLM v Director-General NSW Department of Community Services.*[24] Until this decision, Australia,[25] like most other jurisdictions,[26] considered that the Art 13(b) exceptions should be narrowly construed. In *DP*, however, the majority ruled that there is no warrant for:

> '[the] conclusion that reg 16(3)(b) [which implements Art 13(b) of the Convention] is to be given a "narrow" rather than a "broad" construction. There is, in these circumstances, no evident choice to be made between a "narrow" and "broad" construction of the regulation. If that is what is meant by saying that it is to be given a "narrow construction" it must be rejected. The exception is to be given the meaning its words require.'

The majority did, however, add:

> 'That is not to say, however, that reg 16(3)(b) will find frequent application. It is well-nigh inevitable that a child, taken from one country to another without the agreement of one parent, will suffer disruption, uncertainty and anxiety. That disruption, uncertainty and anxiety will recur, and may well be magnified, by having to return to the country of habitual residence. Regulation 16(3)(b) and Art 13(b) of the Convention intend to refer to more than this kind of result when they speak of a grave risk to the child of exposure to physical or psychological harm on return.'

Whether this in itself signals a broader approach to Art 13(b) (which, if so, is difficult to square both with what was intended and with the Recommendations of the Fourth Special Commission)[27] remains to be seen. However, it is evident that, before the English courts at least, Art 13(b) remains an extremely difficult exception to establish. The plea failed in *TB v JB (Abduction: Grave Risk of Harm).*[28] This case was unusual in that the source of the alleged risk to the

---

[23]   That is the database of abduction cases maintained by the Permanent Bureau, established following the recommendations of the Third Special Commission.

[24]   (2001) 180 ALR 402, [2001] HCA 39, reported by Hall in *The Judge's Newsletter* (Vol 3, Autumn 2001, Butterworths) 38–41 and commented upon by McEleavy [2002] IFL 91.

[25]   See eg *Murray v Director, Family Services ACT* (1993) FLC 92 and *Gsponer and Director General Community Services* (Vic) (1998) 12 Fam LR 755.

[26]   See *Re C (Abduction: Grave Risk of Psychological Harm)* [1999] 1 FLR 1145 (England and Wales), *Re Q Petitioner* 2001 SLT 243 (Scotland), *AS v PS* [1998] 2 IR 244 (Ireland), *Friedrich v Friedrich* 78 F 3d 1060 (6th Cir 1998) (USA), *Thomson v Thomson* [1994] 3 SCR 551 (Canada) *A v A* [1996] NZ FLR 529 (New Zealand) and *2 B v R* 1075, order of 15 August 1996 (Germany).

[27]   See Recommendation 4.3 referred to above.

[28]   [2001] 2 FLR 575.

children in question was not their father, the mother's first husband, but the mother's second husband, the father of her youngest child who was not the subject of the proceedings. The mother, who had wrongfully removed the three children by her first husband (plus her child by her second husband) from New Zealand to England, claimed that her primary motivation for leaving was to get away from her second husband (against whom there were allegations of maltreatment both of the mother and of the children) and that she was too frightened to return. The first husband applied for the return of the three older children but at first instance this was refused under Art 13(b) on the basis of expert evidence that the mother was seriously vulnerable to the anxieties created by the second husband and that she was suffering from mild to moderate depression which would be exacerbated by a return. On appeal this plea was rejected. In Law LJ's view, Art 13(b) could only be satisfied in truly exceptional cases of which this was not one. Arden LJ accepted that deterioration of the mother's condition and consequently in her ability to care for her children could be sufficient to satisfy Art 13b, but considered that in evaluating such a risk the court was entitled to expect that the mother would make all appropriate use of orders of the New Zealand courts for her own and her children's protection. In her Ladyship's view, given the New Zealand court's powers to protect the mother and her children, a 'grave risk' could not be said to have been made out. Dissenting, Hale LJ recognised the vulnerability of victims of domestic abuse and did not believe that on these facts the New Zealand courts could realistically protect the mother and therefore the children so that the Art 13(b) exception had been made out.

II   THE PROPOSED REFORM OF THE BRUSSELS II REGULATION

Even before Council Regulation EC 1347/2000 on Jurisdiction and the Recognition and Enforcement of Judgments in Matrimonial Matters and in Matters of Parental Responsibility for Children of Both Spouses, the so-called Brussels II Regulation, came into force in March 2001,[29] it was the subject of reform proposals by France. The French initiative aimed at facilitating, through the abolition of *exequator*, the exercise of cross-border rights of access.[30] Since, as originally conceived, the scope of the proposed Regulation was to be limited to judgments granting rights of access for a period of not less than one day in proceedings caught by Art 1(1)(b) of the Brussels II Regulation and would be by way of derogation from Art 21 thereto, this proposed Regulation was dubbed 'Brussels IIA', or 'II Bis'.

A second, more ambitious initiative, following the adoption by the Justice and Home Affairs Council in November 2000 of a programme inter alia to extend Brussels II as it affected children beyond the divorce context, was by the Commission itself. In September 2001 it presented a proposal[31] for a Council

---

[29]   Discussed in the Annual Review of *The International Survey of Family Law (2002 Edition)*, ed Andrew Bainham (Family Law, 2002).

[30]   OJ 2000 C234/7.

[31]   'Proposal for a Council Regulation on jurisdiction and enforcement of judgments in matters of parental responsibility' OJ 2001 C232 E/269, on which see Karsten, 'Draft EC Regulation on Parental Responsibility' [2001] Fam Law 885.

Regulation which aimed to extend the Brussels II Regulation to all decisions on parental responsibility based on common rules of jurisdiction and on reinforced co-operation between authorities. At that stage the Council concluded that the French initiative on access should be pursued in parallel.[32]

In many ways the Commission's proposal would have made welcome changes to the Brussels II Regulation, not least because it was to apply to *all* civil proceedings relating to parental responsibility and not just to children of both spouses involved in matrimonial proceedings. This would have removed a major complication of the current Regulation and would have enabled all children of the family to have been treated alike. Another welcome proposal was that each Member State designate a Central Authority to assist with the application of the Regulation.[33] Under the proposal, Central Authorities were to be enjoined[34] inter alia to co-operate on specific cases as, for example, by exchanging information, co-ordinating protective measures and 'to promote agreement between holders of parental responsibility through mediation or other means, and organise cross-border co-operation to this end'.

The proposal also contained improved jurisdictional rules, essentially modelled on the Hague Convention on the Protection of Children 1996. Primarily jurisdiction was to be based on the child's habitual residence at the time the court was seized but there were to be exceptions:[35]

(a)   in cases where the child's habitual residence changed after a court had given a judgment on parental responsibility and one of the holders of parental responsibility was still habitually resident in that State, courts of that State were to retain jurisdiction for six months after removal, unless the left-behind parent accepted jurisdiction of the new State;[36]

(b)   there could be prorogation of jurisdiction either in the context of divorce as provided by Art 4(2) of the Brussels II Regulation or where that jurisdiction had been accepted by all holders of parental responsibility and the child had a substantial connection with that State and jurisdiction was in the child's best interests;[37]

(c)   as under the Hague Convention on the Protection of Children 1996, where habitual residence could not be established or, in the case of refugee or internationally displaced children, presence would have been sufficient to found jurisdiction;[38] and

(d)   the proposed Regulation was to have made limited provision to transfer a case to a court of another Member State on what common lawyers would have regarded as the ground of forum conveniens.[39]

---

[32]   Later the two initiatives were brought together in a fresh initiative presented by the Commission in May 2002.

[33]   See Art 16.

[34]   See Art 17.

[35]   See Art 3.

[36]   See Art 4.

[37]   See Art 6.

[38]   See Art 7. Presence would have also conferred jurisdiction to take protective measures – Art 9.

[39]   See Art 13.

Although in many ways the above scheme represented a substantial improvement on the Brussels II Regulation, the great stumbling block of the proposals was that they also included provisions to deal with child abduction. The proposed Art 5(3) stated:

> 'Notwithstanding the exceptions to the obligation to return the child provided in the Hague Convention of 25 October 1980 on the Civil Aspects of International Child Abduction, in case of wrongful removal or retention of a child, and on the basis of an application by a holder of parental responsibility or by a central authority, the courts of the Member State to which the child has been removed or is retained shall order the immediate return of the child to the Member State that continues to have jurisdiction pursuant to para 2, without prejudice to any provisional measures under Art 9 they may consider necessary.'

In sum, what this proposed was that courts of the requested Member State would no longer be able to refuse a return under the 1980 Hague Abduction Convention. Instead, if they were concerned about ordering the child's return, all they could have done was nevertheless to order the child to be returned but, exercising their powers under Art 9(1), make a provisional order delaying that return pending an adjudication by the court of the requesting Member State as to whether and under what conditions the child should return home. Fundamentally, therefore, what this proposal amounted to was a disapplication of the 1980 Hague Abduction Convention to abductions between Member States.

This proposal proved highly controversial[40] and caused a fundamental split of opinion between Member States. As will be seen in next year's *Survey*, this proposal led to protracted discussions throughout 2002 on the best way forward.

III HUMAN RIGHTS AND FAMILY LAW

This brief review of human rights and family law focuses primarily on the activities of the United Nations Committee on the Rights of the Child and the European Court of Human Rights.

(a) The child's right to education

It is well known that there is now almost universal acceptance of the role of the United Nations Convention on the Rights of the Child in establishing the principles against which State action can be measured in furthering the protection of children. An important aspect of the Convention is the role of the Committee on the Rights of the Child in monitoring and advancing States' compliance with these principles. Part of the Committee's remit is to consider and evaluate the position of children within the jurisdiction of each of the States parties, as reported to the Committee by the State and often by non-governmental organisations as well. The Committee dealt with 27 such country reports in 2001. It may be noted that for

---

[40] See eg Lowe 'Article 5(3) of the Draft EU Regulation on Parental Responsibility – Dealing with Child Abduction' [2002] IFL 36, who was highly critical of the proposal. But cf the counter-arguments by Karsten 'Article 5(3) of the Draft EU Regulation on Parental Responsibility – A Reply' [2002] IFL 42.

four States – Bhutan, Oman, Paulau and Saudi Arabia – it was the first time that they had entered into dialogue with a human rights treaty body, underscoring again the extent to which this Convention commands global support (which is not to say, of course, that children's rights are fully upheld around the world). These reports are not discussed here, since they turn on the particular circumstances of the individual States concerned.

However, the Committee also produced two important overviews of aspects of the Convention. In April 2001, it published a 'General Comment on the Aims of Education'.[41] In producing such a 'Comment' on aspects of the Convention, the Committee provides an authoritative interpretation of the scope of the relevant provisions which may be useful to those lobbying for action in individual States, including by means of legal processes. There is a considerable job to be done in this regard – statistics produced by UNICEF in 1990 show that more than 100 million children, 60% of them girls, had no access even to primary schooling and that over 90 million adults, two-thirds of them women, were illiterate.[42] A State's duty to provide education, being a social right, may be rather more difficult to enforce than a political right such as freedom of expression; programmes and good intentions may be frustrated by levels of debt, civil instability and population growth. Unsurprisingly, the terms of Arts 28 and 29 provide ample scope for States to appear to be attempting to comply, while actually being unable to do so. In this regard, it is important to note that the Comment stressed that resource constraints cannot provide a justification for a State's failure to take any, or enough, of the measures that are required.[43]

Article 28 provides that:

'(1) States Parties recognise the right of the child to education ...

(2) States Parties shall take all appropriate measures to ensure that school discipline is administered in a manner consistent with the child's human dignity and in conformity with the present Convention.

(3) States Parties shall promote and encourage international co-operation in matters relating to education, in particular with a view to contributing to the elimination of ignorance and illiteracy throughout the world ...'

The Article specifies a number of particular duties on States to give effect to these general obligations, including the free provision of compulsory primary education, improved access to secondary and higher education, and the encouragement of regular attendance.

Article 29(1) goes on to provide that the education of the child:

'shall be directed to:

(a) the development of the child's personality, talents and ... abilities to their fullest potential;

(b) the development of respect for human rights ...;

(c) the development of respect for the child's parents, his or her own cultural identity, language and values, for the national values of the country in which the child is

---

[41]   CRC/GC/2001/1. The Comment represented the Committee's formal contribution to the World Conference against Racism, held in Durban, South Africa, in 2001.

[42]   Figures quoted by R Wallace, *International Human Rights Text and Materials* 2nd edn (Sweet & Maxwell, 2001) at p 179.

[43]   Paragraph 28.

living, the country from which he or she may originate, and for civilisations different from his or her own;

(d) the preparation of the child for responsible life in a free society ...;

(e) the development of respect for the natural environment.'

The Committee comments that Art 29 adds a qualitative aspect to the basic right set out in Art 28, requiring that education be child-centred, child-friendly and empowering. It notes that 'education' goes far beyond formal schooling, to embrace a range of experiences and learning processes which will fit children to develop their full potential to live a full and satisfying life within society. This sounds laudable, but it may be unfortunate in certain contexts. For example, the failure of the UK authorities to provide 'education' in the narrow sense to a disruptive child kept in 'secure accommodation' (basically, detention) was held not to be a breach of Art 5(1)(d) of the European Convention on Human Rights by the European Court of Human Rights in *Koniarska v UK*[44] and by the English Court of Appeal in *Re K (A Child) (Secure Accommodation Order: Right to Liberty)*.[45] The ruling was on the basis that 'education' must not be equated rigidly with notions of classroom teaching. But whether the 'university of life' constitutes adequate exposure to a range of experiences likely to enable a child to fulfil his or her full potential may be open to question. This will be especially so in the public care context, given the dismal record of the State (in the UK at least) in educating those children who, by reason of abuse or neglect, are removed from their homes to 'better' placements. A clearer statement of exactly what is entailed in and required of 'education' might have been helpful.

An important message contained within the Comment is the view that children do not lose their human rights by virtue of passing through the school gates.[46] How far schools currently respect their pupils' human rights will vary from jurisdiction to jurisdiction. In particular, attitudes to corporal punishment, which is limited, but not completely outlawed, by Art 28(2), may say much about a State's general approach to respecting the rights of children. The Committee on the Rights of the Child has always taken the stance that States should prohibit corporal punishment in schools[47] and reiterates this in its Comment. One argument put forward for this position is that children should (and, implicitly, will) learn about human rights by seeing them implemented in practice, both at home and at school. In that regard, the whole atmosphere and ethos of a school should reflect freedom and the spirit of understanding, peace, tolerance, equality of the sexes, and friendship among all peoples. Furthermore, a school that allows bullying or other violent or exclusionary practices to occur is not one which meets the requirements of Art 29(1).

Inevitably, however, schooling, or an education system in general, will reflect the wider values of the culture and the society in which they are set. The Committee notes that the Convention underlines the importance of respect for

---

[44] Application No 33670/96, 12 October 2000 (unreported). See the discussion in *The International Survey of Family Law (2002 Edition)* at p 19.

[45] [2001] Fam 377. See the discussion by Judith Masson, 'Securing human rights for children and young people in secure accommodation' [2002] CFLQ 77–92.

[46] Paragraph 8.

[47] See further below.

parents, of the need to view rights within their broader ethical, moral, spiritual, cultural or social framework, and of the fact that most children's rights are embedded within the values of local communities. But the Committee recognises that what this may mean in practice is that gender discrimination can be reinforced by practices such as a curriculum inconsistent with the principles of gender equality, or making school an unsafe or unfriendly environment for girls to participate in. Moreover, discrimination is not limited to gender; the Committee adds that 'Discrimination against children with disabilities is also pervasive in many formal educational systems and in a great many informal educational settings, including in the home'.[48] Discrimination is an issue that is discussed further below.

(b)   Violence against children

It may be argued that acceptance that violence against children is not a form of 'discipline', but rather of 'abuse', is one of the most important remaining battles to be won in the fight for the recognition of children as bearers of human rights on a par with adults. It is significant, therefore, that the Committee held a discussion day in September 2001 on violence against children within the family and in schools.[49] The purpose of such days is to help develop a pro-active role in the strategic achievement of the rights set out in the Convention.[50] It will be recalled that Art 19 of the Convention requires States Parties to take all appropriate measures to protect the child from all forms of physical or mental violence, injury or abuse, neglect or negligent treatment, maltreatment or exploitation, including sexual abuse, while in the care of parents, legal guardians, or any other person who has care of the child. While this provision is aimed at the 'usual' forms of abuse against children, primarily arising from those ostensibly caring for them, Art 37 prohibits State violence and abuse in the form of torture, cruel, inhuman or degrading treatment. Article 28(2), as noted above, requires that disciplinary regimes in schools be administered consistently with the dignity of the child (and the Committee noted the need for the authorities to recognise that bullying and violence between pupils constitute problems as well). The combination of provisions addressing both public and private abuse is particularly important for children, given their vulnerability to violence in the home, but the balance to be struck between intervention to protect the vulnerable child, and interference in the legitimate control of parents over their children in accordance with their cultural, social and religious values, is of course a very fine one. To counteract the argument that the Committee might be advocating a more interventionist stance, it reiterated the importance of using separation from the family only as a last resort

---

[48]   Paragraph 10.

[49]   D Fottrell, 'UN Children's Committee Discusses State Obligations Regarding Violence against Children' [2002] IFL 66–69.

[50]   Previous discussion days have been devoted to children and armed conflict (1992) (leading eventually to the optional protocol passed in 1999); the economic exploitation of children (1993); the role of the family in protecting children's rights (1994); the girl child (1995); the child and the media (1996); children with disabilities (1997); HIV/AIDS (1998); and State violence against children (2000).

under Art 9, and that the best interests of the child dictate that the best outcome must be achieved by the least invasive intervention possible (Art 3).

The Committee adopted a series of recommendations intended to establish a framework for action both by States and by the United Nations itself. The Secretary-General was to be asked to conduct a study of violence against children in accordance with Art 45(c) of the Convention, which would identify the causes of violence and their contributing factors, and document the prevalence and types of violence suffered by children. In addition to seeking to develop a coherent set of policies designed to combat violence at the United Nations level, the Committee also recommended States Parties to pass legislation to prohibit all forms of violence against children, however light, within the family and in schools; to provide sanctions for those guilty of violence, and compensation for the victims; to repeal any legislation permitting violence; and to review child protection legislation to ensure that there is effective protection with intervention tailored to individual circumstances and, where possible, utilising the least intrusive method of protection. States should conduct careful monitoring of their legislation to ensure that it is effective and supplemented by extensive education and training which must be adequately resourced. They should also conduct their own studies into the nature, causes and consequences of violence on children, which should be disseminated and used as the basis for national programmes of public information, awareness raising, training of teachers and social workers, with the goal of reiterating the importance of non-violent methods of discipline. The Committee also drew attention to the particular vulnerability of children with disabilities, to patterns of vulnerability to violence based on gender discrimination (eg sexual violence against girls, physical violence against boys), and to the importance of providing means of enabling child victims to recover from their experiences, bearing in mind their right to privacy under Art 16 and their right to express their views under Art 12 (the Committee stressed the importance of getting children's views of their experience of violence in developing strategies for tackling the problem).

The Committee also proposed a range of strategies, including the training of all professionals working with children in the detection of symptoms of abuse and possible ill-treatment, the establishment of effective reporting systems where abuse is suspected and the protection of whistle-blowing staff when such allegations are made.

These recommendations do not, of course, have the force of law, but they do show States Parties the direction of the Committee's thinking, and provide a framework for action to those who are serious about tackling the issue addressed. They also provide a benchmark against which States' compliance with the Convention may be measured in future reviews of State Party reports. It is likely that most States will be found wanting in this regard.

(c) Child abuse

Turning now to human rights jurisprudence, we can examine the cases dealt with by the European Court of Human Rights in 2001. As part of its annual case-load concerning complaints raising issues relating to the family, the court continues to deal with individual instances of the failures of States to deal adequately with violence and abuse against children. Inevitably, given the focus of the European Convention on Human Rights on State action, instances of abuse and neglect against children reach the court only where there has been some alleged failure on the part of the State to strike the right balance between intervention to protect a child and interference with the privacy of the family, rather than by means of a direct complaint against a family member.

In such instances, the European Court has continued to maintain its existing view that strict scrutiny is required to justify the curtailment of family relationships. Usually, the court will accept that an initial removal of a child is proportionate (within the requirements of Art 8(2) of the Convention) to the aim of protecting the child in a situation of risk. However, the court now assesses such initial removals more closely, and has begun to condemn situations where the child is removed at birth, because of concerns in respect of the parents' care of other siblings, as disproportionate interference with the parents' right to respect for their family life. An example may be found in *K and T v Finland*.[51] This was a case referred by the Finnish government to the Grand Chamber of the Court, after a finding by a Chamber of the Fourth Section of the court that there was a breach of Art 8 regarding the State's action in taking children into public care and refusing to take proper steps to reunite the family (including removing a child immediately after birth from the mother, who was psychiatrically disturbed). The Grand Chamber upheld the finding of a violation of Art 8 in respect of the emergency care order for the newborn baby, but *not* regarding the similar emergency order obtained in respect of an elder child. This may have been something of a Pyrrhic victory for the parents, since the Chamber's finding of no violation regarding the making of *full* care orders was upheld. But the Grand Chamber reiterated the guiding principles in such cases – the mutual enjoyment by parent and child of each other's company constitutes a fundamental element of family life, and domestic measures hindering such enjoyment amount to interference with the Art 8(1) right to respect for family life. In determining whether such interference is justified, the child's best interests are of crucial importance in every case. While the court accepted that stricter scrutiny applies to measures that effectively curtail relations between parents and child than when taking a child into care, it regarded the State's action as highly disproportionate in removing the newborn baby, and commented that there must be 'extraordinarily compelling reasons before a baby can be physically removed from the care of its mother, against her will, immediately after birth as a consequence of a procedure in which neither she nor her partner has been involved. The shock and disarray felt by even a perfectly healthy mother are easy to imagine'.[52] Thus, while the State may have been justified in taking some precautionary measures, it went too far in actually separating mother and child at such an early stage.

Of course, those working in the field of child protection are just as likely to make errors of judgment in *failing* to intervene soon enough. In many instances, the effect of such inaction may ultimately be fatal, with a child murdered at the hands of carers who resisted or avoided scrutiny by social workers until it was too

---

[51]   [2001] 2 FLR 707.

[52]   At para 168.

late. But the obligation on the State to take proper action where suspicions are aroused was confirmed by an important ruling of the European Court in *Z and Others v UK*.[53] Here, the social services department had failed to respond vigorously to repeated reports of concern regarding four siblings who were the victims of neglect and emotional abuse by the mother. The local authority was well aware of reports by police and its own social workers regarding dirty conditions at home, poor clothing, malnutrition and psychological distress. When the children were finally removed from the home, three were found to be suffering psychological disturbance. The Official Solicitor, representing the children, commenced proceedings against the authority for negligence and breach of statutory duty but the domestic courts dismissed the action on the ground that it would not be fair, just and reasonable to impose such a duty of care on the authority. The children accordingly complained to Strasbourg, claiming breaches of their rights under Arts 3 (inhuman or degrading treatment), 8 (respect for family life), 6 (right of access to a court) and 13 (adequate domestic remedy).

The court held that the neglect and abuse suffered by the children reached the threshold of inhuman and degrading treatment required by Art 3. Since the local authority had known of this but had failed to protect the children from serious long-term neglect, there was a breach of Art 3. This is a significant ruling building on previous case-law of the court. It means that ill-treatment at the hands of a *private individual* (which would not usually attract the jurisdiction of the court) may give rise to a breach by the *State* of the victim's human rights, because of the State's failure to take positive action to protect the victim (sometimes known as the Convention having 'indirect horizontal effect'). A similar approach was taken by the court in respect of physical punishment of children, when it ruled, in *A v UK*[54] that the State must, under Art 1, take measures to ensure that individuals are not subjected to inhuman or degrading treatment, including where this is administered by private individuals.

The court also held that violation of such a fundamental right as the prohibition in Art 3 requires that the State provide a proper remedy. As noted above, English law did not permit the bringing of a claim in negligence against the authority, and there was no other effective means of enabling the allegations against the authority to be fully investigated and, if established, of leading to an enforceable award of compensation. The court concluded that there had also therefore been a breach of Art 13.[55]

The converse problem of over-zealous action may be identified in *TP and KM v UK*.[56] A child was taken into care after a social worker and psychiatrist, who had video-recorded an interview with her, had wrongly concluded that she had named her mother's partner as having sexually abused her. Contact between the mother and child was severely restricted for a year. The mother sought access to the video

---

[53]   [2001] 2 FLR 603.

[54]   (1998) 27 EHRR 611.

[55]   English law now provides a remedy, under ss 7 and 8 of the Human Rights Act 1998, which enable the courts to award compensation for breach of a Convention right. See J Miles, '*Z and Others v United Kingdom; TP and KM v United Kingdom*: Human rights and child protection' [2001] CFLQ 431–454 for a full discussion of the issues in this case and in *TP and KM v UK* [2001] 2 FLR 549, discussed below.

[56]   [2001] 2 FLR 549.

tape, but the psychiatrist resisted disclosure. When, eventually, the mother's solicitor finally saw the recording of the interview, it became clear that the child was referring to a different man. The child was returned to the mother, who sued the local authority, the psychiatrist who interviewed the child and the social worker in the case for negligence and breach of statutory duty. Once again, the domestic courts struck out the claim, and the mother and daughter complained to Strasbourg. The court here found breaches of Arts 8 and 13. It held that it is essential that a parent is placed in a position where he or she may obtain access to the information relied on by the authorities in taking measures of protective care. While there is no *right* to see the video recording, there must be careful consideration of whether to disclose it. Since the parent may reasonably not regard the local authority handling the case, or the interviewing psychiatrist, as objective, the question of disclosure should not be decided by the authority or a medical professional. The court therefore placed the onus on the authorities to disclose the relevant material or, if in doubt, to refer the matter to the court for it to decide. The authority's failure to do this had deprived the mother of adequate involvement in the decision-making process concerning the care of her child and thereby of the requisite protection of their interests under Art 8. As in *Z v UK* the court considered that English law in such cases lacked an effective remedy as required by Art 13. Importantly, the court took the view that return of the child to the parent was *not* an effective remedy because it did not provide redress for the psychological damage flowing from the period of separation. Monetary compensation, and not just a finding of maladministration,[57] might be the appropriate remedy in some cases.

The problem in this case arose because of a mistake on the part of those interviewing the child and was compounded by the delay in forcing disclosure of the tape so that the error could be identified. That delay arose because of confusion and uncertainty as to the procedural rights of the parties in the care proceedings, which resulted in one party not having access to essential evidence in the case. This problem has arisen elsewhere. In *Buchberger v Austria*,[58] a Youth Welfare Office took two young children into care after a neighbour reported that they had been left at home unsupervised. The Office sought a transfer of custody from the mother to itself. The district court refused, regarding the mother as capable of looking after the children, but, after various appeals and remittals, the regional court awarded custody to the Youth Welfare Office. In doing so, it took into account evidence as to previous problems with the mother's elder children and allegations of abuse by a former partner, and chaotic and unsatisfactory home conditions. The mother was not shown this evidence nor given an opportunity to rebut it. The Supreme Court rejected her appeal on the basis that it raised no point of law. The European Court of Human Rights held that, by relying on evidence not available to the mother, the Austrian authorities had prevented her from adequately participating in the decision-making process required under Art 8. Moreover, under Art 6, there was a lack of 'equality of arms' – to satisfy the right to a fair trial guaranteed by this Article, each party must have the opportunity to

---

[57]   As could be identified, under domestic law, by an ombudsman investigating such cases.

[58]   20 December 2001, No 32899/96.

have knowledge of, and comment on, the observations and evidence filed by the other.

(d) Fair trial

The two cases discussed above were presented as complaints under both Art 8 and Art 6, because the court has held on many occasions[59] that there is a procedural element to ensuring the right to respect for family life. However, Art 6 is also of direct importance in ensuring a fair trial when family matters may be at stake. In *Pellegrini v Italy*,[60] the applicant married in 1962 in a religious ceremony recognised by the State. In 1987, she petitioned the district court for a judicial separation. In October 1990, the court granted the petition and ordered the husband to pay maintenance. Meanwhile, in November 1987, the applicant had been summoned to appear before the ecclesiastical court without being told why, and she appeared without a lawyer. She then found out that the husband had begun nullity proceedings based on consanguinity because they were cousins. In December 1987, the ecclesiastical court annulled the marriage. She appealed to the Rota. In March 1988, they gave her 20 days to submit observations on the case; at this stage, the applicant was still without legal representation. In April 1988, the Rota upheld the decree and refused to give her a copy of the full judgment or the case file. The case was then referred to the Florence Court of Appeal for a declaration that it could be enforced under Italian law, by virtue of Art 8(2) of the Concordat between Italy and the Vatican, as amended in 1984 and ratified by Law No 121 on 25 March 1985. In November 1991, the Florence Court ruled that the petition was enforceable. The Court of Cassation dismissed the appellant's appeal in 1995, and so she complained to Strasbourg of a breach of Art 6(1).

The court held that, since the Vatican has not ratified the European Convention on Human Rights, the court's role was to examine not whether the proceedings in the ecclesiastical courts were fair but whether the Italian courts had duly satisfied themselves that the relevant proceedings fulfilled the guarantees of Art 6. In other words, the European Court could not directly oversee the fairness of the ecclesiastical proceedings, but could rule on whether the Italian courts, which *are* bound by the Convention, had properly safeguarded the applicant's rights by their assessment of the ecclesiastical proceedings. This may be a significant approach where municipal courts interact with religious tribunals.[61] It provides another example of the *indirect* effect of the Convention in controlling the acts of those who are not directly bound by its terms.

---

[59]   See eg *Scott v UK* 8 February 2000, App 34745/97, discussed in the *The International Survey of Family Law (2002 Edition)* at p 17. There, the court ruled that the mother *had* had a proper opportunity to participate in the proceedings.

[60]   (2002) 35 EHRR 2, Application No 30882/96, 20 July 2001. See N Mole, 'From Rome to Brussels via Strasbourg – Pellegrini v Italy and Brussels II' [2002] IFL 9.

[61]   For example, the Divorce (Religious Marriages) Act 2002 enables an English court to delay the grant of a divorce until requirements for a religious divorce have been complied with. A complainant could argue that, if the religious court's procedures were in breach of Art 6, the English court should not take notice of them and that, in so doing, it had itself broken Art 6.

The court found that the Italian courts had not attached sufficient significance to the applicant's inability to examine the evidence produced by her ex-husband, and thus had failed to attach weight to the right to adversarial proceedings, which is one of the elements of a fair hearing within Art 6(1). Each party to a trial must in principle have the opportunity to have knowledge of, and comment on, the evidence and observations filed, with a view to influencing the court's decision. The court stated that 'what is particularly at stake here is litigants' confidence in the workings of justice, which is based on, inter alia, the knowledge that they have had the opportunity to express their views on every document in the file.'[62] There was a similar breach in respect of the failure of the ecclesiastical court to tell the applicant that she could have a lawyer.

While the ecclesiastical proceedings in *Pellegrini v Italy* were very quick (five months including the appeal to the Rota) the civil proceedings were much slower – the applicant's original claim for maintenance took three years to decide; the proceedings regarding enforcement of the ecclesiastical order took seven years finally to be concluded. The length of proceedings is a perennial complaint to the European Court of Human Rights. A prime example may be found in *Stanciak v Slovakia*.[63] In 1991, the applicant and his wife divorced and the applicant became unable to use their jointly owned property from that time. The divorce was finalised in August 1993 and he sought an order for separation of the marital property. In April 1995, the court appointed an expert to value the movables. The expert's report was not submitted to the court until January 1997. In March 1997, the applicant challenged the judges on the basis of delays in the proceedings and sought transfer to another court. Several hearings and adjournments took place. By the date of judgment by the European Court of Human Rights (12 April 2001), the proceedings were still pending after some seven years and four months. The applicant claimed, inter alia, a breach of Art 6 because of the length of the proceedings. The European Court upheld his complaint, finding that the overall length of the proceedings could not be regarded as reasonable, although it noted his own contribution to the length of the proceedings by twice requesting exclusion of the judges dealing with the case. It held that the reasonableness of the length of proceedings must be assessed in the light of the particular circumstances of the case and having regard to criteria laid down in the court's case-law, especially the complexity of the case and the conduct of the applicant and the authorities in dealing with it, as well as what was at stake for the applicant.[64]

A rather different aspect of the right to a fair trial was raised by two fathers in *B v UK, P v UK*.[65] Article 6(1) provides that:

> 'In the determination of his civil rights and obligations ... everyone is entitled to a fair and public hearing ... . Judgment shall be pronounced publicly but the press and public may be excluded from all or part of the trial ... where the interests of juveniles or the protection of the private life of the parties so requires, or to the extent strictly necessary in the opinion of the court in special circumstances where publicity would prejudice the interests of justice.'

---

[62]   Paragraph 45.
[63]   Application No 40345/98 [2001] IFL 101.
[64]   Paragraph 52.
[65]   (2002) 34 EHRR 19, [2001] 2 FLR 261.

The maxim that justice must be *seen* to be done may be understood literally to require that, in order to safeguard litigants and to ensure the fairness of the system, proceedings should be open to the public and that decisions and judgments should be made known to the public and their reasoning held up to public scrutiny. However, under English law, proceedings relating to children are held in private. Many fathers consider that the courts and the welfare services are prejudiced in favour of mothers when it comes to making decisions as to with which parent a child is to live and the nature and extent of contact with the non-resident father and complain of the 'secrecy' of the system which prohibits the press from attending hearings. The applicants therefore argued that they had suffered a breach of their Art 6 right. The court held that the requirement to hold a public hearing is subject to exceptions; proceedings concerning the residence of a child following parental divorce are prime examples of cases where the exclusion of the press and public may be justified to protect the privacy of the child and the parties and to avoid prejudicing interests of justice. The court considered it essential that parents and other witnesses feel able to express themselves candidly on highly personal issues without fear of public curiosity or comment. It concluded that it is not inconsistent for a State to designate an entire class of cases as an exception to the general rule where considered necessary in the interests of morals, or protection of the private life of parties, or in the interests of juveniles.

As to the delivery of the court's judgment, the court considered that the form of publicity given to this must be assessed in the light of the special features of the proceedings in question and by reference to the object and purpose of Art 6(1). Here, the domestic authorities were justified in conducting the proceedings in chambers and to pronounce judgment in public would to a large extent frustrate the goals of securing the parties' and children's privacy and avoiding prejudicing the interests of justice. The court noted that anyone who could establish an interest was able to consult or obtain a copy of the full text of the orders and/or judgments of the first instance courts and Court of Appeal, and that cases of special interest are routinely published. It concluded that the public can study the manner in which the courts approach such cases and the principles they apply. Here, the court gave States a wide margin of appreciation to determine their approach to this issue, but it is worth noting that the two dissenting judges pointed out that, under the relevant domestic Rules, the court must give leave for disclosure of a judgment delivered in chambers, and that only cases of 'special interest' are likely to be published in the Law Reports. It is interesting to note an increasing trend, in the English courts, to render judgments in public in any event, but the sense of grievance felt by disappointed litigants in family proceedings remains strong.

(e) Discrimination

The complaint of the fathers in such cases is of discrimination against them by virtue of their sex. The issue of the unequal position of *unmarried* fathers and whether such inequality amounts to discrimination under Art 14 of the Convention is one that regularly arises at Strasbourg. At present, until the Optional Protocol 12 comes into force,[66] discrimination can only found a complaint when linked to a substantive right under the Convention. In previous cases, the court has robustly rejected the argument that, by placing unmarried fathers in a weaker legal position than married fathers regarding their children, States are violating their right to respect for family life. The court has argued that there is such a range of circumstances covering the relationship between the unmarried father and his children 'from ignorance and indifference to a close stable relationship' that there is an objective and reasonable justification for the difference in treatment between married and unmarried fathers with regard to their acquisition of parental rights.[67] Where the court *did* find in favour of an unmarried father denied contact with his child, in *Elsholz v Germany*[68] it did so, not on the basis of discrimination allied with Art 8, but under Art 8 alone, since it argued in part that the treatment of the father was no different from that which would have been given to a *married* father.

Usually, where the court finds a breach of a substantive Article such as Art 8, it does not go on to examine the subsidiary complaint raised under Art 14. However, the court's approach appears to be beginning to alter. In three cases heard together, *Sahin v Germany; Sommerfeld v Germany; Hoffmann v Germany*,[69] it was prepared (by a majority) to find that there *had* been a breach of Art 14 taken together with Art 8. In each case, an unmarried father lived as part of the family for a time after the child's birth. The three fathers alleged that subsequent denial of contact by the German courts breached Arts 6, 8 and 14 of the Convention. At the material time, the German statute declared that custody over a child born outside marriage was exercised by the mother, who was entitled to determine the father's right of access, subject to a court decision in the child's interests.[70] Unmarried fathers were also denied a right of appeal from the court's decision. The European Court held that there had been unjustified discrimination against unmarried fathers regarding their right to respect for family life:

> 'The crucial point is that the courts did not regard contacts between a child and the natural father prima facie as in the child's interest, a court decision granting access being the exception to the general statutory rule that the mother determined the child's relations with the father ... there are reasons to conclude that the applicant as a natural father was treated less favourably than a divorced father ...'[71]

Moreover, the failure to grant the unmarried fathers a right of appeal was regarded as a breach of Art 6 (but not in conjunction with Art 14). The Convention does not compel States to set up courts of appeal, but where such courts exist, there must be

---

[66] For discussion of the Protocol, see C McCafferty, 'General Prohibition of Discrimination – the New Protocol to the Human Rights Convention' [2001] IFL 78.

[67] See *Balbontin v UK*, reported as *B v UK* [2000] 1 FLR 1, discussed in *The International Survey of Family Law (2002 Edition)* at p 16.

[68] Discussed in ibid; now reported at [2000] 2 FLR 486.

[69] [2002] 1 FLR 119.

[70] For discussion of the law which replaced these provisions, see R Frank, 'Germany: Parentage Law Reformed' in *The International Survey of Family Law 1997*, ed A Bainham (Martinus Nijhoff Publishers, 1999), at pp 167–182.

[71] At para 55.

effective access to them, and the majority of the court concluded that such access had clearly been denied.[72]

(f) Family life

The fathers in the German cases were all complaining that, by denying them contact, their right to respect for family life had been violated. The cases were instances of the 'indirect horizontal' effect of the Convention. The fathers had failed to persuade the mothers to permit them to have contact. The mothers would not be liable for breach of the fathers' rights guaranteed by the Convention, but the Convention became binding when the German courts – representing the State – failed to enforce the fathers' rights. *Direct* State action, of course, may also disrupt family ties and thus fail to uphold the right to respect for family life where, for example, the authorities seek to deport an individual, who has established family relationships, from their territory. Given the priority attached to firm immigration and settlement rules in the developed world, it is not surprising that complaints against deportation form a regular part of the court's workload.

In *Boultif v Switzerland*[73] the applicant was an Algerian citizen who entered Switzerland on a tourist visa and married a Swiss citizen in 1993. In 1995, he was convicted of robbery and sentenced to two years' imprisonment. On release, the authorities refused to renew his residence permit and they deported him in 2000. He went to stay with friends in Italy. He alleged breach of Art 8, arguing that his wife, who was unfamiliar with the language and culture, could not be expected to move to Algeria and they could not live in Italy as he was unable to obtain a work permit. The court has been inconsistent in its approach to such arguments, sometimes taking a strict line and asserting that the dependent relative can indeed move to the applicant's home country; at other times adopting a more sympathetic stance.[74] The court this time found a breach of Art 8. While there is no right under the Convention for an alien to enter or reside in a particular country, removal of a person from a country where close members of his family are living may infringe the right to respect for family life. The court considered the State's interference disproportionate. It laid down guiding principles to determine whether deportation will be 'necessary in a democratic society' as required under Art 8(2) in such cases. These include the nature and seriousness of the applicant's crime, the length of his stay in the country from which he is to be expelled, the time elapsed since the offence was committed and his conduct during this period, the applicant's family situation, whether there are children of the marriage, and if so their ages, and finally the difficulty the spouse is likely to face in accompanying the applicant to another jurisdiction. Applying these principles to the facts, while the applicant had indeed committed a crime, he had been a model prisoner, his sentence had been a short one and he represented a limited threat to public order. Nor could he

---

[72]   Judge Pellonpaa dissented, arguing that the restriction of access was discriminatory and should have been ruled a breach using Art 14.

[73]   Application No 54273/00, [2001] 2 FLR 1228.

[74]   The concurring Judges Baka, Wildhaber and Lorenzen cited 11 cases where the court has not found a breach of Art 8, even where the applicant has stayed all, or most, of his life in the country and has close family ties there; and five where a violation was found on rather similar facts (see Concurring Opinion).

live his family life outside Switzerland. The wife could not be expected to live in Algeria, having never been there, having no other ties there and being unable to speak Arabic.

The court may be even more sympathetic where the complaint involves children. In *Sen v Netherlands*[75] the Turkish applicant joined his father in the Netherlands in 1977. He married a Turkish wife in Turkey in 1982. Their daughter was born there in 1983. In 1986, the wife joined the applicant in the Netherlands, entrusting their daughter to the care of an aunt. The couple had two further children born in the Netherlands. In 1992, they asked the authorities to permit the daughter to join them. The Dutch authorities refused and argued, inter alia, that she was part of her aunt's family now. The refusal was upheld by the Dutch courts and the applicant complained to the European Court. The court found a breach of Art 8. It held that the daughter had a 'family life' with her married parents from the moment of birth and by virtue of birth. Such a tie cannot be broken other than in exceptional circumstances. The parents had made their lives in the Netherlands, and, although it was their choice to leave their daughter in Turkey, it could not be said that they could never change their minds. It made more sense to let the daughter join the family in the Netherlands than to expect the whole family to go to Turkey, especially as the two other children were used to living in the Netherlands. In refusing to permit this, the court concluded that the Dutch authorities had failed to balance the interests of the family properly against those of upholding the State's immigration policy.

Immigration and deportation decisions are particularly apt to appear arbitrary where State officials attempt to work within rigid rules that politicians have laid down for them. The importance of the existence of a reviewing body able to stand back and assess the reasonableness of the decision taken is not limited to situations arising within the jurisdiction of the European Court of Human Rights. The United Nations Human Rights Committee also has the power to scrutinise such decisions where a State has ratified the Optional Protocol to the International Covenant on Civil and Political Rights. A communication made to the Committee and determined in 2001 provides a valuable example of how a global, supra-national consensus on the application of international human rights norms is being developed. In *Winata and So v Australia*[76] the authors of the communication were a couple who came, independently, to Australia from Indonesia. They formed a de facto relationship and had a son, now aged 13. When their son reached the age of 10, he acquired Australian citizenship, but the parents had overstayed after their visas expired and were refused extensions via a 'protection visa' (based on their alleged fear of persecution as Chinese Christians if they returned to Indonesia). They were advised to seek a 'parent visa', which can be granted only to applicants who are outside Australia, and for which there was a waiting list of several years. Their appeals against refusal of a visa were rejected. In their complaint under the Covenant, they argued breaches of Arts 17, 23(1) and 24(1).

---

[75]	Application No 31465/96 (unreported), 21 December 2001.

[76]	Communication No 930/2000, decision 16 August 2001.

Article 17 provides:

'(1) No one shall be subjected to arbitrary or unlawful interference with his privacy, family, home or correspondence, nor to unlawful attacks on his honour and reputation.

(2) Everyone has the right to the protection of the law against such interference or attacks.'

Article 23(1) states:

'The family is the natural and fundamental group unit of society and is entitled to protection by society and the State.'

Article 24(1) provides that:

'Every child shall have, without any discrimination as to race, colour, sex, language, religion, national or social origin, property or birth, the right to such measures of protection as are required by his status as a minor, on the part of his family, society and the State.'

The Committee ruled that, while aliens may not, as such, have the right to reside in the territory of a State Party, the State is obliged to respect and ensure all their rights under the Covenant. The claim that the State's actions would interfere arbitrarily with the authors' family life related to an alleged violation of a right which is guaranteed under the Covenant to all persons. The mere fact that one member of a family is *entitled* to remain in the territory of a State Party does not necessarily mean that requiring other members of the family to leave involves such interference. But the decision to deport the parents and compel the family to choose whether a 13-year-old child, who had citizenship of the State after living there ten years, either remained alone there or accompanied his parents, was to be considered 'interference' with the family at least where, as here, substantial changes to long-settled family life would follow in either case. The Committee considered that the fact that a child is born, or by operation of law, such a child receives citizenship at birth or later, is not sufficient of itself to make a proposed deportation of a parent arbitrary. But a State's discretion is not unlimited and may come to be exercised arbitrarily in certain circumstances. Here, the son had grown up in Australia from birth, attended Australian schools as an ordinary child would and had developed the social relationships inherent in that situation. In view of the duration of time that had elapsed, it was incumbent on the State to demonstrate additional factors justifying the removal of both parents that went beyond a simple enforcement of its immigration law in order to avoid a characterisation of arbitrariness. In the particular circumstances, the Committee considered that removal by the State of the parents would constitute, if implemented, arbitrary interference with the family contrary to Art 17 in conjunction with Art 23, and, additionally, a violation of Art 24(1) in respect of the son, due to the State's failure to provide him with the necessary measures of protection as a minor.

These cases suggest that there is some degree of agreement amongst the human rights organs that, in striking the balance between permitting States to enforce their immigration and settlement policies and protecting those caught up in the rules, close attention must be paid to the degree of disruption and difficulty that will be caused to individual family members by a decision to remove one of their number from a territory. Domestic authorities should reflect the need for this close scrutiny in their rules and how these are implemented, and should be willing to re-examine cases to ensure that due attention is being paid to the needs of all the individuals concerned.

Finally, it is worth noting a distressing case heard by the European Court of Human Rights against France. In *Pannullo and Forte v France*[77] parents complained of the insensitive treatment they had received from the authorities after the death of their 10-year-old daughter. The child had undergone heart surgery in 1994. Two years later, she went for a check-up and was discharged although she was feverish. A few days later, she returned to hospital where she died in June 1996. The parents complained to the procurator, who opened an inquest to determine the cause of death and whether there was any evidence of negligence (none was eventually found). An autopsy was conducted soon after, but the child's body was not returned to the parents until February 1997. The parents complained that this delay constituted a breach of their rights under Art 8. The complaint was upheld. The court found that the delay was due to inaction and misunderstanding by the judicial authorities of the medical evidence. It ruled that the authorities had therefore failed to strike a fair balance between the right of the parents under Art 8 and the legitimate aim of establishing whether those involved had handled the child's medical treatment properly.

The *Pannullo and Forte* case is a reminder that the right to respect for family life under Art 8 goes beyond the protection of legally recognised family ties; it engages the most sensitive of emotions. It demands of States that they recognise and safeguard the intimacy of human relationships. In so doing, it brings to the forefront the very essence of human rights – the upholding of the dignity and autonomy of the individual against the power of the State.

---

[77]   Application No 37794/97 (unreported), 30 October 2001.

ANGOLA

CHALLENGES FOR THE ANGOLAN FAMILY CODE

Maria Do Carmo Medina[*]

I CONSTITUTIONAL AND POLITICAL CHANGES

The Angolan Family Code was put into force in 1988 by Law no 1/88 and it entirely replaced Book IV of the colonial Portuguese Civil Code relating to family law.

Several principles of a modern conception of family relations were introduced by this Code such as: protection of the family by the State; promoting education, employment, social welfare, leisure, and social insurance; the right of each member of the family to develop his or her own personality and aptitudes; equality of rights and duties between men and women in all domestic relations inside family life and a fair apportionment of responsibilities and tasks at home; equality of every child in relation to the State and the paramount duty of both State and family for his or her protection, whether he or she is born inside or outside wedlock. This was expressed in the preamble and in the Title on Fundamental Principles.

In 1992, Constitutional Law no 23/92, following Constitutional Law no 12/91, changed the political system to a multi-party one and accepted a market economy. After the elections in 1992, Angola suffered a long and very destructive war which we anxiously expect is now approaching an end. The new parliament, the National Assembly, had by Law no 1/98 created the Constitutional Committee composed of members of several political parties represented in it.

Each of those political parties was called upon to present a draft of the new Constitution, as were political parties outside parliament, together with social organisations and citizens.

In 2001 the Constitutional Committee arrived at an agreement on several aspects of the new draft for the Constitution, and one of them was that the customary law should be accepted in the new Angolan positive law. That acceptance can cause great difficulties and contradictions in relation to human rights assured by the Constitution and also by international Conventions ratified by Angola. The most important are the United Nations Covenants on Civil and Political Rights and on Economic, Social and Cultural Rights, and the Convention for the Elimination of All Forms of Discrimination Against Women accepted by Resolution no 15/84 of the earlier People's Assembly.

The Constitutional Law no 23/92, in Art 21°, introduces into the Angolan system of law, all international rules on human rights accepted by Angola as part of internal law and provides for compulsory application by the courts.

---

[*] Professor at the Faculty of Law of the University Agostinho Neto, Luanda.

As it is commonly known, traditional norms, practices and stereotypes legitimise the subordination of women and strongly restrain women's rights in all aspects. To an Angolan History Professor who commented on the political power of traditional authorities, most of their power lay in 'management of Land and Women'. So the introduction of customary law in the family with no restrictions, would be the cause of much antagonism between old and modern conceptions of life. Nowadays, customary law can be applied by courts at municipal level as established by Art 38° of Law no 18/88, which brought into force the Unified Justice System, the Angolan judicial organisation. Usages and customs not codified can be applied in civil actions whenever they are accepted by both parties and if they are in accordance with law. As it is established by doctrine, nowadays customary law can be applied 'praeter legem'.

II THE FAMILY CODE AND CUSTOMARY LAW

In fact some institutions of customary law were introduced in the Family Code such as the Family Council and the de facto union. The Family Council is a judicial body composed of four members of the family, two members chosen by each party in the action; its role is to give advice on the issue under consideration by the court, clarifying the facts. The members of the Family Council may give their evidence on oath but this is not mandatory. The de facto union is, as is commonly accepted, a non-formalised union between a man and a woman who live as husband and wife, outside marriage. Constitutional Law recognises marriage and the de facto union as forms of family (Art 29°).

But other traditional uses of customary law were not protected by the Family Code, although not forbidden. The most widespread of these is the promise to marry, generally an oral and binding contract which seals the agreement *between the families of the bride and bridegroom before traditional marriage.* The offer of *Ilembo* or *alembamento* is made by the bridegroom's family to the bride's family, and acceptance implies marriage and the subsequent deliverance of the woman to the man.

This is looked upon in all traditional ethnic societies throughout Angola as the form of marriage celebration and it generally consists of several gifts made by the bridegroom, or by his family, to the most representative members of the bride's family. Acceptance of the gifts means that the traditional marriage is accepted by both sides and that the young woman must accept all its consequences. Generally the consent of the bride is not necessary and, in order to avoid duress or threats, the Family Code in Art 22° rules that the engagement for marriage is not necessarily binding and does not require the return of gifts if the marriage does not go ahead. Nevertheless, if gifts are returned to the other party, this may be seen as the fulfilment of a moral duty. Damages are restricted to costs incurred in relation to the marriage celebration with the agreement of both parties.

But the most important feature of the Family Code derived from traditional society is certainly the acceptance of the de facto union as a legal form in which to raise a family. The majority of Angolan people live in de facto unions,[1] not only in urban centres but chiefly in rural areas where the proportion of families living in de facto unions is certainly higher.

III   THE DE FACTO UNION IN THE FAMILY CODE

Articles 112° to 126° of the Family Code regulate this institution but it is the application of rules relating to marriage, and termination of marriage by death or by divorce, where the de facto union is recognised, which brings a large spectrum of effects in the personal and patrimonial rights of cohabitants, and in affiliation links to their children.

Extra-marital cohabitation arises for different reasons. The de facto union is accepted as the free establishment of a marital relationship between a man and a woman in an informal manner.

The law establishes that legal recognition of the de facto union depends on three mandatory conditions:

(1)   three consecutive years of cohabitation;
(2)   exclusivity of the relationship;
(3)   capacity of the parties.

The law provides for two alternatives for the recognition of de facto unions: they may arise from mutual agreement between a man and woman, or from a court decision. Recognition by mutual agreement depends on the free agreement by both cohabitants to change their legal position into a recognised de facto union by going through an administrative procedure in the Civil Registrar Office. They must establish their capacity for marriage, that the union has lasted for more than three years, and its exclusivity. The commencement of the de facto union has legal relevance because its recognition by the clerk of Civil Registrars gives it the same effects as those given to marriage, retrospectively from the beginning of the de facto union as long as it satisfied the legal conditions. So, after recognition, the de facto union becomes equivalent to a real marriage in all legal respects. Nevertheless, this form of recognition has not obtained much acceptance by the Angolan people because, generally, cohabitants prefer to celebrate a formal marriage rather than obtain by a written and bureaucratic act legalisation of their cohabitation. This option can also give rise to some difficulties concerning the definition of property acquired during cohabitation but before marriage.

Recognition by the court can occur in the case of death of one of the cohabitants or in the case of termination of the de facto union by the act of one or both of them. The claim must be presented to the court within two years of termination of cohabitation. Standing to bring proceedings is given to both cohabitants or, in the case of death, to their heirs. The court must hear the Family Council and it must be composed of four members, two from the family of the

---

[1]   A study produced by the Angolan Government and UNICEF for the years 1999–2003 ('A future of hope to Angolan children') reveals the following statistics for the adult population aged over 20 in Luanda: married 17%; living in de facto unions 54%; never married 20.3%; separated 5.4%; widowed 2.6%; divorced 0.7%.

man and two from the family of the woman. Generally the Family Council's advice is of great importance to the verdict of the court.

Where the de facto union satisfied the three legal conditions above, the court's judgment will have the same effect as termination of marriage by death or divorce.

The law does not compel people to live in a de facto union which may be ended at any moment by the will of one or both members of the couple. But when it ends, this former union is evaluated in order to consider whether it has fulfilled the three conditions provided by law and, if that is the case, the petitioner may claim these benefits:

–   application for a maintenance order to be paid by the deceased's estate, or in case of inter vivos termination, paid by the ex-cohabitant as long as the termination of the union was not the petitioner's exclusive responsibility;
–   the right to the legal presumption of maternity and paternity of children born to the couple who were cohabiting at the time of the conception period, in the same circumstances as those applying to a married couple;
–   the right to a half share of all property acquired during the cohabitation period in accordance with the law, and also responsibility for payment of common debts;
–   the right to claim occupation of the matrimonial home.

Nevertheless, the protection of the de facto union goes further insofar as the law accords some legal effects to those unions which do not fulfil all the three conditions set out above. In most of these cases, the couple lives in a de facto union but one of them lacks legal capacity to marry because he or she is already married to another person, or in most cases because it is not an exclusive but a polygamous union.

Although the law does not recognise an irregular de facto union, it is to be noted that the petitioner can claim for:

–   the right to the presumption of affiliation given to children born to the couple in the above circumstances;
–   the right to claim occupation of matrimonial home;
–   the right to share property commonly acquired or to have financial compensation for losses due to the relationship of de facto union, as far as the petitioner proves his or her participation in earnings.

IV   JURISPRUDENCE ON DE FACTO UNIONS

The real situation of couples who live outside legal marriage generates a higher demand on the court for settling disputes after the end of a de facto union, generally of a financial nature, relating to property and the matrimonial home and to maintenance of common children.

The Supreme Court, by its Civil and Administrative Chamber, has pronounced some relevant decisions on the subject.

One case concerned a couple, each party divorced from third persons, who had lived together for many years, and had acquired common assets during this period of cohabitation. The man decided to terminate the de facto union and the woman asked the court to prevent any property transfer before the end of the proceedings. The 1990 decision of the Civil and Administrative Chamber of Supreme Court in Process no 21 stated:

> 'The petitioner claims for an enrolment order, having proved real fear of loss of common assets by the respondent, by one side and also her legal connection to this patrimony. Proved that the union between the petitioner and the other party has lasted for many years, a de facto union which came to an end by the actions of the respondent, it must be considered whether the effects of dissolution of marriage by divorce in accordance of Art 113° no 1° of Family Code or only the effects of no 2 of the same Art 113° apply. But, in both cases, that which is stated by the Civil Code relating to a preliminary action before divorce litigation must be applied by analogy.'

In 1996 the Civil and Administrative Chamber of the Supreme Court on Process no 273 stated:

> 'As the identity card of the petitioner proves that he is unmarried as is the respondent, and it is also proved that the couple had lived together for more than ten years in marital cohabitation, from which three children were born, and as it is not proved that the petitioner had established a lasting relationship with another woman, it must be recognised that there was a de facto union according to the law established between them, as stated in Art 113° no 1° of the Family Code. Ownership of the matrimonial home must be given to the respondent who still lives there with their children and the unilateral transfer of the property carried out exclusively by the petitioner declared void.'

One question which arises is how to consider marriage under customary law as a valid de facto union or how it can become converted into a legal marriage. One of the legal conditions for a valid marriage is the mutual agreement of both parties given at the moment of marriage celebration, so the conversion of traditional marriage into a recognised de facto union and consequently into a real marriage will depend on the expressed will of both the man and woman. And, of course, it will also depend on satisfaction of the other legal conditions, ie three years of cohabitation, capacity for marriage and exclusiveness of the relationship. Despite some differences between traditional marriage and recognisable de facto unions we suppose that, in most cases, traditional marriages should be converted into legal marriage.

V ADOPTION

In 1980 the first Angolan Adoption Act, Law no 7/80, was passed which revoked the colonial civil code on the matter. It was considered that the situation of thousands of Angolan children living in abandonment and as orphans as a consequence of war demanded an urgent change. The Family Code introduced in its text much of this law, but after the public consultation which took place before its approbation, it was decided to clarify the institution of adoption and its legal effects. So, adoption appears equivalent to kinship from blood ties, which shows the importance given to it considering that kinship is the most important family link in Angolan society.

Any person under 18 can be adopted, but the law distinguishes two different situations: in cases where the child's parents are unknown or deceased or the child to be adopted has been abandoned, his or her family is not called to come to the court to give their consent. Otherwise, the consent of parents is mandatory. In the absence of parents, consent may be given by other relatives, such as grandparents, brothers or sisters, preferably the relative who lives with the child. Nevertheless, consent can be dispensed with when these relatives cannot be found or are opposed to the best interests of the child. If the child is over ten years old his or her consent is also mandatory. Consent may be given before the court after explanation by the judge of the consequences of the adoption order.

Regarding the prospective adopter, the law demands several conditions. He or she must be at least 25 years old, and more than 16 years older than the child, must have full legal capacity, must show good behaviour in social and family contexts, and must have financial capacity to provide for the upbringing and education of the child. The adoption must be granted by court decision and its aim is the legal, social, moral and affective protection of the child. It creates between the adopter and the adopted an identical link to that which is established between a child and his or her natural parents.

There are two models of adoption regulated in law:

(1)   double adoption made by a couple;
(2)   single adoption made by a single person.

Double adoption can be undertaken by a married couple who live together, or by a couple living in cohabitation who satisfy the legal conditions of a recognisable de facto union.

Single adoption can be carried out by one member of a couple in relation to the child of the other member or by an unmarried person.

The legal effects are not entirely the same for these different forms of adoption. The main consequence is to make adopter and adopted parent and child and to sever the link to the natural parent, which remains only in relation to marriage incapacity. After the decree of adoption, the natural parents will lose their legal tie with the child. Double adoption puts an end to all familial relations between the adopted child and his or her natural family; single adoption by a member of the couple only substitutes the father or the mother as the new parent for the adopted child. On single adoption by an unmarried person, the link to the remaining parent is not broken, but remains in a very restricted way because all parental authority is entrusted to the adopter.

Adoption of an Angolan child by a foreign citizen is subject to authorisation by the National Assembly. In general, before the conclusion of the procedure, the court submits the petition to the National Assembly Committee of Constitutional and Legal Affairs for its opinion. Afterwards it is voted on by the Assembly. The purpose is to protect the Angolan child against illegal trafficking and further loss of Angolan nationality. After the court decision on adoption, it may be transmitted to the Registry Office to enter the adopted child in the register of births; the family name will be changed: in double adoption the child acquires both family names of the adopters, in single adoption only the adopter's family name replaces that of the substituted parent. Where ordered by the court, a new birth certificate must be registered where the adopter or adopters are entered as parents of the adopted child; the original certificate then becomes confidential.

Adoption is not widespread in Angolan society, and several factors can explain this fact. Traditional society practises adoption, although it is not very commonly used. It is necessary to obtain the consent of the adopter's family but, if it is approved, the adoption is accepted and from then on the child becomes a member of the family in every respect.

Otherwise, the meaning of 'child' in traditional society is wider than in the written law. In a general sense, the child of a natural brother or a sister is considered as someone's own child. So, on the disappearance of the natural parents, the extended family, in most cases the eldest brother or sister, or the uncle or the aunt takes care of the orphan. It is the family itself which absorbs its vulnerable members. Another issue is 'de facto' adoption established outside the legal framework and without court participation, creating no formal links with the adoptive family.

The war displaced about 4 million Angolans inside the country and this brought about a terrible impact on family life all over the country: many children lost their parents and other relatives, many were sent to seaside urban centres where they were more protected from the dangers of war though subject to other kinds of danger such as hunger, street life, and so on. Many of them are integrated in relatives' families and also in strangers' families. Rumours are circulating about some people using false declarations of the birth of these children to the supposed parents instead of the true procedure of adoption. It must be explained that the Angolan Government, with UNICEF support, has launched a major campaign for birth registration, free of costs, in order to legalise thousands and thousands of Angolan children who lack civil identification.

VI CONCLUSION

At this very moment of Angolan transition from a long period of war to the peace craved by the great majority of Angolan people, it is not easy to predict what will change in its family law system. Some improvements are, without doubt, necessary to be made such as those on adaptation of the proceedings to the most effective protection of rights and duties regulated by the Family Code, changes on organisation of the judiciary which will allow the Municipal Court to participate in the preliminary mediation of family conflicts, simplification of registration procedures and better professional qualification of registrars' staff. But we would argue that other urgent interventions from the judiciary are required such as putting in working order the Minors Court Act, Law no 9/96, which provides for children in need of social protection and delinquent children, and the drafting and subsequent bringing into force of the law against domestic violence, because both issues are tremendously in need of the efficient and quick intervention of Angolan society.

ARGENTINA

THE SOCIO-ECONOMIC CRISIS AND ITS REPERCUSSIONS FOR CHILDREN AND FAMILIES

Cecilia P Grosman[*] and Ana María Chechile[**]

I INTRODUCTION

It would seem appropriate for us to take this opportunity to comment on the repercussions on the family, and on the laws by which it is governed, of the grave socio-economic situation our country is now experiencing. In particular, we would like to describe the problems of children and adolescents at this difficult time, and the adverse effects on the rights established by the UN Convention on the Rights of the Child, a treaty ranking on a level with the Constitution in our country since 1994.

At the same time, we propose to point to some judgments which are beginning to assert, quite emphatically, the responsibility of the State to give effect to the rights, both economic, social, cultural and civil, set out in the UN Convention on the Rights of the Child.

II THE SOCIO-ECONOMIC SITUATION

The crisis that has blown up in Argentina after years of recession has hit large sections of the population who have no work, and can neither obtain a decent standard of living nor obtain health services. Obviously, the rights of children, invoked with such passion in public speeches, remain mere rhetoric if parents are not given the means of obtaining sufficient income to feed their children, giving them a reasonable home, obtaining care for their health and sending them to school. This is not just an economic problem; unemployment destroys self-esteem and the sense of social inclusion of the parents, who cannot give their children a reasonable education, and often teach them ways to survive in which ethical values are ignored and anything goes.

A few examples suffice to make clear the disruption suffered by Argentine families in all spheres, in the relationship of the couple and in the socialisation of their children. A law (No 25561) declared a public emergency in social, economic, administrative, and financial matters and in relation to foreign exchange. There is,

[*]   Profesora Consulta Titular de Derecho de Familia y Sucesiones, Faculdad de Derecho, Universidad de Buenos Aires, Directora de la Carrera de Especialización (posgrado) en Derecho de la Familia, Investigadora Superior del Consejo Nacional de Investigaciones Científicas y Técnicas (CONICET).
[**]   Profesora de Derecho de Familia, Universidad de la Plata, Provincia de Buenos Aires. Translated by Peter Schofield.

it proclaimed, the existence of exceptional circumstances in the country. In consequence of this, a series of laws were enacted which seriously aggravated the economic depression people were already suffering. According to the National Institute for Statistics and Censuses (INDEC), 53% of the inhabitants of the country – now numbering 36 million in all – live in poverty, and of these almost half are too poor to reach even the minimum nutritional level (ie they are destitute). In some provinces it is even worse, with poverty levels exceeding 70%.[1] Last year more than six million Argentines, many of them from the middle class, joined the 'new poor' as a result of unemployment and the loss of purchasing power caused by the severe increase in prices of products essential for subsistence.[2]

The rate of unemployment runs at 21.5%, to which must be added the 18.6% who have only casual or part-time work. The proportion of men who are unemployed is greater than that of women, since most of the lost jobs were in predominantly male occupations, such as construction, industry and transport, while there is more scope for women in informal occupations, personal services and domestic work.[3] Apart from agriculture and cattle raising, the fall in production affects all sectors, but especially construction, where it reaches 41%.[4] Eight out of ten enterprises are no longer recruiting staff. Exporters alone have potential for expansion.[5]

Among 15- to 19-year-olds unemployment rises to 46.1%. One and a half million young people are denied both education and work.[6] This is the age group that causes most concern, because they are unable to obtain education or employment.

Even those who have work find it hard to cover the needs of the family, as a result of the great devaluation of Argentine currency, which has caused an inflationary process that has hit earnings. Over six months, the currency has been devalued by 360% against the US dollar, resulting in a rise in prices and a corresponding fall in purchasing power. Supermarket prices rose by 74% in eight months.[7] Only 30% of people in work have an income above that required by the cost of basic food and services. The fall in the value of earnings as a result of inflation reached 38% between January and August 2002.[8]

We must add to this impoverishment the effects of the instability and loss of assets felt by people, particularly in the middle class, as a result of the limitations imposed which prevent them from withdrawing deposits and savings from the banking institutions, the so-called *corralito* (little ring-fence). That problem remains unresolved for want of a coherent plan by the Government to enable the economy to be put to rights. In real terms, there has been a confiscation of savings, which amounts for many to the loss of the fruits of years of labour and

[1]   Dirección Nacional de Estadísticas y Censos, Diario, *Clarín*, 22 August 2002.

[2]   Dirección Nacional de Estadísticas y Censos, Diario, *Clarín*, 15 September 2002.

[3]   Dirección Nacional de Estadísticas y Censos, Diario, *Clarín*, 27 July 2002.

[4]   Dirección Nacional de Estadísticas y Censos, Diario, *Clarín*, 20 July 2002.

[5]   Dirección Nacional de Estadísticas y Censos, Diario, *Clarín*, 26 July 2002.

[6]   Del informe del Titular del Consejo de la Niñez, Adolescencia y Familia, Diario, *Clarín*, 11 May 2002.

[7]   Alfredo Sainz, *La Nación*, 26 September 2002.

[8]   Datos registrados, Diario, *Clarín*, 5 September 2002.

serious harm to families, since it violates the legitimate right of those involved to carry through, as intended, their lifetime plans and projects. Also, all dollar deposits held in banks and financial institutions have been converted into national currency, as have debts denominated in dollars. All these decisions are currently challenged as unconstitutional, but a decision of the Federal Supreme Court resolving the matter is still awaited.

The action of the State in response to this situation has been ineffective. It has been left to civil society, the Church, and non-governmental organisations, through networks of solidarity, to play an important part in softening the consequences of this painful emergency. There is active citizen participation and a constantly growing number of highly committed volunteers. However, it must be recognised that relief work, necessary though it now is, is not enough to make an impression on the pattern of poverty and depression. What is needed is a growth in production opening up new sources of employment.

III REPERCUSSIONS OF THE CRISIS ON CHILDREN AND FAMILIES

1 Children of families living in poverty

The socio-economic crisis thus sketched has had a serious impact on children and adolescents. Seven out of eight Argentine children are born in poor households, and of these seven, four live in the greatest poverty.[9] The graphic saying in our country, about the condition of children, is that 'half the poor are children and half the children are poor'. It is no mere tongue-twister; it is the truth.

The most critical situation is that of pre-school-age children – below seven years old – since those who go to school can eat, given that many educational establishments have refectories where children get one or more meals. A high proportion of newborns are malnourished due to underfeeding of their mothers. Research in hospitals in Buenos Aires Province showed that barely 55% of children are born in a healthy condition.[10] One child in two is anaemic and, as one specialist has put it, 'this leaves a permanent scar on body and mind'.[11] Similarly, lack of food affects the health of children, who are more exposed to sickness through the debilitation of their immune system. At this moment, there is public pressure for the passing of a law – called 'the most urgent hunger' – whereby the State would take responsibility for the feeding and health care of 2.3 million children under five and pregnant women living in poverty.[12]

In brief, the present state of children impedes their proper psychological and physical development to the detriment of their fundamental rights to life, health, education and development, recognised in the UN Convention on the Rights of the Child (Arts 6, 18, 24, 27, 28). This harms the rising generation and, by the same token, the future of our society.

---

[9] Dirección Nacional de Estadísticas y Censos, Diario, *Clarín*, 15 September 2002.
[10] Dirección Nacional de Estadísticas y Censos, Diario, *Clarín*, 15 May 2002.
[11] Nora Bär, Diario, *La Nación*, 18 September 2002.
[12] Diario, *Clarín*, 18 September 2002.

This infringement of the economic, social and cultural rights of children results in the destruction of their civil and political rights too, since, as has been affirmed in numerous international documents, over a considerable period, the two types of rights are interdependent and indivisible. When parents cannot maintain a child, he or she risks being abandoned, unable to live with his or her family, becoming a 'street child' or being subjected to sexual or economic exploitation. Often, faced with an abandoned child, the court removes him from his family, to place him in foster care or in an institution, whereas the lack of material resources is not a justification for taking a child from his family. This is a violation of the UN Convention on the Rights of the Child, which permits removal of a child from his parents only when such a step is necessary in the interests of the child (Art 9). As an example, we take a case, similar to a great many that come before the court. A child had been placed in a foster family on the grounds that he was at risk; because his parents lived in extreme poverty, the child was not getting the necessary nourishment and the household did not meet the minimum conditions for him to be allowed to remain there. The parents countered that they never could provide that which was demanded of them, since the shack ('*rancho*') in which they lived did not have water, electricity or a bath, but that they were working and, taking account of their resources, had the fundamental family right to raise and educate their own children. The court ordered the return of the child to his parents and held that 'a child cannot be put into care, depriving him of his fundamental right to his family and identity, unless it be shown to be an extreme situation'.[13] Here the court made the appropriate response, but in many others, when the mother or father do not have legal representation and do not know how to get their children back, they simply lose them for want of resources and of State support.

2   Children and crime

Adolescents and young people who suffer social exclusion often commit crime, because they see no future for themselves, which leads to lack of respect for others, together with feelings of hate and resentment. At the same time, these children are themselves victims of severe institutionalised violence. Recorded data from newspaper reports show that, in 2001, 27% of those killed in confrontations with the police were aged under 18.[14]

3   Abandonment of the family home

Unemployment and lack of resources also break up many homes. Many couples with children are forced to abandon their housing and go to the home of a parent, because they cannot afford to pay the rent or the utility bills. Having to live together in this way, while on the one hand an expression of family solidarity, ever present in these times of penury, represents, on the other, for the family a loss

---

[13]   *C Civ Com Trab y Familia, Cruz del Eje*, 2000/6/14, *Revista La Ley*, Córdoba 2001, p 331.

[14]   Diario, *Clarín*, 18 September 2002.

of space, independence and personal autonomy. Sometimes the return to the family of origin is a strategy of lone mothers caring for children, who cannot afford their upbringing and education.

4 Forced immigration

There are also families that, in the face of lack of work or of an adequate income, have decided to leave the country in search of better living conditions elsewhere. In this way, fathers are separated from children, grandchildren from grandparents. Such forced migrations lead to an emotional loss for the children, who suffer from losing emotional bonds, friends, school and their accustomed surroundings. In a year, 87,000 citizens have left the country, a significant number, considering that, under the last dictatorship that caused so much death and misery, 70,000 people left Argentina.

5 Domestic violence

The many tensions and anxieties of not having the necessities of life increase domestic strife, so cases of violence in the family multiply as people unburden themselves, in the privacy of the home, of the frustration and tension that result from inadequate incomes. Of course, poverty cannot cause such aggression of itself, but it provides the setting in which other personal factors in family interaction can. An aspect worth emphasising is that, because of the lack of work, many households are now kept going by women, since men have only casual employment or none at all. As a result, the men often feel humiliated and their social identity is wounded by their inability to provide for their household. Even though our country affirms the principle of equality and women take an active part in economic and social life, the stereotype persists of the male as the one who should be the main breadwinner. It is reminiscent of the old division of roles: the woman in the home and the man as the earner. This sense of inferiority of the man often gives rise to violence, because he feels undervalued and deprived of status. Not infrequently, he turns to alcohol, unable to see a way forward.

And yet, we should note a paradox. If, on the one hand, as difficulties increase, so does the likelihood of conflict and violence, at the same time the crisis re-establishes the value of the intimate family and makes it, for many, a refuge from the many blows that fall on the Argentines day by day.

6 Marital breakdown

The crisis has also affected the consequences of marital breakdown. While normally separation of a couple means living in separate houses, today, for want of resources, they continue to live under the same roof. Faced with this question, courts have taken two views. One, fortunately in the minority, holds that to rely on the ground of separation, the spouses must live in separate accommodation.[15]

---

[15]   CNCiv, sala L 12/2/93, JA 1995–I–391, ED 154–485.

The contrary view holds that, even when spouses live in the same house, they can still apply for divorce if, despite this, they do not live together in a marital relationship.[16]

7 Maintenance

Conflicts over maintenance have also increased, such as a greater number of non-payments, petitions for reduction of alimony as a result of loss of employment or reduction of earnings of the party paying, and demands for increases due to the rise in the cost of living.

8 Division of assets

Devaluation of the currency has also affected agreements as to the division of assets in divorce cases, since values have been substantially changed, making fresh negotiations necessary and, where there is no agreement, this means more recourse to the courts to amend agreed settlements.

9 Reduction in marriage

The critical situation in the country also has effects on the way couples come together. The marriage rate has dropped markedly and there are more de facto couples.[17] Unmarried couples account for 53% of births in the country.[18] While there are many reasons for the increase in informal cohabitation, on which topic we have commented elsewhere, one reason is the economic difficulty of keeping a household and forming a new home.

10 Hope for the future

We end this brief account of the problems that oppress the country and its families convinced that the resources of Argentina and the cultural level and energy of its people will be able to overcome the critical situation, provided, of course, that it is administered by an efficient government and one free from corruption. The solidarity and the action of the many who are struggling to achieve change in the economic and political system encourage this hope.

---

[16]   Clra CC San Nicolás, marzo 22–1994, *Revista El Derecho*, t 160–122; Juzg Nac de Primera Instancia en lo Civil Nro 77, 17 de diciembre de 1998, *Derecho de Familia, Revista Interdisciplinaria de doctrina y jurisprudencia* Nro 17, Abeledo-Perrot, Buenos Aires, 2000, p 245.

[17]   In Argentina, the Civil Code does not regulate cohabitation or de facto unions. For this reason, cohabitants have no legal rights and duties towards each other. Nevertheless, extramarital children have the same rights as those born in wedlock and their parents have the same responsibilities. Certain rights of cohabitants in relation to housing, property rights and social security have been recognised in some legislation and judicial decisions.

[18]   Dirección Nacional de Estadísticas y Censos Diario, *Clarín*, 28 April 2002.

IV COURTS IN DEFENCE OF THE ECONOMIC, SOCIAL AND CULTURAL RIGHTS OF CHILDREN

The socio-economic situation we have described, detrimental to citizens' rights, has increased judicial activity in support of those rights. A significant strand of current doctrine in Argentina considers that economic, social and cultural rights come within the supremacy of the Constitution and, as such, are enforceable like civil rights, so that the State is obliged to take positive steps to give effect to them. In the case of infants, this means the possibility of claiming from the State a particular service, if non-performance is detrimental to one of the recognised rights of the child and the primacy given to childhood has not been respected.

In this context, a judgment of the National Supreme Court deserves a mention. It ordered the provision of assistance and attention to a handicapped child who had no social support or economic resources. The court ordered an organ of the State, the National Service for the Rehabilitation of the Disabled, to provide basic services for the rehabilitation of a child who suffered from a severe immunological deficiency. The judgment points out that:

> '... on the basis of the provisions of international treaties, which rank on a level with the Constitution, the public authorities have an obligation which cannot be disregarded to guarantee, by positive action, the preservation of health, which is contained within the right to life.'

It goes on to say:

> 'The National State has taken on international undertakings directed to promoting and facilitating the provision of health services needed by minors and cannot validly divest itself of those duties.'[19]

In another judgment, similarly aimed at protecting the child's right to health, on a request for judicial assistance, in a case of failure to provide proper medical attention for a newborn suffering from a serious illness,[20] the court ordered the Government of the City of Buenos Aires to ensure, in an effective and concrete manner, that the child received the treatment clinically required.[21]

The court has also intervened to affirm the child's right to education. The *Asesor Tutelar*, an official who defends children's interests, presented a request for judicial assistance against the Government of Buenos Aires City, for violation of the right to education and for discrimination against children living in a very poor area. The Government of Buenos Aires City had undertaken to build a secondary school in the area, near to an existing primary school. On failure to carry this out, the court ordered the Education Secretary of the Government of Buenos Aires City to build the school forthwith, requiring the presentation of the

---

[19] Corte Suprema de la Nación, 16 de octubre de 2001, *Revista Jurisprudencia Argentina*, 4 de febrero de 2002.

[20] Article 43 of the National Constitution establishes that any person may bring an action for judicial assistance, provided there is no other more appropriate judicial remedy, against any act or omission of the public or private sector authorities which, in a real and urgent manner, infringes, restricts, alters or threatens, with clear arbitrariness and illegality, rights and guarantees protected by the Constitution, by a treaty or by a law. *Asesoria Tutelar v Gobierno Ciudad de Buenos Aires s/ amparo*, exp No 586.

[21] *Asesoria Tutelar v Gobierno Ciudad de Buenos Aires s/ amparo*, exp No 586.

studies and plans and proof of the start of construction within the time fixed in the judgment.[22] In another decision, a judge of the city of Bariloche, Rio Negro Province, dealt with a case of building defects in a school, which put at risk the pupils, teachers and employees, making the normal functioning of the school impossible. To comply with the constitutional right to education, the court ordered the competent authorities to take steps, within 48 hours, to provide facilities for an establishment with reasonable conditions for the pupils of the school to assemble.[23]

Going still farther, in an unprecedented decision based on the extreme poverty that affects many families, in proceedings for judicial assistance brought by the *Defensor* of the *Superior Tribunal de Justicia*, the Court for Minors and Family of Entre Rios Province forced the provincial government to support the three daughters of an unemployed person, ordering a supermarket to supply food to the family each week, and to charge the account to the State. Should the government not pay within 48 hours, the company could use the credit to cancel fiscal debt. Appeal is now pending.

To sum up, these examples show that judges have begun to exercise control over omissions and neglect by the State affecting children's rights. Perhaps, at first glance, these questions may not seem to be part of the normal work of specialist family lawyers. Nonetheless, on consideration, it is seen that many of the aspects affecting family law, matrimonial breakdown, domestic violence, child abuse, non-payment of support or inadequate exercise of parental responsibility arise out of social conditions preventing the family from fulfilling its basic functions of economic and emotional support, and the upbringing and education of children.

It is worth mentioning that the United Nations Committee on the Rights of the Child conducted an observation in Uruguay in 1996 and, on that occasion, expressed 'its concern at the inadequacy of the budgetary estimates for social expenditure, in particular in favour of children belonging to the most disadvantaged groups'. In this connection it recommended that the Signatory State 'adopt all sufficient measures, with the resources available, to allocate an adequate budget to services for minors, especially those related to education and health'.[24]

In this context, a body of opinion, growing in strength, considers that the national budgetary law similarly needs judicial control to decide whether, within the financial resources available to the State nationally, the outline estimates allocate enough resources to cover the economic, social and cultural rights of its citizens. The budget would become irregular if the government were to make an inadequate allocation out of available resources so as to prevent it from giving effect to those rights. The view has been expressed that an individual person

---

22   *Asesoría Tutelar de Justicia Contencioso-Administrativa y Tributaria de la ciudad de Buenos Aires c/ Gobierno de la ciudad de Buenos Aires s/ amparo*, exp No 899/2001.

23   Juzgado Civil de Bariloche, Provincia de Río Negro, setiembre 2000.

24   Quoted in: Juan Faroppa Fontana, Familia y Derechos en las observaciones y recomendaciones del Comité de los Derechos del Niño en las Naciones Unidas, presentación en el Seminario, 'Transformaciones familiares, desempeños sociales y derechos', Universidad de la República del Uruguay y Unicef, Montevideo, Uruguay, 10 de setiembre de 2002.

affected would be able to bring an action for assistance to put a stop to the damage.[25]

Several provisions of the UN Convention on the Rights of the Child compel Signatory States to give parents or carers suitable assistance to carry out their functions in relation to bringing up the child (Art 18) and to give effect to the child's right to an adequate standard of living, where the parents lack resources (Art 27). Add to these the requirements of Art 3, which give a pre-eminent place to children in the allocation of public expenditure. It is logical to see this as giving legitimacy to judicial control against a budgetary law directing resources to objectives not enjoying constitutional priority, ignoring the primacy of the rights of childhood. This means that, even if setting budgetary estimates is an act of the political powers, the courts have the right to keep an eye on whether the allocation of resources takes the Constitution and the international undertakings of the State into consideration. The provisos contained in those treaties – in Art 2 of the International Pact on Economic, Social and Cultural Rights and Art 4 of the UN Convention on the Rights of the Child – to the effect that such rights can only be made effective 'up to the limit of available resources', do not give the Signatory State the right to make arbitrary decisions.

V COURTS IN DEFENCE OF CHILDREN'S CIVIL RIGHTS

So far we have referred to children's economic, social and cultural rights, a particularly sensitive topic in Argentina in 2002. Now, to complete our outline, we wish to comment on a few recent judgments relating to the child's right to identity, to have regular contact with both birth parents, and to claim damages in case of abuse and neglect.

1 Protection of the right to identity

A CHALLENGING PATERNITY IN MARRIAGE

The action to challenge paternity in marriage in Argentine law[26] is aimed at negating the legal presumption of the husband's paternity of children born to a wife after the celebration of a marriage and up to 300 days after its dissolution or annulment, or de facto separation of the spouses.[27]

The action may be brought by the husband or, after his death, his heirs, or by the child. While the child's action cannot be time-barred or lapse, that of the husband or his heirs must be brought within a year from the child's birth registration, unless the claimant can show he was unaware of the birth, in which case time runs from the day he learnt of it. Thus, only two persons may claim: [putative] father and child.

---

[25]   Horacio G Corti, 'El régimen jurídico constitucional de la Ley de Presupuesto, la familia y el carácter expansivo de los derechos humanos', *Derecho de Familia, Revista Interdisciplinaria de Doctrina y Jurisprudencia*, No 22, Lexis-Nexis, Abeledo-Perrot, Buenos Aires, 2002, p 17 y siguientes.

[26]   Articles 258 and 259 of the Civil Code.

[27]   Article 243 of the Civil Code.

Despite the legal text, however, in recent years claims have been brought by the mother, by the presumed biological father and by the Public Procurator, aimed at challenging the paternity of the husband. They were based on the child's right to identity (Art 8 of the UN Convention on the Rights of the Child) and the prohibition of discrimination against women (Art 2 of the Convention on the Elimination of All Forms of Discrimination against Women), both rights with constitutional ranking. Judges have systematically rejected them.

However, recently, there has been a change in this rigid position, some decisions letting in the right of the Public Procurator to bring the action, so broadening the prospect of the child enjoying his true affiliation. One such case culminated in a decision of the National Supreme Court, overturning the decision of the National Civil Appellate Chamber rejecting the claim for filiation brought by the *Defensor de Menores* on behalf of a six-year-old girl. The superior court based its judgment on the detrimental effect of any restriction on the action to challenge the husband's paternity, which prevented the child from claiming her true filiation, since this would hamper her exercise of the right to identity.[28] As a result, the Chamber handed down a new judgment giving the *Defensor de Menores* the right to continue these actions.

The other decision, which allowed the Public Procurator to proceed, was handed down by a first instance judge in the locality of General San Martin, in Mendoza Province.[29] The children whose legal paternity was challenged in the case lived with their mother and biological father. This was why the interest of the minors concerned in obtaining their true relationship was highly relevant. These children knew who their parents were and were cared for by them, but their right to identity was violated, since they were tied to a man who was not their father. This stopped them from using the surname of their biological father who cared for and educated them. In the case, other rights were infringed, since the biological father, not being accredited as such, was denied the exercise of *patria potestas*.

In Argentina, the line of doctrine broadening access to actions to challenge the husband's paternity is progressively gaining relevance, for the benefit of children who, for reasons not desired by them, are held in a situation that contradicts their true biological identity. So much so that, in the current year, various projects have been presented for a law to give the right to bring an action not only to the husband and child, but also to the mother and, in some proposals, to the biological father.

B   THE CHILD'S NAME

The right to identity was also invoked in an adoption application presented in the city of Mar del Plata, Buenos Aires Province, which emphasised the importance for the child of being able to bear the surname of the man who would have been his adoptive father had he not died before the adoption order was made. This was a case of a cohabiting couple who took on the care of a baby, undertaking to marry and adopt him. Note that, in our law, adoption by both members of an unmarried couple is not possible. After steps had been taken with a view both to adoption

---

[28]   CSJN, 13 de febrero de 2001, ED 194–76.

[29]   Xxx (Mza), 12 de setiembre de 2001, en *Revista de derecho de familia. Revista interdisciplinaria de doctrina y jurisprudencia* Nro 20, Lexis Nexis, Buenos Aires, 2002, p 163.

and marriage, the man died. The woman continued with the application and requested that the child bear the surname of the man who was to have assumed the role of father. The first instance judge allowed this, but the *Asesora de Menores* appealed, arguing that the adoptive mother was single and the existing law did not permit children to be given the name of a third party to the adoption. The appellate court confirmed the decision at first instance. It argued that 'it was right to add to the surname of the adopter to that of the deceased, who was her partner when the child was received with a view to adoption, subject to proof of the de facto union, and of the intention to marry and adopt the child, which were prevented by his death'. In the judgment it was held that 'the addition of the surname of the man who, by adoption, was to have become the father speaks to us of an identity, not equivalent to filiation, but integral to the most personal of personal rights. Although the child only lived three months with his proposed adoptive father, this is his family and his history'.[30]

2 The right of children to communicate with both parents

A THE RIGHT TO COMMUNICATE WITH A LESBIAN MOTHER

When spouses separate and the care of their children is given to one, the other parent, who does not live with the child, has the right to reasonable communication with that child or adolescent (Civil Code, Art 264, inc 2). This right is both a duty of the parent and a right of the child (UN Convention on the Rights of the Child, Art 9). In this connection, judicial decisions and doctrine have roundly affirmed the importance of this right, vital for the training, supervision and education of the child,[31] and capable of suspension only when there are grounds of extreme gravity placing in danger the safety of the minor, or his physical or mental health.[32]

We would comment on a recent judgment affirming the right/duty of communication in favour of a lesbian mother. Her visitation rights had been limited to weekly meetings at the office of the *Asesora de Menores*, supervised by a third party. When the dispute reached the Civil and Commercial Appellate Court of San Isidro (First Chamber), it was held that:

> 'the mother's homosexuality is not, of itself, a ground for preventing the minor from having a reasonable pattern of contact with his mother. The relationship of mother and child cannot be impeded or restricted on the ground that she is a lesbian, so long as it does not work against the interests of the child. To stop reasonable contact between a mother and her child, who has strong positive feelings towards her, on the ground that she is a lesbian, would be to disregard the paramount interest of the child envisaged by the Convention on the Rights of the Child, and to discriminate arbitrarily against the mother for her sexual preferences, contrary to all that is established in the anti-discrimination legislation and fundamentally in Art 19 of the National Constitution.'[33]

---

[30] C Civ y Com Mar del Plata, sala 2°, 29/6/2000, JA 2001–I–31.

[31] CNCiv, sala A, 26/6/85; íd, sala C, 25/10/94, JA–III, síntesis, p 163, n 21; íd sala J, 30/11/95, JA 1998–II–síntesis, p 165, n 33.

[32] CNCiv, sala B, 10/4/97, JA 1998–II–476.

[33] Cám 1ra de Apel en lo Civil y Com de San Isidro, 8 de julio de 2002, *www.eldial.com.ar*.

B SHARED CUSTODY

The Argentine Civil Code does not expressly provide for split custody nor does it forbid it.[34] Only doctrine and court decisions opposed it in the past, arguing that it affected the child's stability or was detrimental to his education.

Nowadays, a significant part of doctrine as well as some judgments take a contrary position. They point out the benefits of ordering joint child custody:

(a) permitting the child to keep a close relationship with both parents – advantages to his development;
(b) the active participation of the parents in the child's life increases their responsibility in relation to maintenance – often not complied with by an absent father;
(c) a father's collaboration in child care protects the mother's right to personal and career development, often endangered by the double burden of the woman;
(d) neither parent feels excluded from the process of rearing the child.

Moreover, where both are responsible for the child's care, neither is so likely to criticise the other's actions.

So courts, in their decisions, have begun to accept this form of custody. As a first step, it has only been ordered where both parties agreed to request it. However, lately, going a step further, the judge has sometimes ordered joint custody, even where parties did not ask for it, where, in the court's view, both parents were suitable for assuming the care of their children.[35]

3 Psychological harm to children suffering paternal abuse and neglect

The application of the civil liability rules to family law has raised much discussion, both in doctrine and in decided cases. Starting in the 1980s, courts have handed down decisions in favour of compensation for psychological injury caused where one spouse was guilty of a subjective ground for divorce, that is to say a fault ground and, at the end of that decade, the first judgment was delivered allowing a claim for compensation for psychological harm inflicted by not recognising an extramarital child.[36]

---

[34] Arianna, Carlos, 'Régimen de visitas', *Revista de derecho de familia. Revista interdisciplinaria de doctrina y jurisprudencia*, Nro 2, Abeledo-Perrot, Buenos Aires, 1989, p 119. In this line of thought, CNCiv, sala J, 24/11/98 held that: 'The law does not forbid joint custody, it just does not make provision for it ...'. 'Although Art 264 inc 2 CC could be thought to prevent the granting of joint custody of children to their parents, the provisions of the Convention on the Rights of the Child, in that it establishes as one of its express principles the giving of primordial consideration to the paramount interest of the child, must make a difference to the solution in a case where that kind of custody order is the option that best serves that paramount interest', JA 1999–IV–603. In similar vein, ST Tierra del Fuego, *Antártida e Islas del Atlántico Sur*, octubre 8-997, LL 1998–F–569, with approving note by Martino, Gloria L, 'Un fallo valioso sobre tenencia', LL *Clarín* 1998–F–569.

[35] CNCiv, sala F, 14 February 2002, JA 2002–II–fascículo n 2, p 36; Cciv, y Com Azul, sala II, 4 de junio de 2001, LLBA 2001–1425; ST Tierra del Fuego, *Antártida e Islas del Atlántico Sur*, octubre 8–997, LL 1998–F–569.

[36] Juzg Civ y Com de San Isidro, No 9, 29/3/1988, ED 128–331; Cciv y Com San Isidro, sala 1ra, 13 October 1988, ED 132–473.

Gradually, questions have been posed as to the possibility of compensation in particular aspects of family law such as, inter alia, breach of engagement to marry, harm caused to children in the context of assisted reproduction, and damage caused by domestic violence and non-payment of maintenance.

An interesting decision, in this context of greater acceptance of civil liability in the field of the family, was made on a claim for compensation for damage inflicted on two children through non-performance of the duty to maintain and maltreatment.

It concerned two brothers, whose mother had died, and whose father inflicted physical and emotional violence on them, as well as failing to give them proper attention or to give them what was necessary for their subsistence and education. Because the children were in such a state of neglect the defendant's *patria potestas* was suspended, the children were placed temporarily in care, and a *tutor ad litem* was appointed to represent them.

The designated tutor brought an action to remove the father's *patria potestas* and to demand damages for the brothers for the psychological harm caused to them. The court allowed both actions, finding the deliberate non-performance of the duty of support and the maltreatment of these children fully proved. It ordered the father to pay compensation to each of his children for the mental injury they had suffered.[37] The decision was confirmed in the appellate court.[38]

VI COLOPHON

This concludes our review. After sketching the Argentine crisis, we have tried to show the importance, for the protection of the family, of the initiative of lawyers and the activity of the courts in defence of economic, social and cultural human rights as well as of civil rights.

---

[37] Juzgado de Primera Instancia a cargo de la Dra Mattera, 29 de junio de 2001, unreported.
[38] CNCiv, sala C, 9 de mayo de 2002, unreported.

AUSTRALIA

OF COURTS AND CASH – AUSTRALIAN FAMILY LAW IN 2001

Frank Bates[*]

I INTRODUCTION

Australian family law in 2001 has taken interesting paths in the sense that the apparently inevitable massive case-law regarding children, emanating from the 1995 amendments to the Family Law Act 1975,[1] does not seem to have eventuated. Instead, the law, both case-law and statutory law, has been largely concentrated on curial procedures and financial matters. Controversy regarding the Family Court of Australia has existed, effectively, since the court's inception[2] and the various approaches taken by that court towards spouses' entitlement to the superannuation entitlements of their divorced partners has been a likewise controversial issue.[3] Whilst it cannot be said that all of the problems related to procedures and future financial entitlements have been settled during 2001, developments have been of more than local interest and, from a comparative standpoint, may suggest how other jurisdictions can deal with recurrent family law problems – and, perhaps, how to avoid them.

II COURTS

A Judicial bias

A particular issue which has plagued the Family Court of Australia has been the matter of allegations of judicial bias.[4] Finally, the issue has received the detailed attention of the Full Court of the Family Court of Australia in *Re F: Litigants in Person Guidelines*,[5] which is also important in relation to the continuing problem of unrepresented litigants, a matter which will be considered later in this commentary.[6]

---

[*]   LLM Professor of Law, University of Newcastle (NSW).

[1]   For comment on these significant amendments, see PE Nygh, 'The New Part VII – an Overview' (1996) 10 Aust J Fam Law 4; R Bailey-Harris, 'The Family Law Reform Act 1995 (Cwth): A New Approach to the Parent/Child Relationship' (1996) 18 Adelaide LR 83.

[2]   See L Star, *Counsel of Perfection: The Family Court of Australia* (1966).

[3]   For comment, see D Kovacs, *Family Property Proceedings in Australia* (1992) at 99 ff.

[4]   For comment on some earlier decisions, see F Bates, 'Judicial Bias in the Family Court of Australia' (1997) 16 Civil Justice Q 334.

[5]   (2001) FLC 93–072.

[6]   See text at n 14 ff below.

In *Re F*, the parties had been continually involved in litigation concerning the child of the marriage and financial matters for approximately five years. In all of the proceeding, the wife had been legally represented, whereas the husband, having initially been represented, elected to represent himself in the case. During the trial proceedings, whilst the husband represented himself, he applied to the judge that the judge should disqualify himself. That application was rejected.

In the event, the trial judge made orders in relation to the child and, in so doing, commented that, despite the husband's stated devotion to the six-year-old child, the husband had, because of his antipathy towards the wife, obfuscated his proper attention to the child's best interests.[7] The husband appealed to the Full Court on a total of 17 grounds, eight of which he was allowed to add at trial. The Full Court[8] dismissed the appeal.

On the issue of bias, the court noted[9] that it had been alleged that, by the time the application had been made, the trial judge had made remarks which suggested that he might have been prejudiced against the husband. In addition, it had been claimed that the judge had failed to hear the whole of the husband's case before deciding the issue.[10] In *Re F*, the court pointed out that the test in relation to bias had been enunciated by the High Court of Australia in *Johnson v Johnson (No 3)*.[11] In that case, it had been said that the test was '… whether a fair minded lay observer might reasonably apprehend that the judge might not bring an impartial and unprejudiced mind to the resolution of the question the judge is required to decide'.

The High Court had also continued[12] by saying that judges were not expected to wait until the end of a case before thinking about the issues. 'On the contrary', the High Court stated, 'they will often form tentative opinions on matters of issue, and counsel are usually assisted by hearing those opinions, and being given an opportunity to deal with them'.

On the facts of *Re F*, the court were of the opinion[13] that, although the trial judge had made comments which were indicative of the way in which he was thinking, he had made every effort to warn the husband that he was adopting courses of action which might endanger his case.

B   Assisting the unrepresented litigant

Another ground on which the husband in *Re F* had appealed was that the trial judge had been in breach of the guidelines articulated by the Full Court of the

---

7   The trial judge ordered that a counsellor supervise contact in order to assist the parties to comply with the orders.

8   Nicholson CJ, Coleman and O'Ryan JJ.

9   (2001) FLC 93–072 at 88, 269.

10   The husband relied, inter alia, on the earlier cases of *Rasanayakam and Wallooppilai v Thillanidesam* (1966) FLC 92–696 and *Stiffle v Stiffle* (1988) FLC 91–977. For comment, see F Bates, op cit, n 4 above.

11   (2000) FLC 93–041 at 87, 362 per Gleeson CJ, Gaudron, McHugh, Gummow and Hayne JJ.

12   Ibid at 87, 362.

13   (2001) FLC 93–072 at 88, 270.

Family Court of Australia in the earlier case of *Johnson v Johnson*.[14] There, the court,[15] speaking of cases involving children, had said[16] that, in those cases, '... the court is at all times constrained to act in the best interests of the child. Generally speaking, that obligation imposes upon the court the necessity to conduct as full and complete inquiry into the relevant issues as is possible, and not to be inhibited by restrictive procedures'. Hence, it was necessary to set out the obligations which were considered relevant for trial judges to observe when hearing cases involving unrepresented litigants.

There were, in the court's opinion, eight such obligations: first, the court should inform the litigant of the manner in which the trial was to proceed, the order of the calling of witnesses and the rights which the litigant had to cross-examine those witnesses. Secondly, the judge was required to explain to the litigant in person any procedures which were relevant to the litigation. Thirdly, the judge ought generally to assist the litigant by taking basic information from witnesses, such as home addresses and occupations. Fourthly, if a change in normal procedure is requested by other parties, such as the calling of witnesses out of turn, the judge ought to explain the extent, and possible undesirability, of the interposition of witnesses, to the unrepresented litigant as well as the parties' right to object to that course of action. Fifthly, if evidence was sought to be tendered which is, or may be, inadmissible, the judge should advise the litigant of the rights to object to inadmissible material and to inquire as to whether the litigant objects. Sixthly, if a question is asked, or evidence is sought to be tendered, in respect of which a litigant may have a possible claim of privilege, the judge should inform litigants of their rights. Seventhly, the judge should seek to ensure that a level playing field[17] is maintained at all times. Finally, the trial judge ought to attempt to clarify the substance of the cases presented by unrepresented parties. This was of especial importance where, in the court's own words, it was where because of '... garrulous or misconceived advocacy, the substantive issues are either ignored, given little attention or obfuscated'.

In *Re F*, the court considered[18] that it was necessary to revisit the *Johnson* guidelines as such guidelines were neither immutable nor incapable of revision. In particular, the court in *Re F* referred[19] to a comment in *Johnson*[20] that it was generally undesirable for legal advice to be given to the unrepresented litigant because to do so might be unfair, or appear to be unfair, to other parties and any such advice might be given with free knowledge of the facts. In *Re F* the Full Court stated[21] that the intention of the court in *Johnson* had been to assist both parties and the judiciary without compromising the integrity of the court. In *Re F*,

---

[14] (1997) FLC 92–764. For comment on this decision and its implications, see F Bates, 'Evidence, Procedure, Child Abuse and Fairness in the Family Court of Australia' (2000) 19 Civil Justice Q 56.

[15] Ellis, Baker and Lindenmayer JJ.

[16] (1997) FLC 92–674 at 84, 421.

[17] The phraseology employed by the court, ibid. Not an expression which would be used by the author in most events.

[18] (2001) FLC 93–072 at 88, 273.

[19] Ibid at 88, 275.

[20] (1997) FLC 92–674 at 84, 421.

[21] (2001) FLC 93–072 at 88, 275.

the court relied to a large extent on a report prepared on behalf of the Family Court of Australia,[22] which found the distinction drawn in *Johnson* between information and advice was, in the view of court personnel, logically and practically unworkable and that the *Johnson* guidelines were frequently seen as involving conflict or, at best, being difficult to reconcile with the realities of the court. Thus, in *Re F*, the court stated that, 'Judicial assistance cannot make up for lack of representation without an unacceptable cost to matters of neutrality. However, in our view, the obligation to provide a fair trial has principal significance for a court of law and it must take some steps to assist a litigant in person in order to do justice between the parties with an eye to the reality and prevalence and diversity of litigants in person in this jurisdiction'.

The instant consequence of the court's comment was that they were of the opinion[23] that there could be circumstances which required a judge to give assistance of a legal nature to a litigant in person, even though that assistance might *risk the appearance*[24] of impartiality and neutrality by the other side. In particular, there might have to be intervention or questions from the bench in order to explore whether the litigant's position is understood. That was the more so as the knowledge and skill base of many litigants in person would vary very widely. It followed, the court said,[25] that the giving of such assistance should lie within the discretion of the trial judge and not be circumscribed by mandatory guidelines.[26]

Specifically, the court made four observations: first, they saw no objection to a trial judge drawing the attention of a litigant to the principles applied by the court in examining issues. Secondly, they, likewise, saw no objection to a judge drawing attention to the principles governing the admissibility of evidence. Thirdly, the court regarded it as proper for trial courts to ask questions of witnesses in proceedings involving financial matters, as well as in cases involving the paramountcy principle,[27] where material involves the goal of doing justice between the parties. Fourthly, the court suggested that trial judges might take the view that they should assist in the reformulation of applications which might be made by a litigant in person. These could include, but were not confined to, procedural matters. In that context, the court stated[28] that, 'Subject to the other party sustaining no injustice, we see no objection to a judge reframing the material to properly reflect what the applicant intended. The alternative may be a costly adjournment followed by yet another application.' The court were, likewise, of the opinion that giving advice of that kind was fundamentally different from giving

---

[22]   J Dewar, B Smith and C Banks, *Litigants in Person in the Family Court of Australia – Research Report No 20* (2000) at 2; (2001) FLC 93–072 at 88, 276.

[23]   (2001) FLC 93–072 at 88, 276.

[24]   Court's emphasis, ibid.

[25]   (2001) FLC 93–027 at 88, 277.

[26]   In addition, ibid, the court noted that a number of litigants in person had been using alleged breaches of the guidelines set out in *Johnson* as grounds for appeal. The court did not regard it as appropriate that the guidelines should be used in that way as the circumstances of particular cases varied to a considerable degree.

[27]   See Family Law Act 1975, s 65E.

[28]   (2001) FLC 93–237 at 88, 277.

advice as to a particular litigant's chances of success or advising as to the kind of witness who might best advance a party's case.[29]

It followed that some of the *Johnson* guidelines were in need of revision. Thus, the fourth guideline should be amended[30] so as to read, 'If a change in the normal procedure is requested by the other parties such as the calling of witnesses out of turn the judge may, if he/she considers that there is any strong possibility of such a change causing any injustice to a litigant in person, explain to the unrepresented party the extent and perhaps the undesirability of interposition of witnesses and his or her right to object to that course'. Again, the court considered that the seventh guideline ought to be amended, and, indeed, ought to be the first such guideline, and would read that, 'A judge should ensure as far as is possible that procedural fairness is afforded to all parties whether represented or appearing in person in order to ensure a fair trial'. Lastly, the court considered that an additional guideline should be added. This was that, where the interests of justice and the circumstances of the case require it, judges may draw attention to the law applied by the court in determining issues before it, may question witnesses, may identify applications or submissions which may be put to the court, suggest procedural steps which might be taken by a party and clarify the particulars sought by a litigant in person or the bases for such advice. The court also emphasised that the list was not intended to be exhaustive and there might well be other interventions which a judge might properly make without there being any apprehension of bias.

It remains to be seen how much these revised guidelines will actually benefit the significant number of unrepresented litigants. There is also a risk that represented parties may take exception to their perception of partial treatment of their unrepresented opponents. One simply has to await further developments.

C Evidence

The matter of representation was at issue in the decision of Barlow J of the Family Court of Western Australia[31] in *Pedersen and Pedersen*.[32] That case involved an application by a husband to strike out hearsay evidence contained in affidavits by the wife's next friend and other witnesses.[33] In July 2000, a next friend of the wife had been appointed following medical evidence that the wife was not competent to deal with complex legal and financial matters.[34] The following month, an affidavit sworn by the next friend was filed in support of the wife's application. That affidavit, and affidavits from other persons intended to be relied on by the

---

[29] As the court put the matter, ibid, 'Matters such as these appear to us to be too dependent upon an intimate knowledge of the party's case which goes beyond the material on the record and is thus a function of advocacy rather than assistance or information'.

[30] Ibid at 88, 278.

[31] Section 41 of the Family Law Act 1975 permits States to set up their own Family Courts. Thus far, only Western Australia, for largely geographical reasons, has done so.

[32] (2001) FLC 93–065.

[33] The substantive issues in the case involved cross-applications for property orders and an application for spousal maintenance by the wife.

[34] It appeared that she suffered from a major depressive disorder and cognitive difficulties which caused her to cope very poorly when under stress.

wife, contained hearsay evidence. The husband objected to the admission of that evidence. Thus, the issue for determination was whether, in the peculiar circumstances of the case, the wife should be permitted to rely on the evidence.

The wife argued that the next friend had no choice but to put such evidence before the court because, first, the wife was required to file an affidavit setting out her evidence-in-chief and a detailed financial statement.[35] Secondly, the Family Law Rules provided[36] that the next friend was required to do anything required by the Rules to be done by the party. It was acknowledged by the wife's counsel that there appeared to be no established exception to the hearsay rule permitting the reception of hearsay evidence from a next friend.

In finding in favour of the husband, Barlow J held,[37] first, that, on the appointment of the next friend, it would have been appropriate for an order to have been made discharging the direction[38] requiring the wife to file an affidavit and a statement of financial circumstances. That course, the judge considered, would have resolved any conflict between the direction and the obligations cast on the next friend by the Rules.[39] At the same time, Barlow J was of the view that the exclusion of the hearsay evidence which was sought to be relied on did not necessarily preclude the next friend from presenting in relation to the subject matter of the hearsay evidence. The next friend might obviate the difficulty by locating witnesses to give admissible evidence on the subject matter. In addition, the appointment of a next friend and discharging the pre-trial order did not preclude the wife from swearing and filing an affidavit in support of her application, nor would it preclude the next friend from applying for an order which would permit the wife to give oral evidence at trial. Accordingly, the judge was not persuaded[40] that it would be proper for the hearsay evidence by the next friend, or any other witnesses, to be admitted.

In commenting on the *Pedersen* decision, it should be remembered that it was a decision of the Family Court of Western Australia and, hence, governed by the evidence law of that State. Had it fallen to be decided by the Family Court of Australia, which is a Federal Court, the result might well have been different. It has been suggested[41] that the changes wrought by the Evidence Acts 1995, which govern the law in Federal jurisdictions and the State of New South Wales, have, effectively, abolished the hearsay rule as it was applicable in civil proceedings in those *fora*. Again, to a degree, that is a matter for speculation, although, given the entire circumstances of the *Pedersen* case, more might possibly have been done to assist the wife.[42]

---

[35]   This requirement was the result of a pre-trial direction.

[36]   Order 15, r 11 of the Family Law Rules provides that, 'A person appointed under this Order as a next friend of a party to the proceedings: (a) must do anything required by the Rules to be done by the party; and (b) must do anything permitted by these Rules to be done by the party'.

[37]   (2001) FLC 93–065 at 88, 184.

[38]   See n 35 above.

[39]   See n 36 above.

[40]   (2001) FLC 93–065 at 88, 185.

[41]   See A Palmer, *Principles of Evidence* (1988) at 132. In particular, s 65 of the legislation, it is claimed, has had that effect.

[42]   The relationship between State and Federal matters was discussed by McKechnie J of the Family Court of Western Australia in *Anglicare WA and Anor v Department of Family and Children's Services* (2001) FLC 93–066.

A continuing difficulty in Australian family law proceedings has been the possibility of the parties being able to adduce fresh evidence at an appellate stage. This issue arose in the decision of the Full Court of the Family Court of Australia in *Boege and Boege*[43] where, at the conclusion of the hearing of the appeal, each party was asked whether they wished to adduce any further evidence to enable the court to re-exercise the discretion by reference to circumstances which existed at the time of the trial, should the Full Court allow the appeal. The wife's counsel indicated that the wife desired to adduce further valuation[44] evidence. The argument advanced was the length of time which had elapsed between the trial and the appeal, which was some 16 months. Subsequently, however, it was established that the real reason was that the wife wished to make inquiries as to whether there were any further matters on the issue about which evidence could then be sought. If so, it was intended to obtain the admission of that evidence.

At first sight, it might have appeared that the wife's case had been aided by a *dictum* of Gaudron, McHugh, Gummow and Hayne JJ in the High Court's recent decision in *Allesch v Maunz*[45] where it had been said that, 'If on an appeal by way of rehearing from a discretionary judgement, an appellate court is minded to exercise the discretion in question by reference to circumstances as they exist at the time of the appeal, it is necessary that the parties be given an opportunity as to those circumstances'.

In noting *Allesch v Maunz*, the Full Court pointed out[46] that, in the short time since the decision, it had been a practice of the court to inquire of the parties to an appeal whether, in the event of the appeal being successful, and the court proposed to exercise a discretion to hear it, either party wished to place fresh evidence before the court. 'In our view,' the court said, 'a widespread and well known practice has developed that, while a party wishing to adduce further evidence before the court is not required to have all of the evidence immediately available in admissible form, that party must be able to point to the nature of such evidence'.

The Full Court did not interpret *Allesch v Maunz* as referring, other than in exceptional circumstances, to the deferment of an appeal to enable a party to embark on such an investigation as had been suggested by the wife in *Boege*. The court concluded by saying that it was, '… quite inconsistent with the orderly and expeditious conduct of proceedings that in response to such a request as aforesaid, a party indicates merely that he/she would like the opportunity to investigate whether there may or may not be some further evidence which might be placed before the Full Court for the purposes of determining the appeal'. Whilst being sympathetic to the High Court's views, earlier referred to,[47] as well as Kirby J's comment[48] regarding the necessity to give the parties, '… an effective opportunity to adduce further evidence', it would have been difficult for the Full Court to have

---

[43]   (2001) FLC 93–084.

[44]   For comment on the question of valuation, see D Kovacs, op cit, n 3 above at 181.

[45]   (2000) FLC 93–033 at 87, 517.

[46]   (2001) FLC 93–084 at 88, 445, Ellis, Finn and Warwick JJ.

[47]   See n 45 above.

[48]   Ibid at 87, 521.

decided other than they did on the facts of *Boege*. 'Fishing expeditions'[49] are surely to be discouraged in family law matters as in other areas of law.

The issue of the reception of further evidence also arose in the later decision of the Full Court in the important case of *Re W and W: Abuse Allegations; Expert Evidence*[50] which also involved the use of expert evidence in cases of child sexual abuse in general. On the issue of further evidence, the relevant Department of Family and Children's Services had sought to intervene[51] in the case, asking leave to admit a particular affidavit into evidence. This affidavit had been sworn by a counsellor who had interviewed the husband, and the Department claimed that the counsellor's evidence contained admissions by the husband of inappropriate sexual behaviour which, had they been admitted, might have influenced the trial judge's decision. The Department claimed that it had not intervened at the trial stage because it had expected that the evidence would have been called. The Child Representative[52] indicated that the evidence had not been called because it was believed that, at the time of the trial, the evidence would not have been admissible by reason of statutory provision.[53] The Department now argued that the evidence was rendered admissible both by statutory provision[54] and by the Oath or Affirmation of Office of the Family and Child Counsellor. Inevitably, the husband argued that, by reason of the first provision, the evidence would not have been accepted at trial.

The Full Court unanimously dismissed the application for leave to adduce fresh evidence. Kay J, with whom Nicholson CJ and O'Ryan J agreed, noted,[55] first, that all the Oath which was relied on did was to permit the counsellor to comply with the provisions of the Act dealing with the mandatory reporting of child abuse.[56] The judge was of the opinion that any further investigation raised by a counsellor in response to any such notification was the responsibility of the appropriate authorities to whom the notification was made. Secondly, Kay J stated[57] that the legislation did not render admissible matters which were otherwise the subject of a prohibition as to its admissibility. The second statutory provision[58] had the effect of ensuring that, if the evidence was otherwise admissible, it could only be given by the maker of the notification and not by way of second-hand or hearsay evidence.

That much is predictable and, on a strict reading of the various provisions, is probably accurate, but, perhaps of more importance is the comment of

---

49   See *Air Canada v Secretary of State for Trade* [1983] 2 WLR 494 at 529 per Lord Wilberforce.
50   (2001) FLC 93–085.
51   See Family Law Act 1975, ss 92, 92A.
52   Ibid, ss 68L, 68M.
53   Ibid, s 19N. This section provides that anything said at a meeting or conference conducted by a family and child counsellor, or a court negotiator, or (subject to regulation) a community or a private mediator, marriage counsellor or medical or other professional, is not admissible in any legal proceeding.
54   Ibid, s 67–67B2(4). See text at n 58 below.
55   (2001) FLC 93–085 at 88, 475.
56   Family Law Act 1975, s 70B.
57   (2001) FLC 93–085 at 88, 476.
58   Family Law Act 1975, s 67B2(4).

Nicholson CJ and O'Ryan JJ[59] that it was, '… most unfortunate that the legislation contains no exception to the legislative prohibition to the giving of such evidence in circumstances where its non-receipt may impinge on the best interests of children. This means that a court that is required to make decisions treating the best interests of children as the paramount consideration in determining issues such as residence and contact must do so without having any knowledge of important or relevant facts that could affect such a decision'. That remark must, of course, be thoroughly endorsed.

On the substantive issue, the relevant facts were that the parties had moved abroad and had moved to Australia some four years later. There were three children of the marriage of whom the eldest, who was the child directly involved in the case, was born in 1988 (two years after her parents' marriage), had exhibited behavioural problems from a young age and had been referred to a number of psychologists. Some seven years after the move to Australia, the wife became interested in so-called New Age beliefs and encouraged the eldest daughter also so to be.

In October 1998 the daughter told the wife that she had been sexually assaulted by the husband, who was later charged with two counts of sexual penetration of a lineal relative and four counts of indecent dealing. The husband pleaded not guilty to those charges. However, in addition, according to the wife, the eldest child had observed the husband sexually abusing a younger child and also made the claim that she had been abused by her paternal grandparents.

In November of the same year, the husband began property proceedings seeking orders for residence and property distribution. In essence, the husband argued that the wife's beliefs had influenced the eldest child to make false allegations and that they had adversely affected the wife's ability to parent the children appropriately.

In August 1999, after the eldest child had been extensively cross-examined in the criminal proceedings, the Crown filed a *nolle prosequi* in relation to the charges.

As regards the residence and property proceedings, the trial judge, after a hearing which lasted two days, ordered that the children reside with the husband and that the wife have supervised weekly contact. The trial judge refused to accept the child's allegations of sexual abuse and also made adverse observations as to the wife's credit. *Inter alia*, he held that she had sought to minimise her behaviour in relation to her religious beliefs, which she herself had admitted might be regarded as 'bizarre' and that the wife had actively encouraged the child to become involved with her beliefs which, in turn, had influenced the allegations of sexual abuse.[60] The wife appealed on various grounds, most importantly for the purposes of the present discussion, including that the trial judge had wrongly

---

[59]   (2001) FLC 93–085 at 88, 460.

[60]   Further, the trial judge considered that the wife could not appropriately provide for the emotional needs of the children and, as she continued to accept the veracity of the eldest child's allegations, there was a possibility that she could not attempt to dissuade the child from the belief that sexual abuse had occurred. The judge believed that, were the children to reside with the wife, they might grow up holding the view that the eldest had been sexually abused by their father and paternal grandparents and, hence, there was a danger that they might be subjected to psychological harm.

placed emphasis on the evidence of a psychiatrist called by the husband who had not seen either the wife or the children.

In allowing the appeal,[61] by a majority, the judges all expressed concern about the evidence which had been given by that witness. Nicholson CJ and O'Ryan J stated[62] that a careful reading of the witness's evidence revealed him to have been extremely partisan to the point where the judges found it difficult to accept his professional objectivity. Earlier, the same judges had said[63] that, in their view, the '… case is a classic example of the misuse of expert evidence'. Furthermore, it highlighted[64] the need for reform in the area and referred to the views of Sperling J of the New South Wales Supreme Court, writing extra-judicially.[65] That commentator had urged four courses of action which might be especially applicable to the family law jurisdiction: first, a code of conduct for expert witnesses should be promulgated; secondly, there should be consideration of amending statutes so that breach of a duty of objectivity became professional misconduct; thirdly, there should be greater power to refer out technical issues for determination by an expert referee; and fourthly, there should be amendments to the Rules of Court in respect of matters such as an express power to limit expert evidence to that of a single expert selected by the parties or, in appropriate cases, by the court.

Kay J, although he could find[66] no appealable error in the way in which the trial judge had dealt with the psychiatrist's evidence, added a postscript in which he endorsed the general comments of Nicholson CJ and O'Ryan J regarding the uses and abuses of expert evidence.

Whilst there can be little doubt that the suggestions made by Sperling J[67] would be desirable, one cannot help but wonder whether sufficient utility has been made of existing Rules of Court. Thus, first, Ord 30 r 5 of the Family Law Rules specifies that, of its own motion, the court may call any person before it as a witness. Secondly, by reason of Ord 3A r 3, the court may, at any stage of the proceedings, on an application by a party or of its own motion, appoint an expert as court expert to inquire into and report on any issue of fact or opinion (other than an issue involving questions of law and construction) arising in the proceedings and give directions to extend or supplement, or otherwise in relation to, any such inquiry or report. Finally, Ord 30B r 1 of the Family Law Rules states that the court may call on one or more assessors to assist it in relation to any matter before the court. However, this writer has anecdotal evidence that these existing processes are very rarely used.

---

[61]   In all the circumstances, it was decided, (2001) FLC 93–085 at 88, 470, that a new trial would not be desirable so it was ordered that the matter be listed for directions before the Full Court which heard the appeal.

[62]   (2001) FLC 93–085 at 88, 468.

[63]   Ibid at 88, 466.

[64]   Ibid at 88, 469.

[65]   'Expert Evidence: The Problem of Bias and Other Things' (2000) 4 Judicial Rev 429.

[66]   (2001) FLC 93–085 at 88, 496.

[67]   See text at n 65 above.

III PROPERTY

A The discretion

Section 79(1) of the Family Law Act 1975 provides that:

'In proceedings with respect to the property of the parties to a marriage or either of them, the court may make such order as it considers appropriate altering the interests of the parties in the property, including an order for a settlement of property in substitution for any interest in the property and including an order requiring either or both of the parties to make, for the benefit of either or both of the parties or a child of the marriage, such settlement or transfer of property as the court determines.'

That wide discretion is modified by s 79(2), which provides that an order shall not be made unless the court is satisfied that, in all the circumstances, it is just and equitable to do so, and s 79(4), which sets out seven matters which must be taken into account when exercising the discretion.

2001 saw the decision of the Full Court of the Family Court of Australia in *JEL and DDF*,[68] which represents an important case on the operation of the discretion. The parties had married in 1979 and separated in 1991: there were three children of the marriage and the wife's son from a previous marriage also lived with the parties. The husband was a geologist and had, in 1982, begun employment with Marathon Petroleum Pty Ltd (MPP). During that employment, the husband discovered that MPP was about to terminate a joint venture involving a gold prospect. The husband was of the view that this prospect had a very high exploration potential. The husband pursued this prospect until he, and another person, bought out MPP, the transaction being settled in April 1984. The corporate purchase was made through Pan Australia Mining Ltd (PAM). The husband resigned as general manager of PAM in February 1987 and from the Board in June; at that time, the family shareholding in PAM consisted of seven million shares. The husband sold 6,900,000 of those shares, which produced $30,600,000 and kept the remainder to retain his right of first refusal. In October 1987, the husband sold his right of first refusal for $4,600,000. Hence, it will be readily apparent that large sums of money were involved and, as Kay J put it at the beginning of his judgment,[69] 'Very large money cases are rare in this jurisdiction'.

The trial judge found that, until 1987, the wife had made very significant contributions as a homemaker and parent but, from that date, her contribution had been affected by illness.

During the marriage, the parties developed a company and trust structure known as the L Group which included the JEL Family Trust, the JEL Investment Trust, and L Mining Trust and Bowse Securities. The parties operated a number of activities through those entities.

The trial judge considered the relative contributions of the parties during the marriage but she did not allocate a percentage division based on them. She then considered the factors contained in s 75(2) of the Family Law Act and concluded that it was impossible to understand how they could be used as a basis for allowing the wife an additional percentage. The trial judge concluded that, given

---

[68] (2001) FLC 93–075.
[69] Ibid at 88, 309.

the significant contribution of the wife as homemaker and parent and the contribution of the husband (together with the wife's emotional support) as well as their different abilities and potential to earn income, the appropriate result was that the property (including the various trusts and superannuation) be divided in the proportions of 65% to the husband and 35% to the wife.

On the issue of discretion, both parties appealed against the orders on the grounds that they fell outside the reasonable exercise of the trial judge's discretion. Holden and Guest JJ, in a joint judgment, noted,[70] first, that the discretion granted by s 79 of the Act was very wide and, as such, the powers of an appellate court were limited. The judges then went on to analyse and comment on earlier case-law.[71] In the event, Holden and Guest JJ ultimately distilled[72] nine principles from the cases. These were: first, there was no presumption of equality of contribution or 'partnership'. Secondly, there was a requirement to undertake an evaluation of the respective contributions of husband and wife. Thirdly, although in many cases the direct contribution of one party would equal the indirect contribution of the other as homemaker and parent, that is not necessarily so in each case. Fourthly, in qualitatively evaluating the roles performed by marriage partners, there may arise special factors which attach to the performance of the particular role of one of them. Fifthly, the court will recognise only such special factors as taking the contribution beyond the 'normal range' – in that context, Holden and Guest JJ returned to the comments of the Full Court in *McLay* where it had been said[73] that expressions such as that were not terms of art, but were convenient expressions which represented a practical recognition of the circumstances of many marriages. In particular, their use did not represent a return to any presumption of equality. Sixthly, the determination of an issue of whether or not a 'special' or 'extra' contribution was made by a party to a marriage was not necessarily dependent upon the size of the asset pool, or what Holden and Guest JJ referred to[74] as the 'financial product'. When considering such an issue, care must be taken to distinguish a 'windfall' gain. Seventhly,[75] whilst decisions in previous cases where special factors were found to exist might provide some guidance to judges at first instance, they were not prescriptive, except to the extent that they purported to lay down general principles. Eighthly, it was ultimately the exercise of the trial judge's own discretion on the particular facts of the case which would regulate the outcome and, finally, in the exercise of that discretion, the trial judge was required to be satisfied that the actual orders were just and equitable, not merely the underlying percentage division.

Ultimately, Holden and Guest JJ took the view[76] that the trial judge's determination was above a legitimate exercise of her discretion and re-exercised the discretion to allocate the wife 27.5% based on contribution. In relation to s 75(2) factors, their Honours concluded that, in the context of the case, the

---

[70]   Ibid at 88, 329.
[71]   Notably, *Ferrero and Ferrero* (1993) FLC 92-335; *McLay and McLay* (1996) FLC 92–667; *Strong and Strong* (1997) FLC 92–751.
[72]   (2001) FLC 93–075 at 88, 334.
[73]   (1996) FLC 92–667 at 82, 902 per Nicholson CJ, Fogarty and Desson JJ.
[74]   (2001) FLC 93–075 at 88, 335.
[75]   For an example of such a gain, see *Farmer and Bromley* (2000) FLC 93–060.
[76]   (2001) FLC 93–075 at 88, 337.

differential earning capacities of the parties did not justify an adjustment. However, significant taxation benefits arising from tax losses[77] warranted a further payment of $200,000 to the wife. Kay J agreed[78] with the outcomes proposed by Holden and Guest JJ and discussed approaches to cases involving large amounts of money.

Although *JEL* provided a useful analysis of the process of the exercise of discretion in s 79 cases, it does little to remove a major problem attaching to its operation, that being its perceived lack of predictability.[79]

B   Evidence

Hunt and Hunt[80] involved cross-applications for property orders and an application by the wife for spousal maintenance. The wife had given both oral and affidavit evidence of health problems, which she claimed significantly impacted on her ability to earn. She also filed an affidavit from a general medical practitioner that she was affected by pain and stiffness and swelling of various parts of her body. The husband sought an order that the wife be examined by a consultant rheumatologist of his choice with a view to obtaining a report concerning the wife's health. The husband argued that, in respect of the application for spousal maintenance, the health of the parties was a relevant factor because it represented a correlation with earning capacity. Hence, were the interests of justice to be served, it was crucial that he was able to trust both the wife's claim and her supporting evidence.

Barlow J, of the Family Court of Western Australia, found in favour of the husband. After a consideration of the authorities,[81] he concluded[82] that:

> '... the power to make orders, as sought by the husband, is incidental and necessary to the exercise of the power to make such order for the alteration of property interests, that in all the circumstances are just and equitable and such order for spousal maintenance which the court considers proper in accordance with the relevant provisions of the Act.'

C   Superannuation

A particular difficulty which has plagued Australian family finance and property law has been the treatment of superannuation entitlements. It is safe to say that no coherent approach towards them has been apparent.[83] In 2001, however, the

---

[77]   The tax losses had been discounted for future uncertainties.

[78]   (2001) FLC 93–075 at 88, 309.

[79]   Inevitably, perhaps, there was a *JEL and DDF (No 2)* (2001) FLC 93–083, dealing with overpayment of the award and costs.

[80]   (2001) FLC 93–064.

[81]   See *Parsons v Martin* (1984) 58 ALR 395; *R v Forbes; Ex parte Baron* (1972) 127 CLR 1; *Gilbert and Gilbert* (1988) FLC 91–966; *L v T* (1999) FLC 92–875; *DJL v The Central Authority* (2000) 201 CLR 226.

[82]   (2001) FLC 93–064 at 88, 181.

[83]   The various approaches to be found in decisions of the Family Court of Australia were listed by Purvis J in *Webber and Webber* (1985) FLC 91–648 at 80, 224.

Commonwealth legislature has sought to resolve the issue, albeit in a more than somewhat convoluted manner. This in spite of the Commonwealth legislature having put in considerable effort over approximately a 20-year period.

There are four main elements contained in what is a complex and interacting legislative and regulatory package. These are: the Family Law Legislation (Superannuation) Act 2001; the Family Law Legislation Amendment (Superannuation) (Consequential Provisions) Act 2001; the Superannuation Industry Supervision Regulations; and, lastly, the Family Law (Superannuation) Regulations. A particular difficulty is that much of the detail of the new scheme is to be found in the last set of regulations.

The fundamental reform effected in the legislation is that superannuation is treated as property available for division between the parties. Previously, the situation was most unclear and was, ultimately, dependent on the terms of the relevant deed,[84] although, generally, the court treated superannuation as being a financial resource.[85] Even so, as Kennedy has properly pointed out,[86] courts and practitioners had previously been able to devise a just and equitable outcome, including superannuation, in property disputes. It is provided[87] in the amendments that a superannuation is to be treated as 'property' for the purposes of the definition of 'matrimonial cause' in s 4(1) of the Family Law Act. This basic change will give the parties, or if the parties are unable to agree, the court, a broad range of options in dividing property, now including superannuation entitlements, between them.

The new legislation, which becomes a new Part VIIIB of the original legislation, provides[88] for two main orders: first, a 'splitting' order, which permits the court to split the superannuation interests between the parties in whatever proportions are considered to be appropriate, and secondly, a 'flagging' order which may, first, preserve the superannuation by preventing trustees,[89] by injunction, from paying out an interest pending an order or agreement or to require the trustees to notify the court when an interest becomes payable. These provisions have the immediate effect of permitting the court to make orders in those not infrequent situations where superannuation is the only financial interest of value in the marriage.[90] Under the new s 90MT, the court is given a very broad discretion to split a superannuation interest of a spouse, subject to the 'just and equitable' requirement to be found in s 79(1) of the Family Law Act. In addition, orders, for the first time, will bind third party trustees who will, however, have to be accorded procedural fairness. Such orders are also subject to the provisions of s 79A and thus may be set aside or varied as specified in that provision.

---

[84]   It has been said that the various decisions of the Family Court of Australia had demonstrated no less than eight approaches towards superannuation. See CCH, *Australian Family Law and Practice* (1976) vol 3, para 38–000 ff.

[85]   See Family Law Act 1975, s 75(2) and *In the Marriage of Crapp* (1979) FLC 90–615.

[86]   I Kennedy, 'The Superannuation Reforms' (2001) 15(2) *Australian Family Lawyer* 15 at 18.

[87]   Family Law Act 1975, s 90MC.

[88]   Ibid, ss 90MT, 90MU.

[89]   'Trustees' are defined in ibid, s 90MD, but that definition is somewhat expanded in the Regulations.

[90]   Previously, courts were often required to order a very lengthy adjournment until the interest became available for division; see *In the Marriage of O'Shea* (1988) FLC 91–964.

In the context of splitting orders, note should be taken of the two major types of superannuation scheme which are essentially 'lump sum' schemes, where the level of benefit is directly related to the level of contribution and the investment performance of funds during the period of the beneficiary's membership.[91] Defined benefit schemes, the second type, provide members with a specified level of benefit – either a pension or lump sum or both – based on years of service and the salary earned prior to retirement, as well as contributions and investment earnings.[92] It will be immediately apparent that the latter group are less easy for the law to deal with in the present context because funding will normally only be provided when a member of the scheme becomes entitled to benefit and, hence, the payment which the member will receive depends on future events, such as length of service and final average salary. The value of the interest is not readily ascertainable as it is dependent on the probability of future events and, therefore, has to be calculated actuarially. Nonetheless, if splitting orders may be made in respect of defined benefit schemes, the non-member spouse will receive a proportion of the benefits, which include income by way of pension, when they become available, and the member spouse's contributions will be reduced accordingly. However, the complicated value of the relevant calculation will inevitably be complex and must be calculated actuarially.

It is not only interest, though, which will be splittable. Section 90ME of the Act provides that an 'unsplittable interest' means a superannuation interest prescribed by the regulations for the purposes of the definition. That definition, if such it can fairly be called, brings the Family Law (Superannuation) Regulations 2001[93] into operation: it is prescribed in r 11 that a superannuation interest with a withdrawal benefit of less than $5,000 is an unsplittable interest. Some comment regarding these Regulations is necessary at this point; their purpose, as Bourke puts the matter,[94] being to '... fill the interstitial space left in the primary legislation ...'. They are very complex and detailed and it is hard to reduce them to appropriate form for the purposes of the present commentary.

In addition to unsplittable interests, Part 2 of the Regulations prescribes *payments* which are not splittable. This Part is to be contrasted with an *interest* which is unsplittable under r 11[95] where the whole interest is unsplittable. In respect of Part 2, the interest is splittable, but some particular payments are not.[96] Examples of that kind of payment include[97] payments made on compassionate

---

[91] In September 2000, approximately 87% of Australians who were members of superannuation schemes belonged to accumulation schemes (see Australian Prudential Regulatory Authority).

[92] Benefits are based generally on a multiple of the member's final salary. Of the 13% of superannuants who were not in accumulation schemes, 2% were members of defined benefit schemes and the remainder were in various hybrid schemes which have elements of both. Despite being in apparent decline, defined benefit schemes presently hold almost 50% of superannuation fund wealth in Australia, the reason being that most of them are Commonwealth or State government schemes.

[93] For general comment on these Regulations, see S Bourke, 'Family Law (Superannuation) Regulations 2001' (2001) 15(3) *Australian Family Lawyer* 18.

[94] Ibid at 18.

[95] See text above at n 93.

[96] See Family Law Act 1975, s 90ME.

[97] For a detailed list, see Bourke, op cit, n 93 above, at 18–19.

grounds,[98] payments made on the grounds of severe financial hardship,[99] certain payments made on grounds of incapacity,[100] and payments made to a child or reversionary beneficiary on behalf of a child.[101]

Further, in addition to those payments which are not splittable generally,[102] the Regulations also prescribe payments which are not splittable for particular payment splits. The explanatory statement in respect of the Regulations[103] seeks to explain the reason for the existence of r 14 in the following terms: 'The purpose of the prescription of these payments is to bring to an end a payment split of an interest in favour of a particular separated or divorced non-member spouse where he or she has received the effect of the payment split in some other way at an earlier time than the member spouse's receipt of superannuation benefits'. The payments referred to are largely concerned with transfer and roll-overs of payments, and the prescriptions may be found in r 14.[104]

In addition to splitting orders, flagging orders exist where the fund is not to be immediately split. The so-called flag is an injunction binding on the trustee of the scheme which freezes the fund until the flag is lifted. The parties themselves are able to flag a superannuation interest by way of a superannuation agreement; however, that will require a flag lifting agreement which complies with all the formalities of a financial agreement,[105] to lift the flag and deal with the interest. Alternatively, a flagging order may be made by the court. This device is most likely to be used where the value of a superannuation interest is currently unknown but will be known in the near future – for example, where the member spouse is close to retirement. The legislation[106] states in that context that the court may take into account, in particular, the likelihood that a splittable payment will soon become payable in respect of an interest.

The Regulations deal with payment splitting and flagging by agreement and by court order. Thus, Part 3 of the Regulations deals with matters relating to splitting and flagging as effected by a superannuation agreement.[107] The part also appears to be supported by s 90MJ of the Family Law Act, as amended. Section 90MJ divides superannuation interests into two kinds: first, where the interest is a percentage only interest, any entitlement will be calculated according to the formula to be found in r 19. What this formula does is to separate the superannuation which accumulates after the breakdown of the marriage from the superannuation which had accumulated during the marriage by dividing the accrued benefit multiple at breakdown by that at payment. In the case of interests

---

[98]   See r 12(1)(a).

[99]   See r 12(2)(b).

[100]   See rr 12(1)(a)(i)A, 12(1)(a)(i)(ii), 12(1)(d), 12(1)(e).

[101]   See rr 13(1)(a), (b) and (c).

[102]   See rr 12, 13.

[103]   Attorney General's Department, *Family Law (Superannuation) Regulations 2001: Explanatory Memorandum* (2001) at 4.

[104]   For comment, see Bourke, op cit, n 93 above, at 19.

[105]   Family Law Act 1975, Part VIIIB.

[106]   Ibid, s 90MU(2).

[107]   It is provided, ibid, s 90MJ, that the amount that the non-member spouse is entitled to be paid with a superannuation agreement is to be calculated according to the Regulations.

which are not percentage only interests (and these, according to Bourke,[108] are the most common that legal practitioners are likely to encounter), r 16 points to Division 6.2 of the Regulations,[109] which deals with the calculation of the entitlement where the interest is in the growth phase and r 17 operates similarly in respect of Division 6.3, which deals with the calculation of the entitlement where the interest is in the payment phase. Finally, in relation to Part 3 of the Regulations, r 20 prescribes that the total withdrawal value, for the purposes of s 90MG of the Act, is determined by adding together the withdrawal benefits of each superannuation interest.

Part 4 of the 2001 Regulations deals with payment splitting or flagging by court order. This process is expected[110] to be the most usual form of resolving superannuation matters. In essence, where the interest is a percentage only interest, the entitlement is calculated in accordance with a formula set out in r 26, which operates in an identical manner to the formula in r 19 in Part 3, noted earlier. As regards interests which are not percentage only interests, the same directions exist as in Part 3.

Part 5 of the Regulations deals with valuation. This is important as s 90MT(2)(a) of the Family Law Act states that, if the Regulations provide a method for valuation of an interest, the court must determine the value in accordance with the Regulations. A formula is set out in r 28.[111] Part 6 of the Regulations provides for the entitlement of the non-member spouse where the interest is in the growth phase[112] or in the payment phase.[113] In the first instance, provision is made for an adjustment to the base amount[114] and the payment of the adjusted base amount depending on the circumstances of the payment.[115] Essentially, the principle which applies to these Regulations is that, if there is a sufficient lump sum to pay the adjusted base amount, it is paid out of the lump sum. Where, however, there is no lump sum, or there is an insufficient lump sum, the adjusted base amount is paid as a proportion of ongoing pension entitlements.

Part 7 of the Regulations provides for some general matters; the most important of those being fees,[116] waiver notice[117] and information provision.

One particular issue of especial importance relates to interim provisions: it seems certain that the 2001 legislation will not now come into operation until 28 December 2002. The legislation seems not to have any retrospective effect so that settlements entered into by way either of agreement or court order will not be included in the new legislation, whatever benefits it will prove to have, until that time. The issue, therefore, arises as to what should be done by legal practitioners during that interim period. That issue has been addressed by Watts and Bourke,

---

[108] Op cit, n 93 above, at 19.
[109] See text at n 113 below.
[110] Op cit, n 93 above, at 20.
[111] Ibid.
[112] Family Law (Superannuation) Regulations 2001, Part 6.2.
[113] Ibid, Part 6.3.
[114] Ibid, r 47.
[115] Ibid, rr 48–54.
[116] Ibid, r 49.
[117] Family Law Act 1975, s 90MZA.

who suggest[118] that, first, practitioners should consider whether or not a fair adjustment of property interests can be made without requiring superannuation to be split and, if so, rearrange property without affecting superannuation interests. Secondly, should a client wish to take advantage of the superannuation splitting arrangements, proceedings should be adjourned, or settlement postponed, until 28 December 2002.[119] Thus, if the parties have reached some proposed agreement before that date as to how superannuation can be split, that can be documented in a non-binding form which will be of persuasive effect only on the court. Alternatively, matters may be resolved, at least in part, by financial agreements under Part VIIIA of the Family Law Act. Finally, these writers note that injunctive orders may be necessary to maintain the *status quo* in relation to superannuation interests (particularly in relation to interests in self-managed superannuation funds).

The situation is not easy to foresee, as Bourke has written:[120]

> 'Complexity breeds complexity. The new superannuation scheme will operate in a complex superannuation industry and the design of the scheme has attempted to capture all eventualities, making it complex as well.'

The year 2003 may bring all kinds of creature, undreamt of by the legislation, or this writer, into the light.

IV   CHILDREN

A case which concerns the operation of Part VII of the Family Law Act 1975, as amended in 1995, is the decision of Nicholson CJ of the Family Court of Australia in *Re Nathan (Limited Contact Consent Orders).*[121] The contested proceedings involved allegations of sexual abuse against the father, who strongly contested the allegations. The matter was part-heard and, at the time of the adjournment, the Chief Justice indicated that he could not avoid making an order for supervised contact in the short term. The mother had indicated that she was not unhappy with such an order on a regular and, indeed, frequent basis. However, on the matter being resumed, minutes of consent orders were handed up which provided for a limited form of contact.

In making orders which were in accordance with those minutes, the Chief Justice expressed[122] the concern, '... that children do have a right to know and love their fathers and have contact with them'. He was, thus, concerned that the consent orders unduly inhibited that prospect. Nicholson CJ went on to say[123] that the contact which had been agreed was a very much more limited contact than he

---

[118]   G Watts and S Bourke, 'Superannuation – What to do between now and 28 December 2002' (2001) 15(3) *Australian Family Lawyer* 7 at 11.

[119]   Should some interim distribution of property need to be made in the meantime, that must be achieved by way of interim orders. The new legislation provides that, if a s 79 order (other than an interim order) is in force on 28 December 2002, then the benefit of the new law will be lost.

[120]   Op cit, n 93 above, at 21.

[121]   (2001) FLC 93–078.

[122]   Ibid at 88, 360.

[123]   Ibid at 88, 361.

himself would have ordered. In all the circumstances, however, he considered that the situation represented, '... a classic case of where what is essentially private law limits the ability of the court to make orders in the form that it would prefer, in that the husband cannot be forced to have contact if he does not wish it or wish to pursue it ...'. Nicholson CJ is, of course, correct in that s 60B(s)(a) of the Family Law Act 1975, as amended in 1995, states that, '... children have the right to know or be cared for by both parents, regardless of whether their parents are married, separated, have never married or have never lived together ...'. On the other hand, problems which attach to allegations of sexual abuse are too well known as to need documentation.

Nathan apart, 2001 has not been an especially interesting year so far as the operation of the Family Law Act is concerned. We may have to wait until the full effect of the 1995 amendments is felt.

V MARRIAGE

There can be no doubt that a major landmark has been established by the decision of Chisholm J in *In re Kevin (Validity of Marriage of Transsexual)*.[124] At the outset, it must be said that the judgment is extraordinarily comprehensive and scholarly and its conclusions, for those reasons alone, will be difficult to refute on appeal, which is being heard at the time of writing.[125]

In *Kevin*, the applicants, who had gone through a ceremony of marriage in 1999, had applied for a declaration that their marriage was valid. The issue was whether the husband, who was a female-to-male transsexual, was male at the time of the marriage. The Commonwealth Attorney-General had intervened[126] and submitted that the husband was not male for the purposes of the Family Law Act[127] and, hence, that the application ought to be dismissed on the basis of the decision of Ormrod J in *Corbett v Corbett (otherwise Ashley)*.[128]

The pertinent facts were that the husband was identified as a girl at birth and appropriately named. His genitalia and gonads were female and he had, and continues to have, female chromosomes. On the other hand, he had, for as long as he was able to remember, perceived himself as being male, so that, despite pressure to dress and behave as a girl, he wore boys' clothes whenever he could. He had many masculine attributes and saw himself as a boy when growing up. At school, he was harassed at times because of his male appearance and attitude and had described his adolescence, with the consequent feminisation of his body, as a time of 'pain and stress'. During that time and in his early adult years, he mainly kept his thoughts to himself and felt extremely alienated from people.

From 1994, he generally presented as male, though, in 1995, he saw an article about sex reassignment surgery and had feelings of excitement and relief when he read of other people in his situation and how they had, '... discovered medical

---

[124] (2001) FLC 93–087.
[125] Late February 2002.
[126] See Family Law Act 1975, Part IX.
[127] Ibid, s 43(a).
[128] [1971] P 83.

means to express their true sex as men'. He then embarked on hormone treatment which led to the growth of coarse hair on his face, chest, legs and stomach, as well as a deeper voice. In 1997, he had surgery to reduce his breasts to male size and, during the following year, he had further surgery consisting of a total hysterectomy and bilateral oophorectomy. These procedures constituted 'sexual reassignment surgery' for the purposes of relevant State legislation.[129] In effect, the surgery meant that he could no longer function as a female, especially for the purposes of reproduction and sexual intercourse.

The parties met in 1996, when the husband told his future spouse of his predicament. She regarded him as male and strongly supported his wish to 'bring his body into harmony with his mind'. The following year, they began living together and agreed to marry. Later in the year, the husband changed his given name to Kevin and, some months later, the couple applied successfully to an IVF programme, and the wife became pregnant through an anonymous sperm donor. The expert team involved in the IVF programme concluded that the husband should be considered male biologically and culturally and the parties be considered as being a 'heterosexual couple with infertility consequent to absent sperm production'.

In 1998, the wife changed her family name to that of her husband and, later in that year, the husband obtained a new birth certificate on which his sex was shown as male. The wife gave birth to a male child in November of that year. Prior, however, to that, they were married by a civil marriage celebrant, after having disclosed the preceding history to that person. A relevant certificate was issued. It appeared that, at the date of the marriage, the husband's secondary sexual characteristics were such that he would have been subject to immediate ridicule had he attempted to appear in public dressed as a woman – he could not, for instance, have entered a woman's public lavatory and he was eligible to be given an Australian passport which showed his changed name and which stated his sex as male. It appeared that he had been treated as male for various legal and social purposes including by his employer, Medicare, the Australian Taxation Office, and other public and private authorities including banks and clubs. There was also evidence from numerous family, friends and work colleagues who testified to his general acceptance as being male and to his role as husband and father. Finally, psychiatric examination of the husband revealed that there was no evidence of psychosis or delusional disorder and that he presented as 'an intelligent, emotionally warm man who would be accepted socially as completely masculine'; further his 'brain sex or mental sex' was male and that he was 'psychologically male and that this had been the situation all his life'.

Expert medical evidence had been tendered by the applicants from a number of sources regarding transsexualism and related matters and it was, hence, submitted that that evidence indicated that brain or mental sex was an important, or even definitive, factor in determining a person's sexual identity. The Attorney-General argued that the evidence did not permit any such conclusions to be drawn. Thus, the instant issue was whether the word 'man' ought to be given its ordinary and contemporary meaning. This view could be contrasted with the submissions made on behalf of the Attorney-General where it was claimed that the

---

[129]   Births Deaths and Marriages Registration Act 1995 (NSW), s 32A.

word ought to be that given to it as at the date of the Marriage Act 1961 and that meaning had been formulated in *Corbett.*[130]

Chisholm J granted the declaration which the applicants had sought and, in so doing, discussed medical evidence in relation to transsexualism and like matters and considered legal developments in various jurisdictions. The judge, first of all, took the view[131] that, for the purpose of ascertaining the validity of marriage under Australian law, the question whether a person is a man or a woman must be determined at the time of the marriage. Chisholm J then turned his attention to the *Corbett* decision and concluded[132] that he did not find the reasoning in that case to be persuasive or substantial. Secondly, he took the view[133] that, unless the context required a different interpretation, the words 'man' and 'woman' as used in legislation had their ordinary and *contemporary*[134] meaning to Australian usage. That meaning included post-operative transsexuals in accordance with their sexual reassignment. In reaching that conclusion, Chisholm J applied[135] the decisions of the New South Wales Court of Criminal Appeal in *R v Harris and McGuiness*[136] and of the Full Court of the Federal Court of Australia in *Secretary, Department of Social Security v SRA.*[137]

Of course, an immediate issue was whether special considerations pertained to marriage law, as opposed to criminal law or social security law with which the earlier Australian cases had been concerned. Chisholm J rejected that view emphatically and commented[138] that he had not 'found any discussion that identifies any considerations that might compel the result that marriage law should resist the humane and practical trend to accept the reality of gender reassignment'.

Ultimately, Chisholm J concluded[139] that, in the present case, the husband, at birth, had female chromosomes, gonads and genitals but was a man for the purpose of the law of marriage, at the time of the marriage, especially having regard to six particular matters. These were, first, that the husband had always perceived himself as being male. Secondly, he had been perceived as male by those who had known him since he was a young child. Thirdly, prior to the marriage, the husband had gone through a full process of transsexual reassignment which involved hormone treatment and irreversible surgery which had been carried out by appropriately qualified medical practitioners. Fourthly, at the time of the marriage, in appearance, characteristics and behaviour he was perceived and accepted as a man, by his family, friends and work colleagues. Fifthly, he had been accepted as a man for various social and legal purposes, including his name, admission to the artificial insemination programme, and events subsequent to his marriage. Finally, his marriage as a man was accepted, in full knowledge of the circumstances, by his family, friends and work colleagues.

---

[130] See n 128 above.
[131] (2001) FLC 93–087 at 88, 536.
[132] Ibid at 88, 542.
[133] Ibid at 88, 545.
[134] Author's emphasis.
[135] (2001) FLC 93–087 at 88, 545 ff.
[136] (1988) 17 NSWLR 158.
[137] (1993) 118 ALR 467.
[138] (2001) FLC 93–087 at 88, 569.
[139] Ibid at 88, 576.

It will be apparent that *Kevin* is an important decision, whatever its ultimate outcome. The scholarly and detailed nature of the judge's analysis and conclusion is surely bound to have considerable, and proper, effect, outside its jurisdiction of origin.

VI CONCLUSIONS

2001 represents some of the major difficulties with which legislatures, policy makers and the Family Court have been grappling for some time. The issue of judicial bias, often the result of erroneous allegations by unrepresented litigants, has arisen more than one would like. In turn, the position of the ever-increasing number of unrepresented litigants is proving a justifiable cause for concern. In property matters, the nature of the discretion conferred by s 79 of the Family Law Act has been a source of dispute from fairly early in the Act's operation.[140] Superannuation has likewise caused serious problems since Fogarty J's decision in *Crapp (No 2)*.[141] One can only wait to see whether developments in 2002 will resolve any or all of these continuing issues. One matter, though, is quite certain – evidentiary problems in family law in Australia will continue, as they have always done.

---

[140]   See *Mallett v Mallett* (1984) 156 CLR 605; cf *Wardman and Hudson* (1978) FLC 90–466.

[141]   (1979) FLC 90–615.

BRAZIL

SAME-SEX COUPLES

Maria Berenice Dias[*]

I INTRODUCTION

Questions of sexuality always were, and still are, surrounded by myth and taboo and so-called 'sexual deviations' are seen as an insult to morals and decency. They are deeply rejected by society. Anything outside the established model is 'abnormal' – contrary to established norms – as not fitting the patterns of a polarised and very limited vision.

In Brazil, as in practically all countries of the world, an attempt is made to deny that affective bonds exist between persons of the same sex and this produces an institutionalised prejudice. This majority attitude inhibits the legislature from creating rules for situations that do not fit moral stereotypes, for fear of the hostility of conservative elements, and engenders stigma, both politically and electorally.

This attitude is mirrored in the courts. As well as an inactive legislature, we have an extremely timid and conservative judiciary, refusing to recognise relationships of persons of the same sex. For want of legal norms, judges find themselves prevented from granting rights or enforcing obligations based on homosexual bonds.

But turning a blind eye does not make reality disappear. Legislative omission and judicial timidity only foment discrimination, giving rise to injustice, unjust enrichment and the exacerbation of prejudice.

II IN THE CONSTITUTIONAL SPHERE

The Federal Constitution, dating from 1988, sets up a state of democracy under law. The core of the current legal system in Brazil is respect for human dignity, based on the principles of freedom and equality.

The Magna Carta emphasises, as the fundamental aim of the Federal Republic of Brazil:

'to promote the welfare of all, without discrimination based on origin, race, sex, colour, age or any other grounds.'

---

[*] Chief Judge of the Tribunal of Justice of Rio Grande do Sul; Vice-president of the Brazilian Institute of Family Law (IBDFam); author of 'Homosexual Union: Prejudice and Justice', *www.mariaberenicedias.com.br*. The editor wishes to thank Peter Schofield for assistance with the translation of this article.

Although it is essential to recognise that this ban on sexual discrimination extends to discrimination against homosexuality, neither the guidelines nor the principles of the general law are wide enough to ensure respect for freedom of sexual orientation. In face of this, human rights movements have long sought to have the phrase 'sexual orientation' added to our Magna Carta. However, the Project for Constitutional Amendment, dating from 1995, has yet to receive approval.

III   IN THE LEGISLATIVE SPHERE

Among the several Bills presented so far one only (No 1.151/95) is being proceeded with, its name having been changed from 'civil union' to 'registered civil partnership', the alteration having been approved so as not to confuse it with marriage.

All it proposes is to authorise the formulation of a written pact, registered in the appropriate book in the Office of the Notary for the Civil Registration of Natural People. As the statement of objectives of the Project says, it is not intended to give homosexual partnership the same status as marriage. It seeks to help same-sex partners by way of a guarantee of the priority of their civil rights.

This legislative proposal recognises same-sex partnerships. Without requiring the existence of an affective relationship between the partners, the Project clearly aims to protect homosexual relationships, creating a legal bond giving rise to consequences not only of a proprietary, but also of a personal nature, which cannot be set exclusively in the framework of the law of obligations.

Note that only the unmarried, widowed or divorced can enter into such a pact, in the form of a public document to be submitted for registration in the *registro cartorario*. It has the effect of an impediment to the alteration of the partners' civil status while it remains in force, and nullifies any such contract with more than one person. In either case, breach amounts to the crime of ideological falsehood (*falsidade ideológica*) punishable by one to five years' imprisonment.

The signing of such a pact does not authorise changes of surnames.

There is a free choice of proprietary regime, which can take effect retroactively. It is possible to impose duties, impediments and mutual obligations, but there is an express prohibition on dispositions regarding adoption, tutorship or care of children or adolescents, even if these are children of one of the partners.

Subject to certain limitations, the social welfare and succession rights of the partners are guaranteed. The right to a usufruct – manifestly protective in nature – is obviously aimed at providing maintenance, and serves to demonstrate, emphatically, that this is a form of family relationship. This being so, there is no justification for omitting a maintenance provision, since maintenance is provided for in the event of death, but not if the relationship breaks down. There is, however, nothing to stop the parties including a maintenance provision in their pact.

The Project provides for equal division, if the assets in the deceased's estate arose as a result of activity in which the surviving partner collaborated. The effect of the provision is far from clear, because it necessitates proof of common effort, but it does establish equal division of the property. Moreover, the partner takes precedence over ascendants and descendants, depriving these of the use of the assets. So long as the survivor does not enter a new partnership pact, s/he is accorded the usufruct of a quarter of the estate if the deceased had children, and of half if there are no ascendants. This also lacks clarity, given that, in another article, the survivor is accorded the entire inheritance, absent descendants or ascendants.

Likewise when a trustee is to be appointed (in cases of incapacity) the partner takes precedence over relatives. The integrity of the common home and, in the case of foreigners, nationality rights are guaranteed. Also there is an option of declaring the partnership for income tax purposes, and the income of both partners can be taken into account for the purchase or renting of immovable property.

Partnership ends on death or on court order, on the grounds of breach, or of the allegation that either party no longer wishes to continue it. Even if the partners consent, a court order to end the partnership is necessary. This last requirement is unjustifiable in this type of union, given that extramarital (heterosexual) relationships – so-called stable unions – can be dissolved without judicial intervention. Only in the case of dissolution of a marriage should the stamp of judicial power be required.

Even though the Project has been regarded as timid in comparison to legislation in other countries, it has been a dozen times listed for voting without being approved. In any event, it has little prospect of earning early approval. Despite the fact that the 'GLS' (gays, lesbians and sympathisers) movements are very articulate and active, the forces of conservatism in the National Congress, to which all the religious groups have allied themselves, form a practically immovable obstacle. So it seems improbable that Brazil will get any legislation to regulate such relationships, which are still regarded as 'marginal'.

Where there has been proliferation is in local legislation to ban discriminatory actions, with some State Constitutions inserting the right to freedom of sexual orientation in their texts, under the heading of fundamental rights.

IV   IN THE COURTS

Even where the law is surrounded by an aura of preconception, the judge must not be afraid to do justice. The judge is there to protect rights, not to block them simply because particular postures do not accord with conventional 'correctness'. Having a lifestyle not provided for in legislation does not mean living on the margin of the law, much less being deprived of rights. The mere fact that the law does not provide for a situation is no justification for denying access to justice or for trying to use the law to manage people's lives.

The lack of legislation covering the emergent rights involved in homosexual relationships has not prevented certain questions from being raised in the courts.

Because of the difficulty in obtaining recognition of the existence of an affective relationship as the basis of claims before a court, the rights obtained have been restricted and the benefits granted few, and this across a very limited range.

We must now examine the state of judicial decisions in Brazil in this field.

A   The jurisdiction of the courts

Regardless of what rights are the subject of the claim, actions based on the existence of a homosexual, affective bond rely on this fact as a ground of the suit. However, in almost all the decided cases, the most that has been recognised is a de facto partnership – a matter confined to the law of obligations – in no way envisaged as creating a family situation comparable to a stable heterosexual union. This characterisation prevents the application of the whole range of effects which can only be found in family law.

Resistance to regarding same-sex bonds as a family relationship has meant that claims based on such relationships have been allocated to the Civil Court and not the Family Court. The ground-breaking decision of the Family Division of the Court of Justice of Rio Grande do Sul, dated June 1999, held that the Family Court has jurisdiction to hear the case of a homosexual relationship (OH no 599.075.496), taking the first step to recognising the relationship's family status.

In the light of this decision on jurisdiction, at least in this State of the Federation, all actions concerned with relations between persons of the same sex have been transferred from Civil Court to Family Court. Likewise, appellate jurisdiction in such cases is attributed to the Family Division of the Court of Justice. It is worth noting that this is the only State where the appellate court sits in specialised divisions whose jurisdiction is determined by the nature of the case. For this reason, 'gaucho justice' is beginning to be regarded as the most progressive, in the field of family law in general, and particularly in relation to same-sex couples.

B   Alimony

Even where cases are being heard in Family Courts, homosexual unions are still considered to fall outside the scope of family law, which keeps out actions for maintenance payments.

The only known judgment on the matter is Agravo de Instrumento no 70000535542, reported by Judge Antonio Carlos Stangler Pereira, in the 8th Civil Chamber of TJRS, rejecting by a majority a claim for interim maintenance on the ending of a relationship of eight years' duration.

C   Division of assets

The most common cause of litigation on the ending of an affective relationship is the division of property acquired while the relationship continued.

In cases concerning the ending of a same-sex relationship, faced with the choice between making an unjust decision or one that conflicts with taboos and prejudices, the very most a somewhat timid judiciary will do is to recognise the right to proportionate sharing.

As no consideration is given to the nature of the relationship of the parties, the matter falls to be determined under Art 1.363 of the Civil Code, dealing with de facto partnership:

'Persons entering a partnership contract mutually undertake to apply their efforts and resources to achieve common objectives.'

Consequently, the basis for granting a division of assets is not the recognition of co-ownership resulting from a commonalty of life, but repugnance at unjust enrichment.

This means that both partners must have participated in the activity in which the assets were acquired, and calls for evidence identifying the economic contribution of each in this to establish the proportional share of each. This solution, while attempting to prevent the impropriety of the one with formal title profiting himself exclusively, in the overwhelming majority of cases produces results which are far removed from justice, whether because the relationship was conducted with such a degree of discretion that evidence is hard to come by, or because only a financial contribution is deemed worthy of consideration. Personal care and mutual devotion are not recognised, nor are domestic activities carried out by one of the pair who does not go out to work. This means we are treating as a partnership de facto, something that is neither more nor less than an affective partnership.

D Succession rights

On the death of a partner, as a rule – and even then not in a large number of cases – all the court considers is the survivor's share of assets acquired in partnership, not the deceased's entire estate. The aim is to divide equally on the basis of a de facto partnership, not to deal with succession rights as would be the case in a family situation. Even in the absence of heirs, the right to succession as heir or successor is not raised.

The decisions vary, but in most the claim is rejected in the face of the enormous difficulty in establishing the existence of a de facto partnership. The partner is systematically refused the status of an heir, excluding him from the rights and duties of heirship.

The Superior Tribunal of Justice, in its judgment in a special appeal, laid down that the partner has the right to receive half the property acquired by common effort where a de facto partnership is found to exist (REST 148897/MG).

The result of such decisions is to give an undeserved benefit to distant relatives, who had often rejected, shunned and ridiculed the deceased's sexual orientation. In other cases, for want of relatives, the estate goes to the State as bona vacantia, rather than to the person who should have been recognised as having the right to inherit.

Moreover, there was no development of the line of judicial reasoning.

The pioneering decision which went so far as to treat such relationships as a true family entity was also handed down by the Court of Justice of Rio Grande do Sul on 14 March 2001. By majority, the 7th Civil Chamber – of which I have the honour of presiding – in Civil Appeal no 7000138898 (the reporting judge was Appellate Judge José Carlos Teixeira Georgis) held as follows:

'HOMOSEXUAL UNION, RECOGNITION, DIVISION OF ASSETS, CONTRIBUTION OF THE PARTNERS, EQUAL SHARES. The pharisaism of refusing to recognise that unions between persons of the same sex exist and to give legal effect to the rights that result from them is no longer permissible. Although the object of pervasive prejudice, they are realities judges cannot ignore, however reluctant they may be to accept change. They have consequences similar to those of other affective relationships, to be found by application of reasoning by analogy and of the general principles of law and in reliance on the constitutional principles of human dignity and equal treatment. On his basis, property acquired in the course of such a relationship should be shared as in the case of a stable union, the best model from which to work deductively. Appeal allowed in part, so that division be made between the partners. Voted in favour.'

Faced with a gap in the law, the court applied by analogy the legislation governing extramarital unions. Seeking support in laws which apply to stable unions, on the presumption of mutual collaboration, the court ordered equal division of assets acquired while living together.

Following this decision, similar rights have been recognised in more than three States. Justice has removed the blindfold from its eyes in granting the partner an equal share. Once this development of seeing such relationships as affective bonds becomes consolidated, we shall have gone a long way towards softening society's aversion to them. There is a tendency to accepting as right that which the courts hold to be so.

So judges have shown courage in exercising their function of renewal and, through decided cases, models of general conduct are being established. Even in dealing with the case of which he is seised, the judge acts as the agent of social transformation. The fact that they are of the same biological sex should not of itself prevent rights and obligations from flowing from the fact that two people live together, undertaking duties of mutual assistance, in a true community of love and mutual respect. So there is an irreversible trend towards regarding an affective relationship as a family entity meriting State support and protection, irrespective of the sex of the partners.

E   Status as dependant

Cases in which the dependent status of a same-sex partner has been recognised, giving entitlement to welfare and social work support, are few and far between.

This gives enormous significance to proceedings commenced by the Federal public prosecution service intended to have general effect (erga omnes). On the basis of violation of constitutional dogma and the contravention of the principle of equal rights, forbidding sexual discrimination, preliminary recognition was given to the dependent status of the companions of homosexual members of the federal social insurance system, guaranteeing support and protection and the receipt of a pension on the death of the insured.

This preliminary ruling, which has since been confirmed at each appellate level, led the National Institute for Social Security to issue Normative Instruction no 25/2000 which establishes, with the force of a judgment, steps to be taken to grant benefits to homosexual companions.

Although of an administrative character, this is the first regulatory measure which considers homosexual relations – the first move to launch them in the legal sphere.

So, until there is a final decision on the merits of the case, welfare rights are guaranteed in Brazil on the ending of a relationship, even if this predated the measure.

V ADOPTION

The most controversial question to arise, and the one that has most divided opinion, is that of the right of same-sex partners to adopt. The major doubt on which objection to allowing adoption is based, whether by an individual or by a homosexual couple, centres on anxiety as to the healthy development of the child.

There is great resistance for fear of possible harm to the child through lack of role models, which could lead later to psychological problems. People ask whether the child could become confused as to his own gender identity, unable to refer to the way a carer of each sex relates to the other, with the risk of becoming homosexual also. There is apprehension too at the risk that the child might be rejected in his social milieu or abused by contemporaries and neighbours, which could, in theory, produce psychological disturbance. There is also a tendency to regard such relationships as promiscuous and immoral leading to sexual activity in the minor's presence, or abuse of him by one of the parents.

These worries are confidently dismissed by those who have made a study of this type of family. Essentially, no differences were found in the gender identity, sexual behaviour or sexual orientation of such children. In face of these findings the myth that living with parents of the same sex can compromise the emotional stability of the child cannot be supported. Therefore the assertion that the child who is raised in a homosexual household will be socially stigmatised and his development will be put at risk, or that he will suffer from the lack of heterosexual role models or that his gender identity will be confused is not substantiated.

So we are forced to conclude that current scruples are based on prejudice. Principles must be overturned, values reviewed, and an opportunity made for new discussions and the dismissing of objections, so that adoption by individuals or by homosexual couples can be allowed. Resistance to this results in preventing a considerable number of children who could benefit from a life surrounded by affection and care from being taken out of a marginal existence.

Personal attitudes and subjective convictions of a moral order cannot be allowed to impede the recognition that a child without parents or home would have an upbringing more suited to the needs of life if integrated into a family, whether of persons of different sex or not.

The law dealing with questions of children and adolescents dates from 1990. This is the Statute for Childhood and Adolescence, surely one of the most progressive laws on the protection of minors, and places no restrictions on the possibility of adoption. The right is given to men as also to women, jointly or individually, making no reference to the adopter's sexual orientation.

However, adoption orders are rarely made in favour of homosexuals when they do not conceal their situation. Magistrate Siro Darlan de Oliveira is practically alone in finding a homosexual applicant capable of adopting and making an order in his favour, and was upheld on both points by the Tribunal of Justice of Rio de Janeiro (AC14,332/98 and AC14,979/98). Now this State is conducting a campaign to encourage homosexuals to adopt children who have been abandoned in institutions. Even so, adoption is ordered in favour of an individual alone, even if he or she has a companion who will be living with the child.

This resistance cannot be justified even by reasons of registration. The legal decision to name the adopters as parents in the birth registration, in simple substitution for the birth parents, cannot be a justification for opposing the possibility of adoption by two persons of the same sex. There is no reason why two men or two women should not be registered as parents. Even if the law did not contemplate adoption by a homosexual couple, there is no justification for obstructing this.

Despite the lack of grounds for the restriction, we know of no adoption application being made by, and still less of any order being granted to, a homosexual household and this can only create unjust situations to the disadvantage of the child in particular.

The fact is that children do live in homosexual households. Allowing only one of the partners to adopt ensures the child's rights to maintenance and benefits as well as succession rights only from the adopting partner. When a relationship with no registered tie ends – on separation or the death of a partner – this limitation brings about unjustified loss, depriving the child of rights in relation to the other partner who also stood in the relationship of father or mother to him.

We are driven to conclude that, paradoxically, while intending to safeguard and protect the child, we end up depriving him of the possibility of benefiting from what is his by right, a restriction which contravenes the Constitutional Charter which the law aims to establish.

Difficulties of every kind – existing or potential – make it necessary to seek other ways in which to consolidate a family in relation to children. What usually happens is that a lesbian couple has the ovum of one partner fertilised *in vitro*, using donor sperm, placed in the other's uterus and so carried to term. As the child will be registered solely in the name of the birth mother, and not the genetic mother, the latter has no legal bond – not even contractually – with the child which is hers after all. Registration in the name of only one mother gives rights and duties only in relation to her.

Male couples use the so-called 'rent-a-womb' system; the woman is impregnated by artificial insemination using a mixture of semen from the pair, so neither can be identified as genitor. The baby is regarded as the child of both. Again, in such cases, the impossibility of a joint adoption stops the child having any rights in relation to the non-adopting partner who is equally regarded as his father.

A recent decision, giving custody of a 10-year-old to the (woman) partner of the child's deceased mother, caused a major reaction. The biological mother, a well-known singer, never concealed her lesbian relationship over many years, regularly speaking of her concern for her partner in media interviews. During the 16 years they lived together, this popular singer gave birth to a son fathered by a man who died before the birth. The child was registered in the mother's sole name. He always lived with both women, regarding as mother the partner who looked after him while his biological mother was working in shows on tour. When she died, the paternal grandfather applied for the custody of his grandson, but, respecting the mother's wishes, this was actually given to the woman who had been fulfilling the maternal role.

VI   INCLUSION AS A HUMAN RIGHT

It is essential to recognise that sexuality is an integral part of the human condition. Self-realisation and assurance of respect for liberty come only with freedom of sexual orientation.

As rights are categorised according to degree, we must recognise that sexuality is a first degree right, since it concerns sexual freedom as well as equal treatment, whatever one's sexual tendency. It is a matter of individual liberty, the freedom of the individual being, as are the other first degree rights, inalienable and imprescriptible. It is a natural right that a human being has from birth since it arises from human nature itself.

Nor can we omit to treat sexual orientation as a second degree right, a part of a social category that has to be protected. Deprivation cannot be understood only in economic terms. There is social and legal deprivation when the legal system is inadequate. Victims of deprivation include women, the elderly, those handicapped in their senses, blacks, Jews and, of course, also homosexuals, who, like the others, have always suffered social exclusion.

Likewise, the right to sexuality is moving forward towards inclusion as a third degree right. Among third degree rights are rights forming part of human dignity, diversely attributed to individual subjects and solidarity rights diversely attributed to their objects. These are human rights by nature, among which is included the free exercise of sexuality. There can be no contravention of the fundamental freedom of every human being in relation to his sexuality, which is part of the right of privacy and must remain unqualified.

VII   THE NEW CIVIL CODE

After 27 years in the legislative process, despite much controversy, the new Civil Code which was approved in the current year came into force on 10 January 2003. This Code was out of date already by the time it was approved, since it was drafted before the passing of the Law of Divorce in 1977 and the Federal Constitution, promulgated in 1988, which have revolutionised in particular the field of family law.

So it is quite inappropriate that the new Civil Code is silent on ties which are not defined in terms of the sexual difference of the members of the couple. As the legislature has had a Project before it for more than five years to pass a law to give legal recognition to the so-called 'registered civil partnership', there was no justification for excluding this from the recently approved Code.

There is no constitutional obstacle to recognising such unions as a form of family, as appears from the justification of the new Code. Article 226, subs 3 of the Federal Constitution says:

> 'To give effect to the protection of the State, a stable union between a man and a woman is recognised as a family entity, and their marriage must be facilitated by law.'

However, the Constitutional Charter does not say that a tie between two men or two women is not to be considered a family entity. At most, it could be said that there was no requirement that the law should facilitate their marriage. Unions with diverse characteristics exist as family entities, so the law must provide for them.

The fact is that, while there is a lacuna in the law, there should be a search for a means of correcting this omission which is clearly based on prejudice. Only this will give social efficacy to the constitutional guarantee of equality, prerequisite of individual liberty and basis of the democratic rule of law.

VIII HOMOSEXUAL UNIONS

In their comfortable way, courts try to see nothing and to grant nothing. At most they resort to subtle devices using the law of obligations, identifying what is no more and no less than an affective partnership as a de facto partnership. Excluding such relationships from the scope of family law results in a denial of the rights that flow from family relationships, such as equal shares of assets, inheritance, housing, maintenance and welfare benefits among many others.

Relegating such questions to the law of obligations at least creates a paradox, since family judges end up applying a different branch of the law, outside their own jurisdiction.

It is no use continuing to think in terms of prejudices, that is with predetermined concepts permeated with conservatism. It is necessary to think in judicial concepts, and that means thinking new concepts.

This is the fundamental mission of judicial reasoning, which must play its part as a transforming agent on stagnant social concepts. Just as in the case of the stable union, where the alteration of the social concept of so-called 'concubinage' was led by those applying the law, who drew legal consequences from such relationships, we have to go to the source of the Constitution to get homosexual relationships recognised as a family entity.

At least until the legislature follows the trail of justice and sets fire to the State's neglect in failing to regulate such relationships which, in Brazil as much as in other countries, need regulation, it is up to the judicial power to take responsibility.

Although the Constitution has come, in modernising vein, to give State protection to the family, regardless of the celebration of marriage, it still ignores the existence of family entities formed by persons of the same sex. Now there is no longer discrimination between families based on whether there is a marriage. Protection is not confined to situations where there are children, and one-parent families are also protected. If neither issue nor the ability to procreate are essential for the cohabitation of two people to be legally protected, it is inappropriate to exclude from the concept families based on homo-affective relationships.

If all the characteristics of a family are present – life in common, affective bonds, shared expenses – the same rights must be accorded as to heterosexual relationships with those characteristics. Where there is a lacuna in the law, for want of a rule, the judge must have recourse to Art 4 of the Introductory Law of the Civil Code, which calls for application by analogy and reference to the general principles of law. Analogies can be drawn with other affective relationships such as marriage and stable unions.

As long as the law does not keep up with social development, the changes in mentality and the evolution of morality, no one, least of all those who apply the law, can close their eyes to such developments and perpetrate injustice in the name of discriminatory and prejudiced concepts. Legal questions must not be confused with moral or religious ones.

The courts have accepted the same responsibility in relation to extramarital unions. They must now show the same independence and courage for homosexual unions. Both are affective in nature, based on loving commitment, and it is essential to recognise that stable unions exist in forms which include both heterosexual and homosexual unions. Both deserve the same protection and, so long as legislation does not come forward specifically to regulate them, the legislation relating to family ties should be applied.

It is essential to recognise that homo-affective ties – much more than homosexual relationships – form a social category that must no longer be discriminated against or marginalised by prejudice. It is time for the State that wishes to be democratic and which enshrines the major principle of respect for human dignity, to advance to a recognition that all citizens have the right of individual freedom, to the social right of choice, and to the human right of happiness.

CANADA

CHILDREN, SAME-SEX MARRIAGE AND COHABITATION

Martha Bailey[*]

I INTRODUCTION

This report focuses on children and on cohabiting couples of the same and the opposite sex, which were the subjects of important judicial decisions and legislative reforms over the past year.

The Supreme Court of Canada addressed the significance of race as a factor in determining the best interests of the child and the standard of appellate review for custody and access cases. The Ontario Court of Appeal, in a more controversial decision that will probably be appealed to the Supreme Court of Canada, ruled that the 'reasonable chastisement' defence to a charge of assault on children in one's care does not violate the constitutional rights of children.

In regard to same-sex couples, the most important judicial decisions were lower court rulings in two of the three constitutional challenges to the exclusion of same-sex couples from marriage that have been launched in the provinces of British Columbia, Ontario and Quebec. The courts were split, and this issue will remain at the centre of debate on family law reform over the next year.

The most important legislative reforms took place in Quebec and in Saskatchewan. In Quebec, legislators unanimously passed a broad 'civil union' law that permits same-sex and opposite-sex couples who register to obtain the same legal rights and obligations as married couples in matters within provincial legislative jurisdiction. Saskatchewan also enacted extensive reforms to equalize the position of married and cohabiting couples of the same or opposite sex. Manitoba enacted some limited reforms in 2001, and in 2002 introduced two further pieces of legislation that will extend marital rights and obligations that are within the legislative authority of the province to same-sex or opposite-sex couples who either cohabit for a requisite period or register their 'common-law partnership'. Alberta also introduced a Bill that extends further rights and obligations to 'adult interdependent partners' on the basis of cohabitation or contract. In assessing these legislative initiatives, an important theme is the extent to which couples should be able to choose legal rights and obligations by marrying or registering their union or entering into a contract rather than having legal rights and obligations extended willy nilly to couples who cohabit for a requisite period.

Spousal status as a burden thrust upon those who cohabit is a theme in the key decision on cohabiting opposite-sex couples, a public law case on the issue of entitlement to social assistance payments as a 'sole support parent'. The definition

[*] Associate Professor, Faculty of Law, Queen's University, Kingston, Ontario.

of 'spouse' in Ontario's social assistance statute, which was broad enough to capture relationships that were not spousal in nature and which had the effect of reducing the number of persons entitled to public support, was successfully challenged on the grounds that it discriminated against single mothers on the basis of sex, marital status and receipt of social assistance.

II CHILDREN

A Race and custody

The Supreme Court of Canada has in the past stated that race is a relevant factor to consider in a custody dispute involving a mixed-race family but is not determinative and that its importance will depend on the circumstances of each case.[1] In *Van de Perre v Edwards*, the Supreme Court confirmed this principle and also clarified the standard of appellate review in custody cases.[2]

The mother in this case was an unmarried white Canadian. The father was a married black American with a wife and twin daughters. The parties carried on an 18-month sexual relationship in Vancouver, where the mother lived and the father, a professional basketball player, resided during the basketball season. The mother gave birth to a son in June 1997. When the child was three months old, the mother brought proceedings against the father for custody and child support. In February 1999, the trial judge awarded custody to the mother with access to the father. The father appealed. During the hearing of the appeal, the Court of Appeal invited the father's wife to apply for admission as a party. The wife did so and requested joint custody with the father. The wife's application and the request for joint custody were granted. The mother was granted generous access.

The Court of Appeal found that the trial judge had erred in failing to consider the bonds that existed between the child and the father's wife and other children and the father's extended family, putting too much emphasis on the attitude of the parties towards each other and the father's various extra-marital affairs, and basing his decision on stereotypical views including the tender years doctrine.

The Supreme Court of Canada stated that there was no basis for the Court of Appeal's conclusion that the trial judge had erred. The trial judge did consider the father's family to the extent that evidence was available. The attitude of the parties towards each other was relevant because the child should be with someone who fosters the relationship between the child and the non-custodial parent. That the father and his wife blamed the mother for the affair and believed the mother to be a 'gold-digger' might be relevant in this respect, and it was not an error for the judge to consider this. In regard to the father's extra-marital affairs, the trial judge appropriately considered these only to the extent that they affected the father's ability to parent and the support network he would have as custodial parent. In the Edwards household, the wife carried primary responsibility for raising the children and the father's parenting experience and abilities were limited, in part because of

---

[1]   *H (D) v M (H)* [1999] 1 SCR 328. The judgments of the Supreme Court of Canada are available online at *http://www.scc-csc.gc.ca/home/index_e.html*.

[2]   *Van de Perre v Edwards* [2001] 2 SCR 1014.

the time he devoted to his social life. The father's marriage was weak because of his extra-marital affairs. The wife was a good mother, but marriage breakdown would negatively affect the father's parenting support system. Even if his marriage were stable:

> 'A trial judge cannot give custody to a father merely because his wife is a good mother ... Here it is Mr Edwards' personal capacity to exercise custody that must be considered, and the support provided by his wife is but a factor to be weighed in assessing these parental abilities.'[3]

Finally, the Supreme Court stated that there was no indication that the trial judge had acted on stereotypical views regarding the role of mothers or fathers, black people in general, or black basketball players in particular.

The Supreme Court addressed at length the importance of race in determining custody of a mixed-race child. The three interveners, the African Canadian Legal Clinic, the Association of Black Social Workers and the Jamaican Canadian Association argued that race is a critical factor in custody cases and that it is important to determine which parent will best be able to contribute to a healthy development of racial identity. The Supreme Court took the view that the importance of race in custody cases depends on the circumstances of each case and should be weighed with other relevant factors.

The Supreme Court distinguished between the role of race in adoption cases and in custody cases. In adoption cases, 'the situation might arise whereby the court must make an either/or decision; in other words, the child is either granted or denied exposure to his or her own heritage,' but in custody cases involving the two biological parents the child will normally be exposed to both sides of the child's racial and cultural heritage.[4] However, 'even in adoption cases where it might play a more important role, race is not a determinative factor and its importance will greatly depend on the facts'.[5]

The Supreme Court noted that 'it is generally understood that biracial children should be encouraged to positively identify with both racial heritages' and that 'it is important that the custodial parent recognize the child's need of cultural identity and foster its development accordingly'. Therefore, said the Supreme Court, evidence relating to race in custody cases is relevant and should be accepted, but its significance must be carefully assessed by the trial judge. The Supreme Court noted that general information may be useful but is often contradictory, and it 'may not be sufficient to inform the judge about the current status of race relations in a particular community or the ability of either applicant to deal with these issues'.[6] In this case the parties had not placed much emphasis on the issue of race at trial. The trial judge had not erred in failing to address the issue of race in more detail, given the paucity of evidence on the issue presented at trial; rather the Court of Appeal had erred in giving disproportionate emphasis to the race issue. The Supreme Court stated that 'without evidence, it is not possible for any court,

---

[3]   *Van de Perre v Edwards*, para 30.
[4]   Ibid, para 39.
[5]   Ibid, para 39.
[6]   Ibid, para 40.

and certainly not the Court of Appeal, to make a decision based on the importance of race'.[7]

The Supreme Court's unsurprising conclusion was that race is a relevant factor to consider in a custody dispute involving a mixed-race child and should be considered along with all other relevant factors, but that race is not determinative and its importance must be assessed on a case-by-case basis. The Supreme Court also commented on the error of the Court of Appeal in inviting the father's wife to make a custody application. Even if the Court of Appeal had been correct in initiating the application, which was not the case, it further erred in awarding the father and the wife joint custody without sending the issue of such joint custody back to the trial judge for a hearing.

Van de Perre v Edwards is most important for its clear articulation of the standard of appellate review for custody cases. The British Columbia Court of Appeal had overturned the trial judge's order granting custody to the mother, reasoning that the standard of appellate review is broader in custody cases than in others, and that 'the interests of the child, being paramount, must prevail over those of the parties and of society in finality, and appellate courts must do more than "rubber-stamp" trial judgment unless serious errors appear on their face'.[8] The Supreme Court noted that the notion that an appellate court should make its own determination of the best interests of the child even absent a material error on the part of the trial judge was expressed even more clearly in a subsequent decision of the British Columbia Court of Appeal:

> 'To have a child's future depend on whether an error of law has been shown in a trial judgment, or on whether the trial judge has committed a "palpable and overriding" error in fact-finding, instead of simply being wrong, seems contrary to the principle, which has been stated over and over again by Canadian courts, that the best interests of the child is the primary consideration.'[9]

The Supreme Court rejected this approach and made very clear that appellate courts must put aside the inclination to exercise their own discretion in substitution for that of the trial judge in the absence of material error, saying that 'the narrow power of appellate review does not allow an appellate court to delve into all custody cases in the name of the best interests of the child where there is no material error'.[10]

The Supreme Court dismissed the notion that custody appeals should be treated differently: 'the scope of appellate review does not change because of the type of case on appeal'.[11] An appellate court may overturn a custody order only in the case of a material error, a serious misapprehension of the evidence or an error of law. A narrow scope of appellate review promotes finality, which is important for the parties and the children in custody disputes, and recognizes that the discretion to determine what custody and access arrangements are in the best interests of the child is vested in the trial judge who is able to make a balanced

---

[7]   *Van de Perre v Edwards*, para 43.

[8]   *Van de Perre v Edwards* (2000), 4 RFL (5th) 436 (CA) at para 6.

[9]   *L (A) v K (D)* (2000), 190 DLR (4th) 108 (BCCA) at para 23 (cited in *Van de Perre v Edwards* [2001] 2 SCR 1014 at para 12).

[10]   *Van de Perre v Edwards* [2001] 2 SCR 1014 at para 12.

[11]   Ibid, para 14.

evaluation of the various relevant factors. Failure to address specifically factors that are relevant to the custody determination in reasons for judgment amounts to material error only if such a failure 'gives rise to the reasoned belief that the trial judge must have forgotten, ignored or misconstrued the evidence in a way that affected his conclusion'.[12] The Court of Appeal in *Van de Perre v Edwards* had erred in overturning the trial judgment in the absence of any indication of material error, and therefore the Supreme Court granted the appeal and restored the trial judgment.

Since the Supreme Court's ruling, several provincial appellate courts have applied the principle of appellate review enunciated in *Van de Perre v Edwards* in dismissing appeals of custody orders.[13] In two cases, the Ontario Court of Appeal, applying the *Van de Perre v Edwards* standard of appellate review, granted appeals of custody orders on the basis of material errors on the part of the trial judges.[14] It seems that *Van de Perre v Edwards* will be effective in promoting finality in custody cases, while allowing for the correction of material errors on the part of trial judges.

B   Corporal punishment

Canada's Criminal Code defines the crime of assault as 'the intentional application of force to another person, directly or indirectly, without the consent of that person.'[15] The *de minimus* defence to assault is accepted by Canadian courts and has been successfully invoked by parents and teachers charged with assault of children in their care.[16] Teachers and parents who assault children in their care are provided with an additional, 'reasonable chastisement' defence to the crime of assault in s 43:

---

[12] *Van de Perre v Edwards*, para 15.

[13] *Ryan v Ryan* (2001), 1999 NSR (2d) 401 (CA); *Cox v Brody* [2002] NJ No 111 (CA); *Watson v Tully* [2001] SJ No 613 (CA); *TD v DC* [2001] JQ No 6193 (CA); *Scheiber v Phyall* [2002] BCJ No 1462 (CA); *Brown v Brown* [2002] OJ No 862 (CA); *TM v M* (2002), 165 BCA 88.

[14] See *Johnson v Cleroux* (2002) 23 RFL (5th) (Ont CA), a relocation case, in which the mother was seeking a variation of the custody and access arrangements so that she could move with her children a few hundred kilometres to be with her husband. The Court of Appeal found that the trial judge, who had placed great weight on the expert's report in deciding the case in favour of the father, had made a material error in refusing to admit evidence relevant to the best interests of the child that arose after the expert's report had been prepared and in refusing to allow the mother to cross-examine the expert who had filed a report. The second case was *Segal v Segal* [2002] OJ No 2564 (CA), where the Court of Appeal ruled that the trial judge materially erred in: refusing to admit evidence predating the existing custody order; ordering a change from sole mother custody to joint custody after having determined that a change in custody would traumatize the children; focusing on the best interests of the parents rather than the children; ordering joint custody without addressing the serious communication problems that existed between the parents; issuing an order that was unclear with regard to the responsibilities and rights of each parent and that was bound to lead to conflict; and by ordering unsupervised access by the father contrary to the evidence of the therapist on what arrangements would be in the best interests of the children and without addressing that evidence.

[15] Criminal Code, RSC 1985, c. C-46, s 265. The statutes, regulations, bills and other legislative material of Canada and the provinces and territories are available online at *http://www.acjet.org/cdn_law/LegislativeMaterials.cfm*.

[16] See, eg, *R v Ocampo* [1997] OJ No 4936 (Pro Div) (teacher charged with several counts of assault against several pupils acquitted on all but one count on basis of *de minimus* defence).

'Every schoolteacher, parent or person standing in the place of a parent is justified in using force by way of correction toward a pupil or child, as the case may be, who is under his care, if the force does not exceed what is reasonable in the circumstances.'[17]

Section 43 has been successfully invoked to acquit those charged with assaulting children. An example of a recent case is *R v Bell*, where a father who hit his 11-year-old son with a belt, leaving a bruise on the boy's thigh that matched the shape of the father's belt buckle, was acquitted of assault.[18] There are also cases in which the s 43 defence has been rejected, on the grounds that the assault was not 'by way of correction' or that the force used 'exceeded what was reasonable in the circumstances'.[19]

The Canadian Foundation for Children, Youth and the Law, a not-for-profit organization that advocates on behalf of children, brought an application to challenge the constitutionality of s 43. Supporting the application was the Ontario Association of Children's Aid Societies, the umbrella organization of agencies responsible for child protection, which intervened in the application. The respondent was the Attorney General of Canada, and the Canadian Teachers' Federation and the Coalition for Family Autonomy intervened to argue in support of the constitutionality of s 43. The application did not arise from a specific charge of assault in which s 43 was raised as a defence, and the parties presented their arguments in general terms rather than in reference to a specific factual situation.

The applicant's constitutional argument was based on ss 7, 12 and 15 of the Charter of Rights and Freedoms,[20] which provide as follows:

'7.   Everyone has the right to life, liberty and security of the person and the right not to be deprived thereof except in accordance with the principles of fundamental justice.

12.   Everyone has the right not to be subjected to any cruel and unusual treatment or punishment.

15.   Every individual is equal before and under the law and has the right to the equal protection and equal benefit of the law without discrimination and, in particular, without discrimination based on race, national or ethnic origin, colour, religion, sex, age or mental or physical disability.'

The rights and freedoms set out in the Charter are not absolute. Section 1 of the Charter provides that:

'The Canadian Charter of Rights and Freedoms guarantees the rights and freedoms set out in it subject only to such reasonable limits prescribed by law as can be demonstrably justified in a free and democratic society.'

Laws that violate the rights and freedoms guaranteed by the Charter and that are not 'saved' by s 1 may be declared of no force and effect by the courts, and the applicant was seeking such a declaration in regard to s 43. The judge at first

---

[17]   Criminal Code, s 43.

[18]   *R v Bell* [2001] OTC 380 (Sup Ct).

[19]   See, eg, *R v JOW* [1996] OJ No 4061 (Prov Div) (s 43 defence rejected where mother slapped 13-year-old daughter in face and hit her 17-year-old daughter all over her body, pulled her hair, kicked her, and perforated her eardrum).

[20]   Canadian Charter of Rights and Freedoms, Part I of the Constitution Act 1982, being Schedule B to the Canada Act 1982 (UK), 1982, c 11.

instance dismissed the application, and the Ontario Court of Appeal dismissed the appeal.[21]

The Ontario Court of Appeal primarily addressed the argument that s 43 violates s 7 of the Charter, ie the argument that s 43 infringes the security of the child's person in a manner that does not accord with the principles of fundamental justice. The parties agreed and the court accepted that s 43 infringes the physical security interest of the child by justifying conduct that would otherwise constitute an assault. But the respondent claimed that the infringement is 'in accordance with the principles of fundamental justice' and therefore does not violate s 7 of the Charter, and the court agreed with the respondent.

The court stated that the state 'has clearly and properly determined that [physical punishment of children] is bad' and is 'vigorously pursuing educational programs to discourage and if possible eradicate physical punishment of children' but that 'there is an important state interest to be achieved by not criminalizing the specified conduct'. The 'important state interest' is 'to avoid harm to family life'. The court accepted the views of experts who gave evidence that criminalizing assault of children by parents and teachers 'would have a negative impact upon families and hinder parental and teacher efforts to nurture children'. The court did not satisfactorily explain why the state has an important interest in providing a defence to conduct that would otherwise be an offence and that the state has determined is bad and that the state is trying to eradicate, except by pointing to the experts' views and by pointing out that there are child welfare laws that deal with child abuse.

The court did state by way of reasons for its conclusion that not all violations of personal security violate the principles of fundamental justice,[22] that s 43 is a matter of substantive not procedural law and so the fact that the child has no standing to oppose its application does not violate the procedural dimension of fundamental justice,[23] that the 'best interests of the child' is insufficiently precise in this criminal law context to serve as a principle of fundamental justice,[24] and that s 43 does not violate the principles of fundamental justice by being vague and overly broad.[25]

On the last point, the court stressed the fact that s 43 'decriminalizes only non-abusive physical punishment of children by parents or teachers where the intention is to correct, and correction is possible'.[26] On the issue of what is abusive and what is non-abusive physical punishment, the court accepted the findings of the lower court on the matters of consensus among experts, which included the following:

(1)	corporal punishment of a child under the age of two is wrong and harmful;

(2)	corporal punishment of teenagers is not helpful and potentially harmful;

---

[21]	*Canadian Foundation for Children, Youth and the Law v Canada (Attorney General)* (2002), 57 OR (3d) 511 (CA). The decisions of the Court of Appeal of Ontario are available online at *http://www.ontariocourts.on.ca/appeal.htm.*

[22]	*Canadian Foundation for Children, Youth and the Law v Canada (Attorney General),* para 33.

[23]	Ibid, para 35.

[24]	Ibid, paras 37–40.

[25]	Ibid, paras 42–47.

[26]	Ibid, para 29.

(3)   corporal punishment using objects such as belts, rulers, etc, is physically
        and emotionally harmful and should not be tolerated;
(4)   corporal punishment should never involve a slap or blow to the head;
(5)   corporal punishment that causes injury is child abuse;
(6)   spanking is not recommended, and at best leads to short-term compliance,
        but is not child abuse.[27]

Parents or teachers who used physical punishment on their children that falls
within the court's category of 'abusive', eg by hitting a child with an object or by
causing injury, have successfully invoked the s 43 defence.[28] But the court said
that the fact that 'there have been cases in the past where s 43 was applied to
excuse applications of force that, in light of today's standards and the
unprecedented body of expert evidence filed in this proceeding, should rightly be
characterized as assault' does not mean that s 43 sets a standard that is too vague
or that it is unconstitutional.[29]

The court expressed concern that, in the absence of s 43, parents or teachers
who used 'mild or moderate forms of physical discipline' or who engaged in such
actions as 'putting an unwilling child to bed, removing a reluctant child from the
dinner table, removing a child from a classroom who refused to go, or placing an
unwilling child in a car seat', could be found guilty of assault.[30] The court said it
was 'very significant' that these 'commonly accepted forms of parental discipline
would become criminalized without s 43'.[31] The court did not explain why
common acceptance of physical discipline, accepting, *arguendo*, that such
acceptance exists, justifies violation of the child's security of the person. The
court did not distinguish between moving a child and hitting a child.[32] Nor did it
explore the possibility that teachers and parents may need to move or restrain
unwilling children but do not need to hit them, and that s 43 may be unnecessarily
broad by excusing both types of conduct.

The court expressed the view that s 43 permits parents and teachers to carry
out their important responsibilities. But other groups face similar challenges to
those facing parents and teachers, eg those who provide care to mentally disabled
adults, and manage to do so without being exempted from the general laws of
assault in relation to their charges. In the leading Supreme Court of Canada case
on s 43, *R v Ogg-Moss*, the argument that s 43 should provide a defence to a
caregiver who 'corrected' a 21-year-old mentally disabled man who had spilt milk
by hitting the man repeatedly on the forehead with a metal spoon was rejected,

---

[27]   *Canadian Foundation for Children, Youth and the Law v Canada (Attorney General)*, para 8.
[28]   See, eg, *R v Bell* [2001] OTC 380 (Sup Ct), cited above (father who hit 11-year-old son with belt
        acquitted of assault), and *R v Dunfield* (1990), 103 NBR (2d) 172 (QB) (foster mother who hit
        9-year-old girl with ruler, breaking the ruler, acquitted of assault).
[29]   *Canadian Foundation for Children, Youth and the Law v Canada (Attorney General)*, para 44.
[30]   Ibid, para 23. The quoted words were those of the judge at first instance, who was quoted with
        approval by the court.
[31]   Ibid, para 23.
[32]   The court in *R v Collins* (1996), 192 AR 71 (Prov Ct Crim Div) distinguished between using
        physical force to punish a child and using it to restrain or move a child, and canvassed cases
        involving the latter.

and the court ruled that s 43 must be strictly construed and is limited to chronological children only.[33]

The UN Committee on the Rights of the Child has repeatedly recommended that States prohibit all forms of corporal punishment of children, however light,[34] and, in response to Canada's report to the Committee on measures taken to comply with the Convention on the Rights of the Child, specifically suggested that Canada review its penal legislation allowing corporal punishment of children by parents and teachers.[35] In its most recent report to the Committee, Canada stated that it was reviewing s 43.[36] In the light of the confirmation by the Supreme Court of Canada in *Baker v Canada* that the values reflected in international human rights conventions that have been ratified by Canada may be used as an aid to the interpretation of domestic statues and the Charter,[37] it is notable that the court did not give more attention to the human rights conventions in interpreting the Charter provisions invoked in this application.

The court cited only the Convention on the Rights of the Child and no other relevant human rights treaties and mentioned only Art 19 (right to protection from all forms of physical or mental violence) of the Convention on the Rights of the Child. The court did not refer to the other provisions of the Convention that are inconsistent with Canada's s 43, ie Arts 2 (right to protection from discrimination), 3 (right to protection of the best interests of the child), 12 (right to express views and have views given due weight), 28 (right to school discipline administered in a manner consistent with the child's human dignity), 37 (right to protection from cruel, inhuman or degrading treatment or punishment). Without analysis, the court simply said that Art 19 of the Convention does not explicitly provide that all

---

[33]   *R v Ogg-Moss* [1984] 2 SCR 173. It is permissible, however, to use corporal punishment on mentally disabled children: *R v Park* (1999), 178 NFLD & PEI 194 (Newf SCTD) (teacher who slapped 9-year-old girl with mental disability not guilty of assault because of s 43).

[34]   See, eg Committee on the Rights of the Child, 'Violence Against Children Within the Family and in Schools', September 2001, Report, 28th Sess (CRC/C/111).

[35]   The Committee on the Rights of the Child stated in its concluding observations on Canada's Report, 20 June 1995: '14. Further measures seem to be needed to effectively prevent and combat all forms of corporal punishment and ill-treatment of children in schools or in institutions where children may be placed. The Committee is also preoccupied by the existence of child abuse and violence within the family and the insufficient protection afforded by the existing legislation in that regard', and further: '25. The Committee suggests that the State party examine the possibility of reviewing the penal legislation allowing corporal punishment of children by parents, in schools and in institutions where children may be placed. In this regard and in the light of the provisions set out in Art 3 and 19 of the Convention, the Committee recommends that the physical punishment of children in families be prohibited. In connection with the child's right to physical integrity as recognized by the Convention, namely in its Art 19, 28 and 37, and in the light of the best interests of the child, the Committee further suggests that the State party consider the possibility of introducing new legislation and follow-up mechanisms to prevent violence within the family, and that educational campaigns be launched with a view to changing attitudes in society on the use of physical punishment in the family and fostering the acceptance of its legal prohibition'. Reports to the Committee, responses of the Committee, and other relevant documents are available online at the United Nations Human Rights Committees website: *http://www.unhchr.ch/tbs/doc.nsf/Documentsfrset?OpenFrameSet*.

[36]   Canada has also told the UN Committee Against Torture, both in 1993 and again in 2000, that it is reviewing s 43: see *Concluding observations of the Committee against Torture: Canada*, 26 June 1993, A/48/44, para 307, and Canada's *Report to the UN Committee Against Torture, Convention against Torture and Other Cruel, Inhuman or Degrading Treatment or Punishment*, CAT/C/34/Add.13, 31 May 2000, para 104.

[37]   *Baker v Canada* [1999] 2 SCR 817.

forms of physical punishment should be criminalized, and asserted, 'While the Committee [on the Rights of the Child] recommended that corporal punishment of children be prohibited, it nowhere required that this be done by an extension of criminal sanctions', and that, 'where this has been done elsewhere, it has been done by civil law provisions, not criminal law provisions'.[38] The court's cursory mention and summary dismissal of international human rights values is unfortunate, and its stated assumptions about the laws in other jurisdictions are somewhat misleading.

The position of the Committee on the Rights of the Child that the 'reasonable chastisement' defence to assault conflicts with the Convention on the Rights of the Child has been repeated over many years and has been expressed within Canada as well. For example, in *R v James*, a case of assault by a father against his child, the judge stated that there is a conflict between s 43 and both the Charter and the Convention on the Rights of the child and said, 'I think this is an area that begs for legislative reform'.[39] Regardless of the nature of the recommendations of the Committee on the Rights of the Child, it was inadequate for the court simply to state that the government of Canada is not *required* by its treaty obligations to repeal s 43 (and it should be noted that Canada is never bound by the recommendations, however explicit, of treaty-monitoring bodies).[40] The question for the court was not whether the government was bound by its international obligations to undertake legislative reform but rather how to interpret the provisions of the Charter invoked by the applicant, taking into account the relevant provisions of the Convention on the Rights of the Child and other human rights conventions. The court did not advert to all of the relevant humans rights norms and did not use such norms in interpreting the Charter in this application.

The States cited by the court as having prohibited corporal punishment by civil or family law provisions only and not with criminal laws and that use educational campaigns to change attitudes also have criminal assault laws and do not have 'reasonable chastisement' defences for parents and teachers who assault children.[41] One of the countries mentioned by the court, Sweden, when outlining

---

[38]   *Canadian Foundation for Children, Youth and the Law v Canada (Attorney General)*, para 22.

[39]   *R v James* [1998] OJ No 1438 (Ont Ct of Justice, Prov Div), para 19.

[40]   In *Promises to Keep: Implementing Canada's Human Rights Obligations*, Report of Canada's Standing Senate Committee on Human Rights, December 2001, the Committee makes this point and further notes that the political effect of recommendations from treaty-monitoring bodies 'is diminished by the fact that there is no formal or public process in Canada that is dedicated to following up on the observations, findings, and recommendations of these bodies with respect to Canada's human rights performance'. This Report is available online at: *http://www.parl.gc.ca/ 37/1/parlbus/commbus/senate/com-E/huma-e/rep-e/rep02dec0--e.htm#i)%20The%20Effect%20of %20International%20Human%20Rights%20Law%20on%20Canadian%20Law*.

[41]   Cyprus specifically criminalizes all acts of violence within the family, not only imposing a penalty for violating the prohibition against physical punishment of children but also for committing violence against another family member in the presence of a child: *Cyprus, Report to the Committee on the Rights of the Child*, CRC/C/8/Add.24, 3 February 1995, paras 82–83. The court did not include Israel in its list of countries that have prohibited physical punishment of children, and apparently was unaware of or chose not to mention the decisions of the Israeli Supreme Court striking down the 'reasonable chastisement' defence to assault of children on the part of parents and teachers, which Israel reported on in detail in *Israel, Report to the UN Committee on the Rights of the Child*, CRC/C/8/Add.44, 27 February 2002. See also Rhona Schuz's critical discussion of the Israeli Supreme Court's decisions, 'Israel: Child Protection in the Israeli Supreme Court: Tortious Parenting, Physical Punishment and Criminal Child Abuse',

the measures it has adopted to deal with the problem of corporal punishment of children, expressly refers to its criminal assault provisions in its most recent report to the Committee on the Rights of the Child.[42] This is not to say that Sweden's extensive program to combat corporal punishment has focused on extending penal sanctions against those who use corporal punishment on children; on the contrary, the emphasis has been on changing attitudes. But assaults of children, as with the case of assaults generally, may be prosecuted in accordance with Sweden's prosecutorial policies. An extensive study was conducted on the effects of Sweden's ban of corporal punishment by Joan Durrant, who outlined in detail the manner in which prosecutions for assault of children are carried out and statistics relating to such prosecutions.[43] Durrant's study makes clear that Sweden's prohibition of corporal punishment has not resulted in an increase in prosecutions against parents or other caregivers for assault, but that penal sanctions may be imposed and that there is no defence of 'reasonable chastisement'. The court's stated assumption that prohibition of corporal punishment in other countries 'has been done by civil law provisions, not criminal law provisions'[44] is not fully accurate.

The court concluded on the s 7 argument that s 43 does not infringe the security of the child's person in a way that violates the principles of fundamental justice but rather 'fairly balances the individual and state interests at stake'.[45] The court's dismissal of the applicant's arguments in regard to s 12 of the Charter, the guarantee against cruel and unusual treatment or punishment, was very brief. The court said that s 43 does not subject the child to any treatment or punishment by the state and that therefore s 12 was not engaged.[46]

In regard to the argument under s 15 of the Charter, which prohibits discrimination on the basis of age and other enumerated and analogous grounds, the court proceeded on the basis that s 43 does violate s 15 but ruled that this discrimination is justified under s 1 of the Charter as a 'reasonable limit prescribed by law as can be demonstrably justified in a free and democratic society'. In order to satisfy s 1 of the Charter, the government must show that the objective of the legislation is 'pressing and substantial' and that the means chosen to attain this objective are 'reasonable and demonstrably justifiable in a free and democratic society'.[47] The court ruled that the objective of s 43, to allow parents and teachers to use 'corrective force' so that they can carry out their responsibilities 'to train

---

in *The International Survey of Family Law (2001 Edition)*, ed A Bainham (Bristol: Family Law, 2001), pp 165–186.

[42] *Sweden, Report to the Committee on the Rights of the Child*, CRC/C/65/Add.3, 11 February 1998, para 426: 'From the penal viewpoint, mention can also be made of the provisions of the Penal Code concerning assault, which cover physical violence and the infliction of more tangible forms of mental suffering'.

[43] Joan Durrant, *A Generation Without Smacking: The Impact of Sweden's Ban on Physical Punishment* (London: Save the Children, 2000) (available online at *http://www.endcorporalpunishment.org/pages/frame.html*).

[44] *Canadian Foundation for Children, Youth and the Law v Canada (Attorney General)*, para 22.

[45] Ibid, para 52.

[46] Ibid, para 54.

[47] *Egan v Canada* [1995] 2 SCR 513.

and nurture' children without risking criminal sanctions, is 'undoubtedly pressing and substantial'.[48]

One may have difficulty in accepting that the responsibility of training and nurturing children must include the right to use corporal punishment or that the government's objective of protecting parents and teachers from penal sanctions for using corporal punishment, conduct the government is trying to eradicate, is pressing and substantial. If so, one will also have difficulty understanding from the court's analysis why children, one of the most vulnerable groups, should not receive the same protection of criminal assault laws that is available to every other Canadian, at least in relation to assaults by the people most likely to assault them, their parents and teachers.

If the Supreme Court of Canada grants leave to appeal in this case, the constitutionality of s 43 may receive additional careful consideration by the judiciary.[49] It is likely that there will continue to be debate on the corporal punishment issue in the political arena as well. The federal government, having determined that corporal punishment is bad conduct that should be eradicated, may soon be ready to take the step of eliminating the 'reasonable chastisement' defence, even in the absence of a ruling by the Supreme Court of Canada that s 43 is unconstitutional.

III   COHABITING COUPLES

A   Same-sex marriage

In Canada the federal government has exclusive jurisdiction over 'marriage', while the provinces have exclusive jurisdiction over 'solemnization of marriage in the province'.[50] This means that provincial legislatures may enact laws governing the formalities of marriage only, while the federal Parliament alone may enact laws on all other aspects of marriage, including the capacity to marry. Marriage can be formalized through a religious or a civil ceremony, and provincial laws set the rules for solemnization by a religious authority pursuant to a licence or to the publication of banns or for solemnization in a civil ceremony by a designated state authority pursuant to a licence.

Canada's Parliament has not enacted comprehensive legislation governing the capacity to marry or recognition of foreign marriages. There are some federal statutes on capacity to marry, notably the Marriage (Prohibited Degrees) Act, 1990 which substantially reduced the restrictions on marrying relatives.[51] In 2001, in regard to the province of Quebec only, the federal Parliament enacted legislation dealing with capacity to marry that includes the following provision:

---

[48]   *Canadian Foundation for Children, Youth and the Law v Canada (Attorney General)*, paras 59–60.

[49]   Application for leave to appeal to the Supreme Court of Canada was filed on 14 March 2002: [2002] SCCA No 113 (QL).

[50]   Constitution Act, 1867 (UK), 30 & 31 Vict, c 3, s 91(26) (gives exclusive jurisdiction over 'marriage and divorce' to the federal government) and s 92(12) (gives exclusive jurisdiction over 'solemnization of marriage in the province' to provinces).

[51]   Marriage (Prohibited Degrees) Act, SC 1990, c 46.

'Marriage requires the free and enlightened consent of a man and a woman to be the spouse of the other'.[52] In the other provinces, most aspects relating to capacity to marry are governed by the law in force in each province prior to its admission to Canada. In the result, the common law definition of marriage as 'the voluntary union for life of one man and one woman, to the exclusion of all others' enunciated in *Hyde v Hyde and Woodmansee* has continued to apply in common law Canada, and the notion that same-sex couples have the right to marry has been rejected in past cases.[53]

Three Charter challenges to the exclusion of same-sex couples from marriage have been launched, in British Columbia, Ontario and Quebec. Information on the cases and copies of the pleadings are available at the website of EGALE, an advocacy group supporting equality for lesbian, gay, bisexual and transgendered people and their families and that has intervenor or party status in each of the three cases.[54] The decisions of the courts of first instance have been handed down in British Columbia and Ontario. The Quebec court, which reserved its decision, will probably hand down its decision before the end of 2002. The decisions handed down to date are subject to appeal to the appellate courts of each province and after that to the Supreme Court of Canada.

In the British Columbia case, *EGALE Canada Inc v Canada*, the proceedings were brought by EGALE and by same-sex couples who wished to marry.[55] Each couple had been refused a marriage licence by the provincial authority on the grounds that two persons of the same sex were not permitted by law to marry. The petitioners then applied to the court for a declaration that the marriage of two persons of the same sex is not legally prohibited and that the provincial authority may issue marriage licences to same-sex couples; and for an order requiring the provincial authority to issue the requested marriage licences. The petitioners applied in the alternative for a declaration that any legal prohibition on same-sex marriage violates the Charter and is of no force and effect. The British Columbia Supreme Court dismissed the application.

The court confirmed that marriage is defined by the common law as a legal relationship between two persons of opposite sex and is not open to same-sex couples. The court took the view that judges should make only incremental changes to the common law, and that changing the common law definition of marriage to include same-sex couples was far beyond the power of incremental change that could properly be exercised by a judge. Therefore, any change to the common law definition of marriage would have to be made by legislators, not judges.

The court also held, however, that the federal Parliament is constitutionally prohibited from altering the common law definition of marriage, and that therefore Parliament cannot legalize same-sex marriages. The court acknowledged that, pursuant to their legislative jurisdiction over property and civil rights in the

---

[52]   Federal Law–Civil Law Harmonization Act, No 1, SC 2001, c 4, s 5, in force 1 June 2001.

[53]   *Hyde v Hyde and Woodmansee* (1866), LR 1 P & D 130. Canadian cases that have accepted the common law definition of marriage and ruled against same-sex marriage are *Re North and Matheson* (1974), 52 DLR (3d) 280 (Man Co Ct); *C(L) v C(C)* (1992), 10 OR (3d) 254 (Gen Div); and *Layland v Ontario* (1993), 104 DLR (4th) 214 (Ont Div Ct).

[54]   See http://www.islandnet.com/~egale/index.htm.

[55]   *EGALE Canada Inc v Canada* [2001] BCJ No 1995.

province, provincial legislatures have authority to formalize and recognize same-sex relationships by some other means than marriage. But the court suggested that neither federal nor provincial legislators have the constitutional authority to enact same-sex marriage legislation. The federal government, although given the exclusive legislative jurisdiction over the capacity to marry under the Constitution, does not have the legislative jurisdiction to open up marriage to same-sex couples without a constitutional amendment.[56] The court stated that the word 'marriage' in Canada's Constitution carries a meaning – the traditional common law meaning – entrenched at the time of confederation, and furthermore that one part of the Constitution, ie the Charter, may not be used to impugn or to amend another part, ie the term 'marriage'. This reasoning has been much criticized, was rejected by the Ontario Divisional Court in its decision in the second same-sex marriage challenge, and will almost certainly be rejected by the appellate courts.[57]

The court gave a detailed account of the enactment of federal and provincial legislation that extends to same-sex couples most of the rights and obligations traditionally reserved for opposite-sex or married couples.[58] The court noted, however, that there remain some differences in the legal rights and obligations of same-sex couples and those of opposite-sex couples, eg in the areas of federal immigration and evidence law. The court also stated that 'in most if not all cases, common-law and same-sex couples only acquire their rights and obligations following a period of conjugal co-habitation that may vary from province to province', while those who are married 'acquire their rights and obligations forthwith upon marriage'.[59] The court rejected the argument of the respondent that the broad inclusion of same-sex couples within the legal framework traditionally reserved for cohabiting opposite-sex couples meant that same-sex couples were no longer in a disadvantaged position. Instead the court ruled that, if the definition of marriage were subject to a Charter challenge and could be amended by Parliament (and in the court's view this was not the case), the exclusion of same-sex couples from marriage would constitute discrimination on the basis of sexual orientation in violation of s 15 of the Charter. But the court also stated that the traditional definition of marriage would be saved by s 1 of the Charter as a reasonable limit prescribed by law demonstrably justified in a free and democratic society.

The second same-sex marriage case was decided by a three-member panel of the Ontario Divisional Court in early July 2002.[60] The application was brought by same-sex couples who had gone through a form of marriage in the Metropolitan Community Church of Toronto. Ontario's Marriage Act requires that couples who

---

[56]   See *EGALE Canada Inc v Canada*, para 10: 'Parliament was given exclusive legislative jurisdiction over marriage, a specific kind of legal relationship. By attempting to change the legal nature of marriage, Parliament would be self-defining a legislative power conferred upon it by the Constitution rather than enacting legislation pursuant to the power. Parliament would be attempting to amend the Constitution without recourse to the amendment process provided by the Constitution Act, 1982.'

[57]   The second same-sex marriage decision was *Halpern v Canada* [2002] OJ No 2714 (Div Ct). For a thorough discussion of the issue of the constitutional authority to amend the definition of marriage, see Mark D Walters, 'Incorporating Common Law into the Constitution of Canada: *EGALE v Canada* and the Status of "Marriage"', forthcoming (2002) *Osgoode Hall Law Journal*.

[58]   *EGALE Canada Inc v Canada*, paras 47–67.

[59]   Ibid, para 68.

[60]   *Halpern v Canada (Attorney General)* [2002] OJ No 2714 (Div Ct).

wish to marry obtain a marriage license or have banns published.[61] The applicants had married under the authority of the publication of banns and were given a marriage certificate by the officiating clergyman, but Ontario's Registrar refused to register the marriages. The Metropolitan Community Church of Toronto joined with the couples in bringing the application, and EGALE, granted intervenor status, supported the application. The applicants sought orders that would require government clerks to issue marriage licences to gay, lesbian and bisexual couples and that would require Ontario's Registrar to register marriages solemnized in a church under banns.

The three-judge panel agreed that the common law as it stood did not permit same-sex marriage, that the common law rule discriminated against gays and lesbians contrary to s 15 of the Charter, and that the infringement of s 15 could not be demonstrably justified in a free and democratic society and therefore could not be saved by s 1 of the Charter. As well, the three judges rejected the argument, which had been accepted by the British Columbia Supreme Court in *EGALE*, that the federal Parliament does not have the legislative jurisdiction to open up marriage to same-sex couples without a constitutional amendment.

Although they agreed that the common law definition of marriage violates the Charter, the judges differed on the question of the appropriate remedy. Smith ACJSC and Blair J agreed in ordering a declaration that the common law definition of marriage was constitutionally invalid and inoperative and that the declaration be suspended for a period of 24 months to enable legislators to bring the law respecting marriage into line with the requirements of the Constitution. Blair J went further in stating that should legislators fail to amend the law accordingly within the 24-month period, there should be a declaration that the common law definition of marriage be reformulated as 'the lawful and voluntary union of two persons to the exclusion of all others'. Furthermore, Blair J ordered that if legislators failed to amend the law in accordance with the court's decision, the applicants would be entitled to the orders of mandamus they had requested. The third judge, LaForme J, took the view that this was not an appropriate case for the court to defer to Parliament and that the definition of marriage should be reformulated by the court as 'the lawful and voluntary union of two persons to the exclusion of all others'. LaForme J stated that marriage licences should be granted to the applicant couples, declared that the marriage of the applicant couples were valid marriages, and ordered Ontario's Registrar to register the marriages.

In the result, the common law definition of marriage was declared unconstitutional, and a 24-month suspension of the declaration was granted to permit legislators to amend the law accordingly. Blair J explained his deference to legislators in this case by pointing to possible legal reforms that would bring the law into conformity with the Constitution other than by opening up civil marriage to same-sex couples. Blair J also stated that, if opening up marriage to same-sex couples was the appropriate method of correcting the constitutional violation, legislators were better positioned to craft a law that would address the various questions that arise in relation to legalizing same-sex marriage.

In his discussion of alternatives to legalizing same-sex marriage, Blair J drew on an important report published in 2001 by the Law Commission of Canada,

---

[61] Marriage Act, RSO 1990, c 3, ss 5 and 17.

Beyond Conjugality, which questioned whether conjugality is an appropriate 'marker' for determining legal rights and obligations.[62] The report recommended, *inter alia*, that the federal Parliament and the provincial legislatures enact laws enabling adults to register their relationships for the purpose of being considered a couple for public and private law rights and obligations and 'move toward removing from their laws the restrictions on marriages between persons of the same sex'.[63] Blair J suggested that a carefully crafted registration scheme might survive constitutional scrutiny but that such schemes may be vulnerable to Charter challenges.

Many same-sex marriage advocates reject the alternative of registration schemes, even those that provide all the legal rights and obligations of marriage, on the grounds that this would at best create a 'separate but equal' status[64] and argue that marriage has great symbolic significance as the ultimate form of recognition by the state.[65] Of course, the Canadian government will not be able to provide complete equality to same-sex couples either by a registration scheme or by legalizing same-sex marriage, in part because it is likely that most countries in the world would refuse to recognize either status. But the question is whether the constitutional guarantee of equality requires not just the extension of all the legal rights and obligations of marriage that are within the power of Canadian legislators to provide but marriage status as opposed to registered partnership status as well.

Both the British Columbia and the Ontario decisions will presumably proceed through the appeals process.[66] In the meantime, provincial and federal legislators will continue the law reform process to address discrimination against same-sex couples, and efforts to do so over the past year are discussed in the next section. The federal government has been studying the issue of same-sex marriage and registration schemes for some time, and the Charter challenges have increased pressure to move ahead with reforms.

B   When should spousal status be a choice?

Over the past several years, federal and provincial legislation has been enacted that extends to unmarried opposite-sex and same-sex couples who have cohabited

---

[62]   Canada, *Beyond Conjugality* (Ottawa: Law Commission of Canada, 2001), available online at *http://www.lcc.gc.ca/en/themes/pr/cpra/report.asp*.

[63]   Ibid, recommendations 31 and 33.

[64]   In *Brown v Board of Education*, 347 US 483, 74 S.Ct 686 (1954), the US Supreme Court ruled that in the field of public education the doctrine of 'separate but equal' had no place, and that racially segregated educational facilities were inherently unequal. Commenting on the effects of racially segregated classrooms on African–American public school children, the court said at 494 that this practice 'generates a feeling of inferiority as to their status in the community that may affect their hearts and minds in a way unlikely ever to be undone'.

[65]   See, eg, EGALE, 'Equal Marriage Q & A', posted at *http://www.islandnet.com/~egale/ documents/Equal MarriageQandA.htm*.

[66]   EGALE and other advocates of same-sex marriage have criticized the government for appealing the *Halpern* decision and argue that the government should simply proceed with legislative reforms: EGALE, Press Release, 29 July 2002, 'EGALE Condemns Government Decision to Appeal Same-sex Marriage Judgment' available online at *http://www.islandnet.com/~egale/ index.htm*.

for a requisite period most of the rights and obligations traditionally attached to marriage, particularly since Supreme Court of Canada rulings that marital status and sexual orientation are prohibited grounds of discrimination under s 15 of the Charter.[67] Some rights and obligations have been reserved for marriage, and in particular, legislators have hesitated to extend the application of family property statutes to unmarried cohabitants who have not formally signalled their consent to an equal division of their property.[68] Respect for the autonomy of the parties is often cited as a reason not to impose marital rights and obligations on unmarried opposite-sex couples.[69] Courts and legislators are now considering whether family property statutes can or should be limited to those who choose to marry or register their unions and whether failure to include unmarried couples in the family property statutes unjustifiably discriminates on the basis of marital status.

The constitutionality of family property statutes that extend only to married persons the presumptive right to an equal share of a couple's property in the event of separation or death was the issue raised in *Attorney General of Nova Scotia v Walsh*, which was heard and reserved by the Supreme Court of Canada in the spring of 2002.[70] Ms Walsh applied for a share of the property of Mr Bona, with whom she had cohabited outside of marriage for 10 years, and sought a declaration that Nova Scotia's family property statute was unconstitutional in failing to provide her with the same entitlement to an equal division of family property that she would have had if she and Mr Bona had been married. After the Nova Scotia Court of Appeal decided in favour of Ms Walsh, declaring the definition of 'spouse' in the family property statute was of no force and effect but suspending the ruling for 12 months to give legislators an opportunity to cure the Charter violation,[71] Nova Scotia legislators enacted legislation that provides, *inter alia*, that cohabiting couples of the same or opposite sex may register as 'domestic partners' and that extends to registered domestic partners the rights and obligations of the family property statute.[72] Those in Ms Walsh's position, ie cohabitants who are not registered as domestic partners, are not entitled to bring a claim under the family property statute. The question for the Supreme Court of Canada is whether the Nova Scotia Court of Appeal erred in declaring the family property statute definition of 'spouse' of no force and effect. If the declaration is

[67] *Miron v Trudel* (1995), 13 RFL (4th) 1 (SCC) (marital status); *Egan v Canada* [1995] 2 SCR 513 (sexual orientation).

[68] Note, however, that an unmarried partner has the right to claim a share of the other's property under the common law doctrine of unjust enrichment or the Civil Code provisions on partnership, contract or unjust enrichment: *Peter v Beblow* [1993] 1 SCR 980; *De L'Isle v Carton* [1997] QJ No 1693 (QCA) (QL), application for leave to appeal dismissed with costs, 4 December 1997: [1997] SCCA No 451 (QL).

[69] For example, then Quebec Minister of Justice Serge Ménard explained to the National Assembly of Quebec that the province did not previously include unmarried couples within its scheme of marital rights and obligations out of respect for the autonomy of those who do not wish to submit themselves to the legal regime of marriage: Quebec, Debates of the National Assembly, 18 June 1998.

[70] *Attorney General of Nova Scotia v Walsh* [2000] SCCA No 517, heard and reserved 14 June 2002.

[71] *Walsh v Bona* (2000), 5 RFL (5th) 188 (NSCA).

[72] An Act to Comply with Certain Court Decisions and to Modernize and Reform Laws in the Province, SNS 2000, c 29, ss 32–45 (in force 4 June 2001).

upheld, the further question arises of whether the creation of a registered domestic partner scheme remedies the Charter violation.

In Saskatchewan as well, there was a ruling that the province's family property statute violated the Charter by excluding unmarried couples,[73] but the province did not appeal the decision or wait for the Supreme Court of Canada ruling in the *Walsh* case and instead proceeded with broad reforms in 2001. Saskatchewan now includes cohabiting couples of the same or opposite sex in the definition of 'spouse' for matters that are within the legislative authority of the province, including adoption, change of name, succession, pensions, support and family property.[74] For matters such as support, succession and family property, only those who have cohabited continuously for at least two years are included in the definition of 'spouse'. Saskatchewan has used the traditional common-law Canadian approach of linking rights and obligations to cohabitation, and the province may be vulnerable to criticism for going too far in this direction and undermining the autonomy of the parties. Another problem with Saskatchewan's approach is that it does not provide a registration scheme, and there is no way for a same-sex couple to acquire immediately the rights and obligations that are based on cohabitation for a requisite period. This problem will presumably have to be addressed if same-sex marriage is not legalized.

One year after Nova Scotia's domestic partnership law came into force, permitting couples of the same or the opposite sex to register their unions and thus become entitled to most of the same rights and obligations as married couples enjoy under provincial law,[75] Quebec's similar but broader civil union law was enacted and came into force.[76] Quebec has not previously extended private family law rights to unmarried couples on the basis of cohabitation, as have the common law provinces, because of a reluctance to thrust the private law rights and obligations of marriage on those who have not chosen to marry.[77] Quebec's civil union law respects the autonomy of the parties by extending private family law rights and obligations only to couples of the same or opposite sex who register their union, but it also expands the rights of unregistered cohabiting couples of the same or opposite sex in such matters as consent to health care for an incapacitated partner. Quebec's reforms are distinct from Nova Scotia's in that they are broader, and include the rules relating to filiation and adoption. The other notable aspect of Quebec's reforms was the wholehearted support for same-sex couples and their children expressed by the National Assembly in the debates on the Bill.[78] In contrast with the sometimes grudging manner in which reforms have been enacted

---

[73]   *Watch v Watch* (1999), 182 Sask R 237 (Sup Ct).

[74]   Miscellaneous Statutes (Domestic Relations) Amendment Act, 2001, SS 2001, c 50;
        Miscellaneous Statutes (Domestic Relations) Amendment Act, 2001 (No 2), SS 2001, c 51.

[75]   An Act to Comply with Certain Court Decisions and to Modernize and Reform Laws in the
        Province, SNS 2000, c 29, ss 32–45 (in force 4 June 2001).

[76]   An Act Instituting Civil Unions and Establishing New Rules of Filiation, SQ 2002, c 6 (in force
        8 June 2002).

[77]   In 1998, then Minister of Justice Serge Ménard stated: 'Lorsque le législateur a révisé le droit de
        la famille, tant en 1980 qu'en 1991, il s'est interrogé sur l'opportunité de prévoir des
        conséquences civiles aux unions de fait. S'il s'est abstenu de le faire, c'est par respect pour la
        volonté des conjoints: quand ils ne se marient pas, c'est qu'ils ne veulent pas se soumettre au
        régime légal du mariage': Quebec, Debates of the National Assembly, 18 June 1998.

[78]   Quebec, Debates of the National Assembly (on Bill 84), 6 and 7 June 2002.

in common law provinces, often with heavy hints in the title of statutes or in press releases that the courts have forced the hands of the legislators and public statements or statutory assurances that the province supports the traditional definition of marriage,[79] Quebec legislators, proud almost to the point of chauvinism of the province's record on protecting gay rights, eagerly spoke up in support of reforms, eliminated the Civil Code limitation of marriage to a man and a woman[80] (this has no legal effect because the federal government has exclusive legislative authority over capacity to marry) and passed the Bill unanimously. In the light of Quebec's proud and principled approach to this issue, the extensive public consultation that was part of the law reform process, and Quebec's status as a distinct society within Canada, it is difficult to imagine the province introducing further reforms to extend family property rights and obligations to couples who are not married or registered, regardless of the Supreme Court of Canada's ultimate ruling in *Walsh*.

In 2001, Manitoba enacted reforms in response to the Supreme Court of Canada's ruling in *M v H* that spousal support laws that include opposite-sex but not same-sex cohabitants are unconstitutional. The province included cohabiting same-sex couples in a limited range of laws, including laws relating to pensions, support and workers' compensation benefits.[81] In 2002, Manitoba introduced two Bills that go further in eliminating discrimination against opposite-sex and same-sex couples.[82] Bill 34 extends additional spousal rights and obligations within the legislative authority of the province to opposite-sex or same-sex couples who have cohabited for a requisite period, and for the first time extends to cohabiting same-sex couples the right of joint adoption. Bill 53 creates a registration scheme for 'common law partners' and for the first time extends family property rights and obligations to common law partners who have either registered or cohabited for a requisite period.

In the spring of 2002, Alberta also introduced legislation that will extend to those in 'adult interdependent relationships' rights and obligations relating to such matters as support, wrongful death damages, change of name and succession, but it is more limited than the reforms enacted or proposed in other provinces over the past year, and, in particular, does not address the issue of family property rights raised in the *Walsh* case.[83] The Bill is distinctive in extending rights and obligations on the basis of contract as well as cohabitation and in including non-conjugal couples – an 'adult interdependent partner' is defined as a person who has lived in an interdependent relationship at least three years or for less than three

---

[79] See, eg, Ontario's Amendments Because of the Supreme Court of Canada Decision in *M v H*, 1999, SO 1999, c 6, or the press release issued by Alberta, 'Legislation Addresses Needs of Albertans in Committed Interdependent Relationships', 7 May 2002, in which Alberta's Justice Minister is quoted saying: 'The Alberta government believes that marriage is fundamentally a union between a man and a woman. Alberta law will continue to recognize this. The Adult Interdependent Relationships Act ensures that Alberta legislation is constitutional, and at the same time recognizes and preserves the values of Albertans.'

[80] An Act Instituting Civil Unions and Establishing New Rules of Filiation, s 22.

[81] Act to Comply with the Supreme Court of Canada Decision in *M v H*, SM 2001, c 37.

[82] Legislative Assembly of Manitoba, 3rd Sess, 37th Legis (2002), Bill 34, The Charter Compliance Act, and Bill 53, The Common-Law Partners' Property and Related Amendments Act.

[83] Legislative Assembly of Alberta (2002), Bill 30, Adult Interdependent Relationships Act.

years if the interdependent relationship is of some permanence and if there is a child of the relationship by birth or adoption, or a person living or intending to live in an interdependent relationship who has entered into a written adult interdependent partner agreement. The preamble of the Bill includes Alberta's affirmation 'as a fundamental principle that marriage is a union between a man and a woman to the exclusion of all others'. It is certainly possible that, in the event of legalization of same-sex marriage, Alberta would invoke s 33, the 'notwithstanding' clause, of the Charter that permits legislators to enact statutes that violate the Charter and would refuse to amend provincial laws to include same-sex marriages.[84]

Legislators have been very active over the past year in addressing discrimination against cohabiting opposite-sex and same-sex couples, and will continue to be so. The schemes that have been introduced vary in the terminology used – 'spouse', 'civil union spouse', 'domestic partner', 'common-law partner', 'adult interdependent partner' – and in other details. The broad trend, however, is to equalize the rights and obligations of married and unmarried couples. It seems clear at this point that legislators will need to eliminate the remaining distinctions between same-sex couples and unmarried opposite-sex couples that are susceptible to a Charter challenge and enable same-sex couples to obtain status not just after cohabitation for a requisite period but immediately by marriage or by registration (although it is not clear that a registration scheme and not marriage would survive constitutional scrutiny). Whether rights and obligations relating to certain matters such as family property can constitutionally be limited to those who marry or register remains to be seen. The Supreme Court of Canada's ruling in the *Walsh* case will address that question.

C   Spousal status and social assistance payments

In Ontario, as in most jurisdictions, eligibility for social assistance benefits takes into account spousal relationships. Payments are made to individuals or couples in need. If two persons are in a spousal relationship, their entitlement depends on whether they as a couple are in need. In *Falkiner v Ontario*, the definition of 'spouse' in Ontario's social assistance statute was successfully challenged on the grounds that it discriminated against single mothers on the basis of sex, marital status and receipt of social assistance, contrary to s 15 of the Charter.[85] In the same decision, the Ontario Court of Appeal dealt with the appeal of Paul Thomas, and ruled that, in the case of a person who is receiving social assistance payments because of a disability that renders the person unemployable, the interpretation of 'spouse' must take into account the disability.

The definition of 'spouse' in the social assistance benefits legislation and regulations, which had been amended in 1995 by the provincial Conservative government, included those who had made a self-declaration that they were in a spousal relationship, those who were required to pay support under a court order

---

[84]   Alberta has announced this determination in the past: see, eg, Jill Mahoney, 'Alberta Government Decides to Say No to Same-sex Marriages' *The Globe and Mail* (19 March 1999).

[85]   *Falkiner v Ontario (Ministry of Community and Social Services, Income Maintenance Branch)*, [2002] LJ No 1771 (CA).

or agreement, or those who had cohabited for at least three years. In addition, 'spouse' was defined to include:

'(d) a person of the opposite sex to the applicant or recipient who is residing in the same dwelling-place as the applicant or recipient if:

(i) the person is providing financial support to the applicant or recipient;

(ii) the applicant or recipient is providing financial support to the person; or

(iii) the person and the applicant or recipient have a mutual agreement or arrangement regarding their financial affairs, and

the social and familial aspects of the relationship between the person and the applicant or recipient amount to cohabitation.'[86]

In order to satisfy any of the three, disjunctive parts of the definition of 'spouse' set out in paragraphs (i), (ii) and (iii), there had to be a relationship of 'cohabitation'.

In *Falkiner*, only one part of the definition of spouse, s 1(1)(d)(iii), which had been added in 1995 by the Conservative government, was impugned as violating s 15 of the Charter. It is important to emphasize the narrow nature of the constitutional challenge. There was no challenge to taking spousal relationships into account in determining entitlement or to using couples as the benefit unit but only to one part of the definition of 'spouse' that was considered problematically broad. In the *Thomas* appeal, there was no constitutional challenge, but the appellant argued that as a matter of statutory interpretation he was not in a relationship of cohabitation.

In *Falkiner*, the problem with s 1(1)(d) was that it deemed to be spouses those who had cohabited for less than three years and who had no support obligations to one another, provided the cohabitants had 'a mutual agreement or arrangement regarding their financial affairs'. This definition was broad enough to include relationships that lacked the meaningful financial interdependence that characterizes spousal relationships. As a result of this broad definition, from the moment a single mother on social assistance began cohabiting with a man, she risked losing her entitlement to social assistance and being forced into dependence on a man who had no legal obligation to support her or her children. This was particularly problematic, noted the court, for the many women abused by partners in the past – 'forcing them to become financially dependent on men with whom they have at best try-on relationships strikes at the core of their human dignity'.[87]

The unchallenged portion of the definition of 'spouse' included only those receiving or with a legal right to claim support from a cohabitant. The impugned portion of the definition was defended by the government on the grounds that single mothers who married were immediately included as spouses for the purpose of determining entitlement to social assistance and that those who cohabited instead of marrying should not be given preferential treatment.[88] But married

---

[86]   Family Benefits Act Regulations, RRO 1990, reg 366, s 1(1)(d). The legislation was subsequently appealed, in part to include a definition of 'same sex partner' that was parallel to the definition of spouse, but no amendments affected the issues raised in the *Falkiner* appeal.

[87]   *Falkiner v Ontario*, para 101.

[88]   The conservative press made the same argument. An editorial critical of the court's decision published in the *National Post* of 16 May 2002, asked, 'Why should shacked-up welfare recipients receive more government money than their similarly situated married counterparts?'.

couples are legally obligated to support one another, while those who have cohabited for less than three years are not. The court acknowledged that it may be appropriate to have a definition of spouse in social assistance legislation that is different from the definition of spouse in a spousal support statute, because the purposes of social assistance laws and private spousal support laws are different. But s 1(1)(d)(iii) did not achieve the purpose of treating married people and people in a marriage-like relationship the same for the purpose of social assistance entitlements; rather it was so broad as to include relationships that lacked a sufficient degree of financial interdependence to be considered marriage-like.

The constitutional challenge in *Falkiner* was based on discrimination on the basis of an 'interlocking set' of personal characteristics. The court ruled that the s 1(1)(d)(iii) portion of the definition of 'spouse' was unconstitutional because it discriminated against single welfare mothers because of their sex and marital status and, in addition, on the novel ground of 'receipt of social assistance'. Section 15 of the Charter prohibits discrimination on the basis of enumerated grounds or on grounds that are analogous to those enumerated. 'Sex' is enumerated in s 15, and the Supreme Court of Canada has previously ruled that 'marital status' is an analogous ground.[89] The court in *Falkiner* ruled that 'receipt of social assistance' is another analogous ground, and whether the Supreme Court of Canada will confirm this ruling remains to be seen. The court acknowledged the ruling was 'controversial' because of 'concerns about singling out the economically disadvantaged for Charter protection, about immutability and about lack of homogeneity', but determined that recognition of 'receipt of social assistance' as an analogous ground was justified in order to further the purpose of s 15 of the Charter, which is the protection of human dignity.[90]

The court's ruling that the impugned definition of 'spouse' discriminated on the basis of sex was based on the statistical evidence that showed that women and single mothers were disproportionately adversely affected by the definition: 'although women accounted for only 54% of those receiving social assistance and only 60% of single persons receiving benefits, they accounted for nearly 90% of those whose benefits were terminated by the definition of spouse'.[91] The conclusion in regard to discrimination on the basis of marital status was based on the fact that 'while married people on social assistance receive benefits in accordance with a benefit unit that reflects their actual economic position, the definition of spouse puts the respondents and singles like them into a benefit unit that does not accurately reflect their economic situation'.[92] Single people not on social assistance were free to have 'try-on' relationships without risking any state-imposed penalty. Single mothers on social assistance, however, were not; the result for them of 'try-on' relationships was adverse state-imposed penalties, ie the reduction or loss of their social assistance payments.

The court rejected the government's argument that the violation of s 15 of the Charter was a 'reasonable limit prescribed by law as can be demonstrably justified in a free and democratic society' and thus saved under s 1 of the Charter. In

---

[89]   *Miron v Trudel* (1995), 13 RFL (4th) 1 (SCC).
[90]   *Falkiner v Ontario*, para 84.
[91]   Ibid, para 77.
[92]   Ibid, para 80.

reaching this conclusion, the court found that 'the only possible positive effect of the definition is cost savings' while the 'negative effects are considerable and include reinforcement of dependency, deprivation of financial independence and state interference with close personal relationships'.[93] The court upheld the lower court's declaration that s 1(1)(d)(iii) was invalid. In the result, single social assistance recipients will have a three-year 'grace period' of cohabitation before being deemed to be spouses for the purpose of determining their entitlement to benefits.

While the successful constitutional challenge in *Falkiner* has received the most attention from the legal community and the press, the ruling on the correct interpretation of 'cohabitation' in the related *Thomas* appeal was also important. As noted above, any of the extended definitions of 'spouse' for the purpose of determining social assistance entitlement in s 1(1)(d) required that the social assistance applicant or recipient be residing with a person of the opposite sex and that 'the social and familial aspects of the relationship between the person and the applicant or recipient amount to cohabitation'. It was impermissible under the regulations for the government to investigate or consider sexual factors, and it was instead 'the social and familial aspects of the relationship' that were the relevant factors in determining whether the relationship amounted to cohabitation. In *Thomas*, the appellant argued that as a matter of statutory interpretation he was not a 'spouse' because he was not in a relationship that amounted to 'cohabitation', ie he and his friend were not living together in a conjugal relationship.

Mr Thomas was mentally disabled and permanently unemployable. He had lived for 10 years with a woman he described as a friend and caregiver. Mr Thomas was considered to be a 'spouse' within the meaning of s 1(1)(d) and denied social assistance benefits because his friend's assets were greater than the cut-off point for eligibility. In this case, Mr Thomas and his friend spent almost all their spare time together – they ate together, shopped together, vacationed together, visited friends and each other's families together, and Mr Thomas's friend did his laundry. The government accepted that Mr Thomas's disability was the reason his friend shopped and cleaned for him, but took the view that the fact that the couple spent most of their spare time together indicated that their relationship was a marriage-like relationship of cohabitation.

The court agreed with Mr Thomas's argument that cohabitation means more than spending time together and must include interrelating with friends, family and the community as a couple. The court reasoned that two people may spend almost all their time together because of 'close friendship, economics or simply a lack of alternatives'.[94] The court ruled that it had been an error to focus on the amount of time Mr Thomas and his friend spent together rather than considering whether they interrelated as a couple in a relationship that was marriage-like. The difficulty of distinguishing between a close friendship and a marriage-like relationship, when in both cases the couple live together, are financially interdependent, eat together, spend most of their time together, and visit friends and family together, was adverted to by the court:[95]

---

[93] *Falkiner v Ontario*, para 112.
[94] Ibid, para 33.
[95] Ibid, para 34.

'The line between what amounts to cohabitation under the definition and what is no
more than close friendship may be difficult to draw in some cases, especially as the
Director is precluded for reasons of privacy from investigating or considering sexual
factors. But the difficulty of drawing the distinction is not an excuse for ignoring it.'

The court did not offer assistance in drawing the distinction between a close
friendship and a marriage-like relationship, only ruled that it was a mistake not to
do so.

The court also agreed with the appellant that the interpretation of
'cohabitation' must take into account Mr Thomas's disability. The government
had accepted that Mr Thomas's disability was the reason his friend shopped and
cleaned for him, but the government should also have considered whether they
spent most of their time together for the same reason. The court said:[96]

'Certainly persons with disabilities are capable of forming spousal relationships and
capable of doing so with persons who are not disabled. But the Board should have
considered whether Mr Thomas' disability explained the social and familial aspects of
his relationship with Ms Papizzo, aspects that in another context might well amount to
cohabitation. The evidence before the Board suggested that Mr Thomas needed a
caregiver and that he could not live on his own. Either may have provided a plausible
alternative explanation for why he and Ms Papizzo were together all the time.'

In the result, the court allowed Mr Thomas's appeal and ordered that he receive
social assistance payments as a single permanently unemployable person.

It will be difficult to apply the court's reasons for judgment when determining
whether a relationship is a close friendship or marriage-like. The *Thomas* case
points up the problem of using the couple rather than the individual as the benefit
unit for the purpose of social assistance payments. Mr Thomas's friend testified
that she would not live with Mr Thomas if she had to support him. With his social
assistance payments, Mr Thomas was able to live with his friend and have the
benefit of her companionship and much-needed assistance. If the court had ruled
that the relationship of Mr Thomas and his friend amounted to cohabitation,
Mr Thomas would have been forced to separate from his friend, a result that
seems undesirable from all points of view. Perhaps a system that does not make it
more difficult for persons with disabilities who are permanently unemployable to
attract and keep a spouse would be preferable to one that imposes financial
penalties for doing so. Perhaps, at least in the case of persons with disabilities, the
individual should be the benefit unit, but this issue was not raised or explored in
this appeal.

IV LOOKING FORWARD

Same-sex marriage and civil unions will be the major subjects of family law
reform over the next year. There will be further court rulings, Parliamentary
consideration and widespread public debate on the issue of same-sex marriage.
Canada may well become the second country in the world to open up civil
marriage to same-sex couples. Regardless of whether marriage is opened up to

---

[96]   *Falkiner v Ontario*, para 36.

same-sex couples, both federal and provincial legislators will give further attention to civil unions and to extending rights and obligations to unmarried couples of the same or opposite sex on the basis of cohabitation for a requisite period.

Human reproductive technologies will also be the subject of much debate over the coming year. The government introduced Bill C-56, An Act respecting Assisted Human Reproduction (AHR) on 9 May 2002.[97] If passed, the law will prohibit activities that the government has determined are unacceptable, including: reproductive and therapeutic human cloning; creating *in vitro* embryos except to create a human being or to improve on or teach AHR procedures; creating an embryo from the cell or part of a cell of an embryo or foetus for the purpose of creating a human being; sex selection, except to address sex-linked diseases; altering the genome of a cell of a human being or *in vitro* embryo in a way that is capable of being transmitted to descendants; and commercial surrogacy. In addition, Bill C-56 makes it an offence for anyone to carry out a 'controlled activity' without a licence and requires these controlled activities to be carried out in accordance with the regulations. The controlled activities include: altering human reproductive material to create an embryo; altering or using an *in vitro* embryo; and acquiring, storing, transferring, importing or exporting sperm or ova to create an embryo, or of an *in vitro* embryo for any purpose. Previous efforts to regulate in this area have not been successful, and Bill C-56 has already generated much controversy, in part because of its use of criminal law to regulate in this area.

---

[97]   Bill C-56 and a helpful summary and discussion of the Bill are available online at
http://www.parl.gc.ca/common/Bills_ls.asp?lang=E&Parl=37&Ses=1&ls=C56&source=Bills_ House_Government.

CROATIA

THE CANONIC MARRIAGE – REVISION OF CROATIAN FAMILY LAW AND ITS CONFLICT OF LAWS IMPLICATIONS

Vesna Tomlijenovic[*]

I CANONIC MARRIAGE AND THE CROATIAN LEGAL SYSTEM

Following its declaration of independence in 1991, Croatia has faced numerous changes to its legal system. Some of these changes, especially in family law, have been initiated with a newly established relationship between Croatia and the Holy See.

Deciding to regulate their relations on the basis of several agreements, and not on the basis of the Concordat,[1] the Holy See and the Republic of Croatia started intensive negotiations in 1993,[2] as a result of which several treaties were concluded in the period from 1995 to 1998.[3] Our attention will be focused on the Treaty Concerning Legal Questions (hereafter 'the Treaty') concluded in 1996, which the Croatian Parliament ratified on 25 February 1997. The Treaty is of utmost importance because it defines the basis of mutual legal relations between Croatia and the Catholic Church.

Even before its ratification, the Treaty's provisions caused public and legal debate.[4] Some authors questioned its constitutionality, arguing that it was in principle contrary to the Croatian Constitution because of the creation of discriminatory effects towards religious groups other than Catholics.[5] Some argued that the Treaty contravenes the rule of law because of a doubtful

---

[*] Assistant Professor, Faculty of Law, University of Rijeka.

[1] After the Second Vatican Council, the practice of the Holy See has been to define legal and other relations with individual States on the basis of several agreements rather than on the basis of one agreement, usually called the Concordat. See for detail, N Eterović, *Treaties between Holy See and Republic of Croatia* (hereafter '*Treaties*'), Zagreb, 2001, p 16. The Concordat is an agreement between representatives of the highest Church and State powers concerning the legal position of the Catholic Church in one State in general or concerning settlement of some ecclesiastical–political issue: see Lanović, *The Concordat between Yugoslavia and Vatican*, Belgrade, 1925, p 28.

[2] Eterović, *Treaties*, pp 5–8.

[3] Treaty between the Holy See and Republic of Croatia concerning Co-operation in Matters of Education and Culture (*Official Gazette* – International Treaties, 23/97), Treaty between the Holy See and Republic of Croatia on Religious Assistance to the Catholic Members in Military Forces and of the Police (*Official Gazette* – International Treaties, 2/97, 8/97), and Treaty between the Holy See concerning Commercial Questions (*Official Gazette* – International Treaties, 18/98).

[4] M Alinčić, 'Treaties between The Holy See and Croatia concerning marital disputes are unconstitutional', *Globus*, 7 February 1997.

[5] See for details A Uzelac, 'From Liberalism to Catholicism: Some Aspects of the Legal Regulation of Church and State Relations in Croatia – The New Marital Law', in *Collective Papers of Zagreb Law Faculty*, 49(3–4), 1999, pp 341–374.

dichotomy between State and church authorities[6] and, finally, because it seemed to pierce the constitutional principle of State control over family matters.[7]

We will direct our attention to the legal implications of Art 13 of the Treaty, which, among others, regulates specific aspects of concordat or canonic marriage. Some of the most important legal questions and debates, as well as private international law issues, will be highlighted concerning the relation between Art 13 of the Treaty and the provisions concerning religious marriage in the Croatian Family Act (hereafter FA),[8] which entered into force in 1999.

II CANONIC MARRIAGES AND THE CROATIAN LEGISLATION *DE LEGE LATA*

While Croatia was a part of the Socialist Federal Republic of Yugoslavia (hereafter SFR Yugoslavia), a canonic marriage was not legally regulated, and thus recognized as a legal institution. The Croatian Law on Marriage and Family Relations (hereinafter the LMFR),[9] which had been applied in Croatia before the FA entered into force (1 June 1999), contained no provisions concerning canonic marriage. At the time the LMFR was adopted in 1978,[10] family law was influenced by socialist policies and values, and consequently any religious influence in family law was *a limine* excluded.

However, before World War II, canonic marriage had an important role and place in Croatian legal history. While Croatia was a part of the Austro-Hungarian Empire, and later on a part of the Kingdom of Yugoslavia, Austrian Law as well as Italian law were applied on its territory. Thus, according to the Austrian Concordat of 1855, which applied in Croatian territory, marital disputes were under the exclusive jurisdiction of the religious courts, while competent civil courts decided upon the civil effects of marriage. Numerous provisions concerning canonic marriage were contained in the Cesarean Patent brought in order to enforce Art X of the Austrian Concordat in 1856, and especially, in the Marital Law for Catholics (Annex I of Patent) as well as in the Guidance for Religious Courts in Matrimony Matters (Annex II of Patent).[11] All those legal acts, recognizing canonic marriage, have been applied on Croatian territory. Likewise, the Kingdom of Yugoslavia in 1914 concluded the Concordat with the Holy See,

---

[6]   M Alinčić, 'Which constitutional provision can be considered as the basis for division of power between the Catholic Church and the State of Croatia concerning the procedure for conclusion of marriage', *Vjesnik*, 23 January 1998.

[7]   According to Art 61 of the Constitution of the Republic of Croatia (*Official Gazette*, 44/01; 55/01) on the one hand, a family enjoys special legal protection and, on the other, the same provisions provide that institutions like marriage, and marital legal relations, common law marriage and families, have to be regulated by law.

[8]   Family Act (Obiteljski zakon), *Official Gazette* No 162 of 1998, entered into force on the eighth day after it was published in the *Official Gazette*. However, its application was postponed until 1 June 1999.

[9]   The Law on Marriage and Family Relations (Zakon o braku i porodičnim odnosima), *Official Gazette* 11/78.

[10] Since the LMFR was adopted as republican law and not federal law it was not necessary, after Croatia declared its independence in 1991, to introduce that law as Croatian law.

[11] For more detail about the legal history of canon law on Croatian territory, see B Eisner, *Family Law*, Zagreb, 1950, p 22 et seq; Uzelac, 'From Liberalism to Catholicism', op cit, pp 345–356.

which allowed concordat (canonic) marriage between a Catholic and a member of another religious group (Art 12), recognizing exclusive jurisdiction of church courts to decide upon marital disputes.[12]

After World War II, when Croatia became one of the socialist republics of SFR Yugoslavia, canonic marriage disappeared from the Croatian legal scene. More than 50 years later, due to the Croatian Treaty's ratification, religious marriage reappeared and became legally recognized as an institution of Croatian family law. The newly adopted Croatian FA in 1999 reconfirmed the validity of all religious marriages. However, the FA imposes one general condition for the recognition of religious marriages. According to Art 9, a marriage solemnized before the minister of a religious community has civil effect only if mutual legal relations between the Republic of Croatia and the respective religious community are regulated. This precondition is fulfilled only in relation to the Catholic Church concerning canonic marriage, since the Holy See and the Republic of Croatia have concluded the already mentioned package of Treaties thus creating the legal framework for a mutual relationship.

The FA provides for the solemnization of marriage in religious form, enumerates conditions that have to be fulfilled in that respect and defines the moment from which such marriage produces the same legal effect as marriage solemnized in civil form (Arts 8, 20, 21, 22 and 23). These provisions will be analyzed later.

III THE PURPOSE AND SCOPE OF ARTICLE 13 OF THE CROATIAN TREATY

Article 13 of the Treaty reads as follows:

'(1) From the moment of its solemnization, canonic marriage produces civil effects according to the provisions of Croatian law if there are no civil impediments on the part of the spouses and if legal conditions provided by Croatian legislation are met.

(2) Legislation of the Republic of Croatia regulates the method and the time limits for entering canonic marriage in a state marriage register.

(3) Preparation for canonic marriage includes instructions to the future spouses on church views concerning marriage as a sacrament, especially about its unity and indissolubility, and about the civil effects of marriage according to Croatian law.

(4) Church court decisions on annulment of marriage and decisions of the Supreme Church Authority on a dissolution of marriage have to be handed over to the competent State court for applying the civil effects of religious decisions, in accordance with the Croatian law.'

The cited provision regulates recognition of the civil effects of a canonic marriage, on one hand, and on the other, recognition of the civil effects of church decisions on annulment and dissolution of canonic marriage.

Although adopted by the Croatian Parliament after the Treaty's ratification, the new Croatian FA does not contain the necessary guidelines which could help with interpreting the Treaty's provisions laid down in Art 13. What the FA left

---

[12]   B Eisner, *Family Law*, op cit, pp 24–25.

completely unclear is the understanding of the provision in para 4 of Art 13 providing for the recognition of civil effects of religious decisions concerning annulment and dissolution of canonic marriage.

On what basis can canonic marriage and its effects be recognized by State authorities? It is a well-established principle in Croatian law that the State's paramount interest is to secure a marriage and family relations. The Croatian Constitution contains provisions on marriage and the family in Part III, which is dedicated to fundamental freedoms and human rights. Constitutional provisions establish principles of special State protection for marriage and the family (Art 61), and of maternity, children and the State as guarantor of social, cultural, substantial and other conditions which are necessary for realization of the right to a dignified life (Art 62). Moreover, the principle that marriage, marital and family relations are regulated by the law is expressly provided in Art 61. Consequently, in order to be recognized as legally relevant within the Croatian legal system, a canonic marriage needs to be subject to State control. That is what the FA, through its relevant provisions, does affirm. The same State control principle should apply to church decisions on annulment and dissolution of canonic marriage. It is interesting to analyze whether, and in what degree, such control is enforceable.

A   Religious form of marriage

Since Croatia became part of SFR Yugoslavia in 1945, a civil solemnization of marriage has been the only legally recognized form in which a marriage could be concluded. One of the constitutional principles on which the LMFR was based required marriage, in order to be valid, to be solemnized before the competent State authority (the form of the obligatory civil marriage).[13] Consequently, when solemnized before church authorities, a marriage was without any legal effect, if spouses had not first solemnized their marriage in civil form, even to the extent that a fine or imprisonment was contained in criminal legislation for those who solemnized a marriage according to the religious rules before civil solemnisation.

However, during the nineties, this strict rule on civil solemnization was subject to criticism as being contrary to the constitutional freedom of religion and expression of faith.[14] The need for mitigation was more than obvious. The turning point in this respect was the decision of the Constitutional Court of the Republic of Croatia in 1994,[15] which abolished Art 27 of the LMFR. This Article was struck down as unconstitutional because, according to this provision, a marriage,

---

[13]   According to Art 28 of the LMFR, a marriage not solemnized before the competent State authority was without legal effect at all: see Uzelac, 'From Liberalism to Catholicism', op cit, p 356; M Alinčić/D Hrabar, 'Family Legislation in the Period of Creating a New Legal Order', *The International Survey of Family Law 1995*, ed A Bainham (Martinus Nijhoff Publishers, 1997) at 118.

[14]   Decision of 12 May 1992 of the Constitutional Court of the Republic of Croatia concerning commencing proceedings for unconstitutionality of Art 27 of the LMFR, *Official Gazette* no 41/92.

[15]   Decision of February 1994 of the Constitutional Court of Republic of Croatia, *Official Gazette* 25/94.

in order to be valid, had to be concluded first in civil form.[16] Such a solution was considered to be contrary to the constitutional principle of freedom of religion guaranteed by Art 40 of the Constitution of the Republic of Croatia.[17] By its decision, the Constitutional Court introduced the possibility for the spouses to solemnize their marriage before the minister of a church community prior to its civil solemnization. However, civil solemnization of marriage was unavoidable, because the Constitutional Court did not allow religious marriage to become an alternative form of marriage. There was no possibility for spouses to choose between a civil and religious marriage. The Constitutional Court allowed only the possibility of celebrating marriage first before religious, and then before civil, authorities. Civil solemnization was still necessary for a marriage to have legal effect.

The Treaty's ratification in 1997 radically changed the legal position of a canonic marriage in the context of Croatian law. According to Art 13(1) of the Treaty:

'... from the moment of its solemnization canonic marriage produces civil effects according to the provisions of Croatian law if there are no civil impediments on the part of the spouses and if legal conditions provided by Croatian legislation are met.'

The canonic marriage, according to the Art 13, para 1 of the Treaty, has legal effect, however, upon two conditions: (i) that there are no impediments on the part of the future spouses; and (ii) that all conditions provided for in Croatian legislation are fulfilled.

Consequently, in order to conclude a valid canonic marriage the required conditions have to be fulfilled in both canonic and Croatian family law. In other words, a marriage can be solemnized in religious form only if it can be solemnized in civil form too.

The FA expressly reconfirms this principle, containing provisions regulating the procedure and conditions for granting civil effect to religious marriage. Even by-law provisions were adopted to ensure due process of recognition of marriages celebrated in religious form.[18]

Moreover, in order to celebrate religious marriage, the bride and groom have to provide a document issued by the registrar of civil status proving that all conditions necessary for the celebration of civil marriage, according to the FA, are fulfilled (Art 20, para 1). This document has to contain a formal statement indicating that both future spouses agree upon their surname, as well as a statement proving that all legal forms of marital property regimes recognised by the law are well known to them. Moreover, it must be proven that a minister has

---

[16] Article 27 of the LMFR reads as follows:
'Religious solemnization of marriage is not allowed before marriage is solemnized according to the provisions of this Law.'

[17] The Constitutional Court of the Republic of Croatia justified its decision saying that religious communities had constitutional rights to practise their religious ceremonies. Since solemnization of marriage according to the LMFR was without legal effect, if performed before or after civil solemnization, it was in its nature just a religious ceremony, and therefore the State was not allowed to limit it: see in detail the Constitutional Court of the Republic of Croatia decision of 16 February 1994.

[18] Regulation concerning the content and form of the certificate for the conclusion of marriage, *Official Gazette* No 53 of 28 May 1999.

familiarised them with all marital rights and obligations (Art 20, para 2 of the FA). Once issued, this document is valid for a three-month period (Art 20, para 3 of the FA).

However, it is important to emphasise that the minister has to draw the future spouses' attention to the fact that a religious marriage has civil effect only if evidenced in a State civil registry (Art 20, para 4 of the FA).

The official of the religious community before whom the marriage is solemnized has to hand over to the State registry a certificate signed by the wife, husband and witnesses, and by the minister who solemnizes the marriage, which confirms that the marriage has been solemnized (Art 21 of the FA).

In other words, before religious solemnization, a State registrar has to determine whether all preconditions for civil marriage are met. Additionally, a minister of a religious community, after solemnization, has to provide the State registrar with the certificate of solemnized marriage. That is why there are some authors who point out the fact that there is no real dichotomy between the civil and religious forms of marriage,[19] since, in the case where civil preconditions for marriage are not fulfilled, religious celebration is not possible.

Does a civil registrar, even after religious solemnization, additionally control whether the necessary conditions imposed by the civil law are fulfilled? A minister of a religious community who is entitled to celebrate marriage in religious form has to inform a civil registrar in writing by sending a certificate confirming that a religious marriage has been celebrated (Art 21, para 1 of the FA). Such a certificate has to be sent no later than five days after the day of marriage celebration (Art 21, para 2 of the FA). The registrar is obliged to inscribe solemnization of a religious marriage into the register of civil status within three days from the day he receives the certificate (Art 22 of the FA).

The question is whether such registration can be considered as a formal condition for granting civil effect to canonic marriage, or in other words, whether a registration of marriage in the civil register is of a constitutive nature regarding recognition of the civil effects of a canonic marriage?

According to Art 13, para 1 of the Treaty, a canonic marriage has civil effect if all provisions of family legislation are fulfilled and there are no impediments affecting the spouses. A registration of canonic marriage in a State registry of civil status is required, but not expressly as a condition for its civil validity. However, the same Article expressly provides that canonic marriage has civil effect from the moment of its celebration, and not from the moment of its registration in a register of civil status. The same solution is adopted in the FA. According to Art 23, marriage solemnized in religious form, if concluded in accordance with Art 8, 20, para 2, 3, has civil effect from the day of its solemnization.

Article 13, para 2 of the Treaty indicates that the method and time limits for registration are to be determined by Croatian legislation. The FA in Art 23 provides that a marriage celebrated in religious form has the same civil effects as a marriage celebrated in civil form if all provisions of Art 20 of the FA are fulfilled: ie if prior to religious celebration, the civil registrar issues a certificate concerning

---

[19] M Alinčić, 'A Civil Marriage Entered Into According to Government Regulations and a Religious Ceremony', in *Collective Papers of the Faculty of Law Zagreb*, 47(6) 1997, p 666.

fulfilment of conditions for religious celebration. If such a certificate is issued, canonic marriage has civil effect from the moment of its solemnization.

However, a canonic marriage has to be entered into a register of civil status. Although, the civil effects of canonic marriage derive from marriage solemnization (Art 23 of the FA), and this is the standpoint of the Croatian doctrine, its registration has to be considered as having constitutive effect. Such a solution is adopted in Polish as well as in Italian law.

According to Croatian doctrine, registration of religious marriage in the register of civil status is not a precondition for canonic marriage to have civil effect.[20] If, for the marriage solemnized in religious form, the preconditions provided in Arts 8 and 20 of the FA are not fulfilled, the officer of civil status is not allowed to register such a religious marriage in the registry of civil status.[21] Such a marriage can produce only the effects of canon law. In fact one can conclude that registration of religious marriage in the registry of civil status is of a constitutive nature because, if registration does not occur, a religious marriage has no civil effect at all. Consequently, the civil registrar has the ultimate control over marriage solemnized in religious form.

Much more comprehensible in that respect is the wording of Art 10 of the Concordat concluded between Poland and the Holy See in 1993,[22] which expressly provides that canonic marriage has civil effect from the moment of solemnization if, inter alia, canonic marriage is entered in a register of civil status within five days of its celebration.[23] There is another interesting condition for the recognition of civil effects of canonic marriage provided for in the Polish Concordat. The civil effects of canonic marriage are recognized if both spouses, at the moment of the conclusion of marriage, clearly manifest their common intention to be bound by its civil effects.

In Italian law, a registration of canonic marriage in the State registry is of a constitutive nature[24] and this is also the viewpoint of relevant scholars.[25] Civil

---

[20] Alinčić and others, *Commentary on Family Act*, Zagreb, 1999, p 16.

[21] Alinčić and others, *Family Law*, Zagreb, 2001, p 81.

[22] The Concordat between the Holy See and the Republic of Poland signed on 28 June 1993, published in *Official Gazette* 51.

[23] Article 10 of the Polish Concordat reads in the Italian language as follows:

'*1. Dal momento della celebrazione, il matrimonio canonico comporta gli effetti del matrimonio contratto secondo la legge polacca, se:*

(1) *fra gli sposi non esistono impedimenti previsti della legislazione polacca,*

(2) *in occasione della celebrazione del matrimonio essi fanno una concorde manifestazione della volontà di produrre tali effetti, e*

(3) *la celebrazione del matrimonio è stata trascritta nei registri civili su notifica trasmessa all'Ufficio dello Stato Civile entro cinque giorni della celebrazione del matrimonio; questo termine verr prolungato, qualora non fosse stato osservato a causa di forza maggiore, fino al momento della cessazione di essa.*'

[24] According to Art 8, para 1 of the Italian Treaty (Treaty between the Holy See and the Republic of Italy concerning the Amendments of the Lateran Concordat, 1984), civil effects of canonic marriage are recognized if the latter is registered in the civil register of marriages and if it was, before celebration, announced at the municipal office: see Eterović, *Treaties*, op cit, p 183.

[25] 'Per costituire una valida forma di celebrazione, il matrimonio canonico deve essere perfezionato con tutte le prescrizioni stabilite dall'articolo 8 n 1, dell'accordo fra l'Italia e la Santa Sede … Dovrà poi seguire, per completare l'efficacia del procedimento, la trascrizione … In mancanza di trascrizione, il matrimonio celebrato in forma religiosa non avrà valore …': T Ballarino, 'Il

effects for canonic marriage are recognized in Malta, according to the Treaty between Malta and the Holy See,[26] if canonic marriage is registered in the marriage registry and if it was previously announced according to the civil family law.[27] The same solution can be found in the Estonian Treaty with the Holy See, according to which the civil effects of canonic marriage are recognized as long as the letter is validly registered (Art 8).[28]

The Croatian Treaty, as well as relevant provisions of the FA, has to be interpreted in the same way. Canonic marriage produces civil effects within the Croatian legal system only if all requirements provided by Croatian family law are fulfilled on the part of the spouses, and when the religious solemnization is entered into a civil register of marriages. Ultimate State control over family matters is in that way respected.

B Religious decisions on nullity and dissolution of canonic marriage

The second aspect of canonic marriage regulated by Art 13 of the Croatian Treaty relates to the issue of religious courts' decisions in marital disputes.

According to Art 13, para 4 of the Treaty, religious courts have to hand over their decisions to competent State courts in order to apply civil effects to the latter. The provision reads as follows:

> '(4) Decisions of church courts on nullity of marriage and decisions of the Supreme Church Authority on a dissolution of matrimonial relations, must be handed over to a competent State court for applying civil effects to these decisions, in accordance with the provisions of Croatian law.'

Compulsory State control over family matters, which is required by the Croatian Constitution, means that, before attributing civil effects to such a decision, the latter has to be, necessarily, subjected to ultimate State control. Unfortunately, Art 13, para 4 does not provide the method and criteria for imposing State control, and that is why this provision has caused extensive debates on legal doctrine. Unanimous doctrinal opinion is that its unclear legal language disables its application. Moreover, it is surprising that the Croatian FA, which was adopted after the Treaty had been concluded and entered into force, contains no provisions which could clarify all legal uncertainties concerning recognition of a church decision, although legal doctrine tries, with its interpretation of Art 13, para 4 of the Treaty, to point out its practical inapplicability.

---

matrimonio concordatario nel diritto internazionale privato', *Rivista di diritto civile*, pp 829–831. See also F Santousso, *Il matrimonio*, 1987, at pp 130, 136.

[26] 'Marriages celebrated in the Catholic Church, upon registration and for which a certificate of marriage has been issued by the civil registry office, have civil effect': Art 8 of the Treaty between the Holy See and the Republic of Malta concerning Canonic Marriage of 2 February 1993, AAS 89 (1997), pp 679–694.

[27] See Eterović, *Treaties*, op cit, p 184.

[28] 'Marriages celebrated in the Catholic Church, upon registration and for which a certificate of marriage has been issued by the civil registry office, have civil effect': Art 8 of the Treaty between the Holy See and the Republic of Estonia adopted in Tallinn on 23 December 1998 and in the Vatican on 15 February 1999. See Eterović, *Treaties*, op cit, p 132.

There are two important questions deriving from Art 13, para 4 of the Treaty. First, it is not apparent what was meant by the words 'Decisions of church courts ... must be handed over to a competent State court to apply the civil effects of the religious court decision ...'. It is not clear whether a special procedure is needed in order to recognize the civil effects of church court decisions or whether recognition could be granted automatically. Secondly, it is not transparent which civil effects enter within the scope of the cited provision.

1 RECOGNITION PROCEDURE

As previously stated, the Croatian FA is completely silent regarding the possible attribution of civil effects to church court decisions in marital disputes. However, as we have seen, Art 13, para 4 of the Treaty speaks of attributing civil effects to church court decisions. In ratifying the Treaty, Croatia binds itself to attributing civil effects to church court decisions, although this possibility is not provided for in the FA. Therefore, it is very important to establish the real meaning of Art 13, para 4 of the Treaty.

Legal doctrine strongly opposes any practical enforcement of this provision. There are several grounds on which the doctrinal standpoint is based.

(1)   The attribution of civil effects to religious courts' decisions lacks constitutional justification.[29] According to the Croatian Constitution, judicial power in Croatia is vested in the State courts, which make decisions applying the Constitution and laws (Art 115). Religious courts are not part of the Croatian judicial system,[30] and therefore decisions of religious courts are, within the Croatian legal system, of no legal effect.

(2)   If canonic marriage derives its validity from religious as well as civil law, the same duality principle must govern marriage termination. Whether canonic marriage is legally terminated depends primarily upon civil family law. Article 35, para 4 of the FA provides that the civil termination of religious marriage by a State court decision on nullity or divorce does not affect the obligations of the spouses imposed on them by the religious law according to which the marriage was celebrated. If one concludes *argumentum a contrario*, termination of a religious marriage based on the religious court's decision does not affect the civil validity of the same marriage.

(3)   Moreover, it is very unclear what is meant by the words 'must be handed over to a competent State court for applying civil effects to these decisions'. What was meant by words 'applying civil effects'?

The use of the words 'applying civil effects' has no real meaning since a court applies no civil effects, but, for example, laws. As is correctly emphasized in legal doctrine, decisions, however, cannot be applied but can be enforced.[31] If we are talking about foreign decisions, their enforcement is, according to Croatian law, conditioned by their recognition in a special procedure.

---

29   Alinčić, 'A Civil Marriage Entered Into According to Government Regulations and a Religious Ceremony', in *Collective Papers of the Faculty of Law Zagreb*, 47(6), 1997, pp 668–669.

30   Hlača, 'Cessation of Marriage in the Actual Legal Problem Area', op cit, p 62.

31   Uzelac, 'From Liberalism to Catholicism', op cit, p 369.

This leads us to the question whether 'applying civil effects to religious court decisions' means in fact a recognition of such decisions. Does it mean that church court decisions in marital disputes are, in the context of the Croatian legal system, foreign decisions? There is no doubt that religious decisions from the Apostolic Seat, that is by the Pope himself, are foreign decisions with respect to the Croatian legal system. Do we have to consider religious courts in Croatia foreign? Since religious courts are not part of the Croatian judicial system, religious court decisions could be considered foreign. Therefore, the only way to attribute civil effects to those decisions would be through their recognition. However, the Croatian Treaty in Art 13, para 4 does not speak of recognition of religious decisions but only of applying to them civil effects. If we interpret these words literally, it could mean that these decisions have to be automatically recognized, which is, in the context of Croatian law, impossible.

(4)   Which civil effects can be attributed to religious decisions? Another obstacle for the application of Art 13, para 4 is, according to the doctrine, the fact that 'to apply civil effects to' religious courts' decisions could mean recognition of the legal consequences of marriage annulment or divorce. However, legal consequences are differently regulated in civil and canon law. First of all, it is not clear what civil effects are envisaged by the Treaty. Legal doctrine points out that the FA does not define the term 'civil effects' at all. However, it includes both the legal consequences of annulment of marriage and divorce, which are as articulated in doctrine different with respect to spouses and minor children.[32]

It is very doubtful whether religious decisions could be recognized in Croatia because the content of the civil effects of religious decisions is not clear. The Croatian Treaty speaks of two kinds of religious decisions: marriage annulment (*causae ad matrimonii nullitatem declarandum*), and dissolution of marital relations (*processus ad dispensationem super matrimonio rato et non consumando*). There are no corresponding decisions in Croatian family law. Croatian family law regulates the annulment of marriage but with different effects from those in canon law.[33] While in Croatian law the decision of annulment of marriage is constitutive, annulment of marriage in canon law is a declaratory decision, which means that the marriage was never concluded.

On the other hand, State courts could not enforce religious court decisions because it would be contrary to the FA, which provides a unique regime for the termination of civil marriages as well as for religious marriages. The FA in Art 35(1) expressly provides that, regardless of the form in which a marriage is solemnized, it terminates by: death of one of the spouses; declaration of death of a missing spouse; annulment; or divorce. The second paragraph of the same Article which provides for the moment of termination is important. This is the moment when the State court decision of divorce and nullity becomes *res judicata*. In the case of the State court's annulment and dissolution of religious marriage, the FA

---

[32]   M Alinčić, 'Civil Marriage Entered Into According to Government Regulations and a Religious Ceremony', op cit, p 669.

[33]   Uzelac, 'From Liberalism to Catholicism', op cit, p 370; Hlača, 'Cessation of Marriage in the Actual Legal Problem Area', op cit, p 63.

does not enlarge the legal consequences for the obligations of the spouses imposed on them by regulation of the religious community within which the marriage is concluded (Art 35, para 4). Only by a uniform legal regime for the termination of marriage can we ensure realization of the constitutional principle of equality of all citizens before the law (Art 14 of the Constitution). The equality principle becomes more relevant in the context of different religious communities and their respective religious marriage regulations.

(5)   A sound argument, which speaks against attributing civil effects to religious decisions, is that there is no national implementing regulation in this respect. Notwithstanding the truth of this argument, one has to bear in mind, first of all, that by ratifying the Treaty, its provisions were integrated into Croatian national law, and thus Croatian courts have to apply them. Moreover, according to the Croatian Constitution, the provisions of international Conventions are superior to national law.[34]

(6)   According to some authors, in everyday life there would be no need for recognition of the civil effects of church decisions[35] and therefore the problem in itself is more theoretical than practical. Although recognition of the civil effects of church decisions will be required very seldom in practice,[36] this does not deny the possible application of Art 13, para 4.

(7)   Finally, an argument opposes the application of Art 13, para 4 because it could seriously impair or violate constitutional principles of the independence of the courts, on the one hand, and on the other, equality of citizens before the law.[37]

All the above arguments, with which Croatian doctrine opposes the application of Art 13, para 4, have to be analyzed in the light of similar solutions present in comparative law. What effects, if any, are recognized for church court decisions in marital disputes in other countries?

2   RECOGNITION OF RELIGIOUS DECISIONS IN COMPARATIVE LAW

In comparative law one can find different solutions for granting civil effects to church court decisions. However, if recognition is given, then final State control is generally required.

Relevant in this respect is the Italian law concerning the issue of recognition of the civil effects of religious decisions on nullity and dissolution of canonic marriage. Without going into details[38] it is necessary to point out that in Italian law there were different solutions concerning the civil enforcement of religious decisions.

---

[34]   According to Art 140 of the Constitution of the Republic of Croatia, a ratified international treaty has supremacy over national law.

[35]   Hlača, 'The Cessation of Marriage in the Actual Legal Problem Area', op cit, p 76.

[36]   One of the reasons why spouses would seldom apply to religious courts is the fact that the Croatian FA is much more liberal with respect to marriage annulment. The conditions upon which religious courts can annul marriage are much stricter than the ones contained in family law: see Uzelac, 'From Liberalism to Catholicism', op cit, p 371.

[37]   Uzelac, 'From Liberalism to Catholicism', op cit, p 367.

[38]   See, in detail, N Hlača, 'Legal Regulation of Marriage in the Republic of Italy', *Collection of Papers of the Faculty of Law Rijeka*, 1998, pp 173–193.

The system of *separatio imperfeta*, the Concordato Laterano from 1929 and respective national legislation characterize the first period which lasted from 1929 to 1984. Religious decisions on nullity of canonic marriage were enforced through the procedure of official and automatic recognition.[39] Such automatic recognition was a consequence of the exclusive jurisdiction which religious courts had concerning annulment and dissolution of concordat (canonic) marriage.[40]

The system of automatic recognition of the civil effects of canonic marriage and of religious courts, affirmed by the Concordat of 1929, was strongly criticized. Under the influence of the Italian judicature, which abolished the principle of automatic recognition, the Concordat was revised in 1984.

The new Agreement of Villa Madama was formulated under the influence of the practice of the Constitutional Court as well as that of the Court of Cassation whose decisions almost eroded completely the independent religious court system. According to Art 8(2) of the new Agreement, State courts must recognize the enforceable character of religious decisions on annulment of canonic marriage in the same manner in which Italian courts recognize the effects of foreign decisions within the Italian legal system.[41]

The analogy which is drawn between religious decisions on the annulment of canonic marriage and foreign court decisions stems from the principle of separation of these two systems (civil and religious).

Concurrence between two systems is the main principle underlying the new Italian Agreements which regulate relations between Italy and the Holy See. However, it is a system of separation but not an absolute one. The Constitutional Court considered the very issue of the relation between the two systems in its decision no 18 of 1982. If a legal relation to which civil effects are recognized, is created by canon law, and canon law regulates its validity, it is logical that disputes concerning validity fall within the jurisdiction of the same legal order. However, those decisions concerning validity have to be enforced through special enforcement proceedings in order to secure uniformity for all citizens and legal security.

Therefore, the system, which today actually defines legal relations between the Catholic Church and the State, is a system of *separazione imperfetta*. Canon and civil family law are two separate, independent systems of laws. However, separation is not complete (it is imperfect) because canonic marriage can have civil effect only if the parties can conclude civil marriage, on the one hand, and on the other, religious church courts' decisions on the annulment of marriage are

---

[39]   F Finocchiaro, 'Sentenze ecclesiastiche e giurisdizione dello stato sul matrimonio "concordatario" nell' accordo 18 febbraio 1984 fra l'Italia e la Santa Sede', *Diritto processuale*, 1984, 4, str 406 et seq.

[40]   The relation, which was established by the Concordat from 1929 with the Catholic religious community, was in fact delegation of State sovereignty to a certain degree to one religious community and was enforced by exclusive jurisdiction of the religious courts to decide upon marital disputes. In 1982 the Constitutional Court insisted on the principle of State sovereignty, and in decision nos 16 and 17 of 1982 abolished Art 1 of Law no 810 and Art 17 of Law no 845, since those provisions restrained the Italian Court of Appeal from deciding upon recognition of religious court decisions on the annulment of marriage. See: Santosuosso, *Il matrimonio*, op cit, at p 172.

[41]   Ibid at p 411.

enforceable within the Italian legal system only if the decision in that respect is given in a special recognition procedure (*procedimento di delibacione*) .

Religious decisions have no automatic civil effects as was the case before 1984. The system of *separazione imperfeta* means also that religious courts have no exclusive jurisdiction regarding the nullity of concordat marriage, as Concordato Laterano considered it to be in 1929. An Italian or any other State court can also annul canonic marriage. It is up to the parties to choose between the State or religious court. Moreover, if proceedings are commenced before the State court while between the same parties and on the same subject matter proceedings are pending before the church court, the State court will continue its proceedings and the religious decision will not be recognized.

According to the reformed Concordats, church courts lost their exclusive jurisdiction to decide the validity of canonic marriage. The new Agreement equates decisions of church courts with decisions made by foreign States' courts. This brings us again to the principle of *separazione imperfeta* between the two systems of law: religious and secular.

This principle is expressly provided in Art 8(2)(a) and (b) of the new Agreement of 1984, providing that the Italian court has to determine whether the church court is competent (if, for example, the subject matter of dispute is canonic marriage) and that during the proceedings before the church court, the parties have a possibility to act and to defend their rights as they would have in State court proceedings.[42] Those rights must not differ from those provided by the fundamental principles of Italian civil procedure.

But these are not the only requirements for granting civil enforcement of religious decisions. According to subparagraph (c) of the same Article, in order to enforce the civil effects of a religious decision, it is necessary to determine also if 'other requirements required by Italian legislation for the recognition of foreign court decisions are met'.[43] This means that the Italian court has to find that the religious decision is not contrary to the Italian *ordre public*, that it is not contrary to any decision made by an Italian court, and finally that there are no proceedings pending before an Italian court between the same parties and on the same subject matter, commenced before the religious decision becomes final.

Without going into detail, State control over religious decisions is required in some other countries.

Very similar to the Italian provisions are provisions of the Maltese law combining the religious court's decisions concerning annulment of canonic marriage, as well as a decision of the Holy Father concerning dissolution of marriage.[44]

---

[42] Very interesting in this context is the judgment of the European Court of Human Rights of 20 July 2001, in the case of *Pellegrini v Italy* (no 30882/96). Pellegrini brought an action before the European Court claiming that Art 6(1) of the European Convention on Human Rights was violated by recognition of the ecclesiastical court decision on nullity of marriage because, in the procedure before the ecclesiastical court, her right to a fair trail had been violated.

[43] Finocchiaro, 'Sentenze ecclesiastiche e giurisdizione dello stato sul matrimonio "concordatario" nell' accordo 18 febbraio 1984 fra l'Italia e la Santa sede', op cit, p 412 et seq.

[44] State courts in Malta must determine whether in the same dispute the decision has already been made in the civil court on the same basis as that before the religious courts (Art 5 of the Treaty between the Holy See and the Republic of Malta concerning Canonic Marriage signed on 3 February 1993, AAS 89 (1997) pp 679–694).

According to the Treaty concerning Legal Questions of 1979 between the Holy See and Spain, any ex-spouse is authorized, after a religious decision is made, to apply for civil effects of the religious decision. However, the religious decision is recognized only if the State court finds that the religious decision is in accordance with civil law.[45]

According to the Portuguese Concordat, final religious decisions in marital disputes approved by the Supreme Court of the Apostolic Seat, will be by diplomatic means sent to the Portuguese Supreme Court, which will enforce them and order their entry in the civil register.[46] Portuguese State courts recognize decisions of the Supreme Apostolic Seat and enforce those decisions.

As already mentioned, the Polish Concordat of 1993 adopts a solution which avoids these problems. The provisions of the Concordat provide for separation of jurisdiction between religious and State courts. Ecclesiastical courts have exclusive jurisdiction concerning the validity of canonic marriage and concerning other matrimonial disputes provided by canon law (Art 10, para 3). Matrimonial disputes concerning the effects prescribed by Polish law fall within the exclusive jurisdiction of the Polish courts (Art 10, para 4). This system is similar to the system which was applied in Italy under the Concordat of 1929. Because of the exclusive jurisdiction of the religious courts to decide upon the validity of canon marriage, their decisions are automatically recognized. The Polish Concordat provides only for the compulsory notification of decisions made by religious courts.[47]

IV   POSSIBLE DE LEGE FERENDA SOLUTIONS

Taking into consideration the above doctrinal standpoints concerning the practical applicability of Art 13, para 4 of the Croatian Treaty, we are of the opinion that automatic recognition of the civil effects of church court decisions is not possible. The main reason has already been mentioned. Article 35 of the FA clearly refers to separation between Church and State concerning the decision on nullity or separation of a religious marriage. Consequently, church decisions could not be recognized automatically.

However, there is some logic in considering religious court decisions as foreign decisions. Being considered foreign, these decisions could produce effects within the Croatian legal system only if recognized by a Croatian court.[48]

Recognition of foreign judgments in Croatia is regulated by the Croatian Private International Law Act (PILA).[49] The question arises whether these provisions can be applied by analogy to the enforcement of civil effects of church court decisions?

---

[45]   See Eterović, *Treaties*, op cit, p 184.

[46]   Article 25, *Concordatos II*, pp 347–348.

[47]   The procedure of notification will be according to Art 27 of the Concordat.

[48]   There are some authors who advocate such an approach to religious court decisions, see Hlača, 'The Cessation of Marriage in the Actual Legal Problem Area', op cit, p 62.

[49]   Law on Private International Law (Zakon o rješavanju sukoba zakona s propisima drugih zemalja u određenim odnosima), *Official Gazette* 53/91.

The answer to this question is twofold. On the one hand, it presupposes that church decisions are regarded as foreign decisions, and on the other hand, that the recognition conditions enumerated in the PILA are by their nature applicable to 'religious decisions'.

Is a religious decision on nullity of marriage a foreign decision?

The answer depends on whether religious courts in Croatia can be regarded as foreign courts. Since, as mentioned previously, religious courts are not part of the Croatian judicial system they can only be considered to be foreign.

According to the PILA, foreign decisions are to be recognized only if there is no exclusive international jurisdiction in that matter (Art 89), if the foreign decision is *res judicata* (Art 87), if the parties have had a right to act and to defend their interests and if there are no errors in *procedendo* (Art 88), if there is reciprocity (Art 92), if the foreign decision is not contrary to the *ordre public* (Art 91), if there is no decision of a Croatian court in that respect or if there are no proceedings instituted before the Croatian court between the same parties and upon the same subject matter (Art 90), and, finally, if the foreign decision does not differ substantially from solutions provided by Croatian family law (Art 93).

If the recognition of foreign judgments procedure provided by the PILA could be applied to the enforcement of religious decisions too, application and interpretation of these conditions would be very difficult, especially the condition on public policy, and the other more subtle condition that a foreign decision concerning the personal status of a Croatian national does not in its solution differ substantially from the solutions of Croatian law.

Since there are some differences between the causes for annulment of marriage in canonic and Croatian family law, the question is whether those differences will be considered as contrary to Croatian public policy or whether substantial difference with respect to Croatian law would be invoked.[50] What would be considered contrary to public policy and what religious decisions would be considered as decisions whose solutions differ substantially from solutions of Croatian law is something which is open to doubt.

Very interesting in this respect is the solution introduced in the Italian *Protocollo addizionale* in Art 4, subpara (b), according to which:

> '... in order to apply Arts 796 and 797 of the Italian Code of Civil Procedure,[51] one has to take into consideration the specificity of the system of canon law which regulates canon marriage, which in fact originates from the latter ...'

---

[50] The enforcement of religious decisions will cause no problem in cases where the system of marital impediment is almost the same in canon and civil law. The situation is different where causes for annulment provided by the canon law are invoked such as non-consummation of marriage, unilateral mental reservation, ordine sacro, cultus disparitas or when marriage is contrary to bonus sacramenti.

[51] At the time the Additional Protocol was concluded, recognition and enforcement of foreign judgments was regulated by the Code of Civil Procedure (Arts 796–797). From 1995 a new Private International Law Act has been in force in Italy (*Rivista di diritto internazionale privato e processuale*, 1995, 4) which regulates the procedure of recognition and enforcement of foreign decisions. This change in regulation also has its implications in the sphere of enforcement of religious decisions.

Such definition is given with the purpose of facilitating recognition of religious decisions despite differences between canon and civil law with respect to the annulment of marriage.

Taking into consideration the conditions for recognition of foreign judgments provided for in the Croatian PILA, it would be very difficult to recognize religious court decisions on nullity of marriage. However, Croatian legal doctrine is considering the revision of the PILA and some theses have been already published.

It is the author's opinion that it would be appropriate to reconsider the possibility of formulating a special recognition regime for religious court decisions in marital disputes, as has been done in Italy.

V SOME PRIVATE INTERNATIONAL LAW ASPECTS OF CANON MARRIAGE

Private international law regulations are relevant whenever a disputed relationship has connections with two or more legal systems. This can be the case with canonic marriage too where a foreign element can be manifested through the place of celebration (ie where canonic marriage is celebrated abroad), or through the fact that at least one of the future spouses is a foreigner.

When canonic marriage is concerned there are three issues in connection with which conflict of laws issues can arise. These are:

–   the form and formal conditions for marriage solemnization;
–   the capacity to marry; and
–   the preconditions for entry into marriage.

The form of marriage within the private international law context poses the following dilemma: whether the domestic canon regime would apply to marriages celebrated abroad in a religious form. This leads to another question – whether the canon law has extraterritorial effects.

Advocates for the extraterritorial nature of the Concordat argue that canon law regulates marriage as a sacrament, which is of universal value and therefore, by its nature, excludes any territorial character.[52] Canonic marriage has sacral character which finds its basis in universal values and which excludes any territorial limitations.[53] On the other hand, some authors argue that the Concordat is an international treaty which regulates relations between the State and the Holy See, and therefore regulates relations arising out of a specific State territory.[54] The author agrees with the second opinion, namely that a concordat regime has to

---

[52]   F Finocchiario, 'Matrimonio', in *Enciclopedia del diritto*, vol XXV, 1975, p 859; see also L Christians, 'Le droit canonique internormatif. Conflits de lois et de jurisdiction avec les systèmes étatiques et les autres systèmes religieux en droit matrimonial', *Revue critique de droit international privé*, 198, 2, pp 217–249.

[53]   T Ballerino, 'Il matrimonio concordatario nel diritto internazionale privato', op cit, at p 821.

[54]   In legal theory, some argued that the Concordat cannot be treated as an international contract because of the lack of its legal nature, since its basis is moral and not legal obligation: see M Falco, *Concordato ecclesiastico, Nouvo digesto italiano III*, Torino, 1938, at p 656.

apply to relations originating on the territory of the State with which the Concordat is concluded.

Whether a canonic marriage celebrated in some other country between a Croatian and a foreigner can be, regarding its form, considered valid in Croatia, or whether foreigners can choose canonic marriage as the form of marriage and celebrate such marriage in Croatia is the question.

Under the religious law of certain Churches, ministers of such Churches are entitled to solemnize marriages without territorial limitation in any particular country.[55] States which accept such universal competence do recognize marriages of their nationals solemnized outside their country. Such attitude towards canonic marriage, as well as towards religious decisions, was adopted in Italy according to Art 34(4) of the Concordat of 1929.[56] Today when, according to the reformed Concordat of 1984, there is no such automatic recognition of canonic marriage, a different approach is adopted towards recognition of canonic marriage solemnized outside Italy. Although there is no unanimous opinion, the dominant opinion is that such recognition is not possible.[57] On the other hand, some authors find such recognition appropriate, and in the same vein is the Court of Cassation, which in some of its decisions favors such recognition.[58] If a marriage is celebrated by a minister of the Catholic Church outside Italy, between two Italians, or between an Italian and a foreigner, according to some opinion, such marriage is valid after being subjected to a special regime of concordat marriages. This means that such a marriage has to be inscribed in the Italian register of civil status.

It is traditionally accepted in comparative private international law that a form of marriage is subject to *lex loci actus* (*lex loci celebrationis*) which means that marriage is valid in its form if it is valid according to the law of the State where it is celebrated. Such a solution is accepted in the Croatian PILA (Art 33). Where religious marriages are concerned, there are some exceptions to that rule. The validity of canonic marriage is subject to numerous procedural and material requirements, such as registration of such a marriage. In that case, its validity, where its form is concerned, depends on later recognition of that marriage through inscription in the registers of civil status. An important factor is also the fact of whether the country where the marriage is celebrated recognizes or does not recognize the religious form of marriage. Therefore, if the marriage is validly contracted in a foreign country in religious form, such marriage should be recognized as valid, but in order to produce civil effects in Croatia, it should be entered into the registers of civil status. If, on the contrary, in the foreign country the civil form of marriage is obligatory, then a marriage celebrated in religious form cannot be recognized as valid according to Croatian law.

---

[55] L Pållson, 'Marriage and Divorce', *International Encyclopedia of Comparative Law*, vol III, *Private International Law*, ch 6, at p 40.

[56] That was the case with Italy during the application of the Concordat from 1929, when canon marriages and religious decisions were automatically recognized, even where celebrated or issued outside Italy: see Ballarino, 'Il matrimonio concordatario nel diritto internazionale privato', op cit, p 822.

[57] Vitali, 'In tema di matrimonio canonico dei cittadini all'estero', *Rivista di diritto internazionale privato e processuale,* 1996, pp 513–518; Ballarino, 'Il matrimonio concordatario nel diritto internazionale privato', op cit, p 822.

[58] For more details about judicial practice, see Pållson, 'Marriage and Divorce', op cit, p 40.

Another question in the sphere of the private international law of canonic marriages refers to the question of capacity to marry. Capacity of physical persons is traditionally subject to the national law of the person in question. *Lex nationalis* is applicable for substantial elements of canonic marriage as well.[59]

Assuming that a Croatian national and a foreigner would like to enter into marriage in Croatia and they choose religious solemnization, concerning the issue of preconditions for the existence of marriage or marital prohibitions, besides the application of canon law, the law of the spouse's nationality also has to be applied. Since the minister of the Catholic Church will apply canon law, it will be for the State authorities to determine whether all provisions of national law are satisfied.

A solemnization of canonic marriage does not exclude application of private international law provisions regarding capacity to marry and regarding conditions for material validity of canonic marriage, especially if those conditions are ignored by canon law, or canon law regulates them differently.

When will application of private international provisions be relevant? At the moment of entering in the register of civil status the fact that a canonic marriage was solemnized, the competent registrar will have to determine whether all conditions provided by the *lex nationalis* are satisfied. According to the *de lege lata* solution of the FA, this will also have to be before celebration of canonic marriage, because a registrar will have to issue a document stating that there are no impediments with respect to the spouses. If the spouses are foreigners, those preconditions for entering into marriage will have to be checked according to their *lex nationalis* and, for some preconditions, Croatian provisions are the rules of immediate application (existence of previous marriage, prohibited degrees, natural incapacity) (Art 32 of the PILA).

---

[59]   Ballarino, 'Il matrimonio concordatario nel diritto internazionale privato', op cit, p 828.

THE CZECH REPUBLIC

ADOPTION IN THE CZECH REPUBLIC: REFORM IN THE LIGHT OF THE CHILD WELFARE LAWS

Zdeňka Králíčková[*]

I INTRODUCTION

Adoption is one of the traditional institutions of family law. It is understood as an institution of substitute family care and as a service for the minor child (especially an orphan) in most laws. As regards the legal regulation of adoption in the Czech Republic, it has its roots in Roman law. Nevertheless, the contemporary law of adoption is marked by a tendency to respect human rights and child welfare and to establish the rule of law in the country. The main steps have been taken by passing new Acts, not only in the field of constitutional law but also in the sphere of private law, especially family law, by signing International Conventions, and by introducing a totally new approach to adoption.[1]

II CURRENT LEGAL REGULATION OF ADOPTION

A National law

Adoption is not only a matter of family law. Regarding the new conception of rights of the child and because of the child's new legal status in the family and society, it is necessary to look first at the constitutional position. The Charter of Fundamental Rights and Freedoms (which is part of the constitutional order of the Czech Republic) is based on the theory of *ius naturale* protecting man, woman, child and natural family.[2] The whole legal order, including family law norms,

---

[*] Assistant lecturer at the Faculty of Law, Masaryk University, Brno, the Czech Republic, and former assistant to the Justice of the Supreme Court of the Czech Republic.

[1] The tendency to regard adoption as an institution serving the best interests of the child was already introduced in the 1970s. See A Chloros: 'Adoption in Creation of Relationships of Kinship, in Persons and Family', in *The International Encyclopedia of Comparative Law*, Vol IV, chapter 6, 1976, p 12.

[2] Two judgments of the Constitutional Court of the Czech Republic may serve as proof that the Czech Republic takes the protection of the rights of the child seriously.

  (a) First, the Constitutional Court dealt with the problem of depriving the child of his legal family by administrative decision. Because of the so-called 'negative law making', the Constitutional Court struck down Art 46 of the Family Act of the Czech Republic. This provision enabled the separation of the child from his/her parents against their will by a 'preliminary' administrative act of the former district national committee (district council). According to the new regulation, which is in harmony with the international standards for the protection of the rights of the child, the minor child can be separated from its legal family against the will of the parents only by court determination, in accordance with

must be created, interpreted and applied in light of the Charter as a whole and be guided always by the principle of the best interests of the child and that of the child's participation.

The above-mentioned Charter of Fundamental Rights and Freedoms (No 2/1993 Coll) provides fundamental guarantees for the protection of family, partnership, and children (Art 32, para 1). The Charter expresses explicitly that the care and upbringing of the child is the right of the child's parents and that children have the right to be cared for by their own parents. The 'natural family' is then protected by a provision declaring that the rights of parents can be limited and minor children can be separated from their parents against their will only on the basis of a court's determination in accordance with applicable law (Art 32, para 4). All the institutions of substitute family care, including adoption, need to be understood according to the literal meaning of the word as 'substitution' for the natural family.

The main sources of substantive law in the Czech Republic include the Act on the Family (*Zákon o rodině*, Act No 94/1964 Coll, abbreviated here to 'Czech AF') and the Civil Code (*Občanský zákoník*, Act No 40/1964 Coll, abbreviated here to 'Czech CC'). The essential changes in family law (including matrimonial property law regulated in the Civil Code) were made by the so-called great amendment to the Family Act (Act No 91/1998 Coll). Then the Act on the Social and Legal Protection of Children (the so-called 'Children Act', *Zákon o sociálně-právní ochraně dětí*, Act No 359/1999 Coll) was passed which represented a turning point in the legal protection of the rights of the child. Due to this Act, new forms of co-operation (mediation) in respect of adoption (including inter-country adoption) are regulated.

Owing to the fact that adoption can be granted only by a court, the Act on Civil Judicial Order (*Občanský soudní řád*, Act No 99/1963 Coll), as the basic source of civil procedure law, has to be mentioned. The process of adoption is governed by special rules (Arts 181–185).

B   International law

As far as adoption with international aspects is concerned, the Act on International Private and Procedural Law (*Zákon o mezinárodním právu soukromém a procesním*, Act No 96/1963 Coll) is applied as the basic source of international private law in the Czech Republic. The regulation is traditional. However, the importance of the Act has increased with the spread of international contacts since 1989.

---

applicable law and procedures, ensuring that such separation is necessary for the best interests of the child. See Judgment of the Constitutional Court of the Czech Republic No 72/1995 Coll.

(b)   The Constitutional Court then expressed its opinion on the matter of adoption of an adult person. On the basis of constitutional motions, the Constitutional Court considered whether the Family Act discriminated against adult persons in permitting adoption only for minor children. The Constitutional Court ruled that the equality of subjects of law is not an 'absolute' category. Then it explained in the judgment that a child (by reason of his physical and mental immaturity) needs special safeguards and care and has to be protected by special measures. The institution of adoption is one such measure. See Judgment of the Constitutional Court of the Czech Republic No 295/1996 Coll.

As regards international documents, it is necessary to distinguish between declarations, universal International Conventions and regional International Conventions signed by the Czech Republic in recent years.[3]

1 DECLARATIONS

Among declarations, the Declaration on Social and Legal Principles relating to the Protection and Welfare of Children with special reference to Foster Placement and Adoption Nationally and Internationally (adopted by the United Nations General Assembly Resolution No 41/85 of 3 December 1986)[4] has to be mentioned.

2 UNIVERSAL INTERNATIONAL CONVENTIONS

The most important universal International Conventions include the following.

UN Convention on the Rights of the Child

The Convention on the Rights of the Child was adopted by the United Nations General Assembly Resolution No 44/25 of 20 November 1989 as the first international document devoted exclusively to children. It is considered as the 'Magna Carta' of the rights of the child as it includes a full catalogue of the rights of the child from birth to maturity. The best interests of the child, as the ruling principle of the Convention, is to be a primary consideration in all actions concerning children (Art 3, para 1).

The right of the child to grow up in a family environment, in an atmosphere of happiness, love and understanding is expressed in the Preamble to the Convention. The child's own family is considered to be the natural environment for the growth and well-being of the child. But the child temporarily or permanently deprived of his/her natural family environment, or the child who cannot be allowed to remain in such an environment for his/her best interest, should be entitled to special protection and assistance provided by the State (Art 20, para 1). It is emphasised that, when considering possible solutions, due regard is to be paid to the desirability of continuity in the child's upbringing and to the child's ethnic, religious, cultural and linguistic background (Art 20, para 3).

Regarding the institution of adoption, the Convention pays great attention to many aspects of the matter in question. First of all, the Convention views adoption as a 'substitute' measure for solving problems of the non-functional natural family. The adoption of a minor child is to be authorised only by competent authorities who determine, in accordance with applicable law and procedures and on the basis of all pertinent and reliable information, that the adoption is permissible in the light of the child's status concerning parents, relatives and legal guardians, and that, if required, the persons concerned have given their informed

---

[3] It is necessary to state that the Czech Republic harmonised its legal order with international standards even before signing the International Conventions, mainly by passing the so-called great amendment to the Act on the Family (Act No 91/1998 Coll) and the Act on Social and Legal Protection of Children (the so-called 'Children Act', Act No 359/1999 Coll).

[4] This Declaration is not legally binding, but its principles were taken into account in the preparation of the International Convention on Protection of Children and Co-operation in respect of Inter-country Adoption.

consent to the adoption on the basis of such counselling as may be necessary (Art 21, para a).

As regards inter-country adoption, this is to be considered an alternative mechanisim for the child's care when the child cannot be placed in a foster family or an adoptive family or cannot in any suitable manner be cared for in the child's country of origin (Art 21, para b). The Convention attempts to prevent any misuse of the institution of adoption and mainly improper financial gain due to inter-country adoption (Art 21, para c).

The Czech Republic is a State Party to the Convention.[5] The former Czech and Slovak Federal Republic signed the Convention on 30 September 1990 and the Convention came into force on 6 February 1991. The Convention was published as No 104/1991 Coll.

In this context, the Constitution of the Czech Republic (Constitutional Act No 1/1993 Coll) should be considered. According to its tenth provision, the ratified and published International Conventions on human rights and fundamental freedoms which are binding on the Czech Republic are immediately applicable and have priority over Czech laws.[6] This means that the United Nations Convention is directly applicable in the Czech Republic by courts and administrative bodies.

Hague Convention on Protection of Children and Co-operation in Respect of Inter-country Adoption

The Hague Convention on Protection of Children and Co-operation in Respect of Inter-country Adoption was adopted by the Hague Conference of Private International Law on 29 May 1993 as Convention No 33 with the aim of preventing abduction, the sale of, or traffic in children, and the commercialisation of inter-country adoption.

The Convention recognises, as does the Convention on the Rights of the Child, the right of the minor child to grow up in a family environment, in an atmosphere of happiness, love and understanding. The Convention prefers the upbringing of the child in his/her family of origin but recognises that inter-country adoption may offer the advantage of a permanent family to a child for whom a suitable family cannot be found in his/her State of origin. The Convention attaches importance to the continuity of the child's upbringing and his/her ethnic, religious and cultural background (Art 16, para 1, sub-para b).

The Convention lays down a strict condition[7] for inter-country adoption. It is expressly stated that each Contracting State has to designate a 'Central Authority'

---

[5] See *www.un.org*.

[6] See the recently amended Art 10 of the Constitution of the Czech Republic which came into force on 1 June 2002 and which provides as follows:

'The published International Conventions which the Parliament has agreed with and which the Czech Republic is bound by become part of the legal order. If an international Convention provides something contrary to the Act the Convention shall apply.'

[7] It is necessary to stress that the adoption must take place within the scope of Art 4 of the Hague Convention on Protection of Children and Co-operation in respect of Inter-country Adoption, which provides that the competent authorities of the State of origin:

(a) have established that the child is adoptable (which means 'legally free');

(b) have determined that inter-country adoption is in the child's best interest;

to discharge the duties which are imposed by the Convention upon such authorities (Art 6, para 1).[8] The procedural requirements for inter-country adoption,[9] recognition, and effects of adoption[10] are the subject of special provisions.

The Czech Republic signed the Convention on 11 February 2000 and ratified it on 1 June 2000. The Convention was published as No 43/2000 Coll of international conventions and came into force on 1 June 2000.[11]

3 REGIONAL INTERNATIONAL CONVENTIONS

The European Convention on the Adoption of Children is one of the most important regional International Conventions. The Convention was signed by the member states of the Council of Europe in Strasbourg on 24 April 1967 as Convention No 58. The Convention was passed bearing in mind that, although the institution of the adoption of children exists in all member countries of the Council of Europe, there are in those countries differing views as to the principles which should govern adoption and differences in the procedure for effecting, and the legal consequences of, adoption. The establishing of common principles and practices with respect to the adoption of children was the key aim[12] of the Convention, which was to help to reduce the difficulties caused by those differences and, at the same time, promote the welfare of children who are adopted. The Convention emphasises the principle that adoption should be in the interests of the child (Art 8, para 1) and that adoption should provide the child with a stable and harmonious home (Art 8, para 2). Special attention is paid to

---

(c) have ensured that the persons, institutions and authorities whose consent is necessary for adoption have been counselled and duly informed of the effects of their consent, their consents have been given freely and in the required legal form and have not been induced by payment or compensation of any kind, and the consent of the mother has been given after the child's birth;

(d) have ensured, having regard to the age and degree of maturity of the child, that the child has been counselled and duly informed of the effects of the adoption and of his or her consent to the adoption, where such a consent is required, and consideration has been given to the child's wishes and opinions.

[8] See Chapter III entitled 'Central Authorities and Accredited Bodies' (Arts 6–13), of the Hague Convention which provides that a Contracting State must designate a Central Authority to discharge the duties which are imposed by the Convention. The Central Authorities must then take all appropriate measures to prevent improper financial or other gain in connection with an adoption.

[9] See Chapter IV of the Hague Convention that contains provisions entitled 'Procedural Requirements in Intercountry Adoption'.

[10] First of all it is necessary to say that recognition of an adoption aims at establishing the legal parent–child relationship between the child and his/her adoptive parents and the parental responsibility of the adoptive parents for the child (Art 26 of the Hague Convention). From Chapter VI of the Hague Convention 'General Provisions', it is necessary to point out the prohibition of contacts between prospective adoptive parents and the child's parents (Art 29 of the Hague Convention), the requirement to preserve all information obtained, namely the identity of the child's parents as well as the medical history (Art 30 of the Hague Convention), and prevention of any improper financial or other gain from an activity related to an inter-country adoption (Art 32 of the Hague Convention).

[11] See *www.hcch.net*.

[12] For details, see V Novotná: 'O Evropské úmluvě o osvojení' ('Concerning the European Convention on the Adoption of Children'), *Náhradní rodinná péče*, 1999, No 1, p 16.

anonymity in adoption,[13] although generally it is possible to say that the recent trend seems to be to replace anonymity with openness. This relates to the fact that the institution of adoption is to be regarded as a 'service' for the child.[14] It is interesting that the new Russian law strictly preserves the anonymity of adoption by even allowing, for the purpose of anonymity, to change of the date of birth and the birthplace of the child.[15]

The Czech Republic signed the Convention on 15 December 1999 and ratified it on 8 September 2000. This Convention was published as No 132/2000 Coll of International Conventions in the Czech Republic. Moreover, it came into force on 9 December 2000. The Czech Republic made a reservation[16] to the Convention to the effect that it will not apply Art 7, para 1 of the Convention. Nevertheless, it is possible to state that the legal order of the Czech Republic was put into conformity with the Convention by passing the so-called great amendment to the Act on the Family (by the Act No 91/1998 Coll).

III TERMINOLOGY AND CLASSIFICATION OF ADOPTION

Adoption (*osvojení*) is traditionally understood as acceptance of a stranger's child as one's own and as a voluntary assumption of parental obligations by an individual who usually is not the biological parent of the person adopted. It can be

---

[13]   In this context we may note that Art 20 of the European Convention on the Adoption of Children states *expressis verbis* that:
   '(1)   Provision shall be made to enable an adoption to be completed without disclosing to the child's family the identity of the adopter.
   (2)   Provision shall be made to require or permit adoption proceedings to take place *in camera*.
   (3)   The adopter and the adopted person shall be able to obtain a document which contains extracts from the public records attesting the fact, date and place of birth of the adopted person, but not expressly revealing the fact of adoption or the identity of his former parents.
   (4)   Public records shall be kept and, in any event, their contents reproduced in such a way as to prevent persons who do not have a legitimate interest from learning the fact that a person has been adopted or, if that is disclosed, the identity of his former parents.'
   We may ask if the above-mentioned provisions are not contrary to the UN Convention on the Rights of the Child. It is necessary to point out the following provisions of the Convention:
   –   Art 7, which provides that the child has the right to know his/her parents,
   –   Art 8, which provides that the child has the right to preserve his/her identity, including nationality, name and family relations.
   In practice, all the above-mentioned principles should be harmonised so that the best interest of the child should be followed in each case. On this problem, see J Švestka in M Hrušáková and coll: *Zákon o rodině. Komentář* (*Act on the Family. Commentary*) (2nd ed, CH Beck, Praha, 2000), p 262.

[14]   See M Garrison: 'Law making for baby making: an interpretative approach to the determination of legal parentage', *Harvard Law Review*, 2000, No 4, pp 889–891.

[15]   See J Haderka: 'Nové ruské rodinné právo' ('New Russian Family Law'), *Právní praxe*, 1997, No 4, p 237.

[16]   Article 7, para 1 of the European Convention on the Adoption of Children establishes that 'a child may be adopted only if the adopter has attained the minimum age prescribed for the purpose, this age being neither less than 21 nor more than 35 years'.

viewed as an 'imitation' of a biological relationship (*adoptione natura imitatur*).[17] This conception applies in the Czech Republic.

Adoption can be classified according to many criteria. Regarding the position of the minor child in his/her new adoptive family, it is possible to distinguish full adoption (*adoptione plena*) and simple adoption (*adoptione minus plena*). The conception of full adoption is characteristic in Czech law. It means that the child joins legally the new adoptive family and obtains all the rights of the child born in lawful wedlock,[18] including hereditary rights.

With regard to establishment and revocation of the legal relationship between the adopter and the adopted child, it is possible to classify the adoption according to whether it was based on contract or on an administrative or judicial act. The adoption based on a contract between the parties, and as a device primarily intended to perpetuate a family, seems to be a relic of the past.[19] Adoption based on a court decision is the modern type of adoption which has the child's welfare as its principal purpose. The law in the Czech Republic now follows this conception.

As to revocation, we may distinguish revocable adoption and irrevocable (permanent) adoption. The law in the Czech Republic allows both types, although the revocation of adoption is considered an exceptional case available only on serious grounds. If adoption is to fulfil its aim, it must provide the minor child with a long-lasting family environment, and it is necessary to pay great attention to the mutual suitability of the prospective adopter and the child, to the professional preparation of the prospective adopter, and to the proper procedural requirements of adoption.[20]

Regarding the possibility of re-adoption, we should distinguish adoption with re-adoption from adoption without re-adoption. The Act on the Family in the Czech Republic enables re-adoption, but only in the case of irrevocable adoption.

As to the number of adopters, there is individual adoption and joint adoption. The law in the Czech Republic recognises both types. Joint adoption is possible only for couples.[21]

Regarding the future residence of the child there is the possibility of:

(a)   inner-country adoption;
(b)   adoption from abroad; and
(c)   adoption abroad.

---

[17]   Of course, this definition cannot apply when the adoption serves for 'producing an heir or securing succession to a title', or even for the 'legitimation of children born out of wedlock'. For details see A Chloros: *Adoption*, op cit, p 12.

[18]   The term 'child born out of wedlock' has been acknowledged by Czech law since 1949 when the Act on Family Law was passed. It was inspired by the Soviet model.

[19]   According to the Czech historical position (Austrian Civil Code, ABGB, 1811) adoption was established and terminated by a contract. As a residual feature of this conception, the possibility of terminating adoption by a contract made between adopters and adult children was preserved in both the Act on the Law of Family (1949) and the Act on the Family (1963). The amendment to this second Act (1998, only in the Czech Republic) allowed termination of adoption only on the basis of the court's decision.

[20]   As to this problem, see the new detailed provisions in the Act on the Social and Legal Protection of Children (the so-called 'Children Act', Act No 359/1999 Coll).

[21]   Joint adoption is allowed in the current law only for spouses. See also the European Convention on Adoption of Children, Art 9(2)(b).

The current Czech laws regulate all the above-mentioned types of adoption while taking the first steps towards harmonisation of Czech laws with those of the countries of the European Union.[22]

IV   THE PURPOSE OF ADOPTION

As a natural right of the child, expressed in a long line of national and international documents,[23] we should emphasise the child's right to be cared for by his/her own parents, to grow up in their care and under their parental responsibility. Provided that the parents cannot (owing to objective or subjective reasons and circumstances) or do not want to provide comprehensive care for the child, the State is supposed to take adequate measures commensurate with the scale of the problem in the natural family. Depriving the child of his/her original family and his/her placement in substitute care is to be considered the strongest measure for solving the crisis between the child and his/her parents. Each substitute placement should be understood as a 'substitute' in its linguistic meaning and primarily as a 'service' for the child. Each form of substitute care should be oriented towards the child. The best interests of the child should be followed in each step taken by administrative and juridical authorities.

It is necessary to mention that the so-called socialist law always regulated adoption as an institution of substitute family care, as a 'service' for the minor child. Contrary to this, some laws traditionally viewed the institution of adoption from different perspectives. Those laws enabled adoption of an adult person for the purpose of producing heirs, securing succession to a title, etc (Germany, Austria). However, modern trends follow the conception that adoption is oriented towards the minor child, and to his best interests,[24] to the protection of the natural family, to the protection of the parent in difficulty (especially unmarried or minor mothers), and to the protection of the rights of the so-called 'putative' father.[25]

V   GROUNDS FOR ADOPTION

Regarding the essential grounds for adoption, not all of them are expressed *expressis verbis* in the law; some of them arise only from the nature, purpose and aim of the institution of adoption. However, if one of the following conditions is absent, the institution of adoption cannot be used, adoption is not granted and the child has to be provided for by some other means of substitute care.

---

[22]   The present position is a result of the signing of the Hague Convention on Protection of Children and Co-operation in respect of Inter-country Adoption. In the Czech Republic the passing of the Act on the Social and Legal Protection of Children (Act No 359/1999 Coll) was the crucial turning point in this field.

[23]   The UN Convention on the Rights of the Child, namely Art 9, which declares the right of the child not to be separated from his/her parents against their will, should be mentioned.

[24]   'Replacing' anonymity of adoption with 'openness' is a general trend which is connected with the new approach to adoption as a 'service' for the child. See M Garrison: 'Law making for baby making: an interpretative approach to the determination of legal parentage', op cit, pp 889–891.

[25]   See J Haderka: 'Případ Keegan versus Irsko' ('The case of Keegan versus Ireland'), *Právní rozhledy*, 1995, no 8, pp 311–313.

A Inappropriate, unavailable, hostile or missing family environment

The institution of adoption is generally considered to be the best form of substitute family care, especially where a child has become an orphan. Nevertheless, the institution of adoption does not take place only in that situation, but very often when a child is abandoned. In that context, we speak of 'social' orphans. In this respect the increasing number of neglected, abused and misused children has to be mentioned. It is a cruel reality that child abuse happens behind 'closed doors' – in families. This phenomenon is a product of domestic violence and aggression in society.

As mentioned above, the child has the right to know and primarily be cared for by his/her parents. The child has the right to grow up in his/her natural family and has a legal claim on his/her parents to provide him/her with a stable and harmonious environment and the right to a rounded upbringing.

As a concomitant of the right of the child to live with his/her parents in the natural family, we should mention the right of the parents to have their children in their care, bring them up, and fulfil their parental role. These rights can be exercised according to the concept of 'parental responsibility' (*Rodičovská zodpovědnost*) in the Czech Republic.

Parents are allowed to 'renounce their rights' by giving their consent to adoption.[26] But this right belongs only to the parent who has full capacity and 'parental responsibility' according to Czech law. This right is only held by the parent when he/she is the so-called legal representative of the child. Whether the child is in the parent's actual care or not makes no difference.

To enable adoption, the law requires the consent of both parents as legal representatives. The consent has to be expressed personally, explicitly and directly. Where the child has both parents, consent has to be given by both of them.[27] It is possible to give consent to a prospective adopter or an anonymous adopter (so-called 'blanket consent'). The consent is invalid if given before the birth of the child. The parents are not allowed to give consent before six weeks have elapsed since the child's birth (Art 68a, Czech AF). Revocation of consent is possible, but only before the child is passed to the care of prospective adopters in the case of blanket consent (Art 68a, Czech AF).

The consent of both parents, if they are legal representatives of the child, is not required in three cases according to the Czech AF (Arts 68 and 68a). These are as follows:

(a)   so-called '**lack of interest**':
        the consent of the parents is not required when, for the period of at least six months, they have not showed as much interest in the child as they should have shown as parents;[28] or

---

[26]   Historically, the law did not pay much attention to consent and revocation. Theory and practice were different in the Czech Republic. Nevertheless, the view prevailed that consent could be revoked only before passing the child into the pre-adoption temporary care of prospective adopters.

[27]   For details, see O Planková: *Osvojenie dieťaťa* (*Adoption of the Child*) (Bratislava, 1979), p 66.

[28]   In any case, it is necessary to examine whether the parents have shown a real interest in the child and whether they are able to take appropriate care of the child. In considering 'lack of interest', it is necessary to take into consideration all the obstacles which have prevented the parents from showing a true interest in the child and to consider their character (objective, subjective or even

(b)   so-called '**absolute lack of interest**':
      the consent of the parents is not required when, in the two-month period
      after the child's birth, they have shown absolutely no interest in the child,
      although no serious obstacle has prevented them from showing such
      interest;[29] or

(c)   so-called '**blanket consent**':
      the consent of the parents is not required when they have already expressed
      their consent 'in advance' regardless of the existence of any specific future
      adopter.[30]

The court must examine all the circumstances for applying the concepts of 'lack of
interest', 'absolute lack of interest' and 'blanket consent' at a special hearing (the
so-called 'incidental proceeding'). This special procedure aims at determining
whether the child is 'legally free' (and available for adoption) or not. The court
has to deal primarily with the above-mentioned matters before the prospective
adopter applies for adoption (see Art 68, para 3, Czech AF).

The so-called great amendment to the Act on the Family in the Czech
Republic (Act No 91/1998 Coll) brought about an improvement of the legal status
of the minor parent even where he/she is not the legal representative of the child.[31]
The new law says that the consent of the minor parent is required for the intended
adoption of the child (see Art 67, para 2, Czech AF; since 1998 there is no age
limit). Thereafter the law provides that the concepts of 'lack of interest', 'absolute
lack of interest' and 'blanket consent' apply even if the parent is minor (Art 68,
para 2, Czech AF).

Finally, the so-called great amendment to the Act on the Family in the Czech
Republic (Act No 91/1998 Coll) also introduced an improvement in the legal
status of the so-called 'putative' parent. A man who declares that he is the father
of the child is allowed to initiate a court procedure in order to determine his

---

speculative aspects which might count against the prospective adoption). It is necessary to
examine not only 'lack of interest' shown but also the potential in the parents to consolidate their
personal, family, social and living conditions in order to be able to take personal care of the child
(Art 68, para 1(a), Czech AF).

For a critique of the previous law, see JF Haderka: 'Dopad norem Rady Evropy na moderní
rodinné právo' ('The impact of the norms of the Council of Europe on modern family law'),
Právní praxe, 1994, no 9, p 516.

[29]   The term 'absolute lack of interest' was introduced into the Czech AF by the so-called great
       amendment to the Act on the Family (1998). The lawmaker reacted by passing the new provision
       after long-standing calls from practising lawyers for an effective law. The new provisions help to
       solve the situation of newborn, abandoned children as soon as possible. A period of two months
       has to elapse after the child's birth (Art 68, para 1(b), Czech AF).

[30]   Consent to the adoption has to be given by the parents in advance (before initiating court
       proceedings). The parents have to be personally present before either the court or the body of
       social-legal protection of the child. The so-called great amendment to the Act on the Family
       (1998) established a stringent condition for so-called 'blanket consent' regarding newborn
       children. In harmony with the European Convention on the Adoption of Children, the law
       provides that the consent of the parents who are the child's legal representatives must not be
       accepted before six weeks have elapsed since the child's birth. The new provision aims to protect
       both the newborn child's mother in a difficult situation and the child's right to be brought up in
       his/her natural family.

[31]   The legal position of the minor parent was very weak for a long time in the Czech Republic. The
       courts dealt with minor parents as they would with 'participants' in hearings and their view was
       respected only when they exercised the proper personal care of the child and there were no
       grounds for depriving them of parental responsibility.

fatherhood (according to the amended Art 54, para 1, Czech AF). In addition, the legal status of such a biological father has been improved by the new conception of adoption. According to the new provision (Art 70a, Czech AF), the adoption of the child is not to be granted before the court's decision has been given in the proceedings on fatherhood started on the initiative of the 'putative' father.[32]

In the case of so-called blanket consent, the revocation of the parents' consent is allowed only before passing the child to the care of prospective adopters (Art 68a, Czech AF). Nevertheless, there is no law governing revocation in general in the Czech Republic. Both the doctrine and court practice follow the view that revocation of consent is possible up until the adoption becomes definitive.

B   The best interests of the child

In relation to adoption, the Act on the Family in the Czech Republic is fully in accordance with the key principle of the UN Convention on the Rights of the Child 'that the best interest of the child shall be a primary consideration'. All the other conditions of adoption which these sources of law mention focus on fulfilling this essential condition as well as the aim and purpose of adoption.

According to the international documents and according to the Acts mentioned above, only a minor child may be adopted. Legal sources take the position that the institution of adoption is that of substitute family care which should provide the minor 'orphan' child with care, upbringing and parental responsibility, first and foremost in a family environment. The main aim of the institution of adoption is 'full incorporation' of the minor child in the new, adoptive family. That is why very small children (of pre-school age) are the most suitable for adoption. Children of this age are generally able to adapt to a new family. Regarding the adoption of older children in practice, after marriage the new spouses of their parents very often adopt them (so-called 'step-parent adoption' – which is full adoption). The adoption of the 'nasciturus' is not allowed.

The Czech AF lays down the duty for the court to examine the state of health of the child and familiarise both the prospective adopter and the legal representatives of the child with the findings. The court must obtain a report from a specialist on both the physical and the mental health of the child, including a prognosis. However, the interpretation of this provision should not lead to 'discrimination' against handicapped (disabled) children. Nevertheless, one has to foresee possible problems which might be caused by hereditary diseases or the HIV virus.

---

[32]   The so-called great amendment to the Act on the Family in the Czech Republic (1998) was influenced not only by practical and theoretical demands but especially by Strasbourg case-law. See J Haderka: 'Případ Keegan versus Irsko' ('The case of Keegan versus Ireland'), op cit, pp 311–313.

C   Consent of the minor child

The Czech AF formulates this condition as follows: 'consent is necessary when the child is able to understand the effects of adoption unless the purpose of adoption would be thereby frustrated' (Art 67, para 1, Czech AF). The interpretation of this provision is rather difficult. In practice, the Article is often applied, for instance, when the child has been living in a foster family since his/her early years and has not known his/her original parents, when the foster parents seek to convert foster care into adoption. Nevertheless, in this context the so-called 'participation' rights of the child, grounded in the UN Convention on the Rights of the Child, have to be recalled. According to these rights, the child who is capable of forming his/her own views has the right to express those views freely in all matters affecting the child, and these views are to be given due weight in accordance with the age and maturity of the child. For this purpose, the child must in particular be provided with the opportunity to be heard in any judicial and administrative proceedings affecting the child, either directly, or through a representative or an appropriate body, in a manner consistent with the procedural rules of national law (Art 12 of the Convention). The terms of the above-described 'participation rights' in the Convention have been introduced recently in the Czech AF (see new Art 31, para 3).

It is necessary to add that there is no 'principle of anonymity' of adoption expressly set out in the sources of Czech law.

Czech law does not establish any age limits for taking the child's views on adoption into account.[33]

D   Eligible and suitable prospective adopter and his/her wish to adopt the child

The personality of the prospective adopter plays the essential role in adoption. It is up to him/her whether the adoption will be successful and in the best interests of the child. That is why it is necessary to examine not only his/her 'desire' for the child but also his/her character, personal disposition, motivation for adoption, lifestyle and other circumstances (finances, property, housing, etc). The prospective adopter should ensure a stable and harmonious environment for the child and his/her growth.

Czech doctrine and practice take the position that there should not be such a family relationship between the child and the prospective adopters which would render adoption inappropriate. This condition is not established by law but is a consequence of the nature of adoption. Generally, it is thought that adoption is not desirable between relatives in direct line or between siblings.

---

[33]   European laws regulate this issue differently. The Austrian Civil Code (ABGB, Art 181) recognises the child's 'right to be heard' where the minimum age is five years. According to the French Code Civil (CC, Art 345) the child older than 13 years has always to agree personally with adoption. The German Civil Code (BGB, Art 1746) establishes the age of 14 years for the child to express an opinion on the adoption. Dutch law provides for the child's 'veto' on the intended adoption when he/she is 15 years old.

According to the law, the prospective adopter has to be an adult and has to have full capacity for legal acts in order to be able to exercise the role of the legal representative of the child and protect his/her interest.

The Act on the Family in the Czech Republic lays down *expressis verbis* that the court has to examine, on the basis of a medical report and other necessary investigations, the state of health of the prospective adopter and to judge whether it is not incompatible with the aim of adoption (Art 70, Czech AF). The prospective adopter's state of health should be good enough for him/her to be able to provide the child with a long-lasting and generally suitable family environment. The prospective adopter should be able to become a provider, educator and role model for the child. The court has the duty to make known its findings to the prospective adopter and the legal representatives of the child.

The law finally provides that there has to be a sufficient difference in age between the prospective adopter and the child (Art 65, para 1, Czech AF). The Act on the Family does not establish, however, any age categories or any age limits.[34] Both the law and legal practice interpret the term 'adequate difference in age' as such a difference as is the normal difference in age between natural parents and their children.[35]

The Act on the Family in the Czech Republic lays down *expressis verbis* that the child can be jointly adopted only by persons married to each other (Art 66, para 1, Czech AF). The husband and wife are allowed to adopt the child simultaneously or successively. In these cases, the court has to examine the length of the marriage, its course and 'quality'[36] besides other conditions and aspects. Even where only one of the couple is to adopt the child, the Act requires the consent of the other spouse. This condition has to be fulfilled even in a case where the couple have not been living together. The consent of the spouse of the adopter is not required when that spouse lacks full capacity for legal acts or when there is an obstacle to consent which is difficult to overcome (Art 66, para 2, Czech AF).

Czech law books use the term 'step-parent adoption' when the child is adopted by the new spouse of his/her parent. This form of adoption does not provide the child with a 'new family' but, in fact, puts the *de facto* relationship in harmony with the legal one. Nevertheless, even this kind of adoption is a full adoption.

---

[34] According to the traditional Austrian Civil Code (ABGB, 1811), the adopters had to be less than 40 years old and the adopted child had to be at least 18 years their junior (Art 180).

The European Convention on the Adoption of Children provides that the adopter has to reach a minimum age prescribed for the purpose, this age being neither lower than 21 years nor higher than 35 years (Art 7, para 1). There are, of course, exceptions for the husband of the child's mother and for some other exceptional circumstances. It has already been noted that the Czech Republic had made a reservation in relation to this Article.

For discussion of some problems, see L Macháčková: 'Náhradní rodiče ve vyšším věku – diskriminace v zákoně o rodině?' ('Older substitute parents – discrimination in the Act of the Family?'), *Právo a rodina*, 2000, No 8, p 8 ff.

[35] See Judgment of the Czech Supreme Court No 49/1976, and Art 8 of the European Convention on the Adoption of Children.

[36] See Art 9(2)(b), (c) of the European Convention on the Adoption of Children. Joint adoption is usually allowed only for spouses. Some laws even demand a certain minimum period of marriage, for instance French law requires a marriage of at least five years' duration.

E   Obligatory pre-adoption temporary care

In order to ensure that the adoption will be in the best interests of the child, the Czech AF provides that the child has to be passed to the care, and at the expense, of the prospective adopter for at least a three-month period[37] immediately before the court decision (Art 69, Czech AF). The requirement of pre-adoption care is focused on creating a real relationship between the prospective adopter and the child and provides the new 'family' with a period in which to prove its suitability. It should give a chance to both parties to get to know each other, to prevent a possible revocation of the adoption in the future.

F   Additional conditions for 'irrevocable' adoption

As it is not possible to revoke an 'irrevocable' adoption, the law in the Czech Republic requires for such an adoption some additional conditions besides those above. These are as follows.

(1)   Only a child aged over one year can be adopted by 'irrevocable' adoption (Art 75, Czech AF). The law follows common sense and general knowledge that when the child reaches the age of at least one year, it is possible to predict his/her development, especially as far as health is concerned.

(2)   Another specific aspect of Czech law is that this type of adoption is available first for spouses, or for the spouse of the child's parent, or for the spouse of the child's deceased parent, or for the spouse of the child's adopter (Art 74, para 2, Czech AF). There is one exception to the effect that a single person can adopt a child but only if it can be foreseen that the adoption will be in the best interests of the child (Art 74, para 2, Czech AF).

(3)   Registration is the next condition which is required after 'irrevocable' adoption according to Czech law (Art 74, para 1, Czech AF). The child will obtain a new 'record of birth' with the names of the adopters as his/her parents without the fact of adoption or the identity of his/her former parents being expressly revealed (see Art 20, para 3 of the European Convention on the Adoption of Children). According to the new legal regulations in the Czech Republic, and according to international standards, the public record should be kept in such a way as to prevent persons who do not have a legitimate interest from learning the fact that a person has been adopted or the identity of his/her former parents (see Art 20, para 4 of the European Convention on the Adoption of Children). Nevertheless, as a result of compliance with the Convention on the Rights of the Child, which guarantees the right of the child to know his/her parents (Art 7, para 1), the Czech law regulating public records gives the child who has reached the age of 18 the right to inspect all facts entered in the registers. This means that the adopted child has a legal claim to know his/her origin and the names of his/her original (natural) parents.

---

[37]   Although some jurisdictions regulate obligatory temporary pre-adoptive care more strictly (the Netherlands: one year; France: six months), the Czech law can be considered as adequate and fully in harmony with the aims of adoption and practical demands.

VI ADOPTION PROCEEDINGS

The legal regulation of the institution of adoption and of adoption by administrative and judicial proceedings has seen a large number of changes since the signing and ratifying of the International Conventions in the Czech Republic.

Adoption can be granted only by a court in the Czech Republic. Nevertheless, a special administrative 'proceeding' before 'the authorities of social and legal protection of the child' has to precede the court decision-making in the Czech Republic. The legal regulation of co-operation is in accordance with the International Conventions mentioned above. The new Act on Social and Legal Protection of Children (the so-called 'Children Act', Act No 359/1999 Coll) is the main legal source. The special proceeding (co-operation) concentrates on the mutual suitability of the child and the adopter (Art 20 ff of Act No 359/1999 Coll). The procedure can be started only on the basis of the application of the person seeking to become the adopter. He/she has to apply to the District Authority which keeps all the documentation about the children and prospective adopters. The District Authority has to pass a copy of the documents to the Ministry of Labour and Social Policy. The Ministry keeps the so-called 'central records' which contain, in addition to the documents passed by the District Authority, the so-called 'professional judgements' and the child's opinion obtained by the Ministry before starting their own process – searching for a suitable 'match'.

When a suitable 'match' appears to be found, the prospective adopter has the right to get to know the child and be granted so-called 'obligatory pre-adoption temporary care' (see above). He/she is allowed to put the motion for adoption to the court only after three months have elapsed.

As for inter-country adoption, becoming a party to the Hague Convention on Protection of Children and Co-operation in Respect of Inter-country Adoption can be considered a turning point. According to the Convention, adoption proceedings are started when the prospective adopter applies to the Central Authority in the State of his/her habitual residence. If the Central Authority is satisfied that the applicant is eligible and suitable to adopt, it must prepare a report and transmit it to the Central Authority of the State of the child's origin. The report must include information about the applicant's identity, eligibility and suitability to adopt, background, family and medical history, social environment, reasons for adoption, ability to undertake an inter-country adoption as well as characteristics of the child for whom he/she would be qualified to care. If the Central Authority of the State of the child's origin is satisfied that the child is adoptable, it must transmit its report on the child to the Central Authority of the applicant, proof that the necessary consents have been obtained, and the reasons for its determination on the placement, taking care not to reveal the identity of the mother and the father if, in the State of origin, these identities may not be disclosed. Both Central Authorities must take all necessary steps to obtain permission for the child to leave the State of origin and to enter and reside permanently in the receiving State (Arts 14–22 of the Convention).

The Office of International Legal Protection of Children (*Úřad pro mezinárodněprávní ochranu dětí*) is the Central Authority in the Czech Republic (in Brno) under the Hague Convention on Protection of Children and Co-operation in Respect of Inter-country Adoption and the new Act on the Social and Legal Protection of Children (the so-called 'Children Act', Act No 359/1999 Coll). Before passing the new Act there existed no such legal regulation in the country. Nevertheless, the Ministry of Labour and Social Policy managed to facilitate adoptions for children placed in institutional care in the Czech Republic.[38] Now the Office of International Legal Protection of Children follows the International Conventions and considers adoption abroad only when children cannot be adopted or placed in foster families in the State of origin, viz in the Czech Republic. The Office ensures that inter-country adoption is a *subsidiary* solution and takes measures to ensure that it is realised in the best interests of the child and with respect to his/her fundamental rights, thus preventing the abduction or trafficking in children. Special proceedings are then started according to administrative rules. Nevertheless, adoption must be granted by the court abroad in the State of the habitual residence of the prospective adopters, as it is not within the jurisdiction of courts in the Czech Republic.[39] This applies vice versa when the child from abroad is to be adopted in the Czech Republic.

Finally, adoption itself is granted by the court on the application of the prospective adopter. The future adopter (or adopter's spouse), the child to be adopted, and his/her parents (but only when their consent to the adoption is required) are party to the court proceedings. The child has to be represented by a custodian.

The court proceedings are regulated by the former Czechoslovak Federal Republic's Act on Civil Judicial Order in the Czech Republic (Act No 99/1963 Coll, Arts 181–185).

VII   EFFECTS OF ADOPTION

As has been already mentioned, the most significant effect of adoption is to be seen in the 'total incorporation' of the minor child into a new adoptive family in the Czech Republic.

According to the Czech AF, the child obtains the same rights in the new family as if he/she were born there, including rights in the law of succession.

The adopters in the Czech Republic will assume 'parental responsibility' (*Rodičovská zodpovědnost*) and will be legal representatives of the child. The adopters will have to provide the child with maintenance, and the child will acquire 'ex lege' the surname of the adopter or the adopter's spouse.

As for the name of the child, it cannot be changed in the court proceedings in the Czech Republic. Nevertheless, the new Czech law regulating public records, names and surnames makes it possible for the adopters to choose a new name for the adopted child in substitution for, or in addition to, his own within the period of

---

[38]   On the experience with inter-country adoption, see an article by the director of the Office of International Legal Protection of Children: R Záleský: 'Realizace mezinárodního osvojení' ('Realisation of inter-country adoption'), *Náhradní rodinná péče*, 2001, II, p 9.

[39]   See Art 41 of Act No 97/1963 Coll, on International Private and Procedural Law.

six months from the day when the court decision became effective.[40] The child older than 15 years has to be counselled.

As an effect of 'irrevocable' adoption under Czech law, the name of the adopter (or adopter's spouse) is substituted for the name of the child's parents in the official register. The child will then be given new documents.

The adopted child will acquire citizenship of the Czech Republic provided that at least one of the adopters is a citizen of the Czech Republic, which follows from International Conventions.[41]

VIII REVOCATION OF ADOPTION

The institution of adoption under the law of the Czech Republic (except for simple adoption) is understood as a 'fiction' of the biological relationship. That is why it does not cease to exist either when the child reaches the age of maturity or on the adoptive parents' death (inheritance law is applied to the child then).

The institution of adoption is generally considered as an institution for long-lasting or permanent substitute family care. The new legal regulation for co-operation and careful selection of future adopters should prevent crises in new families. The court is allowed to revoke adoption only on serious grounds when the harmonious relationship between the adopter (adopters) and the child which normally exists between natural parents and children has not been established.[42] The reasons for revocation may relate to the adoptive parents as well as the adopted child. The revocation has legal consequences *ex nunc*. Nevertheless, the effect of revocation is that the child legally returns to his/her family of origin. The 'old' rights and duties in this natural family are 'resurrected' including the duty to maintain and rights of inheritance. The surname of the child will also be changed.

From the literal meaning of the term 'irrevocable' adoption, it follows that this type of adoption cannot be revoked. Nevertheless, re-adoption is allowed but only while the child is still a minor.

IX CONCLUSION

The institution of adoption was viewed by the former socialist law from the perspective of the minor child. Although even today there are some calls for allowing adoption of adults, it is not likely that the present traditional conception of adoption will be abandoned in the re-codified Czech family law. As described above, this institution serves the best interests of the minor child, who is mostly abandoned or an orphan, and aims to provide a 'definitive' solution to the child's critical situation.

---

[40] In the Czech Republic, the new Act No 301/2000 Coll was passed dealing with registers, names and surnames, which allows the adoptive parents to choose both another name or an additional name for the child.

[41] As for granting citizenship in the Czech Republic, see Act No 40/1993 Coll.

[42] It is not long since Czech law made it possible to revoke adoption by a contract made between adopters and the adult child. See footnote 19.

It is necessary to emphasise that the Czech Republic has harmonised its national laws of adoption in accordance with high international standards, first by signing and ratifying the above-mentioned International Conventions and also by passing a large number of Acts and amendments to add to the existing ones.

As has been mentioned many times before, the child has the constitutional right to grow up in an atmosphere of happiness, love and understanding in his/her own family. Only when the environment of the child's origin is inappropriate, unavailable, hostile or missing, should some of the institutions of substitute family care apply.[43] Nevertheless, each form of substitute family care should be oriented to the child's welfare.

---

[43]   In the Czech Republic the following institutions of substitute care are regulated:

1   Collective care:

1.1   Institutional care (Art 46, Czech AF).

1.2   Institutional protective care (Arts 84–86, Criminal Code).

2   Family care:

2.1   Adoption (Arts 63–77, Czech AF)

2.2   Foster care (Art 45a–d, Czech AF).

2.3   Care exercised by a third person (Art 45, Czech AF).

2.4   Guardianship (Arts 78–82, Czech AF).

For details, see M Hrušáková, Z Králíčková: *České rodinné právo (Czech Family Law)* (2nd ed, MU and Doplněk, Brno, 2001), and M Hrušáková a kol: *Zákon o rodině. Komentář (Act on the Family. Commentary)*, op cit.

ENGLAND AND WALES

THE INFLUENCE OF HUMAN RIGHTS AND CULTURAL ISSUES

Mary Welstead[*]

Any survey of family law inevitably involves selectivity on the part of the author, unless it is to be a mere perfunctory glance at the events of the year. I have, therefore, chosen to take a thematic approach in focusing on what I perceive to be the dominant issues in family law in England and Wales in 2001. Two major and sometimes overlapping factors have forced family law out of its secure parochial world and into a wider cultural arena. It was, of course, reasonably predictable that the Human Rights Act 1998 would continue to play a role, although its impact on the expansion of a rights-based legal culture in the family context remains questionable.[1] What is, perhaps, more surprising is the significant number of decisions facing the courts relating to multi-cultural issues which reflects the cultural diversity of society today.

In the following analysis of the law, it becomes evident that both these factors have increased the tensions inherent in family law. Judicial demands for legal certainty (including new legislation where necessary) compete with an acceptance by certain members of the judiciary that the majority of family law matters do not lend themselves to certainty (even with new legislation). Determining the precise 'catchment area' of a specific human right, balancing the demands of those who wish to claim that right, and resolving the competing merits of culturally alien conduct, all challenge judicial discretion to its limits. The dividing line between judicial discretion and the imposition of judicial value judgments thus becomes blurred. It is rare for this dilemma to be openly recognised, acknowledged and discussed.

Critics of reviews of family law have tended to draw attention to the emphasis placed on the law relating to children rather than its involvement in adult familial relationships. I have attempted to address that criticism in an examination of non-genetic fatherhood, validity of marriage, and familial financial disputes. All these issues demonstrate the same elusive search for legal principles, and the obfuscation between discretion and value judgments outlined above.

I CONFIDENTIALITY IN ADOPTION AND HUMAN RIGHTS LEGISLATION

Article 8 of the European Convention for the Protection of Human Rights and Fundamental Freedoms provides for the right to respect for private and family

---

[*] Director of Centre for Multi-Cultural Studies in Law and the Family, University of Buckingham.

[1] See eg *Payne v Payne* [2001] EWCA Civ 166, [2001] 1 FLR 1052 at 1064.

life.[2] Judicial interpretation of Art 8 was considered in three decisions involving birth mothers who wished to protect their privacy when giving up their children for adoption. The decisions illustrate the difficulties in determining what constitutes family life and whose family life or privacy should prevail where there is a conflict of interest between several members of the same family.

In *Z County Council v R*,[3] the court took a broad approach in its interpretation of Art 8. The mother had concealed her pregnancy from her family and was most adamant that they should not learn of it. The local authority respected her wishes. However, the guardian ad litem, concerned about the impact of Art 8, sought the court's guidance as to whether she should contact the mother's siblings to ask if they would be prepared to care for the child and thereby protect the child's right to family life. The court acknowledged that, although the domestic law did not impose a duty on the local authority or the guardian ad litem to consult with the mother's wider family, it did give them the power to do so if they wished.[4]

With respect to Art 8, the court maintained that a 'family life' could exist between a child and its extended family merely by virtue of a blood tie, and regardless of whether any psychological relationship existed between them.[5] However, the right to that family life must be balanced by the mother's right to respect for her own private life. Here the balance came down in favour of respecting the mother's confidence. She had desired to make a new life, which would enable her to make discreet, dignified and humane arrangements for her child's birth and adoption without the knowledge of her family. Holman J recognised that to deny mothers their rights to privacy might put their health at risk, in that they might seek abortions or give birth secretly. The child had already spent his first year with his future adoptive parents; it would be too disruptive to him to explore the possibility of placing him in his mother's extended family to which his mother was totally opposed.

In *Re H; Re G (Adoption: Consultation of Unmarried Fathers)*,[6] two unmarried mothers had concealed their pregnancies from both children's fathers, and from their own families. They had given up their children for adoption and refused to disclose the identities of the fathers. The local authorities in both cases had applied to the court for guidance as to whether the fathers should be consulted in the adoption proceedings.

The mother in *Re H* had cohabited for a short time with the father and had given birth to a son; that relationship had ended prior to the birth. The father, however, maintained the child and had contact with him. One year later, after a brief resumption of the relationship, the mother gave birth to their second child whom she immediately gave up for adoption. She feared that, were the father to find out about this second child, it would cause a deterioration of his relationship with the first child, and also delay the adoption process. The child had lived for

---

2   See Swindells et al, *Family Law and the Human Rights Act 1998* (Family Law, 1999) at para 6.52.

3   [2001] 1 FLR 365.

4   See Children Act 1989, ss 17, 22, 23, Sch 2, Pt 1; Adoption Act 1976, ss 6, 65; Adoption Agency Regulations 1983, reg 7, Parts I, III–V; Adoption Rules 1984.

5   See *Marckx v Belgium* (1979–80) 2 EHRR 330.

6   [2001] 1 FLR 646.

four months with foster parents and nine months with the adoptive parents prior to the court hearing.

The court ordered the local authority to take steps to identify the father and consult with him. In its consideration of Art 8 of the Convention, the court emphasised the evolving culture of greater involvement on the part of children's genetic families in the adoption process. The court gave great weight to the rights of the unmarried father to learn of the existence of his child and be consulted as to the child's future. It held that the father was part of an existing, albeit estranged, family, which included the adoptive child's sibling. The mother's right to privacy had little more than lip service paid to it. Indeed, the court stated that:

> '... it ought not, in the majority of cases, deprive the father of his right to be informed and consulted about his child.'

The decision raises serious questions about the rights to privacy of any mother who wishes to have her child adopted. It also has important consequences for adoptive children, in that the children's future stability will be threatened as the adoption process will become more prolonged. Child psychologists are agreed that the sooner after birth a child is placed with its adoptive parents, the better the chance of bonding and a stable childhood.[7] As a result of the decision in *Re H*, changes in current legislation will be required. At present, unmarried fathers who have not obtained a parental responsibility order have minimal rights to be consulted and no right to consent to, or refuse consent to, adoption.[8]

By contrast with *Re H*, the decision in *Re G* did protect the mother's right to privacy. Her child had been placed in short-term foster care immediately after birth, 6 months prior to the court hearing. The court found that the mother was no longer in contact with the child's father after their 7-year non-cohabiting relationship. Although the couple had discussed the possibility of children, the court ruled that their relationship had been insufficiently stable to create family ties for the purposes of Art 8.[9]

II   ETHNIC DIVERSITY AND FAMILY LAW

The decisions in this section illustrate how multi-cultural issues weave their way throughout so many areas of family law.[10] The judiciary has been forced to confront, often with sensitivity and empathy and sometimes with creativity, cultural backgrounds and beliefs which do not fit easily into the prevailing values of present day society.[11] There is, however, a danger of a naïve interpretation of ethnic questions and the substitution of judicial paternalism for the valid beliefs of the litigants, particularly in determining what is in the best interests of children.

---

[7]   Goldstein, Freud and Solnit, *Beyond the Best Interests of the Child* (London, Collier Macmillan, 1973) at pp 12 ff.

[8]   Adoption Act 1976, s 72(1), Children Act 1989, Sch 10, para 30(7).

[9]   See also *Keegan v Ireland* (1994) 18 EHRR 342.

[10]   Cf Gillian Douglas, *The International Survey of Family Law (2001 Edition)*, ed Andrew Bainham (Family Law, 2001) at pp 84 ff. For a wider discussion of ethnic issues in family law, see David Pearl, 'Ethnic Diversity in English Family Law', in Cretney (ed), *Family Law: Essays for the New Millennium* (Family Law, 2000).

[11]   See eg *Al Habtoor v Fotheringham* [2001] EWCA Civ 186, [2001] 1 FLR 951 at 970 ff.

A   Removal from the jurisdiction

In *Re L (Removal from Jurisdiction: Holiday)*,[12] the court considered Art 8 of the Convention against the background of the Islamic cultural and religious beliefs of the family. The mother was from Pakistan and separated from her husband; she wished to take their son on holiday to the United Arab Emirates, which was not a signatory to the Hague Convention on International Child Abduction.[13] She requested the court's permission. The father feared that she would not return the child and opposed her request. The court demanded a security deposit of £50,000, and also asked the mother and all the relevant members of her extended family to enter into solemn declarations on the Koran that the child would be safely returned.[14] The court stressed the right to family life of the child as the first priority. However, as is so frequently the case, the exercise of this right involves the interdependent rights of the child's family. By allowing the mother to take the child on holiday to visit grandparents, and, at the same time, ensure his return for the benefit of his paternal extended family, the rights of all were protected.[15]

Relationship breakdown between partners who originate from different countries may create problems involving the future residence of their children. Decisions relating to a change of residence have become more frequent.[16] In *Payne v Payne*,[17] the mother was from New Zealand and the father from England. The mother wished to return to New Zealand with her 4-year-old daughter. The father claimed that such a move would infringe the right to respect for his family life under Art 8 of the Convention.

The court first applied the domestic law following the approach outlined in *Poel v Poel*,[18] which stressed the paramountcy of the child's welfare. The court held that there is no legal presumption in favour of granting the application of the parent with care of the child. Nevertheless, the court's decision suggests that, de facto, the latter will almost certainly succeed. Thorpe LJ realistically acknowledged:[19]

'In a broad sense the health and well-being of a child depends upon emotional and psychological stability and security. Both security and stability come from the child's emotional and psychological dependency upon the primary carer.'

The mother's psychological and emotional stability would be affected if her application to leave the jurisdiction were to be denied; this would, of course, impact on her child.

---

12   [2001] 1 FLR 241.
13   Hague Convention on the Civil Aspects of International Child Abduction 1980.
14   See also *Note: Re T (Staying Contact in Non-Convention Country)* [1999] 1 FLR 262; *Re A (Security for Return to Jurisdiction) [Note]* [1999] 2 FLR 1.
15   See also *Re S (Leave to Remove from Jurisdiction: Securing Return from Holiday)* [2001] 2 FLR 507.
16   See eg *MH v GP (Child: Emigration)* [1995] 2 FLR 106; *Re A (Permission to Remove Child from Jurisdiction: Human Rights)* [2000] 2 FLR 225 and *Re C (Leave to Remove from Jurisdiction)* [2000] 2 FLR 457; Rebecca Bailey-Harris [2000] Fam Law 813.
17   [2001] EWCA Civ 166, [2001] 1 FLR 1052; see also *Re X and Y (Leave to Remove from Jurisdiction: No Order Principle)* [2001] 2 FLR 118.
18   [1970] 1 WLR 1469.
19   [2001] EWCA Civ 166, [2001] 1 FLR 1052 at [30].

In his consideration of Art 8, Thorpe LJ maintained that human rights legislation did not necessitate a change in approach to that applied by domestic law to relocation applications over many years.[20] He explained that, once family breakdown has occurred, the right to family life of all members of the family becomes a right for each of them to a fragmented family life. In balancing the rights of all, the child's welfare came first. The court maintained that as the mother's proposal was reasonable and genuine and not in conflict with the paramountcy principle, and it was not her intention to relocate to end the child's contact with her father, she should be allowed to return to New Zealand. The father's right became a limited right to participate in the child's life to the extent permitted by the circumstances.

B   Change of name

Where an inter-cultural marriage ends in divorce, there will inevitably be additional conflict on divorce with respect to the future of the children.[21]

In *Re S (Change of Names: Cultural Factors),*[22] a Muslim wife divorced her Sikh husband and became reconciled to her family of origin. She wished to bring up their son in the Muslim faith and change his three Sikh names to two Muslim ones. The court accepted, once again, that the well-being of the child was inextricably bound up with his mother's emotional security. She needed to reintegrate herself into her Muslim community, and perhaps remarry within it. She was granted permission to bring the child up as a Muslim and change his names informally for the purpose of day-to-day communication. The child should, however, be allowed to keep his Sikh names as they represented an important aspect of his paternal heritage.

C   In the best interests of the child

Perhaps the most important, and the most difficult, cultural and ethical decision facing the Court of Appeal in 2001 was that involving the separation of conjoined twins.[23] The twins' parents were Maltese and fervent Roman Catholics. They came to England for the birth of their children because the necessary medical expertise and facilities were not available in Malta. The twins were joined at the lower abdomen, in a way which meant that the weaker child could only remain alive at the expense of the stronger twin, who had a healthy functioning heart and lungs. The latter would die if the former were not separated from her. However, separation would inevitably bring about the death of the weaker child. The hospital wished to carry out the surgery against the parents' religious and cultural beliefs.

---

[20]   [2001] EWCA Civ 166, [2001] 1 FLR 1052 at 1057, 1063 ff.

[21]   See also *Re J (Specific Issue Orders: Child's Religious Upbringing and Circumcision)* [2000] 1 FLR 571.

[22]   [2001] 2 FLR 1005.

[23]   *Re A (Conjoined Twins: Medical Treatment)* [2001] 1 FLR 1.

The decision raised a serious moral dilemma for the court. Unusually, it agreed to accept written submissions from the leader of the Catholic Church in England, and from Pro-Life Alliance. The court acknowledged the rights of parents to give or withhold consent to medical treatment for their children but held that, in so doing, they must take into account the best interests of the children. The court may override the parental beliefs and wishes, no matter how genuinely they are held, if they are contrary to the children's best interests.[24]

The first issue for the court to resolve was what were the best interests of the children. The operation was clearly more in the best interests of the stronger twin but not in those of the weaker one, although there remained considerable uncertainty about the prognosis for the stronger twin. According to Ward and Brooke LJJ, the surgery would give the twins bodily integrity, which would be of little benefit to the weaker twin, who would die. However, they accepted that surgery would be the lesser of two evils – the immediate death of one rather than the slower death of both.[25] Robert Walker LJ held that it would be in both children's best interests to be separated because to prolong the weaker twin's life in a conjoined state for a few extra months would not benefit her. He also held that both twins would benefit by having their bodily integrity given to them.

The second issue facing the court was that the surgery would be murder[26] unless a defence could be found.[27] Ward LJ held that a plea of quasi-self defence could apply, in that the stronger twin could maintain that the weaker twin was killing her. The operation would rescue her from that fate. Robert Walker and Brooke LJJ held that the defence of necessity applied.

This decision draws attention to the limitations of law in the extremely complex ethical situation of life for one at the expense of death for another. The court showed considerable sensitivity to the parents' views which, in the light of the culture they came from and would return to, could hardly be faulted. The judgment fails to show how the court's substitution of its view, of what was in the best interests of the children, for that of the parents, was legally justifiable. The judgment was one of morals, and rather hazily defined ones, and not of law.

D   Children and mothers in prison

Statistics demonstrate that Afro-Caribbean and African mothers are over-represented in the prison population. The majority of these prisoners are single mothers, imprisoned for drugs-related crimes.[28] Their extended families are more often than not abroad with the result that imprisonment and separation from their children is likely to have more serious consequences for all members of their families than for other imprisoned mothers and their families.

---

[24]   See eg *Re T (A Minor) (Wardship: Medical Treatment)* [1997] 1 WLR 242.

[25]   See eg *Birmingham City Council v H (No 2)* [1993] 1 FLR 883.

[26]   Robert Walker LJ did not accept that it would be murder; he considered that the decision in *R v Woollin* [1999] AC 82 did not apply in circumstances where the killer's motive is good and cannot be achieved without bad consequences.

[27]   The surgery could not be regarded as an omission nor could it be put into the category of the treatment in *Airedale NHS Trust v Bland* [1993] AC 789.

[28]   See *Home Office Prison Statistics* 2000, at p 120.

The future of children from ethnic backgrounds, whose mothers were in different prisons for drug offences, was considered in *R (P and Q and QB) v Secretary of State for the Home Department and Another*.[29] The two mothers applied for judicial review. They challenged, under Art 8 of the Convention, the lawfulness of the prison service policy, which demanded that babies leave their mothers when they reached the age of 18 months. Both mothers had children aged 20 months who were in separate prisons' mother and baby units; they wished to have the children remain with them until their sentences ended.

Q's mother succeeded in her claim that the prison service policy had to be justified under Art 8 of the Convention. The court held that the prison service must consider whether its policy in interfering with the right to family life is proportionate to the pursuit of its legitimate aims. In circumstances as grave as this which involved the separation of a young child from its mother, the more compelling must be the justification.[30] The prison service must balance the welfare of the individual child, the necessary limitations on the mother's freedom, and the extent to which allowing the child to remain with the mother would be problematic for the discipline of other prisoners. At the date of Q's release, her child would be aged between 3 and 4 years old. The nature of the prison and the provision of facilities locally, meant that it was feasible for the child to remain with Q until release. Q was a Roman Catholic and her child was of mixed Anglo-Indian and African-Caribbean descent. The court accepted that there was no Catholic, non-white or mixed race family close to the prison who would be satisfactory as a foster family for the child. The potential harm to the child of being placed with an alternative family without any of these characteristics was held to outweigh all other considerations.

P, however, failed in her claim. She was from Jamaica and her child would be aged between 4 and 5 years when she was due for release. It was held that the prison in which she was incarcerated was an inappropriate environment for her child. A 'culturally appropriate' black foster family had been found for her.

The somewhat simplistic emphasis on the skin colour and religion of an appropriate family was fortuitous for Q's child but not for P's. It resulted in differential treatment for two children facing the potential of similar psychological trauma caused by separation from their mothers. In this instance, the acknowledgment of the importance of ethnicity, although rather narrowly viewed, led to a differentiation, which is worrying. The evidence relating to separation of children of this age from their mothers is overwhelmingly against separation. Sheila Kitzinger, an expert witness in child–parent separation, referred to the potential damage in taking young children from a person with whom a close attachment has been formed, as emotionally mutilating for both the mother and child.[31] Yet the court held somewhat disingenuously that:

'... it would be difficult to conclude that the harm done to [P's child] by separation would be sufficient to outweigh all the other relevant considerations.'

[29] [2001] EWCA Civ 1151, [2001] 2 FLR 1122.
[30] Ibid at 1146.
[31] Ibid at 1139.

The consultant psychiatrist, a second expert witness, suggested that there should be a significant reduction in custodial sentences, and an increase in alternatives to custody, for pregnant women and mothers of young children.[32]

E   Domestic violence

Victims' responses to domestic violence frequently depend on cultural values. Personal embarrassment, acceptance of male domination, fear of loss of children, worry about uncertain immigration status and concern at bringing shame on the family may all deter, or delay, women from reporting acts of violence to the police, or from bringing a civil action. Such was the immediate response of the victim in *A-A v B-A.*[33]

The decision will do little to encourage women from ethnic communities to voice their concerns. It illustrates the rather worrying distinction between sentencing for rape in a criminal prosecution and sentencing for contempt of court for breach of a domestic violence injunction involving rape.[34] The husband and wife were Muslims and Moroccan in origin. They were part of an extended family and subject to its pervasive influence. The husband eventually became the subject of a court order to leave the family home, and refrain from harassing or behaving in a violent or threatening manner towards his wife. During a meeting of the extended family to discuss the marriage, the husband seized the wife and raped her. She, initially, felt unable to report the matter to the police or talk to her family about what had happened because she was too ashamed. Later threats and intimidation towards the wife were a clear breach of the injunction and the husband was found guilty of contempt. He was sentenced to 12 months' imprisonment for the rape and to a shorter term for the other acts of harassment, and threats.

The husband appealed; he maintained that 12 months was too long a sentence for contempt. His appeal was dismissed. Had the husband been charged with the criminal offence of rape, he could have expected a much longer sentence.[35] In the light of the seriousness of the acts, which triggered the contempt, it is surprising that the maximum sentence of 2 years for contempt was not awarded.[36]

F   Asylum

Asylum seekers have been to the forefront of the political and legal agenda throughout the last year as increasing numbers of them seek to settle in the UK. In

---

32   [2001] EWCA Civ 1151, [2001] 2 FLR 1122 at 1139.

33   [2001] 2 FLR 1.

34   Ward LJ, at 4, explained the duality of the process of sentencing for contempt; first, there is the need to ensure that court orders are obeyed and to punish the act which contravenes the order. Secondly, the punishment reinforces the protection given by the original order. See also *Hale v Tanner* [2000] 2 FLR 879.

35   See Sentencing Advisory Panel, *Advice to the Court of Appeal-9, Rape*, in which a revision of current sentencing guidelines, laid down in *R v Billam and Others* (1986) 8 Cr App R (S) 48, was proposed.

36   Contempt of Court Act 1981, s 14 (1).

a claim made by one asylum seeker to the right to family life under Art 8 of the Convention, the court considered ethnicity in a somewhat bizarre and generalised manner, which resulted in the effective deportation of three British citizens and a possible denial of their rights of freedom of movement.[37]

In *R (Mahmood) v Secretary of State for the Home Department*,[38] the applicant, a Pakistani citizen, had been refused leave to remain in England as the husband of a British citizen.[39] He appealed against the Secretary of State's dismissal of his application for judicial review of the refusal. Human rights legislation was paid what might be described as a somewhat disingenuous regard. The applicant had originally entered the country illegally, applied for asylum but was refused. He subsequently married a British citizen of Pakistani origin; two children were born to the couple. The Secretary of State claimed that account had been taken of Art 8 of the Convention and concluded that any interference with family life could be justified in the general public interest of enforcing immigration law.[40] He maintained that the applicant's wife could reasonably be expected to leave England and live in Pakistan whether she wished to do so or not.

The Court of Appeal dismissed the appeal.[41] Lord Phillips of Worth Matravers MR maintained, inter alia, that Art 8 does not impose any general obligation on the State to respect the married couple's choice of residence. Further, if there are no insurmountable obstacles to the family living together in the applicant's country of origin, even if family members experience hardship, Art 8 will not necessarily be infringed; length of residence in England by the applicant's spouse will be an important consideration in these decisions. According to Lord Phillips, the wife knew when she married that her future husband's rights of residence were uncertain.

The decision pays little more than lip service to the Convention. It forces a British citizen, whose marriage was not a sham, to leave the country with her two children, also British citizens, because she married an asylum seeker. It creates two categories of British citizens who marry asylum seekers; those who have family links, however tenuous, with countries whose citizens are likely to seek asylum, and those who do not. The decision would appear to be discriminatory and potentially racist.

III NON-GENETIC FATHERS

A significant number of children are not the genetic offspring of the men whom they believe to be their fathers. Scientific authorities vary in their estimates of misattributed fatherhood but it is generally accepted to be between 5% and 10%

---

[37] See Art 2 of the Fourth Protocol of the European Convention for the Protection of Human Rights and Fundamental Freedoms 1950. The Protocol has not yet been ratified by the UK, however; see the dicta of Thorpe LJ in *Payne v Payne* [2001] EWCA Civ 166, [2001] 1 FLR 1052 at 1064 ff.

[38] [2001] 1 FLR 756.

[39] See also *R v Secretary of State for the Home Department ex parte Isiko* [2001] 1 FLR 930.

[40] Strictly speaking, the Secretary of State did not have to consider the Convention, as it had not been implemented at the time of the decision.

[41] It remains uncertain whether this decision is compatible with the decision in *B v SSHD* [2000] Imm AR 474.

depending on wealth and status. It is less likely to affect high status men.[42] The rights of non-genetic fathers in relationship to their children have been the innovative subject matter of three fascinating decisions.

In *Re D (Parental Responsibility: IVF Baby)*,[43] an unmarried couple sought IVF treatment, using anonymous sperm, from the Reproductive Medicine Unit of a hospital. They indicated to the hospital that they were a stable couple and having signed the appropriate consent forms were accepted for treatment.[44] Section 28(3) of the Human Fertilisation and Embryology Act 1990 provides that, in these circumstances, the man shall be treated as the father of the child.[45] The couple's treatment was unsuccessful and they separated. The woman acquired a new partner but failed to mention this when she returned to the unit for further treatment. She deceived the hospital and relied on the earlier consent. A daughter was born and the woman's first partner, relying on his paternal status under the Act, applied for contact and a parental responsibility order. The Official Solicitor, representing the child, accepted the couple's agreement that any question as to whether the situation came within s 28(3) of the Act would not be explored. The judge was informed and assumed jurisdiction to decide the issues of contact and parental responsibility; thus, the implications of the section were not considered. He saw the father as a stabilising influence in the child's future and gave him indirect contact. He suggested that he might be prepared to give direct contact in three years' time. The man appealed.

The Court of Appeal held that 'sleeping dogs should be allowed to sleep' and that the parties should be allowed to try and improve the situation between them. That might result in the mother agreeing to direct contact, rather than being bound by a court order. Dame Elizabeth Butler-Sloss urged patience on the applicant maintaining that:

> '... it is worth remembering that children have 18 years of minority: they are rather more rewarding as they become older than they are when they are extremely young, a relationship with them when they are grown up can be equally valuable. This father will want to have a relationship with his daughter for the rest of their lives. The rest of their lives is more important than the next year.'

The applicant was also refused a parental responsibility order but was assured that he would be kept informed of any future applications relating to the child, which might adversely affect his position.

It is unfortunate that the court did not assume jurisdiction to interpret s 28(3),[46] although it did urge that the Human Fertilisation and Embryology

---

[42]   See Oliver Curry and Helen Cronin, *The Evolved Family*, Centre for Philosophy of Natural and Social Sciences, LSE, London, January 2001; R Baker, in *Sperm Wars: The Science of Sex* (New York, Basic Books, 1996) at pp 124ff; L Betzig, 'Where are the Bastards' Daddies?', *Behavioural and Brain Sciences* (16)(2) 284–5.

[43]   [2001] EWCA Civ 230, [2001] 1 FLR 972.

[44]   The Human Fertilisation and Embryology Authority recommends the following wording 'She and I are being treated together and that I will become the legal father of any resulting child'. The father here had signed such a consent.

[45]   See Andrew Bainham, 'Sex, Gender and Fatherhood: Does Biology Matter?' [1997] CLJ 512; Craig Lind, 'Fatherhood and the Unmarried Fertile Man' [1997] NLJ 196. See also Human Fertilisation and Embryology Act 1990, ss 28(4), 29.

[46]   See Mason and McCall Smith, *Law and Medical Ethics* (Butterworths, 1999) at pp 63ff.

Authority be asked to look at this issue and, in particular, the wording of the consent form. The embryo was not placed in the mother's uterus in the course of treatment services provided for her and the applicant together; he was no longer part of her life at that time. This man, although the court referred to him throughout as the father, was neither the biological father nor the psychological father to this child. He had not bonded with her; indeed, he had never seen her. In these circumstances, there would seem little point in giving him hope that the court might order direct contact or grant parental responsibility in the future. To adhere to a dubious legal construct of paternity and allow even a quasi-paternal role in terms of indirect contact would not appear to serve the best interests of a young child. This concept of parenthood ignores psychological explanations, which suggest that, unlike an adult, a child has no concept of a genetic (or legally imposed) parental relationship until much later on in his or her development. A child is rationally and emotionally unaware of the events leading to his or her birth. What concerns the young child most is the day-to-day communications with the adults who love and care for him or her and who become the psychological parent figures to whom the child is attached.[47]

A contest between a child's mother (supported by her husband, the child's non-genetic father) and his genetic father, who was applying for DNA testing to establish paternity, came before the court in *Re T (Paternity: Ordering Blood Tests).*[48] The decision demonstrates the importance the courts attach to the biological link between children and fathers even where the child has been raised from birth by an alternative father figure. It is one of the first decisions relating to blood testing in paternity cases since recent changes in child support legislation.[49] Prior to the legislation, a person with absolute control over a child had been able to prevent blood from being taken from the child for the purposes of establishing paternity.[50] Now the court may consent on the child's behalf.[51] The decision is of particular interest because the court held that it was in the child's best interests to know the identity of his genetic father even if there was little possibility of that father being permitted contact with him.

The mother had had sexual intercourse with four men to ensure that she became pregnant. Her husband, who appeared to have fertility problems, had agreed to this course of action but wished to believe, albeit unrealistically, that the child was his. Indeed, he had accepted the child as his own and had brought him up for the seven years prior to the court hearing. The husband and wife feared that DNA testing would destabilise their family unit. The applicant, who was unaware of the existence of the three other potential candidates for paternity, relied upon Art 8 of the Convention to demand testing as a preliminary to an application for a parental responsibility order and contact orders.

---

[47] See eg Goldstein, Freud and Solnit, *Beyond the Best Interests of the Child* (London, Collier Macmillan, 1973) at p 12.

[48] [2001] 2 FLR 1190. See also G Douglas, *The International Survey of Family Law (2000 Edition)*, ed A Bainham (Family Law, 2000) at pp 82 ff.

[49] Family Law Reform Act 1969, as amended by the Child Support, Pensions and Social Security Act 2000.

[50] See *Re O and J (Paternity: Blood Tests)* [2000] 1 FLR 418.

[51] DNA testing has become a simple process and courts may have to face the possibility of illegally obtained evidence: see [2001] Fam Law 573 ff.

The court accepted that the child had a right to respect for his private life (in the sense of knowing his identity) and family life. However, his rights were mutually competing, in that knowledge of his identity and a relationship with both his genetic parents competed with his right to a stable family life with his mother and psychological father who also had rights under Art 8. However, it remained questionable whether the applicant, prior to proof of paternity, had a right to respect for family life which encompassed the child. If he did, his right competed, and had to be balanced, with the rights of all the other parties. Where the various Convention rights pulled in opposite directions, the rights and interests of the child were of particular importance. The child's right to know his true identity was held to be the weightiest and proportionate to the interference with the rights of the other parties.[52] The information was already in the public domain; the applicant had publicised his claims that he was the child's father using his citizens-band radio and leafleting the local community. The court believed that it would be better for the child that such behaviour should come to an end by establishing once and for all whether the applicant was the father.

Acceptance is growing that truth about genetic identity is not only important but also difficult to suppress.[53] It is not merely a question of sentimentality but also one of practical importance involving issues of genetic inheritance. However, proof of genetic paternity should remain a separate issue from the grant of paternal rights particularly where the child has established a strong relationship with an alternative father figure.

One of the most interesting judgments in 2001 was that of a preliminary issue of law relating to the tort of deceit claimed by a non-genetic father.[54] The claimant, a man who had been sterilised some years ago, began to cohabit with the defendant. After 3 years together, she became pregnant. Some 9 years later, the woman admitted to the defendant that he was not the child's father. The claimant maintained that he had supported the woman and child for 9 years in the mistaken belief that he was the father. He alleged that the woman had fraudulently misrepresented to him that this was so, and that she was liable for special damages for the tort of deceit in respect of all the financial support he had given her. The court held that the matter could be determined at trial but warned that there was no certainty, even if liability were proven, that the claimant would recover special damages.

The final outcome of this matter is eagerly awaited. In the light of the evidence relating to misattributed paternity, it may be considered advisable that men should obtain DNA testing on the birth of a child which they have been led to believe is theirs.

IV   VALIDITY OF MARRIAGE

Legal exclusion from the status of marriage, either because of sexual orientation, gender categorisation, or a lack of compliance with formalities, has important

---

[52]   [2001] 2 FLR 1190 at 1197.
[53]   See Mathew Parris in *The Times*, 25 May 2002.
[54]   *P v B (Paternity: Damages for Deceit)* [2001] 1 FLR 1041.

social and legal consequences.[55] Three decisions illustrate judicial thinking as to who should be excluded from, or included in, that status and why.

A Transsexuals

A breakthrough was made in the judicial debate relating to the rights of transsexuals to marry, albeit in the rather minimalist form of the dissenting judgment in *Bellinger v Bellinger*.[56] The applicant, a post-operative transsexual female was correctly registered as a male at birth, in accordance with the criteria established in *Corbett v Corbett (Otherwise Ashley)*[57] (ie the three biological criteria, chromosomal, gonadal and genital were all congruent and indicative of male gender). There was ambiguity about her gender during childhood but she grew up as male and married a woman with whom she had a sexual relationship. She divorced and felt an increasing urge to be a woman. She underwent surgery, married a man, and sought a declaration that their marriage of 20 years was valid because she was female for the purpose of the Matrimonial Causes Act 1973, s 11(c). She contended that *Corbett* was incorrectly decided and should be reconsidered in the light of medical knowledge and social conditions.

The majority decision and the dissenting judgment demonstrate the conflict between devotees of parliamentary legislation and those who support judicial discretion as a valid means of legal change. Mrs Bellinger's application was dismissed by the majority. The court accepted that the criteria for determining gender were more complex than suggested in *Corbett*, and that social attitudes and medical knowledge had changed. However, it viewed *Corbett* as having the advantage of certainty, and that any change in the law would involve major issues of public policy. Therefore, it was for the legislature to act and not the judiciary.

Thorpe LJ, in a most sympathetic dissent, drew attention to judgments of the European Court of Human Rights, which emphasised the need for the law relating to transsexual marriage to be kept under review in the light of new scientific developments.[58] He accepted that there was now major new evidence, which was expertly documented in *Bellinger*.[59] Furthermore, he felt that marriage needed redefining in the light of the multi-racial, multi-faith society of today. He suggested that marriage should be:

> '... a contract for which the parties elect but which is regulated by the state, both in its formation and in its termination by divorce, because it affects status upon which depend a variety of entitlements, benefits and obligations.'

He noted that, although the inter-departmental working group set up by UK government reported in 2000, there was no evidence of an intention to legislate. In those circumstances, Thorpe LJ maintained that the family justice

---

55   See Alison Diduck and Felicity Kaganas, *Family Law, Gender and the State* (Hart, 1999) at pp 34 ff.
56   [2001] EWCA Civ 1140, [2001] 2 FLR 1048. Cf *W v W (Nullity: Gender)* [2001] 1 FLR 324.
57   [1971] P 83.
58   *Sheffield and Horsham v United Kingdom* [1998] 2 FLR 928; *The Cossey Case* [1991] 2 FLR 492; *X, Y and Z v United Kingdom* (1997) 24 EHRR 143.
59   [2001] EWCA Civ 1140, [2001] 2 FLR 1048 at 1076.

system must be humane and ready to recognise transsexuals' rights to human dignity and freedom. He believed it to be a legitimate objective of the court to indulge in judicial law-making and interpret the word 'female' in s 11(c) of the Matrimonial Causes Act 1973 to include a male-to-female post-operative transsexual and recognise the appellant's marriage as valid.[60]

He concluded by adopting the persuasive words of Lord Reed, a judge of the Court of Session and High Court of Justiciary in Scotland, in a lecture delivered in 2000:[61]

> 'In those societies which do permit it, it seems to me difficult to justify a refusal to recognise that successful gender reassignment treatment has had any legal consequences for the patient's sexual identity ... But for the law to ignore transsexualism, either on the basis that it is an aberration which should be disregarded, or on the basis that sex roles should be regarded as legally irrelevant, is not an option. The law needs to respond to society as it is. Transsexuals exist in our society, and that society is divided on the basis of sex. If a society accepts that transsexualism is a serious and distressing medical problem, and allows those who suffer from it to undergo drastic treatment in order to adopt a new gender and thereby, improve their quality of life, then reason and common humanity alike suggest that it should allow such persons to function as fully as possible in their new gender.'

B   Presumption of marriage by cohabitation and repute

Where a marriage does not comply with the relevant formalities laid down by law, it may, nevertheless, be rescued by a concept known as presumption of a valid marriage by cohabitation and repute. The concept has a long history,[62] but has not often been pleaded in recent years.[63] The presumption has been defined as:

> 'Where a man and woman have cohabited for such a length of time and in such circumstances, as to have acquired the reputation of being man and wife, a lawful marriage between them will be presumed [to have taken place], though there be no positive evidence of any marriage having taken place.'[64]

In 2001, two relationships based on this concept were held to be valid marriages. In *Pazpena De Vire v Pazpena De Vire*,[65] the petitioner, a woman of German origin sought a decree of divorce. She maintained that she had been married for 35 years to a man born in Argentina. There was no direct evidence of a marriage having taken place. The petitioner claimed that she and the respondent had used a

---

[60]   [2001] EWCA Civ 1140, [2001] 2 FLR 1048 at 1088. Thorpe LJ commented that in his experience it is hard 'for any department to gain a slot for family law reform by primary legislation'. See *Fitzpatrick v Sterling Housing Association Ltd* [2000] 1 FLR 271, where, in a different context, the House of Lords interpreted the term 'member of a family' as including a homosexual partner; Mary Welstead, '*M v H* Financial Support in Same-Sex Relationships – a Canadian Constitutional Solution' [2000] CFLQ 73.

[61]   [2001] EWCA Civ 1140, [2001] 2 FLR 1048 at 1092.

[62]   The earliest decision is *Wilkinson v Payne* (1791) 4 Term Rep 468.

[63]   See eg *Re Taylor (deceased), Taylor v Taylor and Another* [1961] 1 WLR 9; *Mahadervan v Mahadervan* [1964] P 233; *Chief Adjudication Officer v Bath* [2000] 1 FLR 8. Cf *R v Bham* [1966] 1 QB 159.

[64]   See *Rayden and Jackson's Law and Practice in Divorce and Family Matters* (Butterworths, 17th ed, 1997).

[65]   [2001] 1 FLR 460.

proxy to whom they had granted a special power of attorney to contract the marriage for them in Uruguay. She had obtained an Argentinean passport on the strength of being married, and had given birth to the respondent's child. The respondent denied that there was a valid marriage; he maintained that he had procured a fraudulent marriage certificate, and that there was no other record of the marriage. His assertion was backed up by strong expert evidence that the certificate might be fraudulent.

However, the court held that there was insufficient evidence to rebut the strong presumption of marriage arising from a long period of cohabitation as husband and wife, and public recognition of them as such. Even if the certificate were a forgery, that did not prove that there had been no later ceremony. The petitioner was, therefore, held to be entitled to seek a petition of divorce.

The female petitioner in *A-M v A-M (Divorce: Jurisdiction: Validity of Marriage)*,[66] sought to divorce (or obtain a decree of nullity from), her husband, alleging that they were validly married, although there was no evidence of such a marriage. The parties were Middle Eastern Muslims. They had undergone a ceremony of marriage in London in a private home, intending it to be a formal Islamic marriage. The wife subsequently learned that the marriage was not valid under English law. She was advised that she should seek to validate it by marrying in a country which permitted polygamy. The couple went to Sharjah, but their status was not regularised even though they attempted remarriage. They returned to England, had children and regarded themselves, and were regarded, as married. The wife became a British citizen and acquired a British domicile prior to the breakdown of the relationship.

The court held that there was a presumption of a valid marriage on the basis of cohabitation and repute; only strong and weighty evidence to the contrary would take that presumption away. The presumption was stronger in circumstances such as here, because the marriage presumed to have taken place could have taken place with minimal formality. A valid polygamous marriage could have been contracted in an Islamic country without a public ceremony and in the absence of the wife if she had signed a power of attorney. Although there was no firm evidence that she had done so, she did frequently sign documents for her husband and it was conceivable that one of these had been a power of attorney.

The decision in *A-M v A-M* illustrates how liberal the doctrine of presumption of marriage is. Once cohabitation and repute to be married is present, little will displace the presumption that a ceremony must have taken place, even where the evidence, as here, tended to point to no valid ceremony of marriage.

Caroline Bridge has explained the importance of the doctrine for immigrants in that:[67]

> 'It is clear that the interests of a culturally diverse population in the UK require that a long-standing marriage should not be lightly struck down for want of compliance with the formalities of local law relied on many years later.'

---

[66]   [2001] 2 FLR 6.
[67]   [2001] Fam Law 96.

V FINANCIAL MATTERS

It is perhaps in the area of familial financial disputes that the most calls for legislative reform have been made, and that the fine dividing line between judicial discretion and judicial value judgments has shown itself to be most blurred.

A Ancillary relief

There has been a constant flow of criticism about the lack of principle and the absence of certainty in decisions relating to ancillary provision on divorce. Section 25 of the Matrimonial Causes Act 1973, although it contains the checklist against which judicial discretion is intended to be exercised, does not make explicit its objective.[68] Demands for its reform are frequent.[69] As a result, a number of judicial rules of thumb, each of which have moved in and out of judicial fashion, have been developed to help courts exercise their discretion and determine spousal entitlement. Thorpe LJ, in *Cowan v Cowan*,[70] justified these rules as necessary:

'... in order to inject some mechanism or yardstick to provide some stepping stone towards a reasonably fair and ascertainable outcome. The judges have also sought to reflect changing social values or expectations. Of course there are advantages in that the judges are available to gauge and reflect social change whilst pressure on the legislative process makes it unlikely that parliamentary reform will be attempted more than once in a generation, at best.'

He acknowledged with regret that the decision of the House of Lords in *White v White*[71] had deprived the courts, at least in the 'big money cases', of one of these 'old but useful tools', the reasonable requirements approach to spousal needs. However, the decision in *Cowan* sought to limit the impact of *White*,[72] yet like *White*, confirms little more than what is judicially perceived to be unprincipled. It illustrates the value-laden nature of the process of calculating financial provision on divorce.

According to the House of Lords, in *White*, the court's task is to achieve a fair solution, having applied the criteria laid down in s 25.[73] Lord Nicholls of Birkenhead wisely recognised that '... fairness like beauty is in the eye of the beholder' and appeals to heart as well as to the mind. In spite of this apperception, he remained undeterred from seeking to capture such an elusive creature. Having

---

[68]   Thorpe LJ, in *Cowan v Cowan* [2001] EWCA Civ 679, [2001] 2 FLR 198 at 202, suggests that in removing the original statutory objective in 1984, Parliament 'placed great reliance upon the exercise of judicial discretion, reasonably enough given the high calibre and acquired expertise of the specialist judiciary'.

[69]   See generally the judgment of Thorpe LJ in *Cowan* at 204 ff, in which he summarises the criticisms and proposals for reform.

[70]   [2001] EWCA Civ 679, [2001] 2 FLR 192 at 206.

[71]   [2000] 2 FLR 981. See also *S v S (Financial Provision: Departing from Equality)* [2001] 2 FLR 246.

[72]   Robert Walker LJ, in *Cowan* at 218, stated that he could not see the decision in *White* as 'some sort of cataclysm which has put a quarter of a century's family jurisprudence into antediluvian obsolescence'.

[73]   [2000] 2 FLR 981 at 984.

emphasised that the statutory guidelines gave no support to the reasonable requirements rule, he stressed that fairness required that there must be no discriminatory assessment of the traditional role of the wife as homemaker or of the husband as breadwinner. Lord Nicholls stated:[74]

> 'If, in their different spheres, each contributed equally to the family, then in principle it matters not which of them earned the money and built up the assets. There should be no bias in favour of the money-earner and against the homemaker and the child-carer.'

Finally, Lord Nicholls stressed, by reference to it on three separate occasions,[75] that the court must apply equality of division as a cross-check to any provisional award to prevent the possibility of gender role discrimination. Lord Nicholls recognised that this approach would not always bring about an equal division of assets. [76] After all, s 25(2) contains 14 specific criteria to which the court is directed to have regard. Nevertheless, equality of division did prevail in *White*.

In applying the decision in *White* to *Cowan*, Thorpe LJ decided that, in the absence of parliamentary legislation[77] providing for equal division of matrimonial assets, it was open to the court in the interests of fairness to discriminate between the Cowans' respective roles and make a differential award of 38% to the wife and 62% to the husband. He acknowledged that the husband and wife had been married for almost 40 years. They had commenced married life with minimal resources but the development of a successful business venture by the husband, with an initial contribution by the wife, led to the creation of assets totalling £11.5 million. In Thorpe LJ's view:

> '... fairness certainly permits and in some cases requires recognition of the product of genius with which one only of the spouses may be endowed ... . Whilst no doubt the husband's capacity to devote himself to the expansion of the companies depended in part upon the stability and security of the home and family life which the wife created and sustained, his creativity was not so dependent to the same or perhaps to any degree.'[78]

Mr Cowan's originality extended to the manufacture of plastic bin liners which revolutionised the collection of household waste, and to a certain creativity in his dealings with the Inland Revenue.[79] Mrs Cowan, after initially working in the business, took care of her husband and their two children throughout a long marriage. She had also undertaken the management of the major renovation of a large country house.

---

[74]   Ibid at 992. See also *Vicary v Vicary* [1992] 2 FLR 271 at 289, in which Purchas J refused to accept '... that there is in some way a distinction between those cases in which the wife makes an actual financial contribution to the assets of the family and those in which her contribution is indirect inasmuch as she supplies the infrastructure and support in the context of which the husband is able to work hard, prosper and accumulate his wealth. I can find no justification in logic or authority in law for making an arbitrary distinction of this kind'.

[75]   [2000] 2 FLR 981 at 989 ff.

[76]   Ibid at 989.

[77]   Thorpe LJ's approach in *Cowan* must be contrasted with his dissent in *Bellinger v Bellinger* [2001] EWCA Civ 1140, [2001] 2 FLR 1048 (discussed above) where he sought to justify judicial law-making in the absence of parliamentary legislation.

[78]   [2001] EWCA Civ 679, [2001] 2 FLR 198 at 216.

[79]   Ibid at 222.

Thorpe LJ sought to draw a distinction between what he viewed as Mrs Cowan's inferior domestic position and the important part played by the wife in *White* as a co-worker with her husband on their farm. This approach of the Court of Appeal subverts the decision in *White* with respect to gender role discrimination and denigrates the traditional female role. If followed, it will almost certainly ensure financial discrimination against the many wives who, of necessity, abandon entrepreneurial ventures in favour of creating a stable domestic haven for their so-called genius spouses, and children.

B   Constructive trusts

Differential gender roles were also considered, albeit in the slightly different context of constructive trusts of the family home, in *Le Foe v Le Foe and Woolwich plc, Woolwich plc v Le Foe and Le Foe.*[80] By contrast with *Cowan*, the wife was treated favourably and received a 50% share in the family home as a result of her indirect financial contributions to the family economy. Since the decision in *Lloyds Bank v Rosset and Another,*[81] it has generally been accepted that such contributions, unlike direct financial contributions, do not of themselves give rise to an inference to share the beneficial interest of the property.[82] However, in *Le Foe*, Nicholas Mostyn QC held that the words of Lord Bridge of Harwich, in *Rosset*, were not to be treated as an absolute statement of the status of indirect financial contributions.[83] He held that where such contributions released the legal titleholder from essential household expenditure sufficient to enable him to make the mortgage payments, an intention to share the beneficial interest could be implied. He explained that he had no doubt that in the Le Foe family:[84]

'... the family economy depended for its function on W's earnings. It was an arbitrary allocation of responsibility that H paid the mortgage, service charge and outgoings, whereas W paid for day-to-day domestic expenditure.'

He was further influenced by the fact that the couple had demonstrated throughout a 40-year relationship that they were involved in a joint venture. The wife had always been supportive of her husband in his search for funds and had also made substantial financial contributions to a number of his other commercial property transactions.

---

80   [2001] 2 FLR 970.

81   [1990] 2 FLR 155.

82   Until now, indirect contributions have only given rise to a beneficial interest in property in very limited circumstances. First, where the legal titleholder has shown an explicit intention to share the interest in the property, the provision of indirect contributions by a third party may provide the necessary detriment to ground a constructive trust. Secondly, where there has been a preceding direct financial contribution referable to the purchase of the property which gave rise to a resulting or constructive trust, a later indirect contribution may act as a relevant detriment and, thereby, increase the original share. See eg *Eves v Eves* [1975] 1 WLR 1338; *Cooke v Head* [1972] 1 WLR 518; *Grant v Edwards and Edwards* [1987] 1 FLR 87; *Midland Bank v Cooke and Another* [1995] 2 FLR 915; *Burns v Burns* [1984] FLR 216; Mary Welstead, 'The Deserted Bank and the Spousal Equity' [1998] *Denning Law Journal* 113.

83   [1990] 2 FLR 155 at 163 ff.

84   [2001] 2 FLR 970 at 973.

The decision illustrates a sound and robust approach to the acquisition of a family home. It is an example of judicial creativity in the absence of long-awaited law reform relating to home sharing; the Law Commission's promised discussion paper has not yet appeared. However, it remains to be seen whether *Le Foe* will withstand judicial scrutiny in future decisions relating to constructive trusts.

VI CONCLUSION

Family law has struggled to face the continuing challenges posed by human rights legislation; the multi-cultural diversity of the family; new developments in both genetic tracing and gender identity; and the elusive search for legal principles in financial disputes. At times, the decisions demonstrate empathy and sensitivity on the part of the judiciary, faced with the unenviable task of determining the undeterminable. Inevitably, in a significant number of these decisions, it is clear that the judicial search for legal principles is little more than a chimera and that family justice is often arbitrary and value laden. The questions at issue were frequently ones of a moral, social or emotional nature, which necessitated value judgments rather than legal ones.

Somewhat surprisingly, human rights legislation has affected the outcome in remarkably few decisions. Nevertheless, it has been given considerable judicial attention, which has made an interesting contribution to the debate on the meaning of family life in the twenty-first century.

Whilst the judiciary has continued to draw attention to what they perceive to be the tension between the appropriateness of judicial law-making and the supremacy of parliamentary law-making, the limitations of law in the familial field have been largely ignored. The resolution of family matters may ultimately require an alternative forum involving a wider group of professionals, and it is this issue, and not statutory reform alone, which should be addressed by all those involved in the process of family law.

FRANCE

WORK IN HAND FOR THE REFORM OF FRENCH FAMILY LAW

Sylvie Ferré-André,[*] Adeline Gouttenoire-Cornut,[**] and Hugues Fulchiron[***]

I INTRODUCTION[1]

In the course of a few months, there has been profound upheaval in French family law: legislation on the rights of a surviving spouse, on equality as between children and on the general principles of the law of succession (covered in Section II by SF-A); legislation on parental authority and on the rights of the child (covered in Section III by AG-C); legislation on access to origins (covered in Section IV by AG-C), legislation on the family name (covered in Section V by HF); there is also a proposal for legislation still being debated on divorce. This vast building site of reforms was opened up by the 'pluralist' majority government (socialists, communists and greens) the day after the parliamentary elections of 1997. While Parliament was passing, amid maximum confusion, a law giving a legal status to concubinage (the PACS), two major reports were prepared for the Minister of Justice: one, predominantly sociological, prepared by the Commission presided over by Irène Théry,[2] the other, more strictly legal, drawn up by the Commission convened by Françoise Dekeuwer-Défossez.[3]

Unfortunately, the government's promises of a wholesale reform of family law went unfulfilled. For reasons not only technical, given the breadth of the task and the overload of the parliamentary calendar, but also political, preference was given to splitting the task into partial reforms, which at the same time made it easier for Parliament to put the topics that most appealed to public opinion at the front of the queue. This method did indeed make it possible to pass a number of laws, but it presented a double risk, threatening the coherence of family law on the one hand, and leaving aside urgent and necessary reforms (of the law of filiation, for instance), in favour of texts which, while useful, had no immediate urgency (like the law on the surname, or the law on parental authority). The worst outcome

---

[*] Directeur du DESS de droit notarial de l'Université Jean Moulin, Lyon III, Centre de droit de la famille (Lyon).

[**] Professeur à la Faculté de droit de l'Université Mendès-France, Grenoble II, Centre de droit de la famille (Lyon).

[***] Professeur à l'Université Jean Moulin Lyon III, Directeur du Centre de droit de la famille (Lyon). Translated by Peter Schofield.

[1] Written by Hugues Fulchiron.

[2] *Couple, filiation, parentage*, Odile Jacob (ed), 1998.

[3] *Rénover le droit de la famille, propositions pour un droit adapté aux réalités et aux besoins de notre temps (Renewal of family law, proposals for a law adapted to the needs of our times)*, La documentation française, 1999.

has, however, been avoided, even if the technical quality of some of the provisions leaves something to be desired.

Much has been accomplished in a few years. Indeed, French family law has been revived, borne forward by the dynamic of the principles of freedom and equality, more consistent with the country's international commitments and more respectful of human rights. It is, nonetheless, unfinished business; and the direction to be taken by the new centre-right majority, following the elections of 2002, remains very imprecise. So French family law is like the vast building site of the Sagrada Familia church in Barcelona, with its towers rearing, isolated, towards heaven, its blind porches, and its vaults waiting over the void. It remains to be seen if the group of architects who took over yesterday, and those yet to come, will produce a cathedral or the famous Palais du Facteur Cheval.[4]

II   WHAT RIGHTS HAS THE SURVIVING SPOUSE IN FRANCE AFTER LAW NO 2001–1135 OF 3 DECEMBER 2001?[5]

Under the Civil Code of 1804, the surviving spouse had an unenviable position. In spite of the law of 1891, giving a legal usufruct or, in more residual circumstances, entitlement to outright ownership of the estate, French inheritance rules kept the imprint of the historic concern to keep assets within the blood family, of which the spouse was not a member. Over time, the deceased's free will alone made it possible to compensate for the surviving spouse's lack of succession rights by way of legacies and bequests.[6]

The only real legal protection for the surviving spouse was that which the matrimonial regime provided. In the absence of a prenuptial agreement, the statutory matrimonial regime of community limited to acquests applied. It covered 90% of French people. Under this regime, on the first death, the surviving spouse receives, in addition to succession rights, half the community property, made up of the assets acquired by the couple during their marriage and of their savings.

The exclusion of the surviving spouse from being treated, like the children, as a proper heir did not match the image of the family as lived by French society. For 30 years, the children and the two spouses lived in the most intense form of family life known to the legal system. Succession law, alone, did not see it that way.

Thus, from the middle of the twentieth century, a recurrent social theme has been improving the succession rights of the surviving spouse. In France, each year, at least 240,000 married couples suffer a death. The life expectancy of survivors continues to grow with the passing years. In view of this, surveys indicated that families wanted greater rights for the surviving spouse, even at the expense of the children. However widespread the making of gifts between spouses might be, it was desirable that succession law should incorporate this practice for the benefit of all.

---

[4]   This refers to the somewhat random collection of broken and discarded items cemented together into an 'architectural' monument, curiosity or 'attraction' by one M Cheval, a postman.

[5]   Written by Sylvie Ferré-André.

[6]   French succession law effectively allowed a husband or wife to leave property to the surviving spouse more generously than to any other beneficiary. This type of gift was regarded as an extension of the part normally disposable by will (Art 1094 and 1094-1 of the Civil Code).

Above all, French law was losing its coherence after the divorce reform law of 11 July 1975. Divorced spouses had the right to have their standard of living maintained, whereas a surviving spouse's only enforceable right was to receive maintenance and, where issue survived, a defeasible life interest in a quarter of the estate.

French law had to be reformed in line with other European legal systems, which already gave the surviving spouse more significant rights, by way of usufruct or outright ownership. Some, such as German law and Belgian law, even gave the surviving spouse a reserved share of the estate.

Law n° 2001–1135 of 3 December 2001 'relating to the rights of the surviving spouse, and adulterine children, and modernising certain provisions of the law of succession', in force for the most part from 1 July 2002, has finally achieved this.

It is the culmination of a long process. A project for a law had already been drafted in 1988, then several others in 1991 and 1995, with the aim of reforming the whole French law of succession. These proposals were never debated in Parliament, however. Although the need for reform was generally accepted, there was no consensus on how to reform. Then, after France was condemned by the European Court of Human Rights on 1 February 2001 in the *Mazurek* case, everyone knew there had to be reform, if only to remove discrimination against adulterine children. At this point it was unthinkable to create equality of succession rights between all children without also reforming the rights of the surviving spouse at the same time. True, the law of 3 December 2001 has not reformed succession law completely but it is more than the mere adjustment of details. It plots the course of future reforms.

Taking up earlier projects, for the most part the result of a working party set up 20 years ago led by Professors Jean Carbonnier and Pierre Catala, a proposal for a new law was presented to the Senate on 22 May 2002 with the aim of bringing the development of succession law as a whole to fruition.

For the present, undeniably, the Law of 3 December 2001 is certainly a major work. It creates complete equality between all children. In this it is not innovative, but only catching up on an inadmissible delay. In giving the spouse a more favourable place in the order of succession, it is much more innovative. Until now, the spouse came before only the uncles, aunts and cousins of the deceased, but from now on the spouse shares a reserved share with the descendant heirs or, if there are none, with the ascendants. In principle, the spouse now ousts brothers and sisters.

Promoting the surviving spouse to the head of the line of succession, the law now gives him/her priority over many blood relatives. Improving the spouse's share of assets in the succession marks the victory of alliance over blood, marriage over lineage. Legally, the ties of the heart now come before blood ties.

French law, with these new reforms, has left behind the historical notion of the marginal role of the spouse in the devolution of property. The reform brings in a new image of the family in which the spouse at last has a part, in relation to succession. In the main, the spouse dominates the succession as an heir of the first rank. It is the end of the stem family as the model for succession. This development also gives new recognition to the value of marriage over concubinage. For the first time in France, marriage is the basis of strong rights for the survivor after its ending by death.

Intended for the majority, the idea behind the Law of 3 December 2001 is simple. Family fortunes having largely disappeared, most couples have a legitimate wish to pass on a modest income and a home to the survivor. The expectations of most French people are essentially of a social nature. For the rest, transmission of property still relates to a general strategy for family and property arranged by the notary.

Given this situation, the new law performs its normative role taking account of dominant social expectations. Without sacrificing the orphan, it is generous to the widow.[7] It significantly improves her position with regard to inheritance (see **A** below) and on occasions confers on her intangible rights of a public order (see **B** below).

A   The surviving spouse's place in succession after the Law of 3 December 2001

Up to the present, the existence of issue of the deceased put the spouse in a most unfavourable legal position. Legally entitled to the usufruct of a quarter of the estate, which involved complex valuation, her rights were reduced to almost nothing unless the deceased made a gift to her by will. The inadequacy of the legal rights of a surviving spouse were generally recognised and improvement considered desirable. How to achieve the improvement was the delicate question. Sociologically, in effect, there is no typical surviving spouse, but many different kinds. Young or old, rich or poor, all spouses do not have the same expectations. However, the essential difference is whether there are surviving issue (see 1 below) or not (see 2).

1   THE SURVIVING SPOUSE'S POSITION WHERE THERE ARE HERITABLE ISSUE

In France, as throughout the world, the family that inherits usually comprises the deceased's surviving spouse and issue. In the main, this means issue of the spouse's marriage, even if there are an increasing number of remarriages after divorce. In view of this diversity of family situations, it was hard to choose one pattern of succession to suit all.

The new law made its choice in the new Art 757 of the Civil Code. It says:

> 'If the deceased spouse leaves children or descendants, the surviving spouse receives, according to his/her choice, where all the children are issue of the two spouses, either the usufruct of the whole estate or outright ownership of a quarter of the estate and, where there are one or more children not of both spouses, the ownership of a quarter of the estate.'

Realistically, the new succession law takes account of the plurality of family models. It sets up different succession regimes for families where all of the children are the children of both spouses, and for those where there are other heritable issue. It makes a distinction between:

---

[7]   P Catala, 'Pour une Réforme des successions', *Rép Not Defrénois*, 1999, Art 36.964.

(a)   the rights of the surviving spouse in a traditional family; and
(b)   where there has been a remarriage.

(a)   The legal option of the surviving spouse in the traditional family
Where all of the children are the issue of both spouses, the surviving spouse may choose between receiving the usufruct of all the assets in the estate, or outright ownership of a quarter. Since the survivor is usually an elderly person, the expectation is that the universal usufruct will be chosen.

The choice offered to the surviving spouse between the universal usufruct and outright ownership of a quarter allows a degree of flexibility for the family to balance what may be conflicting interests. It is true, however, that only the spouse may choose. Descendants do not have a choice.

Where there has been a remarriage and not all the deceased's descendants are also the children of the survivor, the family structure is not necessarily suitable to accommodate a universal usufructuary. This is why, legally, it was not appropriate to create a division of property between the usufruct of a 'second' spouse and the reversionary rights of issue.

(b)   Confining the legal rights of the surviving spouse after a remarriage
Where there are issue of the deceased, who are not also children of the survivor, to give a universal usufruct at the option of the spouse could disadvantage the children of the deceased's former union, leaving them bare reversioners after the life interest of a second spouse possibly no older than themselves. As a result, it would be only their own children who could expect one day to receive the inheritance of their grandfather. To allow such a choice would surely contribute little to the harmonious devolution of property, first, since not all remarriages are welcome in the family, and further, and above all, because the law could not impose, even as defeasible rights, that which a donation between spouses could give, for the benefit of the survivor.

Thus, in the presence of issue not common to both spouses, the 2001 legislation does not give an option to the survivor. It confines her to outright ownership of a quarter of the estate. Only the wish of the deceased to benefit the surviving spouse with a universal usufruct in addition to this is effective for this purpose.

Despite the increased legal rights of the surviving spouse, it is expected that gifts between spouses will continue in future to strengthen the inheritance position of the surviving spouse. More often than now, descendants will be entitled only in bare reversion. But it is also true that, with the rise in life expectancy in France, heirs with a reserved share are, in principle, adults advanced in age. Often they have sufficient resources of their own, whereas the surviving spouse will be an elderly widow on a meagre income.

The spouse's position on intestacy is improved even more markedly in the absence of children. The concentration of the family around the married couple and the growing importance of assets acquired during the marriage, rather than of the spouses' personal wealth, have led the Legislature to reconsider the position of the surviving spouse in relation to the deceased's ascendants or collaterals.

Being in the main defeasible, these new provisions leave room for the expression of the deceased's freedom of will.

2   THE SURVIVING SPOUSE'S POSITION IN THE ABSENCE OF HERITABLE
ISSUE

Where the deceased leaves no issue, the surviving spouse sometimes competes
with the deceased's other blood relatives: those of the second order, the father and
mother (see (a) below); brothers and sisters (see (b) below); or those of the third
order, the grandparents. However, in the presence of other collaterals, nothing is
changed by the entry into force of the new law as, since the Law of 26 March
1975, the surviving spouse has come before the ordinary collaterals, the
deceased's cousins, aunts and uncles.

*(a)   The proprietary competition between the surviving spouse and the
deceased's father and mother*
As between the surviving spouse and the parents of the deceased, where the
succession is opened after 2 July 2002, the spouse receives, on intestacy, half of
the estate absolutely. Outright ownership of a half replaces the former right to a
usufruct of a half. This is a fair solution. Certainly, in most cases where the
parents of the deceased are alive, the estate is mainly composed of acquests. It is
unusual for the deceased's assets to include family property. It would seem right
for the spouse's share to be increased beyond what it has been up to now. So, in
addition to her quota share by virtue of marriage, the surviving spouse now
receives half absolutely where previously she would have received only a
usufruct. The father and mother remain heirs with a reserved share of a quarter
each. Their claim is unaffected by the new law, but, as before, the deceased can, if
he wishes, make a gift between spouses, reducing the share of his parents to a
usufruct of a quarter of the estate to each.[8]

Where the spouse is in competition with the deceased's father and mother,
new Art 757-1-1 of the Civil Code makes no other change beyond changing the
nature of the spouse's entitlement from a usufruct to outright ownership.

On the other hand, if either the deceased's father or mother has already died,
the right of the surviving spouse is further strengthened. Henceforth, the spouse
receives the share that the deceased parent would have had. So the spouse gets
three-quarters outright, against the surviving parent's one-quarter, where
previously the spouse got half and the parent the other half. The Legislature has
chosen the solution that conforms to the presumed wishes of the majority. In the
statistically less common cases, where the deceased wishes to benefit his blood
family rather than his spouse, he is still able to dispose of his estate according to
his wishes. Conversely, although there is nothing new in this, spouses can exclude
the mandatory succession law concerning the reserved share of ascendants, by
adopting the matrimonial regime of community of all assets, with a provision that
the survivor inherits the entire estate. By so doing, the surviving spouse would
keep all the matrimonial property.

On the other hand, if the deceased's parents are dead and there are brothers
and sisters of the deceased surviving, as well as the spouse, the Legislature has
acted more boldly. Its preference for marriage over lineage is clearly
demonstrated.

---

[8]   Civil Code, Art 1094, not modified.

(b)   The primacy of marriage over lineage where there are brothers and sisters of the deceased

Under Art 757-5 of the Civil Code, 'in the absence of children of the deceased and of the deceased's father and mother, the surviving spouse receives the entire estate'. Under the former law, in this kind of case, the spouse took only a usufruct of half, and the brothers and sisters took the residue. Now fraternity is ousted from the succession law in favour of 'matrimoniality'.

The model of the lineage family still faces pockets of resistance in certain rural areas in which the stem family and family heritage remain important. For such families, the classic definition of the second order of heirs, consisting of father, mother, brothers and sisters, had to be kept, despite the overturning of their respective rights by the new law. For these families, even if the law provides in principle that the spouse shares in the succession with priority over brothers and sisters, it has to make an exception for family assets in view of the ordinary and customary make-up of their patrimony.

It would have seemed like a second Revolution to these families, attached to their ancestry and ancestral land, to impose the invariable primacy of the spouse in the inheritance of family property. It was a political necessity to include an anomalous succession, based on the origin of the assets, for the benefit of the brothers and sisters of the deceased. Thus new Art 757-3 of the Civil Code provides:

> 'As an exception to Art 757-2, where the parents of the deceased are dead and he leaves no issue, the assets he received from them by succession or gift, which remain *in specie* in the estate, pass, as to half, to the deceased's brothers and sisters or to their descendants who are themselves descended from the predeceased parent or parents from whom the assets originated.'

This right of return by succession applies to half the assets the deceased has received from his father and mother, by gift or by succession, testamentary or by law.

The object of this provision is to bring the assets the deceased has received from his father and mother back home to the family of his progenitors from whom they came. Where family assets are involved, the right of return means that the spouse does not get less than would be the case were the parents still living, that is, a half, while the brothers and sisters receive what their parents would have had, the other half.

This right of return can be exercised only where the assets the deceased acquired by way of gift are still in the estate *in specie*, not converted into another form. What is taken into account is the family property itself, not just its monetary value. So the loss or destruction of the assets bars return, as does alienation, which also includes where the deceased disposes of the assets by will, because the legatee's right vests at the moment of death.

Thus, should the deceased wish to benefit his spouse rather than his family, he is free to bar the right of return by leaving all his property to her. Delicate to set in motion, rarely applied since 1972, the right of return established for the benefit of brothers and sisters rarely creates serious inconvenience for the spouse where the succession has been prepared for her benefit. There is nothing in the new law, apart from the institution of the reserved share for descendants or ascendants, that appears as a rule of public order against the protection of the surviving spouse. To the contrary, the new law sometimes imposes that protection in mandatory terms.

B   Intangible rights of a public order of the surviving spouse under the Law of 3 December 2001

The Legislature has chosen to offer the surviving spouse intangible rights that cannot be overridden, and so advance her in the ranking order of those who can inherit, after much legitimate questioning as to what these rights should be. Other provisions, even though they are defeasible, in particular the right to the home for life, can only be taken from the spouse with strict formalism and determination well beyond the normal. No doubt the Legislature wanted to make it very hard to defeat the right to the home for life, even if it did not give it mandatory status. This enables us to analyse it under the heading of intangible *de facto* rights after the temporary right to the home, of which it is, in any case, only the fulfilment.

Classically, in French law since 1891, the surviving spouse had only one mandatory right: that of the spouse in need to claim maintenance against the estate. The new mandatory rights of the surviving spouse are altogether broader. They take the shape of the classic reserved share in some cases (see 1 below) and of a right to stay in the home which, in most cases, the heritable spouse effectively occupies as the principal matrimonial home (see 2 below).

1   THE RESERVED SHARE OF THE SURVIVING SPOUSE

Studies undertaken over the ten years prior to the enactment of the law generally reported that public opinion was in favour of the guarantee of a minimum share in the estate for the benefit of the surviving spouse. However, the classic notion of a reserved share in the shape of a proportion of the estate was judged unsatisfactory by the authors. At least, the inflexibility of such a system made it unsuitable as a general rule. Where there were descendants, unless the 'dead person's share' of property disposable by will and the amount of property capable of being given away *inter vivos* were to be reduced, the spouse would have had to share with them – a total heresy according to the traditions of the French Revolution. Where there were ascendants, it was inconceivable to sacrifice the progenitors on the altar of the alliance. So, new Art 914-1 of the Civil Code awards the surviving spouse only a subsidiary reserve, failing other reserve heirs. The hierarchy of reserve entitlement remains: first, descendants; secondly, ascendants; and finally the surviving spouse. Even if one does not approve of it, the choice seems to be a balanced one, which does not create too many difficulties.

From now on, the new Art 914-1 of the Civil Code reads:

> '*Inter vivos* and testamentary gifts may not exceed three-quarters of the assets if, there being neither descendants nor ascendants, the deceased leaves a surviving spouse who has not been divorced, against whom there has not been a decree of judicial separation with the force of a *res judicata* and who is not involved in proceedings for divorce or separation.'

The spouse's reserved share certainly cannot avoid being a source of difficulties where, for instance, gifts have been made to nephews. In effect, in any succession opened after 1 July 2002, the spouse's reserve is likely to disrupt what has already been done. The spouse can claim a reduction of the free dispositions if there are not enough assets to cover the reserve.

Naturally, the problem will not affect most cases; it will remain a marginal concern, and French notaries advising families will adapt their advice to the new provisions. However, we still wonder whether so much upheaval was really necessary to create a reserve which will surely satisfy nobody, being too small for some and too inflexible for others.

No doubt the new mandatory right to temporary occupation of the home, as a direct incident of marriage, complemented by a defeasible life interest in its occupancy, does more to achieve the intended protection.

2   THE SURVIVING SPOUSE'S RIGHTS TO THE HOME

The new law creates two kinds of rights to the home for the surviving spouse: one temporary, the other, following in its wake and complementary to it, for life. Both affect the home in which the surviving spouse was living at the time of the death as the main matrimonial home. It is of no account whether the title was in the deceased's name alone or in the joint names of the deceased and the spouse.

The temporary right to the home is of a public order (see (a) below). However, the surviving spouse can enjoy the right to the home for life, on making an express claim to that effect. The life interest follows on from the temporary right. The deceased can only deprive the spouse of this interest under strict formal conditions (see (b) below).

(a)   A temporary right to the home

The temporary right to the home symbolises a great advance for the status of the family home in French law. One could well consider that new Art 736 of the Civil Code establishes protection of the home comparable to a 'primary matrimonial regime *mortis causa*' in favour of the heritable[9] surviving spouse, following on from Civil Code, Arts 212 to 226.

The text provides that:

'If, at the time of death, the heritable spouse is effectively occupying, as the main matrimonial home, a dwelling owned by the spouses or entirely dependent on the succession, he/she has by law, for one year, the right to enjoy that dwelling, free, as well as the contents forming part of the estate with which it is furnished.

If the spouse's dwelling is a rented property, the rent will be reimbursed out of the estate for the year as each payment is made.

Rights provided under this Article are to be treated as direct effects of the marriage, not as succession rights.'

The temporary right to the home is given to any heritable spouse, regardless of matrimonial regime or of status in the succession. In this spirit, the text appears to extend the provisions of Civil Code, Art 215-3 protecting the family home and to be applicable under the same conditions. Like the provisions of the primary regime, the temporary right to the home is treated as a direct effect of the marriage

---

[9]   Civil Code, new Art 732: 'A heritable spouse is a surviving spouse who has not been divorced and against whom there is no separation order having the force of *res judicata*.'

and as of a public order. Spouses cannot block it by means of gifts *mortis causa*. So, should the deceased have made a legacy of the home, the legacy cannot take effect to the detriment of the temporary right. The legatee takes possession only on the expiry of the spouse's right.

Even though it gives the survivor the free use of the home and furniture, the temporary right to the home is in no sense a gift. Being by its nature based on marriage, not on succession, the temporary right to the home benefits the spouse whatever election is made in the succession, and even if the spouse has been disinherited. For the same reason, the temporary right to the home cannot be reduced on the ground of excess. No action for reduction can be brought against it. Classed as a direct effect of the marriage, like the primary matrimonial regime, it would appear to benefit, in private international law, all French spouses wherever resident, and all spouses resident in the territory of the Republic, as a matter of public policy.

In contrast, the life interest in the home, complementing the temporary right to the home, is a matter of succession law.

(b)   A complementary life interest in the home
The life occupancy of the home, complementing the temporary right, is a matter of succession. It is governed by new Arts 764 to 766 of the Civil Code. Thus:

> 'Unless the deceased expresses a contrary intention under the conditions laid out in Art 971 of the Civil Code, the heritable spouse who was, at the time of death, in effective occupation, as the main matrimonial home, of a dwelling owned by the spouses or entirely dependent on the succession, has the right of occupancy over that dwelling until her/his death and the right to use the movable property included in the succession with which it is furnished.'

The aim of the life interest in the home is to ensure maintenance for the surviving spouse. It is a question of being able to live out one's life in familiar surroundings, not having to leave the conjugal residence, and to live there with familiar furniture.

But, as Art 764 of the Civil Code governs the devolution of property forming part of the estate, the surviving spouse gets no life interest under this provision over a home which is only rented. The surviving spouse whose effective main home is a rented property has no rights beyond the use of the furniture in it.[10] The fate of the tenancy is then a matter for the tenancy laws, which also favour the spouse.

In its content, the life interest in the home appears to give the surviving spouse more than a mere right of use and occupancy. It is seen as an intermediate right between that of use and occupancy and that of usufruct. So, unlike the simple right of use and occupancy which the surviving spouse alone can enjoy, property subject to this right can be let by the surviving spouse as if it were a usufruct. Hence, on the basis of Civil Code, Art 764, only dwellings and professional premises are affected. Otherwise, the life interest in the home corresponds

---

[10]   Civil Code, new Art 765-2: 'When the dwelling was subject to a rental agreement, the heritable spouse who effectively occupied it as the principal home at the time of the death receives a right to the use of the movable property with which it is furnished.'

essentially to the rules applicable to a right of use and occupancy. The beneficiary must exercise the care of a *bonus paterfamilias* and pay for its running expenses.

But, to claim the life interest in the home, the intentions of the surviving spouse must be made known within a year from the death; after that, it is too late. Although it is true that the law makes no particular formal requirement for the claim, in view of the conflict of interests between the spouse and the other heirs, it will be hard to avoid arguments over the interpretation to be placed on the spouse's behaviour. It will be necessary to analyse the wishes of the spouse in situations of family conflict, when the spouse does not have a right to the universal usufruct, which could form the basis for a claim to remain in the home. If the spouse maintains silence for a year after the death, he or she will be taken to have renounced the right to a life interest in the home, and might be forced to leave the familiar setting. On the other hand, if the spouse does have a right to the universal usufruct, no problem arises, unless the home has been made the subject of a legacy. The life interest in the home then rests on the inheritance rights of the spouse in the whole estate, which can, in principle, be expressed within 30 years. Where the difficulty arises is when the home has been left to a third party. Then, at the end of a year, when the temporary right to the home runs out, the legacy takes effect in default of the spouse having claimed the life interest.

When the surviving spouse takes a life interest in the home, its value in relation to the assets in the estate is treated in the way that is most favourable to the spouse. Although it is the complement of, and can only come into existence following, the temporary right, the life interest is neither mandatory nor systematic. The law allows the deceased to disinherit the spouse of it by an authentic testamentary instrument.

All the same, the consequences of depriving one's spouse of the life interest in the home are serious, and this should only be done in full knowledge of those consequences and in a notarised will. The means of disinheriting are also technically complex. Under Art 764-2:

> 'the fact that the deceased expressly excludes these rights of occupancy and use under the conditions mentioned in the first subparagraph has no effect on rights of usufruct the spouse receives by operation of law or by gift and these continue to obey their own rules.'

So, disinheriting from the life interest in the home alone is of no use where the spouse has a universal usufruct. What is more, the spirit of the provision leads one to think that indirect disinheritance by making a legacy of the home to a third party would have no effect on the life interest, which would take effect no matter what.

In order to deprive one's spouse of the life interest in the home, one must make an express statement to this effect and, above all, take psychological responsibility for it. Since it is often harder to take away than it is to give, the generosity of the Legislature will not often be called in question, so the surviving spouse's maintenance in a familiar environment is assured.

More than the true reserved share created by new Art 914-2 of the Civil Code, and even more than any other new provisions in the legislation, the real innovation protecting the spouse is the right to the home. Since the home is at the heart of the fortune of most French people, whoever gets this dominates the succession. By possessing the right to the home, the surviving spouse now, in real terms, comes first in the order of heirs. The spouse awarded the family home beats the other heirs hands down.

III THE LAW OF 4 MARCH 2002 CONCERNING PARENTAL AUTHORITY[11]

The Law of 4 March 2002 on parental authority[12] puts the finishing touches to work begun 15 years ago, aimed at enacting the basic principles of co-parenthood and equality in family relationships for parents as well as for children, inspired particularly by decisions of the European Court of Human Rights. Expressly applying to pending proceedings, the Law of 4 March 2002:

(a)   reorganises the rules relating to parental authority around the right of the child to keep links with both parents; and

(b)   puts in place specific protection for minors facing certain dangerous situations.

A   The reorganisation of the rules relating to parental authority

The Law of 4 March 2002 refocuses the rules relating to parental authority around three major principles: the equal status of children with regard to the way in which parental authority is exercised; the maintenance of relations with both parents, regardless of their situation as a couple; and the recognition that certain third parties play a role that particularly merits protection in the child's life.

1   EQUAL STATUS OF CHILDREN WITH REGARD TO THE EXERCISE OF PARENTAL AUTHORITY

The provisions of the Civil Code relating to parental authority as a whole are now grouped into the first Chapter of Title IX of the first Book relating to persons (Civil Code, Art 371 ff). This formal reform gives effect to a substantive reform built on the principle of equality between legitimate and extra-marital children. Whatever the nature of their filiation, the rules of parental authority are the same. Art 310-1 affirms that 'All children whose filiation is legally established have the same rights and the same duties in their relation to their father and mother'.

Parental authority is redefined in terms of its intended objectives. It consists of 'a set of rights and duties having as their purpose the interest of the child', without specifying the means of reaching this result. Reference is no longer made to custody and supervision, which does not mean they no longer exist, but that they are only one means among others to achieve the intended purpose. This is, not only to protect the safety, health and morality of the child, but also 'to ensure his education and permit his development giving him due respect as a person'. The final subparagraph of Art 371-1, by which 'parents take decisions affecting

---

[11]   Written by Adeline Gouttenoire-Cornut.

[12]   H Fulchiron, *L'autorité parentale rénovée*, Defrénois, 2002, Art 37580, p 959.

the child in association with him, taking account of his age and degree of maturity', in particular is indicative of the better recognition of the wishes of the child inspired by Art 12 of the United Nations Convention on the Rights of the Child.

The exercise of parental authority in common is definitively presented as the normal rule, only set aside when the child's filiation is not established within a year of the birth or when it is established by court order.[13] The same rules apply to the exercise of parental authority in common, whether the parents are married or not, whether they live together or not; the requirement that at the time the child is recognised they should be living together has been dropped.

The general rule of exercise of parental authority in common equally extends to the adoptive family since now, where one spouse adopts the child of the other, the biological parent and the adopter can establish the exercise of parental authority in common by making a joint declaration, whereas previously the biological parent alone exercised parental authority.[14]

2   MAINTENANCE OF CHILD'S RELATIONSHIP WITH BOTH PARENTS

The Law of 4 March 2002 is, moreover, based broadly on the principle of keeping the child's relationship with each of his parents. The provisions relating to parental authority are in effect organised in two sections, of which one applies to all children, and the other concerns more particularly the position where parents separate. In cases of separation, the judge can still find that exercise of parental authority by one parent alone is preferable, in the child's interest,[15] but the recent line of judicial decisions suggests that this power will only be used in the most extreme circumstances, where exercise in common would be liable to endanger the child. Removal of parental authority as provided for in Art 373 of the Civil Code becomes exceptional. Abandonment of one's family thus ceases to be an automatic cause for removal of parental authority.

Besides the exercise in common of parental authority, there are provisions for ensuring the effective maintenance of the child's relations with both parents. Art 373-2-6 allows the *juge aux affaires familiales* to 'take measures to guarantee the continuity and effectiveness of the maintenance of links between the child and each of his parents'. Among these measures, the law more precisely invokes noting on the child's passport a prohibition against leaving French territory without the authorisation of both parents. The criminal penalty for failure to produce the child has also been increased, particularly if the child is held outside the national territory,[16] even if the legislature has refused to impose the sanction of automatic withdrawal of parental authority. To improve the campaign against the illicit removal of children, the Law of 4 March 2002 has also set up a judicial specialisation in this field, by providing for a single *tribunal de grande instance* under the jurisdiction of the *cour d'appel* to hear such cases. This judicial specialisation, which at first only concerned proceedings under the Hague Convention of 25 October 1980 on the Civil Aspects of International Child

---

[13]   Civil Code, Art 372.
[14]   Ibid, Art 365.
[15]   Ibid, Art 373-2-1.
[16]   Ibid, Art 227-9.

Abduction, has, at last, been extended to international agreements in relation to the removal of children as a whole.

Other provisions directed at maintaining effective links between the child and both parents include the ability of the judge to order, even if the parents are not in agreement, that the child's residence should alternate between the homes of each of the parents.[17] Likewise there is the obligation of a parent who moves house to keep the other parent informed, so that the latter may apply to the *juge aux affaires familiales* for a consequential modification of the way parental authority is to be exercised.

More generally, Art 373-2-2 affirms that 'the father and mother must each maintain personal relations with the child and respect the links of the latter with the other parent'. This rule is supported by the sanction that, among the elements to be examined by the judge in ruling on parental authority, is 'the aptitude of each of the parents to take on his/her responsibilities and to respect the rights of the other'.[18]

3   THE CHILD'S RELATIONSHIPS WITH THIRD PARTIES

The child's right to maintain relations with both parents, as laid down in the Law of 4 March 2002 is not, however, inconsistent with taking into consideration the child's relationships with third parties, whether family members or not, which particularly merit protection. Art 371-4 lays down the child's right to relations with ascendants, unless there are grave reasons to the contrary. The second subparagraph of Art 371-4 of the Civil Code is even more innovative, since it modifies the criteria for establishing the relationship of the child with a third party 'family member or not'. Whereas the former provision required the existence of exceptional circumstances, the test of the relationship now is the interest of the child, thus favouring the maintenance of the child's relationship with the partner of one of his parents with whom he may have lived for a number of years.

Taking up in part the proposals of the *Dekeuwer-Defossez Report*,[19] the Law of 4 March 2002 also allows parents to share all or part of their parental authority, 'for the requirements of the child's education', with a third party, who, one might reasonably think, could be a step-parent.[20] Where the two parents share parental authority, both need to agree to such sharing with a third party. The third party has the benefit of the presumption by which each of the persons entitled to exercise parental authority is taken to perform usual actions in good faith, so far as third parties are concerned. Such sharing of parental authority must result from a judgment, and the *juge aux affaires familiales* has power to rule on difficulties that may arise from the shared exercise of parental authority, on the application of the parents, of the person with whom exercise is shared, or of the Public Procurator.

---

[17]   Civil Code, Art 373-2-9.

[18]   Ibid, Art 372-11.

[19]   *Rénover le droit de la famille: propositions pour un droit adapté aux réalités et aux aspirations de notre temps,* La documentation française, 1999.

[20]   Civil Code, Art 377-1.

B The protection of the minor in danger

Two specific types of danger are envisaged by the Law of 4 March 2002: that of the minor exposed to prostitution; and that of the unaccompanied foreign minor.

1 PROHIBITION OF PROSTITUTION OF MINORS

The law imposes the principle of the prohibition of prostitution of minors throughout the whole territory of the Republic. It declares also that any minor taking part in prostitution is in danger, and comes within the jurisdiction of the *juge des enfants*. In particular, 'the fact of soliciting, accepting or obtaining, in return for remuneration or the promise of remuneration, sexual relations with a minor who takes part in prostitution, including on an occasional basis' is an offence punishable under Art 225-12-1 of the Penal Code by imprisonment for three years and a fine of 44,000 Euros. Circumstances aggravating recourse to prostitution of a minor are that it is habitual or that it involves the use of a communication network. Further aggravating factors, in common with other offences against minors, are the status of the offender, where the act is committed by a person in authority, and that of the minor, where he or she is aged under 15 years (in the latter case, the punishment is increased to seven years' imprisonment and a fine of 100,000 Euros). Where the victim is a minor, procuring for the purpose of prostitution becomes a specific offence (*infraction*). When the minor is aged under 15, the gravity of the offence is raised to the next level (*crime*). The campaign against paedophilia forms the basis of a further offence (*infraction*) – the possession of a pornographic representation of a minor – where previously it was only an offence to record such a representation for the purpose of distribution.[21] These provisions apply not only to the whole territory of France, but also to persons whose domicile or habitual residence is in France where the offence is committed abroad.

2 UNACCOMPANIED FOREIGN MINORS

The Law of 4 March 2002 also makes provision for improving the situation of the foreign minor who arrives in French territory unaccompanied, with no adult to ensure respect for his rights. Article 35 *quater* of the Ordinance of 2 November 1945 provides that, in the absence of a legal representative accompanying the child, the Public Procurator designates an administrator *ad hoc* who assists him while he is in a holding area and ensures that he is represented in all administrative and judicial proceedings relating to his stay. The law gives the administrator *ad hoc* power to visit the minor in the holding area. Similarly, an administrator *ad hoc* is appointed for a minor when he applies to the OFPRA for refugee status pending establishment of a tutorship for him. This special representation of the unaccompanied child is certainly an improvement to the rights of the child in ensuring those rights are exercised. It also means that the minor receives warning of decisions which may be unfavourable to him, such as to keep him in a holding area, or to take him back to the frontier.

---

[21] Penal Code, Art 227-23.

IV   THE LAW OF 22 JANUARY 2002 ON ACCESS TO ORIGINS FOR ADOPTED PERSONS AND WARDS OF THE STATE[22]

The aim of Law No 2002–93 of 22 January 2002 is above all to reduce the difficulties faced by abandoned children seeking access to their origins, particularly when the birth took place on the basis of anonymity (*'accouchement sous X'*) or where they were entrusted to social services with a request for confidentiality as to the identity of their father and mother. The law does not give a blanket right of access to one's personal origins. As discussed below:

(a)   the right to secrecy of the mother giving birth under anonymity is retained;

(b)   the Law of 22 January 2002 does, however, favour the child's access to his or her origins so far as the rights of the mother permit; and

(c)   the new law greatly improves the situation of the father of a child where the mother gives birth anonymously.

A   Preserving the secrecy of the mother who gives birth anonymously

Following most of the advice in reports[23] on the question, it was never envisaged at the time of drafting the Law of 22 January 2002 that the statutory provisions allowing a woman to give birth under anonymity would be repealed. The right to secrecy of the woman who has given birth did not receive any discussion during the parliamentary debates on the Law of 22 January 2002. It did not repeal Art 341-1 of the Civil Code, by which 'at the time of the birth, the mother can require that her admission and her identity be kept secret'. It did not repeal Art L222-6 of the Code of Social Action and Families providing for the management of cases where women do require this. Nor did it repeal Art 341-1, which makes the anonymity of the birth a ground for rejecting an action to establish maternity.

Giving birth under anonymity is not a peculiarity of French law. It is legislated for in other European countries, such as Luxembourg and Italy, and others, such as Belgium and Germany, are considering adopting similar legislation.[24]

Giving birth under anonymity is soon to be tested for compliance with the European Convention for the Protection of Human Rights and Fundamental Freedoms. The case of *Odièvre v France* is now pending before the European Court of Human Rights in Strasbourg. It is true that the European Court ruled in favour of the right to know one's origins in *Gaskin v France* on 7 July 1986, but subject to respect for third party rights. It is indisputable that breach of the right to know one's origins resulting from giving birth under anonymity is justified by the

---

[22]   Written by Adeline Gouttenoire-Cornut.

[23]   Conseil d'État, *Statut et protection de l'enfant*, La documentation française, 1991; *Rapport du groupe de réflexion sur l'accès des pupilles et anciens pupilles de l'État adopté ou non à leurs origines, présidé par M Pascal remis au ministre des affaires sociales en février 1996; Rapport de la Commission Dekeuwer-Defossez, Rénover le droit de la famille: propositions pour un droit adapté aux réalités et aux aspirations de notre temps*, La documentation française, 1999.

[24]   J Rubellin-Devichi, 'La recherche des origines personnelles et le droit à l'accouchement sous X dans la loi du 22 janvier 2002', Dr fam 2002, chron n° 11.

preservation of the mother's right to privacy, but it remains to be seen how the court will weigh the breach of the child's right to know his origins, arising out of his right to private and family life based on Art 8, against the aim of French law, which is respect for the mother's right to privacy which the same Article protects, inasmuch as it is a question of a situation that arose before the coming into force of the Law of 22 January 2002. It is not certain that the court will find that there is a breach of Art 8 of the Convention, and it seems, in any case, that the Law of 22 January 2002, in facilitating the child's access to his origins while protecting the mother's right to keep her identity secret, conforms to the provisions of the European Convention. Parliament has tried to establish 'a satisfactory balance between the child's right to know his origins and the mother's right to respect for her privacy'.[25]

B   Facilitating access to origins

The Law of 22 January 2002 does not allow access to the identity of a mother who has required secrecy, but facilitates the lifting of secrecy by encouraging the mother to give information which could be passed on to the child and by setting up the National Council for Access to Origins, whose aim is to assist with the provision of information relating to origins, when a case arises.

Article 2 of the Law of 22 January 2002 adds a subparagraph to Art L222-6 of the Code of Social Action and Families by which any woman who asks to take advantage of the provisions regarding anonymity in giving birth should be informed of the legal consequences of doing so and of the importance for everyone to know their origins. She is invited to give information as to her own health and that of the father, the (geographic) origins of the child and the circumstances of his birth, as well as, in a sealed envelope, information as to her identity. She is also told that she may at any time reveal her identity and complete the information she gives at the time of the birth. The names given to the child together with, if appropriate, a mention of the fact that the mother chose these names, as well as a note as to the child's sex, and the date and hour of birth, are written on the outside of the sealed envelope given by the mother containing details of her identity, so that the child to whom it refers can be found. A woman who chooses to lift anonymity, which she is free to do, but never compelled to, is thus offered a very flexible system of disclosure. She can, in effect, decide how much information she will leave for the child, which may only be non-identifying material, or may relate to her actual identity. The mother can also choose the time for the child to be told about his origins, whether she has given the information at the time of his birth or subsequently. This new provision involves one of the officials of the department, who has been informed of the birth under anonymity by the director of the maternity unit, meeting the mother at the unit to give her the information required by the law and to receive the information she eventually decides to leave for the child.[26]

---

[25]   Rapport de V Neiertz, AN n° 3523, 9 janvier 2002, p 5.

[26]   C Neirinck, 'La loi relative à l'accès aux origines des personnes adoptées et pupilles de l'Etat: la découverte de la face cachée de la lune', Rev dr sanit soc 2002, p 189.

The Law of 22 January 2002 sets up the National Council for Access to Personal Origins (CNAOP), under the responsibility of the Minister for Social Affairs, composed of magistrates, representatives of ministries, and of local authority *conseils généraux* and associations, and competent persons.[27] The CNAOP has as its main function the collection and centralisation of the body of available information relating to children's origins and is authorised to act as intermediary between a child born under anonymity who is trying to discover his origins and his birth parents. It receives this information from public and private establishments in which births under anonymity took place, from the various organisations which may have received children under the seal of secrecy or which have been involved in the adoption process, from the Procurator of the Republic who can be required by the CNAOP to provide information appearing on original birth registrations in relation to full adoption (*'adoption plénière'*) and from the organisations managing social benefits which must provide, on the demand of the CNAOP, whatever information they have as to the addresses of the birth parents.

The CNAOP and the president of the *conseil général* are authorised to receive written requests for access to personal origins from children, who have the right to withdraw such a request at any time. The request may come from the child himself, with the consent of his legal representative if he is a minor. It may also be made by the child's legal representative or, in a case of incapacity, by his tutor. After the death of someone born under anonymity, adult descendants in the direct line can also make such a request.[28]

In addition, the CNAOP and the president of the *conseil général* may receive declarations from the mother, the father, one of their relatives in ascending or descending line or privileged collaterals authorising the lifting of the secrecy of his/her own identity. The maker of such a declaration must be told that his/her identity will only be communicated to the person concerned if the latter asks for access to his origins.[29] The father and mother can also ask the CNAOP whether their child has requested access to his origins. It is only at the request of the child that an intervention by the CNAOP to investigate the child's origins can be set in motion. The council simply holds the declarations of the birth parents, and it cannot pass them on to the child unless he asks for them.

Article L147-6 of the Code of Social Action and Families sets the conditions for and the substance of the answer the CNAOP may make to a child's request for access to his origins. The CNAOP may reveal the identity of the mother in the following circumstances:

- when she has made an express declaration lifting secrecy;
- when she has not indicated that she wants to keep her identity secret (in which case the CNAOP must be satisfied of such a desire);
- when, on being approached by a representative of the CNAOP, she has expressly consented to the lifting of secrecy; or

27   *Code de l'action sociale et des familles*, Art L147-1.
28   Ibid, Art L147-2.
29   Ibid, Art L147-3.

- where the mother has died without expressing a desire to keep her identity secret should the child seek to know his origins.

The father's identity can be disclosed to the applicant on the same conditions:

'It is thus if the mother or the father are willing that secrecy be lifted.'[30]

When the mother or the father has died by the time their identity is revealed, a person representing the CNAOP informs the birth family with an offer of counselling. Where the identity of the father or the mother can be disclosed to the child, the law allows the child who has requested access to his origins to be told the identity of their ascendants, descendants, and privileged collaterals, if they have made a declaration to the effect that their identities may be disclosed.

In other cases, the CNAOP may give the child any information it may have acquired, from organisations that were involved when the child was born or adopted, leading to the identification of the birth father and mother. The CNAOP may also send a person to ask the father and mother to disclose such information, while respecting their right to privacy.

Article L147-7 specifies that 'a person's access to his origins has no effect on civil status and filiation. It gives rise to neither rights nor duties on the part of anyone', so confirming a welcome distinction between knowledge of origins and establishment of filiation.

C The improvement of the rights of the father of a child born under anonymity

The Law of 22 January 2002 inserts a new Art 62-1 in the Civil Code by which:

'If it is declared impossible to register paternal recognition, because of the mother's exercise of her right to secrecy, the father can inform the Procurator of the Republic of this. The latter proceeds to investigate the date and place of the registration of the child's birth.'

This provision overturns the rare judicial decisions on the question, which had considered that prenatal paternal recognition was rendered ineffective by a birth under anonymity.[31] If the father knows of the birth of the child – it is enough for him to be aware of the pregnancy – he can establish filiation in relation to the child, and he can even get the help of the Procurator of the Republic in finding the child. A time-limit is, however, imposed on the father's right by Art 352 of the Civil Code, which provides that adoption bars any recognition. One may wonder whether the father's ability to have the child found does not damage, at least in part, the efforts of the Legislature to protect the mother's right of secrecy. The father being *ex hypothesi* aware of the child's mother's identity, it is hard to see how he can be prevented from telling the child with whom he is seeking to establish filiation.

---

[30]   B Mallet-Bricout, 'Réforme de l'accouchement sous X. Quel équilibre entre les droits de l'enfant et les droits de la mère biologique', JCP 2002, I, 119.

[31]   *Riom*, 16 December 1997, JCP 1998, II, 10 147, T Garé; RTD Civ 1998, p 891, obs J Hauser, Dr fam 1998, comm n° 150, obs P Murat.

If the father's right to establish filiation in relation to a child born under anonymity is certainly improved in an appropriate way by the Law of 22 January 2002, he is still not entitled to any right of secrecy, in contrast to the mother. Birth under anonymity is not a ground for rejecting an action to determine paternity.

V   THE REFORM OF THE FAMILY NAME[32]

Equality and liberty: these are the two principles on which the reform of the family name[33] has been constructed.

Equality between men and women

A powerful current of opinion has for some years been pressing for the ending of the last legal discrimination against women. Children born in wedlock had to bear their father's surname, their mother not being allowed to pass on hers. Even in the extra-marital family, a number of rules tended to favour the father. France was almost alone in Europe in keeping such a system. Only Belgium and Italy kept such a patriarchal, even macho, system. This was contrary to major international texts ratified by France,[34] to the line agreed by the Committee of Ministers of the Council of Europe,[35] and to decisions of the European Court of Human Rights[36] (even if the *Burghartz* case, generously quoted in preparatory studies on the law, had no direct bearing on the transmission of the family name to children).

On the other side, voices were raised with equal vigour to insist that the maintenance of the existing rules was perfectly justifiable. There was almost unanimous social acceptance of the immemorial principle of passing on the father's name. As proof of this, although made possible in 1985, the option of combining the name of the parent whose name had not been passed on with one's surname had met with very limited success. In particular, as the Report of the Commission chaired by Françoise Dekeuwer-Défossez emphasised, the historical rule found a new justification in the contemporary development of family law:

'In our society the social bond of maternity is always clearly marked. By contrast the father's position has undergone several decades of profound changes in parallel with the sharing of parental authority and the increase in the number of fathers separated from their children because of the break-up of the couple. Allowing the transmission

---

[32]   Written by Hugues Fulchiron.

[33]   Law n° 2002–304 of 4 March 2002 relating to the family name (JO, 5 mars 2002, p 4159), cf not F Dekeuwer-Défossez, 'Commentaire de la loi relative au nom de famille', *Revue juridique Personnes et familles*, 2002, n°7, p 6; J Massip, 'La loi du 4 mars 2002 relative au nom de famille', *Defrénois* 2002, p 795; adde M Gobert, 'L'attribution du nom: égalité ou liberté?' *Petites affiches* 23 mai 2002, n°102, p 4.

[34]   In particular the UN Convention on the Elimination of All Forms of Discrimination Against Women, of 18 December 1979, Art 16(1)(g).

[35]   Resolution (78) of the Committee of Ministers of the Council of Europe on the equality of spouses in civil law; Recommendation N° R(85) of the Committee of Ministers of the Council of Europe relating to discrimination between men and women based on sex; Recommendation of the Parliament of the Council of Europe relating to discrimination between men and women in the choice of a family name and the transmission of the name from parents to children.

[36]   *Burghartz v Switzerland*, 22 February 1994.

of the mother's name further unbalances the situation and raises the stakes. This may indirectly further undermine the image of paternity.'[37]

The promoters of the law, however, swept aside the argument that 'the mother gives life, the father gives the name' in accordance with the principle of equality. Henceforth we speak not of the 'patronymic' but of the 'family name'. And yet, a trace of inequality survives. In its anxiety for the law to be passed before the parliamentary elections (it was carried in the National Assembly in the final session), the majority was given no choice but to accept what the Senate demanded: that, failing a choice being made by the parents, the child should bear … the father's name.

Equality between children

In fact the rules relating to the name differed according to whether the child was born in or out of wedlock. Paradoxically, the inequality worked to the disadvantage of the legitimate child, who was chained to the name of his father, whereas the name of the extra-marital child could be changed during minority, or even on coming of age. The rules in the two situations still remain different in part. A very simple reality had to be recognised. The filiation of the child born in wedlock is established simultaneously and indivisibly in relation to both parents. That of the child born out of wedlock is divisible, and may be established at different times (and, moreover, not always in relation to both parents). For the child of married parents, the basic principle is quite simple, ie the parents' choice expressed in a joint declaration. Adjustment has to be made for the extra-marital child. Nonetheless, the general rule clearly expresses the egalitarian spirit, applying to legitimate children and to children registered out of wedlock alike, in the title of rules common to legitimate and natural filiation.[38]

Freedom for parents, freedom for children

Naming has long been excluded from the scope of individual autonomy. It has been applied mechanically, leaving little room for the choice of those concerned, and the eventual change has only come under strict legal conditions. The name is a policing institution. It also places the child in a line of ancestry – paternal ancestry. The Law of 4 March 2002 breaks with that tradition. From now on, an essential role is given to the will of the parents, and also to the will of the child during minority and more particularly on coming of age. The result is major upheaval in the relationship between society and the family name, and between the individual and his own name. The Law of 4 March 2002 originated in a variety of proposals put forward by deputies of the 'plural majority'. Strongly supported by the representatives of the Delegation for Women's Rights, it overcame the hostility of the Senate, at the cost, in reality, of important concessions. It reconstructs to a large extent the rules of (1) giving the family name at the time of registration; and (2) changing the family name.

---

[37]   *Report Dekeuwer-Défossez* (see n 2 above), p 68.
[38]   Civil Code, Art 311-21.

1 GIVING THE FAMILY NAME

The general principles set out in Art 311-21 are complemented by special rules for natural, legitimated and adopted children.

General principles

Under Art 311-21 of the Civil Code, 'when a child's filiation is established with regard to both parents, at the latest, by the date of the declaration of birth[39] or subsequently but simultaneously',[40] the parents 'choose the family name which is passed on to him: be it that of the father or of the mother, be it their two names together in the order of their choice, to a maximum of one family name for each of them'. It is further provided that 'where the parents or one of them bear a double family name, they may, by joint declaration, only pass on a single name to their children'.[41]

Parental choice takes the form of a joint declaration before the registrar of civil status at the time of the birth registration or the joint recognition.

The single or double name thus chosen by the parents 'applies to the couple's other children'.[42] This principle of the unity of the family name is quite appropriate, but observing it might be problematical in practice.[43]

One of the most disputed questions was obviously the solution to be applied in the absence of a parental choice. Taking its desire for equality to its ultimate conclusion, the National Assembly had decided that:

> 'In case of disagreement between the parents on the name to be given to the child, he will be given their two names, combined, in alphabetical order, to a maximum of one patronymic from each.'

The Senate vigorously criticised this alphabetical arbitrariness and took the opportunity to restore a little of the paternal pre-eminence, despite the opposition of the Government which claimed that this would take away a large part of the effect of the law. The Senate decided that:

> 'in the absence of a joint declaration before the Registrar of civil status stating the choice of name for the child, the latter takes the father's name'.[44]

Under pressure of time and with its hands tied, as we have already noted, the National Assembly accepted this major amendment.

So the father remains predominant both when the parents disagree and when they are silent. This rule operates only on a subsidiary or provisional basis, however, since the parents together, or the child on coming of age, can always change the name that was thus applied.

---

[39]   This will always be the case for the legitimate child, but also applies to the extra-marital child whose filiation is established by joint recognition or by successive acts of recognition by the father and mother before the declaration of birth.

[40]   Ie if an extra-marital child is the subject of a joint act of recognition.

[41]   Civil Code, Art 311-21-3.

[42]   Ibid, Art 311-21-2.

[43]   Cf J Massip, op cit, n 33 above.

[44]   Civil Code, Art 311-21-1 *in fine*.

Particular situations

For the child born out of wedlock, the principle laid down in Art 311-21 is complemented by the provisions of Civil Code, Arts 334-1 and 334-2, as now amended. By Art 334-1:

> 'The natural child acquires the name of that one of his two parents with regard to whom his filiation is first established.'

The chronological principle was already there in the pre-existing law, but will now have only a subsidiary role. If the child's filiation is established simultaneously with regard to both parents (essentially by joint recognition) before or after the birth declaration, Art 311-21 takes effect. The rule of Art 334-2 only comes into play if filiation, at least on one side, paternal or maternal, follows after the declaration of birth of the child. But it then becomes possible to change the name under Civil Code, Art 334-2, as we shall see.

The benefits of Civil Code, Art 311-21 extend to the child who is subject to a full adoption (*'adoption plénière'*) by a married couple.[45] In the case of simple adoption by a married couple, the child in principle keeps the name of his birth family combined with that of his adoptive family. From now on, it is for the adoptive parents to choose the name to be combined with the original name, whether that of the husband or of the wife, or a double name, in the order of their choosing, up to a maximum of one name for each of them.[46] The child adopted in a simple adoption can thus bear a triple or even quadruple name, if his birth family name is a composite one, although it is true that the judge can, on the adoptive parents' application, order that the child bear only the family names of the adopters.[47]

The rules for the name of the legitimated child[48] and those on the giving of the name[49] have similarly been harmonised with the new egalitarian principles.

2 CHANGING THE FAMILY NAME

If the very heart of the system (changing the name by decree on the application of a person of full age) remains unchanged, the possibilities of voluntarily changing the name during minority on the parents' initiative, and on the child's initiative on coming of age, have been considerably extended.

Changing the name during minority

The new possibility of voluntarily changing a child's name during his minority only applies to extra-marital children who do not come under the general rule of Art 311-21, ie children whose filiation on at least one side was established after the declaration of birth, and not where it has been simultaneously established, as we have seen. These rules which amend Art 334-1 are designed to offer parents a choice not previously open to them.

---

[45] French law does not allow adoption by unmarried cohabitants. Cf Civil Code, Art 357 for the child adopted in France, and Art 357-1 for the child adopted under an order made abroad having the effect of full adoption in France.

[46] Civil Code, Art 363-1.

[47] Ibid, Art 363-2.

[48] Ibid, Arts 331, 334-5 and 334-6.

[49] Ibid, Arts 334-5 and 357.

So, under Civil Code, Art 334-2:

> 'The natural child whose filiation has been established successively in regard to his two parents after his birth takes, by substitution, the family name of that one of his parents with regard to whom his filiation was established on the second occasion if, during his minority, his two parents make the joint declaration before the chief *greffier* of the *tribunal de grande instance.* He can, by the same procedure, take the combined names of his two parents in the order chosen by them and up to a maximum of one family name for each of them.'

If the child is over 13 years old, his consent is necessary.[50]

The traditional recourse to the *juge aux affaires familiales*, provided under Civil Code, Art 334-3, remains a possibility. If the parents disagree, one of them may apply to the judge for the change to be made. Previous judicial decisions held that the term 'change' can mean 'substitution' of one name for another. The legislative preference for a double name would seem to override such a restrictive interpretation.

Change of name on coming of age

Civil Code, Art 311-22 makes a considerable innovation:

> 'Any person to whom the name of one of his parents has been given in application of Art 311-21 may attach in second position the name of his other parent within the limit, in case of plurality of names, of one single family name.'

This facility takes effect by written declaration delivered to the registrar of civil status of the place of birth. It can be exercised at any time between coming of age and the birth of the first child of the person concerned, so as to preserve the unity of the family name.

Even if the freedom thus given to individuals is restricted in that only the combination of one name with another, and not abandonment of one name in favour of another, is allowed, it is nonetheless an upheaval in French law. Up until now, in effect, such a combination was possible but only '*à titre d'usage*' – the name thus added could not therefore be passed on. Now it can. What is more, its bearer may pass on this name alone to his children, under the conditions of choice set out in Art 311-21 of the Civil Code.

Commentators on the Law of 4 March 2002 have heaped criticism on the poor technical quality of a law enacted in something of a rush. As it deals with questions relating to civil status, greater rigour was, indeed, called for. To prove this, the Minister of Justice, concerned that the civil status service should have adequate time to prepare for the implementation of a law which has extremely complex practical implications, has obtained a postponement of its entry into force until 1 September 2003. For the moment, there are already those who are pressing for a reform of the reform.[51]

---

[50]   Civil Code, Art 334-2-2.

[51]   Cf J Massip, *Suggestions pour une modification des règles relatives au nom et au prénom,* Defrénois, 2002, p 1062.

GERMANY

IMPROVING THE POSITION OF WOMEN IN GERMAN FAMILY LAW: THE VIOLENCE PROTECTION ACT OF 2002 AND LANDMARK DECISIONS IN MAINTENANCE LAW

Nina Dethloff[*]

I INTRODUCTION

Last year's developments in the area of family law were largely characterised by new reform laws and ground-breaking court decisions. An important law reform entered into force in 2001 with the new Registered Partnership Law, which significantly improved the legal situation of same-sex partnerships through the creation of registered partnerships.[1] In June 2002, the Constitutional Court held that the Registered Partnership Law is constitutional.[2] In particular, it does not violate Art 6 I of the German Constitution which affords special protection for marriages and families. The special protection of marriage does not prevent the legislator from granting similar rights to both same-sex couples and married couples. The institution of marriage cannot be diminished by establishing another institution which is only accessible to couples who cannot marry. Equally, the Law does not violate the principle of equality protected by Art 3 I of the German Constitution, in stipulating that registered partnership is not open to all unmarried persons regardless of their sex nor to close communities that are based on mutual responsibility between relatives.

The most important law reform of 2002 is the Violence Protection Act, which significantly improves the protection from domestic violence offered to women (discussed in Section II). The Children's Rights Improvement Act also needs to be mentioned: this Act extends the protection from violence offered to children and is intended to produce a few other, limited improvements of their legal status. Fundamental changes have also come about in the area of maintenance law through the new judicature of both the Constitutional Court and the Supreme Court, which will primarily affect the situation of women (discussed in Section III).

---

[*]   Professor Dr, LLM, Chair of Civil Law, Private International Law, Comparative Law and Private European Law at Rheinische Friedrich-Wilhelms Universität Bonn.
[1]   See my overview in the *International Survey of Family Law (2002 Edition)*, ed Andrew Bainham (Family Law, 2002), p 171.
[2]   Judgment of the BverfG of 17 July 2001, *http://www.bverfg.de\.*

II VIOLENCE PROTECTION ACT OF 2002

A Object of the Violence Protection Act

The Violence Protection Act[3] aims to improve the legal status of women, in particular, as typical victims of violence. The Act reforms the civil law protection concerning acts of violence and stalking by complementing the existing provisions of the law of torts with rules allowing their efficient enforcement. The goal of the Act is to afford fast and, above all, pre-emptive protection for victims through enforceable court orders.[4] In order to reach this goal the Violence Protection Act provides for both protective orders (§ 1 VPA) and exclusion orders (§2 VPA and § 1361b BGB).[5] The idea behind both measures is to put distance between the perpetrator and the victim. This method has been shown to be an effective means to break the vicious circle of violence, a case in point being the experiences gained from the recent Austrian Violence Protection Act.[6]

B Protective orders

The courts can make protective orders in cases of unlawful and intentional harm to body, health or liberty of a person (§ 1 I 1 VPA). Unlike German criminal law, the degree of culpability is irrelevant in the case of protective orders. Thus the possible influence of mind-altering substances is immaterial in this regard.[7] In order to ensure effective protection, the Violence Protection Act also includes any harassing actions that fall short of actual injury. The Act lists both threats and stalking as possible reasons for a protective order (§ 1 II VPA). In this context, threats are understood as targeting life, limb, health or liberty. Obviously, such threats will give rise to protective orders only if the judge is convinced that they have a serious basis. Stalking is defined as either trespass or the repeated pursuit of a person against that person's explicitly declared will. Such pursuit may be either physical or effected by means of telecommunications. The use of the term 'repeated' pursuit means that a protective order will not be issued on the grounds of a single such incident.

The victim may seek a protective order each time an action specified in the Act occurs. The Act contains a catalogue of possible protective orders, including an order not to enter the dwelling of the victim, an order not to remain within a

---

3   Gesetz zur Verbesserung des zivilgerichtlichen Schutzes bei Gewalttaten und Nachstellungen sowie zur Erleichterung der Überlassung der Ehewohnung bei Trennung [Law for the improvement of civil court protection concerning acts of violence and stalking and for the facilitation of the relinquishment of the domicile of a marriage in cases of separation], of 11 December 2001 (BGBl I p 3512).

4   Palandt-Brudermüller GewSchG Einl, at 1.

5   As amended by Art 2 VPA; compare Brudermüller, 'Regelungen der Nutzungs- und Rechtsverhältnisse an Ehewohnung und Hausrat', *Zeitschrift für das gesamte Familienrecht* 1999, p 129.

6   Schumacher, 'Mehr Schutz bei Gewalt in der Familie', *Zeitschrift für das gesamte Familienrecht* 2002, p 645; Stormann, 'Schutz vor häuslicher Gewalt – Erfahrungen mit dem österreichischen Bundesgesetz zum Schutz vor Gewalt in der Familie', *Jugendamt* 2001, p 452.

7   § I III VPA.

certain area of the victim's dwelling, an order not to visit specific other places frequented by the victim, an order not to contact the victim (this includes contact via telecommunications) and an order not to facilitate a meeting with the victim. This catalogue is not exclusive. Should an order be breached, the Violence Protection Act provides for criminal penalties of fines or imprisonment for a period of up to one year.

In all of these instances, the orders are subject to limitation by the lawful interests of the perpetrator. A protective order is therefore unavailable if contact with the victim is an unavoidable consequence of the respondent availing himself of a justified interest, for example, visiting a child living with the victim, if the respondent is entitled to such visits, or if the respondent is required to meet the victim for professional or other reasons.[8]

C   Exclusion orders

In instances where violence occurs within the context of domestic cohabitation, courts may order that the jointly used domicile be left to the victim in order to grant the victim, at least temporarily, protection from further acts of violence. The prerequisite for such an exclusion order is that the respondent and victim have shared a household on a long-term basis, ie a 'long-term household'. This term comes from the recently reformed tenancy law.[9] It requires something more than simply living together, though not a bond of relationship or law. It does, however, require an inner bond between the parties. Both heterosexual and homosexual partnerships, as well as communities of elderly people living together, are considered to fall into this category. Although the law is premised upon the idea of a two-person household, there are circumstances in which the law can apply to larger groups cohabiting, provided that they share some form of joint responsibility. Mere roommates, who primarily wish to satisfy their housing needs in a better or cheaper fashion, do not fall into this category.

Entitlement to an exclusion order in accordance with § 2 VPA, like a protective order, requires an existing injury or threat of such injury. If an actual injury has occurred, the victim need only show that he or she lives in a long-term household with the respondent. In instances of an unlawful threat to injure, an exclusion order for the relinquishment of a shared dwelling additionally requires that the measure prevent undue hardship. A particular instance of such undue hardship would be that the welfare of a child living in the communal dwelling is impaired.

An order for the relinquishment of a shared dwelling will be subject to a time limit if the respondent is legally entitled to the dwelling, be it as a result of a lease, ownership or other claim. The law does not proscribe a maximum limit, however, unless the respondent is the sole person with a claim to the dwelling. In such instances, the maximum period for which an order to relinquish the dwelling may be issued, is six months. In exceptional cases, this period may be prolonged for another six months. In cases in which the respondent has no personal claim to the

---

[8]   Compare Palandt-*Thomas* § 823 at 175.

[9]   Schumacher, 'Mehr Schutz bei Gewalt in der Familie', *Zeitschrift für das gesamte Familienrecht* 2002, pp 645, 650.

dwelling, the order will stipulate no time limit. Through these provisions, the Act attempts to maintain a balance between the individual rights of the respondent and the victim. The flexibility of these provisions is also designed to enable the courts to take into account the rights of third parties with claims to the dwelling.

An order for the relinquishment of a dwelling may be refused if there is no imminent danger of further injuries. In these circumstances, the burden of proof is on the respondent. An order may also be refused if the victim does not assert a claim against the respondent for relinquishment of the dwelling in writing. This provision is designed to ensure legal certainty regarding the rights to the dwelling. The fact that a three-month period for the claim is allowed also means that victims may claim relinquishment of the dwelling even if they have fled the dwelling and no longer live there, just as long as the claim is made within three months of the injury being sustained. The aim of this provision is to ensure the victim's rights if the actions of the respondent have already forced the victim to leave the dwelling in order to prevent further acts of violence.

If such a claim is made, the respondent must leave the dwelling. The respondent can also be ordered not to terminate the lease and/or not to take any other actions that may result in no longer being obliged to relinquish the dwelling. The victim will generally be required to compensate the respondent for the right so relinquished if the respondent is, for example, the tenant.

The Violence Protection Act has also changed the BGB's special provision contained in § 1361b regarding the allocation of dwellings to separated spouses or those wishing to separate. Under the new legislation a spouse can claim exclusive occupation of a dwelling should such a step be necessary to prevent undue hardship. In the event of violence or a threat of violence, when for example the welfare of a child may be impaired, the victim is generally entitled to claim for the relinquishment of a dwelling.

D   Children and the Children's Rights Improvement Act

The Violence Protection Act legislates only for the protection of adult victims of violence. It does not apply when children or youths are injured or threatened with injury by their parents or other persons with custodial rights. Rather, such cases fall under the purview of the general provisions of family law. If the victim is a minor, the Family Court may take 'the necessary steps' under § 1666 BGB. Such steps include admonishments, warnings, orders, and revocation of custody. In order to improve the protection of victims who have not reached their majority, the Children's Rights Improvement Act, which passed into law shortly after the VPA, now allows, in accordance with § 1666a BGB, a parent to be ordered to vacate the dwelling.

III   NEW DECISIONS CONCERNING MAINTENANCE LAW

Both the Constitutional Court and the Supreme Court have recently made major contributions in the area of maintenance law. First of all, two landmark decisions of the Federal Constitutional Court relate to the issue of judicial control of matrimonial agreements (discussed at **A**). Furthermore, an important Supreme Court decision, which was later confirmed by the Constitutional Court, concerns the amount of maintenance after divorce where, during the marriage, one of the partners was a homemaker and the other gainfully employed (discussed at **B**).

A Judicial control of matrimonial agreements

In February 2001 the Federal Constitutional Court gave two decisions concerning the judicial control of matrimonial agreements.[10] These decisions dealt with prenuptial agreements in which pregnant women had waived all claims to maintenance in the event of divorce and had agreed to exempt their husbands-to-be from their obligation to pay child support. The court ruled that a partner's freedom of contract on entering marriage was limited in cases where such an agreement does not result from an equal partnership but rather reflects the dominant position of one of the spouses deriving from inequitable bargaining positions.[11] Pregnant women found themselves in such an inequitable bargaining position because the situation of an unwed mother is disadvantageous both legally and in reality. These decisions will have a significant impact on the future of judicial control over matrimonial as well as divorce agreements. Where such an agreement is clearly disadvantageous to one party owing to her inferior bargaining position, the courts will not enforce it. Where a spouse waives all her rights to maintenance, agrees to separation of property without any participation in the accrued gains in the event of divorce, or gives up any share in old-age pension provisions, the courts will closely scrutinise whether or not these disadvantages were imposed on her by exploiting a position of constraint in which the woman may have found herself.

B Levels of maintenance payable after divorce

Recently both the Supreme Court[12] and the Constitutional Court[13] have handed down two more leading decisions, which will be of great importance for the future of the law governing maintenance. In June 2001 the Supreme Court overturned its prior rulings and found that the method it had previously used for determining the levels of maintenance payable did not adequately take into consideration the equal value of homemaking and work outside the family. After divorce a spouse has a right to maintenance if, and in as far as, she or he cannot adequately support her- or himself through gainful employment (§ 1569 BGB). The German Civil Code specifies that gainful employment may not be expected, in particular, when the person in question has been caring for the couple's children (§ 1570 BGB), is elderly (§ 1571 BGB) or is ill (§ 1572 BGB). According to § 1578 BGB, the level

---

[10]   Judgments of the BVerfG of 6 February 2001, and 29 March 2001, http://www.bverfg.de\.

[11]   As already in Schwenzer, 'Vertragsfreiheit im Ehevermögens- und Scheidungsfolgenrecht', *Archiv für civilistische Praxis* 1996, pp 88–113; Dethloff, Note, *Juristenzeitung* 1997, pp 414–415; Büttner, 'Grenzen ehevertraglicher Gestaltungsmöglichkeiten', *Zeitschrift für das gesamte Familienrecht* 1998, pp 1–8.

[12]   Judgment of the BGH of 13 June 2001, *Zeitschrift für das gesamte Familienrecht* 2001, p 986.

[13]   Judgment of the BVerfG of 5 February 2002, *http://www.bverfg.de\.*

of maintenance payable normally depends on the standard of living during the marriage. To the extent that this would be inequitable, especially as concerns the division of labour in, and the length of time of, the marriage, the level of maintenance payable may be measured against the standard of living during the marriage for a limited time only. The future level of maintenance payments may thereafter be based on sustaining an adequate lifestyle. In general, however, the level of maintenance payable is defined by the standard of living during the marriage. This means that both partners are entitled to about half of the income that determined the matrimonial standard of living.

If during the marriage only one partner was gainfully employed and the other took care of the household and children, according to prior case-law the standard of living during marriage was exclusively determined by the income of the gainfully employed partner.[14] If after the divorce the homemaking partner took up gainful employment or worked longer hours than before, the income so gained reduced her or his lack of means, the only result being to lighten the other party's burden of maintenance. The Supreme Court found that this did not conform to the equal value of both partners' contributions during the marriage. Not only the income of the gainfully employed partner, but also childrearing and household work, determine the standard of living during the marriage. After divorce both partners are entitled to share the standard of living that they jointly attained during the marriage. If after the divorce the homemaking partner takes up or intensifies gainful employment, the Supreme Court now considers this employment as a substitute for the homemaking work she or he previously undertook. The monetary value that is to be attributed to the homemaking work undertaken in the past consequently corresponds to the income resulting from this employment. This income no longer only reduces her or his need. Instead the new method used for determining the amount of maintenance now ensures that both partners participate equally in such income – in the same way as both benefited from the homemaking during marriage. The Constitutional Court confirmed last January that the Constitution requires that both partners be able to participate equally in the income.

IV CONCLUSION

Looking back on the development of family law in the past year, we can note that both the legislator, with the Violence Protection Act, and the highest courts have contributed significantly to an improvement of the legal status of women in Germany. Despite these important steps a lot remains to be done to secure equal rights for women and men in family law: although in the past, the numerous provisions in German family law that openly discriminated against women have been abolished, family law still fails to conform with the principle of equality.

---

[14] Compare Judgment of the BGH of 24 November 1982, *Zeitschrift für das gesamte Familienrecht* 1983, p 144; Judgment of the BGH of 27 November 1985, *Zeitschrift für das gesamte Familienrecht* 1986, p 148; Judgment of the BGH of 23 April 1986, *Zeitschrift für das gesamte Familienrecht* 1986, p 783. These decisions were criticised by Büttner, *Zeitschrift für das gesamte Familienrecht* 1999, p 893; Scholz, *Zeitschrift für das gesamte Familienrecht* 1999, p 541; Lorenz, *Zeitschrift für das gesamte Familienrecht* 1993, p 392.

This principle is contradicted not only by those provisions which explicitly cite gender as a relevant criterion, but also by those which typically have a different impact on women than they have on men owing to factual differences between them.[15] In German society there remains a substantial structural inequality between women and men. This derives particularly from the persistence of traditional views on male and female roles in family work.

Although, recently, the Federal Constitutional Court has in principle acknowledged that provisions which have a different impact on men and women due to such factual dissimilarities amount to indirect discrimination and are therefore illegal,[16] in the case in question the existence of indirect discrimination was, surprisingly, denied. The pertinent provision concerning the child's surname does not permit parents to choose a name consisting of both parents' surnames for their children. If spouses keep their own surnames after marriage rather than adopting a joint family name, the birth name of their first child can only be either the father's or the mother's surname, (§ 1617 I 1 BGB). This name must then be used for all subsequent children. The use of a hyphenated name for children being ruled out, parents will, in line with tradition, largely resort to the father's surname. This results in isolating women within the family, and this fact from the outset exerts indirect pressure on them not to keep their maiden name after marriage. Although the provision thus typically has a negative impact on women, because of the factual dominance of the man's surname, the Constitutional Court upheld the provision.[17] In spite of this unfortunate lack of sensitivity to the relevance of a person's name for his or her individuality and personality, and consequently its importance for the achievement of equality, one would hope that in the future the court will resume its important role in promoting equality between men and women.

---

[15] For a more detailed discussion of this problem see Dethloff, 'Reform of German Family Law – A Battle against Discrimination', 3 EJLR 221 (2001).

[16] Judgment of the BVerfG of 30 January 2002, http://www.bverfg.de\.

[17] Judgment of the BverfG of 30 January 2002, http://www.bverfg.de\; criticised by Sacksofsky, 'Grundrechtsdogmatik ade – zum neuen Doppelnamensurteil des Bundesverfassungsgerichts', *Familie, Partnerschaft und Recht* 2002, p 121.

GHANA

FAMILY LAW IN GHANA
UNDER THE CONSTITUTION 1992

Gordon R Woodman[*]

The family law of a state is not normally thought to be closely related to its constitutional law. For Ghana, the relationship might be expected to be quite remote, since the country has had a post-colonial history in which constitutions have proved fragile but the customary family law has continued to be socially powerful irrespective of national politics. On the other hand, the country has come to view the formulation of a constitution as an occasion to review all aspects of its social life. Ready to look critically at their social institutions and to consider continuously the need to adapt them to a changing environment, the citizens of Ghana have, in each of the four constitutions enacted since Independence in 1957, approved provisions with an important bearing on family law. Thus, while the reign of the Constitution, 1992, the Constitution of the Fourth Republic which came into effect on 7 January 1993, may not constitute a distinct era for Ghanaian family law, it is a period which can be conveniently separated for the purpose of this Survey. Accordingly, the first section of this contribution is a brief consideration of the aspects of the current constitution relevant to family law.

Relatively little case-law is accessible for this recent period. The publication of the *Ghana Law Reports* has fallen behind schedule. Only decisions of the Supreme Court are available, principally through the privately published *Supreme Court of Ghana Law Reports.*[1]

A comment is required on the concept of the family in the law of Ghana. The word 'family' in the (official) English language is normally used to translate the word in indigenous languages which refers to the unilineal descent group which is of major significance in each person's social life. Thus 'family' corresponds to the *abusa* or *ebusua* in the Akan languages (of about 50% of the population), which mean matrilineal descent groups. In Akan society, the family:

'... is based upon the common sacred blood that feeds and nurtures the child in his mother's womb, running through all persons male and female in the direct female line of descent from a common female ancestor. Being peculiar to the womb, it is passed on by each female member of the family to all children both male and female born of her; but it dies with every male member.'[2]

---

[*]   Professor of Comparative Law, University of Birmingham, UK.
[1]   SY Bimpong-Buta (ed), Accra: Advanced Legal Publications, PO Box X 222, James Town.
[2]   NA Ollennu and GR Woodman (eds), *Ollennu's Principles of Customary Land Law in Ghana,* 2nd ed, Birmingham: CAL Press (1985), at pp 147–148.

A lengthy account could be given of the law relating to this family: of its membership, its mode of internal government, and its manner of acquiring, holding and disposing of corporately owned land and other property.[3]

However, in the legal literature of which this Survey is a part, family law conventionally does not carry this meaning. Comparison of laws would not be assisted, in an arena in which most contenders are western or western influenced family laws, by an insistence on the African concept of the family. Accordingly, this contribution focuses primarily on the legal regulation of relations between spouses and between parent and child in Ghana. Nevertheless, it is never possible nor justified to exclude the true Ghanaian family from view in considering any social institution such as marriage in the law of Ghana. It will be seen below that the conflict of interest between a person's spouse and his or her family, and sometimes that between a person's child and his or her family, remains potentially acute, especially in cases of inheritance.

I   THE PROVISIONS OF THE CONSTITUTION, 1992 AFFECTING FAMILY LAW

Three types of constitutional provision are especially significant in respect of family law: those setting out the sources of the law of Ghana generally; those which set out general fundamental human rights and freedoms; and those which refer specifically to rights and obligations in family law.

It is provided in Art 11 that the laws of Ghana shall comprise: constitutional and regular statutory provisions; 'the existing law'; and 'the common law'. Statute law, such as the Children's Act, 1998 (Act 560), to be examined later, prevails over the two other types of law in a manner familiar to lawyers accustomed to the modern effects of legislation on other sources of law.

'The existing law' is defined as 'the written and unwritten law' which existed in Ghana immediately before the coming into force of the Constitution. Thus previously enacted statutes, such as the Matrimonial Causes Act, 1971 (Act 367), continue to be valid, except where they are incompatible with provisions of the Constitution. The term 'existing law' would seem sufficient also to maintain in effect the common law received from England and the rest of the common law world, and the customary laws of Ghana. However, these are provided for expressly in the further phrase 'the common law'. Article 11 provides that 'the common law of Ghana shall comprise the rules of law generally known as the common law, the rules generally known as the doctrines of equity and the rules of customary law including those determined by the Superior Court of Judicature'. It is clear that the common law, in the sense of received law, and customary law continue to be parts of the law of Ghana. In extensive areas of the law on the formation of marriage, matrimonial proceedings, parent–child relations, and inheritance, the common law has been largely replaced by statute. However, the statutes on the formation of marriage, primarily the Marriage

---

[3]   Ollennu and Woodman (footnote 2 above), passim; GR Woodman, *Customary Land Law in the Ghanaian Courts*, Accra: Universities of Ghana Press (1996), Chapters 7, 8, 9.

Ordinance,[4] and on matrimonial proceedings including dissolution of marriage, primarily the Matrimonial Causes Act, 1971, generally do not replace the customary law on these subjects but co-exist with it. Consequently, the distinction between the two types of law remains in substance in these fields.

Customary law has been continuously interpreted and adapted for judicial application for more than 150 years, and a large body of case-law has been built. Consequently, 'customary law' for the purposes of the formal legal system means the norms which the courts have enforced or are likely to enforce under this name. These do not necessarily coincide with the norms which are observed in practice among the peoples of the various ethnic groups, although frequently they do.[5]

Despite the categorisation of law in the Constitution, 1992, it is usual and convenient to distinguish in the law of Ghana between: enacted law; customary law; and common law, in the sense of the law determined by courts of law and equity in the common law world. This categorisation is adopted in the remainder of this contribution.[6]

The rules governing the choice of the type of law to be applied in particular cases are of some complexity. While statute law always takes priority, the choice between common law and customary law is governed by general statutory choice of law rules,[7] and sometimes by specific provisions as to the law applicable in stated classes of cases.[8] The effect in the law of marriage is that Ghanaians when contracting a marriage may, by their choice of the manner of celebration, select the law which is to be applied to their marital relationship. Two adults neither of whom is married (unless married to the other under customary law) may opt to marry in accordance with the Marriage Ordinance, in which case their marital rights and duties are regulated by the common law, and the dissolution of their marriage and other matrimonial causes are regulated by the Matrimonial Causes Act, 1971. Adults not married under the Ordinance may opt to marry in accordance with a system of customary law, in which case that customary law generally governs these matters.[9] There was a corresponding division for cases of

---

[4]   Cap 148, Laws of the Gold Coast [Ghana], 1951 rev.

[5]   The issue of the distinction between socially observed customary law and lawyers' customary law has been discussed in: GR Woodman, 'Some realism about customary law – the West African experience' (1969) *Wisconsin Law Review* 128; GR Woodman, 'Judicial development of customary law: the case of marriage law in Ghana and Nigeria' (1977) 14 *University of Ghana Law Journal* 115; GR Woodman, 'Customary law, state courts, and the notion of institutionalization of norms in Ghana and Nigeria', pp 143–163 in AN Allott and GR Woodman (eds), *People's Law and State Law: the Bellagio Papers*, Dordrecht: Foris (1985).

[6]   English 'statutes of general application' which were imported into Ghana at the date when a local colonial legislature was established in 1874, and which formerly constituted part of the received common law, are no longer in force as a category thus defined. A few English statutory provisions are in force by virtue of the Courts Act, 1993 (Act 459), s 119. None will need to be referred to in this article.

[7]   These were in 1993 contained in the Courts Act, 1971 (Act 372), s 49, and have been re-enacted in the Courts Act, 1998 (Act 459), s 45.

[8]   Thus, for example, the Intestate Succession Law 1985 (PNDCL 111) provides for the application of customary law rules in the distribution of specified fractions of an estate in specified circumstances.

[9]   Two exceptions, discussed below, are: (a) an infrequently invoked provision in the Matrimonial Causes Act, 1971, s 41 which permits a party to a customary law marriage to apply to the court to apply the provisions of the Act to a customary law marriage; (b) the possibility that the parties' relationship regarding property rights may be regulated by received common law, as indicated in

intestate succession until the enactment of the Intestate Succession Law, 1985 (PNDCL 111) unified this law.[10] The family law relating to children, on the other hand, has been largely unified by the Children's Act, 1998.

The constitutional provisions setting out fundamental human rights and freedoms (Chapter Five) may for the present purpose be separated into general provisions and those which refer specifically to family law. As to the former, it suffices to note that the Ghana Constitution, 1992, in common with most modern constitutions, enjoins all organs of government to respect and uphold the human rights which are set out, these being the principal human rights recognised and elaborated in international Conventions, without distinction on the grounds of race, place of origin, political opinion, colour, religion, creed or gender.[11] There are clearly implications here for aspects of family law. However, in contrast to some African countries, such as Tanzania and South Africa, where the compatibility of these rights with customary-law polygamy has been debated, Ghana has to date seen no litigation over these issues. A recognition of possible clashes with traditional culture is indicated in Chapter Six, 'The Directive Principles of State Policy',[12] where in an Article which requires the encouragement of customary and cultural values, the State is also required to 'ensure ... that traditional practices which are injurious to the health and well-being of the person are abolished'.[13]

Rights and obligations in family law are explicitly referred to in two Articles. Article 22, in the Chapter on Fundamental Human Rights and Freedoms, provides:

'PROPERTY RIGHTS OF SPOUSES

22 (1) A spouse shall not be deprived of a reasonable provision out of the estate of a spouse whether or not the spouse died having made a will.

(2) Parliament shall, as soon as practicable after the coming into force of this Constitution, enact legislation regulating the property rights of spouses.

(3) With a view to achieving the full realisation of the rights referred to in clause (2) of this article –

    (a) spouses shall have equal access to property jointly acquired during marriage;

    (b) assets which are jointly acquired during marriage shall be distributed equitably between the spouses upon dissolution of the marriage.'

It is arguable that cl (1) was already satisfied by the combined provisions of the Wills Act, 1971 (Act 360) and the Intestate Succession Law, 1985.[14] Parliament

---

cases cited below. Marriage under the Marriage of Mohammedans Ordinance (Cap 129) is extremely rare, since the ordinance applies only to marriages which not only comply with Islamic law in the form of celebration but also are registered under the Ordinance. Virtually no marriages are so registered. This form of marriage is therefore not discussed in this article.

[10] The law is reported upon by MDA Freeman, 'Ghana: Legislation for today', *Annual Survey of Family Law 1987* (1988–89) *Journal of Family Law* 159.

[11] Constitution, 1992, Arts 12–33.

[12] Articles 34–41.

[13] Article 39. In pursuance of this principle, Parliament enacted the Criminal Code (Amendment) Act, 1994 (Act 484) making criminal female circumcision, a practice which was said to be continuing among a few peoples.

[14] Wills Act, 1971, s 13, provides that, inter alia, a spouse of a deceased testator may apply to the court for reasonable provision to be made for him or her out of the estate if the will has failed to make such provision. The Intestate Succession Law, 1985, ss 3 and 4 give the surviving spouse and children a priority right to the household chattels and one house of the deceased; s 5 gives a

has not yet acted on cl (2). Clause (3) has been referred to in case-law which is discussed below.

Article 28, also in the Chapter on Fundamental Human Rights and Freedoms, provides in cl (1) that Parliament shall enact laws to enforce the rights of every child (defined as a person below 18 years of age) to: the special care, assistance and maintenance necessary for his or her development from the natural parents; reasonable provision out of the estate of his or her parents; maintenance and upbringing by his or her parents in co-operation with institutions prescribed by Parliament in a manner which ensures that the interests of the child are paramount; and special protection from physical and moral hazards. The laws are also to ensure that the family is safeguarded in the promotion of the interests of children. Clauses (2) to (4) declare the child's rights to protection from engaging in work which threatens his or her health, education or development, from torture or other cruel, inhuman or degrading treatment or punishment, and from deprivation by any other person of medical treatment, education or any other benefit by reason only of religious or other beliefs. It was to conform with this Article that Parliament enacted the Children's Act, 1998, discussed below.

It might be claimed by critics that the provisions of the Constitution which relate to family law have produced no visible effect other than the enactment of the Children's Act, 1998. It might be replied that in areas of family law other than that relating to children the law of Ghana already complied more or less fully with these provisions, but that in the interpretation of the existing law the courts have found them to provide helpful guidance.

II DEVELOPMENTS IN MARRIAGE LAW[15]

There have been no legislative developments in this field, except for some relating to the marriage of children which will be noted in the next section. Legally monogamous marriage, usually contracted by a Christian ceremony (although a secular, register office procedure is available), has continued to be regulated by the Marriage Ordinance. The great majority of marriages have continued to be contracted under customary law.[16] As noted by Freeman, customary law marriages and divorces were made registrable by the Customary Marriage and Divorce (Registration) Law, 1985 (PCDCL 112).[17] Freeman seems to have interpreted that

---

spouse a proportion of the residue of the estate; and s 12 provides that small estates are to pass to the spouse and children exclusively. Amendments to the Intestate Succession Law, 1985 made by the Children's Act, 1998 strengthening these provisions in the interests of children are mentioned below.

[15] A valuable summary of the existing law is given in Akua Kuenyehia and Esther Ofei-Aboagye, 'Family law in Ghana and its implications for women', in A Kuenyehia (ed), *Women and Law in West Africa: Situational Analysis of Some Key Issues Affecting Women*, Legon: Women and Law in West Africa (1998) pp 23–61.

[16] L Oware Gyekye, Alexina Arthur and EVO Dankwa, 'Family law and customary practices for child maintenance and inheritance in Ghana', in Elizabeth Ardayfio-Schandorf (ed), *The Changing Family in Ghana*, Accra: Ghana Universities Press (1996), p 86, at pp 98–99, 104–105 (although the marriages classified there by respondents as marriages under Moslem law were almost certainly not recognised by the legal system of the State as such: see footnote 9 above); Kuenyehia and Ofei-Aboagye, op cit (footnote 15 above), p 25.

[17] Freeman, op cit (footnote 10 above), pp 160–161.

statute as having the effect that the spouse of an unregistered customary law marriage was excluded from claiming to inherit under the Intestate Succession Law, 1985.[18] There was some judicial and academic discussion of this issue.[19] It was resolved by the Customary Marriage and Divorce (Registration) (Amendment) Law 1991 (PNDCL 263), which provided, with retrospective effect from the date of the principal Act, that the Intestate Succession Law applied to the spouses of unregistered marriages where such marriage was proved 'by oral or documentary evidence'.

Matrimonial proceedings in respect of a 'monogamous marriage', ie an ordinance marriage or an equivalent marriage contracted outside Ghana, are governed by the Matrimonial Causes Act, 1971. This contains provisions which are at most points in substance the same as those of English law at the date when it was enacted, including those introduced by the Divorce Reform Act, 1969 and later consolidated in the Matrimonial Causes Act 1973. It provides that 'the sole ground for granting a petition for divorce shall be that the marriage has broken down beyond reconciliation' (s 1(2)). To establish this ground, the petitioner 'shall satisfy the court of one or more of' a number of facts, the list which follows being almost identical with that in the English statutes (s 2(1)).[20]

Proceedings in respect of customary law marriages are generally governed by customary law. The customary law procedure for divorce entails no court proceedings, but negotiations between the families of the spouses to encourage reconciliation and, if these fail, agreement between the families and the spouses and a formal act (varying according to the particular customary law in issue) to mark the termination of the marriage. The Matrimonial Causes Act, 1971 provides that, on the application of a party to a marriage other than a monogamous marriage, a court is to apply the provisions of this Act, subject to various modifications designed to take account of the customary laws of the parties. There have been few instances of the application of the Act to customary law marriages.[21]

The property rights inter se of spouses have been a principal object of litigation, especially when the marriage has been ended by divorce. The

---

[18]   Ibid, p 161.

[19]   Registration of a marriage was held not to be a necessary condition for inheritance as a 'spouse' under the Intestate Succession Law, 1985 in: *Adade v Dade* [1991] 1 GLR 267; *Essilfie v Quarcoo* [1992] 2 GLR 180; *In re Neequaye (Decd); Armah v Annan* [1991] 1 GLR 496. This was the view put in GR Woodman, 'Ghana reforms the law of intestate succession' [1985] *Journal of African Law* 118 at 123, including note 22.

[20]   This provision corresponds to s 2(1) of the English 1969 Act and s 1(2) of the 1973 Act. The principal differences in the Ghana statute (apart from its more elegant drafting) are: in the case of the fact that the parties have lived apart for two years, the consent of the respondent to the divorce may be dispensed with if it is unreasonably withheld; and the list contains an additional alternative fact, 'that the parties to the marriage have, after diligent effort, been unable to reconcile their differences'.

[21]   Three such instances which have been the subjects of discussion are: *Mensah v Berkoe* [1975] 2 GLR 347, discussed by WC Ekow Daniels, 'Dissolution of customary law marriages by the court' (1977) 9 *Review of Ghana Law* 71; *Adjei v Foriwaa*, digested [1981] GLRD 32, and discussed by GR Woodman, 'The adaptation of customary law to the Matrimonial Causes Act, 1971' (1981 & 1982) 13 & 14 *Review of Ghana Law* 218; *Oparebea v Mensah*, unreported judgment of High Court, 14 December 1989, discussed by Kuenyehia and Ofei-Aboagye, op cit (footnote 15 above), pp 42–43, and the subject of a successful appeal [1993–94] 1 GLR 61, in which the Court of Appeal took a different view of the evidence from that of the trial court.

Matrimonial Causes Act, 1971, s 20, confers on a court in matrimonial proceedings the power:

> '... to order either party to the marriage to pay to the other party such sum of money or convey to the other party such movable or immovable property as settlement of property rights or in lieu thereof or as part of financial provision as the court thinks just and equitable.'

The manner of administration of this power was considered by the Court of Appeal in *Achiampong v Achiampong*,[22] a case arising from an ordinance marriage. The court there held that the section was procedural. It enabled parties to matrimonial proceedings to avoid the need to issue a writ of summons or a summons of some sort to have their claims to property determined. The court's exercise of its discretion to alter the proprietary rights of the spouses in a 'just and equitable' manner must be guided by law. The court gave guidance on the principles of law to be applied. If a wife went to live in a matrimonial home owned by the husband, she did not thereby acquire a proprietary right in that property. However, she acquired a right in rem if she discharged the burden of establishing an agreement between the parties that she should have a beneficial interest in it; or that she directly or indirectly made a substantial contribution in money or money's worth towards the acquisition of the property, as would be the case if she paid for renovation or extensions, or applied her own income for the common benefit of the two of them and the children so as to enable the husband financially to acquire the property. In such circumstances, the spouse in whom the legal title was vested might be required to hold the property on trust for the two spouses. In reaching these conclusions the court referred for authority exclusively to English case-law.

In the period under review, the issue came to the Supreme Court in *Mensah v Mensah*,[23] where again the rights of parties to an ordinance marriage were in issue. The court cited two English cases as authority for 'the principle of the equitable sharing of joint property on divorce', and stated with approval that this principle had been applied in *Achiampong v Achiampong*. The court now had additional authority for taking this view: it held that the principle had been given constitutional effect and force by Art 22(3)(b) of the 1992 Constitution. The result in this case was that the matrimonial home was declared to be the joint property of the husband and wife, to be shared equally. It was ordered that the house was to be valued and sold and the proceeds shared equally between the spouses, but that the wife was to be given the first option to purchase the property.

It is likely that the property rights of parties to an ordinance marriage will be regulated by common law. It is also likely that common law will be applied if a party to a customary law marriage applies to the court for the application of the provisions of the Matrimonial Causes Act, 1971 to the marriage under the provision which permits this.[24] For application in other cases arising from customary law marriages, customary law has or could develop its own principles

---

22   [1982–83] GLR 1017.
23   [1998–99] SCGLR 350 reversing the decision of the Court of Appeal [1993–94] 1 GLR 111 on the interpretation of the evidence.
24   See footnote 20 above. In the three cases cited, the issues crucial to the parties appear to have been claims to property.

regarding the mutual property rights of spouses.[25] However, customary law was not applied in *Sykes v Abbey*,[26] in which the wife of a dissolved customary law marriage issued a writ against the former husband claiming title to a house and a commercial business acquired during the marriage. There appear to have been no matrimonial proceeding nor any application under the Matrimonial Causes Act, 1971. The court decided that the legal title was vested in the husband, but, on the basis of English decisions and *Achiampong v Achiampong*, that an agreement between the parties and the wife's expenditure had created equitable rights in the wife which were enforceable against him. These rights amounted to the entire beneficial title to the house and a share in the business.

While this issue of the choice of law was not expressly discussed, it would seem that the best explanation for the decision is to be found in the statutory choice of law rules. These provide that the law applicable to an issue arising out of a transaction is the law which the parties to the transaction intended or may be taken to have intended to govern the issue.[27] Generally, if the contracting of a marriage may be regarded as a 'transaction' for this purpose, the parties may be taken to indicate by the form of the marriage ceremony the law which they intend to govern all aspects of their relationship. However, there would seem to be little justification for extending this conclusion to every property transaction in which the parties engage in relation to each other. If parties married under customary law choose to deal with property together according to common law principles, it would seem reasonable to give effect to their choice of law. The difficulty here is that the common intention will usually be tacit, and, in cases involving the imposition of a trust on property vested in a spouse for the benefit of the other spouse, contested. It is possible that progress towards what the courts regard as equitable outcomes would be easier if the courts continued to develop customary law principles for application in such cases.[28]

III DEVELOPMENTS IN THE LEGAL RELATIONSHIP BETWEEN PARENT AND CHILD[29]

Statements of the law in this field have been formulated as part of the development of the more general law on children. Ghana was the first country to ratify the UN Convention on the Rights of the Child, which came into force on

---

[25] Such cases as there have been on co-ownership in customary law, including some which involved customary law spouses, are discussed in GR Woodman, op cit (footnote 3 above), pp 342–344.

[26] Ghana Supreme Court Judgments 1996, vol 1, 108.

[27] Courts Act, 1993, s 54(1), r 1.

[28] A summary of judicial developments in this respect, all prior to 1992, is given by Kuenyehia and Ofei-Aboagye (footnote 15 above), pp 32–37.

[29] See, for helpful statements of the law and information on social practice: HJAN Mensa-Bonsu and C Dowuona-Hammond, 'The child within the Ghanaian family', in Ardayfio-Schandorf (ed), op cit (footnote 16 above), p 5; HJAN Mensa-Bonsu and C Dowuona-Hammond (eds), *The Rights of the Child in Ghana – Perspectives*, Accra: Woeli Publishing Services, 1994; Kuenyehia and Ofei-Aboagye, op cit (footnote 15 above), pp 45–60. However, the Children's Act, 1998 was enacted after all of these texts were written.

2 September 1990.[30] The Constitution accordingly contains in Art 28 a provision on children's rights. The parts of this particularly germane to family law read:

'**28** (1) Parliament shall enact such laws as are necessary to ensure that—

(a) every child has the right to the same measure of special care, assistance and maintenance as is necessary for its development from its natural parents, except where those parents have effectively surrendered their rights and responsibilities in respect of the child in accordance with law;

(b) every child, whether or not born in wedlock, shall be entitled to reasonable provision out of the estate of its parents;

(c) parents undertake their natural right and obligation of care, maintenance and upbringing of their children in co-operation with such institutions as Parliament may, by law, prescribe in such manner that in all cases the interests of the children are paramount;

(d) children and young persons receive special protection against exposure to physical and moral hazards; and

(e) the protection and advancement of the family as the unit of society are safeguarded in promotion of the interest of children ...'

The weight of emphasis in this provision is on the principle which gives priority to the interest of the child, although para (e) provides a limited possibility that the law may be administered in a way which takes account of the interest of the family as a whole. Here, as elsewhere, the legislation provides that a child is a person below the age of 18.

The obligation of Parliament was met by the enactment of the Children's Act, 1998, of which Part 1 is entitled 'The Rights of the Child'. This provides that the best interest of the child shall be paramount in any matter concerning a child. It asserts the child's rights: to name and nationality; to grow up with his or her parents unless that would not be in his or her best interest; to reasonable provision out of the estate of a parent 'whether or not born in wedlock'; to education and well-being; to participate in sports and positive cultural and artistic activities and other leisure activities; to express an opinion and to participate in decisions affecting his or her well-being; to protection from exploitative labour; and to protection from torture and degrading treatment. Section 6 on 'Parental duty and responsibility' provides that a parent shall not deprive a child of his or her welfare whether or not the parents are married at the time of the children's birth and whether or not they continue to live together. Every child has the right to life, dignity, respect, leisure, liberty, health, education and shelter from his or her parents, and:

'(3) Every parent has rights and responsibilities whether imposed by law or otherwise towards his child which include the duty to—

(a) protect the child from neglect, discrimination, violence, abuse, exposure to physical and moral hazards and oppression;

(b) provide good guidance, care, assistance and maintenance for the child and assurance of the child's survival and development;

---

[30] *Report of the Committee of Experts (Constitution) on Proposals for a Draft Constitution of Ghana, Presented to the PNDC, 31 July 1991*, p 79.

(c) ensure that in the temporary absence of a parent, the child shall be cared for
     by a competent person and that a child under eighteen months of age shall
     only be cared for by a person of fifteen years and above,

     except where the parent has surrendered his rights and responsibilities in
     accordance with law.'

Both parents' names are to appear on a child's birth certificate unless the father is
unknown to the mother.

A specific provision deals with the treatment of the disabled child, conferring the
right to special care, education and training to develop his or her maximum potential.
Another provision deals with marriage of children:

'14   Right to refuse betrothal and marriage

(1) No person shall force a child—

     (a)   to be betrothed;
     (b)   to be the subject of a dowry transaction; or
     (c)   to be married.

(2) The minimum age of marriage of whatever kind shall be eighteen years.'

These provisions give comprehensive effect to the UN Convention while taking
account of particular problems which are apt to arise in Ghana but which are not
mentioned specifically in the Convention. In respect of the latter, it is noteworthy that
the provision giving a right to freedom from discrimination includes in the list of
grounds of discrimination 'custom' and 'rural or urban background'.

The Act places a duty on District Assemblies, the powerful local government
bodies, to protect the welfare and promote the rights of children within their areas,
acting primarily through their Social Welfare and Community Development
Departments.

Part II of the Act, on 'Quasi-Judicial and Judicial Child Adjudication', provides
for Child Panels to be set up by District Assemblies, with the functions of mediating
in criminal and civil matters which concern children. It provides also for Family
Tribunals, discussed below, as an aspect of jurisdiction in family matters generally.
Part III sets up procedures for the confirmation of parentage of children, the granting
of orders for custody and access, and the granting and enforcement of maintenance
orders, replacing the relatively weak provisions which had previously been in force
with provisions which appear likely to have more impact on the welfare of the
children affected. Part IV provides for formal fostering, and establishes a new
procedure for adoption. It replaces the Adoption Act, 1962 (Act 104), which had been
largely copied from the English Act of its time, and accords with current policies on
adoption in common law countries. Parts V and VI deal with the employment of
children and institutionalised child care, respectively.

The increased attention to the rights of children has produced an amendment to
the Intestate Succession Law, 1985, which itself had been notable for expanding the
rights of spouses and children in comparison with the customary law family of
the deceased.[31] That Law already satisfied for most cases the constitutional
requirement that a child be assured of receiving 'reasonable provision out of the

---

[31]   Freeman, op cit (footnote 10 above), pp 159–160.

estate of its parents'. Nevertheless, the principal section of the Law providing for the distribution of estates was now amended by the addition of the proviso:

'Provided that where there is a child who is a minor undergoing educational training, reasonable provision shall be made for the child before distribution.'[32]

The law thus today gives a child substantial rights to property which was individually owned by a parent at the time of death. The results may not be as far-reaching as might be supposed. A house or other property occupied by a parent at the time of death is frequently in law the property not of the deceased but of the customary law family to which he or she belonged. In the case of an Akan man, his children are not members of that family. Thus the property cannot be inherited as part of his estate, and the children cannot maintain any claim to the property as members of the family which holds title.[33]

The Act, following the Constitution, reiterates the irrelevance of the distinction between birth within and outside wedlock. Provisions of the Act which are explicit in this respect are: the non-discrimination provision which prohibits discrimination against a child on the ground inter alia of 'birth or other status'; the provision on parental duty and responsibility quoted above; and the assertion of the right to parental property. Moreover, the amendments to the Intestate Succession Law, 1985, include the insertion in the definition of 'child' of the words 'whether or not born in wedlock'.[34]

Thus the law in the books has been notably developed to confer rights and protections on children. There is evidence that the law is not entirely effective in practice.[35]

---

[32] Children's Act, 1998, s 125 and Schedule, amending Intestate Succession Law, 1985, s 5.

[33] Relatively recent cases to this effect are: *Yeboah v Kwakye* [1987–88] 2 GLR 50; *Boateng v Boateng* [1987–88] 2 GLR 81.

[34] Children's Act, 1998, s 125 and Schedule, amending Intestate Succession Law, 1985, s 18. Before the Intestate Succession Law 1985 was enacted it was arguable that customary law drew no distinction between legitimate and illegitimate children, and that there were no more than a few instances of illegitimacy introduced by the Marriage Ordinance: see GR Woodman, 'Too many illegitimate children?' (1975) 12 *University of Ghana Law Journal* 51. Under the Intestate Succession Law, 1985 it was arguable that illegitimacy had been abolished with respect to intestate succession: GR Woodman, 'Ghana reforms the law of intestate succession' (1985) *Journal of African Law* 118 at 123, referring to the statutory definition prior to the amendment. This was an elaboration on the definition, also effectively excluding illegitimacy in virtually all instances, in Wills Act, 1971 (Act 360), s 18; it was applied in *Koranteng-Addow v Addo* [1992] 1 GLR 370 to include, as children of a deceased, persons who possibly were not even his natural children but had been treated by him as his children. In *In re Asante; Owusu v Asante* [1993–94] 2 GLR 271 the Supreme Court held that children of a man recognised by him as his children, although born out of wedlock while he was married under the Marriage Ordinance, were entitled to share in the portion of his estate due to all his surviving children. However, two dissenting judgments argued vigorously against the majority view on the ground that it ran contrary to the concept of the 'nuclear [conjugal] family' enunciated in the Intestate Succession Law, 1985. The case was a contested application for letters of administration; it was not certain that dicta on the right of inheritance were part of the ratio decidendi. The latest amendment may have been aimed to remove any lingering doubts encouraged by these dissenting judgments. Other amendments made to the Intestate Succession Law, 1985 by the Children's Act, 1998 appear to be designed to remove interpretative doubts, or to change the specification of sums of money to take account of inflation.

[35] See references given at footnote 28 above, and especially EVO Dankwa, 'The common legal problems of the child in the legal aid clinic', in Mensa-Bonsu and Dowuona-Hammond, op cit (footnote 29 above), p 53, and EVO Dankwa, 'The constitutional provisions of the Fourth Republic – the way ahead', ibid, p 59.

There appear to have been no recent cases in which it has been necessary to analyse the effects of property dealings by or between parent and child during their lifetime. However, earlier case-law suggests that the common law relating to constructive trusts and the presumption of advancement may well be applied here also.[36]

IV   JURISDICTION IN FAMILY CASES

For a long time, the judicial system of Ghana has consisted of a unified hierarchy in which the inferior courts were District Courts and Circuit Courts, and the superior courts the High Court, Court of Appeal and Supreme Court. The regime which followed the overthrow of the Third Republic in 1982 set up a series of tribunals to operate parallel to and to some extent in competition with the normal courts. Under the Constitution, 1992 these have become largely assimilated to regular courts and absorbed into the regular court structure. At each level below the Court of Appeal, jurisdiction is now shared between a court and a tribunal of equivalent status: Community Tribunals are at the same level as District Courts, Circuit Tribunals as Circuit Courts, and Regional Tribunals as the Divisions of the High Court.[37] The Courts Act, 1993 is the principal courts statute. However, jurisdiction in matters concerning children was revised in the Children's Act, 1998. Furthermore, the Courts (Amendment) Act, 2002 (Act 620) will effect further important changes in the courts system and allocation of jurisdiction, abolishing the Circuit Tribunals and replacing the Community Tribunals with District Courts; it has not yet been brought into force.[38]

Under the Courts Act, 1993, jurisdiction in matrimonial causes depends on the law applicable. Community Tribunals have jurisdiction 'in divorce and other matrimonial causes or matters ... where the law applicable is exclusively customary law'.[39] These are the lowest ranking tribunals. A panel consists of a Chairman (who 'preferably' should have legal experience) and two to four other members who are resident in the area of jurisdiction. Traditional rulers are, wherever possible, to be appointed to serve as panel members.[40] There is no other express mention of matrimonial causes in the Act, but the Matrimonial Causes Act, 1971 confers jurisdiction under that Act on the High Court and Circuit Court. Thus these courts have jurisdiction in matrimonial causes and matters where the applicable law is not exclusively customary law.[41]

---

36   Eg *Asantewaa v Ansong* [1992] 1 GLR 550.
37   A general account of the court system is given in GR Woodman, 'Ghana', in Herbert M Kritzer (ed), *Legal Systems of the World: A Political, Social, and Cultural Encyclopedia*, ABL-CIO (2002), vol III, p 590.
38   The Act is to come into force 'on such date as the Attorney-General and Minister for Justice may in consultation with the Chief Justice by executive instrument specify' (s 9).
39   Courts Act, 1993, s 47(1)(f).
40   Courts Act, 1993, s 46.
41   Under the Courts (Amendment) Act, 2002, s 5, replacing ss 39–53 of the principal enactment, District Courts, each consisting of a single magistrate who must be a lawyer of not less than three years standing, will replace Community Tribunals. A District Court will have jurisdiction 'in divorce and other matrimonial causes or matters ...' This jurisdiction will not be expressly limited to cases in which customary law is applicable, but it seems likely that the Matrimonial

Claims under the law of succession, which frequently involve issues of family law, are subject to the jurisdiction of Community Tribunals, Circuit Courts and the High Court according to the value of the property in issue.[42]

The Children's Act, 1998 confers jurisdiction on Family Tribunals. These are Community Tribunals established under the Courts Act, in which the panel includes a social welfare officer.[43] A Family Tribunal has jurisdiction 'in matters concerning parentage, custody, access and maintenance of children'. It is to sit in different premises or on different days from other courts, public access is excluded, and its proceedings are to be 'as informal as possible and ... by enquiry and not by adversarial procedures'. A child has a right to legal representation and to give an account and express an opinion, and is not to be identified in any published information.[44]

It should also be noted that cases concerning Ghanaian family law are increasingly arising in courts in Europe and North America. Large numbers of Ghanaians live and work for extended periods in these countries, while continuing to observe, especially in their family relations, many of the laws and cultural practices of Ghana. Consequently, under the rules of private international law courts are required from time to time to ascertain and apply the laws of Ghana. Moreover, in other cases where the law of the forum is applied, it is sometimes necessary to take into account aspects of Ghanaian family culture, for example in custody cases when determining what is required by the best interest of the child under English law.[45]

CONCLUSION

Recent development in the family law of Ghana has tended towards various modifications of customary law. Perhaps because of globalising influences, in marriage law there has been an enhancement of the rights of spouses, especially wives, in contrast to the rights of the customary family, and a trend to apply more frequently common law rules in the determination of claims to property acquired during a marriage. Similarly, in the law relating to the parent–child relationship there has been an enhancement of the rights of children. But globalising influences

---

Causes Act, 1971 will continue to have the effect of conferring exclusive jurisdiction on the High Court and Circuit Court in causes brought under that Act.

[42] This will continue to be the case under the Courts (Amendment) Act, 2002, subject to the replacement of the Community Tribunals by District Courts (s 5).

[43] Children's Act, 1998, ss 33–34, and (amending the Courts Act, 1993), s 125 and Schedule.

[44] Children's Act, 1998, ss 35–39. The Courts (Amendment) Act, 2002, s 5, will replace s 50 of the Courts Act, 1993 with a section which reads: 'A District Court also has jurisdiction to hear and determine any action that arises under the Children's Act, 1998 (Act 560) and shall for the purposes of that enactment be the Family Tribunal and exercise the powers conferred on a Family Tribunal under that Act and any other enactment'.

[45] See eg *McCabe v McCabe* [1994] 1 FLR 410 (a matrimonial cause in which there was a question as to the validity of a marriage contracted under Ghanaian law). On this case see: GR Woodman, 'Essentials of an Akan customary marriage. *McCabe v McCabe*' (1993) *Journal of African Law* 199; KY Yeboa, 'Formal and essential validity of Akan and Ghanaian customary marriages' (1993–95) 19 *University of Ghana Law Journal* 133. There appears to be no very recent published case report or comment, but the writer can vouch from personal experience as an expert witness that there is a steady flow of such cases in the English courts.

can move in different directions, and one aspect of the present picture is the transplantation of Ghanaian customary law to other lands by Ghanaians responding to economic globalisation by spending part of their working lives outside Ghana. Moreover, the developments just examined do not amount to a trend for customary law to be replaced by imported legal principles. The evidence of the cases, and even more of social activity in general, is that overwhelmingly Ghanaians choose to marry and to govern their family lives according to customary law.

HUNGARY

HUNGARIAN MATRIMONIAL PROPERTY LAW

Martha Dóczi*

I PROPERTY IN MARRIAGE

After very great change in Hungary, the 'old' Hungarian Family Act (adopted in 1952, and amended in 1974 and 1986) is still in force.

The Hungarian Family Act established the complete equality and individual rights of spouses; with respect to nationality, choice of name, residence, exercise of parental rights, property rights and in decision-making concerning children and other questions of family life. Equality of the sexes was made a constitutional principle in Art 67 of the Hungarian Constitution of 1949.

The Family Act pursuant to these fundamentals, provides simply, in Art 72:

> 'Questions concerning the children's upbringing and other questions of family life shall be decided by the spouses jointly. Each of the spouses shall be free to select his occupation, profession, and place of residence.'

Equal rights to possess, use and dispose of joint property are established in Art 27, and equal rights and duties between father and mother with respect to their children in Art 72. When there is a dispute between the parents with respect to the upbringing of the children, Art 73 provides that in the absence of agreement the disputed question shall be resolved 'by the agencies of guardianship with the participation of the parents'. Article 77 provides that the spouses should live together, be loyal to one another, be considerate and respectful of one another and help each other. Article 75 provides that both spouses have the duty of caring for the children and the management of the household, and Art 32 adds the joint duty of contributing to the needs of the household.

Under communist ideology in Hungary, only the state's property was recognised as the basis of the economy. Private property took on a secondary importance. Civil legislation included many rules restricting private individuals' rights to their possessions. For instance, only one house and one car belonged to each family.

The traditional systems of male dominance, and of difficulty or absence of divorce were swept away by revolution. When the Communists took power they quickly repealed or treated as abolished the old bourgeois laws. As repeal left no explicit regulation, separation of assets had to be assumed to be the new system. Equality of husband and wife was therefore achieved.

The marital property system that has been adopted is primarily that of community of acquests. It is thought to correspond to the practice of the working

---

* Judge of the Appeal Court of Budapest.

class. Deferred community is found unsuitable as it is thought to be a system designed for marriages of capitalist entrepreneurs. The existence of a community fund, which under socialist laws is managed jointly by both spouses, expresses the spirit of solidarity, and thus is supposed to further the aim proclaimed in all the socialist states, of preserving and promoting the family. In the West, schemes of sharing acquests are being attacked as a remnant of a society in which women were maintained economically by marriage. Sharing is blamed for concealing the economic dependence of the housewife, and thus holding back the realisation of or delaying achieving the ideal of marriage, based on love and respect, which has been extolled by the fathers of socialism. Such thoughts seem not to have deterred the socialist countries.

In the socialist countries the difficult problem of how to combine community property with equal rights of husband and wife is solved by providing for the joint management of the community fund by both spouses together. Where (for example in Hungary) private property is limited to goods for use and consumption, enterprise capital cannot enter a marital community fund. Under socialist laws on marital property, a third party in good faith may assume that the party with whom he is dealing is acting with the consent of his spouse in dispositions of community assets.

As in all systems of community of acquests, those of the socialist countries designate as the community fund that part of a married couple's property which is acquired during marriage through gainful activity, while property brought into the marriage or acquired during marriage gratuitously is owned separately by each spouse. Property gainfully acquired during the marriage is commonly designated by law as the separate property of one spouse, if it consists of objects which by their nature serve the personal needs, or the exercise of a trade or profession, of that spouse, at least where their value is not disproportionately high in relation to the common income and property.

The very idea of community of acquests in general, and of its socialist version in particular, implies that the fruits of labour are to be the common fund of both spouses. But on the other hand free disposition of earnings is an effective incentive. Besides, an employer is little inclined to deal with anyone but his individual employee. In Hungary, as in most of the other countries, the dilemma is solved in the following way. The claim to wages as yet unpaid is separate property. The pay does not become an asset of the community until it is placed into a common pool or turned into savings. So unpaid earnings are technically part of the community, but the earning spouse has full power to dispose of them.

For obligations incurred by him, either party is liable in relation to his separate assets as well as the share of the community fund that is his when that fund is partitioned. Partition of the community fund before termination of the marriage can, it seems, be brought about by a creditor who is unable to obtain full satisfaction out of the separate assets of his debtor.

In all the socialist countries, a marriage can be terminated easily when it has ceased to function. Upon termination of the marriage, the community fund as a general rule is divided equally. But partition in unequal parts may be judicially decreed in special circumstances. In Hungary, however, the Law on marriage, family and guardianship does not mention the possibility of an unequal division. (Article 31 of this Law sets forth the principle of equal division. Matrimonial property law does not discuss whether there are possible cases of unequal division.) Alimony may be granted to either party in a divorce, but in general it is only available for the period needed by a healthy individual for return to the labour market, or for periods of child care, and permanently in exceptional situations of illness or old age.

A married couple presents itself, for many purposes, as a unit. But the unit consists of two persons. A married couple is viewed as living under such marital regime, and the incidents of their property affairs are determined by it.

Property acquired during cohabitation is equally divided (Art 27). Both husband and wife have equal rights in the possession and the management of family property.

Both parties must co-operate in the control of the community fund but, in everyday transactions, a third party in good faith may assume that the other spouse has given a power of representation to the spouse with whom the third party has been dealing (Art 30).

The Family Act laid the foundation for the system of separate property between spouses. Each spouse owns and controls his or her own property during the marriage and, on dissolution, each takes out what belongs to him or her (Art 28).

Separate property is property which belongs to each of the spouses. In conformity with Art 28 regarding the separate property of spouses, the following matters are considered:

–   possessions before the marriage;
–   property presented to one of the spouses during the marriage;
–   property inherited by a spouse during the marriage;
–   individual possessions for personal use;
–   according to s 31, the spouses may voluntarily divide their property themselves. In this case, they would not go to court. Such a decision by the spouses must be certified by a lawyer or notary. After dividing common property, it becomes separate property.

If the marriage is terminated by death, the surviving spouse, in addition to his or her one-half share in the community fund, takes as the sole heir if there are no descendants or ascendants. But if there are such relatives of the descendant, or if there are brother and sisters, or descendants of brothers and sisters, the surviving spouse takes with them as a co-heir, or as a usufructary of the estate which passes to the children. But in Hungary the rule of ancestral estate still survives.

If the marriage is terminated by death, the property rights of the surviving spouse will depend on whether the deceased left a will.

The systems under discussion here are characterised by the fact that, as far as the ownership and control of property are concerned, one starts out from the premise that husband and wife are independent of each other. What each spouse owned before marriage and what he or she acquires after marriage remains his or her separate property, except assets which the spouses chose to hold in co-ownership. However, the independence of the property of the husband and the wife can be, and often is, qualified by the existence of limited property interests of the other spouse.

In addition, the existence of marriage between the spouses affects their property situation indirectly in a number of ways. There are duties of support and rights of succession upon death. One spouse's creditors may, in certain circumstances, resort to assets belonging to the other spouse. Like people who are not married to each other, spouses may make agreements by which they establish co-ownership of some specific asset or assets. Like others, spouses may jointly engage in business as a partnership, of which they may be the only partners or partners together with other persons.

According to the Hungarian family law (Art 31), where one spouse completes a transaction it is considered that he or she operates with the other spouse's consent. Some transactions require an obligatory notarisation. For these transactions, the consent of the other spouse must be expressed in written form. In other cases, the other spouse's consent may be expressed verbally. If a spouse completes a contract in connection with common property without the consent of the other spouse, the deal may be held invalid by the court. Other than that, it is imperative that the other party to the transaction was aware that the other spouse did not give his or her consent.

Transactions between spouses in Hungary are allowed, but these contracts require an obligatory notarisation. A marital contract is enforceable only if a notary or a lawyer has certified it.

Until 1986, persons without a settlement would contract marriages. Nowadays, there is only one type of 'marriage settlement': the prenuptial property contract. According to Art 27, spouses acquire the right to determine a matrimonial property regime different from the automatic legal one. Thus, spouses are entitled to transfer their separate possessions to their common property. On the contrary, if, according to the law, property is considered common property, they may, by mutual consent, consider it separate. Spouses are entitled to agree to voluntary division of their property. If the spouses have concluded a marriage contract, the division of property on dissolution of the marriage is carried out according to the conditions of the contract. A marital contract is enforceable only if a notary or a lawyer has certified it.

Most property disputes between spouses do not occur during marriage, but on marriage breakdown when the court in proceedings for divorce has wide and flexible discretionary powers under Art 31 to make property adjustment orders.

The court can make the following property adjustment orders:

–   transfer of property order;
–   sale of property order;
–   termination of co-ownership order.

The Civil Code, s 147 provides that:

> 'Any of the co-owners may demand termination of co-ownership; waiver of this right shall be null and void.'

Section 148 says:

> '(1) Objects of co-ownership shall be divided primarily in kind.
> (2) Objects of co-ownership, or a part thereof, may be given by the court into the ownership of one or several co-owners on payment of the appropriate counter-value, if it is justified with regard to the conditions of the co-owners. This requires

the agreement of the co-owner acquiring ownership, except for the case where part of real property is that placed in the ownership of the co-owner who is a resident of the real property, and this does not injure the justified interests of the resident.

(3) If co-ownership cannot be otherwise terminated, or division in kind would cause a significant decrease in value, or would prevent proper use, the objects of co-ownership must be sold and the sale price must be duly divided among the co-owners. Co-owners have the right to prevent sale which is effective against third parties.

(4) The termination of co-ownership, which is objected to by all co-owners, must not be effected by the court.'

II COHABITATION WITHOUT MARRIAGE

Although many couples live together as cohabitants (ie as husbands and wives in the same household, but without going through a ceremony of marriage), Hungarian law does not give them the same rights and responsibilities as spouses. This may have certain advantages (for example, there is no mutual duty of maintenance), but it also has several disadvantages. On relationship breakdown, cohabitants are often in a particularly vulnerable position, as any property dispute must be determined according to the general rules of property law. There is no discretionary jurisdiction to adjust the property rights of cohabitants as there is for spouses on divorce. On the death of a cohabitant who dies intestate, the surviving partner is not treated as favourably as a spouse.

With increasing numbers of couples cohabiting and more children being born outside marriage, perhaps legislation should be enacted to give cohabitants more rights and remedies, although to do so might undermine the institution of marriage.

Unmarried people living together as husband and wife do not usually have the status of a married couple. But under the law, the resources and requirements of an unmarried couple living together are aggregated for the purposes of claiming social security benefits under the Social Security Act 1975.

There are no rules in the Hungarian Family Act relating to cohabitation. Rules regarding cohabitation can be found in other codes, for example the Civil Code, Act II of 1975 on Social Insurance, etc.

Earlier – until 1977 – there was no rule with regard to cohabitation. The first step was taken in the modified Civil Code, which is still in force today. This provides under s 685/A:

'Cohabitants are two persons living together in the same household in emotional and economic community without contracting marriage.'

So we can see that, according to Hungarian law, cohabitation occurs when cohabitants – not only a man and a woman, but two persons, live together in the same household in emotional and economic community without a contract of marriage. However, although sociologists and others who research cohabitation can make do without a precise formal definition, the law needs to be more precise: cohabitation is a stable, more or less permanent, relationship between two persons who are not married to each other (though one or both may be married to someone else) and who share living facilities. They may have children, she may not take his surname, but they may have entered into a formal contractual relationship. The statistical data show that there is more cohabitation today than ten years ago.

Cohabitants, during their relationship and on relationship breakdown, are subject to the general law of property. Ownership of personal and real property of cohabitants is determined by the general law of contract, so that the cohabitant who contracts to buy property owns that property, the cohabitant whose name the bank account is in owns the money, and the cohabitant whose name is on the conveyance owns the property, unless in each case a contrary intention is proved, for example that the property should be jointly owned.

Most property disputes between cohabitants are over a house or land, etc. It may be necessary, for the non-owning cohabitant, to establish an interest on relationship breakdown or to defeat the claims of a third party (for example a mortgagee) to possession of the house. To establish an interest, the non-owning cohabitant can apply to the court for a declaration that he or she has a beneficial interest under an equity.

Section 578/G of the Civil Code says:

'Cohabitants – shall acquire joint property during their cohabitation in proportion to their contribution to acquisition.'

It is worth considering what the results would be where a housekeeping allowance was paid by one cohabitant to another. It is not so easy to infer an intention to share everything in a cohabiting relationship as it is in a marriage. Where the man has given the woman partner a housekeeping allowance, and the woman made savings, or purchased property from money derived from the allowance, then it could be argued that, as donee, she merely held the balance saved or property purchased on resulting trust for him. Where the allowance is given only for housekeeping purposes, but the recipient with the donor's knowledge saves money and buys items in her own name for the home, which they jointly use, then it could be argued that the parties should have a joint beneficial interest in such items, the donee being duly rewarded for thrift by the award of an equal interest. It is the donor's money which is used to purchase the item, but it is the donee's saving which has made the expenditure possible at all. Such a construction of a joint interest may be easier where it is the woman who has made the saving, since thrift is assumed to be a female quality.

In relation to other household goods bought by the parties, the general rule for married couples is that, on divorce, orders can be made transferring rights from one party to the other, although sometimes such action may be too late. Where the couple have had joint funds in joint bank or building society accounts, then the balance on the death of one party accrues to the survivor, and this applies whether the couple were married or cohabiting. Similarly, upon breakdown, the fund would be split between the parties.

Unlike married couples, cohabitants have no right to be considered for compensation for the loss of the possibility of acquiring some future benefit, or for the loss of continuing benefits. So, where the cohabitant works in her partner's business without remuneration, she is unlikely to receive anything by way of reward for work done, or compensation for future loss of benefits. On the other hand, if the cohabitant should later marry her partner, the possibility of receiving compensation will be much greater, even if the marriage only lasts a short time.

Cohabitants have no statutory rights of occupation of the quasi-matrimonial home, unlike spouses who have rights under the Family Code. A cohabitant's right of occupation therefore depends on whether he or she possesses a right of ownership (which usually carries with it a right of occupation) or a right to occupy it under a tenancy.

A cohabitant, like any other person, has complete freedom to leave his or her property on death to whomsoever he or she wishes provided the will complies with formalities laid down in ss 624–635 of the Civil Code. A cohabitant can therefore make a will leaving property to the other cohabitant and/or children. On intestacy the position is different, for the surviving cohabitant, unlike a surviving spouse, is not entitled to the other partner's property, as the rules of intestacy do not apply to cohabitants, although their children are entitled to succeed to property.

According to Hungarian law, a cohabitant has no right of succession from his or her cohabitant; only spouses have this right.

REPUBLIC OF IRELAND

THE CHILD AND THE STATE

*Paul Ward**

I INTRODUCTION

The developments in Irish family law since the last contribution to the Annual Survey have been particularly important, especially child law issues which form the focus of this contribution. But perhaps the most significant recent development was the holding of the 25th Amendment of the Constitution referendum which once again attracted international media coverage of Ireland's oldest, prickliest and morally charged legal thorn, namely abortion. This long-running saga in Irish constitutional law[1] was put to the people for the third time in 20 years. The issue was whether the decision in the X case should be curtailed to remove the threat of suicide as a basis upon which it would be constitutionally permissible to terminate the constitutionally protected right to life of the unborn child where there was a 'real and substantial' risk to the life of the mother, including a risk of self-destruction.[2] The people had rejected this very same proposal in 1992 following the decision of the Supreme Court in the X case. The 2002 referendum intended to amend the Constitution by incorporating into Art 40.3 the text of the Human Life Pregnancy Act 2002 ('the 2002 Act') which would govern the circumstances in which a termination was permissible. The referendum, if passed, would have afforded the 2002 Act constitutional standing and could only have been amended by referendum.

On 6 March 2002, ten years and one day after the Supreme Court decision in the X case was handed down, during which period no legislation was enacted detailing the circumstances for a permissible termination, the people rejected the government proposal, thereby opting to retain the suicide basis for termination. The referendum statistics are interesting in clearly evidencing national division on the issue and in turn reflecting the urban/rural divide. The referendum was defeated by 10,550 votes or 0.84%.[3] These statistics mirror very closely the 25 November 1995 divorce referendum percentages.[4]

---

* College Lecturer, University College Dublin.

[1] See P Ward, 'Ireland: "Abortion, 'X' + 'Y' = ?!"', vol 33, no 2 *University of Louisville Journal of Family Law* 385–407 for a discussion of the background to abortion and the 1983 and 1992 referenda on this issue.

[2] [1992] 1 IR 1.

[3] 1,247,526 votes were cast, of which 629,039 voted against and 618,489 voted for, representing 50.42% against and 49.58% for the proposal. There was a 42.89% turn out from a total electorate of 2,924,430.

[4] 1,628,576 votes were cast, of which 818,837 were in favour and 809,739 against (50.28% and 49.72% respectively), with a margin of 9,098 in favour of divorce being introduced. For further details see *www.refcom.ie.*

Other notable developments in the judicial sphere that have been discussed in previous contributions concern nullity and the recognition of foreign divorces. In *PF v GO'M*[5] (*PF*) the Supreme Court upheld the High Court decision[6] where a decree of nullity was refused in circumstances where the petitioning husband claimed he had not given a full, free and informed consent to his marriage owing to his 'defective knowledge'.[7] The defective knowledge in *PF* was simply that the respondent wife had conducted a sexual relationship with a fellow employee prior to and after the marriage of which the petitioner was unaware at the time of the marriage. The petitioner claimed that had he been aware of the respondent's relationship, he would not have married her. The Supreme Court rejected the argument that conduct of this nature could form the basis for annulling the marriage. The effect of the decision is to curtail the development of the 'defective knowledge' ground which as formulated would have provided great potential to annul marriages in novel circumstances. To this extent the Supreme Court has clarified the law in this area and signalled very clearly that future development of this ground is not possible by restricting the leading authority of *MO'M v BO'C*[8] to its particular facts. This trend in restricting the role of nullity at a time when divorce is available is likewise evidenced in the Supreme Court decision of *PMcG v AF*[9] (*PMcG*) which upheld the High Court's refusal to allow the court-appointed psychiatrist to interview four friends of the parties to the proceedings and the petitioner's brother. Denham J[10] held that the interviewing of third parties was beyond the role of the expert medical witness for a number of evidential reasons. First, such would amount to a preliminary hearing of persons other than the parties. Secondly, this would cause difficulties in cross-examining the witnesses and the operation of the hearsay rule. Thirdly, the weight to be attached to the medical inspector's opinion could be undermined by claims and counter-claims by both parties of failing to interview additional witnesses.[11] Denham J went on to endorse the High Court's reasoning.[12]

Since the decision in *GMcG v DW (Divorce Recognition)*,[13] which held that a foreign divorce could be recognised in this jurisdiction on the basis of either party's residence, as opposed to domicile, in the jurisdiction granting the

---

[5]   [2001] 3 IR 1.

[6]   See P Ward, 'Family Law Issues in the Superior Courts', *The International Survey of Family Law (2001 Edition)*, ed A Bainham (Family Law, 2001) 147 at 160 where the High Court judgment is discussed.

[7]   *MO'M v BO'C* [1996] 1 IR 208 accepted that the failure by the respondent to disclose the fact that he had attended a psychiatrist during his laicisation prevented the petitioner from giving a full, free and informed consent to the marriage. The case is discussed by Ward, 'Defective Knowledge: A New Ground for Nullity', in *The International Survey of Family Law 1996*, ed A Bainham (Martinus Nijhoff, 1998) at 215–235.

[8]   [1996] 1 IR 208.

[9]   [2001] 1 IR 599.

[10] Murray and Geoghegan JJ concurring.

[11] [2001] 1 IR 599 at 605–606.

[12] Unreported, High Court, 24 January 2000, Budd J holding, first, that there was no provision in the Rules of the Superior Courts for interviewing individuals other than the parties to the petition, and secondly, that the respondent had agreed to attend the psychiatrist on the understanding that no person other than the petitioner would be interviewed. The third reason given related to the evidential difficulties outlined by Denham J.

[13] [2000] 1 IR 96.

divorce,[14] the Supreme Court has handed down two further decisions on foreign divorce recognition but did not address the issue of residence as a valid basis. In *AS v RB*[15] and *PK v TK*[16] the Supreme Court addressed the issue of recognition of foreign divorces exclusively on the domicile of the parties without any reference to residence as a basis for recognition. In the former case this resulted in the marriage between the parties being void, as the respondent wife's German divorce was not capable of recognition in this jurisdiction owing to the fact that she was domiciled in Ireland at the time she applied for the divorce. In the latter case, the wife's application for an Irish divorce under the Family Law (Divorce) Act 1996 was rejected as the divorce she sought and was granted in New York was capable of recognition owing to her domicile in New York at the date on when the divorce application was instituted. What is clear from these two decisions is that the law on recognition was categorically stated to be dependent upon the domicile of either of the parties at the time of the application for a divorce. The clear inference to be drawn from this is that domicile is the only basis for recognising a foreign divorce.

II EDUCATION

Sinnott v The Minister for Education and Others[17] is a case of considerable importance concerning the right of mentally and physically disabled children to free primary education.[18] *Sinnott* defines the State's constitutional obligation to provide for the right to education, and more importantly, where it is denied, how that right is to be enforced. As with the plight of severely disturbed children,[19] the State's inaction in bringing forward legislation and providing facilities has been the catalyst for major cases like *Sinnott*.

A brief historical review is needed to place *Sinnott* in perspective. In *O'Donoghue v Minister for Education*[20] the plaintiff suffered from both physical and profound mental handicap. Aged two, he received one hour of physiotherapy and occupational therapy every two weeks. At the age of three, he was receiving conductive education. At the age of four, his mother made three requests for a place in one of the State-funded voluntary organisations providing full-time education to both the physically and mentally disabled. These requests were

---

14 See P Ward, 'Republic of Ireland: Family Law Issues in the Superior Courts', *The International Survey of Family Law (2001 Edition)*, ed A Bainham (Family Law, 2001), 147 at 153.

15 Unreported, Supreme Court, 19 December 2001, Keane CJ *nem diss.*

16 Unreported, Supreme Court, 5 March 2002, Murphy J *nem diss.*

17 [2001] 2 IR 545.

18 Article 42.4 of the Constitution provides: 'The State shall provide for free primary education and shall endeavour to supplement and give reasonable aid to private and corporate educational initiative, and when the public good requires it, provide other educational facilities or institutions with due regard, however, for the rights of parents, especially in the matter of religious and moral formation'.

19 See Section III below and *The International Survey of Family Law 1997*, ed A Bainham (Martinus Nijhoff, 1999) at 355–377, *The International Survey of Family Law (2000 Edition)*, ed A Bainham (Family Law, 2000) at 207 and *The International Survey of Family Law (2001 Edition)*, ed A Bainham (Family Law, 2001) at 147.

20 [1996] 2 IR 20.

refused owing to the lack of places, and the plaintiff's mother then attempted to provide education at home. Subsequently a concessionary but limited place was made available to the plaintiff at the age of six. Whilst other mildly to moderately handicapped children were provided with free transport to the school, the plaintiff's mother had to provide transport. Dissatisfied with this situation, judicial review proceedings were instituted in February 1992 seeking a declaration that the State had breached the plaintiff's constitutional right to free primary education, an order of mandamus compelling the State to provide such education and damages.[21] The High Court held that Art 42.4 imposed upon the State an obligation to provide free primary education to all children. The court was of the view that the plaintiff was educable[22] and the expression 'free primary education' in Art 42.4 was not confined to standard scholastic or academic education that able children receive in accordance with the national primary education curriculum or that which is capable of being provided in the home by parents.[23] O'Hanlon J based his decision on the earlier precedent of *Ryan v The Attorney General*,[24] a case of considerable constitutional importance[25] in that it defined the term 'education' in Art 42 of the Constitution as involving more than education of a scholastic nature[26] and amounted to '... the teaching and training of a child to make the best possible use of his inherent and potential capabilities, physical, mental and moral'.[27] Thus O'Hanlon J was of the view that the teaching and training of basic,[28] expressive[29] and leisure skills[30] fell within the definition of 'education' that the State was obliged to provide free to the plaintiff. O'Hanlon J awarded damages and the declaration sought, but declined to grant an order of mandamus compelling the State to provide the education the plaintiff required[31] on the understanding that the State would honour its obligation in light of the declaration made.

---

[21]   The plaintiff sought to recoup IR£7,645.71 expenses incurred in travelling abroad for and providing home educational services for the plaintiff.

[22]   Ibid at 65 O'Hanlon J found the respondent's contention that the plaintiff was not capable of being educated as unsustainable in the light of both governmental and international research on the educatability of the physically and mentally disabled. Three separate Department of Education Reports in 1965, 1983 and 1990 made recommendations for the provision of education to children with physical and mental handicap across all degrees of handicap. O'Hanlon J also relied upon the report of Hogg and Sebba: *Profound Retardation and Multiple Impairment* (Hester Adrian Research Centre, University of Manchester, 1986).

[23]   Article 42.2 provides: 'Parents shall be free to provide this education in their homes or in private schools or in schools recognised or established by the State'.

[24]   [1965] IR 294.

[25]   The case concerned the introduction of fluoride into the drinking water provided in the Dublin area in the early 1960s. Mrs Ryan objected as this infringed her parental constitutional right physically to educate her children. Whilst her claim was rejected, the High Court and Supreme Court provided a definition of the term 'education'.

[26]   [1965] IR 294 at 310. Kenny J in the High Court limited the term to education of a scholastic nature.

[27]   Ibid at 350.

[28]   Such as washing, dressing, feeding, toileting, sensory awareness and simple household tasks.

[29]   Such as gestures, simple language and sign language.

[30]   Such as play with toys, other children and adults, participation in simple games and physical activity.

[31]   [1996] 2 IR 20 at 71.

The State appealed the decision to the Supreme Court, but the matter was compromised in a somewhat unsatisfactory manner. Indeed, in *Sinnott* Barr J criticised the appeal in *O'Donoghue* as a deliberate attempt to delay the implementation of that decision.[32] On appeal, the Supreme Court substituted the High Court order whereby the State acknowledged that the plaintiff had a constitutional right to free primary education but did not accept the manner in which the High Court had interpreted this obligation. The plaintiff similarly refused to acknowledge any error in the manner the High Court interpreted the State's obligation.[33] Whilst the plaintiff ultimately succeeded in his action, the consequence of the Supreme Court order was to render the High Court decision ineffective from the State's perspective.

The plaintiff in *Sinnott*[34] was born in 1977 and was almost 23 years old at the date of the High Court hearing. In 1978 he was diagnosed as suffering from autism with consequent physical and profound mental disability. Between 1978 and 1999 the plaintiff received two years of primary education and training appropriate to his needs. For the remainder of the period, the educational and training services provided by the State were inadequate or inappropriate.[35] The plaintiff's mother attempted personally to provide appropriate educational and training services for the plaintiff by taking him in 1978 and 1980/1981 to the Disfunctioning Child Centre at the Michael Reese Hospital, Chicago, from which the plaintiff greatly benefited. On returning to Ireland on each occasion, and due to the lack of facilities, the plaintiff regressed,[36] whereupon the plaintiff's mother attempted to provide the specialist therapy herself. What education and training the plaintiff did receive came to an end in 1997 and it was proposed to move the plaintiff to an institution providing education and training for profoundly mentally handicapped young adults, a course of action which the plaintiff's mother considered wholly inappropriate for her autistic child, a view corroborated by expert medical opinion.[37] On the basis of the decision in *O'Donoghue v The Minister for Health*,[38] the *Sinnott* claim would appear unremarkable.

The significance of *Sinnott,* however, lies in the reliefs claimed and granted by the High Court. In addition to seeking a declaration that he had been denied his constitutional right to education, the plaintiff claimed damages for breach of his constitutional rights, negligence and breach of duty by the State. The plaintiff also sought a mandatory injunction directing the State to provide him with lifelong education appropriate to his needs, subject to a review in 2003. The plaintiff's mother also sought a declaration that her constitutional rights had been breached and damages for breach of her constitutional rights, negligence and breach of duty

32   [2001] 2 IR 545 at 580.
33   See the reporters' note, [1996] 2 IR 20 at 72.
34   [2001] 2 IR 545.
35   Ibid at 557: by way of example, in January 1980, the plaintiff was assessed as requiring services five days a week but only received two hours a day one, two or three times a week. The service provided amounted to nothing more than a form of baby-sitting. The facilities were either understaffed or overcrowded.
36   To the extent that he lost the ability to walk.
37   [2001] 2 IR 545 at 562.
38   [1996] 2 IR 20.

by the State. These reliefs gave rise to considerable argument in the High Court
and provided the basis for the appeal to the Supreme Court.

Barr J adopted the reasoning set out in *O'Donoghue*[39] and applied it to the
present case in granting the reliefs sought. The State conceded that the plaintiff
was entitled to free primary education to the age of 18 but denied that it was
constitutionally obliged to provide such education indefinitely. The State argued
that its constitutional responsibility ceased when the plaintiff reached the age of
majority. Barr J identified the fact that the wording of Art 42.4 did not specify any
age limit at which the right to primary education should cease. Further, to interpret
Art 42.4 as imposing an age limit would nullify, through regression, any benefit
an individual derived from primary education in the form of specialist training and
education.[40] The ultimate consequence would be to negative the benefits of the
plaintiff's constitutional right to education and that would amount to a
constitutional injustice. In this regard, Barr J was of the opinion that the State's
obligation to the plaintiff was open-ended and based upon need, rather than age.[41]

The plaintiff succeeded in his claim and was granted the declarations sought
and awarded damages[42] for the period from 1981 to the hearing of the action and
into the future. Barr J subsequently granted the plaintiff a mandatory injunction
directing the State to provide free primary education, specifying the nature of the
education, which order was to be reviewed in 2003.[43] Whilst the issue of punitive
damages did not arise in the present case, Barr J sounded a note of caution for the
State in relation to the outstanding cases.[44]

The plaintiff's mother also succeeded in her claim.[45] The essence of the
mother's claim was that, as a consequence of the State breaching her son's
constitutional right to education, she suffered anguish at witnessing her
son's progress squandered by Departmental failure to provide appropriate free
education to the plaintiff in addition to the distress and indignity of dealing with
the plaintiff's mobility and continence difficulties whilst at the same time battling
fruitlessly against Departmental inaction and disinterest.

The State appealed the decision, challenging three aspects of the High Court
ruling: first, the State claimed that its constitutional obligation to provide free
primary education ceased when the plaintiff reached the age of 18; secondly, that
the High Court exceeded its jurisdiction in both granting a mandatory injunction
directing the State to provide free primary education to the plaintiff and by
imposing a review date in 2003, the latter of which presumed that the State would
not meet its obligation declared by the High Court; thirdly, the State challenged
the award of damages to the plaintiff's mother arising from the State breaching the
plaintiff's constitutional rights, its negligence and breach of duty.

---

[39]   Ibid.

[40]   [2001] 2 IR 545 at 582–584.

[41]   Ibid at 584.

[42]   The plaintiff was awarded damages of IR£225,000, comprising IR£107,000 for specialist
       education and training and IR£115,000 for breach of constitutional rights, negligence (some
       19 particulars of negligence were cited by Barr J) and breach of duty causing suffering, distress
       and loss of enjoyment of life.

[43]   [2001] 2 IR 545 at 598.

[44]   Ibid.

[45]   Ibid, the plaintiff's mother was awarded IR£55,000.

In short, the State succeeded on appeal, but the seven judgments vary in approach and interpretation of the issues, mainly due to the State conceding certain aspects of the High Court ruling.

A majority[46] ruled that the obligation imposed by Art 42.4 to provide free primary education was owed to children and not adults, and thus the obligation ceased when a child reached the age of 18. The general opinion was that Art 42.4 was child-centred, and not adult-centred. Murray J indicated that if the plaintiff's contention was correct, then Art 42.4 would have expressly provided for primary education for adults on a need rather than an age basis.[47] Hardiman J succinctly and logically reasoned that the interaction between Arts 41[48] and 42[49] led only to the conclusion that free primary education was to be provided to children and not to adults, as the provider of education was the adult parent and the recipient was the child of the parent, and not a person of adult status.[50] By contrast, Murphy J, dissenting, held that the constitutional right to free primary education ceased at the age of 12.[51] The Chief Justice adopted an entirely different approach in upholding the High Court decision on the indefinite right of the plaintiff to free primary education. Keane CJ's reasoning is based primarily upon the State's approach to the appeal. The State conceded the plaintiff's right to the award of damages, which was calculated on the basis of a breach of his rights from 1981 until the hearing of the action when the plaintiff was 22, but did contest the obligation on the State to provide primary education beyond the age of 18. It was not possible for the State to concede the award of damages, thereby conceding a constitutional right to primary education, importantly based upon need rather than age, and then argue that the obligation ceased at the age of 18. Keane CJ described the contention as involving 'a feat of mental legerdemain of which I am incapable'.[52]

Further, from the plaintiff's perspective, the education he was receiving and would require in the future could be described only as primary education. The

---

[46]   Denham, Murray, Hardiman, Geoghegan and Fennelly, JJ.

[47]   [2001] 2 IR 545 at 681.

[48]   Article 41 of the Constitution is entitled the Family and the relevant provisions state:

   '**41.1.1** The State recognises the Family as the natural primary and fundamental unit group of Society, and as a moral institution possessing inalienable and imprescriptible rights, antecedent and superior to all positive law.

   41.1.2 The State, therefore, guarantees to protect the Family in its constitution and authority, as the necessary basis of social order and as indispensable to the welfare of the Nation and the State.'

[49]   Article 42.1 provides:

   'The State acknowledges that the primary and natural educator of the child is the Family and guarantees to respect the inalienable right and duty of parents to provide, according to their means, for the religious and moral, intellectual, physical and social education of their children.'

[50]   [2001] 2 IR 545 at 690. This was the case on the interpretation of both the English and Gaelic (Irish) versions of the Constitution.

[51]   Ibid at 674–675 reasoning that the term 'primary education' could not be interpreted to encompass the form of education (assistance from therapists, teaching staff, paediatricians, psychiatrists, social workers, family therapists and psychotherapists) that the plaintiff required, but rather it amounted to scholastic education as provided by teachers in schools to children aged between six and 14. Further, toilet training was an intimate matter in which the State could not intervene.

[52]   Ibid at 636 stressing that the Supreme Court would not entertain or deliver declaratory judgments. The other members of the court disagreed, Hardiman J at 694 stating that the State was asserting its original opinion that the obligation owed was limited to children. See also Geoghegan J at 722.

plaintiff's requirements would not cease merely because he turned 18 and attained the age of majority. The practical reality of the plaintiff's situation was that he would require ongoing specialist training and education. Owing to the plaintiff's autism, it could not be said that he had or would pass from childhood to adulthood. From the foregoing, Keane CJ stated that there was no principled basis either in law or the evidence that the plaintiff ceased to be in need of primary education at the age of 18, 22 or at any age in the future.[53]

Perhaps the most important issue for the Supreme Court to determine was the granting of injunctive relief against the executive. This highly contentious issue had arisen in *TD v The Minister for Education and Others*.[54] The Supreme Court categorically decided that the use of mandatory injunctive relief against the executive was inappropriate as infringing the fundamental constitutional doctrine of the separation of powers. The nature of the order made by the High Court was described as 'unusual and far-reaching'.[55] The leading judgment on this issue was delivered by Hardiman J who questioned the High Court's jurisdiction to grant an order directing the provision of detailed and specific education for the plaintiff based exclusively upon a general constitutional right to education as opposed to the provision of education based upon a legislative structure.[56] The High Court had effectively made a decision and imposed that decision upon the executive, thereby stripping the executive of its roll in determining policy and tethering its discretion in the provision of education, matters which fell exclusively within the executive's domain as part of democratic government and constitutional propriety.[57] The order, in effect, transgressed the constitutional boundary separating the judiciary, the executive and legislature.[58] Further, it stated that injunctive relief should not have been granted and that a declaratory order was appropriate in the circumstances.[59] Keane CJ,[60] Denham[61] and Geoghegan JJ[62] indicated that the court did retain the authority to grant mandatory relief against the executive in appropriate circumstances, the present case not being such. Likewise, the review date set by the High Court, having given final judgment, presupposed that the State would not honour its obligation under a declaratory judgment and exceeded the court's jurisdiction. Keane CJ noted that in the event

---

[53] Ibid at 638–639.

[54] [2000] 3 IR 62 in which Kelly J granted the applicant, a troubled child, an injunction against the Minister for Education to facilitate the building and opening of a high support unit. See below for the Supreme Court's response.

[55] Ibid at 697 per Hardiman J.

[56] The plaintiff's claim was instituted prior to the enactment of the Education Act 1998, which now embodies a statutory scheme for the provision of education.

[57] [2001] 2 IR 545 at 699–708. Hardiman J relied upon the seminal judicial pronouncements on the doctrine of the separation of powers by the Supreme Court in *Buckley and others (Sinn Fein) v The Attorney General* [1950] IR 67, Costello J in *O'Reilly v Limerick Corporation* [1989] ILRM 181 as approved by the Supreme Court in *MacMathuna v The Attorney General* [1995] 1 IR 484 and re-iterated in *Riordan v An Taoiseach* [2000] 4 IR 542.

[58] Ibid at 710.

[59] Ibid at 640, 656 and 711, per Keane CJ, Denham and Hardiman JJ, respectively.

[60] Ibid at 640.

[61] Ibid at 656.

[62] Ibid at 724.

of future disregard of the plaintiff's constitutional right, the powers of the court would be 'as ample as the defence of the Constitution requires'.[63]

The award of damages to the plaintiff's mother was also overturned by a majority of the court.[64] Keane CJ noted that the claim of the plaintiff's mother was unsustainable, as it would logically entitle all members of a family to an award of damages where one member of the family had had his constitutional rights breached.[65]

Whilst *Sinnott* has clarified the constitutional obligation to provide free primary education, litigation in this area remains extant. Barr J in *Sinnott* noted that there were hundreds of similar claims.[66] One such case of interest is *Downey v Minister for Education*[67] which concerned an injunction to direct the Minister of Education to provide a sum of money to meet the plaintiff's education needs prior to the hearing of the plaintiff's substantive action for breach of his constitutional right to education, or in other words an interim payment pending the hearing. Smyth J rejected the application on the basis that liability had not been conceded by the defendants and that the plaintiff's parents had altered the *status quo ante* the litigation by unilaterally deciding a particular course of education for the plaintiff.[68]

III THE CHILD AND THE STATE

The saga surrounding troubled children continues.[69] The saga, briefly, concerns two fundamental issues: first, the absence of statutory authority for civil detention of children in need of special care. The Child Care Act 1991 did not contain any provision to detain children in high support units where their welfare so required. This position has now been remedied by the Children Act 2001. Section 16 of the Children Act 2001 inserts a new Part IVA into the Child Care Act 1991, providing now in s 23B for the making of a special care order,[70] which authorises a health board to place and detain the child in a special care unit. The problem of the absence of statutory authority to detain children was compounded by the lack of secure and high support detention places in the jurisdiction. The second issue stems from the first, in that to place a child in need of special care in a secure

---

[63] Ibid at 640 citing O'Dalaigh CJ in *The State (Quinn) v Ryan* [1965] IR 70 at 122.

[64] Denham J dissenting. It should be noted that the Minister for Education agreed to pay the plaintiff's costs of the appeal irrespective of the outcome, and the Minister allowed the plaintiff's mother to retain the damages awarded in the High Court on an *ex gratia* basis.

[65] [2001] 2 IR 545 at 641.

[66] Ibid at 571.

[67] [2001] 2 IR 727.

[68] Ibid at 734. In addition, the application was not well grounded as the purpose of the application was an award of monies rather than injunctive relief.

[69] For the background to this, see *The International Survey of Family Law 1997*, ed A Bainham (Martinus Nijhoff, 1999), at 355–377, *The International Survey of Family Law (2000 Edition)*, ed A Bainham (Family Law, 2000), 200 at 207 and *The International Survey of Family Law (2001 Edition)*, ed A Bainham (Family Law, 2001), at 147.

[70] Section 23B(1)(a) provides: 'the behaviour of the child is such that it poses a real and substantial risk to his or her health, safety, development or welfare; and (b) the child requires special care or protection which he or she is unlikely to receive unless the court makes such an order'.

environment, health boards[71] were forced to resort to juvenile prisons to accommodate such children. This course of action required the sanction of the High Court, relying upon its inherent jurisdiction, to declare that it was constitutionally permissible to place children in juvenile prisons to safeguard their welfare. In *DG (a minor) v The Eastern Health Board and others*,[72] the Supreme Court reserved its opinion on the constitutional validity of detaining children in penal institutions where their welfare so required. It held, on the application before it, that the High Court had, on the basis of its inherent jurisdiction, the authority to make the order. The Supreme Court stressed that such an order was to be made only in rare and exceptional circumstances and for a limited period of three weeks.

The Departmental response to the Supreme Court decision was to acquire sites and attempt to build and staff high support units in which children could be placed and given appropriate education and services. The problem then became the progress of completing the plans to provide high support units. The matter ultimately came to a head in *TD v The Minister for Education and others*[73] whereby the Minister for Education was compelled by injunction to provide funding and facilitate the opening of specific high support units around the country. The making of such an order against a minister was unprecedented and he duly appealed.

The Supreme Court determined the appeal in favour of the minister and discharged the injunction.[74] The case is of considerable importance dealing with both the existence and enforcement of fundamental constitutional rights of children. The basis for granting the injunction was the vindication of the unenumerated constitutional rights of the applicants. The right in question is 'the right to be placed and maintained in secure residential accommodation so as to ensure, as far as practicable, his or her appropriate religious and moral, intellectual, physical and social education'.[75] The appeal proceeded on the basis that such a right was assumed to exist and the issue as to the validity of such a right was not argued before the court and the statements made therein are purely *obiter*. The significance, however, of the opinions cast should not be discounted, as these judicial opinions indicate considerable resistance to the very existence of such rights.

Chief Justice Keane noted that Geoghegan J in *FN v Minister for Education and Others*,[76] (*FN*), a broadly similar case, had declared such a constitutional right to exist[77] but the Chief Justice reserved his opinion on the correctness of

---

[71]   Health boards are statutorily responsible for the welfare of children in their areas.

[72]   [1997] 3 IR 511.

[73]   [2000] 3 IR 62.

[74]   Unreported, Supreme Court, 17 December 2001.

[75]   Ibid, per Keane CJ at 38.

[76]   [1995] 1 IR 409.

[77]   Ibid, relying upon Art 42.5 of the Constitution which provides:

   'In exceptional circumstances, where the parents for physical or moral reasons fail in their duty towards their children, the State, as guardian of the common good, by appropriate means shall endeavour to supply the place of the parents, but always with due regard for the natural and imprescriptible rights of the child.'

   And the statement by O'Higgins CJ in *G v An Bord Uchtala* [1980] IR 32 at 55–56:

Geoghegan J's pronouncement,[78] assuming it to be correct. He did, however, categorically indicate that if he were asked for his opinion on the matter, he had 'the gravest doubts as to whether the courts at any stage should assume the function of declaring what are frequently described as "socio-economic rights" to be unenumerated rights guaranteed by Art 40'.[79]

Murphy J was less reticent in his opinion. He rejected the existence of the right claimed and dismantled the constitutional foundation for the existence of such a right. He noted that the Constitution provides for expressly guaranteed constitutional rights which fall within the civil and political category. The exception is the right to education which was a socio-economic right. Otherwise there were no expressly guaranteed socio-economic rights and in particular no express right to accommodation, medical treatment or other socio-economic benefits.[80] Murphy J noted that Art 45 of the Constitution reserved exclusively to the Oireachtas (Parliament) the authority to make laws regarding social policy which are expressly not answerable to any court under any provision of the Constitution.[81] Murphy J acknowledged that constitutional jurisprudence had developed unenumerated rights but the very basis for the right the applicants were relying upon was rejected. Murphy J's concerns were threefold. First, the right the applicants claimed, as established in *FN*, was based upon a dictum by O'Higgins CJ in *G v An Bord Uchtala*[82] which dictum it was observed was entirely *obiter* and had no bearing on the sole issue before the court. Secondly, there was no unanimity that the natural rights, as described by O'Higgins CJ were equatable with constitutional rights.[83] Thirdly, Murphy J noted that both O'Higgins CJ and Parke J dissented from the judgments of the majority in *G v An Bord Uchtala*. Such reasoning removed the constitutional basis for the right the applicants claimed. Murphy J further indicated that such rights are desirable but should be statutorily, rather than constitutionally based.[84]

'The child also has natural rights. Normally, these will be safe under the care and protection of its mother. Having been born, the child has the right to be fed and to live, to be reared and educated, the opportunity of working and of realising his or her own full personality and dignity as a human being. These rights of the child (and others which I have not enumerated) must equally be protected and vindicated by the State. In exceptional circumstances, the State, under the provisions of Art 42, s 5, of the Constitution, is given the duty, as guardian of the common good, to provide for a child born into a family where the parents fail in their duty towards that child for physical or moral reasons. In the same way, in special circumstances, the State may have an equal obligation in relation to a child born outside the family to protect that child, even against its mother, if her natural rights are used in such a way as to endanger the health or life of the child or to deprive him of his rights. In my view this obligation stems from the provisions if Art 40, s 3 of the Constitution.'

[78] Unreported, Supreme Court, 17 December 2001 at 42.
[79] Ibid, wholly endorsing the dissenting opinion of Murphy J.
[80] Unreported, Supreme Court, 17 December 2001 at 3–4.
[81] Ibid at 5.
[82] [1980] IR 32.
[83] Ibid, per Kenny J at 97.
[84] Unreported, Supreme Court, 17 December 2001 at 13, Murphy J stated:
  'It is, of course, entirely understandable, and desirable politically and morally, that a society should, through its laws, devise appropriate schemes and by means of taxation raise the necessary finance to fund such schemes as will enable the sick, the poor and the underprivileged in our society to make the best use of the limited resources nature may have bestowed on them. It is my belief that this entirely desirable goal must be achieved and can only be achieved by legislation

The Supreme Court also found that the order made by Kelly J in the High Court offended the doctrine of the separation of powers. A majority[85] discharged the High Court order for reasons stemming essentially from a strict adherence to the constitutional imperative of the separation of powers doctrine. Keane CJ, Murray and Hardiman JJ all emphasised the constitutional importance of the doctrine of the separation of powers, with particular regard for the equal authority which each of the constitutional organs exercised and the fundamental need for mutual respect by and for one another.[86] The High Court order directed the taking of all steps necessary to facilitate the building and opening of secure and high support units in a list of places around the country. As in *Sinnott*, the mandatory nature of the order was inappropriate and a declaratory order was considered sufficient. The Chief Justice observed that once the High Court declares a constitutional right to exist, there is a corresponding constitutional obligation on the executive to vindicate that right. In the event of a failure to do so, the courts would be obliged to declare that there had been a positive failure to vindicate that right.[87] In this regard, the courts possessed the necessary jurisdiction to grant a mandatory order against the executive.[88] Murray J indicated that a mandatory order could be granted against the executive, without, however, specifying the means or policy to fulfil the obligation, in exceptional circumstances where 'an organ or agency of the State had disregarded its constitutional obligation in an exemplary fashion'.[89] 'Disregard' was described as 'a conscious and deliberate decision … accompanied by bad faith or recklessness'.[90] Hardiman J agreed with Murray J adding that a mandatory order was a measure of '… absolutely final resort in circumstances of great crisis and for the protection of the constitutional order itself'.[91] The circumstances of the present case did not warrant such a mandatory order.

Further, by specifying the detail and manner of how the ministerial plans were to implemented, the High Court had effectively assumed the role of the executive, which was constitutionally impermissible. Murray J highlighted some of the constitutional difficulties that would arise from the mandatory order. First, executive policy would fall within the remit of the High Court. Secondly, any alteration in policy would require court approval. Thirdly, the High Court would be adopting the role of policy decision-maker. Fourthly, the answerability of the executive to Parliament would be wholly undermined.[92] Each and all of these reasons constituted a fundamental breach of the doctrine of the separation of powers.

---

and not by any unrealistic extension of the provisions originally incorporated in Bunreach na hEireann.'

[85]   Keane CJ, Murray and Hardiman JJ. Murphy J did not give an opinion on the matter, and Denham J came to the conclusion that the order was valid.

[86]   Citing the authorities relied upon in *Sinnott*, see footnote 41 above.

[87]   Unreported, Supreme Court, 17 December 2001 at 52–53.

[88]   Ibid, per Keane CJ at 48.

[89]   Ibid, per Murray J at 24.

[90]   Ibid.

[91]   Ibid at 74.

[92]   Ibid at 21.

Denham J upheld the High Court order. She acknowledged the fundamental constitutional importance of the doctrine of the separation of powers but also placed significant emphasis upon the court's constitutional obligation to uphold and vindicate the constitutional rights of the child applicants, which necessitated the court, as guardian of the Constitution, to make the order in question.[93] In balancing these fundamental and conflicting constitutional principles, Denham J noted 14 factors of persuasive significance in upholding the High Court order.[94]

Denham noted the exceptional nature of the case, referring to Art 42.5 and the State's obligation towards children whose parents had failed in their duty. Denham J stated that the essential issue for the court's determination was the balancing of the State's constitutional duty towards the applicants and the enforcement of the doctrine of the separation of powers, at the fulcrum of which was the nature of the order made. The judge noted that if individual orders in relation to each applicant had been sought and granted directing specific places for each individual, rather than requiring the ministers to abide by their general plans to provide such places, then the State could not object to such an order as infringing the constitutional demarcation between the organs of government.[95] Denham J concluded that the court had not just a right to make the order but a duty to do so and that the granting of further adjournments would have amounted to an abdication of judicial responsibility.[96]

One final issue of interest that arose was the *locus standi* of the applicants to seek and obtain the relief ordered. The Chief Justice and Denham J were satisfied that the applicants had *locus standi* to maintain the action notwithstanding the reality that if the places were made available to the applicants, they could not benefit from the places, having reached the age of majority. The Chief Justice felt that this issue related to the form of relief the applicants were seeking, rather than the issue of *locus standi*. In any event, the State's failure towards the applicants in the past was sufficient to afford them *locus standi*.[97] Hardiman J and Murray J concurring, disagreed and reasoned that because the facilities directed to be built within the time specified would not meet the needs of the applicants, they had no *locus standi* to seek the relief granted.[98] Murphy J did not cast an opinion on this issue but one would assume that he was of the view that the applicants had no *locus standi* as they had no constitutional right to enforce.

---

[93] Ibid at 16–23.

[94] Ibid at 31–33 which were: (1) the applicant children were in State care; (2) their welfare required the provision of secure high support units; (3) Art 42.5 constitutionally mandated the State to provide for the applicants' education; (4) the applicants had constitutional rights; (5) those rights were not challenged; (6) the applicants were children whose rights required immediate protection; (7) there was culpable delay; (8) delay would cause irreparable harm to the applicants' rights; (9) Kelly J had extensive and personal knowledge of the applicants' and others' positions; (10) the parties had co-operated in informing the court of the ministerial proposals; (11) the applicants were prejudiced by not pursuing their case on the understanding that the proposals would be honoured; (12) the respondent had benefited from lengthy adjournments on informing the court of its proposals; (13) Kelly J suggested the matter, owing to the delay, proceed by way of injunction; (14) Kelly J merely endorsed and enforced a ministerial policy consistent with the applicants' rights and was not creating or determining policy.

[95] Ibid at 34.

[96] Ibid.

[97] Unreported, Supreme Court, 17 December 2001 at 45.

[98] Ibid at 42.

No doubt the respondents in *TD v The Minister for Education* were satisfied with the outcome, but the State's obligations towards severely troubled children, and more particularly their failure in this regard, have been highlighted by the European Court of Human Rights judgment in *DG v Ireland*[99] (*DG*). Briefly, *DG* concerned a claim that Ireland had breached DG's human rights by detaining him in a juvenile prison in circumstances where he had committed no criminal offence, had not been prosecuted or convicted. The Supreme Court, upholding the High Court, authorised his detention on a temporary basis in July 1997 in a juvenile prison.[100] The Supreme Court decision arose from judicial review proceedings compelling the Eastern Health Board and the Attorney General to provide suitable accommodation for his needs. DG was a severely troubled adolescent with suicidal tendencies, who posed a threat to others and had a string of criminal convictions. At the time, March 1997, there was no high support therapeutic unit in the country and efforts were being made to find suitable accommodation in the United Kingdom. That place never materialised and upon DG's release from the juvenile prison in August 1997 until July 1998, when he turned 18, various temporary arrangements were made for him and reported to the High Court. In October 1998 DG harmed himself resulting in hospitalisation, after discharge from which he was arrested and charged with various offences including having threatened his uncle with a knife.

DG successfully alleged a breach of Art 5 that he had been deprived of his liberty.[101] The ECHR rejected the State's claim that the deprivation of liberty was justified as educational supervision under Art 5§1(d)[102] and in so doing succinctly described the kernel of the difficulty in this area as '... if the Irish State chose a constitutional system of educational supervision implemented through court orders to deal with juvenile delinquency, it was obliged to put in place appropriate institutional facilities which met the security and educational demands of that system in order to satisfy the requirements of Art 5§1(d)'.[103] The court noted that DG, being 17 at the time, was not obliged by law to receive education and, further, that the services available in the penal detention centre were entirely voluntary. Indeed, from DG's prison file, the only activity he participated in was playing football.[104] Further, as the detention did not fall within the *Bouamar v Belgium*[105] exception, namely an interim custody measure preliminary to a future regime of supervised education, the court concluded that Art 5 had been breached.[106]

---

[99]　(2002) 35 EHRR 33.

[100]　[1997] 3 IR 511. See P Ward, 'Children: Detention and Abortion', in *The International Survey of Family Law 1997*, ed A Bainham (Martinus Nijhoff, 1999), at 355–377.

[101]　(2002) 35 EHRR 33, at para 73.

[102]　Article 5§1(d) provides for 'the detention of a minor by lawful order for the purpose of educational supervision or his lawful detention for the purpose of bringing him before the competent legal authority'.

[103]　(2002) 35 EHRR 33, at para 79.

[104]　Ibid at para 81.

[105]　(1989) 11 EHRR 1.

[106]　(2002) 35 EHRR 33, at para 85. DG sought €63,500 but was awarded €5,000 plus costs.

DG also alleged a breach of Art 3 of the Convention[107] which the court rejected, primarily, as the detention order was motivated to protect DG's welfare rather than to punish him.[108] Further, detention in a penal institution without trial and conviction could not of itself amount to inhuman or degrading treatment. Apart from being subject to prison discipline and handcuffing at court appearances, which the court considered a reasonable restraint in the light of DG's tendency to harm himself and others, the regime DG was subjected to was neither inhuman nor degrading and was in any event affected by specific directions ordered by the High Court concerning access to, assessment of and reporting on DG.[109] Ultimately DG's allegation of a breach of Art 3 failed for want of supporting evidence that detention impacted upon his mental or physical condition.[110] The court also dismissed allegations of violations of Arts 8[111] and 14.[112]

The *TD* and *DG* cases may now be only of academic interest. The introduction of the Children Act 2001 has provided the courts with the necessary jurisdiction to detain children where their welfare so requires thus making it no longer necessary for the High Court to grant declarations authorising such detention. It is also evident from the *TD* and *DG* cases that considerable and relatively successful efforts have been made to provide the necessary premises in which appropriate care, education and welfare services can be given to such children. The wider substantive issue as whether and to what extent such troubled children have a constitutional right to have their welfare provided for by the State arising from High Court declarations remains an open question in the light of the judicial opinions expressed in *TD*. In this regard, it appears unlikely that either the Supreme Court or the ECHR is likely to revisit this area owing to the discretion now conferred upon health boards where special care orders are sought under s 23B(7)(a) of the Child Care Act 1991 to provide temporary accommodation other than in special care units.[113]

IV THE CHILD, THE STATE AND THE FAMILY

The above cases evidence the growing importance of the rights of children in both the domestic and international arena. As Ireland has a legal system based upon a written Constitution, the contesting of such issues is not unexpected. No more so is the case of *The North Western Health Board v HW and CW*[114] (*NWHB v HW*

---

[107] Article 3 provides: 'No one shall be subjected to torture or to inhumane or degrading treatment or punishment'.

[108] (2002) 35 EHRR 33, at para 96.

[109] Ibid at para 97.

[110] Ibid at para 98.

[111] The right to respect for private and family life.

[112] The right not to be discriminated against.

[113] Section 23B(7)(a) provides: 'Where a special care order is in force, the health board may: (a) as part of its programme for the care, education and treatment of the child, place the child on a temporary basis in such other accommodation as the board is empowered to provide for children in its care under section 36'. As of October 2002 no ministerial order has been made bringing into effect this and the other sections of the 2001 Act.

[114] [2001] 3 IR 622.

and CW). The case concerned whether a child has a right to have carried out a PKU test[115] where the parents object. The test, whilst an innocuously invasive medical procedure, does require consent to be carried out. The test is commonly acknowledged as highly beneficial and important to children and parents alike in both arresting and treating any potential illness that a child might develop and providing peace of mind where a test is negative. The test is carried out throughout the western world but is nowhere compulsory. The preferred method of testing is by blood sample.

The case arose from the health board's concerns about its statutory obligation under the Child Care Act 1991, to provide for the welfare of children, and in particular in accordance with the Health Acts 1947 to 1986 and the Health (Amendment) Act 1987.[116] In short, the health board considered itself statutorily obliged to carry out the PKU test on all children resident in its area and feared its potential liability if it failed to do so where parents refused to consent to the procedure. To alleviate this fear, the plaintiff had sought care orders and directions under the Child Care Act 1991[117] from the District Court, the effect of which authorised the plaintiff to consent to the test being carried out. Indeed, the defendant's fourth child had been the subject of such a care order and direction. In another case the Circuit Court on appeal from one such application reversed the District Court decision causing the plaintiff to cease to rely upon this avenue and created a degree of legal uncertainty. It should be stressed that the plaintiff health board had no cause for concern about the welfare of the child as provided for by his parents, and the only issue of concern was the conducting of the PKU test.

The defendants refused consent to the PKU test by blood sample but did volunteer a sample of hair or urine as an alternative method. The refusal was not based upon religious grounds, which would have further complicated the constitutional issues involved, but upon a profound personal belief that it was wrong to harm or injure another person.

In these circumstances, the plaintiff instituted declaratory and injunctive proceedings seeking to clarify its legal position. The plaintiff could not rely on any statutory framework to ground the declaration and injunction but relied exclusively upon the court's inherent jurisdiction to protect and vindicate the constitutional rights of the child. By a four to one majority,[118] the Supreme Court refused the declaration and injunction sought. The central issue for determination was whether and in what circumstances the State through one of its statutory bodies could override a parental objection to medical screening of children by invoking the court's jurisdiction. This issue in turn involves the interaction of and resolution of potentially conflicting statutory and constitutional principles dealing

---

[115] This is commonly referred to as the 'heel prick test' which screens newborn children for one endocrine condition (hypothyroidism) and four metabolic conditions (phenylketonuria, galactosaemia, homocystinuria and maple syrup urine disease), all of which can cause mental handicap or life-threatening illness but are treatable if detected.

[116] Section 3(4) of the Child Care Act 1991 imposes this responsibility.

[117] Section 18(3)(b)(ii) of the Child Care Act 1991 provides that, where a child is in the care of a health board, the care order confers the authority to give consent to any necessary medical or psychiatric examination, treatment or assessment with respect to the child.

[118] Denham, Murphy, Murray, Hardiman JJ; Keane CJ, dissenting.

with the rights and duties of the three parties and yet another return to the doctrine of the separation of powers.

At the centre of the conflict is the child whose personal constitutional rights conferred by Art 40.3.2 of the Constitution[119] were in issue. The personal right in question can be broadly classed as the right to life or, more accurately in the context of the PKU test, to protection against a threat thereto. Relevant also, however, is the unenumerated right to bodily integrity[120] which, to prevent infringement, would require consent to the conducting of the PKU test. As noted by Denham J[121] such consent cannot be given by a minor but may be provided by a parent or guardian.

In the light of the statutory obligation imposed upon the plaintiff and the view that the child's constitutional rights were being disregarded, the plaintiff sought to have those rights vindicated against the express and firmly held opinion of the defendant parents. The resolution of the conflict between the plaintiff and defendants was determined by the majority not so much on the basis of whether the child's rights had been infringed but rather by addressing who was the proper person to determine how the child's rights should be safeguarded. In support of their polarised positions the parties advocated as their fundamental concern the paramountcy of the child's welfare, if such is not a contradiction in itself. The plaintiffs in this regard relied upon their statutory obligation under the Child Care Act 1991 to provide for the welfare of children residing in their area, the vindicating of the child's personal constitutional rights and Art 42.5,[122] which constitutionally justifies the State intervening to provide for the welfare of children where parents have failed to do so. The defendants similarly advocated the promotion of their child's welfare, but from the more advantageous constitutional position of parents and, more importantly, that of the family.[123] The significance and importance of Art 41 should not be underestimated in the context of the authority, autonomy and sanctity of the family, as a number of statutes have been declared unconstitutional in offending its provisions.[124] Whilst the court acknowledged the child had constitutional rights as an individual, it also noted that

---

[119] Article 40.3.2 provides: 'The State shall, in particular, by its laws protect as best it may from unjust attack and, in the case of injustice done, vindicate the life, good name, and property rights of every citizen'.

[120] Identified by Finlay P in *G v An Bord Uchtala* [1980] IR 32 as an unenumerated constitutional right of the child and cited by Hardiman J in his judgment at [2001] 3 IR 622 at 754.

[121] [2001] 3 IR 622 at 717, citing herself in *In Re a Ward of Court (withholding medical treatment) (No 2)* [1996] 2 IR 79 at 156.

[122] See footnote 77 for the text of Art 42.5.

[123] The relevant provisions of Art 41 of the Constitution are 41.1.1 and 41.1.2 which provide:

'(1) The State recognises the family as the natural primary and fundamental unit group of Society, and as a moral institution possessing inalienable and imprescriptible rights, antecedent and superior to all positive law.

(2) The State, therefore, guarantees to protect the family in its constitution and authority, as the necessary basis of social order and as indispensable to the welfare of the Nation and the State.'

[124] See for example: *In Re Article 26 and the Matrimonial Home Bill 1993* [1994] 1 IR 305 in which an Act purporting to confer on spouses an automatic joint interest in the family home was declared unconstitutional; *Murphy v the Attorney General* [1982] IR 241, where tax legislation that treated married couples less favourably than cohabiting couples was declared unconstitutional and likewise social welfare payments in *Hyland v The Minister for Social Welfare* [1989] IR 624 and the privilege afforded to spousal communications in marriage guidance counselling in *ER v JR* [1981] ILRM 125.

the child had constitutional rights, both individually and collectively as a part of the constitutionally protected family.[125] Further, as Denham J noted, there exists a constitutional presumption that the welfare of the child is to be found within the family[126] and more particularly that married parents of a child had the superior constitutional authority, status and privilege to make an informed but here an unwise[127] decision concerning the welfare of their child. In these circumstances the plaintiff's attempt to override the parents' wishes would constitute an unwarranted interference with the authority of the family.[128] Murphy J placed this concept in perspective by indicating that the court was being invited to exercise a power and make a decision in a role that was, in terms of constitutional priority, 'clearly subsidiary to that of the parents'.[129] Murray J identified the issue more directly and strongly stated that the authority of the family was 'superior even to the authority of the State itself'.[130] Within these purely constitutional parameters, this was a one-sided battle with only one winner, namely the family, as a unit and as individuals. As the matter was determined exclusively in this constitutional setting, the court did not have to consider the wardship jurisdiction and in particular some persuasive English authorities relevant to the issue[131] which would have enabled the court to determine the issue solely on an application of the 'best interests' test.

Denham and Murphy JJ identified the consequences of holding otherwise. The former indicated that the overriding of the parents' decision would threaten to weaken the bond between parents and child.[132] The latter felt a decision in favour of the plaintiff would lead to further court applications where bodies such as the plaintiff considered a parental decision misguided. Such applications would damage the child's long-term interests by eroding parental concern for and performance of their duties.[133] Further, it was noted that authorising the PKU test in this case would lead to compulsory testing of all children.[134]

The court's decision rests upon a balancing of the child's rights and the notion that a child's protection was best provided for by his parents. Central, however, to the child's rights in this case was the unanimous and unquestioned medical evidence. The medical evidence, however, could not be the sole criterion in determining the issue. Murphy J noted that, scientifically and medically, conducting the PKU test was in the child's best interests but that such an approach was too simple.[135] Denham J identified that the resolution of the dispute required

---

[125]   [2001] 3 IR 622 at 725, per Denham J.

[126]   Ibid at 724, citing *In Re JH (inf)* [1985] IR 375, and Hardiman J echoing similar sentiments at 755 and 764, stressing the importance of such a presumption in the absence of any statutory basis for the plaintiff's application.

[127]   Ibid, per Keane CJ at 705, per Murphy J at 733 and per Murray J at 741 who noted that the parents' decision had no rational basis.

[128]   Ibid at 725.

[129]   Ibid at 732.

[130]   Ibid at 738.

[131]   See, in particular, the succinct reasoning of Murphy J at 731–732 where he distinguishes *In Re T (A Minor)* [1997] 1 WLR 242, CA, and *In Re C (A Child) (HIV Testing)* [2000] Fam 48, Fam D.

[132]   [2001] 3 IR 622 at 725.

[133]   Ibid at 733.

[134]   Ibid at 724, per Denham J.

[135]   Ibid at 729.

the balancing of the constitutional rights of the parties involved.[136] Part of this balancing process involved an assessment of the medical evidence. Of significance here was the fact that the child's other siblings had tested negative, indicating that there was no more than a remote possibility of the child having or developing the diseases for which the child was to be tested.[137]

The medical evidence is thus significant for three reasons. First, there was no factual basis for a threat to the child's constitutional rights. Secondly, in those circumstances, there was no basis for overriding the parents' wishes. Thirdly, it logically followed that there was no basis for relying upon the default provision of Art 42.5 of the Constitution which would authorise the State to intervene to act in the place of parents where there had been a failure of parental duty. In this regard, the court did indicate in what circumstances court intervention would be appropriate. Denham J identified 'an imminent threat to life or serious injury' as a basis for a court making a decision contrary to the wishes of the parents.[138] Murphy J[139] and Murray J[140] expressed similar but more broadly based sentiments as to when it was appropriate for the State to intervene. Of considerable interest is on what constitutional basis the court might so intervene. Such a threat, it would appear, could invoke either Art 40.3, which obliges the State to protect and vindicate the personal constitutional rights of the citizen, or Art 42.5, to override a parental decision. From the judgments it would not appear necessary to establish both a threat to the constitutional rights of the child and a parental failure towards a child authorising State intervention with the family. Murphy J clearly indicated that the constitutional basis for overriding a parental decision could rest upon either Art 40.3 or Art 42.5.[141] Hardiman J expressed the same view,[142] but indicated that an application such as the present required some statutory basis, and that the absence thereof was fatal to the plaintiff's application.[143] In Hardiman J's opinion, the essence of the plaintiff's application was to seek to compel parents to submit their children to medical testing on the basis of a constitutionally mandated right of the child as declared by the court rather than emanating from a legislative base. The consequences of such a declaration would be to bypass the legislative process whereby the court determined, as a matter of policy, that mandatory

---

[136] Ibid at 725.

[137] Ibid at 723, 741 and 746, per Murray and Hardiman JJ, respectively.

[138] Ibid at 727.

[139] Ibid at 733, stating: 'In my view the subsidiary and supplemental powers of the State in relation to the welfare of children arise only where either the general conduct or circumstances of the parents is such as to constitute a virtual abdication of their responsibilities or alternatively the disastrous consequences of a particular parental decision are so immediate and inevitable as to demand intervention and perhaps call into question either the basic competence or devotion of the parents.'

[140] Ibid at 740–741, stating: 'It seems, however, to me, that there must be some immediate and fundamental threat to the capacity of the child to continue to function as a human person, physically, morally or socially, deriving from an exceptional dereliction of duty on the part of parents to justify such an intervention'.

[141] Ibid at 730–731, stating: 'The moral and constitutional dilemma is whether the parents having declined to avail of the service, the State, either because of its obligation to vindicate the personal rights of the child involved or the default obligation under Art 42.5, is bound to ensure that the available service is indeed availed of.'

[142] Ibid at 758–759.

[143] Ibid at 761.

PKU testing was in the public interest. This would have the twofold effect of depriving the legislature of considering and determining whether such a policy was appropriate and establishing in constitutional jurisprudence the principle that the right of the child warranted such a development without being subject to challenge in adversarial litigation.[144] Significantly in this regard, Hardiman J reserved his position as to whether any such legislation compelling a PKU test was valid, but he did unequivocally consider the use of the child care legislation to compel PKU testing as 'quite inappropriate'.[145]

The Chief Justice dissented and his judgment is worthy of discussion. Keane CJ approached the issue by first determining whether the granting of the order in favour of the plaintiff health board would in effect constitute a breach of the separation of powers in the judiciary legislating for compulsory PKU testing of all children. The Chief Justice rejected this proposition stating that each refusal by a parent would require individual judicial consideration and determination.[146] Further, he argued that the sole issue before the court was whether there had been a failure to vindicate the child's constitutional rights. The issue was not what the perceived consequences of the decision in favour of the plaintiff was, but rather whether, in vindicating the child's constitutional rights, the court had the authority to grant the order sought. The Chief Justice was definitively of the view that the court had a constitutional duty to protect and vindicate the child's rights where there was a risk posed to them.[147]

On this issue, the Chief Justice, in light of the uncontroverted medical and scientific evidence, assessed the issue as whether the failure to carry out the test was to 'gravely endanger his right, so far as human endeavours can secure it, to a healthy and happy life …'.[148] Keane CJ felt that the risk of not conducting the test was a 'violation of those individual rights to which he is entitled as a member of the family and which the courts are obliged to uphold'.[149] Of particular interest is the approach and comments of the Chief Justice. He clearly viewed this issue primarily from the child's perspective and gave full weight to the child's rights as an individual but was also cognisant of the child's rights within the family. The primary constitutional consideration was the welfare of the child, which was a matter of paramount concern for the court to the extent that it was not possible to allow the parents' 'irrational' objections to take precedence over the welfare of the child on the basis of Art 41 conferring a constitutional status on the family in its authority and constitution.[150] The effect of respecting the parents' decision would be to endanger the right to a healthy and happy life. In support of this conclusion, Keane CJ cited with approval the dictum of Waite LJ in *In re T (A Minor) (Wardship: Medical Treatment)*[151] concluding that the parental objection, which

---

[144]   Ibid at 762.
[145]   Ibid at 744.
[146]   [2001] 3 IR 622 at 704–705.
[147]   Ibid.
[148]   Ibid at 706.
[149]   Ibid.
[150]   Ibid at 705.
[151]   [1997] 1 WLR 242, CA, at 254 stating: 'All these cases depend upon their own facts and render generalisations – tempting though they may be to the legal or social analyst – wholly out of place. It can only be said safely that there is a scale, at one end of which lies the clear case where

was described as 'represent[ing] the infliction of harm, however, minimal, on their child and that this was wrong in principle', was unsustainable in light of the medical evidence, the best interests principle and the child's constitutional rights.

This pragmatic approach is also evidenced in another Supreme Court decision. *The Western Health Board v Karen M*[152] (*Karen M*) concerned an unusual application to the District Court under the Child Care Act 1991. The issue in this case was an apparently simple one, namely whether the District Court could make an order placing a child with foster parents who lived outside the jurisdiction. The respondent mother suffered from a psychiatric condition which the applicant health board considered sufficiently severe to warrant taking the child into care. The respondent mother accepted that she was not able to care for her child and supported the foster placement but objected to her child being placed outside the jurisdiction. The proposed foster parents, one of whom was a cousin of the respondent, had been approved as foster parents by social services in England. The evidence to the court was that fostering was the most appropriate form of care for the child and the more so because it would be with relatives. The court was clearly of the view that the placement was in the best interests of the child's welfare and no issue arose in this respect, notwithstanding the mother's objection. The difficulty was whether such was legally possible under the Child Care Act 1991.

An extensive and in-depth analysis of the 1991 Act is not possible here. The 1991 Act imposes a statutory obligation on health boards to promote the welfare of children who are not receiving adequate care and protection.[153] This duty is fulfilled by recourse to a variety of orders and directions that a health board may seek which entitle the health board to take a child into care[154] or arrange supervision[155] of the child in the home. Once the child is in the care of the health board, s 36 authorises the health board to provide for various types of care for the child, including foster care, but it would not be statutorily possible for a health board to place a child in foster care outside the jurisdiction. The Supreme Court, was, however, satisfied that such a placement was possible by recourse to s 47 which enables the District Court, of its own motion or by application by any person, to give such directions or make such order on any question affecting the welfare of a child. McGuinness J held that s 47 should be given a purposeful interpretation to enable the District Court to make an order authorising the health

---

parental opposition to medical intervention is prompted by scruple or dogma of a kind which is patently irreconcilable with principles of child health and welfare widely accepted by the generality of mankind; at the other end lie the highly problematic cases where there is genuine scope for difference of view between parent and judge. In both situations it is the duty of the judge to allow the court's own opinion to prevail in the perceived paramount interests of the child concerned, but in cases at the latter end of the scale, there must be a likelihood (though never of course a certainty) that the greater the scope for genuine debate between one view and another the stronger will be the inclination of the court to be influenced by a reflection that in the last analysis the best interests of every child include an expectation that difficult decisions affecting the length and quality of its life will be taken for it by the parent to whom its care has been entrusted by nature'.

[152] Unreported, Supreme Court, 21 December 2001, McGuinness J, *nem diss.*

[153] Section 3 of the Child Care Act 1991.

[154] Sections 17 and 18 respectively provide for an interim care order and a care order.

[155] Section 19.

board to place the child in foster care outside the jurisdiction.[156] Further, McGuinness J stated that the court had a duty to protect and enforce the constitutional rights of children,[157] here the child's future welfare, and that this could be achieved by invoking s 47 where the order in question was in the best interests of the child.[158] This approach to safeguarding the rights of the child and in particular the constitutional rights of the child accord precisely with views expressed by Hardiman J in *NWHB v HW and CW* where he advocated the necessity of a legislative base where a court was being called upon to protect and vindicate the constitutional rights of an individual.[159]

Whilst the practical effect of the decision was to remove the child from the jurisdiction, the Supreme Court stressed both that the health board should continue to have responsibility for the child's welfare and that the court retain its supervisory function to the greatest degree possible. In this regard, such an order should only be made 'rarely and with considerable caution'.[160] Such an order is clearly highly unusual and thus must be approached with great attention and caution by the court. McGuinness J identified a non-exhaustive list of factors, which a court should consider in such applications.[161] Here a highly beneficial and practical proposal to secure the child's welfare was not thwarted by a statute which did not specifically provide for the making of an order of this nature. The result was achieved through a combination of a broad and purposeful interpretation of the 1991 Act with the imposing and influential presence of the Constitution filling any legislative lacuna.

A significant consequence here, however, was that the mother's express wishes were overridden by the court. The mother was not married, whereby she would not be considered a family and thus could not benefit from the protection which Art 41 of the Constitution confers. Whilst s 24 of the 1991 Act requires a court to have regard to the rights of parents, constitutional and otherwise, in making orders under the Act, their wishes or objections cannot override the court's consideration of what is in the child's best interests.

V CONCLUSION

The above examination and discussion reveals that, whilst children possess various constitutional and statutory rights, the extent of such and who determines

---

[156] Unreported, Supreme Court, 21 December 2001, McGuinness J at 23.

[157] Section 24 of the 1991 Act specifically obliges a court to consider the welfare of the child as the first and paramount consideration in any proceedings before the court in addition to considering the rights and duties of parents under the Constitution or otherwise.

[158] Unreported, Supreme Court, 21 December 2001, McGuinness J at 26.

[159] [2001] 3 IR 622 at 761.

[160] Unreported, Supreme Court, 21 December 2001, McGuinness J at 26.

[161] These included: the constitutional rights of the child and his parents; the parameters of the law of the jurisdiction to which the child is to be sent, including the applicability of the paramountcy of the child's welfare principle and the principle of the comity of the courts; whether the jurisdiction in question is a signatory to the Hague and/or Luxembourg Conventions on Child Abduction; the existence of a scheme of co-operation between the respective child care agencies in the jurisdictions; whether access to the child by the parents is practical; and the use of undertakings and mirror orders similar to those utilised in child abduction cases.

how such should be exercised depend upon a number of factors. The position of a child within a marital family differs considerably from that of a child born to a single parent. Married parents possess considerable decision-making powers in relation to their children whereas unmarried parents are rendered impotent in rights terms by comparison with their marital counterparts. No more so is this highlighted than by *NWHB v HW and CW* and *Karen M* decisions. Both cases evidence parental concern in the decision-making process for their children where there is an attempt by the State to interfere with the parent–child relationship. In the former case, the right of the child is presumed to be safeguarded by his parents. This decision, however unwise, is constitutionally based and presumed to be in the best interests of the child. In the latter, the reality is that the court makes the decision as to what is in the child's best interest, despite the real and genuine maternal objection, which is of little weight in deciding the child's best interests, owing primarily to the statutory basis for court intervention.

In between these cases lies the position of children to whom the State owes a constitutional obligation to protect and vindicate their rights. The *Sinnott*, *TD* and *DG* cases evidence the State's obligation towards the disabled and disadvantaged. In these cases, it should be remembered that the State, in a parental-type capacity, is positively obliged to provide education and special care services respectively. In the light of this clear obligation, particularly that arising as a default parent under Art 42.5, the question has to be asked whether the State has itself failed in its moral parental duty, as opposed to its legal or constitutional duty, and indeed whether it has itself shown adequate concern and interest in its children.

ITALY

POST-MORTEM ARTIFICIAL INSEMINATION IN ITALY: A CASE STUDY

Antonello Miranda[*]

I INTRODUCTION

Questions prompted by artificial insemination have given rise, from a legal point of view, to various, more and more complex, issues; cases are so unpredictable and dramatic that it is difficult for the law to keep pace with them. Probably this is the position all over the world, but it is particularly true of the Italian legal system where the judge is obliged, in making a decision, to apply only the statutory law, having a very narrow discretionary power to construe and extend the application of the rules to a new case.

In Italy, furthermore, notwithstanding the adaptability of our legal doctrine and the interpretative and reconstructive efforts of the judiciary, it is the body of family law, a massive and very important part of our law, which seems antiquated and out of date: even the expression 'family law', bearing in mind developments in society, today sounds misleading. It might be better to speak of a 'law of families'. And 'in a country such as Italy where only the "traditional" (two-parent) family has strong constitutional and legal protection, this is a very difficult question to solve'.[1] Thus, family law appears to be the area in which doctrinal debate is most vivid and intense and in which, more and more often in a painful way, judges have been called upon to make decisions in the absence of precise, exhaustive and up-to-date rules of law. Furthermore, this is a matter in which the legislator's work appears more and more lacking in influence, if not harmful. This reflects inertia brought about by ideological conflicts as is demonstrated by the 15-year-long parliamentary debate on an Artificial Insemination Act (no statute is yet enacted!).

The point is that family law represents a kind of 'traditional law', spontaneous in nature and far from the idea (typical of jurists belonging to technologically advanced societies) of a law created through some artificial procedure, whether a Bill, or a decision which sets a precedent, or an essay by a prestigious scholar; family law is, for the most part, a spontaneous law of advanced societies which excludes 'any decisional intervention by any authority, and any condition which would limit society's power to choose'.[2] It is especially interesting to note

---

[*]   Full Professor of Private Comparative Law and European Law, Faculty of Political Science, Palermo University.

[1]   See, A Miranda, *State Intervention and 'New Families' in the Italian Law: 'Coming back to the past' shifting from status to contract?* at *http://www.jus.uio.no/ifp/isfl/miranda_antonello.rtf*.

[2]   R Sacco, *Introduzione al diritto comparato*, Torino, 1994, p 26, who suggests how 'the study of ethno-law could induce us to study the spontaneous law of advanced societies again'. A

that when such complex elements (as, in particular, artificial insemination) are involved, statute law, especially if it is prohibitive, can really do little: referring to the artificial insemination cases, in my opinion, any 'prohibitive' law cannot be an effective obstacle to new questions and cannot solve those which have already arisen (but will only draw people towards those countries where it is allowed, as has happened and continues to happen in the case of abortion); furthermore, even if prohibitive legislation were enacted, there would remain the problem of punishment of those involved – the doctor? (but what if he is from a different nation?); the surrogate parents?; the biological parents? – and, of course, there would be the problem of guaranteeing protection to the most innocent party, the child.

As I have argued elsewhere,[3] this characteristic aspect of family law makes the subject unique within the Italian (perhaps within the whole of the civil law) juridical panorama, because we are witnessing a substantial negation of the 'positive' superiority of the legislative formant (which is typical of civil law) in favour of doctrinal and juridical ones: in other words, in contemporary family law, what takes on particular importance are not so much the rules of law (which are too complex and out of step with modern times), but more significantly reconstructions and, most of all, interpretation and actual enforcement of the law by jurists and judges.

Thus, if, for instance, the work of the courts has contributed to the discipline, albeit in a limited way, by recognising phenomena such as *de facto* families (by extensively interpreting the Constitution – particularly Art 2 which protects 'human rights' generally – and the Code and by taking advantage of the gaps left by the legislator), on the other hand, it has fed uncertainty, since the courts must in any event formally comply with statutory rules drafted in circumstances and utilising concepts which today have not only disappeared, but have sometimes even been overturned. That is, for example, the case with legitimate filiation, which in Italy is regulated by a series of legislative dispositions which, today as in the time of ancient Rome, presume the impossibility of tracing paternity (*mater semper certa est, pater nunquam*). These are no longer justified, at least in their present formulation, in a society which, thanks to the development of technology, is able to ascertain genetic descent with certainty.

Therefore, we find ourselves facing a field in which, today, case-law is the main source for rules; but if, on the one hand, this is natural, functional and reassuring in common law systems, on the other hand it is incongruous and therefore disruptive in a civil law system, in which, like it or not, the judge (and the jurist) are, no matter what, always subject to statute law and may only move within its narrow confines; in a very dramatic way, the judge is called upon to make a decision even where there is no statute at all or where there is a statutory provision but it is applicable to a different question. This is so much so as to force judges even to distort and overthrow the *ratio legis* (and sometimes common sense) in order to reach a decision of some sort, as we shall see shortly.

---

translation in English of Sacco's essay is: 'Legal Formants: a dynamic approach to comparative law', in Am Journ Comp Law, XXXIX, 1991, pp 1–34 and 343–402.

[3]   A Miranda, *Toward a New 'Privatistic' Approach to Family Law: the Italian Model* at *http://www.jus.unitn.it/cardozo/Review/Persons/Miranda.htm*.

II THE RECENT CASE OF MRS C

The legislative limits described above have led more than one of our judges to decide on the practicability of artificial insemination contracts with reasoning which is, to say the least, unusual.

Judge D'Antoni was recently[4] asked to solve a particular case of post-mortem insemination. In that case – it seems to be a very curious mixture of two very famous American cases: *Davis v Davis* and *Hecht v Kane*[5] – Mr S (a jailed mafia boss) and his wife, Mrs C, agreed with the Palermo Centre of Reproductive Medicine to proceed with *in vitro* artificial insemination of three ova of Mrs C with the sperm of her husband. The need for artificial insemination was a consequence of the impossibility of Mr S meeting his wife (he was subject to a protection scheme as a witness in mafia cases).

The three fertilised ova were cryo-preserved in the state of 'blastocyst' in the expectation of future implantations in the uterus. Just a few days after the first, unsuccessful, implantation, Mr S died. As a consequence, the Medical Centre refused to proceed with further implantations in accordance with deontological principles and with the Self-regulatory Code of Conduct of Italian Artificial Reproductive Centres.

Mrs C applied to the judge for an urgent order under Art 700, CPC,[6] and for specific performance, an order that the Medical Centre should carry out its promise of 'professional services' by immediately starting to transfer and implant the fertilized ova until such time as Mrs C should become pregnant.

It is very interesting to note that the Medical Centre was a kind of 'non-party': even though formally it was the party breaking the contract, the Centre itself suggested and supported Mrs C's action, offering immediately to carry out performance even before the judge had made a decision. In fact, the Medical Centre was seeking a judicial order *imposing* specific performance of the contract thus absolving itself from moral or legal responsibility.

Mrs C's action was, obviously, completely successful. The judgment, nevertheless, was based on reasoning which leaves numerous doubts. And in fact, it is obvious enough that, in this case, the judge was first forced to choose the less traumatic solution and then, and only then, look for a technical justification in the light of the reconstruction of the general principles of the legal system. This judgment on the one hand avoids the destruction of fertilized and cryo-preserved ova (thereby resolving the ethical problem of the fate of embryos 'looking for a mother') while on the other hand it avoids arguments about the mother's rights in a very difficult assisted fertilization case.[7]

---

[4]   Decree of 8 January 1999, Tribunale di Palermo, in *Il diritto di famiglia e delle persone*, 1999, p 226 ff.

[5]   See A Miranda, 'The Legal Status of the Pre-Embryo: Some Comparative Considerations Prompted by *Davis v Davis*', in JW Harris (ed), *Property Problems. From Genes to Pension Funds*, Kluwer, 1997. It is interesting to note that, in some measure, the case under analysis is similar to the well-known *Blood* case.

[6]   Civil Procedure Code.

[7]   In truth, the probability that, in this case, a pregnancy would result and would continue to term was extremely low.

The reasoning turns on four main points.

(1)   Even if in Italian law specific performance may be ordered only when performance is not personal or need not be carried out by the promisor in person, as in this case, the lack of an obligation to do something in the Medical Centre is not an obstacle to an order of specific performance where a party has already declared itself ready to execute the contract spontaneously. However, if that party should refuse, a claim for damages suffered by the other party would remain unprejudiced.

(2)   The medically assisted artificial reproduction (MAAR) contract, even if it has been entered into by a 'complex contractual party' (ie Mr and Mrs S jointly) would remain effective only in relation to the surviving partner. In fact, the will of the woman should be pre-eminent on the one hand in relation to her right to physical integrity which could be damaged if the implantation were not executed, and on the other hand bearing in mind that the existing relationship, between the fertilized ova and the surviving partner herself is a proprietary one. In other words the fertilized ova would be 'body parts' which, as the 'natural fruits of the mother', are in her possession.

(3)   The right 'of the surviving parent not to see the process of life initiated with the contribution of their own gametes terminated, at least not without her own express consent' must be recognised. Such a right would be in accordance with constitutional dispositions (Arts 2 and 32 of the Italian Constitution) as well as with the rules (even international rules) protecting the right to life, and the integrity of the embryo's health (the Abortion Act, Statute of 22 May 1978, n 194).

(4)   Notwithstanding that Art 234 of the Civil Code provides that a child is 'legitimate' only if he was *conceived* during the marriage and if he *is born* not more than 300 days after the dissolution of the marriage or after the death of one of the spouses, the 'doubts' about the status of the child eventually born and the problems of succession law, are not an obstacle to the execution of the MAAR contract. Indeed, by interpreting and reconstructing Arts 234 and 462 of the Italian Civil Code in an 'evolutionary' way, ie regarding as conception the process of homologous artificial insemination, the child could be considered as legitimate and able to succeed his parents.

III   INITIAL COMMENTS

The judgment certainly deserves a detailed analysis for its numerous implications and inferences: the lack of a clarifying and redeeming statutory intervention by the national legislator, faced with numerous statutory rules enacted by other legal systems in *subjecta materia*, is significant. Nevertheless we want to limit ourselves here to some very short first impressions.

I believe that the most difficult question is to establish with precision the rights of the 'aspirant' mother in relation to the pre-embryo's rights and whether the rights of the mother have pre-eminence over the rights of the pre-embryo or vice-versa.

It seems in fact, on reading the judgment, that on the one hand the two fertilised and cryo-preserved cells were considered as 'subjects' of law and in particular as holders of a right to life or to be born (or, perhaps more correctly, of a right to try to come into the existence) and, on the other hand, the right of the woman to a 'responsible' maternity and to physical and psychological integrity, ie her right to choose to become (or not to become) a mother, was defended. The court, in fact, regarding the artificial insemination process as equal to conception, first said the pre-embryo has the right to be born (as does every human being), but at the same time found that the pre-embryo is a 'body part' of his 'mother', even if separated from her. Later, the court affirmed that statute law grants to the mother the right to a responsible maternity (ie the right to abort is pre-eminent over the right of the foetus or embryo to be born) and also the right to physical integrity, but at the same time the court found that she has the right to recover her 'body parts' and proceed with implantation: the refusal to allow further implantations in her uterus of the fertilized ova would amount, according to the judge, to a violation on the one hand of her right to become a responsible mother and on the other of her right to preserve her physical integrity.

Here, in my opinion, a line of interpretation has been followed which has substantially distorted the meaning of the legislation and in particular the meaning of the Abortion Act 1978 which, far from acknowledging a 'right to maternity' at all costs (one should then ask oneself who the person under the correlative duty would be), instead permits 'non-maternity', if the right to life of the unborn child (already implanted in the uterus) were to be sacrificed, in order to uphold the mother's right to physical and psychological integrity.

According to the Abortion Act 1978 and relevant constitutional provisions, our legal system provides a gradation of protections and acknowledgments which must be observed: the mother's right to health is more significant and stronger than the right of the foetus to be born; the right of termination and the choice of the mother prevails over the right to life of a foetus which has not yet reached three months from implantation; the right of each parent not to procreate prevails over the right of the unborn child.

As a consequence, the mother has only a qualified right, in certain circumstances, to terminate the pregnancy. In other words, the legislator has acknowledged a woman's right *not* to be a mother, and not, conversely, as the court stated, her right to be one.

IV   THE MOTHER'S RIGHT TO PHYSICAL INTEGRITY

In the same way, in the opinion of Judge D'Antoni, it is not persuasive to refer to the woman's right to physical integrity which would have been infringed by preventing her from bringing to maturation ... that embryo which ... constitutes a natural fruit and therefore is an integral part of the mother (by analogy with Art 820 of the Italian Civil Code whose object is the individual right of the owner of fruit or animals).

In fact it is true that, metaphorically, it is possible to draw an analogy with the concept of natural fruits:[8] this could be analogous to what the Italian legal system provides in relation to separated parts of the body. But, first and distinct from the common law approach, Italian law needs to establish not only if there is 'legal ownership' of the body and body parts[9] and who is the 'legal owner', but also in which legal mode this ownership was acquired.[10] Thus, in the case of body parts, or sperm or ova, we must first establish how this property may be acquired.

In my opinion, only the scheme of 'fructification' is entirely applicable to the matter in question, ie to body parts. Indeed, the old concept of *ius in se ipsum* is inapplicable because it would not be possible to bring within the sphere of self-ownership those parts which, once separated, have been joined to others of different origin to create something new and different. Nor is the concept applicable which would consider these parts *res nullius* as a consequence of *derelictio* and therefore subject to acquisition by occupation: in this case, in fact, that would lead to the absurd result of acquisition by those who are interested in using them, that is the doctor or health service involved.

On the contrary, consistent with the scheme of fructification, we should consider as fruits all those goods – even ova, sperm, body parts, etc – whose existence 'derives from the mother and which, consistent with this origin, have the character of new goods, that is an independent good, as a structural entity and source of exploitation'.[11]

Regarding entitlement to the property, we may refer to Art 821 of the Italian Civil Code which provides that the 'fruit' is originally acquired by separation from the mother and consequently admits, in the abstract, the possibility of 'co-ownership' in a situation like the one under examination, giving a symbolic and not exclusive or selective meaning to the literal reference to the right of property. On this basis, the fertilized ova would be available as the single ovum, the single seed, the blood or an organ (parts considered 'viable', but not living, and composed of cells containing the genetic make-up of a human being); but their availability would be subject to the co-ownership of the parties who contributed to fertilization.

---

[8]   See G Criscuoli, *L'acquisto delle parti staccate del proprio corpo e gli artt 820 e 821 cc*, in *Rivista di Diritto delle Persone e della Famiglia*, 1985, p 266 ff; A Miranda, *The Legal Status of the Pre-Embryo: Some Comparative Considerations Prompted by Davis v Davis*, in JW Harris (ed), *Property Problems. From Genes to Pension Funds*, Kluwer, 1997, p 39 ff.

[9]   G Criscuoli, in *L'acquisto delle parti staccate del proprio corpo e gli artt 820 e 821 cc*, in *Rivista di Diritto delle Persone e della Famiglia*, 1985, asserted: 'There is no obstacle in the consideration of body as "thing" or "mother thing" because this term, as used in the rules, has a clearly metaphorical meaning referring to every entity, living or not, capable of productivity'.

[10]   According to Italian law, a person may become owner of a thing (whether movable or immovable) both by direct and original purchase or 'derivative' purchase. The latter is the most common way: A acquires the ownership of a thing from B as a consequence of a sale or as a gift, or by succession. The former mode of acquiring property is more complex: ownership is acquired through an original title where this title is independent of prior ownership. As in Roman Law, we distinguish between the case of acquisition by occupancy (of *res nullius*), by finding, by accession (improvement or natural growth of property) and fructification, by continued and uninterrupted possession over a long period of time.

[11]   G Criscuoli, *L'acquisto delle parti staccate del proprio corpo e gli artt 820 e 821 cc*, in *Rivista di Diritto delle Persone e della Famiglia*, 1985, p 272.

For this reason it is undoubtedly true that, in the present case, the two fertilized ova were 'property' totally separated from the mother and acquired by direct and original purchase as a result of fructification and therefore, by definition, 'external' and 'separated' from the mother's body (and from the father's body, too!).

It follows that not proceeding to implant the ova could hardly cause damage to the physical integrity of the mother. Again, in this case, it seems that the court has upset the normal sense of the rule: the protection of physical integrity exists to avoid something being compulsorily taken from or inserted into a body; not in order to ensure the right to accomplish such an implantation.

V   THE PRE-EMBRYO'S RIGHT TO LIFE

As regards the other argument, that is to say the acknowledgment of the pre-embryo's 'right to life', the 'legal status of the conceived' is not helpful (even if it represents interesting and significant proof of the degree of circulation of foreign models among our younger and more attentive lawyers). Nor is the reference to international legislation and to Arts 2 and 32 of Italian Constitution, in order to justify the validity of the right of the surviving parent not to see the process of life initiated with the contribution of their own gametes terminated, at least not without their own express consent or the 'right to maternity'. This is so for a long series of reasons.

In the first place, because all national and/or international rules enacted to protect 'maternity' are aimed at situations in which implantation has already taken place (whether naturally or artificially) they are intended to protect a 'responsive' and 'aware' maternity in respect of the physical and psychological integrity of the woman, but certainly not, as I have already said, to guarantee a 'right to be a mother'.

Secondly to invoke Art 2 of the Italian Constitution, which merely affirms 'the acknowledgement and grant of sacred human rights' is, in a technical sense, completely misleading as the character of the Article is simply declaratory: justifying the subsistence of an individual's right by reference to the rule which affirms in a merely generic way the right of all individuals is tautological.

Thirdly, because the rules protecting the 'legal status of the conceived' or of the embryo rest on a completely different basis from that of the case under consideration where, scientifically and technically speaking, we are not talking of a human being, nor of an embryo, nor of a conceived being (and perhaps not even of a *concepturus*). To equate naively a fertilized cell, which has been preserved in the state of blastocyst (that is to say doubly divided) with a pre-embryo or an embryo is equivalent to equating what is vital to what is alive, what is a human being to a human organ, what is a human being to a cell.

Even if this is not the place to debate the point in any depth, perhaps it is sufficient to remember that each human organ (liver, heart, lungs, etc) is in itself 'vital' but not 'living', while each cell of our body includes our whole genetic make-up so that it is (no longer) an abstract hypothesis to clone an individual just starting from that cell. If a cell, even if differentiated from the state of blastocyst, is equated with an individual asserting its 'life', we should have to admit that any cell of our body is abstractly capable of replicating a new individual, is itself a person and is therefore the subject of rights: a conclusion that is frankly not plausible.

Fourthly, if it is possible to admit that the right to life of the embryo may be restricted only with the corresponding right of the mother, we must not forget that such rights of the 'mother' follow the real and effective implantation in the uterus when we can technically say that pregnancy has started: pregnancy, in fact, does not start at the moment of fertilization but more exactly on implantation which is something which nowadays may be artificially postponed for a long period.

Before a pregnancy is achieved (and, again, a pregnancy occurs when the fertilized ovum is implanted in the uterus) the right of the father (and also of the mother) not to procreate must be recognized and considered paramount;[12] I think for instance of the situation in which, after assisted fertilization, the mother refuses to proceed to implantation or the father seeks to prevent it. In these cases, I do not believe that it is possible to admit of a right to life for the 'pre-embryos' as superior to the right not to procreate which is logically preceding and pre-existing. Here, the circumstances of the case under examination are singularly similar to those of the well-known case of *Davis v Davis* decided by the Court of Appeals of Tennessee in 1990.[13] In that case the judges had to determine to whom, as between husband and wife then divorced, belonged 'custody' of, and the right to take care of and make decisions about, seven ova fertilized by a homologous process and cryo-preserved pending a possible implantation in the uterus.

In that case, the judges focused on the fact that the fertilized and cryo-preserved ova, however potentially vital or viable, were not 'living', and could not be considered, from a narrow legal point of view, in the same way as a person, treating them rather as biological material. The judges underlined the pre-eminence of the right of the father not to procreate until implantation. The court, asserted that both parties, the woman and the man, have the same interests in fertilized ova and, consequently, both the custody and the right of control and disposition must be exercised jointly by both of the persons who contributed to the fertilization. Thus, in the absence of consent by both the 'aspirant' parents, the court refused to allow the implantation. This conclusion is, in my opinion, extremely advisable and sustainable even in the Italian legal system.

VI   OTHER CONSIDERATIONS

Last, but not least, we have to take into consideration one more aspect: the possibility of an evolutionary interpretation of the rules on legitimate filiation and on succession matters according to Arts 234 and 462[14] of the Italian Civil Code.

---

[12]   See A Miranda, 'Live and let die: tre questioni di vita e di morte', in *Vita not*, 1991, 716 ff.

[13]   Tennessee Ct of Appeals, 13 September 1990.

[14]   '**Article 234**

Each of the spouses and their heirs may prove that the child, born after three hundred days from the annulment, the dissolution or the cessation of the civil effects of the marriage, has been conceived during the marriage. They can also prove conception during cohabitation where the child is born after three hundred days from the pronouncement of judicial separation, or from the consensual separation, that is from the date of the court appearance of the spouses before the

The statute law, indeed, allows each spouse to prove that the child who was born more than 300 days after the dissolution of the marriage (for example, when one of the spouses dies) was conceived during the marriage.

According to the judge in the case under examination, *in vitro* fertilization may amount to 'conception during marriage' if it is a homologous fertilization and if both the spouses were alive at the time of fertilization. This allows the possibility of considering the child who is born thanks to this kind of medical assisted fertilization as legitimate and capable of inheriting from his father even if the father has died in the meantime (ie during the 300 days from fertilization/conception).

We agree with the attempt of the judge to broaden the sense and application of the statutory rule which would, otherwise, be a victim of its time. Nevertheless, as I said before, it is juridically and technically incorrect to equate 'conception', ie the moment when there is the implantation in the uterus, with the moment of 'fertilization' (whether *in vitro* or natural).

Furthermore, in this respect, it seems rather imprecise (if not wrong) to refer to the rules of legitimate filiation which are aimed at other, different situations, while those relating to natural filiation would be more suitable for this purpose. Hence, as to the rules of succession, more than to Art 462[15] of the Italian Civil Code, clauses 1 and 2 – which are difficult to apply to the facts and the circumstances of this case – it is preferable to look at the third clause of Art 462, ie to the rule that allows the *concepturus* to succeed by will (of a deceased person); in the presence of a will in favour of the 'test-tube' baby, in my opinion, it is absolutely correct to apply that provision drawing on the express wishes of the testator to the effect that he wants to continue with the artificial insemination process after his death.

Nevertheless, we are aware of the difficulties that our judges face in such a complex and difficult case: so, notwithstanding the discrepancies and gaps in the reasoning of the judgment, I think it is highly praiseworthy that the judge had the courage to confront the 'tragic choices' and give a decision.

---

judge when the same judge has authorized them to live separately. In any case, the child can propose an action in order to claim the status of a legitimate child.'
'**Article 462**
All those born or conceived at the time of the succession taking effect are able to succeed (Cod Civ 1, 594 ff, 600, 784). A child is presumed conceived, in the absence of evidence to the contrary, up to the time of the opening of the succession, who is born within three hundred days from the death of the person whose succession is in question (Cod Civ 232). Moreover the child of any named person living at the time of the death of the testator may receive by last will and testament, although not yet conceived (Cod Civ 643, 715, 784).'
[15] See note 14.

JAPAN

TURNING TO THE POINT WHERE SOCIETY NEEDS TO 'CO-OPERATE' AND 'CO-ORDINATE' FOR THE 'COMMONWEAL' – DEVELOPMENTS IN FAMILY LAW IN JAPAN 2001

Teiko Tamaki[*]

I INTRODUCTION

During the year 2001 in Japan, there have been many developments in every area of family law including new legislation. First, the Guardianship for Dependent Adults Act 1999,[1] as previously described in detail by K Niijima,[2] and some new developments in the treatment of dependent adult cases, as a result of the Act, were seen in 2001. Secondly, the law for the Prevention of Spousal Violence and the Protection of Victims came into effect on 13 October 2000, with a husband being arrested, as the first case under the Act, in the very next month. Thirdly, since the Prevention of Child Abuse Act 2000 took effect, new cases of child abuse were reported almost every day. This Act was arguably a turning point which helped to bring the problem of child abuse to the surface in Japanese society.

In this paper, I will try to describe developments in the above family law topics with reference to a number of notable cases. Other research trends and general developments in the field of family law are examined in the latter part of the paper.

II THE GUARDIANSHIP FOR DEPENDENT ADULTS ACT 1999

Since the Guardianship for Dependent Adults Act 1999 (the GDA Act) was enacted in April 2000, its effects have been seen both in statistical data and a number of new cases. The GDA Act provides new terms and sets out conditions under which dependent adults may take legal decisions and manage their property.

---

[*] Research Assistant, Faculty of Law, Niigata University.
The author gratefully acknowledges the editorial assistance of Dr Benjamin Goold.

[1] Each Act has two dates which it might be appropriate to describe as the date when the particular Act took effect under the legislative system in Japan. The first date is the day when the particular Act got through Parliament and was officially announced (*koufu*), and the second date is the day when the Act began to be applied to actual cases (*shikou*). Normally there is about a six-month gap between the two dates and, for this reason, to specify the year of the particular Act coming into force might be not clear where two dates cross over two years. In this paper I use the date of announcement (*koufu*) to refer to the coming into force of each Act.

[2] K Niijima, 'Guardianship for Adults', in *The International Survey of Family Law (2001 Edition)*, ed A Bainham (Family Law, 2001).

The Act aims at abolishing discrimination against dependent adults by calling them 'incompetent (*kinchisansha*)' or 'quasi-incompetent (*jun-kinchisansha*)', and focuses on the importance of rights of self-determination. In addition, the Act provides for the additional protection of individual privacy under a new records system, requiring individual applications under the GDA Act to be registered in an independent registration book (and not in a Family Registration Book (*koseki*) as under the old system).

For these reasons, the hope is that the GDA Act will function as a flexible and practical system, a fact that appears to have been borne out given that the number of claims made to family courts concerning the guardianship of dependent adults has almost doubled since the new Act came into effect.[3] In particular, court cases dealing with General Aid (*Hojo*), a newly created category of Adult Guardianship, discussed the issue of self-determination in relation to the persons in need of General Aid.

It is also pointed out that a practical discussion of how the GDA Act would apply to both cases of foreigners residing in Japan and Japanese citizens living abroad is required in order to prepare for various anticipated cases in this cosmopolitan society.[4] With reference to registration of Guardianship, the importance of the role played by notary publics (*koushounin*) was also examined in its practical application by a notary public in active service.[5]

A   Statistics

According to statistics published by the Family Bureau of the Supreme Court,[6] the total number of Adult Guardianship classification claims was 9,007 for the year 2000. The breakdown of claims dealing with validity of guardianship were:

(1)   Guardianship (*Koken*) 7,451 cases (2.5 times more than the year 1999);
(2)   Curatorship (*Hosa*) 884 cases (1.3 times more than the year 1999); and
(3)   General Aid (*Hojo*) 621 cases (a new type of protection).

Under the new Act, the claimant is required to follow a certain process; first, settle on an Adult Guardianship agreement and register, then select his or her guardian. The procedure takes some time, and, during the period under consideration the number of Adult Guardianship cases was 801, suggesting that the number of claims for selection of guardians will increase gradually from now on.

The statistics also suggest that the average length of proceedings for each claim went down, and that 43% of all claims were processed within three months (29% in the year 1995), and that 14.6% of all cases were taking more than six

---

3   Family Bureau, 'Overview of the Adult Guardianship Cases between April 2000 and
        March 2001', *Kagetsu* (Monthly Bulletin on Family Courts), vol 53 no 9, 2001, at 135–154 and
        vol 54 no 1, 2002, at 141–150.

4   See M Yamada, 'On the Adult Guardianship Cases involving Non-Japanese', *Kagetsu*, vol 53
        no 9, 2001, at 1–32. Yamada suggests the GDA Act should apply to non-Japanese and Japanese
        abroad, especially in the light of International law.

5   Y Matsuno, '*Ninikoukenkeiyakuteiketsu no jitsujo to mondaiten* (Current Circumstances and
        Problems of Adult Guardianship's Voluntary Agreement)', *Case Kenkyu* vol 270, at 3–29.

6   Family Bureau, op cit.

months (35.3% in the year 1995). In addition, the length of time taken for the evaluation of dependent adults shortened, such that 44% of all cases were processed within a month, and 40% in less than two months.[7] The figures also show that the average cost of evaluation went down, and that 89.8% of all evaluations cost less than 100,000 yen (38% in the year 1995, 28.4% cost more than 200,000 yen) in accordance with the reduced time for evaluation.

B   Cases

As mentioned in the above paragraph, two cases at the Sapporo High Court relating to General Aid (*Hojo*) were dismissed, mainly because the appointment of a guardian was clearly against the person's will in both cases.[8] The decision of 25 December 2000 noted that the person in question expressed a clear intention to withdraw the claim requesting General Aid (*Hojo*), and the court therefore applied s 10(1) of the Act on Guardianship by Agreement to the effect that there was no particular reason for the person's interest. The decision of 30 May 2001 simply focused on the fact that the person did not wish to receive General Aid (*Hojo*).

The other two cases at the Tokyo High Court adopted a similar approach to the interpretation of the former Act on Adult Guardianship, arguing that it is not acceptable to examine claims for selection of a guardian and commencement of guardianship separately.[9] Referring to the fact that there is no provision for the register of a complaint against the decision for selecting a guardian (s 27(2) of the Practice Rule for Family Law Litigation provides for a right of complaint against commencement of guardianship), both complaints about the selection of a guardian were dismissed.

III   DOMESTIC VIOLENCE

The background to domestic violence (DV) and related issues in Japanese society was described in a previous International Survey,[10] which noted that Japan was still awaiting the enactment of a specific law for protection of victims of DV. Before the Prevention of Spousal Violence and the Protection of Victims Act 2001 (the DV Act), the Civil Code, the Criminal Code, and the social welfare law were the major legal bases for the bringing of domestic violence cases, which provided primarily 'a remedy' as resolution of DV problems rather than 'prevention'.

In September 2000, the Prime Minister's Council for Gender Equality insisted on the need for new legislation for the prevention of violence against women. Following this, an internal project team of the House of Councillors produced a

---

[7]   There is no equivalent data for this in the year 1995.

[8]   Sapporo High Court, 25 December 2000 (*Kagetsu* vol 53 no 8 at 74) and 30 May 2001 (*Kagetsu* vol 53 no 11 at 112).

[9]   Tokyo High Court, 25 April 2000 (*Kagetsu* vol 53 no 3 at 88) and 9 September 2000 (*Kagetsu* vol 53 no 6 at 112).

[10]   S Minamikata and T Tamaki, 'Developments in Japanese Family Law During 1998 – Domestic Violence Reforms', in *The International Survey of Family Law (2000 Edition)*, ed A Bainham (Family Law, 2000), at 231–238.

draft Domestic Violence Bill, which was submitted to the Parliament, with the result that the DV Act began to be applied to real cases in October 2001. The DV Act aims at protecting both male and female victims of domestic violence. However, it is also true that the majority of reported victims of domestic violence were women,[11] so that victims are now almost always assumed to be female.[12]

The meaning of the term 'spousal' for the purpose of the DV Act includes various categories of partners – such as a common-law wife/husband and a cohabitant – in order to deal with domestic violence cases flexibly and to ensure that the Act reflects changes in family form and structure. The main feature of the new Act is that, the court can now issue a protection order against a repeat offender in a domestic violence case if there is a grave threat of renewed spousal violence constituting significant harm to life or physical conditions. The protection order has two parts: the order to prohibit an approach to a victim and the order to vacate the home. The former order is designed to prohibit the offender from approaching the victim and loitering in the vicinity of the victim's domicile, workplace and so on for a six-month period. The latter order requires the offender to vacate the home for a two-week period. In addition to this, the Act provides for the punishment of individuals who violate a protection order, either with imprisonment, with labour of up to one year, or a fine of not more than one million yen.

Unfortunately, the problem with this new system is that the procedure for seeking a protection order is excessively complicated and intrusive. Under the DV Act victims of domestic violence must set out their circumstances in detail and state whether they have sought advice and support from officers of the Spousal Violence Advice Centre or police officers (if not, the victims have to see a notary public to have their statement sworn). Although the aim of this system is to discourage individuals from making false statements, it is unrealistic and impractical to require such complicated procedures for those who are in pressing need of help and in imminent danger. Moreover, it has been argued that despite the enactment of the DV Act there is still a shortage of places to protect victims (there are currently only about 35 private shelters in Japan). The Cabinet Office reported in its survey of shelters that 80% of the shelters are inadequate in terms of safety and guard facilities owing to a lack of funds.[13] As these shelters are meant to be used for temporary protection, it is necessary to arrive at an urgent solution to the above problems.

The DV Act allows for the revision of its provisions (s 3 of the supplementary provision) at least once in every three years, so it is expected that new measures to meet the more practical needs of domestic violence may be produced in the future.

---

[11]   92.3% of the DV cases in which arrests were made were cases with female victims (see fn 14 below).

[12]   Accordingly, many publications provided by the Cabinet Office Gender Equality Bureau – such as an English manual for the new DV Act – assume that the DV offender is 'a husband'. See 'Eradication of Spousal Violence' (Pamphlet) at *http://www.gender.go.jp/english_contents/ndex.html.*

[13]   *Nihon Keizai Shinbun* (newspaper), 20 December 2001.

A   Statistics

The number of cases of domestic violence exposed by the police during the year 2001 was 1,444 cases, which is a significant increase since 2000.[14] The figure includes murder (191 cases), bodily injury (1,097 cases) and assault (156 cases). In addition, 1,333 cases out of the total (92.3%) involved violence against a wife by a husband (including a cohabitant), and 111 cases (7.7%) involved violence against a husband by a wife.

According to the survey conducted by the Ministry of Health, Labour and Welfare, the number of requests for advice about domestic violence has also been increasing, from 7,352 cases in 1999 to 9,176 cases in 2000.[15]

B   Cases

As yet, there have been no published court decisions under the DV Act, although the following cases were reported in Japanese newspapers shortly after the DV Act came into force.

(1)   The Osaka District Court placed a husband under both protection orders, prohibiting him from approaching his wife and children for six months and requiring him to vacate their home on 19 October 2001.[16]
(2)   The Takamatsu-Minami Police Station of the Kagawa Prefectural Police, arrested a 24-year-old company employee who violated a protection order prohibiting him from approaching his wife, after he broke into his wife's parents' house where she had sought refuge.[17]

IV   CHILD ABUSE

It was rather striking to see so many reports of child abuse in the Japanese media over the last year. Hardly a day went by when there was no news on child abuse in Japanese newspapers. The Prevention of Child Abuse Act 2000 (the 'PCA Act') took effect on 17 May 2000 and has been in force since 20 November 2000.[18] Although it might be premature to suggest that this increase in the disclosure of child abuse cases in the media is a result of the PCA Act, it is possible to argue

---

[14]   White Paper 'FY 2001 Annual Report on the State of the Formation of a Gender Equal Society' and 'Policies to be Implemented in FY 2002 to Promote the Formation of a Gender Equal Society' at 24, see *http://www.gender.go.jp/english_contents/index.html*.

[15]   *Nihon Keizai Shinbun* (newspaper), 5 September 2001. The survey also reported the figure for consultations on domestic violence by each prefecture. The urban cities had higher portions, such as Tokyo (1,495 cases), Kanagawa (1,265 cases) and Fukuoka (624 cases). However, it is inappropriate to judge that victims of domestic violence are much more concentrated in the urban cities only from the data at this stage, because it might be assumed that those victims of domestic violence in rural areas may find it difficult to take action or to ask for advice from others.

[16]   *Nihon Keizai Shinbun* (newspaper), 20 October 2001.

[17]   *Nihon Keizai Shinbun* (newspaper), 14 December 2001.

[18]   For the introduction of the PCA Act see S Minamikata and T Tamaki, 'Family Law In Japan During 2000', in *The International Survey of Family Law (2002 Edition)*, ed A Bainham (Family Law, 2002) at 221–223.

that the PCA Act has drawn greater attention to the issue of child abuse generally. Whereas these child abuse cases might have been hidden in the past, even prior to the passing of the PCA Act it had become much more common to view suspicious cases involving children as a form of child abuse. According to official statistics on child abuse cases dealt with by local Child Welfare Offices in the country, some apparent changes before and after the PCA Act can be identified as detailed below. Looking generally at incidents of child abuse reported in the media during the year 2001, a common feature is that some of the cases involved multiple offenders within a single family.[19] Furthermore, many of those parents perpetrating violence against their children appeared to do so for their own 'selfish' reasons, such as in response to the children being less attached to the parents.

A   Statistics

The Ministry of Health, Labour and Welfare released the Annual Report of Child Abuse Consultation Case Proceedings during the financial year 2000 (April 2000 to March 2001).[20] This report was based on a survey of 174 Child Welfare Offices (*Jidosodanjyo*), spread over the whole of Japan. The number of cases in which advice on child abuse was requested totalled 17,725 in the financial year 2000. This was 1.5 times more than the previous year (11,631), and 16 times more than 10 years ago (1,101) when the government began to record such statistics. The report suggests the reason for this apparent increase is largely a result of the PCA Act 2000 and other indirect effects of the Act which led people to consult and report on child abuse matters. The increased figures which may relate to an application of the PCA Act included:

(1)   channels of information (reported child abuse cases);
(2)   cases of entry and inspection of the residence; and
(3)   temporary protection (custody) of the abused child.

As for (1), the number of contacts from the neighbourhood, child welfare centres, public health centres, police and schools during 2000 increased considerably when compared with those of the previous year. This suggests that people in local areas have become more willing to report potential child abuse cases, and that the above institutions have acquired legal grounds to ensure that their actions are based on the PCA Act. Secondly, it has been argued that to enter and inspect on the spot a family who seems to have a child abuse problem is not easy, as many of the child victims' parents, the suspicious perpetrators of child abuse, tend to refuse to allow entry to local Child Welfare Officers and try to hide the facts. Because of the introduction of new powers granted to the public institutions – giving them

---

[19]   An extreme case was where four members of a family committed abuse of a 3-year-old boy and killed him in Chiba, in February 2001. They were the child's stepmother, step-grandparents, and step-great-grandfather, and were sentenced differently. The child's father was also arrested for abandonment of parental responsibility. See *Nihon Keizai Shinbun* (newspaper), 8 April, 5 July and 20 November 2001.

[20]   Equal Opportunity and Child Welfare Department, Ministry of Health, Labour and Welfare, 14 November 2001. See *http://www.mhlw.go.jp/houdou/0111/h1114-3.html*.

authority to enter and inspect those households – the number of cases in 2000 was 96 and the number of children involved was 132 (as compared with figures of 42 cases and 64 children in 1999). The number of temporary protection (custody) orders based on Art 33 of the Child Welfare Act also increased during 2000 to 6,168 cases. This suggests that, along with the general increase in cases involving calls for advice on child abuse, serious cases requiring a separation of children victims from their parent(s) may have also increased.

The impression may have been given that in the media offenders in child abuse cases can vary, including the mother/father, stepmother/father, girl/boyfriend (partner) of the victim, and so on. However, the statistics reveal that it was mothers who constituted 61% of the principal perpetrators of child abuse, whereas fathers constituted 23.7% in the year 2000. The figure for mothers as the major perpetrators is also increasing year by year.

B Cases

In order to provide for the legal protection of a suspected victim of child abuse, an application under s 28 of the Children Welfare Act 1947 is now available. As the provision allows for intervention by the public authority with the consent of the Family Court even in cases where there is no consent from the child's parents, the Head of the Child Welfare Office (*Jidosodanshocho*) is now enabled to exercise the right to place the child victim in temporary custody. The Hiroshima Family Court declared that a suspected victim of child abuse could be placed under protection in a Child Welfare Home without there being a need to specify the major perpetrator of abuse (whether the child's mother or father).[21] Cases heard at the Osaka Family Court (2 April 2001), the Fukuoka Family Court (23 April 2001) and the Sapporo Family Court (11 June 2001) all reached the same conclusion. Children who had been placed under the temporary custody of the Head of the Child Welfare Office (*Jidosodanshocho*) were to be admitted to the Child Welfare Homes, provided it was clear that it would affect the children's welfare and harm their interests if they continued to be looked after by their own parents.

Referring to s 834 of the Civil Code, the Sasebo Branch of the Nagasaki Family Court declared that an abusing father forfeited his rights and duties (*shinken*) over his three children who were the victims of sexual abuse and bodily harm.[22] The Kokura branch of the Fukuoka Family Court also provided a new interpretation of 'an abused child', which included children not likely to be personally abused but kept in the same environment as their abused siblings, on the grounds that being kept in that environment could amount to mental abuse.[23]

It has also been pointed out that one of the major difficulties of dealing with these child abuse matters is the problem of fact-finding, particularly because it is difficult to investigate domestic matters of this kind. However, contrary to past

---

[21] Decree of the Hiroshima Family Court, 28 July 2000 (*Kagetsu* vol 3 no 1 at 95).

[22] Decree of the Sazebo Branch of the Nagasaki Family Court, 23 February 2000 (*Kagetsu* vol 52 no 8 at 55). See F Tokotani's commentary in *Hanreitaimuzu*, no 1046 (February 2001) at 86–88.

[23] Decree of the Kokura Branch of the Fukuoka Family Court, 1 December 1999 (*Kagetsu* vol 52 no 6 at 66). See F Tokotani's commentary, ibid at 85–86.

trends in the Child Welfare Office – which tended to avoid conflicts with parents – both the Child Welfare Office and the Family Court are now likely to reach a positive decision in order to serve the interests and protect the welfare of abused children.

V   RESEARCH TRENDS, CASES, AND OTHER ISSUES IN JAPANESE FAMILY LAW

A   Research

Research in the area of family law in Japan over the last year has tended to broaden and become much more complicated. This said, the overall research trend was much the same as in previous years, particularly regarding issues relating to the application of DNA testing to parent–child relationship determination and Gender Identity Disorder. A lot of discussion on testamentary succession and wills emerged in the area of succession law (ss 882–1044 of the Civil Code). Along with the new legislation, studies concerning each topic and Act were also published. In addition, a considerable number of commentaries on matrimonial property were prominent in 2001, and significantly the Family Lawyers Conference (an associate society of the International Society of Family Law in Japan) chose legal issues on child abuse problems at its 17th Annual Meeting.[24]

As already noted in the previous survey, the function and needs of the Japanese family court have now been questioned and the issue has become more pressing not only among family law academics but also practitioners, such as family court officers.[25] The trend also echoes the theory that all litigation of personal affairs should only take place in family courts. Whereas, under the current legal system, this litigation is dealt with by the district court, as the second tier where mediation at a family court has failed to resolve the dispute.

B   Cases

The cases discussed here were heard during the period and are indicative of some key characteristics of Japanese culture and common ideas.

(1)   Concerning the questions of parental rights, duties of care, and control over the child, the Tokyo High Court declared that it is not appropriate to judge the necessity of parental financial support for one's child simply by reference to the fact that the child was healthy and had

---

[24]   The topic of how to address child abuse issues was discussed in the Annual Meeting. Comparative studies on the child abuse problem in Germany, England and Japan were also presented. See *'Kazoku <Shakai to Ho> (Socio-Legal Studies on Family Law)'* no 7, 2001 October at 19–198 for further details.

[25]   The 16th Annual Meeting of the Family Lawyers Conference was entitled 'Fifty Years of the Family Court in Japan'. The papers were read and the discussions heard in the conference were printed in *'Kazoku <Shakai to Ho> (Socio-Legal Studies on Family Law)'* no 16, 2000 October at 38–245.

reached 20 years old.[26] The case concerned the situation of a university student who claimed parental support for tuition fees and other living expenses. Although the original judgment dismissed the claim (Yokohama Family Court, 27 September 2000), the Tokyo High Court created a major precedent and concluded that distinguishing between a child in need of parental financial support and a child regarded as a financially independent adult cannot be decided by the application of a single test, and that the court is required to take all kinds of detailed factors into consideration, such as the actual income of the student and the reasons for a shortage of funds. The decision might be difficult to understand for people in other countries where children over 18 years old, or 20 years old, are automatically regarded as adults and where they have a different financial system on higher education.[27]

(2) Among the succession law cases, the Hiroshima High Court included in the definition of a successor a person in charge of the family customary events (*saishikeishosha*) such as the worship and upkeep of their ancestors' tomb,[28] and the Tokyo District Court defined the distribution of mementoes (keepsakes) of a deceased person (*katamiwake*) in respect of inherited property.[29] The former case held that both tombs and connected burial grounds belong to the inherited property of the family,[30] and where there is no particular indication of the deceased selecting a person to be in charge of the family customary events, successors have no such right to select the person by themselves. In the latter case, a judge declared that the *katamiwake*, requiring successors to remember the deceased, does not affect s 921(3) of the Civil Code, which states that a person who deliberately hides inherited property cannot become a lawful successor. However in the instant case, one of the successors, who renounced the right of succession, took almost all the valuable items left by the deceased including clothes, shoes, and carpet. It was found that this exceeded the extent of the *katamiwake* so that s 921(3) of the Civil Code applied.

C Other developments

Apart from the above topics, the following issues have also received considerable attention, especially in the media.

(1) The legitimacy of surrogate mothers and the legal right to have a child through the use of in-vitro fertilisation with a third person's involvement. A private maternity clinic in Nagano Prefecture carried out an arranged birth by in-vitro fertilisation in which the sister of a couple provided the

---

[26] Decision of the Tokyo High Court, 5 December 2000 (*Kagetsu*, vol 53 no 5 p 187).

[27] In general, it is not common for students in Japan to take out bank loans (even in the exceptional cases, banks would require a proper guarantor), and grants and scholarships for university students are not widely available. As a consequence, many parents of Japanese university students assist their children financially.

[28] Hiroshima High Court, 25 August 2000, see *Hanreijiho* no 1743 at 79 and its case review by Y Sato in *Hanreitaimuzu* no 1068 (November 2001) at 114.

[29] Tokyo District Court, 21 March 2000, see *Hanreitaimuzu* no 1054 (May 2001) at 255–260.

[30] Section 897(1) of the Civil Code.

fertilised egg. A report by the council of the Ministry of Health, Labour and Welfare in December 2000 suggests such births should be prohibited; thus the Ministry announced that they aim to prepare and submit a Bill, which includes a prohibition on the use of surrogate mothers, to Parliament without delay.[31] Discussion of this issue continued throughout the year, especially with reference to the related news of a 60-year-old woman who gave birth to a child by in-vitro fertilisation using an American woman's egg. Particular attention in this case focused on the *shinken* (parental rights and duties) and the larger question of who would be the child's 'legal mother'.

(2)   Law reform governing the use of separate family names by married couples, which states that couples are required to choose just one family name, either the husband's or wife's, at the time of marriage registration under the current Civil Law.[32] This reform has been eagerly awaited, especially by those women who found it hard to maintain their maiden names at work and wished to maintain their privacy by changing their family names both at marriage and on divorce. Along with a stream of developments in the area of sex and gender issues, this law reform first appeared in 1991, with the advisory committee for the Minister of Justice later submitting a report recommending the introduction of a system of separate family names in 1996. The issue has been raised on and off, and in August 2001, it appeared from a survey that a majority agreed with the system. However, despite a discussion of actual revision of the Civil Code, slow progress has been made and the final decision to introduce a system of separate family names has not been reached.

(3)   Division of matrimonial property on the breakdown of marriages between middle-aged couples. Change in the area can be viewed as a further development of the rules on division of matrimonial property at the time of divorce, such that they now include pensions and retirement pay.[33] In particular, consideration has been given to the establishment of a new system of measurement under which, if a couple agrees to the division of a husband's Welfare Pension at the time of divorce, the wife can also receive the Pension in future.[34]

(4)   The gap between ideas of equality of the sexes and reality, especially in the field of equal opportunities to employment. It was found in a survey during 2000 by the Ministry of Health, Labour and Welfare that more than 30% of women had been victims of discrimination in their job interviews as a result of their marriage plans. On the other hand, cases also dealt with a new provision relating to a child's sex difference in terms of the calculation of

---

[31]   *Nihon Keizai Shinbun* (newspaper), 19 and 20 May, 1 and 11 June 2001.

[32]   The proportion of married couples who chose the husband's surname was 97% according to the recent statistics of 2001. The figure is not published, although the statistics are included in the *Heisei 13 nendo Jinkodotaitokei* (*Vital Statistics of Population* 2001), and the data was gained through the Vital and Health Statistic Division, Vital Statistics and Information Department, Ministry of Health, Labour and Welfare.

[33]   S Minamikata and T Tamaki, op cit, 2002, at 225.

[34]   *Nihon Keizai Shinbun* (newspaper), 10 November 2001. The Welfare Pension is to be paid to the husband of a wife who is not working, with the payment equal to a sum to cover both of them as a couple. England introduced a system for dividing pensions at divorce in 2000, following pioneering schemes in countries such as Canada and Germany, *Nihon Keizai Shinbun* (newspaper), 17 October 2001.

isshitsu rieki, a form of compensation for loss of income where a child is killed in a car accident (decrees of the Nara District Court July 2000 and the Tokyo District Court March 2001). According to the new provision, the compensation is to be worked out on the basis of the average wage of both men and women. It used to apply different figures for men's average wage and women's average wage depending on the case.

VI CONCLUSION

As witnessed by the increasing numbers of family law cases being processed by the family courts, Japanese family courts are currently under pressure to put new reforms into action. In order to meet the serious needs of people facing family relationship problems including marriage and divorce, family courts should be centralised for the purpose of family law litigation.[35] Because disputes are resolved through the use of mediation (*chotei*), it has been argued that such procedures will be much more effective if in-court mediation (*kajichotei*) and the litigation of personal affairs (*jinjisosho*) are conducted in the same place.

Moreover, it has been said that reform of the judicial system in Japan should focus on creating a system that is familiar to ordinary citizens. In particular, although people need better access to lawyers, it is also true in reality that lawyers are rarely needed in family law matters. Therefore, there is a pressing need to establish a system which ensures people can obtain necessary legal advice and support at a serviceable level, as well as access at a low cost. The three Bar Associations in Tokyo (*Tokyo, Tokyo Daiichi* and *Tokyo Daini Bengoshikai*) have begun to look into setting up a co-operative legal advice centre for family law matters, which will aim to assist people with family problems who need prompt legal advice from lawyers in the community. A similar plan might be welcomed in other local communities as well.[36]

All the above topics in the Japanese family law area in 2001 have led to similar tasks being pursued as a next step, namely:

(1) to establish networks in local communities to provide mutual assistance;
(2) to train various experts/specialists in family law matters; and
(3) to create practical and up-to-date manuals specifically dealing with family problems.

As for (1), it has been repeatedly pointed out that, despite changes in the law resulting from the PCA Act, there is still a lack of close co-operation in child abuse cases. Child Welfare Officers, police, teachers at school and kindergarten and neighbours all need to co-operate in discovering victims of child abuse and

---

[35] The Justice System Reform Council, Interim Report, 20 November 2000, see *http://www.kantei.go.jp/jp/sihouseido/report/naka_houkoku.html#4seidoteki*.

[36] See M Tanamura, '*Kajijiken o meguru shihokaikakuseido no genjo to kadai* (Current situation and problems concerning a reform of the Japanese Judicial System with reference to family matters)', *Houritsujiho*, vol 73 no 7, at 91–95. As for the Legal Advice Centre of Family Matters of the three Bar Associations in Tokyo, there has been progress (*Nihon Keizai Shinbun*, 1 August 2001) although it is said that practical problems persist such as disagreements over its intended location.

preventing them from being harmed.[37] However, it may still be difficult to draw a line between a necessary intervention and an unjustified interference with an individual's privacy.

There is also a need to broaden the definition and category of professionals who deal with problems concerning family law. Traditionally and institutionally, family court welfare officers have played a key role in processing family law disputes. Nonetheless, these officers have no special skills and qualifications for dealing with family matters, as special training is generally not required. It is important to train people who deal with family law matters in order to ensure that appropriate solutions can be found in cases of child abuse and domestic violence.

Finally regarding point (3), given the growing diversity of family forms and structures, and because issues relating to the family have become more complicated, it might be appropriate to say that existing approaches to the resolution of family disputes in Japan may now be out-of-date. Any new approach to family problems and arguments over family matters must take all factors into consideration, such as a broad conception of the 'family'. We have seen various new issues raised in individual cases in the making of the new legislation, and as such it is necessary to set up concrete measures to ensure that the next stage in family law in Japan is the right one.

---

[37] Y Iwasa suggests, from a lawyer's practical viewpoint, that there are some differences in the tackling of the child abuse problem depending on factors such as the geographical location of the Child Welfare Office and the different tasks carried out by the profession relating to child welfare. Y Iwasa, '*Bengoshi kara mita jidogyakutaijiken* (Child abuse cases observed by a practising lawyer)', *Kagetsu* vol 53 no 4 at 1–32.

THE NETHERLANDS

BUMPER ISSUE: ALL YOU EVER WANTED TO KNOW ABOUT DUTCH FAMILY LAW (AND WERE AFRAID TO ASK)

*Ian Sumner and Caroline Forder**

I INTRODUCTION

In the 2002 edition *Survey* article for the Netherlands attention was focused exclusively upon marriage and marriage-like relationships. This time we have sought to provide an overview of the main developments across the entire field of family law. A number of important developments in the field of private international law are discussed (the private international law consequences of opening up marriage to same-sex couples, the Act on conflicts of law arising in cases of pension adjustment, the Act on conflicts of law in cases of determination of parentage by descent and the Bill on conflicts of law in adoption). The review of family property which is taking place in the Netherlands now includes two new Acts: the Act on the Rights and Duties of Spouses (and registered partners) and the Act on Contractual Participation Clauses. We discuss case-law on maintenance issues (termination of maintenance liability in the event of cohabitation of the person entitled to maintenance with a third party, and the maintenance liability of the mother's same-sex partner for a child which they brought up together). Selected case-law on parenthood issues is included, as well as a discussion of the Act on Storage and Dissemination of Information regarding Gamete Donors. An overview of recent developments in custody and access law is provided, featuring the position of step-parents and the position of the parent who does not have custody following divorce. An item on recent research on the use of mediation in custody and access disputes is included. Finally, the review concludes with a discussion of recent important developments in child protection cases (supervision orders and the position of foster parents, the case for introduction of a new measure aimed at preventing child abuse, the new Act on Child Abuse Advice and Reporting Centres and the Bill to reform the Child Assistance Act).

* The first author is a PhD researcher at the Molengraaff Institute for Private Law, Utrecht University. He is currently writing a PhD on the private international law aspects of the emerging forms of registered partnership within Europe especially within Belgium, England and Wales, France and the Netherlands. The second author is Professor of European Family Law at the University of Maastricht, the Netherlands.

II MARRIAGE AND PARTNERSHIP

A Opening up marriage to same-sex couples: private international law aspects

On 1 April 2001, it became possible for the first time for couples of the same sex to celebrate civil marriage ceremonies before the Registrar of Births, Deaths and Marriages.[1] The historical aspects of the legislative process itself have already been described in detail in the last three editions of this Survey.[2] However, since the 2002 edition, the Dutch Standing Committee on Private International Law (the *Staatscommissie*) has furnished a report outlining its insight into the possible private international law problems and solutions arising from the opening up of marriage to couples of the same sex.[3] At first sight, it might seem that for couples of the same sex, marriage could be treated in the same way as a registered partnership.[4] Although there are many similarities between the two institutions, there are fundamental differences. On the one hand, registered partnership is a new and young institution that is relatively limited in its recognition, whereas marriage, on the other hand, is a consolidated, traditional and pre-existing institution.[5] In the field of private international law this has the result, according to the *Staatscommissie*, that registered partnership deserves new rules whilst the question remains open as to how far the existing rules relating to marriage are also applicable to same-sex marriages.

The formal requirements of the Dutch legislation allow same-sex marriages to be celebrated between non-Dutch nationals, so long as one of the parties has a permanent place of residence in the Netherlands.[6] This increases the chance that there will be a foreign element in the marriage, consequently increasing the chance that rules of private international law will need to be invoked. The recognition of a same-sex marriage in other countries was the first question posed by the *Staatscommissie*. In dealing with the question, the *Staatscommissie* rightly stated that this cannot be answered by resorting to Dutch legislation, but instead must be referred to the country where recognition is sought.

The Netherlands, Luxembourg and Australia are currently the only three signatories to the 1978 Hague Convention on the Celebration and Recognition of the Validity of Marriages, which lays down, *inter alia*, a set of choice of law rules

---

[1]   The Registrar in the Netherlands is also responsible for the registered partnerships register.

[2]   *The International Survey of Family Law (2000 Edition)*, ed A Bainham (Family Law, 2000) at 240–253; *The International Survey of Family Law (2001 Edition)*, ed A Bainham (Family Law, 2001) at 301–304; *The International Survey of Family Law (2002 Edition)*, ed A Bainham (Family Law, 2002) at 278–282.

[3]   *Advies inzake het internationaal privaatrecht in verband met de openstelling van het huwelijk voor personen van hetzelfde geslacht* (Staatscommissie, 2002).

[4]   For more information on the Dutch registered partnership, see W Schrama, 'Registered partnership in The Netherlands' (1999) 13 *International Journal of Law, Policy and the Family* 315–327.

[5]   *Advies inzake het internationaal privaatrecht in verband met de openstelling van het huwelijk voor personen van hetzelfde geslacht* (Staatscommissie, 2002), p 2.

[6]   Article 2a, Wet Conflictenrecht Huwelijk, *Staatsblad 1989*, nr 419.

relating to the recognition of foreign marriages.[7] The Convention imposes a requirement upon the 'recognising' signatory state to recognise, subject to a public policy exception, all those marriages concluded in accordance with the law of the *lex loci celebrationis* (the law of the place where the marriage was celebrated). The *Staatscommissie*, however, was divided on the question whether the Dutch same-sex marriage actually falls within the scope of the Convention. The 1978 Convention is no different to any other Hague Convention in that the definition of the key term, 'marriage', is notable in its absence. It is stated:

> 'The Special Commission has not attempted to qualify or to reduce the scope of the term "marriage" in the preliminary draft Convention by definition, and this term when used in the Convention should be taken to refer to the institution *in its broadest, international sense*.'[8]

The division in opinion centred on the understanding of the phrase 'in its broadest, international sense'. Some of the members of the *Staatscommissie* believed that the stress should be placed on the word 'international' and not on the word 'broad'. At present, the opening up of civil marriage to couples of the same sex seems likely to continue to be a uniquely Dutch phenomenon. Although recent developments have sparked a debate in the Belgian Chamber of Representatives concerning the introduction of similar legislation,[9] the trend is certainly not towards a greater general European or world-wide phenomenon. Therefore, the understanding of the word 'international' must, *per se*, be restrictive. Only those institutions that can be compared on the basis of minimum requirements would fall within the applicability of the Convention (thus excluding same-sex marriages). The rest of the *Staatscommissie* believed that the stress should instead be placed on the word 'broadest' and therefore encompass all relationships that are considered to be marriages according to national law.[10]

The *Staatscommissie* report also deals with issues relating to matrimonial property,[11] the applicable law on the ending of a marriage, divorce jurisdiction and the recognition thereof, maintenance, adoption, joint parental authority and inheritance law. Each of these aspects are obviously also worth attention, but in this Survey, time and space restrict detailed explanation of the problems and solutions encountered and proposed.[12]

---

[7]   *Tractatenblad 1987*, nr 137 (14 March 1978). Ratified by the Netherlands and came into force through the Wet Conflictenrecht Huwelijk, *Staatsblad 1989*, nr 392.

[8]   Author's own emphasis, *Actes et Documents de la Treizième Session, Tome II*, p 292 § 9.

[9]   Discussions in the Chamber of Representatives, 1999–2000, 0692/001. Wetsvoorstel tot wijziging van de artikelen 144, 162 en 163 van het Burgerlijk Wetboek; Discussions in Chamber of Representatives, 1999–2000, 0861/001. Wetsvoorstel tot wijziging van het Burgerlijk wetboek betreffende het homo-huwelijk; Discussions in the Chamber of Representatives, 2000–2001, 1011/001. Wetsvoorstel tot aanvulling van artikel 144 van het Burgerlijk Wetboek betreffende het huwelijk van personen van hetzelfde geslacht; Discussions in the Chamber of Representatives, 2001–2002, 1692–001. Wetsontwerp van wet tot openstelling van het huwelijk voor personen van hetzelfde geslacht en tot wijziging van een aantal bepalingen van het Burgerlijk Wetboek.

[10]   LThLG Pellis, 'Het homohuwelijk: een bijzonder nationaal product' (2002) 6 *Tijdschrift voor Familie- en Jeugdrecht* 162–168.

[11]   Governed in the Netherlands by the Wet conflictenrecht huwelijksvermogensregime, *Staatsblad 1991*, nr 628.

[12]   For more information, see the report itself and Pellis, op cit, n 10 above.

B   Other aspects of opening up marriage to couples of the same sex

1   RELIGIOUS MARRIAGES

During the debate surrounding the opening-up of same-sex marriage, the issue of religious marriages was brought to the forefront. According to Art 1:68 of the Dutch Civil Code, a religious ceremony is not allowed to take place before the parties have assured the minister of religion that a civil marriage ceremony has previously taken place before the Registrar of Births, Deaths and Marriages. This provision must also be considered in combination with Art 449 of the Dutch Criminal Code, which makes it a criminal offence for a minister of religion to solemnise a marriage before a civil marriage has taken place. Some commentators believe that the Art 1:68 ban is contrary to the parties' freedom of religion.[13] It has been said that, since the opening-up of same-sex marriage, the inherent and fundamental nature of marriage has changed. All those couples who now wish to enter into a civil marriage must opt for the 'new opened form' of marriage (ie one which is also open to same-sex couples). It has consequently been argued that the prohibition on legally recognised religious marriages should now also be abolished.[14] However, the State Secretary has stated that there remains enough justification for the maintenance of Art 1:68 of the Dutch Civil Code and Art 449 of the Dutch Criminal Code.[15] It seems, therefore, that for the foreseeable future, the distinction between church and state marriage will remain. It is the author's opinion, however, that the objections brought against Art 1:68 are far-fetched. Whilst marriages are now solemnised between couples of the same sex as well as opposite sexes, the 'fundamental nature' of marriage remains the same: the public display of commitment between a loving couple irrespective of gender or sexuality.

2   CIVIL SERVANT DIFFICULTIES

Since the summary in the last edition of the Survey,[16] two Dutch municipalities have refused to perform marriages between couples of the same sex on grounds of conscientious, religious objection.[17] The law itself provides no solution for the religious objections of Registrars to performing same-sex marriages, and the municipalities must deal with the situation themselves. Registrars with conscientious, religious objections are allowed to hand these cases to another Registrar either in the same municipality or in a neighbouring municipality. The two municipalities in question stipulated that all Registrars were compelled to solemnise all marriages regardless of the gender of the parties. The Commission on Equal Treatment held that, although the requirement contained no form of

---

13   'Kerkelijk huwelijk voor burgerlijk huwelijk blijft strafbaar' (2001) 43 *Nederlands Juristenblad* 2118–9.

14   S Roes, 'De scheiding van Kerk en Staat en het huwelijk' (2001) 11 *Tijdschrift voor Familie- en Jeugdrecht* 111–113.

15   Kerkelijk huwelijk voor burgerlijk huwelijk blijft strafbaar, op cit n 13 above.

16   *The International Survey of Family Law (2002 Edition)*, ed A Bainham (Family Law, 2002) at 281–282.

17   'Gewetensbezwaarden hoeven geen homohuwelijken te sluiten' (2002) 13 *Nederlands Juristenblad* 696.

direct discrimination on grounds of religion, there was, however, a form of indirect discrimination since people with a religious background would be more frequently affected by such a requirement. The General Law on Equal Treatment[18] requires that all forms of indirect discrimination are objectively justified. Since there were enough Registrars in the two municipalities in question who had no conscientious, religious objections to solemnising marriages between couples of the same gender, these marriages could be celebrated without problem. Therefore, there was no objectively justified reason for the compulsory requirement imposed on the Registrars. The Commission on Equal Treatment therefore concluded that the requirement imposed on the Registrars was a form of indirect discrimination which could not be objectively justified and consequently allowed Registrars with conscientious, religious objections to refuse to perform same-sex marriages.[19]

3 LIGHTNING DIVORCES

With the introduction of the same-sex marriage legislation, two new articles were introduced into the Civil Code, providing for the conversion of a registered partnership into a marriage and vice versa.[20] In this article, reference will be made to a conversion from marriage into registered partnership, but of course the same process is also valid in the opposite direction. The procedure itself states that if two people have notified the Registrar of Births, Deaths and Marriages (hereafter referred to as 'the Registrar') that they wish their marriage to be transformed into a registered partnership, the Registrar of the place of residence of one of the parties may draw up an instrument of conversion. It would seem that this Article provides the Registrar with a discretionary competence to refuse to draw up such document. However that is not the case. The Registrar is allowed to refuse to draw up such an instrument only on the grounds listed in Art 18b of Book 1 of the Dutch Civil Code.[21] The future registered partners must live in the Netherlands (although not necessarily together)[22] or one of them must possess Dutch nationality.[23] In the latter case, the conversion must take place at the Registry of Births, Deaths and Marriages in the Hague. It is also stated that the conversion shall constitute a termination of the registered partnership and cause the marriage to commence on the date upon which the deed of transformation in the register of marriages is drawn up. Importantly, the provision also states that conversion does not affect any pre-existing family law relations with children born prior to the conversion.[24] The mirror procedure to convert a registered partnership into a marriage is elucidated in Art 1:80g of the Dutch Civil Code.

---

[18] Algemene Wet Gelijke Behandeling.

[19] Equal Treatment Commission, 15 March 2002, Decision nr 2002–24.

[20] Article 77, Book 1, Dutch Civil Code provides for the conversion of a marriage into a registered partnership and Art 80g, Book 1, Dutch Civil Code provides for the reverse.

[21] These grounds are that the parties have not complied with the grounds listed in Art 18, Book 1, Dutch Civil Code or on grounds of public policy.

[22] Article 83, Book 1, Dutch Civil Code had imposed a cohabitation condition, but has since been repealed.

[23] SFM Wortmann, 'Rechtsontwikkelingen in het personen- en familierecht: flitsscheidingen en verrekenbedingen' (2002) 6477 *Weekblad voor Privaatrecht, Notariaat en Registratie* 165–172.

[24] Article 80g §3, Book 1, Dutch Civil Code.

One would imagine that the issue of conversion would have been heavily discussed in both academic and legislative circles. However, it appears that the issues surrounding the conversion procedure were not thoroughly thought through and many consequential problems now need to be addressed.[25] For example, imagine that a woman in a heterosexual marriage becomes pregnant. The couple decide that they would like to convert their marriage into a registered partnership. After the conversion is complete, the child is born. This has the consequence that, assuming the father has not recognised the child before the birth, the father of the child acquires no automatic paternity rights over the child, even though the child was conceived during a marriage and the same parties are still connected in a state-regulated institution which is equated in all but a few respects to that of marriage. Is it really justifiable that the father must then seek parental authority under the Art 252 procedure?[26] These issues have rarely been addressed in Dutch literature, and it is the author's opinion that this legal loophole needs to be tightened, or at the very least addressed by the legislature.

The possibility of such a conversion procedure allows for a married couple (whether of the same or different sex) effectively to divorce, if both parties are in agreement, within twenty-four hours. The question arises whether this form of dissolution is simply a form of administrative divorce.[27] Recent figures indicate a quadrupling in the number of heterosexual registered partnerships which coincides with the introduction of the conversion procedure from marriage to registered partnership.[28] Little research has been conducted in this field, although the Dutch Central Bureau for Statistics has agreed to look into whether it is possible to maintain statistics on the number of couples utilising this procedure.

The Minister of Justice has the impression that the number of dissolutions of a registered partnership after the conversion into a marriage is increasing. Nevertheless, he does not believe that the conversion of a marriage into a registered partnership necessarily leads to an impulsive divorce. After all, the only way to dissolve a registered partnership speedily is by an agreement to terminate.[29] The President of the Association for Family Lawyers has also stated that the number of such lightning divorces is on the decrease.[30]

---

[25] See C Forder, 'Spieghel Matrimoniael' (1999) 32 *Nederlandse Juristenblad* 1559–1560 and Wortmann, op cit, n 23 above; I Sumner, 'Transformers: Marriages in Disguise?' (2003) 1 *International Family Law* 15.

[26] Before being able to use the Art 252 procedure, the father must first recognise the child in accordance with Art 204, Book 1, Dutch Civil Code. He must apply under Art 253c, Book 1 but is not regarded as the father until he has recognised the child. The Art 252, Book 1 procedure requires both the parents of the child to register together with a county court registrar. It requires no court intervention, and the Registrar has only limited competency and cannot determine whether the parental authority order is in the best interests of the child. For more information, see the last *Survey* article *The International Survey of Family Law (2002 Edition)*, ed A Bainham (Family Law, 2002) at 278–282.

[27] See, *inter alia*, PMM Mostermans, 'De wederzijdse erkenning van echtscheidingen binnen de Europese Unie' (2002) 3 *Tijdschrift voor het Nederlands Internationaal Privaatrecht* 263–273.

[28] The number of heterosexual registered partnerships in 1998 was 1,616; in 1999, 1,495; in 2000, 1,322; 2001, 2,691; and up until July 2002, 3,445 heterosexual registered partnerships have already been celebrated.

[29] As provided for under Art 80c(c), Book 1, Dutch Civil Code in conjunction with Art 80d, Book 1, Dutch Civil Code.

[30] 'Flitscheiding stuk minder populair', *Algemeen Dagblad* (15 August 2002).

C Sham marriages

The Prevention of Sham Marriages Act, as discussed in earlier Surveys,[31] introduced into the Second Chamber on 28 October 1999, came into force on 1 April 2001.[32]

III PROPERTY RIGHTS ARISING THROUGH MARRIAGE OR REGISTERED PARTNERSHIP

A Act on the Rights and Duties of Spouses

The provisions of the Act on the Rights and Duties of Spouses are described in the 2001 Survey.[33] The Act[34] came into force on 22 June 2001.[35] The proposal in the Bill to amend the law regarding liability of spouses *inter se* for household costs[36] was abolished by amendment on 9 October 2000.[37] The government followed arguments put forward by academics that the proposed new Art 84 caused more problems than the old one. In particular, the new proposal was considered unduly complicated, especially in comparison with similar, but generally more global, provisions in neighbouring countries. It was not very likely that couples would understand the new rules.[38] Moreover the new rules could cause injustice when the husband was the main earner and the wife worked part-time, spending the majority of her time on child-care and home-making. Were the wife in this situation to inherit property under an exclusion clause, so that it was her own and not community property, the new rules could nevertheless require her to make her inheritance available to defray the household expenses. Under the present rules, which indicate the incomes of the spouses as the primary source for discharging household expenses, her inheritance would not normally be vulnerable. The government accepted the point that this change would achieve an unfair result.[39] The government accepted that it was attractive to try to find a way of recognising unpaid contributions made by a spouse who worked in the home

---

[31] *The International Survey of Family Law (2000 Edition)*, ed A Bainham (Family Law, 2000) at 240–253; *The International Survey of Family Law (2001 Edition)*, ed A Bainham (Family Law, 2001) at 301–304; *The International Survey of Family Law (2002 Edition)*, ed A Bainham (Family Law, 2002) at 278–282.

[32] *Staatsblad 2001,* nr 160, Besluit van 27 maart 2001 tot inwerkingtreding van de Wet van 13 december 2000, *Staatsblad 2001,* nr 11, tot wijziging van de regeling in boek 1 van het Burgerlijk Wetboek met betrekking tot het naamrecht, de voorkoming van schijnhuwelijken en het tijdstip van de totstandkoming van de scheiding van tafel en bed alsmede van enige andere wetten.

[33] Dutch report, *The International Survey of Family Law (2001 Edition)*, ed A Bainham (Family Law, 2001) at 306–312.

[34] Act of 31 May 2001, *Staatsblad 2001*, nr 275.

[35] Ibid, Art III.

[36] Dutch report, *The International Survey of Family Law (2001 Edition)*, ed A Bainham (Family Law, 2001) at 309–310.

[37] Second Chamber, 2000–2001, 27 084, nr 6.

[38] Gr Van der Burght (2000) 6409 *Weekblad voor Privaatrecht, Notariaat en Registratie* 493–501, especially at 498.

[39] Second Chamber, 2000–2001, 27 084, nr 5, p 11.

rather than in paid work, but could not find any satisfactory legal form for achieving this through adjustment to Art 84.[40] Finally, it was recognised that Art 84 had in many cases little or no practical significance.

In debate in the Second Chamber, objections continued to be raised against the abolition of the duty of spouses to live together.[41] These arguments were expounded in the 2001 Survey.[42] This issue was also extensively discussed in the First Chamber.[43] The government maintained its position on this point that abolition of the duty of spouses to cohabit was in accordance with the modern, somewhat business-like way in which marriage is regulated in law.[44]

There was fierce debate about the proposed abolition of Art 85. Article 85, Book 1, Dutch Civil Code makes spouses jointly and severally liable vis-à-vis third parties for each other's debts incurred in the course of the 'ordinary running of the household'. That provision, and the proposal for its abolition, is described in the 2001 Survey.[45] Against abolition it was argued strongly that the protection offered to third parties was not a dead letter; there was even a tendency in case-law to extend the provision to, for example, dental and medical treatment. Third parties might be more ready to extend credit in doubtful cases if they knew that both spouses would be liable.[46] An amendment to reinstate the joint liability of spouses was accepted by the Second Chamber.[47] Arguments on behalf of the government that the provision secured an outdated protection of the more economically vulnerable married woman in the 1950s[48] did not carry the day. The question why this special protection should be available to third parties dealing with a married person, whilst not extended to a third party dealing with an unmarried (though cohabiting) person, was not answered.

B   Act on Contractual Participation Clauses

This Act is the second is a series of three concerned with modernisation of the law of matrimonial property. The first is the Act on the Rights and Duties of Spouses, discussed above. The third will amend the basic matrimonial system of property which applies in default of any contractual provision and will introduce an

---

[40]   Second Chamber, 2000–2001, 27 084, nr 5, pp 12–13; nr 10, p 15 (Cohen).

[41]   Second Chamber, 2000–2001, 27 084, nr 7 (Van der Staaij and others); nr 10, pp 3–4, 9–11 (Van der Staaij (SPG) Schutte (RPF/GPV)); Second Chamber, 32–2721–2 (Van der Staaij).

[42]   Dutch report, *The International Survey of Family Law (2001 Edition)*, ed A Bainham (Family Law, 2001) at 308–309.

[43]   First Chamber, 2000–2001, 27 084, nr 152a and 152b; First Chamber, 22 May 2001, 30–1377–1382.

[44]   Second Chamber, 2000–2001, 27 084, nr 10, pp 12–15 (Staatssecretaris Cohen); Second Chamber, 6 December 2000, 32–2723–2726; First Chamber, 22 May 2001, 30–1382–1387 (Staatssecretaris Kalsbeek).

[45]   Dutch report, *The International Survey of Family Law (2001 Edition)*, ed A Bainham (Family Law, 2001) at 311.

[46]   Second Chamber, 2000–2001, 27 084, nr 10, p 5 (Vos, VVD), 15; Second Chamber, 6 December 2000, 32–2723.

[47]   Second Chamber, 2000–2001, 27 084, nr 9 (Vos); Second Chamber, 12 December 2000, 34–2815 (votes).

[48]   Second Chamber, 6 December 2000, 32–2724 (Cohen).

alternative basic system. The Act on Contractual Participation Clauses was passed on 14 March 2002,[49] and came into force on 1 September 2002.[50]

The Act introduces a statutory system for contractual participation claims between spouses and registered partners. The statutory regulation of participation in the profits accumulated during marriage is abolished, and the new regulation takes its place in the Civil Code in Book 1, Title 8, s 2. The system which was abolished was a specific form of contractual participation, by which the spouses, who owned no common or joint property during the marriage, bound themselves in contract to share any increase in value in their respective goods. The reform introduced by the Act responds to a change in practice of married couples. In the 1950s and 1960s, only 8% of couples-to-be entered a marriage contract regulating property rights at all; the vast majority allowed their property rights to be regulated by the statutory community of property system which applies in default. At the end of the 1970s, pre-marriage contracts regulating property became more popular; in 1970, 10.5% of couples made such a contract, but in 1996, the number was 28%. Within that group of couples concluding a pre-marriage contract excluding the system of community of property, the most popular construction was total exclusion of all community of property. In 1970, 61% of couples concluding a pre-marriage contract did so in order to exclude all community of property. At that time contractual participation schemes were used in 14% of all cases of couples concluding a pre-marriage contract. But after 1975, contractual participation schemes became more popular: in 1996, 73% of all pre-marriage contracts featured contractual participation schemes.[51]

The attraction of exclusion of community of property is that it ensures that inherited property does not leave the family via marriage (and, in particular, marriage followed by divorce) and it protects one spouse in the event of bankruptcy of the business of the other. However, one serious disadvantage is that a spouse who is not economically active during the marriage can end up empty-handed at the end of the marriage. To deal with this problem, notaries developed clauses which excluded community of property but provided for some participation in the profits accrued by both spouses during the marriage. This rejoices in the name of the 'Amsterdam contractual participation clause', of which a new version, developed in the 1950s, is also extant. In the original Amsterdam clause the parties would divide all surplus assets present at the end of the marriage, not being assets brought in by inheritance or gift. This scheme received the blessing of the Dutch Supreme Court in 1944.[52] In the new Amsterdam clause the division of surplus assets should take place on an annual basis. It was realised even then that spouses probably would not insist on division of assets at the end of each year. But it was considered important that each had the possibility to request

---

[49]   *Staatsblad 2002*, nr 152 (K 27 554).

[50]   Besluit van 3 juli 2002, houdende vaststelling van het tijdstip van inwerkingtreding van de wet van 14 maart 2002, tot wijziging van Boek 1 van het Burgerlijk wetboek (regels verrekenbedingen) (*Staatsblad 2002*, nr 152), *Staatsblad 2002*, nr 370.

[51]   MJA Van Mourik, 'De ontwikkeling in de praktijk der huwelijkse voorwaarden', (1998) 6302 *Weekblad voor Privaatrecht, Notariaat en Registratie* 17; Second Chamber, 2000–2001, 27 554, nr 3, p 5.

[52]   Dutch Supreme Court, 21 January 1944, *Nederlandse Jurisprudentie* 1944, 45 (Van de Water-Van Hemme).

such division. Where division did take place it had the dual effect of enabling each spouse gradually to build up some private resources and furthermore it gave the spouse who was not in paid employment a measure of independence. The Amsterdam clause is an example of a final contractual participation clause (because participation only happens at the end of the relationship) and the new Amsterdam clause is an example of a periodic contractual participation clause. In both cases there is no community of property. The clauses described represent a broad general form; in notarial practice an infinite number of permutations are possible.

The new provisions are divided into three sections: Part One regulates general rules regarding contractual participation schemes. Parts Two and Three cover periodic and final contractual participation clauses respectively. The Civil Code only regulates matters regarding contractual participation clauses which can apply to all cases: aspects which vary from case to case are not provided for in the Civil Code. For example, the Civil Code does not specify whether the contractual participation applies to earned or unearned income; that is a matter for the parties to each marriage to decide. The provisions included in the Code are thus applicable to all forms of contractual participation clause, whether relating to earned or unearned income.[53] Most of the provisions may be excluded expressly or implicitly by the pre-marriage contract. Furthermore, it is provided that certain matters can be varied by simple contract; the parties are not bound in this case to the formal requirements applying to the making of a pre-marriage contract. Thus, in the situation of divorce, the parties can vary by simple contract the moments in time suggested in Art 142 of Book 1, Dutch Civil Code for determining the extent and content of the property in which both spouses are to participate. A number of provisions cannot be varied by the parties. These are: first, the power to request from the other spouse an annual, written overview of assets.[54] If this provision is excluded, the whole operation of participation can be thwarted. Secondly, the power to request termination of the obligation to participate cannot be excluded; nor can the power to request damages.[55] Thirdly, the power to request a payment provision[56] may not be excluded. This applies when one spouse is in financial difficulties and requires a special arrangement to spread or otherwise ease the burden of the payments. Fourthly, the limitation period applicable to contractual participation claims[57] cannot be excluded. Fifthly, the power to request a description of goods subject to the participation scheme[58] cannot be excluded. Just like the first provision, an exclusion of this provision would undermine the whole scheme.

Contractual participation clauses have generated considerable case-law in the last few years. Most persistent have been disputes regarding what should happen when the spouses, contrary to the contractual provisions, have not periodically shared in the increase in value of their respective properties, but wish to do so

---

[53]   Second Chamber, 2000–2001, 27 554, nr 3, p 11.
[54]   Article 138(2), Book 1, Dutch Civil Code.
[55]   Article 139(2) and (3), ibid.
[56]   Article 140(1) and (2), ibid.
[57]   Article 141(6), ibid.
[58]   Article 143(1)–(3), ibid.

when the relationship breaks down. The Dutch Supreme Court held in 1985 that the clause could be complied with by the man saving all the assets in his name throughout the marriage; a reasonable interpretation of the clause implied that these savings should be divided on breakdown.[59] Similarly, if the parties had contracted under the new Amsterdam clause, but had not divided any assets during the marriage, the Dutch Supreme Court held it was reasonable to make the division at the end of the marriage.[60] Difficult questions were raised in various cases regarding the applicability or not of various provisions in the Civil Code when one or other Amsterdam clause was used.[61] There was uncertainty as to whether, if the division of assets did not take place, the spouse who had invested his property was also liable to share the profits of investment as well as the assets themselves.[62] The Dutch Supreme Court had to lay down limits regarding the validity of a clause which provided, when periodic division of assets was stipulated by the parties but had not taken place, for lapse of the right to request division.[63] It is expected and hoped that the codification of this case-law in the new provisions will provide some clarity regarding the limits of contractual freedom in this field and, at the very least, will not lead to any increase in the work-load of the judiciary.[64]

A brief exposition of the general principles which apply to contractual participation clauses under the new rules follows. These provisions may be deviated from in the pre-marriage contract. The provisions from which deviation is not possible have already been mentioned. The starting point is that of mutuality; both parties must have equal access to the assets subject to the duty to divide.[65] The underlying idea is that the assets should benefit the spouses equally. The same rationale underlies the provision that the division should be equal.[66] A spouse who, in the process of division, deliberately conceals property which should be divided, is obliged to compensate the other spouse.[67] The participation scheme applies only to property acquired during the existence of the duty to divide; thus property already existing before the marriage and inherited and gifted property is not subject to the scheme.[68] A testator or benefactor is entitled to

---

[59] Dutch Supreme Court, 15 February 1985, *Nederlandse Jurisprudentie 1985*, 885, annotation Luijten.

[60] Dutch Supreme Court, 7 April 1995, *Nederlandse Jurisprudentie 1996*, 486, annotation Kleijn (Vossen-Swinkels); Dutch Supreme Court, 19 January 1996, *Nederlandse Jurisprudentie 1996*, 617, annotation Kleijn (Rensing-Polak); Dutch Supreme Court, 28 March 1997, *Nederlandse Jurisprudentie 1997*, 581, annotation Kleijn; Dutch Supreme Court, 3 October 1997, *Nederlandse Jurisprudentie 1998*, 383, annotation Kleijn (Bal-Keller).

[61] Dutch Supreme Court, 23 October 1981, *Nederlandse Jurisprudentie 1982*, 256, annotation Luijten; Dutch Supreme Court, 7 April 1995, *Nederlandse Jurisprudentie 1996*, 486, annotation Kleijn (Vossen-Swinkels); MJA van Mourik, 'Het periodiek verrekenbeding op orde gebracht', (1995) 6188 *Weekblad voor Privaatrecht, Notariaat en Registratie*.

[62] Dutch Supreme Court, 3 October 1997, *Nederlandse Jurisprudentie 1998*, 383 (Bal-Keller).

[63] Dutch Supreme Court, 18 February 1994, *Nederlandse Jurisprudentie 1994*, 463, annotation Kleijn; Dutch Supreme Court, 19 January 1996, *Nederlandse Jurisprudentie 1996*, 617, annotation Kleijn (Rensing-Polak).

[64] Second Chamber, 2000–2001, 27 554, nr 3, p 10.

[65] Article 133(1), Book 1, Dutch Civil Code.

[66] Article 135(1), ibid.

[67] Article 135(2), ibid.

[68] Article 133(2), ibid.

provide that the property he or she gives is not to be subject to any contractual participation obligation between the spouses.[69] Provision is made for the circumstances in which an asset which should have been divided has in fact been alienated. If the alienation takes place for value, the goods which are bought with that money may in some circumstances be brought under the duty to divide.[70] In principle, the division should take place with money, but in certain circumstances a division of goods in kind may take place.[71] In particular, it might in some circumstances be unacceptable to sell the matrimonial home in order to satisfy the obligation to divide. This might occur where one spouse needs the home in order to bring up the children and that spouse is able to pay the outgoings and continue the mortgage repayment whilst the other spouse has no special reason to insist on sale.[72] A division of goods in kind can only be requested by one spouse, or imposed upon the other spouse, if the circumstances are such that a payment in money would be unacceptable in the light of standards of reasonableness and fairness.[73] One spouse is not liable to the other for the way in which he or she manages his or her property. Poor management of property does not give rise to any liability to pay damages.[74] A corollary of this lack of responsibility for management is that it must be possible for one spouse to terminate the duty to share if the other spouse is incurring unreasonable debts, wasting assets or failing to provide information regarding the property.[75] In these circumstances, the disadvantaged spouse does have the right to be compensated by the other for his or her losses.[76]

The Dutch Supreme Court's case-law regarding the situation when division has not taken place when it should have done, is codified in Art 141, Book 1, Dutch Civil Code. In principle the property which should have been divided, but has not been, will be the subject of a division at the end of the relationship: a periodic participation clause is thus treated in these circumstances as a final participation clause. However, other property might be included in this later division if such is required by considerations of reasonableness and fairness.[77] The obligation to divide is not extinguished earlier than three years from the end of the marriage. The parties cannot agree to a shorter period.[78] Because divorce can be a very emotional period, a period for consideration of such an important matter as division of assets accumulated throughout the marriage should not be subject to shortening.[79]

---

[69]   Article 134, Book 1, Dutch Civil Code.
[70]   Article 136, ibid.
[71]   Article 137, ibid.
[72]   Second Chamber, 2000–2001, 27 554, nr 3, p 15.
[73]   Second Chamber, 2001–2002, 27 554, nr 5, pp 10–11; nr 6.
[74]   Article 138(1), ibid.
[75]   Article 139, ibid.
[76]   Article 139(2), ibid.
[77]   Article 141(3), Book 1, Dutch Civil Code; Second Chamber, 2001–2002, 27 554, nr 5, pp 12–13; nr 6.
[78]   Article 141(6), Book 1, Dutch Civil Code.
[79]   Second Chamber, 2000–2001, 27 554, nr 3, pp 17–18.

Many of the criticisms of the Act on Contractual Participation Clauses[80] are connected with the complexity of putting a relatively simple idea into practice. The kind of complexity is illustrated by recent case-law of the Dutch Supreme Court. On 2 March 2001 the Dutch Supreme Court gave judgment in a fishing business case.[81] The parties had contracted to exclude all community of property, but had provided, on the basis of the Amsterdam clause, that there would be division of the assets built up by the parties during the marriage. The assets had not been divided during the marriage. The court accepted that the husband's assets, which included active shares in his fishing business, should be brought into the division. The question was how this should be done. The duty to divide includes not only assets accumulated, but also the profits of any investments made with such assets. The Dutch Supreme Court held that a clause purporting to exclude reliance upon a claim to divide assets after a period of time had elapsed, could only be relied upon where such was fair and reasonable. The court rejected the husband's claim to invoke that clause; there were no circumstances justifying reliance upon it. However, the court stressed that the spouses' liability to divide was always subject to the principles of reasonableness and fairness. This meant, in particular, that the wife could not expect the husband to sell his business in order to achieve maximum realisation of his assets. (The wife had led the unprepossessing argument that the husband was the oldest fisherman in the fleet and could therefore be expected to retire.) A crucial argument was the method by which the value of the fishing business should be calculated. The wife argued for liquidation value; this would be the maximum valuation. But since the court had rejected the argument that the husband should be expected to cease his business, it was logical to reject the argument that his liability to divide assets should be founded on a valuation which assumed that he had sold the business. The valuation preferred by the court was the yield value. This was the lowest valuation. The court held that it was necessary to use this conservative valuation as the husband's earnings were determined to a decisive extent by fishing quotas. The amount of these fishing quotas were impossible to predict as they were determined by European Union and national fishing policy. Furthermore, considerations of reasonableness and fairness meant that the wife's claim to division could never extend so far that the husband would be required to make a payment which would place the husband's source of livelihood in jeopardy. In applying this principle, it was reasonable to take account of any future developments possibly causing a decrease in the yield of the business, in particular, a possible lowering in fishing quotas in the future.

In a case decided by the Dutch Supreme Court on 26 October 2001, the dispute was about the date at which the goods to be divided should be valued.[82] The parties were married under exclusion of all community of property, but they

---

[80] For critical comments on the Act, see: LCA Verstappen, 'Naar nieuwe verrekenstelsels (I)' (2000) 6387 *Weekblad voor Privaatrecht, Notariaat en Registratie* 67–72, and (2000) 6388 *Weekblad voor Privaatrecht, Notariaat en Registratie* 92–95; Gr van der Burght, 'Wetsvoorstel nieuw huwelijksvermogensrecht: Beter laat dan nooit, maar toch te vroeg (I)' (2001) 6437 *Weekblad voor Privaatrecht, Notariaat en Registratie* 251–259, (2001) 6438 *Weekblad voor Privaatrecht, Notariaat en Registratie* 277–280.

[81] *Nederlandse Jurisprudentie 2001*, 583 and 584, annotation Wortmann.

[82] *Nederlandse Jurisprudentie 2002*, 93, annotation Kleijn.

had contracted an Amsterdam clause, which required them to divide from time to time the assets acquired during the marriage. No division had ever taken place. During the marriage the parties had bought their first house in the husband's sole name and financed by a mortgage in the husband's name. The first house was sold for a price far above the price originally paid; partly with this profit the couple bought their second house which was in both names. The question arose as to the date at which the property should be valued; in particular whether the increase in value of the first house should be included in the division of assets. The general principle that the relationship between the parties is governed by the principles of reasonableness and fairness does not provide a good indication for the answer to such a specific question. The Dutch Supreme Court noted that, although the parties were bound to share the assets accumulated during the marriage on an annual basis, they had not done so. Nor had either of them kept a track of their financial matters in order to facilitate such division at a later date. The court held that the principles of reasonableness and fairness implied that the parties are bound to divide, in accordance with the contractual participation clause, assets acquired during the marriage when it cannot be established that the parties or a third party had the intention that that asset should be in the sole property of one of the spouses. In principle, it is reasonable to assume, if the parties have made no provision to the contrary, that the property was acquired in consequence of investment of income which should have been divided. In practice, this meant that the husband was obliged to share the extra value of the first house with his wife. The Supreme Court remarked that the first house, although transferred into the husband's name, was bought on a mortgage paid off by their joint incomes.[83] Moreover, the profits made on sale of the first house were used to buy a second house in joint names. In these circumstances, the Supreme Court could see no indication that the parties had any other intention than that the profits of the house should ultimately accrue to husband and wife jointly.

C   Act on Conflicts of Law arising in cases of Pension Adjustment

On 1 May 1995, new pension adjustment rules after divorce came into force.[84] Under the old law, upon the death of a spouse, the surviving spouse had an automatic right to a share of any pension accumulated during the lifetime of the deceased.[85] The Pension Adjustment After Divorce Act (hereafter called the PAADA) extended these rules to divorced couples, albeit only with limited rights being extended to the divorcée on the pension accumulated during the marriage by the other spouse. However, in many cases the question concerning the applicable law began to arise when spouses, either by virtue of their nationality or by virtue of their place of residence, had connections to a country other than the Netherlands. Take a married couple, married in accordance with the law of a country other than the Netherlands, who move to and take up residence in

---

[83]   This conclusion was remarkable, as neither the court of first instance nor the Court of Appeal had concluded this from the facts.

[84]   Wet verevening pensioenrechten bij scheiding, *Staatsblad 1991*, nr 628.

[85]   *Tractatenblad 1988*, nr 130 (14 March 1978). Ratified by the Netherlands and came into force through the Wet Conflictenrecht Huwelijksvermogensregime, *Staatsblad 1991*, nr 628.

the Netherlands. They begin working there and build up their pension schemes in the Netherlands. What is the applicable law regulating the pension adjustment after divorce? According to the original pension scheme rules, the answer was left open. However, since the enactment of the Act on the Conflict of Laws arising in cases of Pension Adjustment,[86] based on proposals of the *Staatscommissie*,[87] new provisions lay down rules to deal with these situations. A new Art 10a, PAADA provides that, in the case of a divorce where one party has the right to a share of the pension scheme built up by the other spouse, the applicable law is the same as that applicable to the matrimonial property scheme. The Act came into force on 1 March 2001. The law deals only with marriages;[88] the international private law aspects of registered partnership are to be dealt with separately.[89]

IV MAINTENANCE OBLIGATIONS

A Marriage is the basis of the maintenance obligation

When is a marriage not a marriage? For some purposes, in particular immigration, the civil status registrar may refuse to register a marriage contracted with no other objective than to obtain a right of residence. Furthermore, such marriage may, even after it has been contracted, be declared null and void.[90] But it is no defence to an action for spousal maintenance that both parties contracted the marriage with no other intention than to evade immigration laws by providing the husband with a right of residence, even though there was no consummation and the parties never lived together. The Dutch Supreme Court held on 1 February 2002 on these facts that as long as the marriage had not been declared null and void it was valid for the purposes of bringing a maintenance obligation into existence.[91] The Supreme Court rejected an argument that the maintenance obligation came into effect only if the spouses could be shown to care for one another, to live together or otherwise run a joint household. And it was certainly not the case that it was necessary to demonstrate that there is a causal connection between the way in which the parties have organised their lives during the marriage and the reduced earning capacity of the partner seeking maintenance support. Those factors were all relevant for determining the extent of the obligation, in value and in time, but were not relevant for determining whether there was any obligation at all.[92] The Supreme Court was unimpressed by the fact that the administrative court had concluded

---

[86] Wet conflictenrecht pensioenverevening, Wet van 13 december 2000, *Staatsblad 2000*, nr 4.

[87] Advies inzake pensioenverevening (Staatscommissie, April 1998).

[88] Since the Dutch definition of marriage has been altered in Art 1:30, this provision is equally valid for same-sex marriages, as for opposite-sex marriages.

[89] Advies inzake geregistreerd partnerschap (Staatscommissie, May 1998).

[90] Articles 51 ff, Book 1, Dutch Civil Code. See Dutch report, *The International Survey of Family Law (2001 Edition)*, ed A Bainham (Family Law, 2001) at 304–306 and Dutch report, *The International Survey of Family Law (2000 Edition)*, ed A Bainham (Family Law, 2001), at 252–253.

[91] *Nederlandse Jurisprudentie* 2001, 171.

[92] See also Dutch Supreme Court, 9 February 2001, *Nederlandse Jurisprudentie* 2001, 216, annotation Wortmann.

that the marriage was a sham for immigration purposes and for the purposes of social security liability. The orders of the administrative court did not in any way undermine the fact that the marriage was valid for civil law purposes unless and until declared void. The defendant argued that, since the declaration by the immigration court that he should leave the Netherlands, he was obliged to live in the underworld and that he had no access to the employment market. It was therefore unreasonable, argued the defendant, for the civil court to order him to pay maintenance. In the Supreme Court's view, this point was relevant to the extent of liability, but not to the existence of the obligation.

B   No termination of ex-husband's maintenance obligation in consequence of cohabitation with a married man

According to Art 160, Book 1, Dutch Civil Code, the liability of an ex-spouse to pay partner maintenance terminates automatically when the ex-spouse in receipt of maintenance marries or registers a partnership, or lives with another person as if they were married or had registered a partnership. The approach of the Dutch Supreme Court to the question whether the ex-spouse is living together with another within the meaning of Art 160, is, in the light of the very drastic consequences, notoriously restrictive.[93] Thus, the Dutch Supreme Court recently held that, if a wife who is in receipt of maintenance starts living with a married man, she cannot be said to be living with another person as if they were married. The Supreme Court reiterated its earlier position that cohabitation within the meaning of Art 160 implies that the cohabitants have an emotional relationship of enduring character and that the partners care for each other, live together and have a joint household. In short, the relationship should have the characteristics of commitment associated with a normal marriage.[94] The intention of the parties in this case was not to live together permanently, but merely to provide the married man with accommodation in a period during which he was looking for a new place to live. The very short period of living together – a total of four months – and its limited purpose indicated that in this case the comparison with marriage was inappropriate. Furthermore, the parliamentary history of Art 160 indicated that the purpose of including under Art 160 the situation in which the person in receipt of maintenance was living with another, was to avoid such a person having an incentive to cohabit rather than to re-marry. However, if the new partner is married, the wife in receipt of maintenance has no option but to cohabit, since her chosen new partner is simply unavailable for marriage. In this case the new partner had no intention of divorcing his wife, who was a psychiatric patient.

The Dutch Supreme Court pointed out that the fact that the wife is living with another man is a circumstance which the court is entitled to take into account when determining the extent of her need for maintenance in accordance with Art 157 of Book 1. Moreover, the court has power, under Art 401 of Book 1,

---

[93]   Article 160 is discussed in the Dutch Report, *The International Survey of Family Law 1994*, ed A Bainham (Martinus Nijhoff, 1996), at 355–356.

[94]   Dutch Supreme Court, 2 April 1982, *Nederlandse Jurisprudentie 1982*, 374; conclusie A-G Franx in Dutch Supreme Court, 10 April 1981, *Nederlandse Jurisprudentie 1981*, 348; Dutch Supreme Court, 25 November 1994, *Nederlandse Jurisprudentie 1995*, 299, annotation de Boer.

Dutch Civil Code, to adjust maintenance liability in the light of changed circumstances affecting the needs of the person in receipt of maintenance. The court added that it was preferable to take account of it in this way, rather than under Art 160, as the court is able to take account of all the specific circumstances of the case and to reach a decision in the light thereof.[95]

Given that the court has this flexible jurisdiction under Art 401 of Book 1, Dutch Civil Code to take account of any new developments indicating a change in the needs of the person receiving maintenance, it is far from evident that Art 160, Book 1 is needed at all. Moreover, the restrictive interpretation of Art 160 by the Dutch Supreme Court in the above case and a list of other cases has reduced it more or less to a dead letter. Many other legal systems do quite well without such a provision.[96] The Dutch government has said, in response to remarks in Parliament during the introduction of legislation on marriage, that it will review the operation of Art 160, Book 1, Dutch Civil Code.[97] Advice is now being sought from the Dutch Society for Case-Law and the Dutch Order of Advocates.

C   Maintenance obligation of mother's female partner

The Dutch Supreme Court passed judgment on 10 August 2001 on the question whether the mother's female partner could be held liable to pay maintenance in respect of the child born five years earlier to the mother. The two women had had a relationship of ten years' standing and, after five years, they had together arranged the conception and birth of the child who was born to the plaintiff, and they had together brought up the child for five years. When the couple separated the defendant denied that she was liable to pay maintenance. According to Art 394, Book 1 of the Civil Code, a man who consents to his female partner receiving artificial insemination treatment can be sued for maintenance of the child. Because that provision refers to a 'man', the birth mother's female partner who consented to artificial insemination cannot be sued for maintenance. The Supreme Court noted that the question had already been raised in Parliament when the Bill was being debated, and that the Parliament was informed that the provision did not include a woman. The Dutch Supreme Court confirmed that there was no provision of international law leading to another result. The court maintained the argument that, in the absence of provision by the legislator, a maintenance obligation could only be based upon marriage or partnership or a blood tie or something which could have been a blood tie.

The Supreme Court rejected an argument that there was relationship of 'family life' within the meaning of Art 8 of the European Convention on the Protection of Human Rights and Fundamental Freedoms (ECHR) between the two women. Family life was alleged to arise from the fact that the women had lived together as partners for more than ten years and had given birth to and cared for a child together for more than five years. The interpretation of family life by the

---

[95]   Dutch Supreme Court, 13 July 2001, *Nederlandse Jurisprudentie 2001*, 586, consideration 3.5.

[96]   For example, Sweden: A Agell, 'Samenwonen zonder huwelijk', in CD Saal and CJ Straver (eds), *Samenleven in meervoud, juridische en sociologische aspecten van het samenwonen zonder huwelijk* (1981, Samson sociale en culturele reeks, Alphen aan de Rijn/Brussel) at 192–214.

[97]   First Chamber, 2000–2001, 27 084, nr 152a, p 2.

Dutch Supreme Court such that the lesbian co-parents are excluded is highly questionable. Despite the fact that the issue concerned maintenance, and therefore did normally fall within the scope of 'family life' in Art 8 of the ECHR, the court allowed itself to be distracted by the lesbian character of the relationship which the court saw as a reason to negate 'family life'. Because the Supreme Court concluded that the relationship did not fall under the protection of Art 8 of the ECHR, the Supreme Court did not have to consider the discrimination argument based on Art 14 of the ECHR. Article 14 of the ECHR does not apply to a situation of fact not falling within the scope of another Article of the Convention.[98] It is regrettable that the applicants did not allege violation of Art 26 of the International Covenant on Civil and Political Rights (ICCPR), which is an independent discrimination provision applicable regardless of whether the subject-matter of the claim falls under another Article of the ICCPR.[99] It is equally difficult to appreciate why the Supreme Court did not apply Art 26 of the ICCPR of its own motion.[100] In our view this question should be run again under the Twelfth Protocol of the ECHR when it comes into force.[101] That protocol provides protection from discrimination in situations of fact not covered by another Article of the ECHR.

The Swedish Commission on Children in Homosexual Families recommended in 2001 that, if the female partner of the birth mother consents to donor insemination which results in the birth of a child and subsequently the partner denies that she is the child's parent, it should be possible for the birth mother to apply to the court for an order establishing that the partner is the parent of her child or establishing liability for maintenance.[102]

V PARENTHOOD BY DESCENT

A Right to know one's origins

The Bill on Storage and Disclosure of Information on Gamete Donors, described in the 2000 Survey,[103] was passed on 25 May 2001[104] and will be brought into force in stages by statutory instrument. The provisions of Art 3 regulating disclosure of identifying information about the donor[105] will come into force on 29 May 2004.[106]

---

[98] Dutch Supreme Court, 10 August 2001, *Nederlandse Jurisprudentie 2002*, 278, annotation Jan de Boer.

[99] Opened for signature in New York on 18 December 1966.

[100] Annotation Jan de Boer, under the Supreme Court's decision in *Nederlandse Jurisprudentie 2002*, 278.

[101] Opened for signature on 4 November 2000, *Tractatenblad 2001*, nr 18. Ratification by the Netherlands is pending (K 28 100(R 1705)).

[102] SOU 2001:10, p 14.

[103] Dutch report, *The International Survey of Family Law (2000 Edition)*, ed A Bainham (Family Law, 2000), 256–261.

[104] *Staatsblad 2002*, nr 240.

[105] Article 3(2), second sentence, and (3)–(5).

[106] Act of 25 May 2002, *Staatsblad 2002*, nr 240, Art 14.

In the 2000 *Survey*, it was mentioned that the government would commission research to examine the likely effects upon prospective sperm donors of disclosure of identifying information regarding the donor.[107] This research was submitted to the Second Chamber of Parliament in September 1999.[108] At present, there are some 500 sperm donors in the Netherlands: 433 'A' donors (anonymous) and 71 'B' donors (who disclose their identity). The research shows a difference in the motives for the men to become sperm donors. Category 'B' donors, in contrast to category 'A' donors, are more frequently single, and have themselves no children and often do not wish for them. Regarding all donors and potential donors,[109] the most commonly given reason for being a donor was to help someone else to have a child. The research tried to estimate what the effect would be upon the willingness of men to come forward as donor after introduction of the Act on disclosure of information regarding sperm donation. Of those interviewed, who are at present acting as sperm donors, 50% said that after the Act had come into force they would not be prepared to be a sperm donor any more. One third of those presently acting as sperm donors said that they would be prepared to continue acting as donor after the Act came into force. The results also indicate that the provisions of the Act are not well known or well understood. A publicity campaign may have a positive effect upon the willingness of men to act as sperm donors.

B   Act regulating conflicts of law in cases in which parenthood by descent is at issue

In cases where parenthood by descent is at stake, current practice refers all cases to a judge whose answer is characterised by the use of unwritten rules and an absence of argumentation. However, on 14 March 2002, the government passed a long-awaited codification of the private international law rules related to such issues.[110] The aim of this codification was to fill the lacuna for the Registrar of Births, Deaths and Marriages and to codify the current case-law in the field. The Act itself, as suggested by a report written jointly by the *Staatscommissie* and the Permanent Commission for cases involving civil status and nationality,[111] is divided into 13 Articles, subdivided into five chapters. The first chapter deals with the situation of parenthood by descent in relation to married or divorced couples; the second with parenthood by recognition or judicial determination of fatherhood; and the third with parenthood by legitimation.

Article 1 lays down a three-tier hierarchical system for the applicable law in cases where the parenthood of a child is in question. Since the birth mother is

---

[107]   Dutch report, *The International Survey of Family Law (2000 Edition)*, ed A Bainham (Family Law, 2000), 261.

[108]   M den Otter, M Trommelen and G van der Veen, *Bereidheid tot donatie van sperma bij opheffing van anonimiteitswaarborg* (September 1999, ZorgOnderzoek Nederland/Zon, SWOKW).

[109]   This was simply a random selection of men whose names were chosen from the telephone directory and who were in the relevant age group: p 17 of the report.

[110]   A number of cases (Dutch Supreme Court, 31 January 1992, *Nederlandse Jurisprudentie 1993*, 261, and Dutch Supreme Court, 7 November 1997, *Rechtspraak van de Week 1997*, 217) highlighted the need for legislation in this field.

[111]   Second Chamber, 2001–2002, 26 675, nr 3.

under Dutch law always considered to be the legal mother,[112] this Article really in effect only refers to questions relating to fatherhood. If the man and wife have a common nationality then this is to be regarded as the applicable law.[113] In its absence, the applicable law will be the law of the state where the man and woman have their habitual residence, or if this is also absent then the state of habitual residence of the child. The same law is also to be applied to the question of whether such a decision can be annulled.[114] If the parties are not married then the parenthood of the child is determined according to the law of the birth mother's nationality.[115]

In cases involving the recognition of a judicial determination of paternity, a similar hierarchical system of applicable law is applied. Reference is made in the first place to the law of the state of the man's nationality, followed in its absence by the law of the state of the habitual residence of the child. If this is also absent, then the law of the state of the child's nationality determines questions relating to parenthood.[116]

The legitimation of a child by reason of the marriage of one of his or her parents, or by reason of a subsequent decision of a legal or another competent authority, is determined by reference to the 1970 Rome Agreement.[117] An irrevocable foreign legal decision, whereby the parenthood by reason of parentage is determined or changed, will always be recognised in the Netherlands, unless:

(1)   there appears to be insufficient connection with the Netherlands to found the jurisdiction of the Dutch judge;
(2)   there is evident lack of research or argumentation undertaken; or
(3)   the recognition of the decision would be contrary to the public policy of the Netherlands.[118]

Such an Act is long overdue and provides the necessary clarity needed in this field, even if it is slightly unfortunate that such a complicated system of hierarchical conflicts of law rules has been chosen. The decisions previous to the Act had brought a somewhat arbitrary feeling to this field of law, which this Act will hopefully begin to dispel.

C   Mixed case-law on the establishment of parenthood

As already stated in the previous section, motherhood is almost always ascertainable. Fatherhood, on the other hand, is a more complicated issue. The new parentage rules introduced on 1 April 1998 have created a system of legal

---

[112]   Article 198, Book 1, Dutch Civil Code.
[113]   If the husband and wife have more than one common nationality, then Art 1(3) determines that they are deemed to have no common nationality.
[114]   Article 2(1), Wet conflictenrecht afstamming, *Staatsblad 2002*, nr 153.
[115]   Article 3(1), ibid.
[116]   Article 4(1), ibid.
[117]   *Tractatenblad 1972*, nr 61 (10 December 1970).
[118]   Article 9(1), Wet conflictenrecht afstamming, *Staatsblad 2002*, nr 153.

paternity which gives strong emphasis to the blood link.[119] The new rules, as discussed in previous Survey reports,[120] extended the father's rights in a number of determinate fields. For example, old Art 224(1) had required a father to obtain the mother's consent before he was able to recognise the child. Article 204(3) codified the case-law from the Dutch Supreme Court and gave the court the power to substitute the mother's consent. This provision has recently been tested in two Supreme Court cases.

In a case before the Supreme Court on 16 February 2001, the parties had had a relationship from October 1995 until the end of 1997, during which time they had cohabited for one and a half years.[121] In 1998, after the break-up of the relationship, a child was born. The father, who wanted to recognise the child, submitted a claim on the basis of Art 1:204(3) of the Dutch Civil Code.[122] The district court allowed the request and the mother appealed. The Court of Appeal in Amsterdam stated that:

> 'The father of a child, who is born outside of a marriage, is he who recognises the child. For a recognition to be valid the father needs the permission of the mother. Art 1:204(3) of the Civil Code grants the man, who is the begetter of the child and to whom the mother bestows no permission, a procedural right. The begetter can, when the conditions of Art 1:204(3) of the Civil Code are satisfied, request that the permission be substituted by that of a district court. The basic assumption in this procedure is that both the child and the begetter are aware that the recognition will have consequences for their parentage relationship. It is in this light not reasonable for the mother to ban the father from the child's life.'[123]

The mother made three claims in her appeal case of which the first is of most interest. She claimed that the Court of Appeal had misunderstood the weighting of the interests of the child, the mother and the father. Reference was made to Art 204(3), Book 1, where it is stated that the mother's permission can be substituted by the court if the recognition would not prejudice the interests of the mother or child. The Court of Appeal had, however, mentioned a number of situations where the best interests of the mother would be preserved by a refusal of substituted permission, eg in instances of rape. However, a similar situation was here not evident. The Supreme Court agreed with the Court of Appeal in Amsterdam, and the appeal was subsequently rejected. It is interesting here to see the Supreme Court's reasoning in allowing the father to recognise the child quite regardless of the quality of the relationship with the mother or the child. Previous to this decision it was a widely held opinion that the father would have to prove 'family life' within Art 8 of the ECHR.

---

[119] For further information, see SFM Wortmann, 'Nieuw afstammingsrecht' (1997) 12 *Tijdschrift voor Familie- en Jeugdrecht* 282–287.

[120] Dutch report, *The International Survey of Family Law (1997 Edition)*, ed A Bainham (Martinus Nijhoff, 1999), at 259–308.

[121] Dutch Supreme Court, 16 February 2001, *Nederlandse Jurisprudentie 2001*, 571.

[122] This provision allows for a district court to substitute its permission for the mother's permission in a recognition procedure.

[123] Author's own translation.

The application of this Article was subsequently brought under review on 31 May 2002.[124] A begetter[125] wished to recognise his child, which had been born outside marriage. The mother refused to consent to the application. The father requested substituted permission, which the district court subsequently granted. The mother appealed; however, before the decision of the Court of Appeal, the mother's spouse, with the permission of the mother, recognised the child. The biological father requested that this second recognition be disregarded by the court since he had already requested substituted permission and proceedings were still pending. The Court of Appeal held the recognition to be invalid. The mother appealed. The Supreme Court held that, from the moment when a request for substituted permission by the biological father has been granted, the mother can only grant conditional permission to another for recognition. This conditional permission therefore has effect only when the request for substituted permission is judicially refused. The case is striking since it gives an *a priori* right to biological parentage over and above parentage established by dint of marriage. It is also surprising that the issue of bad faith on the mother's part was not discussed.

Another area which has been heavily discussed concerns DNA-testing. In a case brought to the Court of Appeal in The Hague in May 2001,[126] a child had been born in 1996 to a married couple who divorced in 1998. The father had signed the birth certificate and was registered as being the father. The mother applied for a declaration of non-paternity. The mother stated that she had had an extra-marital relationship and in this period had become pregnant with the child. She believed that it was in the best interests of the child to know who her real biological father was. It was common knowledge, according to the mother, that her husband was not the father, and she wanted to prevent the child hearing this from a third party. The father refused to have a voluntary DNA-test. The mother requested that the Court of Appeal order a DNA-test. The father continued to assert that he was the child's biological father and denied that he had ever said that he was not the biological father. The Court of Appeal, with reference to previous case-law, held that a declaration of non-paternity can be made only when circumstances indicate that the father cannot reasonably be the biological father of the child. The burden of proof lies with the claimant, in this case the mother, to prove such allegations, which she had failed to do. A DNA-test results in a serious infringement of the physical integrity of the father, which can only be justified if there were already reasons to believe that the father cannot plausibly be the father of the child. Therefore, the Court of Appeal held that a declaration of non-paternity would not be granted. This case can be seen in stark contrast with the Supreme Court case of 22 September 2000 where the decision revolved around an application for paternity recognition instead of non-paternity.[127]

The parties had had a relationship from April 1995, during which period they also lived together for just under a year. They separated but remained in contact.

---

[124]   Dutch Supreme Court, 31 May 2002, *Nederlandse Jurisprudentie 2002*, 470, annotation de Boer.

[125]   The term *verwekker* in Dutch refers to the biological father who provides genetic material through sexual intercourse. This therefore excludes a biological father who provides sperm via sperm donation.

[126]   Court of Appeal, The Hague, 16 May 2001, case number 955-R-00; (2001) 9 *Tijdschrift voor Familie- en Jeugdrecht* 246.

[127]   Dutch Supreme Court, 22 September 2000, *Nederlandse Jurisprudentie 2001*, 647.

In May 1998 a child was born which the mother claimed to be the child of her ex-partner. The man denied the allegation and refused to recognise the child as his own. The mother subsequently requested the district court to establish the biological fatherhood of her child. The case pivoted on the DNA-tests that needed to be undertaken. The district court undertook expert research, which the Court of Appeal confirmed. The fact that the man could well be the begetter of the child can be reason enough for the ordering of DNA-tests. The district court judge was, held the Supreme Court, justified in holding that expert DNA-tests be undertaken even if this was to have an impact upon the bodily integrity of the man himself. This case serves to reinforce the current position under Dutch law, that if a man could be a possible begetter of the child, then the judge is justified and competent to order DNA-tests to be undertaken.[128] If the father were to refuse to submit to the tests, adverse conclusions could be drawn.

D Procedural position of minors in parentage litigation

Even though the Dutch legislature has consistently avoided confronting the question whether an independent right to bring proceedings for minors should be introduced,[129] there is continued debate and disagreement as to its desirability.[130] Since 1995, a number of individual pieces of legislation have increased the right of a minor to bring his or her own case before the court, but it is still the case that a minor is normally treated as incompetent to commence legal proceedings and therefore needs a representative. In a number of special family law procedures, the child plays a central role. Examples are the annulment of the recognition of a child,[131] an application procedure for a declaration of non-paternity,[132] or the legal declaration that a man is the child's father.[133] The question therefore arises whether the child can play an independent role in such proceedings, or must he or she be represented by a representative?

If the request is made by the father or mother, then the child is treated as an interested party and earns the right to be represented by a court-appointed curator.[134] However, if the minor child requests an alteration in his or her own legal parental status, then the child is represented by a court-appointed curator who is treated as the claimant.[135] It was decided in 1995 that the increased juridicalisation of family arguments was not desirable and therefore the possibility for children to bring claims themselves should, as far as possible, be kept to a minimum. However, as compensation, the rights and duties of the *curator bonis* were extended.

---

[128] A Heida, 'Vaderschapsprocedures en DNA-onderzoek' (2002) 5 *Tijdschrift voor Familie- en Jeugdrecht* 122–129.

[129] Second Chamber, 1989–1990, 21 309.

[130] P Vlaardingerbroek, 'De bijzondere curator en het afstammingsrecht' (2001) 4 *Tijdschrift voor Familie- en Jeugdrecht* 101–107.

[131] Article 200, Book 1, Dutch Civil Code.

[132] Article 200(4), ibid.

[133] Article 199d, ibid.

[134] Article 250, ibid.

[135] Article 212, ibid.

In emergency procedures, where the fundamental rights of a minor child are in issue and the appointment of a special court-appointed guardian cannot be delayed, it is clear that the child should in principle be represented by a special court-appointed curator, if the interests of the child are contrary to those of the parents.[136] It seems that in parentage cases the child's interests are required to be represented by a court-appointed curator. The case-law on whether a special court-appointed curator is able to request a declaration of non-paternity, the annulment of recognition of the child or the legal declaration that a man is the child's father if the child is younger than 12, is contradictory.

In a recent case in the district court in Rotterdam,[137] a child requested the annulment of a recognition, stating that the man was not his biological father.[138] The claim was, however, made by the mother of the child in her position as an interested party in the case. The minor requested a DNA-test be undertaken to establish parentage. The district court decided that, in accordance with Art 7(1) of the UN Convention on the Rights of the Child,[139] a child has the right from birth to know who his or her parents are. The district court in its judgment implied that the minor has the right to know whether his or her legal parents are also his or her biological parents. Stemming from the provisions of the Convention on the Rights of the Child, the Rotterdam district court also held that this implied that it needed to be sure that the child was financially capable of bringing such a claim. If that be the case, and the child is a party to the case, then this places the obligation on the Kingdom of The Netherlands to pay for the costs of the case.[140] This must be seen in contrast to the case discussed above at C before the Court of Appeal in The Hague on 16 May 2001, where the DNA-test was refused. In the present case, there were factors indicating that the defendant might not be the father.

VI ADOPTION

A Intercountry adoption

Adoption has been possible in the Netherlands since 1956, but to this day there remains an evident lack of rules concerning the private international law issues relating to adoption cases falling outside the scope of the 1993 Hague Convention on Adoption.[141] A Bill on conflicts of law rules in adoption cases has, therefore, now been sent to the Dutch Council of State.[142] The Bill regulates which law a

---

[136]   Article 250, Book 1, Dutch Civil Code. P Vlaardingerbroek, 'De bijzondere curator en het afstammingsrecht' (2001) 4 *Tijdschrift voor Familie- en Jeugdrecht* 101–107.

[137]   District Court Rotterdam, 10 July 2000, rek nr 00–203.

[138]   I Pieters, and P Dorhout, 'Jurisprudentie: Afstamming' (2001) 1 *Tijdschrift voor Familie- en Jeugdrecht* 24.

[139]   *Tractatenblad 1990*, nr 46. Came into force in the Netherlands on 7 March 1995.

[140]   Article 182(3), Dutch Code on Civil Procedure; *Airey v Ireland* (1979) 2 EHRR 305.

[141]   Hague Convention on Protection of Children and Co-operation in respect of Inter-country Adoption 1993, *Tractatenblad 1993*, nr 197. This Convention was brought into force in the Netherlands by the Wet van 14 mei 1998 tot uitvoering van het op 29 mei 1993 's-Gravenhage tot stand gekomen verdrag, *Staatsblad 1998*, nr 302.

[142]   Wetsvoorstel Conflictenrecht Adoptie, (2002) 2 *Nederlandse Juristenblad* 107.

Dutch judge must apply in adoption cases in international cases, as well as the conditions for the recognition of foreign adoptions which fall outside the scope of the 1993 Hague Convention. The proposal has no impact on cases that fall within the scope of the 1993 Hague Convention.[143]

According to Art 3(1), Dutch law will apply to all adoptions obtained in the Netherlands except on issues related to the permission, consultation and informing of the child's parents, other people or institutions.[144] These issues will be referred to the law of the child's nationality. If the child is in possession of two or more nationalities then the nationality with which the child has the closest connection will be deemed to be applicable. If this law does not recognise the adoption, then Dutch law will apply in default. In the explanatory notes, it is stated that, at first sight, it might seem strange that a separate Article is deemed necessary when dealing with the legal consequences attached to an adoption order. However, under Dutch law, different private international law rules may apply depending upon the legal issue being discussed. For example, if discussing issues related to the child's inheritance rights, then reference to the 1989 Hague Convention on the Law Applicable to Succession to the Estates of Deceased Persons must be made. Here it is stated that, in the absence of a chosen choice of law, the habitual residence of the testator or testatrix will be applicable. Conversely, if one was discussing the parental maintenance obligations with respect to the child, the law of the child's habitual residence is applicable.[145] The government has consequently opted for an all-encompassing rule to govern all questions related to the legal consequences of adoptions falling under the scope of this Bill.

The third section of the Bill deals with the recognition of foreign adoptions and their legal consequences. The basic assumption and core of the definition is that the decision in question, which creates parental ties between the child and the adoptive parents, must have been made by a competent authority.[146] Currently the vast majority of cases which come before Dutch judges are decided in accordance with unwritten and rather arbitrary rules. By introducing a standardised set of applicable law rules, it is hoped to harmonise the decision-making process and create more certainty in this field.[147]

The Bill makes a distinction between a number of different types of adoption depending on where the parties are habitually resident. The habitual residence is taken to be the habitual residence of the party, both at the time when the request for adoption was made and at the time of the decision. According to Art 6, once it is determined that the decision has been made by a competent authority, a foreign adoption order will be automatically recognised if concluded:

(a)   in a foreign state where the adoptive parents and the child had their habitual residence at the time of the request for adoption and at the time of the decision;

---

[143]   Article 1, Wet Conflictenrecht Adoptie, Second Chamber, 2001–2002, 28 457, nr 2.

[144]   Article 3(2), ibid.

[145]   Hague Convention on the Recognition and Enforcement of Decisions relating to Maintenance Obligations 1973, *Tractatenblad 1974*, nr 86.

[146]   Second Chamber, 2001–2002, 28 457, nr 3, p 12.

[147]   Ibid, p 4.

(b)   in a foreign state where either the adoptive parents or the child had their
       habitual residence both at the time of the request for adoption and at the
       time of the decision.

The decision will, however, nonetheless not be recognised in the Netherlands if:

(a)   no substantial research or consultation has been undertaken;
(b)   if, in the case of Art 6(1)(b), the adoption order is not recognised in the state
       where the child has his or her habitual residence at the relevant time. In
       other words, if the order is obtained in State A (the state of the habitual
       residence of the parents), but not recognised in State B (the state of the
       habitual residence of the child) then it will also not be recognised in
       the Netherlands; or
(c)   if the decision is contrary to public policy.

A complex set of rules has been proposed in relation to the recognition of foreign
adoption orders. However, it is submitted that this is a step towards the avoidance
of limping adoption orders.

B   Article 8 of the ECHR and adoption

A recent case came before the Dutch Supreme Court dealing with the issue of
adoption and the right to family life protected under Art 8 of the European
Convention.[148] The case centred on the application by a stepfather who sought to
adopt the children of his spouse. The biological father did not oppose the adoption
order. The prospective adoptive father was, however, less than 18 years older than
the children he wished to adopt. The Court of Appeal refused the application since
the stepfather had not satisfied the requirements of Art 228(1), Book 1 of the
Dutch Civil Code that there should be at least an 18-year age-gap between him
and the children. The stepfather argued, on appeal to the Supreme Court, that this
was contrary to his right to family life as protected under Art 8 of the European
Convention on Human Rights. The Supreme Court held that, even though Art 8
can lend itself to the protection of family life between adoptive parents and
children,[149] there is no right to be able to adopt a child, without first satisfying the
conditions stipulated by national legislation. Therefore, due to the fact that
the adoption was contrary to the age requirements in Art 228, Book 1 of the Dutch
Civil Code, Art 8 of the ECHR could not be used to support an adoption
application.

The opinion of the Dutch Supreme Court in this case that Art 8 of the ECHR
does not safeguard any right to adopt a child appears to be supported by the
European Court of Human Rights' decision in *Fretté v France* where it was stated
that Art 8 of the ECHR does not guarantee any right to adoption.[150] *Fretté* was,
however, not a case in which there was *de facto* family life between the
prospective adopter and the child. It is moreover understandable, in the light of
the current restrictive policy in Dutch legislation regarding step-parent adoption,

---

148   Dutch Supreme Court, 30 June 2001, *Nederlandse Jurisprudentie 2001*, 103.
149   ECRM, 10 March 1981, Application No 8896/80, D&R 24, p 176 and ECRM, 5 October 1982,
       Application No 9993/82, D&R 31, p 241.
150   Application Number 36515/97, 26 February 2002, § 32.

that the Dutch Supreme Court was not anxious to find a right to adopt in this case.[151]

VII   PARENT AND CHILD LAW

A   Custody

1   JOINT CUSTODY

The Act on shared custody by dint of registered partnership, discussed in the 2001 Survey,[152] came into force on 1 January 2002.[153] That Act is intended primarily to provide for shared custody to arise automatically when a child is born to a woman who has a registered partner or spouse who is also a woman. The Act also applies if a child is born to a woman who has a man as a registered partner; in that case different provisions apply depending upon whether the man has recognised the child before birth or not. Not everyone is convinced that this Act does justice to the position of the mother's female partner. Henstra argues persuasively in her doctoral thesis that the mother's female registered partner or spouse should become the child's legal parent by dint of birth.[154] However, there is much more going on in custody law. Not least is the problem of excessive complexity of all the different provisions[155] and inconsistency.[156]

Another problem is connected with the possibility of obtaining a joint custody order. Parents who have shared custody during the marriage and who divorce after 1 January 1998 have automatically, in consequence of the Act of 30 October 1997,[157] joint custody after the divorce unless one or both request the court to order sole custody in the child's interests. According to a decision of the Dutch Supreme Court on 10 September 1999, the court should only accede to the request for sole custody if there is shown to be an unacceptable risk that the child will be caught between warring parents. Moreover, there must be no reasonable prospect of improvement in the situation. Mere disagreement or communication difficulties between the parents provide insufficient reason for an order for sole custody.[158] Where the circumstances between parents are difficult, the court has the possibility of making an order regulating the child's place of residence without

---

[151]   A new statutory condition of Dutch adoption is that the child cannot expect anything from his or her birth parent as a parent: Article 227(3), Book 1, Dutch Civil Code.

[152]   Dutch report, *International Survey of Family Law (2001 Edition)*, ed A Bainham (Family Law, 2001), at 315–319.

[153]   Act of 4 October 2001, *Staatsblad* 2001, 468. Implementation instrument of 7 November 2001, *Staatsblad* 2001, 544.

[154]   A Henstra, *Van ouderschapsrecht naar afstammingsrecht* (Boom juridische uitgevers, 2002).

[155]   A Nuytinck, 'De complexiteit van de gezagsregeling', *Tijdschrift voor familie- en jeugdrecht* 2002, 190–191.

[156]   J Doek, 'Het gezag over minderjarigen, Iets over een doolhof en het zoeken van (rode?) draden', (2000) *Tijdschrift voor Familie- en Jeugdrecht*, 217–226.

[157]   *Staatsblad* 1997, 506, discussed in the Dutch report, *The International Survey of Family Law 1997*, ed A Bainham (Martinus Nijhoff, 1999), at 284–288.

[158]   *Nederlandse Jurisprudentie 2000*, 20.

necessarily having to make any order regarding the joint custody.[159] It is thus evident that there is a strong policy decision in favour of joint custody. In some circumstances, the court may be unable to order joint custody at the time of the divorce, but circumstances may change so that a later application for joint custody may become appropriate. Under the present provisions, a later order changing an order for sole custody into an order for joint custody can be made only where both parents make an application for joint custody.[160] This restriction is incompatible with the rationale of the joint custody provision, which does not require excellent communication between the parents, but only the absence of unacceptable risk for the child. It has therefore been proposed by Jansen that the law on this point be changed. He has argued that the failure to introduce reform may lead to violation of Arts 8, 6 and 13 of the ECHR, since the parent who is unable even to bring the issue to court is deprived of a vital aspect of his or her family life.[161]

If the parents have joint custody and the child, due to mental or physical challenge, is living with and being cared for by both parents even in adulthood, the Dutch Supreme Court has held that Art 8 of the ECHR is violated by the absence of possibility in the Civil Code to give both parents the power to act in legal matters on the child's behalf.[162] The Dutch Supreme Court held that it was not necessary to refer the matter to the legislator; the Supreme Court declared the provision of joint guardianship to be applicable to this situation by analogy.

2 POSITION OF THE PARENT WHO DOES NOT HAVE CUSTODY

If, following divorce, an order for sole custody is made, or the parents were never married and the father recognised the child but did not obtain an order for custody, the parent who does not have custody is not in a very favourable position. On 13 July 2001, the Dutch Supreme Court was seized of an application for joint custody by a mother who had had sole custody of the child since his birth, and her spouse, who was not the child's father.[163] The child's natural father, who had recognised the child but had never had custody, opposed the application. Article 253t(3), Dutch Civil Code provides that the court should reject an application by the parent with custody to share joint custody with another 'if, also taking account of the interests of the child's other parent, there are reasonable grounds to believe that granting the application will be contrary to the child's interests'. The natural father was trying to establish access with the child; trial access arrangements were not going smoothly. The father's fears that the grant of the application would dash his hopes of establishing a good relationship with the child were not accepted by the Dutch Supreme Court as a reason not to grant the order requested.[164] The Dutch Supreme Court held that parliamentary debate on the provision in question indicated that it was Parliament's intention that the

---

[159]   Dutch Supreme Court, 15 December 2000, *Nederlandse Jurisprudentie 2001*, 123, annotation Wortmann.

[160]   Article 253o(1), second sentence, Dutch Civil Code.

[161]   S Jansen, 'Gezamenlijk gezag na scheiding: over een dubieuze voorwaarde' (2000) *Tijdschrift voor Familie- en Jeugdrecht*, 109–111.

[162]   Dutch Supreme Court, 1 December 2000, *Nederlandse Jurisprudentie 2001*, 390.

[163]   The application for a legal parent to share custody with another person is made under Art 253t, Dutch Civil Code.

[164]   Dutch Supreme Court, 13 July 2001, *Nederlandse Jurisprudentie 2001*, 514.

decisive indication for the question whether the order should be granted was whether the child's interests were undamaged. The interest of the parent without custody only had a subsidiary role. The value choice behind this provision has been criticised by Van Teeffelen. Whereas there is, in general in Dutch family law, a preference for the interests of the natural parents when in competition with social parents, in Art 253t, Book 1, Dutch Civil Code (the application for joint custody of a child's birth parent and a person who is not the child's parent), the preference is reversed. The provision says that the application by the parent with custody and the new social parent (who need not be married to the birth parent) must be granted unless the child's interests are shown to be at risk. This contrasts with the situation in the event of an adoption application by the parent with custody and his or her new partner. If the parent with custody and her new partner wish to adopt the child, the parent without custody has a right of veto. That veto right can only be overridden if the parent without custody has never or scarcely lived with the child or has been guilty of abuse or neglect of the child.[165] Van Teeffelen proposes that Art 253t(3), Book 1 be amended to provide that when deciding whether to grant joint custody to the parent with sole custody and the proposed social parent, account must be taken of the interests of the other birth parent in the continuation of a good relationship with his or her child. The decision should be made which promotes the child's best interests.[166] However, it may be doubted whether this proposal, if adopted, would bring any different result or reasoning than that of the Dutch Supreme Court of 13 July 2001 discussed above. The law is confronted with a dilemma between protecting the position of the social parent and that of the parent without custody. The position of the social parent, most particularly the step-parent, has been the subject of a doctoral dissertation, to which I will now turn.

3   LEGAL POSITION OF STEP-PARENTS

In Dutch law the step-parent has practically no legal status. Considering the increasing frequency of step-parenting, this absence of provision is striking. The step-parent may take advantage of the provision discussed above (Art 253t, Book 1) of applying together with the parent with sole custody for an order for joint custody. It should be noticed that the step-parent only has that possibility if the parent with custody consents to the joint application; the step-parent cannot act on his or her own initiative. Furthermore, the application will be rejected unless the parent with custody has held sole custody for a minimum of three years.[167] If the parent with custody has joint custody with the other birth parent, there can be no shared custody with the step-parent. It was seen in the preceding paragraphs that the policy of the law tends to promote joint custody between divorced parents, thus restricting the scope for the step-parent to apply for shared custody. Furthermore, the parent with custody and the step-parent must have cared for the child for at least one year immediately preceding the application.[168]

---

[165]   Article 228(2), Book 1, Dutch Civil Code.

[166]   P Van Teeffelen, 'Sociaal en biologisch ouderschap, Enige kritische opmerkingen over Art 1:253t BW' (2001) *Tijdschrift voor Familie- en Jeugdrecht*, 133–137.

[167]   Article 253t(2)(b), Book 1, Dutch Civil Code.

[168]   Article 253t(2)(a), ibid.

Notwithstanding the rather minimal opportunity for the step-parent to share custody with the birth parent, the step-parent is liable, for the duration of the marriage or registered partnership, to maintain the child.[169] However, there then appears another peculiarity: the step-parent's liability to pay maintenance for the child terminates on divorce from the birth parent without any possibility of extension. This contrasts with the maintenance liability of the birth parent's partner who obtains custody under Art 253t, Book 1, Dutch Civil Code, which continues after termination of the custody relationship for a period equivalent to the duration of the custody order.[170] In the last situation there is even the possibility of extending the maintenance liability. These and many other anomalies are investigated in Draaisma's PhD thesis. Draaisma proposes that the step-parent, regardless of the type of relationship with the birth parent (marriage or registered partnership, same or opposite sex), should have automatic custody over a child living with and being cared for by the step-parent. The step-parent should be obliged to co-operate with access arrangements between the child and the birth parent without custody. The step-parent should be liable for the child's maintenance and should be liable for torts committed by the child. After termination of the relationship between the step-parent and the birth parent, the step-parent should have a right to apply for access with the child. A change of name to the step-parent's name and step-parent adoption should only be possible in exceptional circumstances. The recent reform of adoption law[171] introduced an extra condition for an adoption, namely, that the child should expect nothing from his or her natural parents. Furthermore, although Dutch courts have the power to order a change of the child's surname to that of the step-parent, in practice they rarely do so.[172]

B   Access

1   CONDITIONS CIRCUMSCRIBING WHO MAY APPLY FOR ACCESS

Not everybody has the right to apply for an order providing for access to a child. A parent (ie the child's birth mother and the man who is married to her or who has recognised the child[173] or regarding whom paternity has been established by court order) has a right to apply under Art 377a, Book 1, Dutch Civil Code for regulation of access.[174] Other persons, in order for their application to the court to be admissible under Art 377f, Book 1, Dutch Civil Code, must prove additionally that they have a relationship with the child of such quality that it may be regarded as 'family life' within the meaning of Art 8 of the ECHR. In the Dutch Civil Code

---

[169]   Article 392 ff, Book 1, Dutch Civil Code.

[170]   Article 253w, ibid.

[171]   Act of 21 December 2001, *Staatsblad* 2001, 10; see Dutch report, *The International Survey of Family Law (2000 Edition)*, ed A Bainham (Family Law, 2000) at 262–264.

[172]   T Draaisma, *De stiefouder: stiefkind van het recht. Een onderzoek naar de juridische plaatsbepaling van de stiefouder* (VU Uitgeverij, 2002).

[173]   Dutch Supreme Court, 26 November 1999, *Nederlandse Jurisprudentie 2000*, 85. As was held in that case, even a sperm donor who has recognised the child (with the mother's consent) is entitled to make an application under Art 377a rather than Art 377f, Book 1, Dutch Civil Code.

[174]   Article 377a, Book 1, Dutch Civil Code.

this family life is expressed as a 'close personal relationship'.[175] Applications under Arts 377a and 377f, Book 1, Dutch Civil Code do not only differ concerning the requirement that extra circumstances be established. An application under Art 377a may only be refused in restricted circumstances, namely: if the access order would cause serious damage to the child's welfare; if the parent is evidently unsuitable to exercise access; if the child, being 12 years of age or older, has indicated serious objections; or other serious considerations affecting the child's welfare obtain (Art 377a(3), Book 1, Dutch Civil Code).[176] An application under Art 377f may be rejected if the access is not in the child's interests or the child, being 12 years or older, objects (Art 377f(1), second sentence, Book 1, Dutch Civil Code).[177]

This rule applies to a begetter who is not married to the mother and has not recognised the child, but also to other persons such as grandparents, foster parents or step-parents. A case before the Dutch Supreme Court on 29 March 2002 concerned an alleged 'social grand-parent'; the applicant did not convince the court that the relationship between her and the child was sufficiently close to qualify as family life.[178] It is sometimes argued that a distinction should be made between the begetter and the other categories of applicant, and that the begetter should not be required to prove extra circumstances in order to have the right to apply for access.[179] So far the Dutch Supreme Court has held that the distinction is compatible with Arts 8 and 14 of the ECHR.[180] The fact that the begetter could in theory have recognised the child – so bringing himself within Art 377a, Book 1 – but did not do so, is not a reason to disregard or adjust the factual circumstances which tend to establish family life for the purposes of the begetter's access application under Art 377f, Book 1, Dutch Civil Code.[181] Courts regularly make mistakes regarding the grounds of refusal to be applied in access applications by begetters, but such an error is not a ground for cassation as it can be corrected by whichever court is seized of the proceedings.[182]

The distinction in the grounds for refusal of access, mentioned in the previous paragraph when applied to the begetter, were at issue in a series of cases against Germany which were recently decided by the European Court of Human Rights. The applications were made by four unmarried fathers who complained of discrimination when compared with divorced fathers. Access applications by an unmarried father can be rejected according to the grounds laid down in § 1711 German Civil Code whereas an access application by a divorced father can only

---

[175] Article 377f, Book 1, Dutch Civil Code.
[176] Article 377a(3), ibid.
[177] Article 377f(1), second sentence, Book 1, Dutch Civil Code.
[178] Dutch Supreme Court, 29 March 2002, *Rechtspraak van de Week* 2002, 62.
[179] De Boer, annotation under Dutch Supreme Court, 15 November 1996, *Nederlandse Jurisprudentie 1997*, 423.
[180] Dutch Supreme Court, 15 November 1996, *Nederlandse Jurisprudentie 1997*, 423, annotation de Boer; Dutch Supreme Court, 26 November 1999, *Nederlandse Jurisprudentie 2000*, 85; Dutch Supreme Court, 25 June 1999, *Nederlandse Jurisprudentie 1999*, 616; Dutch Supreme Court, 19 May 2000, *Nederlandse Jurisprudentie 2000*, 545, annotation Wortmann; Dutch Supreme Court, 29 September 2000, *Nederlandse Jurisprudentie 2000*, 654; Dutch Supreme Court, 8 December 2000, *Nederlandse Jurisprudentie 2001*, 648.
[181] Dutch Supreme Court, 29 September 2000, *Nederlandse Jurisprudentie 2000*, 654 o.w. 3.4.
[182] Dutch Supreme Court, 25 June 1999, *Nederlandse Jurisprudentie 1999*, 616.

be rejected in the more restrictive circumstances mentioned in § 1634 German Civil Code. In *Elsholz v Germany*[183] the European Court stated that it would not exclude the possibility that the difference in treatment violated Art 14 in conjunction with Art 8 of the ECHR but held that on the facts it was not demonstrated that the discrimination had made any difference. However, in *Sahin,*[184] *Sommerfeld*[185] and *Hoffmann*[186] the European Court held that Art 14 in conjunction with Art 8 of the ECHR was violated. The distinction between those two paragraphs is identical to the distinction made in the Dutch Arts 377a and 377f outlined in the previous paragraph. Applicants for access under Art 377a, Dutch Civil Code have a right to access which may only be refused under the conditions circumscribed. By contrast, applicants under Art 377f Dutch Civil Code must prove that the circumstances justify their claim to the right and, furthermore, that right can be excluded in circumstances less restrictive than those specified in Art 377a, Dutch Civil Code. However, the ground of distinction is different. The Dutch access provisions make a distinction between, on the one hand, a 'father', who may be either married to the mother or divorced from her or a man who is not married to the mother but has recognised the child, and, on the other hand, a man who has not recognised the child. This distinction seems much more reasonable than the German distinction between the man who is married to the mother and the man who is not. The German distinction makes an assumption about all unmarried fathers without differentiation.

In the social grandmother case previously mentioned, Advocate-Generaal Moltmaker argued that grandparents by blood possibly should not have to prove additional circumstances in order to apply for an access order. The Advocate-Generaal bases this argument on Art 8 of the ECHR and the European Court's statement in *L v Finland* that the 'mutual enjoyment by ... grandparent and child, of each other's company constitutes a fundamental element of family life and domestic measures hindering such enjoyment amount to an interference with the right protected by Art 8 of the Convention ...'.[187]

These additional circumstances demonstrating a close personal relationship to the child may concern events before the child's birth or events thereafter. Events before the child's birth will relate particularly to the quality of the relationship which the applicant had with the mother. If a man has a relationship with the mother which is comparable to a marriage, through cohabitation or a living-apart-together relationship, then according to the case-law of the European Court of Human Rights, the man has family life with any child born out of that relationship.[188] Other circumstances before the birth may be of relevance to the question as to whether there is family life, such as whether the pregnancy was planned, whether the man cared for the woman during the pregnancy or otherwise adjusted his position. Circumstances of relevance after the birth will be, in

---

[183]   *Elsholz v Germany*, 13 July 2000, para 54–61, ECtHR.

[184]   *Sahin v Germany*, 11 October 2001, para 56–61, ECtHR.

[185]   *Sommerfeld v Germany*, 11 October 2001, para 53–58, ECtHR.

[186]   *Hoffmann v Germany*, 11 October 2001, para 56–60, ECtHR.

[187]   *L v Finland*, 27 April 2000, (2001) 32 EHRR 30; Dutch Supreme Court, 29 March 2002, *Rechtspraak van de Week* 2002, 62, Conclusie van de Advocate-Generaal, o.w.2.10.

[188]   *Keegan v Ireland*, 26 May 1994, ECtHR Series A, vol 290, para 44; *Kroon v The Netherlands*, 27 October 1994, ECtHR Series A, vol 297-C, para 30.

particular, the extent to which the man has been engaged in the care and upbringing of the child. The Dutch Supreme Court's requirements for the proof of family life, whether based on circumstances before or after the birth, are strict.[189] However, the Dutch Supreme Court on 29 September 2000[190] found family life to be established when the man had stayed overnight with the mother very regularly over a period of a year. A further slight relaxation in these high standards was made in a decision of the Dutch Supreme Court on 19 May 2000.[191] The Dutch Supreme Court held that it was possible, in order to establish a close personal relationship, to take circumstances before and after the birth into consideration. The parties had a short-term, difficult relationship, in which the pregnancy was unplanned. But they made preparations for the birth of the baby, and the mother explored whether she would agree to recognition of the child by the father and, for a short time, was prepared to try out whether they could stay together as a family. Five months after the baby's birth, the relationship broke down completely. The circumstances before the birth, taken alone, did not compare to the kind of relationship found in *Keegan* (where the parties had lived together for a year) or even *Kroon* (where the parties had a long-term living-apart-together relationship). Nevertheless, in combination with the circumstances after the birth they did amount to sufficient closeness to allow the man to make an application for access.

2 ENFORCEMENT OF ACCESS

The Dutch Supreme Court has been asked to rule in a number of cases upon the nature and extent of the State's obligation to secure the enforcement of access. On 30 November 2001 the Dutch Supreme Court held that the filming of the father's visits to the children on video was a violation of his private life within the meaning of Art 8 of the ECHR. Accordingly, if the father was not prepared to give his consent to the filming, the videos could not be made unless there was a statutory basis for the action. In that case there was none, so that the child protection authorities had to desist. The decision on this point is just one small illustration of the very difficult relationship between the father and the child welfare authorities, in which the father was the loser. The Dutch Supreme Court upheld the appeal court's decision that access could be excluded because the father's failure to co-operate with the child welfare authorities presented a risk to the children's welfare.[192]

The European Court of Human Rights stated in *Hokkanen v Finland* that Art 8 of the ECHR imposes an obligation upon states to take effective measures to enforce access between parent and child. In that case, Finland was found to have violated Art 8 of the ECHR by a persistent failure of the authorities to enforce contact between Hokkanen and his daughter who lived with her maternal grandparents.[193] But the responsibilities of the State (in particular the courts) are not unlimited. In *Nuutinen v Finland*, the European Court held that the refusal of

---

[189] See the case of Dutch Supreme Court, 5 June 1998, discussed in Dutch report, *The International Survey of Family Law (2000 Edition)*, ed A Bainham (Family Law, 2000) at 264–265.

[190] *Nederlandse Jurisprudentie 2000*, 654.

[191] *Ibid* 545.

[192] Dutch Supreme Court, 30 November 2001, *Rechtspraak van de Week* 2001, 192.

[193] 23 September 1994, ECtHR, Series A, vol 299-A.

the Finnish authorities to deploy the measure of 'fetching' – the forcible collecting of the child – was justified on the facts of the case. The European Court recognised that, although realisation of access is generally in the child's interests, circumstances can be such that the enforcement of access is against the child's interests. The central question is 'whether the national authorities have taken all necessary steps to facilitate access as can reasonably be demanded in the special circumstances of each case'.[194] The Dutch Supreme Court concluded on 29 June 2001, in accordance with the decision in *Nuutinen*, that Art 8 of the ECHR does not impose upon the state the duty to impose forcible measures in order to secure the enforcement of access.[195] Furthermore, the Dutch Supreme Court held that neither Art 8 of the ECHR nor Art 16 of the International Convention on the Rights of the Child (hereafter ICRC) imposes an obligation upon the state such that the court is obliged to order the Child Welfare Authority to supervise and assist in implementation of access.[196] Such activities by the Child Welfare Authority constitute an interference with parental rights within the meaning of Art 8 of the ECHR and therefore require to be provided for by statute. In fact the Child Welfare Authority was not empowered by statute to act in access cases; nor did the court have a statutory power to order the Child Welfare Authorities so to act. The lack of statutory authority meant that any engagement of the Child Welfare Authority in access matters is a violation of Art 8 of the ECHR which cannot be justified under para 2 of Art 8. Everything depends upon the circumstances. The European Court accords the state a wide margin of appreciation in the area of enforcement of access. In accordance with this wide margin of appreciation is the judgment of the Dutch Supreme Court on 13 April 2001. That court held that the imposition of a supervision order in order to secure the enforcement of access can be justified under Art 8 of the ECHR, if the lack of access or the existence of access, or the conflicts arising from the enforcement of access, present a serious threat to the child's mental or physical welfare. A further condition for the application of a supervision order is that other less invasive instruments for enforcing access have failed or may reasonably be expected to fail. The indications for a supervision order in a particular case must be proven to a high standard.[197]

The attitude of the Dutch Supreme Court is underwritten by two decisions of the European Court declaring applications against the Netherlands regarding enforcement of access inadmissible because manifestly unfounded. In *Zander v the Netherlands* the applicant complained that Art 8 of the ECHR was violated by the fact that the court had terminated the applicant's exercise of access with his daughter and that the authorities had not taken sufficient measures to safeguard the applicant's right of access with his daughter. The European Court held the application inadmissible. The European Court held that a wide margin of appreciation was applicable and that the decisions were evidently taken in the

---

[194]   27 June 2000, ECtHR, para 128.

[195]   Dutch Supreme Court, 26 January 1996, *Nederlandse Jurisprudentie 1996*, 355; Dutch Supreme Court, 24 March 2000, *Nederlandse Jurisprudentie 2000*, 356 o.w. 3.4; Dutch Supreme Court, 29 June 2001, *Nederlandse Jurisprudentie 2001*, 598 annotation Wortmann.

[196]   Dutch Supreme Court, 29 June 2001, *Nederlandse Jurisprudentie 2001*, 598 o.w. 3.3.

[197]   Dutch Supreme Court, 13 April 2001, *Nederlandse Jurisprudentie 2002*, 4 o.w. 3.3; Dutch Supreme Court, 13 April 2001, *Nederlandse Jurisprudentie 2002*, 5 o.w. 2.5 (obiter).

child's best interests.[198] In *Troost v the Netherlands* the European Court also held the complaint manifestly unfounded. The applicant had requested the court to impose an unlimited fine on the mother or to reduce the maintenance to which the mother was entitled on the daughter's behalf if the mother failed to comply with the access order. The Dutch national court had imposed the fine but refused to bring the non-payment of the fine into account in order to reduce the maintenance order. The European Court held that the refusal of the national court was reasonable, taking into account the mother's limited financial resources. Moreover the state could not be held responsible for the mother's limited financial resources and thus the unsuitability of imposing upon her the remedies proposed by the applicant.[199] A similar line is followed in *Glaser v United Kingdom.*[200]

C USE OF MEDIATION IN ACCESS AND CUSTODY DISPUTES

In 1998 a number of experimental projects using mediation in divorce cases and access disputes were set up in various parts of the country. In that year, the Ministry of Justice commissioned an investigation into the effectiveness of those projects. The results of those investigations were published in September 2001.[201] This research was preceded by a report of the De Ruiter Commission in 1995, which had examined the role of mediation in achieving simplification of divorce procedure.[202] One of the most important conclusions of that report was that the Commission thought it possible to introduce a form of out-of-court divorce, in which the post-divorce provision would be made in a deed drawn up by an advocate or notary. Mediation has a key role in these proposals, to assist divorcing couples to make the agreements which will be recorded by deed. Hence the Ministry of Justice commenced the above-mentioned mediation projects and the evaluation thereof.

The success of the mediation was measured. There are two measurements to be made: the extent to which the parties were satisfied with the mediation process itself, and the extent to which they were satisfied with the result. The levels of satisfaction differed for the two different types of mediation: namely, divorce mediation and access mediation. Regarding divorce mediation, 78% of those interviewed were satisfied with the mediation process as such; and 75% were satisfied with the outcome. Although those interviewed commented that the mediation process was emotionally very demanding, many considered a great advantage of mediation was that they had managed to negotiate the arrangements themselves without the intervention of a court. The results were less good regarding access mediation. But given the situation at the outset, this is not surprising. Of those couples making use of access mediation 83% described their ability to communicate as poor. In 48% of cases, the court had imposed the exercise of access; in 37% of cases, the parties had themselves agreed to access. Access mediators, in contrast to divorce mediators, are generally not lawyers. In

---

[198] 24 October 2000 and 5 December 2000, ECtHR, *Nederlandse Jurisprudentie 2001*, 384.

[199] 27 April 2000, ECtHR, Application 3764/97, *NJCM-Bulletin* 2001, p 241.

[200] 19 September 2000, (2001) 33 EHRR 1, ECtHR.

[201] B Chin-A-Fat, and M Steketee, 'Evaluatie experimenten scheidings- en omgangsbemiddeling' (2001) *Tijdschrift voor Familie-en Jeugdrecht*, 296–302.

[202] Anders Scheiden, *Rapport van de Commissie Herziening scheidingsprocedure*, 2 October 1996.

41% of cases, the parties were satisfied with the outcome of mediation. In 31%, the mediation failed and the parties returned to court. The courts were not generally prepared to impose a duty on the parties to go to mediation. The research indicated that the parties did not always understand what they could realistically expect from the mediation. For instance, a common reaction was that one party had expected the mediator to be more assertive vis-à-vis the other party.

The most interesting aspect of the results of this investigation concern two questions: first, whether the mediators were able to protect adequately the interests of the weaker party to the divorce, and secondly, whether the children affected by the divorce are adequately involved in the mediation process. Regarding the first question, it is important to notice that economic imbalance of power almost never played a role. That is to say that the mediator was able to compensate adequately for the lack of economic power of one of the parties. But an imbalance of emotional power was a serious problem. For example, if one party had the children living with him or her, the other party felt himself or herself at an emotional disadvantage. It is a challenge for the mediator to manage those imbalances and where necessary to compensate for them.

The second issue concerned the position of children. If there are judicial divorce proceedings, the court is obliged to inform itself of the opinion of any child over the age of 12 regarding access and other arrangements following divorce. Children of a younger age should also be consulted, if they are capable of understanding their interests in the arrangements. Furthermore, children of 12 and over, and younger children if they are able to appreciate their own interests, have a right to approach the court informally, to ask the court to amend custody or access arrangements of its own motion.[203] However, if, as the De Ruiter Commission proposes, there is no court proceeding, then these procedural rights of the child no longer obtain. The question is how to engage the child in the mediation process such that his or her ideas and wishes about the arrangements following divorce can be made known. The research shows that in neither the divorce mediation nor access mediation was the child directly involved in the process. In divorce mediation, 18% of children were involved; in access mediation, the figure was 5%. Many mediators feel that mediation concerns a conflict between the parents and that there is no place for the child. Some, especially the lawyers, were unsure how to talk to children. Insofar as the interests and opinions of children were taken account of, this was done indirectly. For example, the mediators advise and encourage the parents to talk to the children about the divorce and its consequences. The researcher sent a questionnaire to a number of children affected by divorce and asked them whether they would have liked to have been involved in the mediation process: 62% of children responding to the questionnaire considered that the parents had taken account of their wishes and interests regarding access, and 70% thought they had done so regarding the place in which they lived. It emerged that 50% of the parents had spoken with their children about the divorce and its consequences; 25% had never spoken with the children on these matters; and 25% sometimes. Of the children responding to

---

[203]   For more detail, see C Forder, 'Seven steps to achieving full participation of children in the divorce process', in: J Willems (ed) *Developmental and autonomy rights of children* (Intersentia, Antwerp, Oxford, New York, 2002) at 105–140.

the questionnaire, 79% were content with the outcome of the procedure. Nevertheless 36% of those children would have liked to have been involved in the divorce mediation process in some way; and 29% of children would have liked to have been involved in the access mediation. It is therefore not surprising that a major recommendation of this report is that children of 12 years or older should be involved in the mediation process. The point is to give them an opportunity to make their views known. The mediator could hear these views, or could engage another person to interview the children. The child concerned should be free to choose whether he makes those views known orally or in a written form, or whether to do so at all.[204] Furthermore, if out-of-court divorce is introduced, a procedure will have to be created to make it possible for the court to be informed of the child's views and wishes. A further recommendation was that the provision of information regarding mediation should be improved.

The difficulties of hearing children on matters which affect them are not just practical; much greater is the problem of attitude. On 29 March 2002, the Dutch Supreme Court judged an access application by a woman who had acted as social grandmother to a child who had not quite attained the age of 12.[205] It was argued before the Dutch Supreme Court that the lower courts had erred in not hearing the child to find out what she thought of the applicant and whether she would like to see her. The appeal court had refused to hear the child 'because otherwise she might get the idea that she has to take a decision'. In my view it should be possible to make it clear to a child that she may have an opinion, without having to bear any responsibility for the decision; that is, after all, the court's job. According to the Dutch Supreme Court, Art 12 of the ICRC had not been violated by the failure of the lower courts to hear the child. The Supreme Court remarked dryly: 'That Article does not provide that children (younger than 12 years) should personally be heard in all matters which concern them'. The reference to 12 years is clearly wrong. Article 12 does not mention any age-limit, but refers to a child 'capable of forming his or her own views'. It is true that Art 12 does not give the child a right to be heard; it gives the child the right to express his or her views freely. However, it is a minimalistic interpretation of Art 12 to assume that the right to express views freely can be satisfied regardless of whom – if indeed anyone – is hearing those views. The point is made quite clearly in para 2 of Art 12, that the child should be given the right to be heard in any judicial or administrative proceedings affecting him. The final clause of para 2 of Art 12, which provides that the hearing should be 'in a manner consistent with the procedural rules of national law', does not mean that the national authorities are entitled to dispense with the hearing. It is intended to give the national authorities flexibility as to the way in which the hearing takes place. The Dutch Supreme Court miss, in my view, the whole point of Art 12 in its final sentence of the judgment. It reads:

> 'In the present case the requirements of Art 12 ICRC are satisfied by the fact that various representatives and propounders of the child's interests – the mother, the father and the Child Protection Body – have been heard.'

---

[204] L Smulders-Groenhuijsen, 'Omgaan met omgang, een kritische beschouwing' (2002) *Tijdschrift voor Familie- en Jeugdrecht*, 77–82 at p 82.
[205] *Rechtspraak van de Week* 2002, 62.

Article 12 requires the child to be asked for his or her view personally. The views of another person on what the child wants are no substitute for this.

VIII   CHILD PROTECTION MEASURES

A   Public support of upbringing

There is generally a lot of concern at the moment about the adequacy of the child protection system. In June 2000 the Cabinet published a discussion document entitled 'Compulsory measures supporting upbringing'.[206] This document is concerned with two groups of children: namely, those who have committed criminally relevant activities, and those who have been signalled, by schools or social work, as having problems at home, but where the problems are not serious enough to justify child protection measures. The starting-point of these proposals is that it is now known that far more can be achieved with children if intervention is made at an early stage. The numbers of children subject to a supervision order is rising sharply, as is the rate of recidivism: more than 50% of those children subject to a supervision order commit one or more offences in the subsequent 12 months.[207] Furthermore, it is understood that many of the children coming into the child protection system have parents with inadequate resources for upbringing.[208] (In 87% of child protection cases there are said to be problems with upbringing.) It is thus attractive – and that is the aim of this proposal – to investigate which measures might be used in order to stimulate the willingness of parents to make use of the facilities which are offered to increase upbringing skills or otherwise support the family. The measures which come into question are either threats or coercion. A threat is used when the parents are warned that, if they do not accept help offered, they and their child may well be subject to coercive measures, such as a supervision order or even removal of the child from the home. Coercion is used if the court imposes sanctions upon the child and or parent.[209]

The civil law measures which are presently available are: supervision orders, discussed in Section **VIII.B** below; and the removal or suspension of parental rights. The latter two measures are seen as more interventionist than supervision orders; they will be used only when a supervision order has been shown to be unsuitable. Suspension of parental rights is less far-reaching than removal thereof. Parental rights can be suspended, as long as the child's interests will not thereby be damaged, if the parent is unsuitable or unable to care for and bring up the child. Suspension will only be ordered against the parent's will in certain defined conditions:

(a)   where a supervision order has been in place for six months and it has emerged that such order is insufficient to protect the child;

---

[206]   Second Chamber 1999–2000, 27 197, nr 1. Niet-vrijblijvende vormen van opvoedingsondersteuning.

[207]   Second Chamber 2000–2001, 27 187, nr 2, p 1.

[208]   Second Chamber 2000–2001, 27 187, nr 3, p 2.

[209]   Ibid, p 3.

(b)   where the suspension of the rights of one parent is necessary in order to remove the child from the influence of the other parent, in respect of whom parental rights have had to be terminated;

(c)   where the parent is unable, due to mental disturbance, to consent to the suspension;

(d)   where the child has been cared for outside the family with the parent's consent for at least one year, and it is in the child's interests to continue that care as the child will otherwise be at risk.[210]

Removal of parental rights goes a step further, as it terminates the parent's rights altogether. Accordingly the court is empowered to remove parental rights only if the order is necessary in the child's interests and:

(a)   the parent is guilty of abuse of his or her rights, or serious neglect of one or more of the children;

(b)   the parent has a bad lifestyle; or

(c)   he or she has been convicted for an offence against a minor in his or her family or has been convicted of a number of classified offences against any minor.

Furthermore, removal of parental rights may be ordered if:

(d)   the parent has failed to follow the instructions of the family guardian agency if the child was subject to a supervision order or has interfered with a placement out of the home; or

(e)   there is reason to fear serious neglect of the child's interests because there is a risk that the parent will remove the child from the persons presently caring for him or her.[211]

In the Netherlands there is a range of support facilities offered to parents whose children have come into contact with criminal circles or otherwise are having difficulties. The first measure is crisis intervention, which involves giving direct help for a few months. This help is given on the understanding that it is to avert the need for a supervision order. The parents realise that a supervision order will follow if the measure is unsuccessful. Secondly, there is a scheme of video hometraining by which the parents are helped to develop their skills in upbringing. Thirdly, there is a scheme of family psychotherapeutic intervention, as practised currently in the region of Nijmegen. Fourthly, if the child has committed criminal acts, there are schemes by which the child will be steered out of the criminal procedure and given alternative tasks and receive specialised supervision. These last-mentioned schemes are known as 'STOP' and 'HALT'. Parents are involved in these schemes in varying degrees across the Netherlands. There is only one situation in which parents can be subject to a criminal sanction on account of the behaviour of their children: namely, in the case of non-attendance at school. The parent can receive a penalty of a maximum of one month in prison.

Against this background, the Cabinet considered what measures could be done to reach parents who might not be prepared to receive help on a voluntary

---

[210]   Article 268(2), Book 1, Dutch Civil Code.

[211]   Article 269(1), ibid.

basis. The Cabinet was not in favour of introducing the measure now in force in England, by which the parent can be made criminally liable for the child's criminal activities. First, the Cabinet argued that such approach contradicted the principle of criminal responsibility for one's own actions. Secondly, this method had not been shown to be particularly effective. Judges in England are understandably reluctant to use the measure. Thirdly, there is a risk that such measure will put further pressure on an already severely burdened parent–child relationship. However, the Cabinet recommended that parents should be systematically involved in any contact which the child had with the State authorities regarding the child's criminal activities. And the Cabinet resolved to consider further the possibility of introducing a new child protection measure in addition to the measures of supervision order or removal or suspension of parental rights.[212] The objective is to try to reach the parents who do not ask for help with upbringing but who could be expected to benefit from assistance. By definition these are parents of children whose activities are not serious enough to attract any of the existing range of coercive measures (supervision order, suspension or removal of parental rights or criminal intervention with the child).[213]

This proposal has been subject to criticism.[214] The problem is that intervention by the State is quite properly strictly circumscribed. Article 8 of the ECHR imposes strict limitations upon any interference in the relationship between parent and child, and the case-law is becoming increasingly strict. The new measure which the Cabinet is thinking about is intended for cases which do not attract the present range of actions. The likelihood is that there is not sufficient indication for any intervention. And Art 8 of the ECHR prohibits intervention unless it is shown to be 'necessary in a democratic society' and that the means used are proportionate to the aim pursued. Moreover, the intervention must be shown to be effective. The aim – of achieving early support to the family in order to reduce the risk of greater problems later – is worthy and in accordance with Art 8 of the ECHR. But it may seriously be doubted whether the Cabinet will succeed in coming up with a proposal which satisfies the requirements of necessity and proportionality.

B   Foster children and supervision orders

There has been a considerable amount of writing and research into the question of legal regulation of the position of foster children and the supervision orders which are often used to protect them. In the last two years, the Dutch Family Council brought out three reports on foster children.[215] A number of reports from different organisations have examined the legal problems associated with long-term care

---

[212]   Second Chamber 1999–2000, 27 197, nr 1, p 14.

[213]   Second Chamber 2000–2001, 27 197, nr 3, p 5.

[214]   S Wortmann, 'Kroniek van het personen- en familierecht', *Nederlands Juristenblad* 2002, p 1577–8; M Bruning, 'Herziening kinderbeschermingsmaatregelen: over noodzaak en uitstel' (2002) *Tijdschrift voor Familie- en Jeugdrecht* 104; *Nederlands gezinsraad, Als vrijwillig te vrijblijvend is* Den Haag (2001), p 106.

[215]   *Thuisplaatsing van pleegkinderen* (Den Haag, 2001); *Als vrijwillig te vrijblijvend is* (Den Haag, 2001); *Pleegzorg en adoptie in Nederland en Engeland* (Den Haag, 2002).

and supervisions orders.[216] And several investigations have revealed shortcomings in the practical functioning of the system of foster care and supervision orders.[217]

1 WEAK LEGAL POSITION OF THE FOSTER PARENTS

One very serious problem can be summarised as the failure to give foster parents an adequate opportunity to participate in decisions affecting the foster child. This problem arises most acutely when the child is subject to a supervision order and is placed with the foster family by a family guardianship agency.[218] (If the child's parents agree to the placement of the child in a foster family, the placement is usually made by a placement agency. In this situation the parents retain all parental rights and can decide, subject to the restriction mentioned below, when to remove the child from the foster parents.) Alternatively, the child might be subject to a compulsory protection order made by a court. This can be a supervision order, or removal or suspension of parental rights. In the latter two cases, the parental rights over the child will be exercised by the family guardianship agency. That agency can decide to place the child with a foster family and also to remove that child from the foster family to return him or her to the parents, or to place him or her with another foster family. In both cases, ie voluntary placement and compulsory placement of the child with a foster family, the foster parents have a statutory right to resist removal of the child at the initiative of the parents or the family guardianship agency. If the child has lived with the foster family for more than one year, the foster parents can refuse to release the child, and insist that the parents or family guardianship agency apply to the court for an order regarding the child's future residence.[219] However, the court must order removal of the child from the foster family unless there is an indication of serious neglect of the child's interests.[220] Nevertheless, this provision ensures that foster parents have the right to bring the matter to court before they are obliged to release the child. In one situation, the foster parents do not have the right to refuse release of the child pending a court application, namely if the child is subject to a supervision order. This situation has arisen despite a reform of the law in 1995 which was intended to increase the legal protection given to foster parents[221] – a reform which the Dutch Supreme Court had indicated was necessary in the light of the right to respect for family life of foster parents. The Dutch Supreme Court held that if the foster parents had a relationship of 'family life' with the foster child within the meaning of Art 8 of the ECHR, the foster parents have the right to apply to the court for a supervision order and the right to appeal against removal of their foster

---

[216] J de Savornin-Lohman, e.a, *Met recht onder toezicht gesteld, Evaluatie herziening ots-wetgeving*; NW Slot, e.a, *909 zorgen, Een onderzoek naar de doelmatigheid van ondertoezichtstelling* (VU 2001); BO Vogelvang Adviesbureau van Montvoort, *Maatregel ... regelmaat? reconstructie van het (doorbreken van) transgenerationele overdracht van kinderbeschermingsmaatregelen; Probleem ouders, problem kinderen? Een literatuurstudie van transgenerationele overdracht van problemen die tot kinderbeschermingsmaatregelen (kunnen) leiden* (WODC, 2001); AWM Veldkamp, *Over grenzen!* (Ministerie van Justitie, 2001).

[217] ECC Punselie, *Pleegzorg met visie, juridische haken en ogen* (Utrecht, VOG, 2000).

[218] *Gezinsvoogdij-instelling.*

[219] Article 253s, in conjunction with Art 336a, Book 1, Dutch Civil Code.

[220] Article 253s, Book 1 Dutch Civil Code.

[221] Discussed in Dutch report, *The International Survey of Family Law 1995*, ed A Bainham (Martinus Nijhoff, 1997) at 366–367.

child in order to place him or her in another foster family.[222] If the child is subject to a supervision order and is placed with the foster parents by the family guardianship agency, the most invasive action which the family guardianship agency can take is removal of the child. To do this, the family guardianship agency must first obtain court authorisation. The foster parents have the right to request the family guardianship agency to refrain from making the change in the child's residence.[223] Furthermore, if the family guardianship agency does not respond positively to their request, the foster parents can appeal to the court asking for authorisation for the removal of the child to be withdrawn or suspended.[224] Although this appears at first blush a suitable remedy for the foster parents, it is not. This is because the withdrawal of authorisation to remove the child does not create any rights for the foster parents or restore the child to the foster parents; on the contrary, withdrawal of the authorisation restores the child to the natural parents.[225] The foster parents have no recourse to the court, which can result in the court exercising restraint over the decisions of the family guardianship agency. Although the Child Protection Council has a power to bring such decisions to the court, it can only act in time if it is informed by the family guardianship agency of the latter's proposed actions. In practice, the timely information is seldom forthcoming.[226]

The argument given for the weak position of the foster parents when the child is subject to a supervision order is that the supervision order is intended to be a temporary measure. Thus, it is not envisaged that the child will bond with the foster parents; accordingly, it is not thought to be in the child's interests to safeguard his or her home with the foster parents. On the contrary, the idea is that the child will be restored to the natural parents as soon as possible. But, in practice, children often do stay with foster parents for long periods of time. In fact, before the reform in 1995 a supervision order could not last more than two years; since 1995 this restriction no longer applies. It is therefore necessary to accept that the foster parents and foster child can bond, and that this bonding can form 'family life' within the meaning of Art 8 of the ECHR. Accordingly, there is much to be said for the proposal brought by Bruning that if family life has been established between foster parents and child, every change in the child's residence requires a judicial decision.[227]

2 INSUFFICIENT REGARD FOR THE CHILD'S INTERESTS

The Dutch Family Council's investigation into the case management of 28 cases of children in long-term foster care reveals that the interests of the children were

---

[222] Dutch Supreme Court, 10 March 1989, *Nederlandse Jurisprudentie 1990*, 24; Dutch Supreme Court, 23 March 1990, *Nederlandse Jurisprudentie 1991*, 150.

[223] Article 263(2), Book 1, Dutch Civil Code.

[224] Article 263(4), ibid.

[225] AC Quik-Schuijt, 'Het Arnhemse Hof en de rechtspositie van pleegouders', *Tijdschrift voor Familie- en Jeugdrecht 1999*, 75–77.

[226] Dutch Family Council report, *Thuisplaatsing van pleegkinderen* (2001).

[227] M Bruning, 'Pleegouders: verzorgers zonder recht?', *Ars Aequi* 2000, 846–848; M Bruning, 'Herziening ots (nog) geen verbetering voor betrokkenen, hoofdlijnen van de wetsevaluatie ots' (2001) *Tijdschrift voor Familie- en Jeugdrecht* 137–144; *Nederlands gezinsraad, Thuisplaatsing van pleegkinderen* (Den Haag 2001).

seldom, if ever, in the foreground. On the contrary, the legal position of the natural parents is dominant. This attitude is stimulated by the case-law of the European Court of Human Rights, which insists on a very high standard of protection of parental rights. But the position of the child is almost completely overlooked. To make matters worse, children have no procedural protection in these decisions. In many cases their opinions were not asked. In the light of Arts 9 and 12 of the ICRC the procedural as well as substantive law position of children in this area needs revision.

3   ABSENCE OF PRESSURE TO MAKE A DECISION REGARDING THE CHILD'S FUTURE

A second problem with long-term foster care when the child is subject to a supervision order is that the present legislation does not require anybody, at a given moment in time, to make a decision regarding the child's future. The child can thus remain in foster care for years, subject to the uncertainty as to when and if the foster care will end. The child is thus led on by the promise – in many cases, an illusion – that he or she will eventually be returned to the natural parents. In the meantime, uncertainty about the future makes it impossible for the child and foster parents to bond. Since bonding in a loving relationship is essential to the healthy development of the child's personality, it is evident that the present legislation leads to a result which is detrimental to the child's interests.[228] Part of the problem is a sort of inertia, by which the agencies involved with the child prefer to let sleeping dogs lie as long as the child is with the foster parents, and the natural parents do not ask for return of the child. The legal difficulty arises because the measure which has to be sought is removal or suspension of the natural parents' rights. For removal of the parents' rights, the court must be satisfied that the parent is 'unable or unsuitable to care for the child'.[229] But the Dutch Supreme Court has held that, as long as the parent agrees to voluntary placement of the child with the foster parents, it cannot be said that the parents are unsuitable or unable to care for the child. The Dutch Supreme Court stated that the willingness of the parents to allow the child to be brought up by others already shows a sufficient discharge of parental care such that removal of parental rights is not possible.[230] However, the Dutch Supreme Court held that removal of parental rights could be ordered if the parents' decision to allow the child to remain with the foster parents appeared to be uncertain or unreliable,[231] or where the natural parents do not wish to bring the child up themselves, but object to particular foster parents.[232] Some authors, for example Bruning,[233] argue that this attitude of the Dutch Supreme Court sufficiently protects the child and makes further reform unnecessary. But others argue that it is necessary, especially in the light of Art 20

---

[228]   T Weterings, e.a., 'De (on)bruikbaarheid van het huidige maatregelenpakket bij de langdurige pleegzorgplaatsing'(2001) *Tijdschrift voor Familie- en Jeugdrecht*, 66–73.

[229]   Article 268(2), Book 1, Dutch Civil Code.

[230]   Dutch Supreme Court, 7 April 2000, *Nederlandse Jurisprudentie 2000*, 563, annotation de Boer.

[231]   Dutch Supreme Court, 15 June 1990, *Nederlandse Jurisprudentie 1990*, 631; Dutch Supreme Court, 8 May 1992, *Nederlandse Jurisprudentie 1992*, 498.

[232]   Dutch Supreme Court, 4 April 1994, *Nederlandse Jurisprudentie 1994*, 523.

[233]   M Bruning, 'OTS of ontheffing bij pleeggezinplaatsing; een vervolg; is de HR om?' (2000) *Tijdschrift voor Familie- en Jeugdrecht*, 157–160.

of the ICRC, to introduce a statutory requirement to take a decision about the child's future, in order to protect the child from protracted insecurity regarding the future.[234] The Dutch Family Council has for these reasons argued that in many cases an order suspending or terminating parental rights is to be preferred to the protracted duration of the supervision order.[235]

An attractive proposal to regulate the position of long-term foster parents and their foster charges is provided by Bruning.[236] She proposes a series of new measures, which will be outlined. First, she proposes an 'upbringing-support measure', intended to provide intensive practical support to the child and parent in the existing situation. This measure is similar to the present supervision order, with the one difference that it cannot be combined with compulsory placement of the child outside the natural parents' home. It can, however, be combined with a voluntary placement with foster parents. The measure should not last more than one year, with very restricted possibility of extension. The whole purpose of the measure is to provide high quality support to the child's upbringing; thus there should be an upbringing plan in which very concrete objectives are specified. Two variants on this measure are possible. There could be 'upbringing-support for adolescents'. The objectives should be to support the adolescent in attaining independence; there is no question of reunion with the parents (in the physical sense). A second variant, based upon recent Supreme Court case-law (discussed in Section **VIII.B.2** above), would be 'access-support'. This is a measure to provide practical support for the achievement of access between parent and child. This measure could be applied only if the court has determined that the disadvantages of not having access outweigh the disadvantages of an enforcement measure of this kind. Two recent decisions of the Dutch Supreme Court stress that a court should be convinced in the particular case that the measure of enforced access really serves the child's interests.[237]

Bruning's second proposed measure is an 'upbringing-placement'. In this measure the child and parent are physically separated. The measure should only be used if lesser measures are not effective and should last for a maximum of one year. In this measure the ultimate aim should be to restore the relationship between parent and child.

The third category propounded by Bruning is an 'upbringing-placement for unlimited time'. The decision to take such a measure should be made not later than two years after the child was physically separated from the natural parents. Once this measure is in place, it is no longer the objective to restore the (natural) parent–child relationship. The purpose of the measure is to provide the child with the necessary continuity and security. The natural parents do not have to be excluded from having a role in the child's upbringing, but it might be appropriate at this stage to transfer certain parental rights to the foster parents or the family guardianship agency.

---

[234]   Weterings, op cit, n 228 above.

[235]   *Thuisplaatsing van pleegkinderen* (2001).

[236]   M Bruning, 'Herziening kinderbeschermingsmaatregelen: over noodzaak en uitstel, *Tijdschrift voor Familie- en Jeugdrecht* 2002, 102–108'.

[237]   Dutch Supreme Court, 13 April 2001 (two cases), *Nederlandse Jurisprudentie 2002*, 4 and 5.

As an ultimate resort, Bruning suggests termination of parental rights. This would be a reform for Dutch law, which at present has two overlapping measures: the removal and the suspension of parental rights (see Section **VIII.A** above). Considerable confusion exists as to the relationship between these two measures; accordingly, a proposal to unify them can be welcomed. The question whether parental rights should be terminated should be approached from the point of view of the child's needs, not from the point of view of any culpability or otherwise of the parents.

The weak position of the foster parents is reflected in the non-recognition of the financial implications of foster parenting. According to the Dutch Supreme Court on 21 February 2001, the right to respect for family life protected in Art 8 of the ECHR is not violated by Art 19 of the Succession Tax Act. That Article provides that a foster child does not have the privileged position of 'child' for Succession Tax Act purposes unless the child has been cared for by the foster parent to the exclusion of the natural parent for a minimum of five years. According to the Dutch Supreme Court, Art 19 did not, on the facts, place the child in a dilemma which might be prohibited by Art 8 of the ECHR, such that he or she would have to choose between forgoing succession tax advantages and definitively leaving his or her natural parents. In particular, there was no evidence that either the child or the foster parents had felt any restriction in the way in which they lived their family life.[238]

In a letter of 8 June 2001, the Ministers of Health and Welfare and Justice indicated that they intend to implement a number of measures to deal with problems in three areas: the payment system for foster parents, the improvement in the support system for foster parents and improvement of the legal position of foster parents.[239] In a letter dated 19 December 2001,[240] the Minister of Justice expounded a more general range of hot issues relating to child protection. These are:

- Is there a need for a 'lesser' child protection measure than a supervision order? (discussed in Section **VIII.A** above);
- Is there a need to improve the legal position of long-term foster parents by giving them (the right to apply for) custody rights?
- Does the present system of child protection measures satisfy the requirements of the European Convention on Human Rights and the United Nations Convention on the Rights of the Child?
- How should the problems faced in the practice of supervision orders be tackled?

Concrete proposals can thus be expected at a later stage, and will be examined in a later *Survey*.

---

[238] Dutch Supreme Court (tax chamber), 21 February 2001, NJB 2001–13, p 639.

[239] Second Chamber 2000–2001, 27 410, nr 19; Second Chamber 1999–2000, 26 816, nr 27.

[240] Second Chamber 2001–220, 28 000 VI, nr 46, p 5; Second Chamber 2001–2002, 28 000 VI, nr 55 (21 February 2002).

C   Legislative proposal to regulate child abuse advice – and reporting centres

1   BACKGROUND TO THE ACT

In 1972 the government had commenced, by way of experiment, a system of Confidential Doctor Offices to which suspected child abuse could be reported. This experiment was so successful that it was extended to become a national network. In 1989 the Confidential Doctors Offices were brought within the purview of the Child Assistance Act (*Wet op de Jeugdhulpverlening*) (see Section **VIII.D** below). In 1987 a commission was asked to investigate the functioning of the Confidential Doctors Offices. This committee reported in 1991 in its report 'Legal position'; as is clear from the report's title, the committee advised that legal regulation of the Confidential Doctors Offices' position was needed. In 1993 the government reacted by stating that legislation would follow. Around the time that the government took up this position regarding the Confidential Doctors Offices, another debate commenced regarding the need to have a child abuse advice and reporting centre. To examine this issue, the Hermans Commission was appointed in 1994. The proposals in the Bill on Advice and Reporting Centres for Child Abuse (referred to hereafter as reporting centres) is based upon the practices already established in the Confidential Doctors Offices regarding the giving of advice and reporting. The provisions on advice and reporting centres are inserted into the Child Assistance Act.

On 3 July 2001 the government presented to the Second Chamber a Bill to regulate reporting of child abuse.[241] In 1998 the Hermans Commission published the results of its investigations into the reporting of child abuse.[242] In reaction to this report, the government announced that it intended to regulate in legislation the powers and responsibilities of the Centres for advice and reporting of child abuse. The Act, which was passed on 26 September 2002,[243] gives effect to that intention.

2   THE ACT CREATES A POWER NOT A DUTY TO REPORT

The Act deals with three matters: first, it defines the responsibilities of the advice and reporting centres; secondly, it regulates the complicated questions of privacy which arise in the context of reporting of child abuse, and thirdly, it prescribes the procedures to be followed in reporting child abuse. For the avoidance of doubt, in the Netherlands a choice has been made not to introduce a *duty* to report. Instead the law concentrates on giving the reporting centres the *power* to receive and deal with reports which are voluntarily made.[244] The government gave its reasons for not introducing a duty to report. First, experiences abroad suggest that a relatively high level of false reports could be expected. Secondly, a duty to report might discourage individuals from approaching professionals for help. Thirdly, the

---

[241]   Wijziging van de wet op de Jeugdhulpverlening in verband met de advies- en meldpunten mishandeling, Second Chamber 2000–2001, 27 842, nrs 1–2 and 3.

[242]   The Hermans Commission report is discussed in Dutch report, *The International Survey of Family Law 1997*, ed A Bainham (Martinus Nijhoff Publishers, 1999), at 300–301.

[243]   *Staatsblad* 2002, 515. To be brought into force by statutory instrument; to date (14 January 2003) not yet in force.

[244]   Second Chamber 2001–2002, 27 842, nr 5, p 2.

imposition of a duty to report may obstruct the possibility for a professional to resolve the problems in consultation with the family. A power to report gives the professional the opportunity to take the matter further when such an attempt has failed.[245] However, in one situation there is a duty to report. This applies in the case of professionals working with children in the field of child protection. If the executive of a child care institution becomes aware that a person working in the institution is committing child abuse, the executive is obliged to report that fact to the reporting centre. Furthermore, any individual working for such an organisation who becomes aware that another employee is committing or has committed child abuse is obliged to report such fact to the executive.[246] A similar duty to report already applies to the executive of educational bodies and employees of such bodies.

3   FUNCTIONS OF THE REPORTING CENTRES

The reporting centres do not have the functions of prevention, crisis intervention or assistance. The key responsibilities will be the giving of advice, performing consultation, accepting, investigating and forming a judgment upon appropriate action to be taken on a report of suspected child abuse, referral and transfer of cases, co-ordination of assistance, and providing feedback to reporters of child abuse.

The first function concerns the giving of advice.[247] In this case, the reporting centre will only record the personal details of the person seeking advice with that person's consent. In the case of any information recorded, the data protection laws apply without restriction. A difficult situation may arise if, in consequence of information brought by a person seeking advice, the reporting centre becomes aware that there is a situation in which it appears possible or likely that a child is being abused. In this case, the reporting centre should retain a passive attitude. It should try to encourage the person seeking advice to report the suspected abuse. But if the person seeking advice does not wish to report, the reporting centre should not take action on its own initiative. The reporting centre should only act on its own initiative if it is very clear that a child is being abused. This passive attitude is necessary in order to secure the confidence of those seeking advice. A more interventionist approach in these circumstances might deter people from coming to the centre for advice.[248]

The second function of the centre is to receive reports of suspected child abuse. Ordinary members of the public as well as professionals (police, school staff) and persons working in the child care sector may report child abuse. In acute cases in which the reporting centre believes that urgent action is necessary, it may refer the case immediately to the Child Protection Agency without conducting further investigation. The Child Protection Agency may also be approached

---

[245]   Second Chamber 2001–2002, 27 842, nr 5, p 16; Second Chamber 57-3908-9, 19 March 2002 (Vliegenthart).

[246]   Article 34e, Child Assistance Act; introduced by amendment, Arib et al, Second Chamber 2001–2002, 27 842, nr 14 (amendment) (see nrs 9 and 12).

[247]   Article 34a(2), Child Assistance Act.

[248]   Second Chamber 2000–2001, 27 842, nr 3, p 10.

directly in any case in which there is an acute risk and urgent action is needed. All other cases should be brought in the first instance to the reporting centre.

Upon receipt of a report, the reporting centre must investigate the report and decide what action needs to be taken.[249] In order to carry out this task of investigation, the reporting centre may talk with the person who reported the suspected abuse; it may request information from other professional bodies or from the local authority registration system; it may talk with the person whom the report concerns (suspected abuser) or, if different, the child's parents, and with the child concerned, or with others, such as teachers. This procedure should conclude with either a referral to the Child Protection Agency or to a voluntary assistance agency or a decision that no action need be taken. The initiative should be that which is most suited to the child.[250] If the reporting centre concludes that action needs to be taken regarding the parents' rights of custody, the reporting centre must transfer the case to the Child Protection Agency.[251] The reporting centre may refer the case to other bodies, such as the police.[252] If a referral is made, the reporting centre will follow up the case not later than six months after the date of referral, to establish the outcome of the referral.

Finally, the reporting centre should report the outcome back to the person who made the report.[253] Members of the public will only be informed that the matter has been investigated. Professionals will be given details of the problem identified and the way it has been resolved; and child care workers will be informed of the entire case and its outcome. The Hermans Commission stressed the importance of this feedback, which should have the effect of strengthening the willingness of the public to come forward and remove uncertainty about the effects of reporting child abuse.

In order to enact legislation on reporting child abuse it was necessary to provide a definition of child abuse. This is:

> 'Every form of physical, mental or sexual interaction involving violence or threats towards a minor by parents or other persons in relation to whom the child is in a position of dependence or otherwise not at liberty. The action by the parent or other person towards the child may be active or passive and must be such that serious damage is caused or threatens to be caused to the minor in the form of physical or mental damage.'[254]

This definition excludes violence towards children by persons not in a parental or similar position; thus violence by other children is not included, however serious. The definition also excludes violence by persons who have no relationship whatsoever with the child. A crucial element is the element of damage. Particularly in cases of mental damage, where the damage often appears much later in the abused child's life, this requirement of damage is a serious restriction. In debate in the Second and First Chambers, concern was expressed about the fact that the requirement of proof of damage sets a higher hurdle for proof of child

---

[249] Article 34a(1)(b), Child Assistance Act.
[250] Article 34a(1)(c), ibid.
[251] Article 34a(1)(d), ibid.
[252] Article 34a(1)(e), ibid.
[253] Article 34a(1)(f), ibid.
[254] Second Chamber 2000–2001, 27 842, nr 3, p 12.

abuse than in the criminal law.[255] The definition includes inaction; accordingly, neglect is also covered. The definition also includes the failure to take steps to prevent the child from being abused by another person. The reporting centres are only concerned with abuse of children. Other groups, such as mentally challenged or older persons, are not covered by this reporting system.

A difficult issue is the question of anonymity. The Confidential Doctors Offices follow a policy of maximum openness towards the family concerned with the report. However, in practice, it is also necessary to take account of the wish of some reporters to remain anonymous. It is possible for a reporter of child abuse to remain anonymous vis-à-vis the child and the family. The reporting centre is entitled to refuse to disclose this identity to the family and child.[256] However, reports from reporters who will not disclose their identity to the reporting centre will not be accepted. Furthermore, a reporter who is a professional providing services to the family which are connected to the child's upbringing cannot remain anonymous vis-à-vis the family. This includes the family GP. In these circumstances it is reasonable to expect the professional to discuss the matter with the family. A report from such a person, without disclosing that person's identity to the family, can only be accepted if disclosure would put the child at risk, or if disclosure would for some reason damage the relationship between the professional and the family. Other professionals, such as crèche workers or teachers, are entitled to remain anonymous vis-à-vis the family and the child but not vis-à-vis the reporting centre. Whenever possible, also these reporters should talk things over with the family first. But their relationship to the family is generally of a different character to that of, for example, a GP, so that the opportunity for discussion of suspected child abuse is not so evident.

Detailed rules lay down the procedures to be followed by the reporting centres, the interaction between the reporting centres and the Child Welfare Agency, and the circumstances in which a person is entitled to make an anonymous report.[257]

4 THE FUNCTIONS OF THE REPORTING CENTRE AND THE PROTECTION OF PRIVACY

The introduction of child abuse reporting centres raises difficult issues regarding privacy protection. For this reason, a number of exceptions have had to be made in the Data Protection Act. Personal privacy is protected in Art 10 of the Dutch Constitution and in Art 8 of the ECHR. The storage and dissemination of personal information is regulated by the Data Protection Act 2001, which implements the European Directive of 24 October 1995 on the protection of natural persons in connection with storage and dissemination of personal information.[258] In general, the handling of personal information must be done carefully and responsibly. Such data may only be collected for circumscribed, justified purposes. Furthermore,

---

[255]   Article 300, Criminal Code; Second Chamber, 19 March 2002, 57-3919 (Rouvoet (ChristenUnie)); First Chamber 2001–2002, 27 842, nr 295a, p 3 (Groenlinks).

[256]   Article 43(e), Data Protection Act.

[257]   Besluit advies- en meldpunten kindermishandeling, Wet op de jeugdhulpverlening 21 June 2002, Staatscourant 2002, nr 116, p 11.

[258]   Directive 95/46/EG.

every action must be proportionate. In particular, the interference with individual privacy must not be greater than necessary to satisfy the purpose for which storage is made, and must take place in the least interfering manner. Finally, certain categories of information are, because of their extra sensitivity for the individual, subject to extra restrictions. This concerns particularly information regarding health and criminal activities.

In order to investigate a report of suspected abuse, the reporting centre may need to retrieve and store information regarding the child, his or her family members, the informer and the suspected abuser. In principle, this information may only be retrieved and used with the consent of the persons concerned. But the character of the work of the reporting centres requires that exceptions apply. The reporting centre is entitled to retrieve and store information as is necessary to carry out its functions unless, in the circumstances, the rights and freedoms of the individuals concerned should have priority.[259]

In general, the permission of the child should be sought before information regarding him or her is disclosed to third parties. Nevertheless, the reporting centre is entitled to disseminate information regarding the child who is the subject of the report to any person whose co-operation, in a professional capacity, is necessary in connection with protection of the child. This exception extends to the child's legal representatives. If the child is under the age of 16, the child's legal representatives generally have to be asked for permission to disclose information regarding their child. But the reporting centre may, if the circumstances so require, disseminate information regarding the child to the necessary professionals described above without requesting the permission of the child's personal representatives.[260] If the reporting centre discloses information to third parties under these provisions it is obliged by law to inform the persons to whom the information pertains that the disclosure has taken place. In general, this information should be provided at the moment at which the information is taken and stored. However, the reporting centre need not inform the person immediately if supplying the information would place the child at serious risk. In these circumstances, the reporting centre is obliged to delay informing the persons concerned of the storage of information regarding them, for a maximum period of four weeks. This period may be extended by two weeks if such delay is necessary in order to end a situation of child abuse or to investigate reasonably suspected child abuse.[261] This requirement is onerous for the reporting centre. The two-week period requires the reporting centre to justify repeatedly the delay in informing the persons affected. Moreover, it is quite likely that the two-week or four-week periods will run at different times regarding the various persons involved in any particular case. It may happen that a parent or other person has suspicions that an inquiry is running, and makes an approach to the reporting centre to ask whether information is being collected about himself or herself. In general, the law requires such person to be informed immediately if information is being collected. But in this case also an exception applies, to make it possible for the reporting centre to carry out its work. Thus, even when a person makes a direct inquiry

---

[259] Article 8(f), Data Protection Act.
[260] Articles 44(3) and 34c(1), Child Assistance Act.
[261] Articles 34d(1) and (2), ibid.

whether information is being collected about him or her, the reporting centre is entitled to refuse to answer if disclosure would cause serious damage to the child's interests.[262]

Some information is, because of its sensitive nature for the persons concerned, subject to extra restrictions under the Data Protection Act.[263] This concerns, in particular, information pertaining to the health of the child or other persons, and information regarding the criminal record of the child or others. The reporting centres are entitled under existing law to process such sensitive information regarding the child insofar as such processing is necessary for the good treatment of the child concerned. The word 'treatment' is intended to have a broader meaning than simply medical treatment.[264] But the reporting centres may also need to process information regarding the health or criminal record of other persons. The Act gives the reporting centres such power if a report has been made from which a reasonable inference can be made that a child is being abused.[265]

Further provisions regulate the provision of information to the reporting centres. For example, the reporting centre may wish to seek information from the GP or the child's school or crèche. Information from the police, the child's guardian or the child welfare circuit may be needed. Furthermore, the accuracy of this information may need to be checked against the information stored by the local authority. Because disclosure of this information infringes the right to privacy of the individuals concerned, all of these bodies are subject to restrictions regarding the disclosure of the information to the reporting centres. Some of these bodies are subject to specialised legislation regarding the disclosure of information. Insofar as disclosure is not covered by specialised legislation, the Data Protection Act applies. Many of the individuals mentioned in this paragraph are furthermore subject to a professional duty of confidence. According to existing case-law it is already accepted that a person is discharged from the professional duty of confidence whenever a professional is confronted by a conflict of duties and the other duty outweighs the professional's duty of confidence. A doctor is thus discharged from the duty of confidence to his or her patient if the doctor is aware of circumstances relevant to a situation in which a child is being abused and confidential information pertaining to the patient is relevant to that situation of child abuse. The entitlement of the doctor to disclose is not unrestricted; the disclosure is itself subject to further qualifications regarding the manner and timing of disclosure and the persons to whom disclosure is made. The Bill thus codifies existing law by making it clear that a professional may be entitled to disclose information even though the doctor has obtained that information in the context of a professional duty of confidence.[266] In its commentary on the Bill, the Council of State remarked that it did not consider that the proposed reform would lead to any increase in certainty in the law for the professionals concerned. It remains a difficult decision for a professional who, when confronted by the

---

[262] Article 34d(3), Child Assistance Act.
[263] Articles 16–23, Data Protection Act.
[264] Article 21, ibid.
[265] Regarding health matters: Article 34c(2), Child Assistance Act; regarding criminal record, Art 34c in conjunction with Art 21(3), Data Protection Act.
[266] Article 34c(3), Child Assistance Act.

dilemma, must take the decision alone and face the consequences later in case of error. Considerable certainty would be given to professionals were the various professional bodies to give thought to the matter and each work out a code of practice.[267] A further provision places beyond doubt that the local authorities are obliged to supply information to reporting centres insofar as such information is necessary to discharge the responsibilities of the latter.[268] It is of great importance to find a way of creating more security for professionals in this matter; the Hermans Commission was informed that in 27% of cases in which a professional was aware that a child was being abused, the professional nevertheless chose not to disclose the information. It is perhaps necessary to make it absolutely clear to professionals that, where the overriding duty to disclose confidential information obtains in order to avert a situation of child abuse, there is no violation of the duty of confidence. This point is not entirely clear in Dutch law, where the matter rather tends to be presented as if there is a violation of the duty of confidence, but that the violation does not attract liability.[269]

If a local authority discloses information regarding a person (X) to any other person or body, the local authority is subject to a duty to inform X of the disclosure within four weeks.[270] The existing exceptions to this duty do not cover the case of disclosure of information to prevent child abuse. Accordingly, a new provision in the Act entitles the local authority to abstain from disclosing to a person that information regarding that person has been requested and disclosed, if such abstention is necessary in order to end a situation of child abuse or to investigate a reasonable suspicion of child abuse.[271]

The reporting centres have the right to store the information collected under the above-mentioned provisions. However, that right of storage is not indefinite. The information may be stored, when reports have been made regarding several children in the same family, until the youngest child, with whom the reports were concerned, has attained the age of majority.[272] The material may be stored only if the material makes a contribution to the termination of the situation of child abuse in that family or if it is reasonable to assume that the material needs to be used with respect to a possible child protection measure. The reporting centre is obliged to destroy information stored within three months of such a request by the person to whom the information pertains.[273] The reporting centre is entitled to refuse to carry out the destruction if the material is needed in order to protect the interest of another person or if a legislative provision prohibits destruction.[274] A child of 12 years or younger, or a child older than 12 years who is not capable of appreciating his or her own interests in the matter, is not entitled to request destruction of information.[275] In such a case the application may be made by the

---

[267]   Second Chamber 2000–2001, 27 842, nr 3, p 26; Second Chamber 2000–2001, 27 842, A, p 4.
[268]   Article 34c(4), Child Assistance Act.
[269]   I van der Straete and J Put, 'Doorbreking van het beroepsgeheim bij kindermishandeling: een belgisch-Nederlandse vergelijking' (2002) *Tijdschrift voor Familie- en Jeugdrecht* 66–73.
[270]   Article 103(3), Wet gemeentelijke basisadministratie persoonsgegevens.
[271]   Article 34c(5), Child Assistance Act.
[272]   Article 44a, ibid.
[273]   Article 44b(1), ibid.
[274]   Article 44b(2), ibid.
[275]   Article 44b(3), ibid.

child's legal representative.[276] Reporting centres will undoubtedly receive reports which, after investigation, turn out to be false or unfounded. This is one reason why it is important that the persons concerned are informed of the reports made about them; they are entitled to request destruction of the information stored. This aspect may require further attention in the future.

5 EVALUATION OF EFFECTS OF THE ACT

The Committee on the Rights of the Child observed, in reaction to the report submitted by the Netherlands under Art 44 of the UN Convention on the Rights of the Child, that it welcomed the efforts of the Netherlands to establish a network of child abuse reporting and counselling centres and the plans to strengthen child abuse monitoring and reporting systems.[277] The passing of this Act is a significant contribution to the responsibilities of the State under Art 19 of the Convention. That Article requires the State to take measures to protect children from all forms of physical and mental violence, neglect or negligent treatment, maltreatment or exploitation, whilst in the care of parent(s), legal guardian(s) or any other person who has the care of the child. The way that the Act has operated will be evaluated three years after it comes into force.[278] A choice has been made not to introduce a duty to report; that was thought to be counter-productive. But one of the purposes of the provisions is to increase the rate of reporting; according to some figures only one-third of all cases of child abuse are actually reported. The effectiveness of the system in preventing child abuse depends to a considerable extent upon the capacity of the existing services to respond to the referrals which are made by the reporting centres. At the present time there are serious waiting lists for child protection services. If the proposed regulation of reporting centres is successful, an increase in the reporting of child abuse may be expected – an increase of 10% is estimated. But this will lead to further burdening of the child protection services. It would be contrary to the purpose of this legislation were the reporting centres to be tardy, through over-load or other causes, in reacting to reports of child abuse. The statutory instrument allows the reporting centres three months from the date of report of suspected child abuse to conduct their investigation. In the First Chamber there were comments that this period is too long.[279] The government is giving its attention to that problem.[280]

---

[276]   Article 44b(4), Child Assistance Act.

[277]   Committee on the Rights of the Child, Twenty-second session, 26 October 1999, United Nations website CRC/C/15/Add 114, para C 17.

[278]   Artikel IIA: Second Chamber 2001–2002, 27 842, nr 11 (Tweede nota van wijziging) (25 April 2002).

[279]   First Chamber, 24 September 2002, EK 1–8 (Swenker); EK 1–17 (Swenker, Le Poole); 1–19 (Ross-van Dorp).

[280]   Second Chamber 2001–2002, 27 842, nr 5, p 13; Second Chamber 2000–2001, 28 007, nr 1; Second Chamber, 19 March 2002, 57–3913; First Chamber 2001–2002, 27 842, nr 295b, p 3; 24 September 2002, EK 1–13 (Ross-van Dorp); cf Peer Commission Wachtlijsten in de jeudgzorg.

D   Bill on Youth Care Law

1   BACKGROUND TO THE BILL

A Bill regulating the entire field of Child Care Law was introduced into the Second Chamber on 18 December 2001.[281] This Bill is intended to replace the Child Assistance Act which came into force in 1990. The Bill regulates the right to care, access to care and the financing of the care provision services. The field of child care has long been challenged by the multiplicity of different organs providing overlapping or not-quite interlocking services. The Child Assistance Act aimed at achieving co-ordination and co-operation of this vast network of services, but even shortly after coming into force it became clear that the Act did not succeed in that goal. The problem was that a number of organisations, providing various forms of child care, managed to negotiate a position outside the purview of the Act. Thus, organisations concerned with children's mental health, family guardianship agencies and closed institutions remained outside the Act. Furthermore, those organisations fell under the responsibility of the Ministry of Justice, whereas the child care institutions covered by the Child Assistance Act were answerable to the Ministry of Health, Welfare and Sport. The Child Assistance Act did achieve some steps in the direction of cohesion and co-ordination by imposing the obligation upon agencies to co-operate, but the steps taken were not enough to satisfy the stringent demands of an over-stretched sector. In 1994 the two responsible Ministries initiated a child care management policy,[282] which helped to stimulate co-operation in the child care sector. The Child Care Bill codifies that policy and seeks to underpin the interconnection between the various parts of the child care sector.

The reforms introduced in this Bill are not revolutionary, but rather follow an approach which can already be found in countries such as England and Germany. In fact the Kinder- und Jugendhilfegesetz already placed the German child care system at regional and local level in 1990. England and Germany already have an integrated entry-point for determining access to child care services. And in both countries, the integration of services goes further than will be achieved by the Child Care Bill, even if that Bill achieves its objectives. Both countries enjoy the advantage that the child care system falls under the responsibility of one ministry; not two, as in the Netherlands.[283]

2   INTEGRATION AND CO-ORDINATION OF SERVICES

Child care for the purposes of the Bill is defined as 'support of and the giving of assistance to children, their parents, step-parents or others insofar as they care for and rear children within their family, in development or child-rearing problems or the threat thereof and in child protection matters'. The Bill is concerned with situations in which upbringing has become problematic, and with private

---

[281]   Regeling van de aanspraak op, de toegang tot en de bekostiging van jeugdzorg (Wet op de jeugdzorg), Second Chamber 2001–2002, 28 168.

[282]   Regie in de Jeugdzorg, Rijswijk, Den Haag, Ministerie van VWS en Ministerie van Justitie, 1994.

[283]   A Van Unen, 'Concept-Wet op de Jeugdzorg: sluitstuk van en aanzet tot ontwikkelingen in de jeugdzorg' (2001) *Tijdschrift voor Familie- en Jeugdrecht* 213.

(ie non-criminal) child protection measures (supervision orders or suspension or termination of custody).

From an organisational point of view, the Bill provides for one entry-point into the child care system: the child care offices. There will be one child care office in each province. The child care office will be the access-point to all provision of child institutions following a child protection order, most institutions concerned with mental health care for children and the care for mentally challenged children with problems relating to development and upbringing, and other institutions concerned with voluntary child care. However, although the child care offices form the access-point for these institutions, if the bodies concerned are regulated by other statutory regimes, as are the institutions concerned with child protection and children's mental health, those statutory regimes will continue to regulate the bodies as before.

In order to stimulate co-ordination of the various parts of the sector, the Bill creates an obligation to co-operate. Measures are taken in the Bill to ensure that the facilities offered are in accordance with needs. This needs-driven approach contrasts with the approach in the Child Assistance Act which was organised around the characteristics of the providers.

3   DE-CENTRALISATION

The Bill seeks to develop a considerable degree of de-centralisation. Thus, responsibility for financing and organisation of voluntary child care bodies and the family guardianship agencies rests with the provinces. However, the Child Protection Agency and the institutions receiving children pursuant to a child protection order remain under the direct responsibility of the Ministry of Justice. According to the Bill, each province must draw up, in consultation with health insurers, local authorities, the Ministry of Justice, client organisations, the child care offices and the providers, a four-yearly policy plan. This plan must strive to achieve a balance in the need and provision of services, stimulate co-ordination and take account of local policy regarding child care. Since 1994 the provinces have shown that they are capable of assuming these responsibilities; the Bill gives them a legislative basis.

4   A STATUTORY RIGHT TO CHILD CARE

Under the present Dutch law there is no general right to child care. There is a right to mental health care for children and a right to care for developmentally challenged children, because this care is financed by the general health insurance fund.[284] Furthermore, a child has a right to be protected against neglect and abuse. The Child Care Bill introduces a right to child care, insofar as such claim does not already exist under other legislation. The right to child care of children who are placed in institutions pursuant to a child care order will not be secured under the Child Care Bill, because the legal position of these children is regulated in another

---

[284]   Algemene Wet Bijzondere Ziektekosten.

statute.[285] Furthermore, there is no right to child care in respect of general social work services provided for children.[286]

The right to child care gives the child concerned and his or her parents a claim-right to the services which, following screening by the child care office, have been determined to be necessary for the child. If the care indicated cannot be provided, the child and parents have a claim which may ultimately be enforced against the providers or the health insurers in the administrative court. Van Unen argues that the introduction of the right to child care is a much-needed specification of the fundamental social rights to health care laid down in Arts 20–23 of the Dutch Constitution. Without such specification, the rights cannot provide the basis for directly enforceable individual claims.[287] Several courts have indicated that a structural shortage of facilities for certain categories of children is a violation of Arts 3(2) and 20(1) of the United Nations Convention on the Rights of the Child.

5 CHILD CARE OFFICES

The child care offices have the following functions: first, they are the only access point to the child care system. In this capacity, they have responsibility for screening, diagnosing and making referral to the appropriate provider. They should stimulate early action by providing facilities for consultation. They should support and guide the client. They should offer a family guardian or guardian. They should provide a youth probation service. And they should provide an advice and reporting centre for child abuse (see Section **VIII.C** above).

The key position of each child care office in each province requires that the Offices are entirely separate from any providers. Offices which are currently collaborating in an organisational sense with providers will have to end such collaboration.

The decisions taken by the child care offices are subject to judicial review by the administrative courts. Furthermore, the Child Care and Protection Inspection Service will scrutinise, not just whether the Child Care Act is complied with, but also whether the child care offices function effectively.

6 FINANCING

The focus of the reform in financing is to ensure that the providers are responding to identified needs indicated through care programmes.

The use of the provincial child care office as sole entry-point is a serious contribution to coherence in a labyrinth of services. But this approach is not underpinned by the system of financing of the various providers. Thus the voluntary child care and child protection sector is financed by the provinces; the health insurers finance the child mental health services; and the Ministry of Justice finances the institutions receiving children pursuant to child protection measures.[288]

---

[285] Beginselenwet justitiële jeugdinrichtingen.

[286] Welzijnswet 1994, Wet justitie subsidies, Wet collectieve preventie.

[287] A Van Unen, *De wet op de jeugdhulpverlening: overheid of particulier initiatief?* (Lemma Uitgevers, Utrecht, 1996).

[288] Van Unen (2001), op cit, n 283 above, p 209.

7 COMPLAINTS AND MEDIATION PROCEDURES

In 1997 every branch of the care sector was required to introduce a client complaints body. The Child Care Bill now requires each organisation to have a separate client complaints body. There are already a number of practical difficulties with the existing obligations; in particular, it is difficult to find enough persons willing to staff them.

A further difficult point is that many organisations have a mediation procedure. Van Unen argues that the Bill fails to deal with a number of aspects of the use of mediation and client complaints bodies. For instance, it should be made clear that a client is entitled to go directly to the client complaints body, and should not be required first to engage in mediation. Furthermore, the Bill should provide that the mediator should be someone whom both parties have agreed; not a person chosen by the institution against whom the complaint is brought. The Bill should specify time limits within which a complaint should be brought, as institutions at present use differing time limits. It is further necessary that the Bill indicates which persons, apart from the child, his or her parents, step-parents and others exercising custody jointly with the parent, are entitled to complain. Some institutions accept complaints by neighbours, grandmothers; others do not. Finally, Van Unen points out that the right to complain should not be restricted to children who have attained the age of 12; children under that age should also have the right, if they are able to appreciate their own interests in the matter.[289]

E Proposal for a Children's Ombudsman

On 6 December 2001 a Bill to create a post of Ombudsman for the rights of the child was introduced into the Second Chamber by private members' bill (by members Arib and Van Vliet).[290] The Committee on the Rights of the Child remarked in its comments on the last Dutch report, submitted to the Committee on 26 October 1999, that 'it was concerned about the lack of an independent mechanism to monitor the implementation of the Convention'.[291] In a motion brought on 9 May 2000 in the Second Chamber by the members Arib and Ravestein,[292] the Second Chamber had voted to request the government to establish a Children's Ombudsman. The government's view, expressed in a letter of 13 November 2000,[293] was that the functions of such an ombudsman were already – probably – adequately covered by existing agencies. Moreover, the government noted that the functions of the children's ombudsman differed from country to country. The government thus considered that further research was necessary to establish exactly which functions of the Children's Ombudsman were not being covered at present in the Netherlands. The members Arib and Ravestein did not agree that the functions were already covered by existing agencies, and

---

[289] Ibid, pp 212–213.

[290] Voorstel van wet van de leden Arib en Van Vliet tot instelling van een kinderombudsman, Second Chamber 2001–2002, 28 102.

[291] Consideration of reports submitted by States Parties under Art 44 of the Convention, Twenty-second session, The Netherlands, CRC/C/15/Add 114, 26 October 1999, para C 12.

[292] Second Chamber 1999–2000, 26 816, nr 7.

[293] Second Chamber 2000–2001, 26 816, nr 32.

thus presented this Bill to the Second Chamber. The proposed Bill presents the Children's Ombudsman as a watchdog, who scrutinises the activities of all public authorities in the light of children's human rights. The ombudsman should act on his own initiative or on request in all situations in which the rights of children are at issue, in order to give advice to the government. Furthermore, the ombudsman should keep track of government policy regarding youth in such matters as health, schooling, developmental challenge, child care, children at work, etc. The ombudsman should be independent of all ministries. The ombudsman should have three areas of responsibility: first, supervision and implementation of the UN Convention on the Rights of the Child; secondly, giving comment, with or without request so to do, in the light of the human rights of the child, on all aspects of legislation and policy relevant to children's interests; thirdly, receiving and dealing with complaints regarding children's rights. There is already a developed network of complaints procedures regarding, in particular, the clients of child assistance services, children in closed institutions and clients of the Child Welfare Agency. Nevertheless these procedures do not always work optimally. A particular problem is that the complaints bodies are attached to the institution against which the complaint is to be brought; this feature creates a considerable degree of reluctance to bring complaints. Moreover, there are situations in which there is no one body to which a complaint can be brought. The situation would be improved if the ombudsman could act as a body of last resort for complaints.

IX ELIMINATION OF DISCRIMINATION AGAINST WOMEN

On 6 April 2002, the Dutch Parliament approved the ratification by the Netherlands of the Optional Protocol of the Convention for the Elimination of Discrimination Against Women, opened for signature on 6 October 1999 in New York.[294] The ratification by the Netherlands took effect on 22 August 2002.

The Netherlands submitted its third report to the CEDAW (Committee on the Elimination of Discrimination Against Women) in 2000.[295] The Committee found the new Dutch law regarding names to be in violation of Art 16 of the Convention.[296] The problem lies with Art 5(5), Book 1, Civil Code which provides that if the mother and father who are married do not make a choice regarding the child's surname by the date of registration of the child's birth, the child will take the father's surname by default. The Minister of Justice registered disagreement with the position of the CEDAW. The government is of the opinion that the rule applies only within marriage and that this fact provides a justification for the default rule in favour of the father's name. This view shows an assumption about the nature of marriage which appears outdated. Furthermore, the government argues that there is a need for some certainty regarding the child's name.[297] This approach is also debatable; with modern computer facilities it must be possible to

---

[294] Original text of the Convention: *Tractatenblad* 2000, 99; Dutch translation: *Tractatenblad* 2002, 6; Approval of ratification: *Tractatenblad* 2002, 131.

[295] CEDAW/C/NET/3, 22 November 2000.

[296] Paras 38–39.

[297] Brief van de Staatssecretaris Verstand aan de voorzitter van de Tweede Kamer, Den Haag, 1 October 2001.

make some provision pending a decision by the parents. Finally, the government relies upon the decision of the European Court holding the complaint in *Bijleveld v The Netherlands*[298] inadmissible for manifest unfoundedness. This argument is also unpersuasive. Although that case concerned equal treatment regarding the names given to children of married parents, it was quite a different issue to the one presently under discussion.

---

[298] Application 42973/98.

NEW ZEALAND

FROM PARENTAL RELOCATION, RIGHTS AND RESPONSIBILITIES TO 'RELATIONSHIP' PROPERTY

*Bill Atkin**

I INTRODUCTION

A wide variety of issues came before the New Zealand courts in 2001. Some of these will be noted but one which is becoming more and more a growth industry is the desire of one parent to relocate to another city or country. The principal matter before Parliament in 2001 was reform of the rules relating to property division. The former matrimonial property legislation came in for a major overhaul and many changes were made, including the incorporation of widowed parties into what had hitherto applied primarily to separating and divorced parties. But the change which captured greatest media attention and split the political parties was the inclusion of de facto (including same-sex) relationships in the new code. The new 'relationship' property statute was in fact a substantial amending of the Matrimonial Property Act 1976, even to the extent of a name change. Instead of a completely fresh Act of Parliament, the law passed in 2001 is, rather oddly, found in the Property (Relationships) Act 1976. It came into full effect on 1 February 2002.

II RELOCATION

The question of a parent and children shifting some distance from where they have been living is not new. However, it appears to be attracting more and more attention from the New Zealand courts than in the past, even at Court of Appeal level. The issue can arise when the desire is to move from one part of the country to another, but it is exacerbated when the foreshadowed move is to another country. Because New Zealand is geographically isolated, even a move to near neighbour Australia can cause all sorts of problems for maintaining contact with the other parent. While the parent who wishes to relocate may have understandable reasons for doing so, for example to be near other members of the family or for employment prospects, this may be at a cost. New Zealand has no rule in favour of joint or shared custody, but there are certain political forces which are aiming for this. In a broader sense, there appears to be a greater use of joint or shared custody (although statistics do not exist to bear this out) and a wide expectation that both parents will continue after separation to play significant roles in their children's lives. The Court of Appeal has referred to 'the growth and

* Reader in Law, Victoria University of Wellington.

degree of involvement of both parents in family care, and a clear move in Family Court orders, away from what counsel characterised as older "property" based concepts of sole custody and access, to shared care'.[1] In line with this, the emerging trend in court judgments is against relocation.

The point was tested in *D v S*,[2] a decision of the Court of Appeal which accepted the largely unfettered welfare of the child as the key criterion. The court in reality reaffirmed its earlier decision in *Stadniczenko v Stadniczenko*[3] to the effect that there were no presumptions to help resolve these cases. In the meantime however the Court of Appeal in England in *Payne v Payne*[4] had come up with an approach that, while eschewing any presumptions as such, very much played into the hands of the party wishing to relocate. According to *Payne*, 'great weight' was to be given to the reasonable proposals of the party wishing to relocate and an application to relocate 'will be granted unless the court concludes that it is incompatible with the welfare of the child'.[5] The New Zealand Court of Appeal rejected this approach. It said that 'presumptive or a priori weighing is inconsistent with the wider all-factor child-centred approach required under New Zealand law ... the reasonableness of a parent's desire to relocate with the children is to be assessed in relation to the disadvantages to the children of reduced contact with the other parent, along with all other factors'.[6] Four of the five appellate judges thought that the High Court Judge, Panckhurst J, who found in favour of relocation, had erred in relying on *Payne*. The fifth Court of Appeal judge agreed that *Payne* was not good law in New Zealand but took the view that Panckhurst J had not in fact relied on the case.

The facts of *D v S* involved an Irish mother and a New Zealand father, who met in Ireland, got married and lived in New Zealand for over 10 years. They had three boys and, after their separation, the Family Court made a joint custody order. However, the mother wanted to return to Ireland to be near her family. While the Family Court had made it a condition of the custody order that the children should not leave New Zealand without the court's agreement, Panckhurst J on appeal reversed this. As we have seen, the Court of Appeal upheld the father's appeal but in the meantime the mother and children had already gone to Ireland and had been there for five months. The father's victory in the Court of Appeal was therefore somewhat problematic. The Court of Appeal decided to remit the case to the Family Court in order that the changed circumstances could be taken into account. The thought was that the new status quo, life in Ireland, might be upheld.

Several other cases involving relocation were decided in 2001. These cases indicate that, where relocation is permitted, there are usually special factors to justify the result. For example in *A v A*,[7] there had been false abuse allegations

1   *D v S* [2002] NZFLR 116 at para [36]. A good example of the use of joint custody is *W v C* [2000] NZFLR 1057. But a cautionary note is also sounded by Judge Clarkson in *Allen v Connolly* [2002] NZFLR 49, where the judge refused the father's request for joint custody in a situation of considerable conflict between the parents.

2   [2002] NZFLR 116.

3   [1995] NZFLR 493.

4   [2001] 2 WLR 1826.

5   Paragraphs [85] and [26] per Butler-Sloss P and Thorpe LJ respectively.

6   [2002] NZFLR 116 at para [47].

7   [2002] NZFLR 265.

against the father who was based in Melbourne, Australia. He was granted interim custody in Christchurch, New Zealand, but had to return to Melbourne for his work. He was then granted permanent custody and able to take the children with him. There was a suggestion that the mother might also shift to Melbourne, leading to a possible joint custody arrangement in the future. In *Gray v McGill*,[8] the daughter aged 10 had been with her father since the age of four and the father wished to shift to Queensland. The mother discontinued her application to prevent removal on the eve of the proceedings, thus paving the way for relocation. In *K v B*,[9] a 17-year-old boy had been in foster care. He wanted to shift to Australia to live with his maternal grandmother but the father objected, partly on the ground that the boy would be separated from his younger brother. The court, obviously influenced by his age, granted the boy's wish.

On the other hand, *K v C*[10] was a case where approval to shift to Australia was granted by the Family Court on the mother's ex parte application but reversed by Priestley J in the High Court. The father was a violent man and there was a protection order against him. It was alleged that he said that he had a gun to take the mother and children 'out'. But Priestley J held that it was not appropriate to deal with this kind of case without notice to the respondent. Otherwise, there would not be a proper assessment. The Family Court decision had been made on unverified evidence which had been accepted in an 'uncritical way'[11] and failed to take account of the fact that the mother and children were in the meantime in a 'safe house'. Nevertheless, as in *D v S*, the father's victory counted for little as the mother and children had already shifted to Australia, having assumed a new identity. More straightforward was *Hemer v Eden*,[12] where the mother's application to move to Australia with her new partner was denied. Parenting had been done on a shared basis and there were close bonds with both parents. Commenting on *Payne v Payne* prior to the Court of Appeal's judgment in *D v S*, Judge Inglis QC said that 'there is a dangerous fallacy in the assumption that what is claimed to be in the welfare and best interests of the custodial parent necessarily marches with what is in the welfare and best interests of the child'.[13] Finally the case of *Millist v Millist*[14] is noted. The parents were both Seventh Day Adventist by religion but there was a dispute over schooling. The mother wished to shift within New Zealand from Christchurch to Nelson, quite some distance away, where she had aged parents, and planned to teach the children herself. The court however was not satisfied that her teaching skills were good enough and favoured conventional education through a Seventh Day Adventist School in Christchurch. The court therefore did not approve of the move to Nelson.

8   [2001] NZFLR 782.
9   [2001] NZFLR 1029.
10 [2002] NZFLR 200.
11 At para [68].
12 [2001] NZFLR 913.
13 At para [63].
14 [2001] NZFLR 1085.

III GUARDIANSHIP

Under New Zealand law, a child's parents are usually both guardians of the child. This means that they both have rights and responsibilities with respect to the upbringing of the child. An exception is the unmarried father who was not living with the mother at the time of birth. He can however apply to the court to be appointed a guardian.[15]

Two cases in 2001 illustrate different sides to the guardianship story. In *McDermott v Kena*,[16] the parents had lived together for about a year but the relationship ended one month before the birth of their son in 1999. Under the law, the father was not a guardian. This was by chance, because if they had separated one month after the boy's birth the father would have been a guardian. There was considerable acrimony between the parties and the mother had a protection order against the father. Despite this and with the mother's co-operation, the father had maintained contact with his son, although access changeovers took place at the Barnardos Supervised Access Centre to avoid direct contact between the parents.

The father sought a court order appointing him a guardian. The principal test for determining this question is the welfare of the child. The judge thought that the father had brought the application, not to vindicate his rights as a parent, but out of the normal and proper interests of the child. On the face of it, where a father has a keen and active interest in his child, the law should encourage and reinforce this by establishing the appropriate legal framework. What signals are being sent by a failure to appoint such a father a guardian? The judge thought it likely that the father in this case 'will be appointed a guardian and indeed should be appointed a guardian in due course'.[17] But he noted that there needed to be a good working relationship between the parents which was not currently present and he thought that the appointment of the father as guardian would 'exacerbate the tensions between him and Miss Kena, which will inevitably reflect negatively on Dylan'. The judge therefore made no order but adjourned the proceedings with a review in 12 months' time. The father missed out, but only for the time being.

Contrast *McDermott v Kena* with *B v H*.[18] The father in the latter case was a guardian of his two children but he sought an order for his removal as a guardian. The parents had fallen out long ago and had been litigating since 1990. Both parents harboured strong views against the Family Court and one has the impression that the father's application was more a tactic or a political statement than anything else. The test for the removal of a parent as a guardian is a tough one – either for some grave reason the parent is unfit to be a guardian or is unwilling to exercise guardianship responsibilities (s 10(2), Guardianship Act 1968). On the facts, there was no suggestion that the father was unfit, and he had presented no evidence that he was unwilling to exercise his responsibilities. Judge Boshier thus had no basis for the father's removal. With a touch of frustration, the judge counselled the parties that judicial solutions to their problems were unlikely to be found and that they needed help from outside the law.

---

15   Section 6, Guardianship Act 1968.
16   [2001] NZFLR 954.
17   Paragraph [28].
18   [2002] NZFLR 140.

IV FINANCIAL RESPONSIBILITIES

Under New Zealand law, a parent's financial responsibilities towards the upbringing of a child are captured in the Child Support Act 1991. This scheme was highly controversial when it was first introduced, primarily because it operated retrospectively to dramatic effect. Although the level of controversy is now far less manifest – mainly because the really contentious cases have passed through the system – there still lurks an aura of discontent and a feeling that the scheme may not be entirely fair.

The system is based on a 'formula assessment' of the amount of child support a liable parent should pay. In its simplest form, the formula takes the liable parent's taxable income up to a maximum figure, deducts a 'living allowance' which is adjusted for the number of dependants, with a percentage of the balance being the amount to be paid. Whatever this amount turns out to be, there is a minimum amount which must be paid. Quite a large number of liable parents, especially those on low incomes or in receipt of a social security benefit, pay the minimum.

Two statutory changes were made in 2001. First, the minimum amount of child support was raised from $10 per week to $12.75, with a mechanism for further increases in accordance with the cost of living. Secondly, an amendment was made to the maximum amount of income to be taken into account. Whereas before this 'cap' it had been twice the average wage, Parliament increased it to 2.5 times the average wage. The actual amount moves from year to year with alterations in wage scales. These two amendments do not address any underlying concerns about the scheme. The parliamentary select committee which heard submissions on the legislation pointed out a raft of unsatisfactory features but it determined to do nothing about them.[19]

One other aspect of the scheme came in for scrutiny in 2001, this time by the courts. It is recognised that the formula assessment will not always produce a fair result. The legislation therefore contains a procedure whereby a 'departure' from the formula can be granted in favour of either the liable parent or the recipient. A departure can be granted only if a good ground has been established (including proof that there were 'special circumstances'), a departure is just and equitable for all concerned, and is also 'otherwise proper'.[20] Court of Appeal precedents[21] determined that it is difficult to get a departure. A further issue however had not received much attention. If it was appropriate to grant a departure, how should the court calculate the amount of the departure? The Court of Appeal explored this in *D v C*.[22]

This case concerned several years of child support payments but most of the judgment relates to the year beginning 1 April 2001. The father's income as an orthopaedic surgeon was high – $260,000 per annum – while the mother's was $41,000 as a lawyer. In terms of the 'cap' mentioned above, the husband's income

---

[19] For a fuller discussion of this, see B Atkin and W Parker, *Relationship Property in New Zealand* (Butterworths, Wellington, 2001) para 7.3.

[20] Section 105, Child Support Act 1991.

[21] The leading decision is *Lyon v Wilcox* [1994] 3 NZLR 422.

[22] [2002] NZFLR 97.

above $67,659 was ignored under the formula. The three children were the subject of a joint custody arrangement. This entitled both parents to apply for a child support assessment, with the lower assessment being deducted from the higher one. This meant that, because of his higher income, the father ended up paying the balance to the mother. There was little debate over the merits of granting a departure requiring the father to pay more. The Court of Appeal, rather willingly compared to its earlier decisions, thought that the costs involved in bringing up these particular children were significantly higher than allowed for by the formula and that these high costs represented 'special circumstances'. Likewise, the court thought that the 'level of the husband's income represents a special circumstance taking the case well outside the ordinary run'.[23] The real issue at stake was the extent to which the formula should be departed from.

In the High Court,[24] Durie J developed a principle of proportionality. Under this principle, the parents should pay for their children's needs in proportion to their income. This obviously worked against the father and was challenged. Durie J, in the light of the evidence presented to him, calculated the costs of the three children to be $27,000, a high figure but one which the Court of Appeal subsequently accepted. He then noted that, after combining the earnings of both parents, the father was earning 86% of the total. In the absence of any factors, as Durie J saw it, to lower the burden of the costs which the father should bear, his proportion of those costs was to be 86%. Under the joint custody arrangement, he was already paying for some of these costs directly, and he was also paying child support as assessed under the formula. After doing the mathematics, Durie J ordered the father to pay an extra $4923 per annum.

The approach of the Court of Appeal is somewhat beguiling; for the court rejected Durie J's test of proportionality, yet appeared to adopt it in reaching its own decision in the case. The court was of the view that neither the policy of the Act nor its principles supported Durie J's 'rigid and mathematical approach'.[25] 'The Act gives no suggestion that a mathematical exercise of this kind was to be undertaken, even as a starting point in applying the statutory criteria ... the judge's whole appreciation of the issues before him was infected by this error of approach'. This is a resounding rejection of the principle of proportionality. The court then went on to set its own figure for the departure order. In doing so, it stated that the 'proportionate ability, on a tax paid basis, of the parties to contribute to the extra amount involved in the departure order will usually be a key factor ... [b]ut all aspects bearing on the appropriate outcome must be taken into account'. Thus, proportionate ability appears to be the starting point after all, with allowance being made for such things as intangible contributions to the children's upbringing. The court thought that Durie J had failed to recognise the major contribution that the father was making of a non-financial kind.[26] Taking this into account, the court settled on 80% as the father's share of the

---

[23]   Paragraphs [29] and [30].
[24]   *C v D* [2001] NZFLR 433.
[25]   Paragraph [24].
[26]   Paragraph [32].

children's costs, only 6% lower than Durie J's percentage. In actual dollars, the father was required to pay $3303 extra per annum under the Court of Appeal's ruling.

In his judgment, Durie J acknowledged that there may be factors which justified a deviation from strict proportionate shares and he in fact referred to proportionality as a 'starting point'.[27] In the light of this, it is suggested that the only real difference between Durie J and the Court of Appeal was the ease with which a deviation might be made. In this respect, it is further suggested that the Court of Appeal's judgment did not actually do justice to Durie J's approach. The outcome appears to be that the principle of proportionality, as slightly softened in its application by the Court of Appeal, should be the usual test for determining the level of departures from the child support formula.

One other child support case sheds some light on the scheme. *Mazengarb v Ambler*[28] shows that in circumstances very different from *D v C* differing incomes and a change in custody arrangements can work unfairness for the high earner. As we shall see, any sense of proportionate payment disappears in a situation which does not fit the usual mould.

The mother had had custody of the two children for seven years. She had been earning at a high level, beyond the 'cap' on income under the formula. In return however the father had paid the minimum amount of child support ($10 per week) and latterly had been on sickness benefit from the State. The mother had incurred a considerable debt in order to provide housing for herself and the children. One of the children then went to live with her father and the mother was assessed for child support. Because of her high income, she was assessed to pay $696.50 per month, vastly more than she had received when the father was paying child support.

The Family Court Judge thought that this was an unusual case. Because the mother's payments went to the State to offset the cost of the benefit that the father was receiving, the State was much better off at the expense of the children. The judge granted a departure order, with the effect that the mother had to pay only $200 per month.

V PARENTAL RESPONSIBILITIES AND ADOPTION

Adoption cases still appear not infrequently in the Family Court. Often the less straightforward cases involve an intercountry element or involve older children. Some adoption applications succeed, others fail. *Re application by H (adoption)*[29] is an example of a successful adoption application of two Burmese boys aged 16 and 14. The female applicant was an aunt of the boys and she and her husband had adopted them in Burma according to Burmese law in 1994. They came to New Zealand in 1999. The Department of Child, Youth and Family Services thought that the adoption was being used as a means of getting round immigration rules and the judge recognised that adoption should not be used for such an ulterior

---

[27] *C v D* [2001] NZFLR 433, para [80].

[28] [2001] NZFLR 1009.

[29] [2001] NZFLR 817.

purpose. But here there was a genuine parent/child relationship, the applicants were fit and proper people, and the boys wished to stay with the applicants and saw no future back in Burma. This may be contrasted with *Re C (adoption)*,[30] where the court refused to allow the adoption of a 15-year-old Thai girl. The applicant wife stated in an affidavit that she was a cousin of the girl but it transpired that she was in fact the girl's mother and that Thai birth records had been falsified. An adoption had already occurred in Thailand. The woman had come to New Zealand in 1995 or 1996 and had married a man who had criminal convictions and gang associations. They had tried several forms of employment including running an escort agency but by the time of the hearing they had no income and almost no assets. In these circumstances, an adoption order was not thought appropriate. Judge Clarkson made it clear that there were no lower standards where the adoption was occurring within a family than for a stranger adoption. It also appeared that the girl could stay living with the family and there was no threat of her removal.

Adoption was also denied in *Application by P (adoption)*.[31] A father and stepmother sought to adopt two boys aged 17 and 14. Their mother was dead but there were still links to the mother's family, in particular the boys' maternal aunt who was their testamentary guardian. She refused to consent to the adoption but in earlier proceedings her consent was dispensed with.[32] The boys strongly supported adoption, described in fact as 'strong advocates' and offering 'fervent support' for the adoption.[33] Judge Somerville discussed the advantages and disadvantages of step-parent adoptions in general and then looked more specifically at this case. Adoption would enhance the boys' sense of security and wellbeing by recognising the relationship with the stepmother, would assure them of rights of inheritance from her, and would avoid conflict with the testamentary guardian in the event of the father's death. On the other hand, adoption was irreversible and lifelong, it would sever links with the maternal side of the family, and the stepmother's position could be legally recognised by appointing her an additional guardian. The Department of Child, Youth and Family Services opposed the adoption but counsel appointed to assist the court supported it because of the wishes of the children. The judge took the view that the boys' motive in supporting the adoption was really to promote the stepmother's welfare rather than their own. He saw little real advantage to the boys in the adoption: 'while the adoption may be something that the boys want, it is not something they need or require'.[34] Further, adoption 'is to provide a child, who cannot or will not be cared for by his or her own parents, with a permanent family life. It is not intended to make a step-parent feel part of a reconstituted family or to impress a legal seal of approval on a successful relationship'.

In some ways, the outcome of this case is understandable, especially because of the cutting of legal ties with the boys' birth family. But it is also somewhat troubling. It rides roughshod over the ostensible wishes of the boys and relies on a

---

[30]   [2001] NZFLR 577.
[31]   [2001] NZFLR 673.
[32]   *P v C* [2001] NZFLR 193.
[33]   [2001] NZFLR 673, 679.
[34]   [2001] NZFLR 673, 680.

revisionist reinterpretation of those wishes to be able to side-step them. An adoption here would cut legal ties but the court had already made a statement about those ties by dispensing with the aunt's consent. The adoption would have created new legal ties with the stepmother's family, something additional guardianship would not achieve. These ties could well be said to represent the new reality for these boys.

Adoption procedures came in for intense scrutiny in a judicial review case, *P v Department of Child, Youth and Family Services*.[35] The case was only partially successful but it is an indication that important State functions involving children are far from immune from review by a judge of the High Court.[36]

The case involved an attempt by a New Zealand couple to adopt a child from Thailand. In 1997 the plaintiffs were approved for intercountry adoption and papers were sent to Thailand (but appear to have been buried somewhere there). In due course, the husband went to Thailand and met a two-year-old child from a family who were employed as domestic servants by a business associate. The child was brought to New Zealand where an interim adoption order was sought unsuccessfully. The child stayed on in New Zealand to the consternation of the Department and immigration authorities. The Department began proceedings to have the child declared in need of care and protection because she came from an intact family in Thailand and appeared to be staying illegally in New Zealand for the purposes of adoption. Eventually the child was escorted back to Thailand. In the light of all this, the Department revised its opinion of the plaintiffs. A 'home visit' was made and the plaintiffs were subsequently advised that the Department would no longer support their intercountry adoption application. A 'Home Study Report' dated 10 May 1999 was one of the main subjects of the proceedings.

The plaintiffs challenged the Department on a number of fronts but succeeded on only one. Potter J held that the decision to initiate care and protection proceedings was not unjustified or unreasonable. Further, she held that the evidence did not support the contention that the departmental officers were biased against the plaintiffs nor had predetermined the unfavourable decision in the 1999 report. She nevertheless held that the 1999 Home Study Report was unlawful and invalid. The reason for this was that the plaintiffs had not been provided with another report which existed, setting out the Department's concerns about them and had not been provided with a full and fair opportunity to respond to these concerns. During the 'home visit', they had been confronted with a series of important and difficult issues but this was not the proper environment for the plaintiffs to be heard in their own defence. They had not therefore been treated in accordance with the principles of natural justice.[37]

One other adoption case appears to represent an altered judicial approach. *GMG v MAB*[38] was a case where the birth mother sought revocation of an interim adoption order. The child was born in 1999 and the mother had consented to adoption. She had maintained contact with the adopting parents and the child, but

---

[35] [2001] NZFLR 721.

[36] The judgment can be placed alongside another important judicial review case, *CMP v D-GSW* [1997] NZFLR 1, where Elias J (now Chief Justice) scrutinised procedures relating to children in need of care and protection.

[37] See especially paras [162] and [163].

[38] [2002] NZFLR 241.

this became difficult and she obtained an access order from the court. She later sought revocation of the interim order but this was refused by the Family Court. On appeal, two High Court Judges held that the Family Court Judge had not applied the law correctly. They criticised the judgment for being too 'discursive' and too 'strictured'. The High Court Judges distinguished between two approaches to the revoking of an interim adoption order:

(1)   one labelled 'the irrevocability of consent approach' which gives natural parents little or no opportunity to change their minds; and

(2)   the 'welfare and interests of the child approach'.[39]

In summary, they accepted the latter approach even though it 'could be seen as a major departure in approach to the issues raised in this appeal' where the result is wide open.[40] The position appears to be summed up in this statement:[41]

> 'If the welfare and interests of a child will not be promoted by adoption, given the willingness and ability of the relevant natural parent to care for and bring up that child, logic suggests that an interim order (which, on that hypothesis, ought never crystallise into a final order) ought to be revoked.'

There is no doubt that under s 11 of the Adoption Act 1955 an adoption order cannot be made unless it will promote the welfare and interests of the child. The question is how this is affected when the natural parent who consented to adoption has a change of mind. It is suggested that there is some difficulty with the High Court ruling. If there is such a change of mind, it trumps the adopting parents unless the court is persuaded, despite the natural parent's willingness and ability to care for the child, that the adoption will nevertheless promote the child's welfare and interests. This could place many reputable adopting parents in an intolerable position, even if, as in *GMB v MAB*, they have been bringing up the child for a couple of years.

VI   RELATIONSHIP PROPERTY

One of the major pieces of legislation passed in 2001 was an amendment which transformed the Matrimonial Property Act 1976 into the Property (Relationships) Act 1976.[42] The original Act set in place a deferred community property regime for married people. The 2001 reforms make many changes but the main ones can be summarised as follows:

•   The deferred community property regime in the 1976 Act is extended to de facto relationships. Same-sex relationships are included in this category.

•   It is also extended to survivors where a marriage or relationship comes to an end with the death of one of the parties.

---

[39]   Paragraphs [57] and [58].

[40]   Paragraph [6].

[41]   Paragraph [71].

[42]   For a full discussion of the reforms, see B Atkin and W Parker, *Relationship Property in New Zealand* (Butterworths, Wellington, 2001). The substantial changes came into effect on 1 February 2002.

- It amends the rules which determine what is 'relationship property' (formerly known as 'matrimonial property') and what is 'separate property'. Generally speaking, the Act applies to relationship property, but there are some powers which enable the court to make orders affecting separate property.
- The rule of equal division is strengthened.
- There are new powers enabling the court to compensate one party for being economically disadvantaged as a result of the marriage or relationship.
- There are new rules enabling the court to grant compensation where one party has suffered because of the transfer of relationship property to a family company or a family trust.
- The rules for dealing with debts have been clarified.
- Whereas the High Court and the Family Court used to have concurrent jurisdiction in property cases, now all cases must begin in the Family Court. The Family Court may transfer complex cases to the High Court.
- The ability to 'contract out' of the Act has been strengthened by making it harder for the court to set an agreement aside.

At the same time as amending the 1976 Act, Parliament amended other Acts, primarily to place married and unmarried couples on the same footing. Thus, 'spousal' maintenance is extended to de facto partners, and de facto partners have the same succession rights as married persons (including on an intestacy).

Comments on some only of these reforms will be made. The decision to place unmarried couples on the same basis as married ones was passed by a very narrow margin in Parliament. However, when it then came to the inclusion of same-sex couples within the notion of a de facto relationship, the margin was far greater. One of the concerns of parliamentarians was how to define a de facto relationship. By their very nature, they can come in many different guises and it may be especially hard to determine exactly when a relationship began. The problem is eased to a certain extent by a rule which excludes most de facto relationships of less than three years from the scope of the Act. The thinking here is that, if a relationship has lasted at least three years, it is likely to have revealed sufficient signs to attract a statutory property regime. Shorter relationships will come under the Act only if there has been a child or if one party has made a substantial contribution to the relationship, and in addition there would be serious injustice if no order is made.[43]

Some meaning must nevertheless be given to the phrase 'de facto relationship'. A definition is provided in s 2D. The basic test is that of two people who 'live together as a couple'. The section then gives a non-exclusive list of nine factors which the court should take into account. These include such things as care of children, ownership of property, mutual commitment to a shared life and public reputation. The relationship may be a sexual one but need not be.[44] Again, there may be some mutual sharing of finances but there need not be. The parties may

---

[43]   Section 14A, Property (Relationships) Act 1976. The language is borrowed from Australian statutes.

[44]   In fact, in a trusts case, the Court of Appeal accepted that a longstanding association was a de facto relationship even though for religious reasons the parties had never had sexual intercourse: *Horsfield v Giltrap* (CA 207/00, 28 May 2001).

have a common residence but a de facto relationship may exist even if the parties
have their own residences.

While it may be hard in some cases at the edges to determine whether or not
there is a de facto relationship, the law is now much clearer for those that fall
under the Act. While the courts had developed the law of trusts in order to ensure
some element of justice in these situations, outcomes were always hard to predict.
For example, in some instances the claimant might manage to get a half share of
the property, but often this was not the result. For example, the woman in *Watson
v Taylor*[45] got $275,000 but this represented only 21.8% of the pool of property. In
Buysers v Dean,[46] the woman sought over $200,000 but was granted $58,000 and,
in order to do so, the judge resorted to the principle of quantum meruit to
compensate the woman for domestic housekeeping and childcare services.

The extension of the property regime to cover widowed parties was based on
the premise that a person whose relationship is ended by death should be in no
worse a position than one whose relationship has ended by separation or divorce.
However, a widowed person is not obliged to seek division of property under the
Act, in particular where there is perfectly adequate provision under the inheritance
law. Most survivors will in fact be well provided for under the deceased's will.
However, there will be exceptions and it may be to the survivor's advantage to
seek a half share of the relationship property. Where an application is made under
the 1976 Act, the applicant usually forgoes entitlements under the will or on
intestacy. While the rules for separated and widowed parties are for the most part
the same, there are some special rules which favour the survivor over the
deceased's estate and beneficiaries. First, as a general rule, the estate cannot make
a claim under the 1976 Act, only the survivor can. Secondly, there is a
presumption that property is relationship property with a consequential onus on
the estate to show otherwise. Thirdly, where married persons (as opposed to de
facto partners) separate after less than three years, the equal division rule can be
ousted in favour of division based on contributions to the marriage. This will not
usually occur on death – in a short marriage ended by death, equal division is
much more likely.

One of the main, yet controversial, innovations of the 2001 reforms is the
introduction of powers to grant compensation for economic disparity. Section 15
is a general power enabling the court to order the payment of a sum of money out
of relationship property or the transfer of relationship property from one party to
the other. Section 15A is more specific but with a wider remedy. It relates to the
situation where the owner's actions have increased the value of the owner's
separate property (eg the owner has devoted time and energy to making
improvements to a separate property house), in which case the court can make
orders affecting not only relationship property but also separate property. The
overall effect of these compensatory adjustments is to upset the otherwise equal
division of the property.

These two powers can be exercised only if certain conditions are met. It must
be shown that both the income and the living standards of one party are likely to
be significantly higher than those of the other party. Very importantly, the

---

[45]   [2002] NZFLR 59.
[46]   [2002] NZFLR 1.

disparity must be linked to the division of functions during the period of cohabitation. If it can be explained by some other cause, then no adjustment can be made.

These powers are controversial because of the degree of uncertainty they introduce into the scheme. How easy will it be to satisfy the jurisdictional conditions? Even if they are satisfied, the court has a discretion whether or not to order compensation. What factors will be relevant to this discretion? The Act mentions likely earning capacity and care of children, but adds the open-ended expression 'any other relevant circumstances'. Then, if a court decides to exercise the discretion, how does it calculate the level of compensation? No guidance is given in the statute.

While there has been concern that the equal division rule has not always left the parties to a relationship on an even footing and that it has tended to ignore the real value in higher qualifications and career advancement, the solution is something of a two-edged sword. It remains to be seen how the courts deal with economic disparity but the price in the meantime is a significant degree of unpredictability and the prospect of considerable litigation.

NIGERIA

DEVELOPMENT IN FAMILY LAW AND WELFARE SERVICES IN NIGERIA (1997–2002)

Bolaji Owasanoye[*]

I INTRODUCTION

Since Professor ENU Uzodike's article in the 1999 edition of the *Survey*,[1] there has been no contribution on developments in Nigerian family law. Before that, there was no contribution since 1990. The reason, as stated in her article, was the absence of major developments in the area since 1990. That position has not changed much till now. There has been little or no development in case-law principles since her article, which covered relevant family law issues from the angle of case-law, viz, property rights and inheritance, testamentary capacity and disposition of property, division of property and custody of children on divorce and the view of the Supreme Court on customs recognising marriage between the living and the dead.

On the other hand, statutory law has, since the last contribution, focused on the impact of poverty on the family. There is no gainsaying the fact that poverty affects significantly the perception of rights and cognitive ability and capacity to appreciate or protect rights. Uzodike noted that the origin of statutory intervention was the Family Support Programme (FSP) of the wife of the late military head of state, Maryam Abacha, whose initiative was backed by the Family Support Trust Fund Decree No 10 of 1995. However, there is a forerunner to the Family Support Trust Fund decree. That forerunner is the Nigerian Children's Trust Fund Decree No 30 of 1990 that established the Nigerian Children Trust Fund (NCTF).

The preamble to Decree No 30 of 1990 indicates that it was passed in furtherance of the objectives of the International Year of the Child, an event that occurred in 1979, 11 years before the promulgation of the decree! The delay is a sober reflection of the importance attached to children's rights and family welfare in Nigeria. Since the advent of the decree, however, the world has moved forward significantly with the adoption of the Convention on the Rights of the Child (CRC) in 1989 and the African Charter on the Rights and Welfare of the Child (ACRWC) in 1990.

Although it appears that the Children Trust Fund decree has been overtaken by the CRC and other more recent legislation, we intend to review it, first, because its main objectives remain very relevant in the context of the rights of the child as

---

[*] Associate Research Professor, Nigerian Institute of Advanced Legal Studies, University of Lagos, Campus, Akoka, Lagos.
[1] ENU Uzodike, 'Developments in Nigerian Family Law: 1991–1997', *The International Survey of Family Law 1997*, ed A Bainham (Martinus Nijhoff, 1999), pp 325–344.

a member of the family and as enshrined in the CRC and ACRWC and, secondly, because the last review on Nigeria did not touch on the statute.

II THE NIGERIAN CHILDREN TRUST FUND DECREE

Section 1(1) declares that the main objective of the Trust Fund is to provide integrated welfare services and programmes to Nigerian children. What 'integrated welfare services' means is not defined, therefore it is ambiguous, but in the context of actual programmes for the multitude of poor children in Nigeria it has proved to be an excuse for inaction.

Section 1(2)(a) and (b) provide that the Fund shall consist of such monies as may be contributed by the government of the Federation, a State or a local government and such sums of money as may be raised, from time to time, by the Board by way of contributions or donations from any person (whether corporate or unincorporated).

The funding structure of the Fund is grossly inadequate to fulfil its wide objective, especially since the main source of money into the Fund is subvention from the government, federal, state and local government. Experience shows that money from these sources is never adequate because children and family welfare services have a mere collateral relevance to policy makers. Moreover, reference to the state and local government as contributors to the Fund has turned out to be futile because they hardly get enough from the Federation Account to meet their needs due to the over-centralisation of resources in the federal government contrary to the federal structure the country avows.

During the military era, it was impossible to get the three levels to contribute faithfully to the Fund in spite of the unitary command structure; therefore, it is not likely that the semi-independence given to the lower levels of government by the present federal constitutional arrangement will be able to do better. Furthermore, the state and the local government are reticent in contributing to any fund managed by a federally constituted body. Besides, children as a legislative subject has always been reserved for states under Nigeria's various constitutions.[2] Therefore, states often ignore federal statutes, which mandate them to act one way or another on a matter which is within their constitutional purview without corresponding resource increase from the federal government.

In view of the foregoing, a more definite source of money for the Fund is required. One such possible source is the education tax fund (ETF) established vide the Education Tax Fund Decree No 7 of 1993, which obliges some companies to pay a certain percentage of their profit as education tax. Since the ETF focus is education, which is one of the cardinal objectives of the CTF, it is suggested that the CTF be funded through the ETF.

---

[2]   Children are a residual matter under the legislative lists because they are not mentioned in the exclusive and concurrent lists, which would have given the federal government power to legislate on them. In the case of international Conventions, however, the federal government may domesticate a treaty it executes on behalf of the country, provided that the majority of states consent where the subject matter is reserved for states by the constitution.

Section 1(3) provides:

'In this Act, any reference to a child is a reference to a person who has not attained the age of 16 years and "relief" means any purpose connected with:

(a) the provision of scholarship;

(b) the provision of emergency relief and social assistance, including food stuff, clothing, medical and hospital stores and facilities and means of shelter; and

(c) the amelioration of the condition of any child affected by this Act.'

The definition of child, which applies only to persons under 16 years of age,[3] is at variance with Art 1 of the CRC and the ACRWC, both of which define a child as any person less than 18 years of age. Although the decree was passed before Nigeria ratified the CRC,[4] there was an amendment to the statute in 1993[5] after the ratification of the CRC, which should have been used as an opportunity to amend the definition of child to bring it in line with the CRC.

Section 1(3)(a) is another reason for requesting the NCTF to tap into the ETF because the section defines 'relief' to mean, 'any purpose connected with provision of scholarship'. This is more related to education because scholarship is a matter more closely associated with education. It also implies that the CTF has an obligation to promote any object that will assist the provision of education to children. This is a very wide object and an important function for the fund.

Paragraph (b) of 1(3) adds another important responsibility to the intervention of the fund, ie 'emergency relief and social assistance'. For the purpose of this analysis, we may take the expression as one. The use of the word 'emergency' implies that the Fund may not take preventive measures in the interest of children, but rather, where there is a disaster the Fund may provide emergency relief. This is not salutary although it is understood that it is intended to use the Fund as a supplementary source of resource since it is not the agency with primary responsibility for the social services children need. The assumption is that since other ministries and departments already have responsibility for taking care of children, an emergency relief agency is what is needed for isolated outbreaks of disasters affecting children.

The other point to make in respect of emergency relief and social assistance is that the provision could have been invoked early this year but it was not. The auspicious opportunity was the aftermath of bomb blasts at Ikeja Military Cantonment in Lagos, where old ordnances and bombs kept at the munitions dump went off without notice on the evening of 27 January 2002 till the early hours of the next day. Over 20,000 families were directly displaced by the incident, many of them children. In fact, about nine primary and secondary schools were directly affected by the incident. The schools were virtually razed to the ground. The government directed affected schools to share the premises of other schools not affected by operating a shift system. Although this has not been convenient, the NCTF has not moved in or offered any noticeable assistance either to the children, the schools or the family.

Our next observation relates to what appears to be a conflict of objectives. The two main functions of the Fund, ie provision of scholarship and provision of emergency relief, seem to be incompatible because the first does not admit any

---

[3] Section 1(3).

[4] Nigeria ratified the CRC in 1993.

[5] Nigerian Children's Trust Fund (Amendment) Decree No 72 of 1993.

emergency or danger whereas the second does. However, if provision of scholarship is intended or interpreted to mean educational assistance to children who deserve financial support for education, although education is important, such a need cannot be regarded as an emergency. The open-ended nature of s 1(3)(b) implies that every child deserves scholarship. Ordinarily one would like to support such a beneficial argument that every child should be supported to get education, but this is simply impracticable in the polity as it is. Therefore, it is better to do little effectively than too much ineffectively.

Anyhow, whichever interpretation is adopted is likely to be criticised. If the Fund adopts the wider interpretation of providing scholarship to all children, government will say it is taking on more than was contemplated. If the Fund adopts the narrow argument of providing scholarship only to deserving children, it will discover many qualified children and will still not be able to meet their needs in the context of a severely impoverished population. This will lead to further criticism of its ineffectiveness. Such criticisms dog the gifted children and nomadic education schemes of the Federal Ministry of Education. In view of the foregoing, it is expedient that the ambit of the Fund's function be clearly determined in the light of all necessary practicable parameters.

Finally, on this subsection, is s 1(3)(c) which is also contradictory. It talks of 'the amelioration of the condition of any child affected by the decree'. The expression implies a negative impact of the decree on children, whereas this is not so. What is intended is that the Fund may be used to ameliorate the condition of any child eligible for support in accordance with its provisions.

The management of the Fund was initially vested in a Board with broad membership from different government departments, but is now vested in the National Advisory Council of the National Commission for Women.[6] The confusion which dogged the former Board as established by s 2(2)(a), which listed the membership of the Board to include representatives of federal ministries charged with responsibilities for matters relating to the finance, 'the Fund', education and health amongst others, is removed because it could never be determined which ministry has responsibility for 'the Fund', since other line ministries were specifically mentioned.

One other observation on the Board is that its composition is not balanced because the non-governmental organisation sector, which does a lot for children, is not represented. Unfortunately, the amendment of 1993 does not cure this defect.

An important issue arises from s 2(10), which provides that 'the administrative expenses of the Board shall be borne by the Ministry until such time as the fund is able to bear such expenses from its own resources'. Although this provision is overtaken by the 1993 amendment, which replaces the Ministry with the National Commission for Women, it raises the other problem of resources because the National Commission for Women is a government agency, which hardly gets sufficient subvention for its traditional activities. Taking on the extra responsibility for the NCTF, though statutory, has not increased its subvention. It is our opinion that the NCTF is better situated under the Federal Ministry of Women Affairs and Social Development. The transformation of the NCTF to a statutory body with perpetual

---

[6]   See Nigerian Children's Trust Fund (Amendment) Decree No 72 of 1993.

succession and power to sue and be sued through the 1993 amendment, has not made it more effective in the protection of the rights of children.

The functions of the Board are found in s 3 of the decree but its scope is too wide for the Board to achieve without adequate funding. The broad functions include, inter alia, conduct of a regular assessment of materials and financial requirements of needy children; making grants to NGOs in the federation, organising and implementing programmes contained in National Development Plans for children, devising ways and means of raising money for the Fund. Any Board able to implement all that is contained in s 3 will resolve most of the critical issues affecting children in spite of the position that only needy children in need of emergency relief are contemplated.

Section 3(4) empowers the Board to organise and implement programmes for the welfare of children, especially those who have not attained school age and 'such other programmes as are embodied in any National Development Plan for the benefit of children'. This implies that every child under six years of age is the responsibility of the Board for welfare programmes because they have not attained school age. In addition, programmes contained in any National Development Plan for children immediately become the responsibility of the Board. Although National Development Plans hardly consider children, nevertheless, the Board has quite a handful considering this provision. This is the reason why a recognised and unimpeachable source of funding for the NCTF is critical to its functions.

One final point on the NCTF is that the wide-ranging functions prescribed in s 3 overlap with the existing functions of many other agencies. This multiplicity of functions is one of the underlying banes of child development programmes in Nigeria.

III FAMILY SUPPORT PROGRAMME

The Family Support Programme (FSP) is another statutory initiative introduced to improve the status of families. Decree No 10 of 1995 backed the programme. As stated above, this family social service programme was discussed in the last review on Nigeria, therefore we will not say much about it except that it has been overtaken by another family social service programme, the Family Economic Advancement Programme (FEAP).

FSP while it lasted had no definable guidelines or procedure for the achievements of its objectives until it was overtaken by FEAP.[7] This is besides the fact that it was dependent on donations from influential Nigerians many of who are 'political donors' who make pledges which are never redeemed.[8]

Although the Fund was created by law as a separate trust, it was managed under the office of the First Lady. Therefore, it was not surprising that it could not achieve much given the politicisation of its objectives and operations and its over-centralisation under a unitary system of government.

---

[7] For some of the anomalies of the FSP see Uzodike, op cit, n 1.

[8] See *Guardian Newspaper*, Tuesday, 5 March 1996, at p 4.

IV FAMILY ECONOMIC ADVANCEMENT PROGRAMME[9]

The Family Economic Advancement Programme (FEAP), backed by the Family Economic Advancement Programme (Establishment Etc), followed the FSP Decree No 11 of 1997. The FEAP was designed to cure the anomalies of the FSP, although the FSP decree was not repealed. We intend to make a detailed analysis of the practical application of the FEAP because it was widely touted by government as the much-needed succour to family instability, poverty alleviation and the empowerment of vulnerable members of the family.

The FEAP was a micro-credit initiative proposed mainly as a poverty alleviation and welfare project through the provision of micro-credit for local cottage industries. According to s 2 of its enabling law, it was established to improve the living conditions of Nigerians, in particular low-income earners. Its main objectives were: poverty reduction through improving the standard of living of Nigerians and minimising income disparities between the rich and the poor; encouragement of design and manufacture of machinery and equipment locally so as to provide a solid foundation for industrialisation; encouragement of producers at ward level to form co-operatives; reduction of rural urban migration through the creation of employment opportunities at ward levels; promotion of production and development consciousness through the utilisation of available resources; and promotion of industrial development at every ward in the country.

The FEAP as a model of poverty alleviation programmes for families is a stark pointer to the Achilles heel of government-initiated micro-credit programmes because it was dogged by several dilemmas summarised below.

(1)   Applicants had to be incorporated into co-operatives comprising not more than six people. This meant that one family could not apply. It also implied that potential beneficiaries had to establish joint business ventures even if their sentiments could not sustain it. The requirement conflicted with existing petty trade of a number of potential beneficiary families.

(2)   There was a problem of multiple layers of registration. Each group of applicants had first to register at the state co-operative office. Upon clearing this hurdle, they had to move to the state secretariat to be registered at the Ministry of Women Affairs and Poverty Alleviation. From there, they had to apply for a loan through the bank and from there to the local government for verification. Thereafter, the application went back to the state before the application was taken to Abuja, the Federal Capital Territory to be screened by a Committee. This Committee received applications from all applicants in a federation of 120 million people of whom about 75% are poor and are potentially qualified for the micro-credit!

(3)   The next dilemma was in the documentation that had to be done. The process required each group to apply in writing to the Registrar of Co-operatives to be registered as a co-operative. Forms and Bye Laws were sold to the group for a fee. After registration as a co-operative, a process which might take up to a month, depending on whether or not there was a query, the applicant had to open an account with any of the five designated

---

9   See generally, Bolaji Owasanoye, 'The Family Economic Advancement Programme Micro Credit Scheme in Perspective', forthcoming.

banks in the country. If these banks had no branch office nearby, the applicants had to travel great distances to the nearest bank. Although selected banks were amongst the biggest in the country with more branches, nevertheless, about 60% of the country was not covered by their services. Therefore, restricting applicants to them denied many beneficiaries the facility. However, if a co-operative succeeded in meeting a bank's documentation requirement, it moved to the next stage, ie to collect the FEAP registration forms at the State level. The forms were obtainable upon presentation of minutes of a meeting of the group approving that the loan should be taken. Thereafter, completed application forms were submitted for processing at the State level. Again, this process might take months even if there was no query. If successful, a FEAP Certificate was issued.

(4)   The FEAP Certificate and the original copy of the Co-operative Certificate were then taken to the bank selected to obtain FEAP loan forms. The banks requested that applicants fill a mandate that their account should be debited. Also, they were to provide two referees who had to be acceptable to the bank. How a poor person would get a referee for a loan from a regular bank was not factored into the considerations. Next, the applicant had to take the loan application forms to the Local Government for endorsement. The form passed through at least four tables, ie the Ward secretary, Ward Chairman, Head of Department of Agriculture (HOD Agriculture), back to the Ward Secretary and finally to the Local Government Chairman. This process could take a fortnight and then only after repeated visits. The endorsed application was returned to the Bank. The bank demanded the following: duly completed FEAP loan application forms with original certificates of registration as a co-operative; original registration certificate issued by the FEAP; and the opening of a mandatory savings account with 10% of the loan request as deposit. This implied that if an applicant wanted ₦500,000.00 (about $3500.00) loan, it would deposit from its resources ₦50,000.00 (about $400) with the bank. The applicant also had to open a current account to service the credit. The contradiction in this requirement is apparent in a situation where about 70% of the population live on less than a dollar per day.

(5)   A pro forma invoice of the equipment or machine to be purchased for the cottage industry had to be procured. FEAP guidelines insisted that these invoices be obtained from a select group of vendors. The restriction was a monopoly, which denied applicants the opportunity of shopping for the best equipment at the best prices. An invoice from an unapproved vendor was rejected even if the applicant had struck a better bargain.

(6)   A feasibility study of the cottage industry proposed had to be submitted in a prescribed format provided by the bank. Suffice it to say that the format could only be understood and completed by a chartered accountant. This implied that every applicant had to employ an accountant for a fee to conduct feasibility.

(7)   From this step the bank scheduled an inspection of the project site where the proposed cottage industry was to be carried on. This visit might take from one week to two months to schedule except with relentless pressure. Simultaneously, the bank issued a cash flow sheet to each applicant to project its earnings. This was different from the feasibility demanded earlier. If this was not submitted the application was not processed.

(8)   After site inspection, the bank wrote a recommendation with the application to the FEAP state office. Finally, the form would be taken to Abuja, away from the tearful eyes of an already sapped applicant. Even after an application was approved from Abuja, a bank could impose additional requirements like a cross-guarantee, a pledge on fixed assets and insurance requisition.

There were other problems. The policy requirement that participating banks contribute 30% of their loan portfolio kept many banks away from the scheme because it required them to act contrary to their economic interest. This is why the banks compounded the programme by asking for collateral from the potential beneficiaries. This implied that poor families would never access the loans.

Finally, the centralisation of the decision-making process in the federal government at Abuja was typical of the military but it also implied that the real beneficiaries of the programme had no redress mechanism considering the cost of travel to the city.

The shocking discovery is that after going through the painstaking process described above, several applications were not successful. The FEAP was bedevilled with corruption. By September 1998, it had received ₦5.9 billion, as subvention but only a handful of Nigerian families benefited and these were not poor or needy.

From the above, we find that the avowed commitment of government to the welfare of women and children is found more on paper than in action. The failure of laudable family welfare programmes is traceable to glamorisation of welfare programmes by the wives of previous military rulers starting with the regime of General Ibrahim Babangida 1985–1993. Wives of military heads of state and their state counterparts have since assumed direct responsibility for child and family welfare services as a portfolio of a non-constitutional office of first lady. Although they brought attention to the problems, their style glamorised the subject matter and elevated it to ceremonial events without concomitant concrete action or programmes to improve the condition of women and children.[10] Changes in government often led to programme discontinuity, without this being officially recorded as such.

Another reason for failure is over-centralisation of programmes in the central government. Considering the population, geographical size and ethnic diversity of Nigeria, no welfare programme situated within the central government structure can succeed because it will be too far removed from the grass roots. Such a strategy will fuel corruption and wastage of resources.

Exaggerated bureaucracy is a third reason for programme failure: in the case of the FEAP, the cumbersome processes and conditions spanning local to state to federal government, not to mention the co-operative office, banks and management consultants who were expected to prepare expensive feasibility studies upon which an application was to be considered, all without any assurance that the application would succeed.[11] Not surprisingly, professional touts infiltrated the process, thereby increasing the costs and eroding the benefits.

---

[10]   *Children's and Women's Rights in Nigeria: A Wake Up Call*, National Planning Commission, Nigeria and UNICEF, 2001 pp 242–248.

[11]   Ibid.

Corruption and lack of accountability bedevilled family welfare programmes. The FSP and FEAP were designed to give access to micro-finance; however, remote connection to the grass roots in operation and management allowed operators to use the schemes as sources of free money disbursed to ghost beneficiaries while the real applicants were denied.

The final point to make here is that in spite of past failures, family welfare services remain a necessity. The current regime of President Olusegun Obasanjo scrapped the FEAP as a result of its failure to meet its objectives and for the reasons listed above. His own family welfare programme is called the National Poverty Alleviation Programme (NAPEP). It is not backed by law and is not situated under the office of the first lady but within the political party structure, which implies that non-party members will have a difficult time accessing the facilities. There is not much on record concerning the performance of the programme yet, as it replaced the short-term Poverty Alleviation Programme that replaced the FEAP in 1999. At the moment, there is no concrete evidence that the NAPEP will achieve better results than previous programmes discussed above. But it remains to be seen how effective it will be.

V DISSOLUTION OF MARRIAGE

The decision of the Supreme Court in *Menakaya v Menakaya*[12] provided an opportunity for it to reaffirm the position taken 28 years earlier in *Oviasu v Oviasu*[13] that a petition for the dissolution of a marriage can only be taken in open court as provided in the Matrimonial Causes Act[14] and not in chambers. The facts were that the petitioner, Dr Tim Menakaya presented a petition at the High Court of Anambra State in Eastern Nigeria in January 1993 against the respondent, Ann Okwuchukwu Menakaya for dissolution of the marriage. The respondent filed a cross petition for a judicial separation. When the matter came up in 1994, the parties reported to the court that moves were on to settle the matter out of court.

Before the adjourned date, the parties exchanged correspondence containing counterproposals for the settlement of the issues between them. On the adjourned date, counsel for the parties, both senior advocates,[15] made a joint application to the court to hear the petition in chambers. The judge therefore retired to his chambers to continue the proceedings. The discussion in chambers showed that the parties were agreed on some issues but not all the issues. After hearing counsel briefly, but without taking any evidence, oral or affidavit, on the contentious issues between the parties, the judge adjourned the matter for judgment. In his judgment, the judge dissolved the marriage and made monetary awards on the contentious issues between the parties. Dissatisfied, the respondent appealed to the Court of Appeal.

The majority decision of the Court of Appeal found as a fact that the cumulative effect of s 103(1) and (2) and s 114 of the Matrimonial Causes Act and

---

12   [2001] 43 WRN 1.
13   (1973) 11 SC 315, 8 NSCC 502.
14   No 18 of 1970, now Cap 220, Laws of the Federation of Nigeria, 1990.
15   A Senior Advocate of Nigeria is the equivalent of a Queen's Counsel.

order 1 r 9 of Matrimonial Causes Rules is that proceedings under the Matrimonial Causes Act must be in open court with some defined exceptions. In fact, Niki Tobi JCA, as he then was said:

> 'The relief or order sought in the petition are (a) decree of dissolution of the marriage; and (b) an order for the custody of the children, these two reliefs cut across s 114(a) and (c) of the Matrimonial Causes Act. In the language of order XXIII r 1 of the Matrimonial Causes Rules, while the procedure adopted by the learned trial judge could be justified as it relates to the relief for the custody of three children of the marriage, it is not so in respect of the relief for the dissolution of the marriage. This is because order XXIII r 1 excludes the choice of procedure by the court with the consent of the parties in respect of proceedings for a decree of dissolution of marriage, the trial judge ought not have allowed himself to be led to hear the matter by the unique procedure.'

In spite of this finding, the Court of Appeal disallowed the appeal on the ground that counsel was estopped by his conduct of not only requesting that proceedings be heard in chambers but by making arguments there in favour of his client. On further appeal to the Supreme Court by the respondent, the Supreme Court had no difficulty in reversing the Court of Appeal and following the dissenting judgment of Ejiwunmi JCA (as he then was) at the lower court that a party cannot waive a statutory right. The Supreme Court said that an estoppel by conduct or waiver could not operate to undermine a statutory provision conferring a public right as opposed to individual right.

The Supreme Court also affirmed that the law is mandatory that proceedings in respect of petitions for dissolution of marriage must be in public. By extension, this decision covers proceedings for decrees of nullity, judicial separation, restitution of conjugal rights and jactitation of marriage because s 114(1) of the Act defines matrimonial causes to include these. The court affirmed other associated principles of law, for example, that a judge cannot reach a conclusion without taking evidence from the parties. This is what constitutes a hearing. Furthermore, where parties aspiring towards settlement or a consent judgment fail to reach agreement on any matter, the duty of the court is to call for a trial in order that unresolved issues may be considered through the evidence of the parties.

Although there is no gainsaying the fact that the Supreme Court correctly applied the law as it is, there is no reason why the law should not allow proceedings of the genus listed in s 114(1) to be held in camera if the parties consent to it. As a matter of fact, the law already allows some exception to the present rule, but where there will be no miscarriage of justice the law ought to go beyond its present state. The proceedings in chambers must however be published with the reasons for the judge's decision being clearly stated. In that way the public interest will be served.

VI   ADMINISTRATION OF ESTATES

In *Charles Dele Igunbor v Mrs Olabisis Afolabi (nee Igunbor) and Anor,*[16] the Supreme Court had to decide whether there was a distinction between a 'probate

---

[16]   [2001] 25 WRN 84.

matter' and a 'probate action'. In the case of the latter the court could only be approached by way of a writ of summons while in the former the court could be approached by way of a motion.

The facts were that the appellant, Charles Dele Igunbor, applied by way of motion to be joined as co-administrator to the estate of the late PA Igunbor who was survived by five wives, fifteen children and a younger brother. The eldest child, Mrs Olabisi Afolabi, and the youngest wife, Mrs Mary Oyeyemi Igunbor, had applied for letters of administration without the knowledge of the appellant. On becoming aware of the application, the appellant entered a caveat to prohibit the grant of the letters of administration to the respondents alone. The appellant filed an application by way of motion on notice for an order to join himself and one Mr John Ogunmola Igunbor as co-administrator in respect of the estate of the late PA Igunbor.

The application was opposed on the ground that the applicants should have come by way of writ of summons. The High Court overruled the objection and granted the prayers in the motion on notice. Dissatisfied, the respondents appealed to the Court of Appeal. The Court of Appeal allowed the appeal on the grounds that the motion was not in compliance with the rules and that the defect was fundamental. The appellants appealed against the ruling of the Court of Appeal. The main issue for determination before the court was whether the application before the lower court was a probate matter or a probate action. The Supreme Court found that the Administration of Estate Laws of Oyo State and the High Court Law govern proceedings in respect of administration of estates and the rules made under the law in the same state. Consequently, the High Court (Civil Procedure) Rules 1978 of Oyo State of Nigeria were found to be applicable to the case because it originated from Oyo State of Nigeria. Furthermore, the Supreme Court found that order 35 r 16 of the Rules provides that suits respecting probate or administration of estates must be instituted and carried on, as nearly as may be, in like manner and subject to the same rules of procedure as suits in respect of ordinary claims.

Using the provision of order 1 r 2 of the High Court (Civil Procedure) Rules, the Supreme Court tried to distinguish between the words 'cause', 'matter', 'action', 'probate action' and 'high court'. But on the really thorny issue of whether or not the matter was a probate action or probate matter, the court concluded that an action in administration of estate must be commenced by writ within the definition of the Rules and it will qualify as a probate action. If it is an original proceeding between the plaintiff and defendant it will qualify as a 'cause'. Such probate actions will include matters relating to the grant or recall of probate or letters of administration other than common form business. 'Matter' on the other hand was defined to mean every proceeding in court not a cause, ie every proceeding not an original proceeding between the plaintiff and defendant.

The Supreme Court found support in its earlier decision on the same matter in *Coker v Coker*[17] that an interlocutory application may be made by motion at any stage of any cause or matter within the meaning of s 2 of the Supreme Court Ordinance Cap 211 which is in *pari materia* with order 1 r 2 of the High Court Rules, where 'matter' was defined as 'every proceeding in court, not in a

---

[17]   (1956) 1 FSC 37.

cause'. Considering that the appellant in the present case was not initiating a fresh action or suit, which could be regarded as an original proceeding against a defendant or defendants, the application could not be regarded as an action to be commenced by writ. Besides, the application was not a grant or recall of probate or letters of administration such that it could be classified as an action to be commenced by writ.

The Supreme Court refused to consider in detail the fifth issue in the appellant's appeal which was formulated as a question, namely 'which law applied to the administration of the estate in dispute, is it the Administration of Estate laws of Oyo State or Bini customary law of inheritance?' The question was relevant because the appellant wanted a determination why the estate should not have been distributed in accordance with the customs of the deceased, a Bini man from Edo State of Nigeria. The Supreme Court found that the Administration of Estate Laws of Oyo State applied to the case because s 26 of the law provides that, where the deceased died wholly intestate as to his estate, administration shall be granted to one or more persons interested in the residuary estate if they apply for the purpose.

By implication, once interested persons apply to administer the estate of a person who dies intestate, administration of the estate in accordance with customary law is overtaken by the statute whose provisions must be followed. However, this conclusion cannot be hastily reached because s 49(5) of the Administration of Estates Law provides that, where any person subject to customary law contracts a marriage under the Marriage Act and that person dies intestate leaving behind a widow, a husband or any issue of the marriage, any property that the deceased might have disposed of by will, will be distributed in accordance with the provisions of the law.

In the instant case we are not sure if any of the widows of the deceased was married under the Act, neither was the schedule of property an issue in the matter. It must however be emphasised that, even if the deceased once married under the Act and was never divorced, his taking four other wives, most likely under customary law, was probably not challenged even though it constitutes bigamy,[18] because it is common practice in Nigeria for men married under the Act to take other wives without repercussion. This is because it is widely believed that monogamy is alien to Nigerian culture and monogamous marriage should not be given preference over customary marriage.

VII PROPERTY RIGHTS ON INTESTACY

The Court of Appeal had the opportunity in 2001 in the case of *Ukeje v Ukeje*[19] to affirm an important constitutional provision, ie s 42(2) of the 1999 Constitution,[20] that 'No citizen of Nigeria shall be subjected to any disability or deprivation merely by reason of circumstances of his birth'. The facts were that the plaintiff/respondent filed an action in the Lagos High Court against

---

18 Contrary to s 370 of the Criminal Code, Cap 77, Laws of the Federation of Nigeria, 1990.
19 [2001] 27 WRN 142.
20 Formerly s 39(2) of the 1979 Constitution of Nigeria.

the administrators of the estate claiming that she was the daughter of Lazarus Ogbonnaya Ukeje (deceased) and therefore entitled to share in his estate.

The plank of the defence relevant to this paper was that the plaintiff did not prove that her mother, who was called as a witness, was ever married to the deceased, and, secondly, that under Igbo customary law of inheritance, the plaintiff being female could not inherit landed property.

The lower court found that the plaintiff proved her case and refused to be dragged into requesting proof of the plaintiff's mother's marriage to the deceased. The Court of Appeal said:

> 'the success or failure of the respondent's case does not depend on whether her mother was married to the deceased or not. To so contend is to subject her to a disability based on the circumstances of her birth.'

It was easy for the court to reach this conclusion because the right of a 'child',[21] as opposed to the right of a wife, was involved. As pointed out by Uzodike,[22] even the Supreme Court still gets cold feet when presented with the opportunity to reverse discriminatory customs against women. This is in spite of s 42 of the 1999 Nigerian Constitution,[23] which guarantees freedom from discrimination. Besides, Nigeria has signed and ratified other international Conventions which protect women generally from discrimination, notably, the Convention on the Elimination of All Forms of Discrimination Against Women (CEDAW) and the Convention on the Rights of the Child, which can be used to protect the girl child from discrimination. The problem remains that government has not taken concrete steps to domesticate the Conventions and popularise them. The African Charter on Human and Peoples Rights[24] remains the only relevant treaty domesticated so far.

On the Igbo native law and custom that was pleaded, as disentitling the plaintiff from sharing in her father's estate, the Court of Appeal again had no difficulty in dismissing the claim using two criteria: first by relying on a 1991 dictum of a justice of the Supreme Court that:

> ' ... Any customary law that sanctions the breach of an aspect of the rule of law as contained in the fundamental rights provisions guaranteed to a Nigerian in the Constitution is barbarous and should not be enforced by our court.'[25]

This was buttressed by the recent uplifting decision of the Court of Appeal in *Mojekwu v Mojekwu*.[26] Secondly, because the main property in contention was landed property situated in Lagos, the Court of Appeal held that *lex situs* would apply. Therefore, Yoruba native law and custom, which stipulates that when a man dies intestate his property devolves on all his children who share the same equally, while the eldest child assumes the position of head of the family and manager of the estate on behalf of all the children, will apply.

---

21 Child in the sense that the plaintiff/respondent sued as a child of the deceased although she was already an adult at the time she filed the action.

22 Op cit, n 1.

23 The section is not new. It is the same as s 39 of the 1979 Constitution.

24 Cap 10, Laws of the Federation of Nigeria 1990.

25 Per Wali JSC in *Agbai v Okogbue* (1991) 7 NWLR (Pt 204) 391.

26 (1997) 7 NWLR (Pt 512) 288.

In spite of this decision, it is not yet settled, at least by the Supreme Court, whether or not a woman can inherit landed property under customary law, irrespective of where it is sited on Nigerian soil. It is, however, disturbing that in 1991, in *Agbai v Okogbue*[27] the Supreme Court made its inspirational observation on discriminatory customs and fundamental rights only to get cold feet in 1997 in the case of *Akinnubi v Akinnubi*,[28] when presented with the opportunity to nullify the discriminatory custom which regards a wife of a customary marriage as inheritable property who cannot inherit nor serve as administrator of an estate. It is not clear if the seemingly straightforward case of *Ukeje v Ukeje* will get to the Supreme Court but it is hoped that, if it does, the court will seize the opportunity to develop the law in this area by settling once and for all the contention on customary inheritance rights of women on all fronts whether as widows, wives or children.

VIII   CONCLUSION

From the foregoing, we note that family law and the various welfare services in the period under review, have not improved drastically the lot of the underdogs in the family, ie women and children. Their status remains diminished considering the severely weakened economy and programmatic failure of welfare programmes. The few supportive decisions of the courts have also not made much impact for the same reasons. Placed beside their counterparts in the developed world, therefore, there is not much to celebrate.

More gratifying, however, is that the situation remains on the agenda of public discourse thanks to the work of non-governmental organisations and international development agencies. Due to sustained activity by these, the government in 2000 approved a National Policy on Women to address some of the problems of discrimination and disadvantage affecting women. The policy has chapters on education, science and technology, health, employment, agriculture, industry, the environment, legal reform and legislative protection, politics and decision-making.

As rightly observed by the policy, gender issues in development planning and other fields of policy have hitherto received little attention. Under the newly approved policy, government is expected to improve resource allocation to address problems affecting women and to ensure the mainstreaming of women's issues into all development programmes in a planned and sustainable manner.

Similarly, children are getting attention through the proposed Children's Bill, but the protracted bureaucracy and politics of divergent ethnic views through which the Bill is passing gives much cause for concern. In 1997, Uzodike reported that the decree was ready but not signed.[29] Since then, a lot of water has passed under the bridge. The draft decree was *mutilated* by the outgoing military government to satisfy the sentiments of those who felt that too many rights incompatible with the prevailing

---

27   Above.
28   (1997) 2 NWLR (Pt 486) 144.
29   Op cit, n 1.

customs in some parts of the country, had been given to children.[30] But since the return to civil rule in 1999, the draft began another journey of review which is still continuing. In summary, the Children's Bill, which is expected to introduce far-reaching changes to the rights of children within and outside the family, is pending.

The avowed commitment of government to the welfare of women and children is found more on paper than in action. Government develops commendable policy papers or programmes in support of the rights and welfare of women and children but it fails to pursue the goals it sets for itself.

As noted above, family welfare services, which could have been used to improve the situation of children and women, have suffered severe programmatic failures. The Ministry of Women Affairs and Social Development at the federal and state levels are charged with responsibility for the implementation of child and family welfare services, but these have to compete with the non-constitutional office of the wife of the chief executive at the federal, state and council level for resources and project implementation. The matter reached a deplorable height under the military because the wives glamorised the problems of women and children and turned otherwise concrete action projects into ceremonial events. Although the 'first ladies' brought attention to the problems, their style diminished the seriousness of the situation.

Another reason for the dismal performance of family welfare services was the undue politicisation and over-centralisation within the top echelon of government. The population, geographical size and ethnic diversity of Nigeria does not admit of a unitary style for welfare programmes. Besides, such an approach negates the principle of federalism, which the constitution avows. The local council must be the platform for the design and implementation of welfare programmes irrespective of the sponsor.

---

[30] See Bolaji Owasanoye, 'Implementation of the Convention on the Rights of the Child in Nigeria', paper presented at World Congress on Family Law and the Rights of Children and Youth – Bath, England, 19–22 September 2001.

NORWAY

CHALLENGES TO AN ESTABLISHED PATERNITY –
RADICAL CHANGES IN NORWEGIAN LAW

Peter Lødrup[*]

I THE LEGAL BACKGROUND – BASIC ISSUES

In 2002, the Norwegian Act on Children and Parents of 1981 was dramatically changed in respect of the rules on parenthood. The basic philosophy behind the 2002 reform is that it is in the best interest of the child that the man who is the biological father should also be considered the legal father, even if it means that an existing father's parenthood is challenged. The 2002 reform is a continuation of the 1997 reforms.

In Norway – as in the other Nordic countries – paternity can be determined in three ways: If the mother is married, her husband becomes the legal father of the child; the pater est rule firmly applies, albeit in recent years with a more restricted scope than previously. If the mother is unmarried, paternity is determined either according to the father's acceptance, or by legal judgment. The common question in these three cases is under what conditions can paternity be changed, either by the child acquiring another man as his or her father, or by being left without a legal father.

With the use of present day DNA testing, in operation in Norway since 1992, it is possible, with at least 99.9% accuracy both to exclude a man and to determine who is the father of a child. This has provided us with a method which makes future paternity cases easier in respect of the legal procedures and the obtaining of results, the quickest determination of the paternity of a child of an unmarried mother, and in a legal case dealing with change concerning paternity. Consequently, we have here a means whereby we can confirm or disprove the accuracy of a judgment based on the more inaccurate blood analyses of past years. A DNA test can further confirm or disprove paternity established by the pater est rule determined by a judgment.

Against this background, the following question arises: How far can legislation go in respect of restricting legal action on paternity, particularly legal action which could alter the existing paternity? The question is also relevant for a child without a legal father. Such limitations are partly the time restrictions for legal procedures; partly the material requirements which must be fulfilled before an action for change can be undertaken; and partly the restrictions as to which persons can undertake legal action. Furthermore, there are the regulations in the Act on Civil Procedures regarding the reopening of already determined judgments which contain limitations for changing paternity. Consequently, the basic issue is

---

[*] Professor of Law, University of Oslo.

the extent to which establishing biological paternity should be the ultimate aim, or whether existing legal paternity should be protected against interference.

II   SOME REMARKS ON THE CHILDREN AND PARENTS ACT AS IT WAS BEFORE 1997

The Children and Parents Act of 1981 – as it read prior to 1997 – listed a number of rules which indicated that biological paternity was not fully clarified.

The following persons could be interested in challenging paternity:

–   the child;
–   the mother's husband;
–   the mother;
–   the man who has acknowledged paternity;
–   heirs who, in the event of a change of paternity, would receive a greater inheritance;
–   a third party claiming to be the child's biological father.

(1)   In cases where paternity is based on the pater est rule or an acknowledgement by a particular man according to the rules for the determination of paternity by acknowledgement,[1] the rules were as follows:

   (a)   The child's right has never been contested, and no deadlines have been established as to his or her possibility of entering into legal proceedings in order to change paternity.

   (b)   Furthermore, *the mother's husband* can take legal action in cases where paternity is based on the pater est rule.

   (c)   *The mother has the right to legal action on the same grounds as the father*, in other words, the right to enter into legal action for change both when the paternity is based on the pater est rule and where it is based on acknowledgement.

   (d)   *The man who has acknowledged paternity* can enter into litigation in order to have his paternity annulled.

   (e)   *The heirs of the husband* had, in Norway, the right to take legal action after the death of the father until 1997.

   (f)   Prior to 1997, *a man who claimed to be the father of a child who already had a father*, could not have his paternity tried in court.

(2)   If paternity has been determined by judgment, the regulations are different.

The Act on Civil Procedures states in § 407 no 6 that the reopening of an earlier judgment can only take place in cases in which 'new facts or proof have been presented, which alone or in connection with what has been established on a

---

[1]   A man accepted by the mother may take on paternal responsibility. This is further the case in respect of the man whom the relevant public authority responsible for finding the child's father, claims to be the likely father. As the relevant public authority can require that the man in question, the mother, and the child provide blood tests for a DNA analysis, the man who has tested positively admits to paternity. In practice, this means that the role of the court in paternity cases is eliminated.

previous occasion, clearly would have resulted in a different judgment'. When a request for reopening a case is presented to the court, a preliminary evaluation should take place in respect of whether the case should be retried or not. According to the Act on Civil Procedures § 412 second sentence, the request should be denied if it is evident that the circumstances or proof presented is inadequate. If the request is not rejected according to the second sentence, the case may be referred to a main hearing, or the court can decide on the presentation of proof. The nature of the evidence will then determine if the request is rejected or if the case is to be decided on its merits. Whether the results of the case would then be different, depends on whether or not the conditions in the Act on Civil Procedures § 407 no 6 have been met.

Thus, the reopening of a case takes place in two stages. First, the person who requests a reopening has to meet the requirements of § 412. This accomplished, the case is then passed on to the main hearing, and the requirements for an alteration of judgment are now given in § 407 no 6. With the latter threshold being so high, namely, that new judgment can be given only when the new evidence that has been established, together with that presented previously, would clearly imply a different judgment, this means that it is not easy to obtain agreement in a reopened case.

When DNA testing became available, the courts accepted the results as a reason for reopening earlier judgments where this proved that the judgment was wrong. When the mother, the father, and the child agreed to a blood test in order to obtain the results of a DNA analysis, no problems arose. If the results reconfirm the judgment, the parties are satisfied. However, if the results show that the judgment is wrong, the case is reopened.[2] This is the case when the result shows that the man in question is the father, and when he is not.[3]

It is, however, possible that one of the parties involved refuses a blood test. In this case, the following question arises: is the possibility of a DNA test to be considered as new evidence according to the Act on Civil Procedures § 407 no 6, cf § 412, so that the court, according to the Act § 412 second sentence, contrary to the wishes of one party, can demand that a blood test be taken in order to obtain results showing whether the earlier judgment was valid? The answer provided by the Supreme Court in 1998 was negative.[4] Without the involved parties' consent, the courts could not demand that a blood test be taken and hence establish the validity of the judgment. Consequently, the legal situation was clear: if a DNA test is available, showing that the earlier judgment was wrong, the condition for reopening the case is present. However, when such a test is not available, the court cannot demand that the parties, against their consent, agree to a DNA test being carried out, with the above-mentioned reservation of 1997. Later, the Supreme Court stated that these rules also apply in cases where the child requests the reopening of a judgment.[5]

---

[2]   See, for instance, Rt 1986 p 720, Rt 1996 p 104, Rt 1997 p 413.

[3]   Examples here are Rt 1996 p 104 and Rt 1996 p 1142.

[4]   Rt 1998 p 219.

[5]   Rt 1999 p 308.

III   REFORMS OF 1997 AND 2002

In 1997 and 2002, the rules described above were amended on certain key points. Seen in the light of these rules, Norwegian law, as it relates to the changing of paternity and the reopening of final paternity judgments is in significant ways different from that of other Nordic countries.

The Civil Action regulation was expanded in 1997 to cover a third party who insists that he is the child's biological father. Article 6 s 3 in the Act on Child and Parents read as follows:

> 'The person insisting he is the father of the child, can, until the child reaches the age of three, enter into legal proceedings in respect of paternity if he is able to present information which indicates that he might be the father. The court can by judgment make exceptions to the three-year time-limit when valid reasons are present.'

Based on this, any man could within the given period enter into a lawsuit in order to change an existing paternity based on the pater est rule or acknowledgement. This could not be prevented by the child, the mother, or the father.

Civil action such as this in respect of a third party does not exist in the other Nordic countries, and is an important means for unifying legal and biological paternity. What, then, was the rationale for such a radical change? In a report circulated for hearing, the Ministry for Children and Family Affairs questioned a third party's civil action, though without making a statement in this respect. One was somewhat uncertain about the legal-political aspects and perhaps also the political grounds. From the report it appears that opinions were divided. A third-party right to civil action was supported, among others, by the Ombudsman for Children, the Gender Equality Ombud, the Norwegian Council of Churches, and the Norwegian Society of Rural Women. Among those who were opposed were The Norwegian Bar Association, the Association of Ministers of the Church of Norway, the Gender Equality Centre and the Front for Women.[6] However, the Ministry arrived at the conclusion that such a right of civil action should be introduced, based on a wide consensus that it is 'important for the child that paternity is correctly determined'. In addition to the emotional aspects for the child, it was stated that paternity:

> 'is important in other aspects as well, for instance, in a medical sense, in order to disclose inherited diseases. Further, aspects of legal inheritance are mentioned, in cases where the legal and biological father dies before the child is old enough to institute legal proceedings himself. In cases in which neither of the legal parents wish to contest the paternity issue, it might be an advantage for the child to let a third party have the opportunity to take legal action, in order for paternity to be determined. It is likewise an advantage for the legal parents to know who is the child's right father, rather than having a worrying uncertainty which might be exposed should the parties decide to part company at some future date.'

After having rejected civil action with deliberately disruptive intentions as counter evidence, the Ministry of Children and Family Affairs summed up its views as follows:

---

[6]   See the hearings, Ot prp (1996–97) no 56 p 27 ff.

'After an evaluation of the views and argumentation presented at the hearing, the Ministry has decided that the suggestion of the right of the one who claims to be the biological father to enter into civil action should be proposed. Emphasis is given to the fact that it would be in the best interests of the child to obtain as early as possible knowledge of, and communication with, its biological father, and that the legal relationship as much as possible should reflect the biological situation. Further, the suggestion would represent a practical consequence of equal status of the parents in relationship to the child. Finally, it is emphasized that contrary opinions no longer remain as strong because DNA technology ensures a correct result, and because unsettling legal proceedings are avoided.'

As is evident, the rationale for the right to enter into legal action is fairly limited. The suggestion did not create much of a debate in Parliament and was passed with five contrary votes. It should, however, be emphasized that without the DNA technology and the resultant simplified legal proceedings, such a reform would not have been desirable; in fact, it would have been almost unthinkable.[7]

In 1997, the Ministry also considered whether time restrictions for legal action should be abolished, but came to the conclusion that the one-year time limit should still remain in operation.[8] Similarly, the position was maintained that, if a man in order to have his case heard had to 'provide information which indicated that someone else might be the father of the child', he could introduce a similar request for a third party wishing to enter into legal action in order to have his paternity tried.

The legal situation at the turn of the century was consequently clarified. Norway was provided with new rules in respect of the right of taking an action to court, and the Supreme Court had in 1998 alleviated the problems in respect of reopening cases.

However, this period of calm was not to remain for long.

Parliament questioned the validity of the conclusion reached by the Supreme Court in 1998. Not least in political circles there was a wish to consider changing the rules once again. Consequently, the Ministry of Children and Family Affairs provided for a hearing, in which it was recommended that the conditions and time restrictions for legal action should be removed, and should rather include in the Act on Children and Parents a separate rule in respect of reopening, making it possible to reopen paternity judgments without the strict conditions laid down by the Act on Civil Procedures. The proposal was widely supported during the hearing, and the Ministry's proposal regarding amendments to the Act on Children and Parents § 6 and the new § 28a were sanctioned in December 2002.

With the amendments, the Act on Children and Parents § 6 now reads:

'The child, each of the parents, and a third party claiming to be the father of a child who already has a father, can take a case to court in respect of paternity after marriage or acknowledgement.'

---

[7] It should be mentioned that, in the preparation of the Act on Children and Parents of 1981, there was a negative attitude in respect of making access for demanding change too wide, which was partly due to lack of evidence – as proof is weakened as the years go by (cf NOU 1977: 35 p 35), and one was often uncertain if the new decision was right (cf p 36).

[8] Ot prp (1996–97) no 56 p 31.

We note that all time restrictions concerning the taking of legal action have disappeared, whereas it has not been made a condition for such action that information supported by evidence of a different paternity is presented. Consequently, a man claiming to be the father of a child born in wedlock can take legal action against the mother's husband and the child, and claim that he himself is the father. For legal proceedings to be commenced, the court will require that a blood test be taken together with a DNA analysis. According to Art 9 of the Children and Parents Act, the result of the DNA test will then automatically be the basis of the judgment, and a new judgment can be made without a main hearing. We see that neither the mother, the child, nor the husband can prevent such a commencement of legal proceedings.

But what about the conditions for the reopening of an earlier judgment? The new Art 28a reads as follows:

> 'A final judgment can be demanded to be reopened without regard to the conditions of the Civil Procedures Act §§ 405–408 if there was no DNA test available in the case. If a reopening is agreed to, the court should request that a blood test be taken together with a DNA analysis. When the DNA analysis has been provided, the rule according to § 25 first sub-section is valid.'

According to this, no new proof or facts are required for the case to be reopened. This seems reasonable enough as the courts, when the case is presented, must impose the necessary requirements in respect of blood tests in order to have a DNA analysis. The result of the analysis will determine the outcome of the case. When we know that a great number of older paternity cases were decided by blood type testing which could not determine paternity with any accuracy, and only exclude, and not determine, the father, it is obvious that many of these cases have resulted in biologically incorrect judgments.

In its rationale for these amendments, the Ministry expands on the views on which the 1997 reform was based, and has in several respects a different and more liberal point of view than in 1997. Here, it should be mentioned that in 1997 the Ministry found that it would be 'undesirable having no time limit whatsoever'.[9] At the time, this was explained as follows:

> 'Unfortunate results might appear if a man, who had acknowledged paternity in spite of the fact that he possesses information about someone else being the father of a child, is allowed to wait as long as he decides to put aside the paternity issue. This might result in situations where the man, after a break-up following several years of living with the mother, wishes to have his paternity set aside in order, for instance, to have a motive for not paying child maintenance.[10] ... If legal action is not taken prior to the time limit, the person is considered having accepted his paternity "as having legal effect", so that he cannot be released from paternity several years later.'

According to the Ministry, identical views were present in 1997, when paternity was based on the pater est rule:

> 'The one-year time restriction should consequently also apply in these situations. ... It is further assumed that this access [for the court to be exempt from the time restriction] is being used with the same care as at the present time.'

---

[9]   Ot prp (1996–97) no 56 p 31.
[10] This appears to have cohabitation in mind.

For a third party claiming to be the biological father, the three-year time restriction should be relevant, one felt, in 1997:

'The one-year time restriction should also apply to the person claiming to be the child's biological father. In order to protect the child by not breaking into an existing family unit, the right to enter into legal action in such cases should be restricted, so that a time limit of three years after the birth of the child is imposed. "The court's ability to exempt itself from this time restriction is assumed 'in these cases as well'" ... "to be used with considerable care".'

Five years later, the picture has changed. Now all time restrictions and conditions for legal action are to be done away with:

'The consequence of the regulations with time restrictions on all parties, except for the child, to take legal action is that passivity is being "penalised". A man not wishing to disturb the harmony of an established, matrimonial cohabitation by questioning the paternity of the spouse's children might have to accept the situation as final. This is also the case in respect of a mother who does not enter into legal action for change within one year even if she knows that her husband is not the father of the child, or that the wrong man has acknowledged paternity.

Through the press and private inquiries at the Ministry, we know that for a man to be the legal father of a child he doubts is his and without the possibility of having the paternity determined, he could be under considerable strain. We also know a reasonable amount about the difficult situation facing the man who is dependent on the consent of the legal parents in order to determine if he is the father of the child, and possibly to have the paternity changed. If the paternity is not changed, these people often have no possibility of establishing contact with the child, which might lead to a sense of loss and despair.

Doubt in respect to paternity could, regardless of regulations, lead to the child experiencing a sensation of unrest and conflict within the family. The child might hear of the doubt as to who is the real father or mother from the parents themselves or from others. Conditions and time restrictions in respect of initiating legal proceedings in order to change paternity can hardly protect the child from the psychological unrest and doubt about paternity that could be created. The rules also apply in those situations where the "child" is no longer of a young age and the need for protecting the child is no longer a major concern.'[11]

Not much concern is shown to the man who for a long period of time has been the father of the child:

'The earlier legal father loses all rights in respect to the child and vice versa. If the paternity case leads to a break-up of the relationship of the mother and the person who has been the child's legal father, the child might lose contact with the man who has been his or her legal and social father. However, the child will gain the opportunity for establishing contact with his or her biological father.'[12]

In respect of the reopening of cases, the following must be noted:

'The Ministry based its intention of simplifying access to the reopening of cases on the argumentation given for abolishing the conditions and the deadlines for changing paternity based on the pater est rule, referred to above. Considering the suggested break with older legal perspectives (as well as with Nordic law generally), together

---

[11]   Ot prp (2001–02) no 93 pp 7–8.
[12]   Ot prp (2001–02) no 93 pp 7–8.

with the Supreme Court case in 1998, it is surprising that only a few of the bodies present at the hearings expressed an opinion about this suggestion; however, those who did, such as the Norwegian Bar Association and Legal Advice for Women, were supportive. We can therefore confidently state that the suggestion did not provoke any debate. It is thought provoking, however, to note how quickly opinions changed. In 1997,[13] the Ministry found that there was no reason for providing special regulations for the reopening of such cases, and at the time was given parliamentary support. But five years later, opinions were completely reversed.'

IV   FINAL REMARKS

As noted in this article, Norwegian law during the last five years has been 'turned upside down' in respect of a considerable portion of the rules relating to the change of paternity and for earlier judgments concerning paternity. Similar rules have not been considered in the other Nordic countries, and it might therefore be of interest to contrast the new Norwegian rules with some aspects of the way in which Denmark and Sweden have solved these issues.

The new Danish Act on Children and Parents of 2001, which, in spite of its name, is a law relating entirely to parenthood, does not give the parties concerned such wide possibilities for changing existing paternity on an individual basis, without going through an administrative organ. In Denmark, all cases concerning change start at the 'statsamtet' (the county administration), which then determines if the case should be reopened. We must add here that in Denmark the word 'Genoptagelse' (reopening) relates to any new interpretation of paternity, regardless of the method employed, in other words, not only where it was determined by judgment. The interesting thing in this connection is that the Danish Act on Children and Parents[14] still maintains a three-year time limit for legal action where paternity has already been determined by acknowledgement or judgment, cf the Act § 11.[15] Those entitled to enter into legal action are the child, the mother, and the father, or their estates. It is further a condition for reopening that 'information exists about circumstances which one could assume would alter the results of the case, or, at least, provide grounds for assuming that the results would be different'. A three-year limit for contesting the registration of paternity or an acknowledgement, was, however, reduced from three years to six months after the birth of the child. The rationale for this was that the reduction of the time limit would create better conditions for lasting stability in respect of the child. The Danish law also allows for legal action by the third party, which, however, is more restrictive than the new Norwegian Art 6. A man who has had a sexual relationship with the mother during the time when the child would have been conceived, can enter into legal action and claim that he is the father. This must, however, be done within six months of the birth of the child, and is valid, unless the child already has a registered father or the child was conceived during a criminal offence.

---

[13]   Ot prp (1996–97) no 56 pp 32–33.

[14]   Act no 460 of 7 July 2001.

[15]   However, the three-year limit now also applies to the child.

Making reference to Danish law is with the intention of showing that these questions have been raised more or less at the same time in both Denmark and Norway, although with quite different results, and where concern for the stability of the child's circumstances was considered in very different ways. The third party right to legal action was created in Norway in 1997, but has had no impact on the Danish considerations, although a detailed description of this existed in the draft by the Commission on the Law on Children and Parents.[16]

This leads us to examine the current contrast between Swedish and Danish law in respect of third parties generally. Swedish law prevents without exception a third party from entering into legal action in order to be acknowledged as father of the child, whereas we noted that in Denmark this possibility still remains open in the rare cases where the child does not have a father, with a time limit of six months after the birth of the child. In Sweden, the man who announces his paternity to the welfare office has little chance that this office will clarify the paternity question unless the child's mother verifies his paternity. In Norway since 1997, as we have noted, the man who claims to be the father can claim the right to bring a legal action if the public authority (now the county welfare office) dealing with his paternity request sets aside his case. In Sweden, the argumentation for a negative position, for instance, has been that the social office's participation is sufficient, that legal action by the man might weaken the mother's interest in clarifying the paternity issue, or that she might prefer abortion rather than giving birth to the child. It should be emphasized that it appears that Danish and Swedish law is more comparable to European law in this respect. Nonetheless, it is my opinion that Norwegian law appears preferable on this issue, and I am primarily in agreement with the views on which the 'biological' approach is based. Hence, it is encouraging that Swedish authors currently writing on the issue think that an absolute prohibition with respect to children born out of wedlock is going too far.[17] It is interesting to note that in Norway the right to enter into legal action exercised by the man who claims to be the child's father, in those instances where the municipal office has dropped the case, was not challenged during the hearings.

These reflections on certain key rules in respect of changes to Swedish and Norwegian law, and with the occasional glimpse at Danish law, convey, needless to say, a somewhat mixed impression. In addition to major differences in respect of material and procedural rules, they reveal three interesting features:

–   In Norway, the view on major issues has changed radically since the Act on Children and Parents was passed in 1981, and further since 1997.
–   In Denmark, the Norwegian changes have not had much impact on the preparation of the Act on Children and Parents (Børneloven) of 2001.

---

[16]   See 'Betænkning om børns retsstilling' (Report on the position of children), Bet no 1350, 1997 p 126 ff.
[17]   Cf Singer, 'Mannens talerätt vid fastställande av faderskap' ('The man's right to be heard on the determination of paternity'), SvJT 1992 p 549 ff esp p 558 ff, Bull, op cit, p 696. See also Saldeen, 'Något om faderns ställning i svensk rätt' ('Reflections on the father's role in Swedish law'), *Festskrift til Anders Agell* (*In Honour of Anders Agell*), Uppsala 1994 p 545 ff at p 566.

– In Sweden, one has not seen a need during recent years to make changes to the Act on Children and Parents (Föräldrabalken) on issues of major significance.

I again wish to pose the question which I touched on above, but feel unable to answer: Are the Nordic countries so different?

And finally: we have looked above at a number of rules which in our countries provide different answers to a number of questions. But for both Swedish and Norwegian law, international conventions constitute the framework for an individual country's flexibility in the choice of solutions. Here, the European Convention on Human Rights, Art 8 on the right to the protection of one's privacy and respect for family life is of interest, and the UN Convention on the Rights of the Child, particularly Art 7, which, for instance, gives the child the right, to the greatest extent possible, to know its parents, cf also Art 8 in this respect. Could all our different rules be harmonised in the light of our convention obligations? As far as I can see, the question has not been raised during the Norwegian legislative processes in recent years. In the *Kroon* case,[18] the Dutch rule which prevented a third party from bringing legal action in respect of paternity change was set aside as being contrary to Art 8. A long time after the disappearance of her husband, the wife gave birth to a child with her present partner. As the parties were not divorced, the absent husband was, according to the pater est rule, the father of the child. Denying the partner the right to enter into legal action was in conflict with the right to family life. This is an interesting case as regards the right now automatically given a man according to Norwegian law to challenge a 'pater est' father.

---

[18]   *Kroon v The Netherlands*, Series A 297 (1994).

PAPUA NEW GUINEA

INCEST AND MARRIAGE PROHIBITIONS: IMPLICATIONS OF RECENT CHANGES TO THE LAW AGAINST INCEST UNDER PAPUA NEW GUINEA'S CRIMINAL CODE

John Y Luluaki[*]

I INTRODUCTION

In the space of just over five months, provisions under the Criminal Code proscribing incest went through two lots of statutory change. On 11 October 2001, an amendment of ss 223 and 224 of the Criminal Code, Chapter 262,[1] was made extending the existing law against incest to include relations which were previously not covered by the amended law. The changes came about when Lady Carol Kidu MP successfully introduced the Criminal Code (Amendment) Bill 2001. Then, on 28 March 2002, she again successfully introduced the Criminal Code (Sexual Offences and Crimes Against Children) Bill which, *inter alia*, repealed ss 223 and 224 of the Principal Act and replaced them with an entirely new regime. This article discusses these changes insofar as they relate to the definition of incest and the implications they have in respect of the law concerning marriage prohibitions.

The successful passage of the March 2002 Act represents a significant step in protecting the rights of children as provided for by Art 19 of the United Nations Convention on the Rights of the Child. It provides:

> '(1) State Parties shall take all appropriate legislative, administrative, social and educational measures to protect the child from all forms of physical or mental violence, injury or abuse, neglect or negligent treatment, maltreatment or exploitation, including sexual abuse, while in the care of parent(s), legal guardian(s) or any other person who has the care of the child.
>
> (2) Such protective measures should, as appropriate, include effective procedures for the establishment of social programmes to provide necessary support for the child and for those who have the care of the child, as well as for other forms of prevention and identification, reporting, referral, investigation, treatment and follow-up of instances of child maltreatment described heretofore, and, as appropriate, for judicial involvement.'

The incidence of child sexual abuse generally and incest as a form of such abuse is not available in the country although newspaper reports of such cases seem to be

---

[*]   Associate Professor of Law, School of Law, PO Box 317, University of Papua New Guinea, PNG.
[1]   Hereafter 'the Code'.

on the rise. However, that it is increasing and widespread throughout the country received judicial comment in the case of *The State v Arthur Taradi Tamti,*[2] a case of non-consensual incest between father and daughter. Commenting on the increasing prevalence of incest, Jalina J said:

'This year alone I have dealt with a number of incest cases. In *The State v John Elei* ... I sentenced the prisoner who forced his sister to commit incest with him to six years imprisonment in hard labour. In *The State v Pikah Ndrohas* ... I sentenced the prisoner who consensually committed incest with his sister and who had a prior conviction for incest with the same sister to seven years' imprisonment in hard labour. In *The State v Francis Liro* ... I sentenced the prisoner to a total of 13 years' imprisonment for incest with two separate daughters. In *The State v David Daniel and Polin Daniel* ... I sentenced the son to eight years' imprisonment and the mother to two years and six months' imprisonment. [These cases] demonstrate that incest is becoming prevalent and must be stamped out through imposition of stiff penalties.'

In introducing the proposed amendments to ss 223 and 224 of the Code in October 2001, and commenting particularly on the prevalence of sexual violence against women and children in the country, Lady Carol Kidu explained:

'My concern is not about incest between consenting adults, but incest against children who live in the situation of trust and dependency and to protect our children. [I]t is very important for us to protect our children and by passing this amendment today, we are making a very public statement about the rights of children.'[3]

She then proceeded to stress the important role of legislators in responding to the situation of sexual violence and child sexual exploitation and shaping public perceptions and values by making appropriate changes to the criminal law and justice system. The passing of the proposed amendments would clearly indicate a 'moral denunciation of the conduct as unacceptable'.[4]

A significant aspect of the new law is the distinction it makes between incestuous sexual intercourse between consenting adults which it regards as being less serious than when the act involves a dependent child. The change is both welcome and timely, if not overdue. At least now, people who 'grow' their own child victims can expect to be punished more severely than previously. The changes also go a long way to protecting children from this form of child sexual abuse while at the same time maintaining the traditional justifications for the existence of the incest prohibition which are partly biological, partly social and protective of the family, and partly the product only of traditional moral values and attitudes.

II PURPOSE OF THE TABOO AGAINST AND DEFINITION OF INCEST

Every society identifies certain, though not all, forbidden forms of sexual congress as particularly dreadful, attracting both human anger and punishment. Sexual

---

[2]   (1999) N1878.

[3]   *Hansard*, 11 October 2001, p 32.

[4]   Ibid.

relations between parent and child and between brother and sister are, with very few exceptions, universally forbidden and everywhere not mentioned without a shudder. Many theories have been advanced as to the origin and reasons for the observance of the incest taboo. However, there is as yet no universally accepted theory to explain the universality of the rules against incest. Anthropologist Lucy Mair tells us that the theories of incest are of two kinds. One kind asks 'why it is regarded with such horror; [while the other] asks why there is a rule against it in every society'.[5] All of these theories have offered either biological, psychological, sociological, socio-cultural, socio-economic, or evolutionary explanations of the incest taboo.[6] They included the theories of 'instinctive' revulsion against incest, as necessary to prevent the birth of biogenetic defectives caused by inbreeding, and necessary to join families into larger groups to maximize benefits from such co-operation.

This theory, which Leslie White calls the 'culturological'[7] explanation for the existence of the incest taboo, explains the presence of the incest taboo in terms of the socio-cultural and economic contexts of the family or tribe. The theory claims that the incest taboo was necessary not only to ensure that there was stability within the family but it also ensured co-operation between individuals in ways that maximized the economic benefits of co-operation between families or tribes. This in turn ensured the family's collective survival. According to this theory:

> '[T]he prohibition of incest has at bottom an economic motivation ... Rules of exogamy originated as crystallizations of processes of a social system rather than as products of individual psyches. Inbreeding was prohibited and marriage between groups was made compulsory in order to obtain the maximum benefits of cooperation.'[8]

However, incest and marriage prohibitions are not necessarily conflicting conceptions; only different. Incest pertains to sexual congress as such while marriage prohibitions to exogamy, a relationship which cannot be created merely by sexual congress. Exogamy, in this theory, was therefore necessary for the family's very own survival. Either the family survived by forming into larger groupings through the practice of out-marrying or faced extinction. As first noted by EB Tylor in 1888:

> 'Exogamy, enabling a growing tribe to keep itself compact by constant unions between its spreading clans, enables it to overmatch any number of small intermarrying groups, isolated and helpless. *Again and again in the world's history, savage tribes must have had plainly in their minds the simple practical alternative between marrying-out and being killed out.*'[9]

---

5   L Mair 1972, *An Introduction to Social Anthropology*, Second Edition, 84.

6   See D Aberle *et al*, 'The Incest Taboo and the Mating Patterns of Animals', in DW McCurdy and JP Spradley 1979, *Issues in Cultural Anthropology. Selected readings*, 111–122, 112–113.

7   L White, 'The Definition and Prohibition of Incest', in DW McCurdy and JP Spradley (eds) 1979 *Issues in Cultural Anthropology. Selected readings*, 95–110, 100.

8   Ibid at 103.

9   EB Tylor, 'On a Method of Investigating the Development of Institutions; Applied to Laws of Marriage and Descent' (1888) *Journal of the Anthropological Institute*, vol 18, 245–269, 267. Emphasis added.

There is, however, as yet no satisfactory theory of the relationship between the prohibition of incest and the rules of exogamy although it is clear that they are not extensions of the rules against incest between persons who are closely related by blood, such as between parent and child and between siblings. According to one commentator on the matter, 'incest was so dangerous that marriage had to be invented to prevent it!'[10]

Generally, the rules of incest and exogamy are mutually exclusive although they do coincide in some cases, under certain circumstances and for certain categories of relatives. Incest rules compel one to marry outside the family, at least outside the nuclear family. However, the same rules would not apply to certain categories of close relatives outside of this basic unit. Incest and exogamy rules are based on different considerations and reflect different values, although in many instances they do actually coincide. Thus, although in most cases those who are covered by the incest rule cannot also be marriage partners, this is not necessarily so because some categories of relatives who are otherwise considered too close for sexual congress are preferred or even prescribed marriage partners. The marriage of cross-cousins is one such example. Incest rules prohibit sexual connexion, a consideration not necessarily present in marriage. As Lowie notes:

> 'Marriage, as we cannot too often or too vehemently insist, is only to a limited extent based on sexual considerations. The primary motive, so far as the individual mates are concerned, is precisely the founding of a self-sufficient economic aggregate. A Kai [of New Guinea] does not marry because of desires he can readily satisfy outside of wedlock without assuming any responsibilities; he marries because he needs a woman to make pots and to cook his meals, to manufacture nets and weed his plantations, in return for which he provides the household with game and fish and builds the dwelling.'[11]

What is important for our purpose is that the different theories about incest reveal that there is no universal definition of incest although there is agreement that it involves sexual connexion between categories of close relatives traced either lineally or laterally. Although there is agreement that there is no society that does not recognize the taboo as covering the elementary family of parent, child and sibling, there are widespread variations as to the application of the incest taboo to other degrees of relations beyond this basic group. In all cases, however, definitions are constructed to emphasize either social or blood ties and in some cases both. For our purpose, most legal definitions of incest have emphasized the blood link rather than links that are social in nature. It is the relationship of the legal definitions to the area of marriage prohibitions that concern us.

III   LEGAL DEFINITIONS OF INCEST

Prior to the March 2002 law, there was no clear definition of 'incest' under the Criminal Code although the wording of ss 223 and 224 prior to their repeal indicated conformity with the commonly accepted definition of incest – acts of

---

[10]   E Leach, 'The Social Anthropology of Marriage and Mating', in V Reynolds and J Kellet (eds) 1991 *Mating and Marriage*, 91, at p 108.

[11]   RH Lowie, 1920 *Primitive Society*, 65–66.

sexual intercourse performed with parents, siblings, children (of the blood) and other lineal descendants and ancestors. Further, the term 'carnal knowledge' was used in the sections instead of the more popular lay term of sexual intercourse. However, the two terms did not represent different activities. In the case of *R v Brombey*, Philips J stated that

> 'Carnal knowledge means sexual intercourse, and sexual intercourse is complete upon penetration of the female organ by the male organ.'[12]

Section 6 of the Code explains that 'carnal knowledge' or 'carnal connexion' is 'complete on penetration', even if only slightly and the hymen is not ruptured.[13] It is irrelevant that there was no erection of the penis or emission of seed or that the perpetrator intended a result other than sexual gratification[14] such as simply to hurt a woman's feelings, as punishment or to avenge a past wrong.

If incestuous sexual intercourse involves the penetration of the vagina, what constitutes 'sexual intercourse'? Is, or should, penetration be limited to the penetration of the vagina by the penis? Can or should non-penile penetration of the vagina amount to incestuous intercourse? These questions, which could not be answered under the old law, are now answered by s 2 of the 2002 Act (amending s 6 of the Code). This section, which adopts the term 'sexual penetration' instead of the more common term of 'sexual intercourse', defines sexual penetration as follows:

'6 Sexual Penetration
When the expressions "sexual penetration" or "sexually penetrates" are used in the definition of an offence, the offence, so far as regards that element of it, is complete, where there is:

(a) the introduction, to any extent, by a person of his penis into the vagina, anus or mouth of another person; or

(b) the introduction, to any extent, by a person of an object or a part of his body (other than his penis) into the vagina or anus of another person, other than in the course of a procedure carried out in good faith for medical or hygienic purposes.'

This means therefore that for purposes of the crime of incest, it would be committed even if there is no contact between the penis and the vagina. Further, one can also anticipate that sometime in the distant future, the terms 'penis' and 'vagina' will need also to be defined to accommodate changes in technologies designed to reassign biologically determined genitals of an individual to complement the emotional and psychological make-up of the individual.

---

[12]   (1952) QWN 32, at p 36.

[13]   *R v Yoka Kiok* (1970) No 607.

[14]   *The State v John Kalabus* [1979] PNGLR 87.

IV   CATEGORIES OF RELATIONS COVERED BY THE INCEST LAW

A   The old law

Prior to the amendments of 2001 and the Act of March 2002, ss 223 and 224 provided as follows:

'**223   Incest by man**

(1) A person who carnally knows a woman or girl who is, to his knowledge:

(a)   his daughter or other lineal descendant; or

(b)   his sister; or

(c)   his mother,

is guilty of a crime.

Penalty: Subject to s 19, imprisonment for life.

224   Incest by adult female

(1) A woman or girl of or above the age of 18 years who permits:

(a)   her father or other lineal ancestor; or

(b)   her brother; or

(c)   her son,

to have carnal knowledge of her, knowing him to be her father, or other lineal ancestor, her brother or her son, as the case may be, is guilty of a misdemeanour.

Penalty: Imprisonment for a term not exceeding three years.'

Under these provisions, the crime of incest was restricted to persons who were related only by blood, such as between a man and his daughter, sister including a half-sister,[15] mother or other lineal descendant, or between a woman and her son, father or other lineal ancestor. Thus, the criminal prohibition against incest did not apply to situations of sexual contact between a man and his grandmother, between cousins or between a man and any of his nieces.[16] The man also escaped criminal responsibility if he entered into a sexual relationship with his step-daughter.[17] A woman, defined as being a person above the age of 18 years, was similarly restricted from engaging in such relationships. Under the old provision, she was prevented from permitting a person whom she knew to be her brother, son, father or other lineal ancestor to have carnal knowledge of her. No other relatives who are generally regarded as being too close for sexual contact were covered by the Code. Thus, it was not incest if she allowed a person whom she knew to be her grandson, cousin or nephew to have carnal knowledge of her.

---

[15]   *The State v Luke Aidou* [1985] PNGLR 292.

[16]   *In Re Emmanuel Lavaki* (1982) N324 (M).

[17]   *State v Bob Madaha Seneka* (1990) N970 (M).

B   The amendments of 2001

Both ss 223 and 224 of the Criminal Code were affected by the amendments of 2001. The principal purpose of the changes was to extend the category of persons who could be charged and be held criminally liable for incest. Otherwise it did not change the substance of the law on incest.

The amending words to ss 223 and 224 are highlighted in italics below:

'223   Incest by man

(1)   A person who carnally knows a woman or girl who is, to his knowledge:

    (a)   his daughter, *stepdaughter, adopted daughter, whether by custom or otherwise* or other lineal descendant; or

    (b)   his sister; *stepsister, half sister or adopted sister, whether by custom or otherwise*; or

    (c)   his mother, *stepmother, foster mother or guardian to whom the person is wholly dependent for his livelihood and sustainence (sic); or*

    (d)   his niece,

is guilty of a crime.

Penalty: Subject to s 19, imprisonment for life.'

Similar changes were made to s 224 regarding incest by a female. This provided:

'224   Incest by adult female

(1)   A woman or girl of or above the age of 18 years who permits:

    (a)   her father, *stepfather, foster father or guardian to whom this person is wholly dependent for her livelihood and sustainence (sic)* or other lineal ancestor; or

    (b)   her brother; *stepbrother or adopted brother, whether by custom or otherwise*; or

    (c)   her son, *stepson, adopted son, whether by custom or otherwise; or*

    (d)   her nephew,

to have carnal knowledge of her, knowing him to be her father, *step-father, guardian to whom the person is wholly dependent for her sustainence (sic)* or other lineal ancestor, her brother, *step-brother, half-brother, adopted brother, whether by custom or otherwise,* or her *son, step-son, adopted son, whether by custom or otherwise or her nephew* as the case may be, is guilty of a misdemeanour.

Penalty: Imprisonment for a term not exceeding three years.'

The greatest difficulty presented by these amendments concerned the issue of determining if a particular category of 'relatives' described in the amendments existed at the time the alleged incestuous intercourse took place. The difficulties related particularly and only to 'relatives' described as 'customarily adopted daughter, son, sister or brother' and 'foster mother/father or guardian to whom this person is wholly dependent for his/her livelihood and sustenance'. However, as the March 2002 Act has removed these categories, it will serve no useful purpose to consider the issues raised.

C   The Criminal Code (Sexual Offences and Crimes Against Children) Act 2002

Section 13 of the 2002 Act repealed ss 223 and 224 of the Code and replaced them with a single s 223. This provides:

> **'223   Incest**
>
> (1)   A person who engages in an act of sexual penetration with a close blood relative, is guilty of a crime.
>
> Penalty: Imprisonment for a term not exceeding seven years.
>
> (2)   For the purposes of this section, a close blood relative means a parent, son, daughter, sibling (including a half-brother or half-sister), grandparent, grandchild, aunt, uncle, niece, nephew or first cousin, being a family member from birth and not from marriage or adoption.
>
> (3)   No person shall be found guilty of an offence under this section if, at the time of the act of sexual penetration occurred, he or she was under restraint, duress or fear of the other person engaged in the act.'

In comparing the above provisions with the 2001 amendments, the following differences are revealed. First, the 2002 provisions have removed the relationships of stepdaughter, adopted daughter, stepsister and adopted sister as coming within the definition of the crime of incest. Sexual penetration, as defined, of any person in any one of these categories would therefore not constitute incest. However, if the victim is a child under the age of 16 years or is between the ages of 16 and 18 and is in a relationship of trust, authority and dependency with the perpetrator, this would constitute an act of unlawful sexual penetration or conduct under the Act.[18] Secondly, the definition has retained, on the whole, the common definition of incest based on lineal descent except that it has added the non-lineal lateral relationships of aunt, uncle, nephew and first cousin, relationships which were previously not included under the 2001 amendments or the earlier law.[19]

Thirdly, the 2002 law makes a sharp distinction between incestuous sexual intercourse between consenting adults, on one hand, and instances of incestuous sexual connexion in which one party is a child, on the other. A 'child' is defined as being a person under the age of 16 years. A child under this age is not capable of giving consent to an act of sexual penetration.[20] Thus, incestuous sexual connexion with a person under the age of 16 cannot be consensual and therefore amounts to incestuous rape as well as unlawful sexual penetration of a child contrary to s 229A of the 2002 Act. It is also clear that the new Act ranks the interests of children, as vulnerable, physically and emotionally immature and dependent persons, higher than those served by the observance of the incest taboo in society generally. Thus, incestuous sexual penetration of a child is regarded more seriously and attracts a higher penalty than when it occurs between two consenting adult relatives. The penalty for incestuous sexual penetration of a child under the age of 16 years, regardless of whether the child is a blood relative or

---

[18]   Sections 229A and 229E respectively.

[19]   *In Re Lavaki* (1982) N324 (M).

[20]   Section 229F.

not, is up to 25 years' imprisonment[21] or up to life imprisonment if the victim child is less than 12 years old or is in a relationship of trust, authority and dependency, as defined,[22] with the offender.[23] Incest between two consenting adults, by contrast, carries a penalty of up to only seven years' imprisonment.[24] Where consent is absent, and both parties are adults, the conduct becomes rape, and proceedings are to be instituted under separate provisions in the Act.[25]

Fourthly, as mentioned earlier, the 2002 law replaces all references in the Code to the expression 'carnal knowledge' or 'carnal connexion' with the expressions 'sexual penetration' or 'sexually penetrates'. Section 2, which replaces s 6 of the Code, defines 'sexual penetration' as 'the introduction, to any extent, by a person of his penis, an object, or a part of his body into the vagina, anus or mouth of another person' for a non-medical or hygienic purpose. The new law therefore makes unnecessary, but includes, the need for the presence of the act of penile penetration of the vagina before the crime of incest can be committed.

It is also worth noting that prior to the March 2002 Act, the Code categorized male incest differently from that of female incest. Under the Code, if a man, regardless of age,[26] committed incest, it was a 'crime'. It was only a 'misdemeanour' if a female person, above the age of 18 years, committed the act. Under s 223, a female person below the age of 18 years was incapable of committing incest. The penalties were also different. A male person who committed incest might be imprisoned for a maximum period of up to life whereas a female only up to three years. Although history shows that men are more likely to initiate and perpetrate incestuous relations, and that physically women are incapable of having carnal knowledge of a male person, the rationale for these differences was otherwise neither clear nor justified. Why should a woman who knowingly permitted a male person to have carnal knowledge of her or induced a male child to deal improperly with her sexually, whether penile penetration of her occurred or not, attract a lesser punishment than her male counterpart?

Section 13 of the March 2002 Act has eliminated this difference. This has been effected by making 'any person', whether male or female, who commits incest guilty of a crime for which a penalty of up to seven years' imprisonment may be imposed.

V ADOPTION AND INCEST

It is significant that the 2002 Act provides that 'relatives' covered by the incest prohibition do not include persons who become family members following adoption. Does this mean that the law protects a man who sexually penetrates his adopted daughter? It appears that the answer is both yes and no, depending on the factors of the age of the daughter and the presence or otherwise of consent at

---

[21] Section 229A(1).

[22] Section 6A.

[23] Section 229A(2) and (3).

[24] Section 223.

[25] Section 347.

[26] Under s 30(3), however, there is a rebuttable presumption that a male person under 14 years of age lacks the capacity to have carnal knowledge.

the time of the alleged sexual penetration. But we begin with a discussion of the effect of adoption on the law of incest as it was prior to the Act of March 2002.

The extent to which the new legal relationships effected by adoption affected the legal provisions proscribing incest was a matter of some controversy. Here, the law appeared to have made a distinction between adopted persons and those who were related by blood. Thus, while sexual contact between a man and his natural daughter constituted incest, this was not the result if it took place between him and his adopted daughter, even if he had raised and brought them up as twins, because of the absence of the lineal connection.

In *The State v Misimb Kais*[27] and *Sanguma Wauta v The State*,[28] the National Court and the Supreme Court respectively held that sexual intercourse with a customarily adopted daughter did not amount to incest. These conclusions followed a strict interpretation of s 223 of the Code which clearly distinguished between adopted children and children 'of the blood'. Under this provision, the term 'daughter or other lineal descendant' meant 'daughter of the blood' or descendant of the blood and did not extend to a customarily adopted daughter. Support for this conclusion was also drawn from s 37(2) of the Constitution which provides that a 'person may not be convicted of an offence that is not defined by … a written law'. Since s 223 of the Code did not extend the definition of incest to include a customarily adopted daughter, custom could not be applied pursuant to Sch 2.1 of the Constitution even if under the relevant custom, sexual intercourse between a man and his customarily adopted daughter was regarded as being equivalent to 'incest'.[29] Moreover, since the laws dealing with adoption were made subject to any law relating to a sexual offence which distinguished natural children from other 'children'[30] and because s 223 of the Code made such a distinction, it was not proper for the court to go outside the clear terms of that provision.

Nevertheless, even in the absence of such parliamentary intervention then, the interpretation of the effect of adoption as *not* creating the additional relationships of 'father' and 'daughter', in accordance with existing statutory provisions concerning adoption, for purposes of the offence of incest under s 223 of the Code is open to serious legal question and in any event not in harmony with the social reality of the extended family and expectations in the country.

Even though the *Misimb Kais* and *Sanguma Wauta* cases concerned customarily adopted daughters, it appears that the court in each case would have reached the same conclusion if the matters involved statutory adoptions despite the clear terms of s 28 of the Adoption of Children Act, Chapter 275. Under this provision, an adopted child becomes the child of the adopting parents 'as if the child had been born to the adopters in lawful wedlock', and at the same time, the child ceases to be the child of his/her natural parents.[31]

---

[27]   [1978] PNGLR 241.

[28]   [1978] PNGLR 326.

[29]   *Sanguma Wauta v The State* (above).

[30]   Section 27(2), Adoption of Children Act, 1968 (No 8 of 1969).

[31]   On this, see O Jessep and J Luluaki 1994 *Principles of Family Law in Papua New Guinea*, 154–155.

Later decisions have, however, doubted if these decisions can be accepted as necessarily stating the correct legal position at the time. In *The State v Aidou*,[32] for example, the court was asked to consider if sexual intercourse between a half-brother and half-sister amounted to incest as proscribed by s 223 of the Code. It was clear that according to the customs of the Siassi people, sexual intercourse between a half-brother and half-sister was forbidden. To determine if incest had been committed, the court had to be satisfied that the definition of 'sister' under s 223 of the Code included a half-sister. The court decided that since the Code did not provide a definition of the word 'sister', it should provide one. Drawing support from the custom of the Siassi forbidding sexual intercourse between a half-brother and a half-sister, applicable common law principles,[33] and the fact that the Siassi custom was not inconsistent with a Constitutional Law or statute or inapplicable to the circumstances of the country, Barnett AJ concluded that the term 'sister' as used in s 223 of the Code included a half-sister and therefore found the accused guilty of committing incest against his younger half-sister.

Again, in *The State v Peter Burin*,[34] the court was asked to consider if sexual intercourse between first cousins constituted incest within the meaning of s 223 of the Code. According to the custom of the parties, they were regarded as brother and sister and therefore sexual intercourse between them was prohibited. It was held that a sister under s 223 included a cousin sister, and that such a finding depended on custom, whether a first cousin has the status of a sister for the purposes of the section. This assumed, of course, the relationship of 'father' and 'daughter' between uncle and niece whereby an uncle would be guilty of incest if he had sexual intercourse with his niece because he *is* her father and she his daughter.

In the strict legal sense, however, the decision in *The State v Peter Burin*[35] can be challenged. There appears to have been no justification for the court to have confused lineal blood relatives with lateral ones especially when s 223 was framed so as to restrict the offence of incest to people related by blood only. If it had been intended to include also the uncle and niece relationship, it could have easily done so by adding 'lateral' relatives as well. As such, there was no need to define 'sister' and it was therefore not open to the court to extend the definition by what amounts to a legislative act. This view is supported by the fact that under the Marriage Act, Chapter 280,[36] the marriage of first cousins is not prohibited. To think otherwise is to argue the absurd, that first cousins can marry but they cannot have marital sex. If they do, they would be committing incest and risk spending their marriage in prison.

There is a further problem with the decision in *Peter Burin's* case. If this decision is to be accepted as stating the correct legal position at the time, it means

---

32   [1985] PNGLR 292.

33   *R v Thompson* [1933] QJPR 93. In this case, the Queensland Court of Criminal Appeal, when interpreting an identical section in the Queensland Criminal Code, held that a 'sister' included a half-sister who had the same mother as the accused but a different father. This decision obtained the status of a decision of the High Court of Australia when that court refused leave of appeal on this point: *R v Thompson* (1934) 52 CLR 750.

34   [1994] PNGLR 15.

35   Ibid.

36   Hereafter the 'Marriage Act'.

that, depending on the peculiarities of custom, the definition of 'father', 'mother', 'daughter', 'son', 'brother', 'sister' is anything but precise and may include an endless list of categories of persons who may be regarded as 'father', 'daughter', 'sister', 'brother', and so on. Lineal and lateral relatives represent different kinds of relatives but at what point do they cease to have the same meaning and take on different meanings? To the point where sexual intercourse with a 'sister' or 'daughter' in one community will amount to incest and the guilty person be sent to prison, his/her fellow citizen in another community will escape criminal responsibility for incest. Thus, if the facts in *In Re Emmanuel Lavaki*,[37] the case in which the court held that a person who has sexual intercourse with his niece did not commit incest, occurred in Peter Burin's community, he would have been adjudged guilty of incest and punished accordingly. This is a most unsatisfactory situation and must be avoided. These inconsistent decisions militated against the development of a coherent system of legal principles, a result perhaps not intended by the court in that case. The better view however is that the definition of 'mother', 'father', 'sister', 'brother' should be restricted to people related by blood regardless of customary extensions to other 'relatives' and that it is up to the legislature to extend it, by clear express statements to that effect, to include other categories.

The problem the courts faced in the cases of *The State v Misimb Kais* and *Sanguma Wauta v The State* was not helped by the fact that s 223 provided no definition of 'incest' or of the words 'father', 'son', 'daughter' or 'sister'. Such a provision might have extended the definition of these terms to include these newly created relationships. As this was not the case, if the courts decided otherwise, it would amount to a legislative act, a power that only Parliament has the right to exercise. Indeed, Raine DCJ felt that there were good reasons for Parliament to feel it desirable to amend the law. He suggested that 'the present sections should not be fiddled with, and that a completely new section be constituted, dealing solely with girls who have been legally adopted, or adopted in the customary sense'.[38]

To an extent, the legislative amendments Raine DCJ had in mind were effected, almost 23 years to the month later, by the October 2001 amendments to the Code. This controversy appears now to have been given its final legal quietus with the enactment of the March 2002 Act. However, the exclusion of the special relationships effected by adoption in the new definition of incest raises special problems when applying these relationships to the issue of marriage prohibition.

As regards the question whether sexual intercourse between a man and his adopted daughter is protected by the law, the position under the new law is that it is not incest but the adoptive father stands to be criminally charged for any one of two acts of unlawful sexual penetration of a child or not at all, depending on the age of the daughter. If the adopted daughter is a child under the age of 16 years, criminal charges will be laid under s 229A[39] of the Code. If the age of the child is between 12 and 16 years of age, a maximum penalty of 25 years' imprisonment

---

[37]   (1982) N324 (M).
[38]   *Sanguma Wauta v The State* [1978] PNGLR 326, at p 335.
[39]   As amended by s 15 of the Act.

may be ordered. If the child is below 12 years, the maximum possible penalty is life imprisonment. However, if the adopted daughter is between the ages of 16 and 18 years and she is also in a relationship of 'trust, authority or dependency' to the adoptive father, a term of imprisonment not exceeding 15 years will be imposed. By contrast, if the adopted daughter is above the 18 years of age, no offence is committed except that rape charges may be laid if sexual penetration occurred without her consent.[40] Thus, if consensual sexual intercourse takes place between a man and his adult adopted daughter, no offence is committed even though, as mentioned below, he can never marry her.

VI INCEST AND MARRIAGE PROHIBITIONS

Prior to the amendments of 2001, all lineal relatives covered by the incest prohibition under the Code were also recognized as prohibited marriage partners under the Marriage Act, Chapter 280.[41] Apart from the issues raised by the effect of adoption on the incest requirement, as discussed earlier, no other category of relatives was covered by the incest prohibition. This position was subsequently changed by the 2001 amendments and again by the 2002 Act. The new laws on incest have, however, given rise to both positive and negative consequences.

Under the old laws, certain lateral relatives were not covered by the incest requirements even though they were recognized as coming within the marriage prohibition requirements under the Marriage Act. This situation arose in the case of a man and his aunt or niece and a woman and her uncle or nephew. This meant that, while sexual intercourse could take place between them without breaching the laws against incest, they could not enter into a marriage contract under the Marriage Act. This apparent conflict has now been removed by including that category of relatives in the new incest provisions. Unfortunately, the conflict has been continued in the case of first cousins. Under the new law, incest would be committed if sexual intercourse took place between first cousins. It must be stated, however, that some societies in Papua New Guinea recognize first cousins as preferred marriage partners. In others, they are prescribed partners. Unfortunately, the thinking that went into putting together the new incest provisions appears to have missed this point altogether. That this may not be the custom in most societies[42] cannot and should not have justified the enactment of legal provisions having a general application.

Under the Marriage Act, first cousins are allowed as marriage partners. The effect here therefore is that while they can get married, marital sexual intercourse cannot take place between them without also contravening the law against incest. For them, therefore, the choice is between having a sexless married life or spending their married life in prison. The question should therefore be asked whether a successful charge can be brought against the husband for committing incest against his wife.

---

[40] Section 347, *Criminal Code*, as amended by s 17 of the 2002 Act.
[41] Hereafter the 'Marriage Act'.
[42] As occurred in *The State v Peter Burin* [1994] PNGLR 15.

John Y Luluaki

Under s 229G of the 2002 Act, it is a defence to a charge of sexual penetration of a child if, at the time of the alleged offence, 'the child was of or over the age of 14 and the [accused] person was married to the child'. Thus, in order for the accused to escape criminal liability, two elements must be proved. First, it has to be proved that the child had reached the age of 14 years or above, and secondly, the accused was married to the victim child at the relevant time. Marriage, however, is not a defence to a charge of incest under the Act. However, by parity of reasoning with the offence of sexual penetration of a child, it would appear that if the marriage has been freely and voluntarily entered into and solemnized and there are no grounds avoiding it, sexual penetration of one's wife would in law not amount to incest. Sexual intercourse between a husband and wife who are also first cousins would therefore, it is submitted, be protected from criminal prosecution. This interpretation would mean that the legal protection given to parties to customary first cousin marriages would be extended to such marriages under the Marriage Act.

Furthermore, the inclusion of the categories of aunt, niece and first cousin also means that the number of different situations in which incest would be committed if sexual intercourse takes place has been increased. This in turn is likely to have an increasing effect on the incidence of incest cases in the country.

Conflicts between the new criminal laws on incest and the Marriage Act prohibitions also arise in the converse situation. That is, while the Code does not criminalize sexual intercourse between certain categories of relatives, they are not eligible marriage partners under the Marriage Act. Thus, sexual penetration of an adopted daughter or stepdaughter is not incestuous whereas marriage with them is forbidden. This means that if the adopted daughter or stepdaughter is older than 16 years, her adopted father or stepfather can found a family with her and they can live as if they were married, such as in a *de facto* relationship, and there would be nothing criminal or otherwise illegal about their association. With respect, I doubt if the framers of the new law intended such a result.

In law, adoption produces the result that the adopted child becomes the adopting person's child as if he or she was the natural child of the adopting parent. It is for this reason that marriage between adoptive children and parents is prohibited. Unfortunately, the new law does not consider this link as justifying the application of the incest law to this relationship. Under the present law, while an adoptive father may be found guilty of a sexual offence against his dependent adopted daughter who is under the age of 18 years, no offence would be committed if he sexually penetrates her with her consent and she is over that age. This is a most unsatisfactory situation and one which could easily have been avoided by including the special relationships created by adoption as coming within the definition of incest in the new law.

VII CONCLUSIONS

In the last few years, the issue of children's rights and Papua New Guinea's international obligations under the Convention on the Rights of the Child, which it ratified in 1993, has been the subject of much public discussion and concern. Several national gatherings (forums, workshops, conferences, and seminars) have carried the issue of children's rights as their theme. A review of the domestic laws in relation to the rights of children established by the Convention on the Rights of the Child was completed in 2000.[43] Later this year, in September, the 5th Papua New Guinea National Legal Convention, under the auspices of the Papua New Guinea Judiciary in collaboration with the PNG Law Society, the Attorney General's Department and the Law School, University of Papua New Guinea, bearing the theme 'Protecting the Child', will be held. A comprehensive review of the colonial Child Welfare Act, Chapter 278, is also in progress and it is expected that this will go for parliamentary consideration in 2003.

While efforts to locate the issue of children's rights more centrally in the political and governmental processes, and generally increase public awareness of the need to take the issue of children's rights more seriously, have begun and continue, the enactment of the Criminal Code (Sexual Offences and Crimes Against Children) Act, 2002, represents the single most important piece of legislative initiative in that regard since Papua New Guinea ratified the Convention on the Rights of the Child. However, what is perhaps disappointing about the initiative is that it came in the form of a private member's Bill and not, as one would have expected, from those within the Executive and Legislative arms of government responsible for initiating and progressing such legislative enactments and changes in the law. Nevertheless, that the law was unanimously supported without amendment is testimony to the burgeoning of a hitherto absent political interest in this subject and a willingness on the part of the legislature to respond positively to the need to make new laws and change existing ones to make them more suitable to the changing circumstances and needs of this country consistent with the requirements of a world society.

The 2002 Act has changed the laws relating to crimes against women and children in many significant respects although this article has concentrated only on the crime of incest and its relationship to the issue of marriage prohibition under the Marriage Act. Maybe an opportunity to discuss these other areas will become available in the near future. There is of course little doubt that the public has warmly if not enthusiastically welcomed this new law. However, while we wait to see the outcome and effect of the enforcement process, and prediction can be a peculiarly difficult task, it is hoped that the new Parliament[44] will take inspiration from this initial step towards a long-term objective of translating rhetoric into legislative and administrative reality through a combined process of legislative reform and organizational restructure aimed at ensuring that those who need to be protected from sexual and other abuses are provided such protection by the law. However, it also hoped that in its zest to introduce and enforce these important laws, Parliament does not lose sight of the other important need to avoid conflicts

---

[43] *The UN Convention on the Rights of the Child. Legislative Review*, December 2000, Department of the Attorney-General. In relation to the domestic laws dealing with the rights of children to be protected from all forms of abuse, including sexual abuse, the Review, in noting the inadequate and colonial nature of the wording of the provisions in the Criminal Code dealing with sexual offences against children, recommended that the definition of the term 'carnal knowledge' should be widened to include acts of non-penile penetration of the vagina, anus or mouth: pp 169–170.

[44] This is written in election year. Polling for the 2002–2007 Parliament begins on 15 June 2002 and concludes on 29 June 2002.

between laws and for the statutory scheme to be structured in a consistent and coherent manner.

SCOTLAND

SOME DREAMS REALISED, SOME DISAPPOINTMENTS

*Elaine E Sutherland**

I   INTRODUCTION

Regular readers of the *International Survey* may be familiar with the thrust of the contributions from Scotland over the last few years. They have focused on two main themes. First have been attempts to assess whether early optimism regarding the 'great things' the new Scottish Parliament would achieve was well-founded. Secondly, the impact of the Human Rights Act 1998 in, essentially, incorporating the European Convention on Human Rights into the legal systems of the United Kingdom was examined. Discussion to date has focused on child law. This year, priority will be given to other areas of family law and what, if any, impact these two key developments have had. Of course, child law has not remained static and developments in that area are mentioned, albeit briefly.

Certainly, no one could accuse the Scottish Parliament of being inactive. The Scottish Executive has shown a particular enthusiasm for consultation over proposed law reform, sometimes making special efforts to give children and young people a meaningful opportunity to be part of the process.[1] However, there have been some very clear examples of 'feet dragging' and, sadly, nowhere is this more evident than in the field of family law. As long ago as 1992 the Scottish Law Commission made a number of excellent proposals for reform.[2] Some of these found expression in the Children (Scotland) Act 1995[3] but many of them languished, neglected, despite a relatively constant whine from academics and some practitioners. Given the lapse of time, the Scottish Executive felt it should consult again on the Commission's proposals and took the opportunity to raise a number of new issues.[4] In September 2000, it set out its proposals for reform and asked several further questions.[5] Thereafter, and despite promises in the Scottish

---

[*]   LLB, LLM, Reader, School of Law, University of Glasgow, and Professor, Lewis and Clark Law School, Portland, Oregon.

[1]   For example, in discussions about the need for a Children's Commissioner for Scotland, there was extensive consultation with children: see below. Similarly, when reform of the law on physical punishment of children was being considered, the views of children were sought: see below.

[2]   *Report on Family Law* (Scottish Law Commission No 135, 1992).

[3]   Part I of the *Report on Family Law* (above) formed the basis for Part I of the 1995 Act. See Elaine E Sutherland, 'Child Law Reform – At last!' in *The International Survey of Family Law*, ed A Bainham (Martinus Nijhoff, 1995), p 435.

[4]   *Improving Scottish Family Law* (Scottish Executive, March 1999).

[5]   *Parents and Children: A White Paper on Scottish Family Law* (Scottish Executive, 2000). A 'White Paper' is a government document setting out firm proposals for law reform, with the term 'Green Paper' being used for a consultation document. Due to its hybrid nature, this White Paper was a 'white paper with green edges'. The new questions asked related to giving non-marital

Parliament that legislation would be introduced, there was a conspicuous lack of activity. Why the delay? The need for further consultation following the publication of the White Paper is hardly an explanation, since responses were required by 8 December 2000. The real reason may be that, one way or another, the Scottish Executive's plans are guaranteed to offend sizeable groups throughout the country. There is a suspicion (by definition, unproven) that, with elections to the Scottish Parliament scheduled for May 2003, the Executive is reluctant to introduce controversial legislation.[6]

Lawyers throughout Scotland have been on a sharp learning curve with regard to the European Convention on Human Rights and the 'human rights dimension' can be seen throughout the legal system. No law reform proposal is complete without a discussion of the human rights implications and all new legislation is subject to scrutiny for compliance with the Convention. The Convention Rights Compliance (Scotland) Act 2001 sought to effect compliance in a range of areas where problems were anticipated. 'Convention points' are now a regular feature of litigation in the Scottish courts.[7]

II MEDICO-LEGAL ISSUES AND THE FAMILY

Wrongful birth and wrongful conception[8]

Many individuals seeking to avoid conceiving a child (or, as is often the case, another child) enlist the help of the medical profession and undergo a vasectomy (male) or sterilisation operation (female). If the operation is performed negligently, or the advice from doctors as to whether it has been successful is given negligently, should the individual be able to recover damages at all when the very outcome sought to be avoided, the birth of a child, results? If so, should there be any limit on the heads of damage for which recovery is permitted? Does it make any difference whether the resulting baby is healthy or has disabilities? Does it matter whether the individual seeking to avoid the birth is motivated by convenience, economic pressures, his or her own disability or a host of other considerations? While it might have been thought that these questions had been

---

fathers automatic parental responsibilities and parental rights on joint registration of the child's birth; the proposed step-parent agreements; and the merger of adultery and unreasonable behaviour into one ground for divorce.

[6] At the time of writing, it is understood that a draft Family Law (Scotland) Bill will be published late in 2002 but that no time will be allocated to debating it until after the 2003 elections.

[7] See, for example, *S v Miller* 2001 SLT 531, discussed in EE Sutherland, 'Justice for the Child Offender in Scotland?' in *The International Survey of Family Law (2002 Edition)*, ed A Bainham (Family Law, 2002), p 357. See also *S v Miller (No 2)* 2001 SLT 1304. In *Nicol v Caledonian Newspapers Limited*, 11 April 2002, Outer House, unreported, but available on *www.scotcourts.gov.uk/opinions/pat2803.html*, the interaction of Arts 8 (privacy) and 10 (freedom of expression) was explored in the early stages of a rather unusual case where the defender in a divorce action sought damages for defamation from a newspaper which published an article reporting his wife's allegations of his alleged domestic abuse and fraud. A proof before answer was allowed.

[8] For an excellent discussion of the terminology used in some of the cases discussed in this section and the cases themselves, see JK Mason, 'Wrongful Pregnancy, Wrongful Birth and Wrongful Terminology' (2002) 6 *Edinburgh Law Review* 46.

answered,[9] either expressly or implicitly, courts throughout the United Kingdom have devoted considerable energy to revisiting them over the last few years, at least in part due to more general developments in the law of delict (= tort).

Recent Scottish developments begin with *McFarlane v Tayside Health Board*. The McFarlanes already had four children and had decided that their family was large enough. Mr McFarlane underwent a vasectomy. After using contraception for several months, the couple was informed by the hospital that his sperm count was negative and they could dispense with such precautions. It transpired that the medical advice was erroneous and the couple's healthy daughter, Catherine, duly arrived. Readers may recall that *McFarlane* has made two previous appearances in the *International Survey*. In the first, the present author lamented that the Lord Ordinary had embraced the 'joys and blessings' argument in refusing to award damages for either the mother's pain and suffering or the cost of raising the child.[10] The second mention welcomed the McFarlanes' successful appeal,[11] when the Inner House of the Court of Session rejected the 'joys and blessings' argument resoundingly and, applying the ordinary rules of delict, found the hospital board liable for Ms McFarlane's pain, suffering and distress, her loss of earnings, the cost of moving to a larger home and the cost of raising Catherine. It may be stating the obvious to note that the final head of damages, at £100,000, was by far the largest.

Sadly, that was not the end of the story, and two years later the House of Lords substantially overturned that eminently sensible decision.[12] One might be forgiven for having difficulty in extracting a clear ratio from their Lordships' speeches since, in the words of Brooke LJ, 'the five members of the House of Lords spoke with five different voices',[13] but the effect was to deny recovery for the cost of raising a healthy child. If there is any ratio to be found it is that the claim for the cost of raising the child is for pure economic loss and, as such, could only be upheld where it would be 'fair, just and reasonable' or where the defender

---

[9] See, for example, *Emeh v Kensington Area Health Authority* [1985] 1 QB 1012; *Thake v Morris* [1986] 1 QB 644; and *Anderson v Forth Valley Health Board* 1998 SLT 588. As a result of what was thought to be established law, settlements were reached in a number of Scottish cases. See *Pollock v Lanarkshire Health Board* (1987) and *Lindsay v Greater Glasgow Health Board* (1990), discussed in JK Mason and RA McCall Smith, *Law and Medical Ethics* (5th ed, 1999, Butterworths) at p 85.

[10] Elaine E Sutherland, 'From Birth to Death' in *The International Survey of Family Law 1996*, ed A Bainham (Martinus Nijhoff, 1998) at pp 384–386, commenting on *McFarlane v Tayside Health Board* 1997 SLT 211.

[11] Elaine E Sutherland, 'Consolidation and Anticipation' in *The International Survey of Family Law (2000 Edition)*, ed A Bainham (Family Law, 2000), at pp 331–333, commenting on *McFarlane v Tayside Health Board* 1998 SLT 307.

[12] 2000 SLT 154. Their Lordships upheld Ms McFarlane's claim in respect of pain, suffering and other costs associated with the pregnancy and birth.

[13] *Parkinson v St James and Seacroft University Hospital NHS Trust* [2001] 3 All ER 97, at 107. This view did not prevent his Lordship giving a masterly analysis of the various judgments at pp 107–110, something which Hale LJ expanded upon to excellent effect in *Rees v Darlington Memorial Hospital NHS Trust* [2002] 2 All ER 177, at 182–183. Lord Prosser, in *McLelland v Greater Glasgow Health Board* 2001 SLT 446 at 453, commented that while 'their Lordships expressed themselves in markedly different ways', he found this to be 'an aid to construction rather than the opposite'. However, the fact that he spent considerable energy explaining the different reasons for the decision tends to support the more widely held view that the lack of a clear ratio renders the case less than helpful.

had assumed responsibility for the pursuers' economic interest.[14] In addition, some reliance was placed on the notions of distributive justice.[15] The decision of the House of Lords in *McFarlane* was greeted with horror, certainly by most academic writers. In terms of legal analysis, viewing the cost of raising a child, the very thing the pursuers sought to avoid, as pure economic loss, is open to question. That a defender should be absolved of the bulk of liability when his or her negligence had precisely caused the result which could have been anticipated is unprincipled. On a policy level, the fact that one unlucky couple should bear the cost of medical negligence when that cost could have been spread over all health service users is undesirable. Whatever the flaws in their Lordships' reasoning, the fact remains that the House of Lords is the highest Scottish civil court and its decisions are binding on lower courts.[16]

The impact of the decision was felt swiftly in *McLelland v Greater Glasgow Health Board* where, despite being informed that a pregnant woman had a family history of Down's syndrome, the hospital administered only a non-diagnostic screening test rather than amniocentesis, which would have diagnosed Down's syndrome. Believing the foetus to be free of the condition, Ms McLelland proceeded with her pregnancy, rather than having a termination. When her son, Gary, was born with Down's syndrome, she and her husband raised an action against the health board, seeking to recover damages for the suffering and distress they had each experienced, her pain and loss of wages, the cost of raising their son to adulthood, and for his care as an adult. Their initial success in the Outer House[17] was short-lived since the appeal was heard after the House of Lords' decision in *McFarlane*. While upholding the father's claim for solatium, the Inner House rejected the claim in respect of the 'ordinary' costs of maintaining Gary.[18] The McClellands did recover for the additional costs of care attributable to Gary's condition.

Some indication of the lack of enthusiasm for the decision of the House of Lords in *McFarlane* can be seen by the willingness of the Court of Appeal in England to distinguish it. In *Parkinson v St James and Seacroft University Hospital NHS Trust*,[19] a case involving a negligently performed sterilisation, recovery was allowed for the additional costs attributable to the child's disabilities, albeit ordinary maintenance was not recoverable. In *Rees v Darlington Memorial Hospital NHS Trust*,[20] a woman with severe visual impairment who, again, was the victim of a negligent sterilisation operation, was successful in claiming for the additional costs of raising her child, this time occasioned by her own disability. Increasingly, courts are having to show considerable ingenuity in

---

[14] *Caparo Industries plc v Dickman* [1990] 2 AC 605.

[15] As developed in *Frost v Chief Constable of South Yorkshire* [1999] 2 AC 455. Lord Steyn, in a phrase which is already coming back to haunt the courts, referred to 'the commuter on the Underground' and his or her perception of what would be fair.

[16] It would be tempting to claim that Scottish law differed from its English counterpart or that their Lordships had failed to understand it, were it not for the fact that the two Scottish Law Lords, Lord Clyde and Lord Hope, made no such claims and, indeed, reached the same conclusions as their fellow Law Lords.

[17] 1999 SLT 543.

[18] 2001 SLT 446.

[19] [2002] 3 All ER 97.

[20] [2002] 2 All ER 177.

seeking to avoid the otherwise iniquitous results of following *McFarlane*. The distinctions are not entirely convincing and one has some sympathy with Lord Morison's expression of dissent in *McLelland* where he said:

> 'I see no logical ground upon which it could be held, consistently with the defenders' admission of liability, that an award of damages to the pursuers includes part of the cost of maintaining the child but excludes another part.'[21]

Tied as they are to disability, the distinctions are instinctively uncomfortable. Unless or until the House of Lords reconsiders its position, legislation is the only answer. If this means that the Scottish Parliament takes Scottish law to a more just conclusion, then inconsistency within the UK is a price worth paying and the remedy for England and Wales is similar legislation at Westminster.

Assisted reproduction

The various techniques available to assist a person to have a child where the more conventional method is, for whatever reason, not appropriate, are governed by the Human Fertilisation and Embryology Act 1990.[22] Powers of administration and decision-making under the Act lie with the Human Fertilisation and Embryology Authority (HFEA). Recently, controversy has arisen over a number of issues surrounding assisted reproduction and the goal here is simply to alert the reader to developments in Scotland, rather than to engage in an in-depth analysis of the issues themselves.

First, given the fame of Dolly, perhaps the best-known sheep in the world, readers are doubtless aware of the work on cloning carried out at the Roslyn Institute, near Edinburgh. More recently, the Centre for Genome Research at Edinburgh University was given permission by the HFEA for stem cell research using cells from human embryos in its attempts to find cures for life-threatening diseases. Research of this nature is subject to stringent controls but, as elsewhere in the world, this has not prevented huge controversy over the ethics of such work.[23]

A second source of concern has been the storage of gametes for possible future use by the donors themselves. For example, prior to undergoing treatment

---

[21] *McLelland v Greater Glasgow Health Board* 2001 SLT 446 at 457. Lord Morison would have allowed recovery for all maintenance and care costs.

[22] Since the Act was passed, both commercial surrogacy and the posthumous use of gametes have been re-examined: see *Surrogacy Review for Health Ministers of Current Arrangements and Regulation* (1998, Cm 4068) and *Review of the Consent Provisions of the Human Fertilisation and Embryology Act 1990* (Department of Health, 1998), respectively. The latter review was prompted, in large part, by the case of Diane Blood who sought to use sperm extracted from her comatose husband shortly before his death: *R v Human Fertilisation and Embryology Authority, ex parte Blood* [1997] 2 All ER 687. Ms Blood was successful in securing the right to travel to Belgium for treatment and has gone on to have two children. Disputes continue over parental responsibilities and rights in respect of children born as a result of assisted reproduction, particularly where same-sex relationships are involved and/or conception has been effected by do-it-yourself insemination rather than treatment in a facility licensed under the 1991 Act: see below.

[23] Kate Foster and Jason Beattie, 'Scots to pioneer embryo research', *The Scotsman*, 28 February 2002, p 5, and Kate Foster, 'Pro-lifers' bid to stop research on human embryos', *The Scotsman*, 4 March 2002, p 3.

for cancer which might render him sterile, a man might donate sperm with the intention that, if his treatment proves successful, he and his partner would use the sperm to have a child. The donation might also be made in order that his widow could go on to have their child.[24] A malfunction in the storage facilities at one Edinburgh hospital resulted in damage to a number of sperm samples being stored with this sort of use in mind. As a result, couples and widows have been deprived of the chance to have a child using the male partner's genetic material.[25] In the light of the courts' generous attitudes to the medical profession over liability for failed sterilisations and vasectomies, one wonders what the approach will be over the issue of liability for depriving an individual of the opportunity to have a child. Where a couple plan to use their own gametes to have a child together by means of IVF, there has always been the possibility that an error at the storage facility may result in their gametes being given to another couple or *vice versa*. Recent developments in England and Wales suggest that this possibility has become a reality.[26]

To what extent should potential parents be able to select characteristics of their potential child? It should be noted that Art 14 of the European Convention on Human Rights and Biomedicine 1997[27] prohibits sex selection for other than health reasons. The HFEA's most recent Code of Practice simply provides that 'Centres *should not* select the sex of embryos for social reasons'.[28] It is interesting that the Code does not employ one of the more usual legal formulations 'must not' or 'may not' and this suggests that sex selection on social grounds could be permitted in exceptional circumstances. Since sex selection for medical grounds is not mentioned, it can be inferred that there is no objection to the practice. So, for example, it may be allowed where there is a significant risk that a child of one gender, but not the other, would inherit a particular disease. The issue came to the fore in Scotland over the case of a couple, the Mastertons, who had four sons and whose only daughter died in a tragic accident. They wanted to use IVF to ensure that they had another female child. Having failed to obtain treatment in the UK,

---

[24] A couple wishing to keep this option open should ensure the man's written consent to posthumous use in order to avoid the problems experienced by Diane Blood; see n 22, above.

[25] The whole incident was exacerbated by allegations that the hospital's eight-month delay in telling patients amounted to an attempted cover-up and the subsequent enquiry by the Scottish Executive which cleared it of wrongdoing, while finding the delay regrettable. The hospital claimed the delay was due to difficulty in finding a biologist to carry out an internal inquiry and problems in assessing the extent of the damage to individual samples. See Camillo Fracassini, 'Hospital cancer blunder labelled a "whitewash"', *Scotland on Sunday*, 7 April 2002.

[26] In Hampshire, England, a clinic which stored embryos created from couples' gametes for future use by the couples ran into problems over its procedures for identifying particular embryos. It has been suggested that a number of embryos will be destroyed and a number of couples have lost their only opportunity to attempt implantation and parenthood using their own genetic material: Lois Rogers, 'Clinic to destroy embryos', *The Sunday Times*, 17 January 2001, p 26. It has been reported that a gynaecologist and a scientist are to be charged under the 1990 Act: Lewis Smith, 'Two face charges over embryos', *The Times*, 10 January 2002, p 6. What may be one of the clearest cases of a mix-up over gametes came to light when a white couple, who believed their own gametes had been used, were presented with black twin babies: Ian Cobain, 'Court battles start for white couple with black twins in IVF mix-up', *www.timesonline.co.uk*, 9 July 2002.

[27] Properly styled the Convention for the Protection of Human Rights and dignity of the human being with regard to the application of biology and medicine: Convention on Human Rights and Biomedicine. At the time of writing, the UK has neither signed nor ratified the Convention which entered into force (between parties to it) on 1 December 1999.

[28] At para 9.9, emphasis added. The Code was last revised in March 2001.

they travelled to Italy but, to date, have not succeeded in producing a female embryo.[29] It is worth noting that they had not reached the point of being refused permission by the HFEA and their case has not been tested in court. The whole controversy over what the press likes to call 'designer babies' was further fuelled when the HFEA recently gave permission to a couple in England to use genetic screening and IVF to create a child whose tissue would match that of their son. The intention is that stem cells from the blood in the new baby's umbilical cord could then be used in a bone marrow transplant to treat their son's potentially fatal blood disorder, thalassaemia.[30] While one can have nothing but sympathy for a parent's desire to save the life of his or her child, it is at least arguable that to produce a human being for the primary purpose of donating cells to save the life of another amounts to degrading treatment of the donor child, contrary to Art 3 of the European Convention on Human Rights.

Infecting with HIV

It is somewhat surprising that Scotland has no history of successful prosecution for the passing on of a sexually transmitted disease.[31] The first such case arose in 2001, when Stephen Kelly was convicted of recklessly infecting his partner with HIV and sentenced to five years' imprisonment.[32] While in prison previously, Mr Kelly had been informed that he was HIV positive and of the danger of infecting others. After he was released, he met Ms Craig, formed a relationship with her and deceived her about his HIV positive status. The couple had unprotected sex and Ms Craig became HIV positive.

---

[29] Sue Leonard, 'Embryo given away because it is not a girl', *The Sunday Times*, 4 March 2001, p 11.

[30] Nigel Hawkes, 'Couple win right to create life-saving baby', *The Times*, 23 February 2002, p 12. This approach is not new. In 1997, in Portland, Oregon, a five-year-old girl suffering from myelogenous leukaemia received blood cells from her baby brother's umbilical cord after it was found that her parents and other siblings were not suitably matched for bone marrow donation; AP: 'Umbilical blood transplant for leukemia: an Oregon first', *The News Tribune*, 12 January 1997, p B4. However, in a later English case, the HFEA refused permission when parents sought to use IVF to select a baby who would provide an exact tissue match to enable their son to receive bone marrow: William Lyons, 'Couple denied designer baby to help sick son', *The Scotsman*, 2 August 2002.

[31] There have been a number of successful prosecutions for 'culpable and reckless conduct' where, prior to search by a police or prison officer, the accused denied possession of sharp objects and an unprotected syringe was then encountered by the officer: *Gemmell v HM Advocate* 1900 GWD 7-366; *Kimmins v Normand* 1993 SLT 1260; *Normand v Morrison* 1993 SCCR 207; *Donaldson v Normand* 1997 JC 200.

[32] *HM Advocate v Kelly*, High Court at Glasgow, 23 February 2001, unreported. While the trial itself is unreported, a decision on the admissibility of certain evidence can be found on *www.scotcourts.gov.uk/opinions*. The case is also the first successful HIV related prosecution in the UK. Not surprisingly, it attracted considerable media attention; see, for example, John Robertson, 'HIV man jailed for infecting his lover', *The Scotsman*, 17 March 2001, p 4. It is unclear from press reports whether Mr Kelly had developed AIDS but concern about his health was expressed at the sentencing hearing and the court indicated that it would be for the authorities to decide whether he should be released from hospital earlier than normal.

Since so much of Scottish criminal law is presently common law, there is considerable scope for apparently 'new' offences to develop.[33] In practice, this amounts to no more than adapting existing forms of words when charging an individual with a criminal offence. However, there is scope to challenge this sort of development of the criminal law under Art 7 of the European Convention on Human Rights.[34] This problem will be resolved if and when the draft Criminal Code for Scotland is adopted through legislation.[35] In addition, there may be policy problems over criminalising the passing on of HIV.[36] Will it discourage people from being tested? Given that one cannot normally consent to assault, can a person ever assume the risk of infection? If we are to criminalise infecting another with a particular condition, why not take a similar approach to other conditions and diseases? Unless penalties are to attach to using public transport or going to work when one has a cold, where is the line to be drawn?

Adults with incapacity

The Adults with Incapacity (Scotland) Act 2000, a product of the work of the Scottish Law Commission,[37] became the first substantive piece of legislation from the Scottish Executive's legislative programme to be enacted. Essentially, the Act provides a comprehensive code for decision-making about the personal welfare and medical treatment of adults with impaired capacity, as well as the management of their property and financial affairs. It replaces a complicated array of, sometimes ambiguous, common law and statutory provisions which had outlived their usefulness.

The Act provides for a continuing power of attorney, which allows for management of property and finances and a welfare power of attorney, dealing with personal welfare matters, with each being effective only once registered with the Public Guardian.[38] It creates a simple procedure for dealing with the incapacitated person's money to provide for routine matters and a scheme for dealing with the property of persons in hospitals and other registered establishments, like nursing homes. Fundamental to the Act are four principles. First, any proposed intervention must be both necessary and beneficial. Secondly, intervention shall be by means of the least restrictive option. Thirdly, the present and past wishes and feelings of the incapacitated person must be ascertained, if

---

[33]   See, for example, *Khaliq v HM Advocate* 1984 SLT 137, where a shopkeeper was convicted of culpable, wilful and reckless conduct, having supplied children with packages containing glue and polythene bags (the means by which to inhale the glue).

[34]   Article 7(1) provides: 'No one shall be held guilty of any criminal offence on account of any act or omission which did not constitute a criminal offence under national or international law at the time it was committed'.

[35]   The draft Code can be found on *www.law.ed.ac.uk/dccs* and, essentially, it rewrites the criminal law of Scotland. For a child and a family lawyer, the section on sexual offences is of particular interest.

[36]   For a discussion of this issue in other jurisdictions, see *R v Cuerrier* [1998] 2 SCR 371 (Canada); South African Law Commission, *The Need for a Statutory Offence Aimed at Harmful HIV-Related Behaviour* (1998) available on *wwwserver.law.wits.ac.za/salc/salc.html*.

[37]   *Report on Incapable Adults* (Scottish Law Commission No 152, 1995).

[38]   For further information about the Office of the Public Guardian, see *www.publicguardian-scotland.gov.uk*.

that is possible, and account taken of them. There is also provision for consulting other persons like the nearest relative, primary carer and guardian. Demonstrating a refreshing recognition of the reality of human relationships, the Act defines 'nearest relative' to include a same-sex partner.[39] Finally, the adult should be encouraged to develop and exercise his or her own skills in respect of both personal welfare and management of property.

In 1977 the Scottish Law Commission proposed legislation dealing with public authority powers aimed at ensuring adequate protection of vulnerable adults including, but not confined to, persons with a mental disorder.[40] A subsequent review of mental health legislation supported the Commission's proposals insofar as they would apply to persons with a mental disorder (those within its remit).[41] In 2001, the Scottish Executive returned to the issue of protecting vulnerable adults and issued a further consultation paper.[42] The results of that consultation process are awaited but it is anticipated that the Scottish Law Commission's proposals will be endorsed again and that legislation will follow.

III VIOLENCE AND THE FAMILY

Domestic abuse

Violence in the family setting is, sadly, an all-too-familiar problem in Scotland. The common law remedies had long been recognised as inadequate when the first modern attempts were made to address the problem in the Matrimonial Homes (Family Protection) (Scotland) Act 1981. That Act provides spouses with a right to live in the family home and the possibility of having an abusive partner excluded from the home, by court order. It also deals with various ancillary matters, most significantly, an enhanced police power of arrest where breach of a matrimonial interdict (= injunction) is reasonably suspected.[43] Most of the rights available to spouses are also available to heterosexual (but not same-sex) cohabitants, but often on a more limited basis. A further weapon in the arsenal against domestic abuse was added when a new kind of exclusion order was introduced by the Children (Scotland) Act 1995.[44] This order is available only on the application of a local authority and is designed to effect the removal of an adult from the home where that adult poses a threat or danger to a child.[45] While

---

[39]   Section 87(2).

[40]   *Report on Vulnerable Adults: Public Authority Powers* (Scottish Law Commission No 158, 1997).

[41]   *Report on the Review of the Mental Health (Scotland) Act 1984* (Scottish Executive, 2001), available on *www.scotland.gov.uk/health/mentalhealthlaw*.

[42]   *Consultation on Vulnerable Adults* (Scottish Executive, 2001), available on *www.scotland.gov.uk/ consultations/justice/vacp-00.asp*.

[43]   The Act also provides for such matters as enjoyment of the contents of the home, payment of bills in relation to the home, sale of the home, and transfer of tenancy. See further, Eric M Clive, *The Law of Husband and Wife in Scotland* (4th edn, W Green, 1997), chapter 15; Elaine E Sutherland, *Child and Family Law* (T&T Clark/Butterworths, 1999), chapter 12.

[44]   Section 76.

[45]   It was always possible, under the 1981 Act, for a spouse or cohabitant to seek to exclude a partner where the partner was abusing a child of the family or was threatening to do so. However, the

these statutes were important advances in the battle against domestic abuse, significant gaps remained. The range of persons covered was narrow and so, for example, same-sex partners were not included, and interdicts under the 1981 Act terminated on divorce, thus leaving the former spouse unprotected at a time when she might most need protection. In addition, the post-arrest procedure was cumbersome to the point of being unworkable. The Protection from Harassment Act 1997, which might have assisted some of the unprotected individuals, was aimed primarily at stalkers, and was somewhat flawed and unpopular with sections of the judiciary.[46]

The Protection from Abuse (Scotland) Act 2001 sought to remedy the situation. A masterpiece of simplicity, the eight-section Act was drafted by the Non-Executive Bills Unit,[47] and was the first 'Committee' Bill to be passed by the Scottish Parliament.[48] The Act empowers a judge to attach a power of arrest to an interdict for the purpose of protection against abuse provided that the applicant can demonstrate that there is a risk of abuse in breach of the interdict.[49] 'Abuse' is defined widely, as including 'violence, harassment, threatened conduct, and any other conduct giving rise, or likely to give rise, to physical or mental injury, fear, alarm or distress'.[50] The interdicted person must be given an opportunity to be heard and there is provision to void the same person being subject to interdicts under the 1981 Act and this Act simultaneously.[51] On granting a power of arrest, the court must specify its duration (no longer than three years initially, with possible extension of up to a further three years being available)[52] and there is provision for the court to recall a power of arrest.[53] The power of arrest does not come into effect until it, and any other prescribed documents, have been served on the interdicted person[54] and it must also be notified to the chief constable of any police area in which it has effect.[55] The power of arrest allows a police officer to arrest an individual without a warrant where breach of the interdict is reasonably suspected and where the officer considers there is a risk of abuse or further abuse. The person arrested must be informed of the reason for arrest and taken to a police station. He or she will then be informed of his or her right of access to a solicitor and to have one other person informed of the detention, and is then detained until

---

1981 Act exclusion orders are rarely used to this effect, often because the non-abusing partner is afraid of the abuser.

[46]   The Act empowers the court to grant a non-harassment order, breach of which can attract a penalty of up to five years' imprisonment.

[47]   Non-Executive Bills at Westminster were often badly drafted and the Scottish Non-Executive Bills Unit seeks to avoid the problem.

[48]   It was promoted by the Justice and Home Affairs Committee. The Scottish Law Commission pointed out the need for law reform in this area in 1992; *Report on Family Law*, op cit, n 2. The Scottish Executive revisited the issue in 1999 and 2000; *Improving Scottish Family Law*, op cit, n 4, *Proposals for Protection from Abuse Bill* (Scottish Executive, 2000).

[49]   Section 1.

[50]   Section 7.

[51]   Section 1(2)(a) and (b).

[52]   Section 1(3).

[53]   Section 2.

[54]   Section 2(1).

[55]   Section 3. The operation of the power of arrest is not suspended pending notification to the chief constable but, in practice, police officers may be reluctant to use a power of arrest of which they have no notice.

charged or brought before a court.[56] Thereafter, the arrested person will either be subject to criminal proceedings or will be brought before the court in respect of the alleged breach of interdict.[57] In the latter case, the court may order further detention for up to two days, provided it is satisfied that there is both a *prima facie* case of breach of interdict and substantial risk of abuse or further abuse if further detention is not ordered.[58]

The enormous importance of this Act lies in the fact that its provisions are available to anyone who has, or is seeking, an interdict. Thus, for example, it can be used by individuals who have, or have had, a relationship, as well as victims of stranger-stalkers and children being bullied at school. Not only can it be used to protect former spouses in the post-divorce context, but its provisions are available to their future partners or to other family members, should the aggressor turn his attention to them. In addition, the procedure to be followed by police officers responding to allegations of breach of interdict is much clearer than in previous legislation.

In the first project of its kind in the UK, funding has been approved for research into domestic abuse and forced marriages experienced by ethnic minority women in Glasgow, Scotland's largest city.[59] The study will look at the incidence and characteristics of the problems as well as the obstacles to minority women gaining access to assistance and support services.

Violence against children

At the time of writing, it remains quite legal for a parent to inflict violence on his or her child in the name of 'reasonable chastisement'. The present author has expressed the view, at length and with (boring) regularity,[60] that such an approach leaves the legal system in breach of the United Nations Convention on the Rights of the Child. Furthermore, the European Court's willingness to use the UN Convention as an aid to construction of the European Convention,[61] combined with the trend amongst other countries to ban all violence against children, means that it will reach the same conclusion in respect of the European Convention in the not-too-distant future. Permitting any violence against children sends a message to parents that some violence is acceptable and some parents will cross whatever line is drawn by those who believe line-drawing to be possible. Perhaps saddest of all, the legal system sends a message to children that it is sometimes permissible for bigger, stronger people to hit smaller, more vulnerable people. Insofar as members

---

[56] Section 4. There is special provision in relation to detention of a person under the age of 16, for notification to parents and carers and for them to have reasonable access to the child: s 4(4).

[57] Section 5(1)–(3).

[58] Section 5(4).

[59] J Doherty, 'Research to study ethnic abuse rise', *The Scotsman*, 13 February 2002, p 6. The court can grant nullity of a marriage which took place as a result of duress; see, for example, *Sohrab v Khan*, 23 April 2002, see n 97 below.

[60] Most recently, see Elaine E Sutherland, 'Can International Conventions Drive Domestic Law Reform? The Case of Physical Punishment of Children' in eds John Dewar and Stephen Parker, *Family Law: Processes, Practices and Pressures* (Hart Publishing, 2003).

[61] See, John P Grant and Elaine E Sutherland 'Scots Law and International Conventions' in eds Alison Cleland and Elaine E Sutherland, *Children's Rights in Scotland* (2nd edn, W Green, 2002), para 4.43.

of the public are willing to come forward and report cases where they believe a parent has 'crossed the line' (whatever that is), there are encouraging signs of a climate which is becoming less tolerant of violence against children. In a much publicised case, a French tourist was convicted of assault having, according to witnesses, 'punched and kicked' his eight-year-old son after the child misbehaved in a restaurant.[62]

In 1992 the Scottish Law Commission recommended clarification of the rules on reasonable chastisement but not the abolition of the concept. Having revisited the matter,[63] the Scottish Executive proposed reform of the law to clarify the law on 'reasonable chastisement' and to remove the defence altogether in certain circumstances. The issue continued to be controversial and a number of public opinion surveys were carried out. One of the most interesting is that conducted by Save the Children, using questionnaires and focus groups, which involved some 1,300 children and young people.[64] A flavour of the findings can be gleaned from the fact that 74% of those who responded thought that it is fundamentally wrong for an adult to hit a child; 94% thought that other forms of punishment would provide better, less damaging, ways of dealing with problems; and many children felt that physical punishment is irrational and is often prompted by adult anger or frustration.

The Criminal Justice (Scotland) Bill, introduced into the Scottish Parliament in 2002, followed through on the Executive's promise and gives the courts guidance on assessing whether what was done to a child 'was a physical punishment carried out in exercise of a parental right'.[65] The Bill, if passed, would also remove the defence of reasonable chastisement altogether in respect of a child under three years old or where the action involved a blow to the child's head, shaking or the use of an implement.[66] Even these modest reforms have faced opposition, with all kinds of scare-mongering tactics being employed in the attempt to leave the law in its current lamentable and ambiguous state.[67] At the time of writing, the Bill is making its way through the committee stages of the

---

[62]   Frank O'Donnell, 'Frenchman who beat son cites racism', *The Scotsman*, 1 March 2002, p 3. The suggestion that the father was singled out for prosecution because of his nationality is questionable in the light of the, again much-publicised, case of a Scottish father who was convicted of assault having beaten his daughter in a dentist's waiting-room: see EE Sutherland, 'How Children are Faring in the "New Scotland"' in *The International Survey of Family Law (2001 Edition)*, ed A Bainham (Family Law, 2001), at p 363.

[63]   *The Physical Punishment of Children: A Consultation* (Scottish Executive, 2000).

[64]   *It Doesn't Sort Anything: A report on the views of children and young people about the use of physical punishment* (Save the Children, 2002).

[65]   The court is directed to consider the nature of what was done, the reason for it and the circumstances in which it took place; its duration and frequency; the physical or mental effect on the child; and the child's personal characteristics including, but not limited to, the child's sex, age and state of health; cl 43(1).

[66]   Clause 43(3).

[67]   The Christian Institute has attacked the proposed reforms as intrusive and claimed they would divert valuable resources from more serious cases of child abuse: Hamish MacDonell, 'Smack ban "may aid abusers"', *The Scotsman*, 29 April 2002. The Association of Chief Police Officers in Scotland warned of police time being taken up by a deluge of reports of trivial instances: Andrew Denholm and Jeanette Oldham, 'Smack ban will swamp police', *The Scotsman*, 15 May 2002.

legislative process and it can only be hoped that politicians feel able to put the rights and welfare of the children of Scotland before their own political self-interest.

IV   ADULT RELATIONSHIPS

Cohabitation

While it is growing in popularity, heterosexual cohabitation presently receives very limited legal recognition in Scotland. On the one hand, a cohabitant can recover damages for the wrongful death of a partner,[68] and has the right to live in the family home and to have a violent partner excluded, albeit in more limited circumstances than the remedies afforded to spouses.[69] On the other hand, cohabitants are not obliged to support one another financially and, should they separate, no special regime applies to resolving property disputes. While the Scottish Executive returned to the Scottish Law Commission's 1992 proposals[70] in its 2000 White Paper,[71] delay in bringing forward a Family Law (Scotland) Bill means that the very limited proposals for reform lie dormant.

Much of the debate about recognising heterosexual cohabitation centres on the fact that, for many of the individuals involved, marriage is an option. If they have chosen not to marry, so the argument goes, then their choice should be respected and they should not be saddled with the consequences of marriage by a paternalistic legal system. To put it another way, if they have rejected the responsibilities of marriage, they should not reap the rewards. Of course, this argument ignores the fact that some cohabitants are not free to marry while, for others, failing to marry may not be a conscious choice. In any event, individuals are notoriously ignorant of the precise legal consequences of decisions.

This debate is irrelevant, however, when one turns to consider same-sex relationships. At present, marriage is simply not available to same-sex couples in Scotland[72] and there is no concept of the registered partnership as an alternative

---

[68]   Damages (Scotland) Act 1976, as amended by the Administration of Justice Act 1982, s 14(4).

[69]   Matrimonial Homes (Family Protection) (Scotland) Act 1981, s 18.

[70]   *Report on Family Law*, op cit, n 2.

[71]   *Parents and Children*, op cit, n 5.

[72]   Marriage (Scotland) Act 1977, s 5(4)(e). In addition, in Scotland, there is currently no legal recognition accorded to the possibility of a person changing gender: *X, Petitioner* 1957 SLT (Sh Ct) 61. The Court of Appeal in England recently refused to depart from the same stance, established in *Corbett v Corbett* [1971] P 83: see *Bellinger v Bellinger* [2002] 1 All ER 311. However, the dissent of Thorpe LJ in *Bellinger* provides a cogent statement of the reasons for changing the law, in this respect, and it may be that the House of Lords will be persuaded by his reasoning when it considers the case in the pending appeal. That their Lordships will do so seems all the more likely in the light of the decision of the European Court of Human Rights in *Goodwin v United Kingdom*, App No 28957/95, 11 July 2002, where failure to recognise a transsexual's post-operative gender was found to violate Arts 8 and 12 of the European Convention. Recognition that some change in the law was required had already been acknowledged to some extent, in England and Wales: see *Report of the Interdepartmental Working Group on Transsexual People* (Home Office, 2000), available on *www.homeoffice.gov.uk/ccpd/wgtrans.pdf* and *Civil Registration: Vital Change. Birth, Marriage and Death Registration in the 21st Century* (Cm 5355, 2002), available on *www.statistics.gov.uk/registration/whitepaper/default.asp*. Matters

method of recognising personal relationships. Given that so many other countries are embracing the reality of same-sex relationships and making provision for legal recognition, either, like the Netherlands, by opening up marriage[73] or, more often, through the mechanism of registered partnerships or the like,[74] the resolute refusal of both the Scottish Law Commission and the Scottish Executive to address the matter is, to put it mildly, regrettable. It is not, however, wholly surprising. William N Eskridge examined how legal systems arrive at recognition of same-sex relationships and demonstrated that it is often a matter of progressing through various stages:

> 'repealing laws criminalizing consensual sodomy, equalising the age for same-sex and different-sex intercourse, prohibiting discrimination on the basis of sexual orientation, affording same-sex cohabiting couples the same rights and obligations as different-sex couples, recognising same-sex unions as "registered partnerships" or the like, and expressly allowing same-sex partners to adopt children on the same terms as married couples.'[75]

He might have added provision for marriage between same-sex couples at the end of the list. In addition, the Scottish Executive's reluctance to confront the issue squarely may, at least in part, be a product of its bruising battle over homosexuality in the context of education.[76]

---

are now being taken forward by a UK working group in which members of the Scottish Executive are actively involved and, since some of the issues relate to devolved matters (eg marriage, birth registration), while others relate to matters reserved to Westminster (eg social security, pensions, nationality), it is anticipated that a co-ordinated approach will be attempted.

[73] In the Netherlands, the definition of marriage was amended in 2001 to include same-sex couples and, at the time of writing, it is the only country to have done so. For details of the legislation, see, Kees Waaldijk's explanations on *ruljis.leidenuniv.nl/user/cwaaldij/www/NHR/news.htm.*

[74] Denmark led the way with the Registered Partnership Act 1989 and was followed by Sweden, Norway and Iceland. France introduced the *pacte civil de solidarite* in 1999, while Vermont was the first US state to provide for civil unions in response to the constitutional challenge mounted in *Baker v Vermont* 744 A 2d 864 (1999). In both Canada and South Africa, constitutional challenges to different treatment of same-sex couples have also been successful; see, respectively *M v H* (1999) 171 DLR (4th) 577 and *Satchwell v President of the Republic of South Africa and Another*, 26 July 2002, available on *http://www.concourt.gov.za/cases/2002/satchwellsum.shtml*. See also *Du Toit v Minister of Welfare and Population Development*, 28 September 2001, 2001 SACLR LEXIS 157. A further hearing in *Du Toit* took place before the Constitutional Court on 9 May 2002 but no reported decision is available at the time of writing. Constitutional challenges have not always proved successful in the long run. In Hawaii, for example, in *Baehr v Lewin* 852 P 2d 44 (1993) and *Baehr v Miike* 910 P 2d 112 (1996), the denial of marriage licences to same-sex couples was found to be unconstitutional under the Hawaiian constitution, but the legislature responded by amending the constitution to remove that line of argument. The debate in the US is far from over with the Defense of Marriage Act limiting federal and inter-state recognition of same-sex relationships and a constitutional amendment is being proposed in the Federal Marriage Amendment Bill.

[75] William N Eskridge, 'Comparative Law and the Same-Sex Marriage debate: A Step-By-Step Approach Toward State Recognition' 31 *McGeorge L Rev* 641 (1999–2000), at p 647. See also, William N Eskridge, *The Case for Same-Sex Marriage* (Free Press, 1996) and William N Eskridge, *Gaylaw: Challenging the Apartheid of the Closet* (Harvard University Press, 1999). Kees Waaldijk charts a similar progression in 'Civil Developments: Patterns of Reform in the Legal Position of Same-Sex Partners in Europe' (2000) 17 Rev Can Dr Fam 62.

[76] While the Scottish Parliament did finally repeal s 2A of the Local Government Act 1986, which prohibited a local authority from 'intentionally promoting homosexuality' or the 'acceptability of homosexuality as a pretended family relationship', when it passed the Standards in Public Life (Scotland) Act 2000, s 34, there was strident opposition led by a wealthy businessman, who funded a much publicised campaign, and some influential religious leaders.

Recently the Scottish Parliament has made encouraging progress in recognising same-sex relationships. As we have seen, both the Adults with Incapacity (Scotland) Act 2000 and the Protection from Abuse (Scotland) Act 2001 apply to same-sex partners. The Housing (Scotland) Act 2001[77] gives statutory recognition to the decision of the House of Lords in *Fitzpatrick v Sterling Housing Association*,[78] by extending succession to secure tenancies to same-sex partners. The Mortgage Rights (Scotland) Act 2001 allows a same-sex partner of the debtor the same standing to seek suspension of enforcement as of a standard security over the couple's home as is given to spouses and different-sex cohabitants.[79] Case-law demonstrates rather more patchy progress, with isolated examples of same-sex partners gaining recognition. As we shall see, whether they can acquire parental responsibilities and parental rights, similar to those of any other step-parent, is a matter of debate in Scotland at the time of writing.[80] After consultation, the Scottish Law Commission recommended that same-sex cohabitants should be able to recover damages for the loss of a loved one on the same basis as different-sex partners.[81] These are small steps along the road and, in the light of the theory of progressive recognition of same-sex relationships, it appears that Scotland is grappling with Eskridge's fourth stage. It can only be hoped that we move on to full recognition of same-sex relationships rather more rapidly than we have in respect of recognising heterosexual cohabitation. While marriage and marriage-like relationships are devolved matters, the impetus for recognition of same-sex relationships may come, not only from world opinion, but from legal developments in England and Wales.[82]

Marriage by cohabitation with habit and repute

Marriage by cohabitation with habit and repute is the only remaining valid form of irregular marriage (ie marriage without complying with the statutory formalities)[83] in Scotland. Its history and the rules for its application are discussed slightly more fully in the 2000 edition of the *International Survey*.[84] For a valid marriage by cohabitation with habit and repute to exist, the parties must have had capacity to

---

[77] Section 22 and Sch 3.

[78] [1999] 4 All ER 705.

[79] Section 1(2)(c). That statute is a further recognition of the decision of the House of Lords in *Smith v Bank of Scotland* 1997 SC (HL) 111. For a recent application of *Smith*, see *Clydesdale Bank v Black* 2002 SLT 764.

[80] Two recent sheriff court decisions take different views on the granting of parental responsibilities and parental rights to the same-sex partner of a child's parent; see below.

[81] *Report on Title to Sue for Non-Patrimonial Loss* (SE/2002/179, Stationery Office), Recommendation 10. The Report is available at *http://www.scotlawcom.gov.uk/index-1.htm* and was preceded by consultation on proposals contained in a discussion paper, *Title to Sue for Non-Patrimonial Loss* (SLC Discussion Paper No 116, 2001), question 9.

[82] After the introduction of Registered Partnership Bills in the House of Commons and House of Lords in 2001 and 2002 respectively, the matter has been taken up by the Cabinet Office.

[83] Marriage (Scotland) Act 1977.

[84] EE Sutherland, 'Consolidation and Anticipation' in *The International Survey of Family Law (2000 Edition)*, ed A Bainham (Family Law, 2000), at p 329. For a full discussion of the concept, see EM Clive, *The Law of Husband and Wife in Scotland*, at paras 05.019–05.060 and Elaine E Sutherland, *Child and Family Law*, at paras 10.75–10.80.

marry, have lived together in Scotland as husband and wife for a sufficiently long time[85] and have been generally regarded by those who knew them as a married couple.[86] Thus, marriage by cohabitation with habit and repute can be contrasted with the 'open' or 'simple' cohabitation which is popular today. Usually, declarator of marriage is sought after one of the parties has died and the survivor is seeking recognition as a spouse for inheritance or other purposes. In these cases, the claimant may be opposed by the deceased's executors, often relatives of the deceased who, in the absence of a spouse, will succeed to the deceased's property. Less frequently, declarator is sought where both parties are alive and one seeks to set up a marriage, simply as a means of seeking a divorce and, thus, access to the legal regime for division of property available to spouses, but not to cohabitants.[87]

The Scottish Law Commission recommended the prospective abolition of this kind of marriage[88] and that recommendation was supported by the majority of respondents to the Scottish Executive's consultation seven years later. However, the Executive concluded that marriage by cohabitation with habit and repute should be retained since it did benefit a small number of people.[89] Of course, had the Executive implemented the Commission's proposals on giving greater recognition to simple cohabitation, the needs of these people might, at least arguably, have been met.

The Commission's principal objection to the concept was that it created uncertainty and might put a later, regular marriage in jeopardy. In addition, it was unhappy to give advantages to couples who engaged in deception, when such advantages were denied to couples who lived together openly and honestly. Perhaps the real problem is that the older case-law on marriage cohabitation with habit and repute was developed at a time when 'living together without marriage was highly uncommon amongst respectable persons' and the fact that 'social conditions and perceptions' have changed.[90] As a result, in a number of recent cases where the survivor sought to establish a marriage after her partner's death, while the length of cohabitation was sufficient, it was the repute element which proved fatal more often than not.

---

[85]   Only periods of cohabitation when the couple were free to marry can be taken into account. In modern times, some courts have been willing to accept very short periods of time as sufficient; see, for example, *Shaw v Henderson* 1982 SLT 211 (11 months enough); *Mullen v Mullen* 1991 SLT 205 (6 months enough); *Kamperman v McIver* 1994 SLT 763 (6 months not 'necessarily insufficient').

[86]   What is required here is summed up in the classic statement, 'although repute need not be universal it must be general, substantially unvarying and consistent and not divided; *Low v Gorman* 1970 SLT 356, per Lord Robertson at p 359.

[87]   For a recent unsuccessful example of this, see *Walker v Roberts* 1998 SLT 1133.

[88]   *Report on Family Law*, paras 7.1–7.13 and Rec 42. The Commission emphasised that a marriage contracted prior to any legislation implementing its abolition should be valid, whether or not declarator had already been sought.

[89]   *Parents and Children*, op cit, paras 10.4 and 10.5.

[90]   *MacGregor v MacGregor*, 17 January 2001, Outer House, unreported but available on the Scottish Courts website at *www.scotcourts.gov.uk/opinions/TGC2812a.html*, at para 7, where the Lord Ordinary also observed that "living in sin" is no longer a phrase in common usage', albeit that phrase did arise in evidence in the case before him.

In *Ackerman v Blackburn*[91] a woman was unsuccessful in seeking declarator of marriage by cohabitation with habit and repute after her partner's sudden death as a result of a hill walking accident. There was no dispute that they had each been free to marry and had lived together for some four years, thus satisfying the 'cohabitation' element of the test. The issue in dispute related to the 'repute' element of the relationship. As often happens in such cases, when one of the best possible witnesses is no longer available, there was some dispute over aspects of the evidence. Certainly, there were witnesses who encountered the couple and had regarded them as married. However, they were, in the words of the Lord Ordinary 'on the periphery of the acquaintanceship'[92] of the couple. Crucially, the pursuer had not called any witnesses from spheres where the deceased had been particularly active (his church, political party and former employer) and other acquaintances and family members regarded the couple as being engaged[93] or as simply cohabiting. Similarly, in *MacGregor v MacGregor*,[94] divided repute, with negative repute being demonstrated by such factors as refusal to admit Mr MacGregor to the local Orange Lodge because he was 'living in sin' and the fact that Ms MacGregor used her own last name,[95] proved fatal to the pursuer's case.

In *Vosilius v Vosilius*,[96] however, the pursuer was able to establish a marriage by cohabitation with habit and repute. This was so despite the fact that each of the parties was known, by different people, either by his or her own, or by the other's, last name. While some of the deceased's children said they knew their father was not married to the pursuer, her children gave evidence of growing up in the household with him and regarding him as their father and a neighbour of some 29 years' standing supported the repute element of the claim. There was some debate about whether, during the latter years, the couple had lived as landlady and lodger but the Lord Ordinary made clear that, even if this had been established, the period of cohabitation as husband and wife was sufficient to establish a marriage prior to any change in the nature of the relationship.

---

[91] 18 January 2000, Outer house, unreported, but available on the Scottish Courts website at *www.scotcourts.gov.uk/opinions/019_13_98.html*. The very detailed judgment of the Lord Ordinary is particularly interesting, not least because he explores all aspects of repute in detail but examines the possibility that a marriage might be established in this way, regardless of the fact that the relationship subsequently broke down. Of course, were this to be the case, the couple would remain married until divorce or death. The unsuccessful appeal (called a 'reclaiming motion' since the original case was an action for declarator) is reported as *Ackerman v Logan's Executors* 2002 SLT 37.

[92] A similar phrase was used in *Walker v Roberts* 1998 SLT 1133 at 1136, where temporary judge Horsburgh had described the repute there as existing 'only at a peripheral level of social contact'.

[93] The pursuer's claim that the gold band set with diamonds which she wore on her ring finger, was regarded by herself and the deceased as a wedding ring, was rejected by the court.

[94] Op cit.

[95] Reliance on this fact is curious since many women in Scotland (including this author) do not adopt their husband's last name on marriage nor does the law require them to do so.

[96] 2000 SCLR 679.

Marriage

Romantics around the world may be forgiven for retaining an image of Scotland as the home of the runaway marriage, with (particularly young) couples from other jurisdictions racing across the border from England to be married by clasping hands over the anvil in the blacksmith's forge at Gretna Green. Delightful as this picture is, it bears little relation to what is legally possible. Certainly, Scots law permits a person to marry from the age of 16 without parental consent.[97] However, it has long been the case that individuals from abroad may be required to produce a certificate of no incapacity.[98] In addition, marriages cannot normally be solemnised immediately, since the marriage schedule (which authorised the marriage ceremony to be performed) will not usually be issued until 14 days have elapsed from lodging the marriage notices (the forms giving details of each of the parties).[99]

The Marriage (Scotland) Act 2002 removed what had long been regarded as an anomaly on the issue of where the wedding could take place. The couple can choose either a religious or a civil ceremony. If they choose a religious ceremony, then the place of celebration is restricted by the rules of the particular religion and, in some cases, where the individual religious celebrant is prepared to perform the ceremony.[100] Where the couple opted for a civil ceremony, prior to the Act, they were denied this choice of location, since registrars were only permitted to solemnise marriages in the registration office, save with the permission of the Registrar General in exceptional circumstances.[101] It had long been felt that this restriction was unnecessary and, indeed, that it interfered with individual freedom of choice.[102] After consultation,[103] it was decided to remove the anomaly and the

---

[97]   Marriage (Scotland) Act 1977, s 1. That marriage requires the consent of each of the parties is axiomatic. There is a small, but growing, body of case-law where arranged marriages have been challenged on the basis that one of the parties was subject to duress by family members. For a recent example, see, *Sohrab v Khan*, 23 April 2002, unreported but available on *www.scotcourts.gov.uk/opinions/A2756_00.html*.

[98]   Marriage (Scotland) Act 1977, s 3. This certificate should be issued by a 'competent authority' in the foreign person's country of domicile and should indicate that the individual 'is not known to be subject to any legal capacity (in terms of the law of that state)'. Such a certificate is only required if it is 'practicable' to obtain one and a number of national governments do not issue them.

[99]   Marriage (Scotland) Act 1977, s 6. This is not as onerous as it might seem since the marriage notices may be submitted by post or by a third party in Scotland. Thus, the parties do not have to be in Scotland for the 14-day period. Marriage in Scotland is relatively simple to arrange and can be inexpensive. For practical advice on how to do it, see the General Registers for Scotland website at *www.gro-scotland.gov.uk*.

[100] This varies from one religion to another but, certainly, some celebrants will marry the couple at a place of their choosing, frequently an hotel or a private home. This opens up the possibility of a couple choosing to be married at a more exotic location, like the top of a mountain, assuming a suitably willing and agile religious celebrant can be found. A newspaper reported the example of a couple who were married by a Church of Scotland minister in the Edinburgh Dungeon, a rather gruesome tourist attraction devoted to notorious criminals like Burke and Hare: George Mair, 'Couple get married in dungeon', *The Scotsman*, 11 March 2002, p 9.

[101] Marriage (Scotland) Act 1977, s 18. For example, permission would have been given for a registrar to perform the ceremony in a hospital where one of the parties is too ill to attend at the registration office.

[102] The possibility of allowing registrars to perform marriage ceremonies at places other than registration offices was explored in the early 1980s but nothing came of the proposal. It is thought that the opposition of various religious groups to the expansion of the range of venues available to

Marriage (Scotland) Act 2002 now provides for local authorities to approve places where civil marriages may be solemnised within their districts.[104] Extensive regulations[105] supplement the statute and these, in turn, are explained further in Guidance from the Registrar General.[106] The romantics mentioned at the beginning of this section will be delighted to learn that one of the first locations to be so approved was the Old Blacksmith's Shop at Gretna Green.

V CHILD LAW

The child's voice

The United Nations Convention on the Rights of the Child, ratified by the United Kingdom on 19 April 1990, gives the child who is capable of forming views the right to freedom to express those views and requires that account be taken of the child's views when decisions affecting him or her are being taken.[107] Ratification of the Convention can be seen as a starting point of increased appreciation that Scottish law and practice needed to do more if this obligation was to be complied with. Of course, before a person can have an effective voice, he or she needs to know something of what the law provides, how the system operates, and how to utilise the system

Recent developments signal improvements in the child's voice being heard in Scotland. Child-friendly, age-appropriate literature is being produced by the Scottish Executive and various organisations involved with children. The Scottish Child Law Centre has now moved to new, and much improved, premises, with a larger staff and will offer an expanded range of services to children and adults with an interest in child law.[108] The Law Society of Scotland has launched a website giving information to children about relevant law.[109]

After many years of campaigning, the need for a Children's Commissioner in Scotland was addressed by the Education, Culture and Sports Committee. It began its inquiry in 2001, seeking to establish whether there was a need for such an office and, if so, what the role and responsibilities of the Commissioner should be. Central to the inquiry was consultation with young people and their views were gathered through interviews, focus groups and a special event where the

---

registrars was significant in defeating the proposals for reform at that time. With respect, one might ask what the celebration of civil marriages has to do with religious groups.

103 Original consultation was carried out by the General Register Office for Scotland in 1998 and, after proposals for a Private Member's Bill, the Scottish Executive took the matter forward in a White Paper, *Civil Marriages Outwith Registration Offices* (Scottish Executive, 2001), available on *www.open.gov.uk/gros/cmoro.htm*.

104 Regulations will give further details of the criteria to be used in granting or refusing approval and the Act itself provides for a system of appeals to the courts where approval has been refused and in respect of suspension or revocation of approval.

105 Marriage (Approval of Places) (Scotland) Regulations 2002 (SSI No 260/2002).

106 The Registrar General's Guidance to Scottish Local Authorities on the Approval of Places for Civil Marriages (10 June 2002).

107 Article 12.

108 The Centre can be reached on *enquiries@sclc.org.uk*.

109 The site is *www.lawscot.org.uk/childlaw*.

Committee heard from a number of young people. Adults gave written submissions to the Committee. All the hard work proved worthwhile when the Committee's Second Report was published recommending the creation of the office of Children's Commissioner and outlining that person's role,[110] a recommendation which has been accepted, in principle, by the Scottish Executive.

In *Shields v Shields*,[111] the Inner House of the Court of Session took the opportunity to clarify the importance of a court giving the child concerned the opportunity to express his or her views when a decision about parental responsibilities or parental rights was being taken. In that case, married[112] but separated parents were in dispute over the residence of their seven-and-a-half-year-old son.[113] Each sought residence (formerly custody), but the dispute was focused when the mother decided to 'further her career by taking a promoted post in Australia for a period of up to three years',[114] something which would clearly inhibit the father's contact with the child. She sought a specific issue order allowing her to take the child out of the country in the face of the father's opposition. Initially, she was successful before the sheriff,[115] who dispensed with intimation to the child as being 'inappropriate',[116] and that decision was upheld on appeal to the Sheriff Principal. In accordance with the obligation under Art 12 of the UN Convention, the Children (Scotland) Act 1995 requires the court to give the child the opportunity to express his or her views 'so far as practicable' and directs the court 'have regard to' these views in the light of the child's age and maturity.[117] There are a number of mechanisms for doing this. One is by intimating the case to the child, enclosing a form (Form F9), and leaving the onus on the child to respond by completing the form or by some other method. This inexpensive, but often wholly inappropriate, method has been criticised by the present author elsewhere.[118] However, the court has other options and, for example, a report from an independent third party can be ordered by the court, or the judge can see the child in chambers. None of these methods had been employed by the sheriff in this case. Granting the appeal, the Inner House emphasised that the sheriff had erred in failing to ascertain whether the child wished to express his views and stressed that the duty on the court regarding the child's views was one which continued until the order was made. It noted that seeking views by intimation and the use of Form F9 should not necessarily be

---

[110] *Report of the Inquiry into the Need for a Children's Commissioner in Scotland*, 2nd Report of the Education, Culture and Sport Committee (2002), available on *www.scottish.parliament.uk/ official_report/cttee/educ-02/edr02-02-02.htm*.

[111] 2002 SLT 579.

[112] The fact that the parents were married meant that each entered the dispute with full and equal parental responsibilities and parental rights: Children (Scotland) Act 1995, s 3.

[113] By the time of the Inner House decision, the child was almost ten years old and delay in the appeal process continues to be a problem in cases of this kind.

[114] At p 581.

[115] In Scotland a sheriff is a legally qualified judge.

[116] A recent pilot study into the operation of the 1995 Act found that dispensing with intimation to the child was requested in 34% of cases, although this does not tell us how often the request was granted, nor how many children's views were ascertained in other ways: *Monitoring the Children (Scotland) Act 1995: Pilot Study* (Central Research Unit, 2000).

[117] Section 11(7)(b).

[118] Elaine E Sutherland, *Child and Family Law*, op cit, paras 3.45–3.49.

seen as the principal method of ascertaining a child's views, observing, 'where younger children are involved or where there is a risk of upsetting the child, other methods may well be preferable'.[119]

While some progress has been made in hearing the voices of children in a variety of settings, it is increasingly acknowledged that there are significant gaps in, and obstacles to, children having a meaningful input at the levels of policy, law and practice.[120] The recent publication of a two-volume study,[121] conceptualising and evaluating the current position and mapping the need for future research, is, thus, greatly welcomed.

Residence and contact: some interesting cases

Given the space devoted to child law in recent Scottish contributions to the *International Survey*, the initial intention was not to consider residence and contact cases. However, it would be remiss of the author if she failed to alert the reader to interesting developments in two particular areas in this respect.

The first concerns donor insemination, same-sex parenting and conflicting decisions emanating from two courts of first instance. $X v Y$,[122] heard at Glasgow Sheriff Court, concerned a lesbian who had a child as a result of do-it-yourself donor insemination. Both the donor father and the mother's same-sex partner sought parental responsibilities and parental rights in respect of the child. As a 'gay parenting' case, this one had it all, since the donor father was also living in a stable same-sex relationship. As a teaching aid, it is a gem, since the judge at first instance got the law absolutely right in one respect and plum wrong in another. Granting full parental responsibilities and parental rights to the father, the sheriff correctly recognised that he had standing and applied the welfare test under the Children (Scotland) Act 1995. In so doing, she noted the fact that he was homosexual was irrelevant. It was when she turned to the claim of the mother's partner that things began to go wrong.[123] She opined that the mother, her partner and the child did not constitute a 'family unit' for this purpose and, thus, did not gain protection under Art 8 of the European Convention on Human Rights. That

---

[119] At p 583. It is interesting to note that, when the child's views were ascertained, he indicated that he did not wish to go to Australia.

[120] See, for example, Elaine E Sutherland and Alison Cleland, 'How real are Children's Rights in Scotland' and Alison Cleland, 'The Child's Right to be Heard and Represented' in Alison Cleland and Elaine E Sutherland, *Children's Rights in Scotland* (W Green, 2001).

[121] Kay Tisdall, Rachel Baker, Kathleen Marshall and Alison Cleland, *'Voice of the Child' Under the Children (Scotland) Act 1995: Giving due regard to children's views in all matters that affect them* (Scottish Office Central Research Unit, 2002). A summary of the research findings is available on *www.scotland.gov.uk/cru/resfinds/scrf2-00.asp* and the main report is available on *www.scotland.gov.uk/cru/red/voc1-00.asp* and *www.scotland.gov.uk/cru/red/voc2-00.asp*.

[122] 6 March 2002. At the time of writing, the case is unreported but can be found under the less-than-helpful title of 'Pursuer against Defender in the case of Child A' by searching the family law sheriff court cases, using the date and the name of the sheriff (Duncan) on *www.scotcourts.gov.uk/index1.htm*.

[123] While the Human Fertilisation and Embryology Act 1991, s 28 provides rules for husbands and male partners to be treated as the father of a child resulting from assisted conception, the Act is shamelessly hetero-centric. Thus, there is no scope for a woman's female partner to be treated as a parent. In any event, for the rules to apply, treatment must be in a facility licensed under the Act and the arrangement here was of the do-it-yourself variety.

conclusion, while highly questionable, is irrelevant. Any person who 'claims an interest' may apply for parental responsibilities and rights,[124] so it did not matter whether the mother and her partner were, or were not, a family unit. The sheriff went on to make clear that, applying the welfare test, she would not grant parental rights and responsibilities to the mother's partner. There is no doubt from the judgment that the sheriff was, very clearly, most unimpressed by this woman. Just one month later, a rather different view was taken in Edinburgh Sheriff Court.[125] There, two women living in a stable same-sex relationship were given parental responsibilities and rights in respect of each other's children. It is understood that the decision in *X v Y* will be the subject of an appeal, and the decision of a higher court is both necessary for clarification and awaited with interest.

While of long standing in the US and much loved by movie-makers, the idea of a 'witness protection scheme' is fairly new to Scotland.[126] Usually, witness protection involves a prosecution witness being spirited away to a secret location by the police in order to protect him or her from threats from, or harm by, the person against whom the evidence will be given at the latter's trial. Sometimes, it is necessary to provide longer-term protection by helping the witness start a new life, perhaps with a new identity. In some cases, not only the witness but also members of his or her family will require protection if intimidation of the witness is to be avoided and long-term safety is to be ensured. Where a child accompanies a parent into the programme the result may be a disruption of the child's relationship with the other parent, if that parent is not also subject to protection. Courts in the US have experience of dealing with the non-programme parent's complaints over denial of visitation.[127] Scotland had its first such case in 2002 when a child's father sought a court order for contact with his son, who was in the programme along with the child's mother and an older half-sibling.[128] He was successful but contact did not operate smoothly and it is understood that the father is now seeking a residence order, so that his son can come out of the programme and live with him. This will pose an interesting dilemma for the court. How is it to assess 'welfare', in the sense of a continued relationship with his father, against 'welfare', in terms of personal safety?

---

[124]   Children (Scotland) Act 1995, s 11(3)(i).

[125]   Sheriff Noel McPartlin gave his decision in private on 5 April 2002 and, since there is no likelihood of an appeal, the case may well not be written up and, thus, not reported. See Stephen Fraser and Catherine Deveney, 'Lesbian couple win same parental rights as married heterosexuals', *Scotland on Sunday*, 7 April 2002, p 1. It appears that one of the women had a four-year-old son as a result of a previous marriage and the other had an eight-month-old boy by anonymous donor insemination. The four-year-old child's father had not opposed the application.

[126]   While the police have always offered protection to some witnesses on an *ad hoc* basis, the first dedicated witness protection scheme in Scotland was established in Strathclyde in 1996: see Nicholas Fyfe and Heather McKay, *Making It Safe To Speak? A Study of Witness Intimidation and Protection in Strathclyde* (Scottish Office Central Research Unit, 1999).

[127]   They have tended to deny the non-programme parent visitation, albeit awarding damages for interference with the child–parent relationship: *Ruffalo v United States* 539 F Supp 949 (1982) and *Franz v United States* 707 F 2d 582 (1983).

[128]   At the time of writing, no report on the case is available: see Lorna Hughes, 'Police ban dad from seeing son on witness protection', *Sunday Mail*, 14 April 2002, p 2.

VI CONCLUDING THOUGHTS

What, then, is the verdict on the performance of the Scottish Executive and the Scottish Parliament, at least in the family law arena? On the positive side, they can point to their legislative activity in terms of the Adults with Incapacity (Scotland) Act 2000 and the Protection from Abuse (Scotland) Act 2001: two well-drafted statutes which make a real contribution to improving the lives of many. While the Marriage (Scotland) Act 2002 hardly shook jurisprudence to its core, it has increased freedom of choice for the many individuals who opt for a civil marriage, but would like the ceremony to be performed somewhere other than a government office.

The Executive might also point to its extensive consultation on family matters, as a reflection of its commitment both to family law reform and to involving all sections of the public, including children, where appropriate, in shaping that reform. Therein lie a couple of problems. While consultation is highly desirable, it should not provide the excuse for endless procrastination. The delay in introducing the, much awaited, Family Law (Scotland) Bill, which could address so many of the outstanding issues, is completely unjustified on any grounds other than political self-interest.

A further problem with consultation is that it can present an issue as debatable when that is not the case. As we have seen, international law is clear in prohibiting all violence against children. As a result of consultation, the Scottish Executive brought forward its proposals for reform of the law on physical punishment of children in the Criminal Justice (Scotland) Bill. While better than nothing, the Bill fails to extend to children the protection from violence offered to all other persons in Scotland. What is more, it fails to live up to the international standards by which all the jurisdictions in the United Kingdom are bound by virtue of having ratified the United Nations Convention on the Rights of the Child. There is no doubt that some very vocal sections of the adult community in Scotland favour retention of some right for parents to inflict physical violence on their children,[129] but that does not absolve the government of its responsibility to ensure that children's rights are respected. To put it another way, regardless of how many lobbyists supported the introduction of slavery in Scotland, nothing would make its introduction legitimate.

What of the impact of the European Convention on Human Rights? Certainly, the Human Rights Act has brought rights under that Convention more easily within the reach of the Scottish people. While further political commitment to the Convention is reflected in the Convention Rights Compliance (Scotland) Act 2001, the real strength of the 'human rights dimension' lies in the fact that it enables individuals to enforce Convention rights in the courts. This puts these rights beyond the reach of political compromise and political self-interest. As we have seen, the Scottish courts are becoming increasingly familiar with applying the Convention and, as always, the European Court is there to push matters along

---

[129] For example, Simon Calvert of the Christian Institute put the position thus, 'The Executive is trying to force Edinburgh wine bar views on ordinary parents', quoted in Hamish MacDonell, 'Smack ban "may aid abusers"', *The Scotsman*, 29 April 2002.

as it did, so splendidly, in *Goodwin v United Kingdom*.[130] Indeed, that may give us an answer to the questions posed at the outset. It is the combination of the two key factors highlighted – devolution and greater access to enforceable human rights – that offers the hope for the future.

---

[130]   App No 28957/95, 11 July 2002.

SPAIN

DE FACTO UNIONS REVISITED

Gabriel García Cantero[*]

I INTRODUCTION

To bring my report in the 2001 edition of the *Survey*[1] up to date I must refer to laws of four other autonomous communities which, with varying titles, terminology and scope, make regulations for the legal situation of *de facto* unions within their respective territories. In order of date of promulgation, these are:

- Law 2/2000, of 3 July, for legal equality, of the *Comunidad Foral* of Navarre;
- Law 1/2001, of 6 April, by which *de facto* unions are regulated, of the Autonomous Community of Valencia;
- Law 11/2001, of 19 December, on *de facto* unions, of the Community of Madrid;
- Law 18/2001, of 19 December, on stable pairs, of the Balearic Islands.

These laws divide into two groups: one – the laws of Navarre and the Balearic Islands, which are Autonomous Communities with full competence in making law for their territory (*'ley foral'*); the other – those of Valencia and Madrid, which lack competence in family law. The regulation presented by the former group is more extensive. That of the latter is restricted to matters of a social, administrative, fiscal, etc, nature, affecting *de facto* pairs, whereas the laws of the former group have a significant impact on family law. However, there is a fairly similar legal plan, and they coincide on certain points, and in the grounds set out in the Reasoned Justification which accompanies each law.

II NAVARRE

The *Ley foral* of 3 July 2000 of Navarre has been referred to the *Tribunal Constitucional*, by the National Government, but at the time of writing the case has not been decided. It is in three chapters, which deal with the following: General Provisions, Content of the Relationship of the Pair, and Regime for Succession, Fiscal Matters and the Public Service. It has, in all, three Articles, one

---

[*] Emeritus Professor of Civil Law at the University of Zaragoza, Spain. Translated by Peter Schofield.

[1] See Gabriel García Cantero, 'The Catalan Family Code of 1998 and Other Autonomous Region Laws on De Facto Unions', *The International Survey of Family Law (2001 Edition)*, ed A Bainham (Family Law, 2001), p 399 ff.

additional provision, a transitional one, one repealing section and two final provisions.

Article 1 lays down the principle of non-discrimination, by which, in the interpretation and application of the legal system of Navarre, nobody should suffer discrimination by reason of the family group to which he belongs, whether his birth or filiation was in marriage or in the union of two persons living together in an analogous affective relationship, regardless of their sexual orientation. It is likely that it will be found that the constitutional principle of equality and non-discrimination is not an adequate basis for placing such pair relationships on an equal footing. The *Tribunal Constitucional* has ruled that only the situations of marriage and *de facto* (heterosexual) unions are identitical in nature.

By Art 2.1 this law defines a stable union as the free and public union, in an affective relationship analogous to a conjugal one, regardless of sexual orientation, between persons of full age or emancipated minors, not being related to each other by consanguinity or adoption, by descent, or collaterally within the second degree, provided that neither is joined to some other person, in marriage or in a stable pair relationship. By Art 2.2 a pair is stable once conjugal cohabitation has lasted for at least a year, or if the couple have offspring and live together or have expressed their intention of forming such a pair relationship in a public document. Evidence in any form admitted by law is acceptable. In consequence the law treats same-sex and different-sex pairs alike, using as the test the existence of 'an affective relationship analogous to a conjugal one', not an easy legal concept to identify in practice.

Article 4 provides for the dissolution of the stable pair in the following cases:

(1)   on the death or declaration of death of either member;
(2)   on the marriage of either member to another person;
(3)   by mutual consent;
(4)   by authenticated notification to the other of unilateral repudiation;
(5)   by effective cessation of cohabitation for over a year; and
(6)   as set out in public documents.

The regulation of personal and patrimonial aspects may be freely decided in a public or a private document; parties may also, subject to the minimum legal requirements, provide for compensation on breakdown in their pact. In default of a pact, members of a stable pair contribute, according to their ability, to the upkeep of the household and common expenses, in economic form or by personal work. On the ending of the relationship, either member may claim periodical maintenance payments from the other in two cases:

(1)   if the cohabitation had reduced his or her ability to obtain an income; and
(2)   if care of children of the couple prevented or seriously impaired his or her ability to earn.

In default of a pact, if a breakdown occurs during the lifetime of both members, the one who had worked in the common home or for the other cohabitant, without adequate reward, can claim economic compensation for unjust enrichment. These maintenance and compensation rights are subject to strict requirements: claims must be made within a year of the end of the cohabitation; alimony ends after three years, and other payments on the children's majority.

By Art 7 the members of the pair are jointly liable to third parties on contracts for upkeep of the household and maintenance of children of their relationship.

Article 8 allows the pair, whether heterosexual or homosexual, to adopt children. Unmarried couples are equated to married spouses for tutorship, curatorship, incapacity, declaration of absence, and declaration of prodigality (Art 9). When the *de facto* relationship ends, its members can make arrangements convenient to themselves for the care of, and access to their children, subject to the power of the judge to alter them if they are not consistent with the children's interests (Art 10). The authority of the members of the pair in relation to the children on a separation appear to be excessive, not respecting the principle of the integral protection of children of Art 39.2 of the Constitution, nor the UN Convention on the Rights of the Child 1980, ratified by Spain.

The members of the pair are equated to spouses in relation to the universal usufruct the *Ley foral* of Navarre known as 'usufruct of fidelity'[2] (Law 253 of the 1973 Compilation of the Laws of Navarre). They are treated as spouses for the purpose of succession to assets, apart from '*bienes troncales*'[3] (Law 304). They are also treated as spouses in the fiscal law of Navarre; in the law relating to the public service and in the law relating to widows' pensions.

To summarise, it appears that, in this law, Navarre has tried to go against the doctrine of the *Tribunal Constitucional*, which has repeatedly denied that the principle of equality applies between *de facto* pairs and spouses, with particular reference to widows' pensions. It also departs from the general doctrine of Spanish law, which denies homosexuals the capacity to adopt, this being contrary to the interests of the minor, a doctrine recently supported by the European Court of Human Rights in Strasbourg.

III VALENCIA

The Valencian Law of 6 April 2001 is in five chapters, dealing respectively with the following matters: General provisions, Registration of *de facto* unions, Registration of cohabitation pacts, Termination of the union, and Administrative rules. There are eight Articles, completed by two transitional provisions, a repealing section, and three final provisions.

In the Preamble, it says that: 'marriage continues to be the dominant form of union in the West', and that 'marriage and *de facto* unions, since they concern different institutions, are established by and follow personal choices, the differences between which must be respected at a social, as well as at a legal level'. If this argument seems clear and convincing, the next affirmation seems to

---

[2]   This is a typical legal institution of Navarre. The surviving spouse has a universal usufruct over all assets and rights belonging to the deceased at the time of death. It is interesting to note that, under Law 262, the right is lost if the survivor cohabits ('*vive maritalmente*') with another person. This indicates that a surviving member of a stable union would lose the benefit of the *usufructo de fidelidad* on forming another such relationship. The logical conclusion is that the Law of 3 July 2000 goes against the spirit and the letter of the legal system of Navarre.

[3]   Literally 'stem assets'. Assets inherited from parents or grandparents and, by special local law and custom, reverting to source, rather than passing to the normal heir, in default of issue.

be a *non sequitur*: 'Stable and durable cohabitation must be regarded as a reality to which the public authorities with rule-making power owe proper respect. Regulatory rules must be the balancing and equalising mechanism for those people who, through choices freely exercised, may feel discriminated against'. It is not easy to understand how the Valencian Legislature lost sight of the principle of responsibility for one's actions: no one forces you to marry, but should you decide not to, what rational basis can there be for a law that says you must be treated as though you had? Such a law devalues the one form of sexual union the Constitution recognises. On the other hand, the new law is presented as provisional in nature, pending regulation of *de facto* couples by the central authorities. So we shall be faced with an 'anticipatory competence' for which the Constitution does not allow, or with a quite unacceptable 'invitation to the State to legislate'.

The only innovation in the definition of the pair *de facto* is that it is formed by inscription in the Autonomous Community's Administrative Register (Art 1.2). Registration, under the law, involves an administrative procedure, openly and with the opportunity to challenge ('*de caracter contradictorio*') before the official responsible for the Register and two witnesses and subject to regulations. In view of the constitutive effect of the registration, proof of the existence of a pair *de facto* must be proved by reference to a certificate from the official responsible for the Register.

The terms of the cohabitation are to be confirmed in a public document. This shows what the parties agreed on in relation to property matters, and ending the relationship, but it is valid only if it conforms with the law; it cannot limit the equality of the rights of the members nor be seriously against the interests of either (Art 4.1). Such pacts have effect only between the parties and never against third parties (Art 4.3) and must be inscribed in the aforementioned Register in order to be valid (Art 5.1). In default of an agreement, it is assumed the parties make an equitable contribution to meeting expenses, 'in proportion to their resources' (Art 4.2).

As to the grounds for termination, these are much the same as in the other autonomous laws, save that the period of *de facto* separation is only six months (Art 6). The reason for termination must be entered in the administrative register (Art 7).

Further, there is equality with married couples in Valencian administrative law and in the application of public law generally and budgetary matters, subventions, and contributions in particular (Arts 8 and 9).

There is little civil law in this measure, due, as indicated earlier, to the fact that the Autonomous Community of Valencia lacks legislative power over this. What is surprising is the constitutive character given to inscription of the pair in the administrative register.

IV   MADRID

Mutatis mutandis, we can say of the Law of 19 December 2001 of the Community of Madrid what has been said of the Valencian law on which it is modelled to the extent of using it as a precedent. Hence, I shall focus on the (few) differences.

In the Madrid version, inscription in the administrative register is not constitutive, but what Art 3.1 says amounts to the same:

> '*De facto* unions to which the present Law refers take effect from the date of their inscription in the Register of *De Facto* Unions of the Community of Madrid, provided that it is certified that the requirements mentioned in Art 1 are complied with openly and with opportunity for challenge ("*en expediente contradictorio*") before the Officer responsible for the Register.'

The same system of making a pact applies to the *de facto* union, but with the addition of a prohibition: 'Pacts whereof the objective is solely personal or relating to the private life of the cohabitants are void' (Art 4.4). This seems to restrict the content of such pacts to exclusively proprietary matters. These pacts governing cohabitation are registrable, and there is administrative recourse against refusal to register them.

Causes of termination of cohabitation and fiscal and administrative matters, are exactly the same.

V BALEARIC ISLANDS

The Law on Stable Pairs passed by the Parliament of the Balearic Islands on 19 December 2001 differs to some extent, in the Reasoned Justification, from those described above. It relies on the freedom of personal development (Art 10.1 of the Constitution); the Resolution of the European Parliament of 8 February 1994 on equality of rights of homosexuals and lesbians in Europe; on 'a profound legal study' (author unidentified), as well as on various sociological studies and consultation with representative bodies (also anonymous). The Legislature proposes 'recognition of certain effects of the pair relationship in the civil, proprietary, fiscal and public service fields', while warning, 'without it being supposed at any time to be an adulterated copy of the pattern of traditional marriage'. It seems that there was no wish to create an 'alternative marriage', but clearly the stable pair mimics matrimony, and the latter has on many issues been its model. On the other hand, pairs *de facto* also exist that are not subject to this law – the regime governing them being unknown.

The Law is in two titles, one for general provisions and the other for the relationship of the pair. The latter deals quite extensively with the following matters:

–   pacts of cohabitation (Art 4);
–   the economic regime of the pair (Art 5);
–   alimony (Art 6);
–   equality with [married] spouses in some respects (Art 7);
–   causes of termination (Art 8);
–   effects of breakdown or termination while both are alive (Arts 9 and 10);
–   custody and visitation regime for children (Art 11); and
–   effects of termination by reason of death (Arts 12 and 13).

Additional provisions 1 and 2 equate stable pairs to married in the provisions relating to the public service of the autonomous entity, in the field of employment law and, generally, in the rule-making competence of the Balearic Islands. There are three final provisions, one to the effect that in autonomous fiscal matters 'so far as possible' the Autonomous Community will treat stable pairs and spouses alike'.

As this Law is fundamentally inspired by the earlier ones I only note here the particularities.

–   Pacts of cohabitation can be formed orally (Art 4). A surprising rule and one that could give rise to many practical problems.
–   Article 5.4 clearly states that, while cohabitating, each member of the pair retains the ownership, enjoyment and administration of property previously acquired and of that acquired during the cohabitation (without differentiating – both gratuitously and for value). This rule seems to be part of the minimum obligatory content mentioned in Art 4.1, though without much explanation. So, for the cohabitants to own assets in common, an express pact is needed, and this question is the most contentious in practice.
–   Article 6 provides that 'the members of the pair are obliged to provide each other with maintenance and claims for these are to take priority over any other legal obligation'. The drafting is confusing and may conflict with other rules. Supposing one of the members is obliged to make compensatory periodical payments under a divorce judgment, is this postponed for the cohabitant's right to maintenance?
–   There is a 'copy of the pattern of traditional marriage', as the Reasoned Justification puts it, not only in the above-mentioned maintenance (Art 6), matters of tutorship, curatorship, incapacity, declaration of absence and prodigality (Art 7), questions that may be regarded as somewhat secondary or accessory, but also, in particular, in relation to succession, testate as well as intestate (Art 13). How is it argued that this is not interpreted as an 'adulterated copy' of marriage?

VI   SOME CONCLUSIONS

No definitive conclusions can be drawn regarding this phenomenon, which could be called 'legislative haemorrhage' or, perhaps better, 'infection' with a virus that increases its effect each time it is contracted. There are still eight Autonomous Communities that have not legislated on *de facto* pairs, and it is likely some will do so. What is needed is for the National *Cortes* to pass a law and for the *Tribunal Constitucional* to declare its position.

After Catalonia and Aragon differentiated between heterosexual and homosexual couples, the trend has turned towards treating both equally. The resulting interregional conflicts of law may prove insoluble. It is still possible that this legislation will be ruled unconstitutional inasmuch as the Constitution reserves to the State the regulation of marriage in its personal aspects. The topic has given rise to an extensive bibliography in Spain.

BIBLIOGRAPHY

BAYOD LÓPEZ Carmen. 'Parejas no casadas, capítulos matrimoniales y normas de régimen económico matrimonial', RCDI, 1995, p 129 ss.

BERCOVITZ. 'Las parejas de hecho', Aranz Civ, 1993-1, p 1823 ss.

CORRAL GIJÓN Mª del Carmen. 'Las uniones de hecho y sus efectos patrimoniales', RCDI, I, 2000, p 3325 ss, y II, p 559 ss.

ESTRADA ALONSO. *Las uniones extramatrimoniales en el Derecho civil español*, 2ª ed (Madrid 1991).

GALLEGO DOMINGUEZ. *Las parejas no casadas y sus efectos patrimoniales* (Madrid 1995).

GARCÍA RUBIO Mª Paz. *Alimentos entre cónyuges y entre convivientes de hecho* (Madrid 1995).

GAVIDIA SÁNCHEZ. *La unión libre (el marco constitucional y la situación del conviviente supérstite* (Valencia 1995).

GAVIDIA SÁNCHEZ. 'Las uniones libres en la Ley Foral navarra de parejas estables', AC, núm 17, 2001, p 605 ss.

GITRAMA GONZÁLEZ. 'Notas sobre la problemática jurídica de la pareja no casada', *Homenaje a J Beltrán de Heredia* (Salamanca 1984), p 209 ss.

JORDANO BAREA. 'Matrimonio y unión libre', AC, 1999-1, p 181 ss.

LACRUZ BEREDEJO. *Convivencia 'more uxorio'. Estipulaciones y presunciones, en el vol collectivo 'El centenario del Código civil'* (Madrid 1990), I, p 1061 ss.

LÓPEZ AZCONA Aurora. 'La ruptura de las parejas de hecho', Cuadernos Aranz Civ, núm 12, 2002.

MARTÍN CASALS. 'Aproximación a la Ley catalana 10/1998, de uniones estables de pareja', DpyC, núm 12, 1998, p 143 ss.

MARTÍNEZ DE AGUIRRE. 'Las uniones de hecho, Derecho aplicable', AC, 1999-4, p 1095 ss.

PANTALEÓN PRIETO. 'La autorregulación de la unión libre', PJ, núm 4, 1986, p 119 ss.

REINA-MARTINELL. *Las uniones matrimoniales de hecho* (Madrid 1996).

TORRES LANA. 'Relaciones patrimoniales a la conclusión de la "convivencia more uxorio"', *Homenaje a Vallet de Goytisolo* (Madrid 1988), V, p 771 ss.

TORRES LANA. 'De Nuevo sobre las relaciones patrimoniales entre parejas no casadas', Aranz Civ, 1993-II, p 2407 ss.

VILAGRAS ALCAIDE (director). *El Derecho europeo ante la pareja de hecho* (Barcelona 1996).

In this bibliographical selection a variety of doctrinal opinions regarding *de facto* unions as well as various jurisprudential and legislative solutions can be found.

Abbreviations used:

AC:	Actualidad Civil (Madrid);
Aranz Civ:	Aranzadi Civil (Pamplona);
DpyC:	Derecho privado y Constitución (Madrid);
PJ:	Poder Judicial (Madrid);
RCDI:	Revista Crítica de Derecho Inmobiliario (Madrid)
RJC:	Revista Jurídica de Cataluña (Barcelona);
RJN:	Revista Jurídica del Notariado (Madrid).

SWEDEN

MINOR AMENDMENTS AND STATUTORY PROPOSALS: BRUSSELS II, SAME-SEX ADOPTION AND OTHER MATTERS

Åke Saldeen[*]

I INTRODUCTION

In my report for the last edition of *The International Survey of Family Law* on the development of Swedish family law in 2000, I mentioned in the introduction two statutory proposals presented during 1999, which I explained in my report for 1999,[1] namely, first, the Ministerial Memorandum Ds 1999:57 presenting the commission report 'Joint Custody for Unmarried Parents and a Linguistic and Editorial Review of Chapter 6 of the Code on Parents, Children and Guardians[2]', and, secondly, the statutory proposal 'New Cohabitant Rules' (Official Government Report – SOU 1999:104), which at the time of writing my report for this edition of the *Survey* (June 2001) had not yet resulted in any legislation. This is still the position, ie at the time of writing (June 2002) no legislation has been passed as a result of these proposals. However, amended legislation entered into force on 1 January 2001 concerning so-called maintenance support in the case of shared residence.[3] This statutory amendment means that parents who are separated are entitled to half of the maintenance support when the child lives alternately with the parents, ie some time with the mother and some time with the father.[4]

In my report for 2000, I also mentioned in the introduction that not much had happened during 2000 in the field of family law. This can also be said of 2001. A number of minor statutory amendments have however been made during the year in question and I shall briefly describe these under Section II. Furthermore, some commission proposals were presented together with some Government Bills which are of interest. I will briefly describe these under Section III.

---

[*] Dean and Professor of Private Law, Faculty of Law, Uppsala University. Translated by James Hurst.

[1] See *The International Survey of Family Law (2001 Edition)*, ed Andrew Bainham (Family Law, 2001).

[2] Sometimes referred to as the Parental Code.

[3] See 'maintenance support' in my report for 1996 in *The International Survey of Family Law 1996*, ed Andrew Bainham (Martinus Nijhoff Publishers, 1998) at pp 481–486.

[4] Full maintenance support comprises SEK 1,173 (€128.00).

II SOME STATUTORY AMENDMENTS 2001

As is known, on 29 May 2000 the Council of the European Union adopted a regulation on the jurisdiction of courts, and recognition and enforcement of judgments in marriage cases and cases concerning parental responsibility for common children, known as the Brussels II Regulation. This entered into force on 1 March 2001 and since then has been directly applicable in Sweden. The regulation in question means that the EU has been transformed into a uniform jurisdictional district in cross-border cases concerning, *inter alia*, marriage and also regarding applications in such cases relating to custody, access and residence of children as regards the common children of spouses. Furthermore, the regulation involves, *inter alia*, ensuring so-called free mobility within the EU for the kinds of judgments it covers.

In 2001, the Swedish Riksdag (Parliament) passed an Act with supplementary provisions on the Brussels II Regulation (Swedish Code of Statutes – SFS 2001:394).[5] The new Act involves provisions dealing with enforcement in the Swedish courts, Svea Court of Appeal and the Supreme Court, and also governs how enforcement of foreign determinations must be implemented. The provisions correspond, *inter alia*, to the supplementary provisions on enforcement proceedings at Svea Court of Appeal and the Supreme Court that were introduced as a consequence of Sweden acceding to the Lugano Convention (1992).

According to the Brussels II Convention (supplementary provisions) Act (2001:394), the rule is thus that the first, initial consideration of a matter shall take place at Svea Court of Appeal by a legally qualified sole judge. Furthermore, among other things, a judge who has dealt with the first consideration is disqualified from dealing with a case concerning reconsideration of the same matter. In order for an action to be eligible for consideration by the Supreme Court, it is required that the Supreme Court has granted the applicant leave to appeal in accordance with Chapter 54, Section 10 of the Code of Judicial Procedure. (According to this statutory provision, leave to appeal may 'only be granted if, first, it is of importance for guidance on the application of the law that the Supreme Court considers the appeal or, secondly, there are extraordinary reasons for such a determination, for example there are grounds for relief for substantive defects, or a grave procedural error has occurred, or the outcome in the Court of Appeal is obviously due to a gross oversight or gross mistake'.) If an application for a declaration of enforceability is granted, the foreign determination may be enforced in accordance with Chapter 21 of the Code on Parents, Children and Guardians. Among other things, this means that enforcement is requested at the County Administrative Court where, in conjunction with an order for enforcement, certain compulsory measures may be taken on matters such as, for instance, an order subject to a fine for default or a decision for collection of a child through the agency of the police. However, the County Administrative Court must in the first instance work to ensure that the determination may be enforced by voluntary means. Unless it is clearly unnecessary, the County Administrative Court must hold an oral hearing. Finally, it may be mentioned that the County Administrative Court can refuse enforcement, *inter alia*, in cases where the child

---

[5]   Government Bill 2000/01:98.

has reached the age of 12 and opposes enforcement, unless the County Administrative Court nonetheless considers that enforcement is necessary with regard to the best interests of the child.

During 2001, the Riksdag also decided on an amendment of the Rules of the Code on Parents, Children and Guardians concerning the maintenance obligation of parents, whereby an interruption of studies no longer results in the parents' maintenance obligation ceasing.[6] According to the main rule, parents are liable for maintenance until a child attains the age of 18. Before the statutory amendment in question, the rule provided that, if the child studied at compulsory school, upper secondary school or corresponding educational institution after the child had attained 18 or *resumed schooling before the child attained the age of 19*, the maintenance obligation lasted as long as the education continued, though at most until the child attained the age of 21. Thus the implication of this was that a child who, *after* attaining the age of 19, wished to resume studies that had been started earlier but discontinued was not entitled to maintenance under the so-called 'interruption rule'.[7] Through the statutory amendment that entered into force on 1 January 2002, the 'interruption rule' has been abandoned, which means that an interruption to studies no longer results in the parents' maintenance obligation finally ending but on the contrary, if the child attends school after attaining the age of 18, the parents are always liable to pay maintenance during the period the education continues, though at most until the child attains the age of 21. The Government Bill concluded, among other things, that the 'interruption rule' was introduced as part of the reform of the maintenance rules that took place in 1978 and that today it is 'much more common for children to have a break in their basic education than it was then. Current developments tend towards more young children deciding to have an interruption in their education and, for example, working abroad'.[8] The disadvantages associated with the interruption rule were now therefore more apparent and manifestly jeopardised the education of more children than previously.

During 2001, the Riksdag also decided to amend the Act on Certain International Issues Relating to Matrimonial Property Relations (1990:272), insofar as the ambit of the Act was basically extended to relate not only to spouses but also to cohabitants (Code of Judicial Procedure – SFS 2001:1141).[9] This statutory amendment entered into force on 1 February 2002.

III SOME STATUTORY PROPOSALS 2001

In February 1999, a parliamentary commission was appointed with the task, according to the Government's terms of reference, to investigate and analyse the situation of children in homosexual families. Furthermore, the commission was to decide on the legal differences between homosexual and heterosexual couples

---

[6] Government Bill 2000/01:134, Maintenance of Children aged 18, and Parliamentary Standing Committee on Civil-Law Legislation Report 2001/02:LU I.

[7] Code on Parents, Children and Guardians, Chapter 7, Section 1.

[8] Government Bill 2000/01:134, p 11.

[9] Government Bill 2000/01:148 and the Parliamentary Standing Committee on Civil-Law Legislation Report 2001/02:LU4. See J Fam L 409 (1991–1992) regarding the Act 1992:272.

regarding the issue of, *inter alia,* the possibility of adopting children. The commission was known as the Commission on Children in Homosexual Families.

At the end of 2001 the commission submitted its final report 'Children in Homosexual Families'.[10] According to the report, the majority of the commission considered that the legal differences concerning the possibility of homosexual and heterosexual couples respectively adopting children could no longer be deemed objectively justified and that registered partners, like spouses, should be afforded the opportunity to be jointly considered as adoptive parents.[11] The majority of the commission also proposed that an opportunity should be created for a registered partner, subject to the same preconditions as for married couples, to adopt the other party's child, so-called 'step-child adoption'. The majority of the commission further proposed that lesbian couples who are registered partners or who live in a cohabitant relationship should, in the same way as heterosexual spouses and cohabitants, gain access to assisted fertilisation (in this case donor insemination) at public hospitals.

In March 2001, following the consultative procedure for prospective legislation, the Government presented the Bill 2001/02:123 'Partnership and Adoption', which was passed by the Riksdag in May 2002. In this Bill, the Government expressed the view that an opportunity for assisted fertilisation at public hospitals for lesbian couples should not be introduced before a final position had been adopted on the issue of how the legal parenthood of the child should be governed. However, the passing of the Bill by the Riksdag also means that registered partners will, when the legislation enters into force, be given an opportunity to be considered as adoptive parents. This, however, further means that it will be possible for registered partners and homosexual people to be appointed as specially delegated custodians to exercise jointly the custody of a child. The Riksdag has delegated power to the Government to decide when the legislation should enter into force. This is because the legislation relating to the adoption issue necessitates Sweden giving notice terminating its membership of the European Convention on the Adoption of Children 1967. I will report in detail on this legislation in next year's report.

As regards adoption, it may also be mentioned that, *inter alia*, the issue of the biological parent's consent to adoption was dealt with in a Ministerial Memorandum submitted in November 2001, namely Ds 2001:53 'Parental Consent to Adoption, etc'. According to Swedish law, there is no formal requirement for consent to adoption by biological parents who do not share the legal custody of the child. However, such person shall, if it is possible, be heard concerning the adoption matter.

According to the practice of the Supreme Court, when determining adoption applications, the issue of the importance of the opposition of the non-custodial parent should be assessed on the basis of what may be deemed to be in the best interests of the child in the individual case (the adoption has the immediate effect of ending the non-custodial parent's right to access with the child). In practice, an important factor when determining the issue of adoption has been the value to the

---

[10]   Official Government Report – SOU 2001:10.

[11]   See registered partnership in my report in *The International Survey of Family Law 1994,* ed A Bainham (Martinus Nijhoff Publishers, 1996), p 441 ff.

child which continued access with the non-custodial parent may be deemed to have. It is proposed by this Ministerial Memorandum, which has not yet (June 2002) resulted in legislation, that the law be amended so that consent for adoption should also be required from a parent who does not share legal custody. However, according to the proposal, refusal of consent will not constitute an impediment to the granting of adoption, provided the adoption is manifestly in the best interests of the child.

It is also proposed by the Ministerial Memorandum that, among other things, a rule should be introduced into the rules of the Code on Parents, Children and Guardians concerning adoption providing that the person or persons who adopt must, as soon as appropriate, inform the child that he or she is an adopted child. In the explanation of the proposal, it was recalled that the child's right to know about his or her parents is prescribed by the UN Convention on the Rights of the Child. The view that an adoptive child should learn about the adoption and about his or her biological origins is clearly indicated in the *travaux préparatoires* to the applicable adoption legislation, even if no rule concerning this has been introduced. It is also pointed out that adoption research has demonstrated the importance for the positive development of the adoptive child that he or she has knowledge of his or her biological and ethnic origin. It is also emphasised that there are in fact good opportunities for an adoptive child to learn of his or her origin through the investigation concerning the prospective adoptive parents' suitability. These investigations are required in connection with adoption applications and are conducted by the Social Welfare Committee under the Social Welfare Services Act, and must also be archived.[12] Even if the majority of adoptive parents share the view that it is in the best interests of an adoptive child to learn about his or her true origin, and also do actually tell the child that he or she is adopted, one cannot, according to the Memorandum, ignore the fact that there may be cases where, for various reasons, it is difficult for the adoptive parents to inform the child. According to the Memorandum, in order to emphasise further the right of the child to learn about his or her origin and support the parents in this connection, a clear rule imposing a duty on the adoptive parents[13] to provide information should be introduced into the legislation.

Finally, let me add the following. My report for 2000 largely dealt with the legal situation in Sweden concerning assisted fertilisation. I mentioned there that neither egg donation nor so-called surrogate motherhood was accepted in Swedish law but that a commission proposal had been presented in a Ministerial Memorandum about permitting egg donation.[14] Such legislation has now been implemented by the Riksdag passing, in May 2002, Bill 2001/02:89 'Treatment of Involuntary Childlessness', which the Government had presented in January 2002.

---

[12] However, in Swedish law a general court (a district court in the first instance) makes decisions on adoption – approximately 1,000 foreign adoptive children come to Sweden each year. In addition, approximately 100–150 Swedish children are adopted through so-called step-parent adoption.

[13] During 2001, a commission was appointed with the task of presenting proposals to reinforce the rights of children in connection with international adoption and which may contribute to reducing the risks of trade in children. It is also a task for the commission to discuss what it is that makes adults good adoptive parents. The Commission should have completed its task no later than 15 December 2002. See Commission Terms of Reference 2001:93.

[14] Ds 2000:51.

I will provide a detailed report on this new legislation, which enters into force on 1 January 2003, in next year's report on developments in Swedish family law.

SWITZERLAND

ABORTION, REGISTERED PARTNERSHIP
AND OTHER MATTERS

Olivier Guillod[*]

I INTRODUCTION

Following the completion of the divorce reform that came into force on 1 January 2000, one would have expected some legislative calm. Instead, two contentious issues have been intensively debated for the last couple of years: abortion (Section II) and registered partnership (Section III). In addition, the unpredictable fate of a Bill on the family name (Section IV) and the ratification of the Hague Treaty on International Adoption (Section V) will be commented upon.

As to case-law, it is too early to draw any firm conclusion on the way courts have interpreted the new divorce provisions. One can merely note that the Federal Court's restrictive view of the grounds allowing one party to get a divorce without waiting for the normally required four-year separation period (Arts 114 and 115 CC)[1] has prompted members of Parliament to suggest an amendment to the two-year-old law on divorce. According to that pending amendment, the required duration of separation allowing one spouse to get a divorce against the will of the other would be reduced from four to two years.[2]

II ABORTION

On 4 June 2002, the Swiss people accepted an amendment to the Criminal Code concerning abortion and rejected the popular initiative entitled 'For mother and child', the purpose of which was to ban almost any abortion.[3]

Since 1942, abortion had been governed by Arts 118 to 121 of the Criminal Code.[4] Those provisions were very restrictive: a woman was allowed to have an abortion only if two licensed medical practitioners certified that abortion was the only means of preventing a life-threatening risk for the pregnant woman or a danger of serious and permanent impairment to her health. In addition, the woman

---

[*]   Professor of Law, Neuchâtel University. I would like to thank Noémie Helle, attorney at law, for her valuable research assistance.

[1]   See for instance ATF 127 III 129, ATF 127 III 342, ATF 127 III 347, ATF 128 III 1 (all the Federal Court's decisions are available in their original language – ie German, French or Italian – on www.bger.ch).

[2]   See *www.parlament.ch/ab/frameset/f/index.htm*, under the Fall session of the National Council.

[3]   For the detailed results, see Feuille Fédérale (FF) 2002 4786, *www.admin.ch/ch/f/ff/2002*. For the text of the popular initiative, see FF 2000 I 207, *www.admin.ch/ch/f/ffr/2000*. For the amendment to the Criminal Code, see FF 2001 1257, *www.admin.ch/ch/f/ff/2001*.

[4]   *Recueil Systématique du droit fédéral* (RS) 311.0, *www.admin.ch/ch/f/rs/c311_0.html*.

(or her legal representative where she was not competent) had to give her written consent. In any other case, the person performing an abortion (physician, midwife, or anybody else) as well as the pregnant woman herself could be punished by a fine or imprisonment.

The Federal Court made some key decisions on various legal issues dealing with abortion, such as the protection of fundamental rights,[5] equal treatment[6] and the legal status of the embryo.[7] However, even though a very liberal practice of abortion developed in most of the 26 Swiss cantons, no criminal conviction has been pronounced for the last 15 years. The gap between a quite liberal practice and the stringent legal provisions on abortion was so big that a reform of the Criminal Code was deemed inescapable.

Reforming the law on abortion is a long story in Switzerland. The first attempt was made in December 1971, through a popular initiative called 'For the decriminalisation of abortion'.[8] In 1974, the Federal Council (ie the Swiss government) introduced a Bill that forbade abortion except where there was a special indication for it, including the so-called 'social' indication that allowed a woman to abort more easily than under the law in force.[9] In 1976, a second popular initiative called 'For the deadline solution' was launched: women could legally abort during the first 12 weeks of pregnancy. That prompted the withdrawal of the previous initiative 'For the decriminalisation of abortion' before a popular vote.[10] In 1977 and 1978, the Swiss citizens rejected first the popular initiative 'For the deadline solution'[11] and then the federal law that would have allowed abortion under specific indications.[12] In 1980, a third popular initiative 'For the right to life' was launched; it asked for a total ban on abortion, except to save the pregnant woman's life.[13] The initiative was also rejected by the Swiss people in 1985.[14]

After a few years, during which politicians did not dare submit new proposals, a member of the Swiss Parliament asked again in 1993 for the 'deadline solution' that would allow abortion during the first trimester of pregnancy. After that deadline, abortion would be allowed only if a doctor affirmed that it was the only way to prevent a risk threatening the mother's life or her physical or psychological well-being. Parliament decided to take up the matter again and to find a solution balancing the woman's right to choose and the protection of the foetus's life.[15] It eventually passed a law amending the Criminal Code in March 2001,[16] on which a

---

[5]   See for example ATF 101 Ia 252: freedom of opinion; 101 Ia 292: right to a hearing; ATF 97 I 893: freedom of expression.

[6]   See ATF 101 Ia 575.

[7]   See ATF 119 IV 207.

[8]   FF 1971 II 2045.

[9]   FF 1974 II 706. The Bill was later passed by Parliament but more than 50,000 Swiss citizens asked for a referendum that was held in 1978.

[10]   1976 I 847 and FF 1976 III 592.

[11]   FF 1977 III 951.

[12]   FF 1978 II 36.

[13]   FF 1980 III 266.

[14]   FF 1985 II 677.

[15]   See FF 1998 IV 4734.

[16]   FF 2001 1257.

group of citizens asked for a referendum.[17] At roughly the same time, a fourth popular initiative was launched, called 'For the mother and child',[18] the purpose of which was to ban abortion altogether (even where pregnancy resulted from rape), except where it was absolutely necessary to save the pregnant woman's life.

On 2 June 2002, the Swiss citizens had to decide at the same time on the amendment of the Criminal Code and on the initiative 'For the mother and child'. They clearly accepted the former and soundly rejected the latter.[19] In short, it took more than 30 years and six tries to amend the law on abortion.

According to the new Art 119 of the Criminal Code, in force since 1 October 2002, a woman can legally have an abortion within the first 12 weeks of pregnancy. She must simply consult with a licensed physician and state that she feels distressed. The woman, or her legal representative if she is incompetent, must make a written request. A minor woman who has discretion within the meaning of Art 16 of the Civil Code (which is usually accepted from 14 years on, although it must be assessed on a case-by-case basis) can decide herself, without any intervention from her parents or her guardian. When the 12-week deadline is over, a woman can still get an abortion if a physician agrees that the termination of pregnancy is necessary either to protect her bodily integrity from a serious risk of impairment or to dissipate a state of deep distress. There is no time limit but the longer the pregnancy the higher the risk must be for the pregnant woman.

III REGISTERED PARTNERSHIP

In November 2001, the Swiss government circulated the first draft of a Bill on registered partnership for same-sex couples.[20] Federal Councilwoman Metzler introduced the proposal with unusual lyricism:

> 'Love, it's when two people have feelings for each other … Love, it's when two women or two men have decided to be together and to help each other in the good as well as in the bad day. Love is at the heart of this Bill.'[21]

According to various estimates, in Switzerland as elsewhere in Western Europe, gay and lesbian people make up 5 to 10 per cent of the population.[22] Although homosexuality is no longer considered an illness, it nevertheless constitutes an important social taboo. For the Federal Council, the legal recognition of homosexuality should contribute to reducing its social stigma. The first draft of the Bill was circulated among cantons, political parties and other interested organisations up until March 2002. To the surprise of many in rather conservative Switzerland, the reaction was overwhelmingly positive: almost everybody agreed that the law ought to allow homosexual couples a framework similar to the one

---

[17]   FF 2001 4464.

[18]   FF 1998 2573 and FF 2000 207. For the position of the Swiss government on that initiative, see FF 2001 633.

[19]   For the detailed results, see FF 2002 4786.

[20]   The proposal and the accompanying report can be found in French, German or Italian on the internet site of the Federal office of Justice (www.ofj.admin.ch).

[21]   Quoted by Michel Montini, 'Gays, gays, enregistrons-nous?', *Plädoyer* 3/2002, p 49.

[22]   For details, see Federal Council report, pp 4–5.

provided by marriage. A minority of answers went even further, asking why marriage should not be open to same-sex couples. In view of that positive stance, a bill should now be formally introduced in Parliament before the end of 2002.

The proposal would create a new legal institution called 'registered partnership' (*partenariat enregistré; registrierte Partnerschaft*). The expression 'registered partnership' is controversial among gay and lesbian associations: indeed, the name reminds many of them of the infamous registers of homosexuals which were set up during the Second World War. It will be up to the Swiss Parliament to decide whether or not to change the name of the Bill.

Unlike the French PACS (*pacte civil de solidarité*), which is open to heterosexual as well as homosexual couples, the Swiss registered partnership would be strictly reserved for same-sex couples (Art 2 of the draft law). The main reason given to explain this limited scope was because heterosexual couples deserved no special protection from the law because they may always choose between cohabitation and marriage. On the contrary, homosexual couples were reduced to cohabiting and were therefore deprived of various entitlements such as inheritance rights or social security benefits.

According to the Swiss government, Art 14 of the Federal Constitution – which protects the freedom to marry and have a family – is based on a traditional conception of the family and should therefore be amended before a law allowing homosexual couples to get married could be passed. Although the latter view is not undisputed among legal scholars, it was certainly politically wiser to create a new legal institution for same-sex couples, separate from marriage but close to it. The regulation of registered partnership is indeed clearly inspired by the legal framework for marriage. On many aspects generally considered as unproblematic, registered partners would enjoy the same legal situation as married people. By contrast, on sensitive issues like those concerning children, sharp distinctions would be made.

If passed, the proposal would bring a long list of improvements to the legal situation of homosexual partners. First of all, gays and lesbians would be free to register their partnership, a move that would involve a modification in their civil status. Previously 'single', they would become 'bound by a registered partnership' (Art 3).

According to Art 4 of the proposal, the partners must be 18 years old and have discretion if they want to enter a registered partnership. In addition, one of them must either be Swiss or live in Switzerland. Each partner should further prove that she/he is not married nor bound by another registered partnership. Legal impediments to registered partnership are the same as for marriage with, however, one additional requirement: the registrar of civil status must refuse to register a partnership which is intended only to bypass the restrictive legal provisions on getting a residence permit (Art 5/2).

Unlike married people who share a common surname, partners would not be allowed to bear a legally recognized common name. However, the Federal Council said that they could have their 'registered name' written on their identity card or passport.[23]

---

[23]   See Federal Council report, p 13.

Once registered, the partners, each according to his or her capacity, would care jointly for the proper maintenance of the community, much like married couples (Art 14; compare with Art 163 CC). But, unlike Art 164 and 165 CC for married couples, the draft law does not provide for any compensation scheme for the partner who has reduced his or her professional activity to keep the household or to help in his or her partner's enterprise. The government explained that the difference was due to the fact that in same-sex couples, each partner usually has a job and earns his or her living, while in married couples, one of the spouses frequently gives up (in full or in part) his or her job in order to look after the children or maintain the upkeep of the household.[24]

The partners' house or apartment is protected: one partner could not sell it, or terminate the lease, or restrict through any other legal transaction the right of use of the abode without the other's express consent (Art 15; compare with Art 169 CC for spouses). Like a spouse (Art 166 CC), each partner would represent the partnership in matters of the current requirements of the partnership during their life in common (Art 16). Both partners would have a mutual obligation to give information concerning income, capital or debts (Art 17; compare with Art 170 CC for married couples). Each partner would be entitled to discontinue the maintenance of the common home for so long as his or her personality or economic security is seriously imperilled by a continuance of life in common (Art 18; compare with Art 175 CC for spouses) and to claim for alimony.

Unlike spouses, who are placed under a matrimonial property system of participation in acquisitions (Art 196ff CC) and may choose another system, registered partners would be placed under a system of separate estates, without any other choice (Art 19). Here again, the main rationale given by the government[25] was that partners had no need for the equivalent of a matrimonial property system because both of them usually had a living and were financially independent. That situation might nonetheless be problematic where a partner has reduced his or her activity to maintain the upkeep of the household.

Registered partners would be barred from adoption and medically assisted procreation (Art 28). In other words, they would be treated like heterosexual cohabitants on both issues (see Art 264a CC and Art 3 of the Federal Act on Medically Assisted Procreation). The Swiss government thought[26] that it was too early to allow homosexuals to raise children, even though it did not go as far as saying that they had poorer educative skills than heterosexuals. In reality, a number of gays and lesbians already have children and bring them up. If a partner has custody of one or several children, Art 29 provides that the other should assist him or her in the exercise of his or her parental duties (parental power, education, maintenance of the child), like a step-parent (see Art 299 CC).

Two of the main improvements in the legal condition of same-sex couples deal with taxation and inheritance rights. With regard to income tax, homosexual cohabitants have been so far taxed separately, each according to his or her earnings. According to the Bill, registered partners are considered to be a single entity for tax purposes, like married people. That will be an advantage where one

---

[24] See Federal Council report, pp 12, 15.
[25] See Federal Council report, p 15.
[26] See Federal Council report, pp 17–18.

of the partners earns considerably more than the other. On the contrary, it will be a disadvantage where each partner earns approximately the same amount. As to cantonal inheritance taxes, registered partners would also be treated like married couples who are usually exempted from such taxes or pay a minimum rate. That would make a huge difference because the inheritance tax rate presently depends on how closely one is related to the deceased person. Today, when a homosexual partner dies, his or her companion is taxed as someone who has no ties with the deceased. The tax rate is consequently very high, reaching in some cantons 40% of the net value of the estate.[27]

The dissolution of a registered partnership is regulated like a divorce, except in two matters. Partners would be entitled to terminate their partnership by mutual agreement just like spouses (Art 31; compare with Art 111–112 CC). But if a single partner wanted to terminate the registered partnership, the required period of separate life would be just one year (Art 32), instead of four years for married people (Art 114 CC). The government explained that difference by arguing that registered partners had no common children who would need protection. Concerning alimony, registered partners would have a more limited right than spouses: it is only where a partner reduced his or her professional activity during the partnership or where he or she had lost other alimony (eg from a previous divorce) by entering the partnership that he or she could claim for alimony (Art 36). Each partner's old-age entitlements accumulated during the partnership would be divided by two, as in a divorce (Art 35, referring to Art 122ff CC). Expenses resulting from the dissolution of the partnership would be shared in a fair way among partners (Art 37). The lease over the partners' apartment could be attributed to either of them, according to the needs of each partner (Art 39; compare with Art 121 CC where the judge in divorce proceedings has the additional power to grant a right of residence to the spouse who does not own the house).

To sum up, one could say that homosexual couples should get a legal status approaching that of marriage, probably in a couple of years. Indeed almost everybody expects Parliament to pass the Bill rather swiftly.[28] A possible popular referendum would certainly approve the law passed by Parliament. The fiercest battle will probably take place over adoption and access to new reproductive technology.

IV   REFORMING THE FAMILY NAME: A SWISS QUAGMIRE

In Switzerland, the family name remains a male stronghold. Although it is somewhat embarrassing, it is not that surprising in a country where women only acquired the right to vote in 1971 after two unsuccessful tries.

According to the provisions that have existed ever since the Civil Code entered into force in 1912, the family name of spouses is, as a matter of principle,

---

[27]   For more details, see Olivier Guillod, 'A new divorce law for the new millennium', *The International Survey of Family Law (2000 Edition)*, ed A Bainhaim (Family Law, 2000), p 368.

[28]   At the very moment when this contribution was sent, the Swiss government forwarded a slightly revised version of the Bill on registered partnership to Parliament.

the name of the husband. When the law on marriage was revised in the 1980s, two minor amendments were brought to that rule: first, a woman getting married could decide to bear a double name made up of her maiden name followed by her husband's name (Art 160/2 CC), but the latter remained the only 'family name'; secondly, an engaged couple could request that the wife's surname be the family name after the wedding if there were grounds worthy of consideration (Art 30/2 CC). Children born to married parents always bear the family name, ie the name of their father, while children born out of wedlock bear their mother's surname, even where paternity is established.

It seems obvious that such a regulation is contrary to the principle of equal treatment of men and women. Parliament nevertheless refused several times to change it in the 1980s and 1990s. The Federal Court (Switzerland's highest court) could not alter the law because, under the Swiss Constitution (Art 189), it has no power to rule on the constitutionality of a federal law passed by Parliament (and possibly ratified by Swiss citizens in a referendum).

The Federal Court had nevertheless to decide an interesting case in 1989 where a man who had agreed to bear his wife's maiden name as family name (according to Art 30/2 CC) asked the registrar of civil status to be allowed to keep his own surname and place it before the family name (according to Art 160/2 CC by analogy). The court refused, arguing that Art 160/2 CC had been introduced to mitigate the general rule that discriminates against women and that if a man wanted to keep his surname, he should simply refuse to bear his wife's maiden name.[29] On appeal, the European Court of Human Rights in Strasbourg reversed the ruling, affirming that the Federal Court decision violated Arts 8 and 14 of the European Convention on Human Rights.[30] The resulting situation was to some extent ludicrous: husbands were entitled to the same, but minor, right as wives (ie bearing a double name) but wives were still deprived of the basic right enjoyed by husbands (ie keeping their surname when getting married).

In order to place men and women on an equal footing as to the name of the family, a female (although not a feminist!) member of Parliament submitted a proposal to amend the Civil Code in December 1994 that was rewritten several times. According to the final proposal, an engaged couple would be entitled to choose as their common family name either the wife's surname or the husband's. If they had a child, she or he would naturally bear their common family name. But an engaged couple could also decide that each spouse would keep his or her surname after the wedding and therefore that they would not share a common family name. If they had a child, they would have to decide which surname he or she would bear. The chosen name would then be the same for all subsequent children.

The proposal raised a disproportionately large controversy in Parliament as well as in the Swiss media. The lower Chamber of Parliament passed it first in 1999. Then in June 2001, the upper Chamber finally adopted the Bill as well, despite a campaign from some newspapers which published editorials against the bill and which mixed all kinds of arguments, making it impossible to ascertain whether they were soundly conservative or genuinely concerned with keeping

---

[29]   ATF 115 II 193.

[30]   *Burghartz v Switzerland*, # 16213/90, February 22, 1994, Series A 280–B.

genealogical lines clear. After decades of unsuccessful attempts, feminists and many other people concerned with equal rights could finally rejoice.

Or so they thought … A few days after the upper Chamber had approved the Bill, the full Parliament had formally to adopt all laws that each Chamber had separately approved previously, which is usually a mere formality. To the astonishment of many, the full Parliament rejected the Bill amending the Civil code provisions on the name of the family. In two minutes, a Bill patiently moved through Parliament for the previous seven years was killed. I guess the surname of the husband is engraved on its tombstone.

V   INTERNATIONAL ADOPTION

Most children adopted in Switzerland come from abroad. In 2000 for instance, out of 808 children adopted, only 198 (ie slightly less than 25%) were Swiss. About as many came from European countries and more than half (420) came from other continents, especially from Asia and South America. Rumours have been circulating about child trafficking and other abuses which prompted the Swiss government to sign the Hague Convention on international adoption, of 29 May 1993.

In June 2001, the Swiss Parliament ratified the Hague Convention and adopted implementing provisions[31] that came into force on 1 January 2003. Several protective measures (Art 17ff) in the federal Act on foreign adoptions will apply not only to adopted children coming from a country that has ratified the Hague Convention but also to other international adoptions. The need for protection is indeed the same for all foreign children adopted in Switzerland. When the adoption was decided abroad and can be recognized in Switzerland, a curator is named for the child in order to assist the adoptive parents who immediately have parental power over the child (Art 17). Where the adoption was decided abroad outside the Hague Convention framework and cannot be recognized in Switzerland, a guardian is named for the child (Art 18) until he or she is adopted according to Swiss law (which requires a one-year[32] stay with the adoptive parents). As soon as the child resides in Switzerland, the prospective adoptive parents have a duty to maintain the child (Art 20), although they do not have, as yet, parental power over him.[33]

When the adoption is governed by the Hague Convention, the matching decision as to the fitness of the prospective adoptive parents will be made by a central authority at the cantonal level (Art 3). The Federal Office of Justice in Bern will be the supervising body (Art 2) in charge of coordinating procedures, issuing guidelines, as well as informing the population.

The Swiss Parliament also took the opportunity to clarify the right of the adopted child to know his biological parents, a right that could be inferred from Art 119 of the federal Constitution as well as from Art 7 of the Convention on the

---

[31]   See FF 2001 2770, *www.admin.ch/ch/f/ff/2001*.

[32]   According to the revised version of Art 264 CC (it was formerly 2 years).

[33]   For more details, see Philippe Meier, Martin Stettler, *Droit civil VI/1, L'établissement de la filiation (Art 252 à 269c CC)*, 2nd ed, Fribourg 2002, p 177ff.

Rights of the Child. Following the rules applying to children born through medically assisted conception (Art 27 of the federal Act on medically assisted procreation),[34] Art 268c CC provides that the adopted child is entitled to know his or her biological parents as soon as he or she turns 18. He or she might even ask for it sooner, if there were material grounds for obtaining the information.

The right to know one's biological parents will however be really effective only for internal adoptions, where the name of the natural (as well as legal, according to Art 252 CC)[35] mother and, possibly, the name of the father are recorded in the register of births. In international adoptions, the implementation of the adopted child's right to know his or her biological parents will of course depend on the legislation of the country of origin.

---

[34] RS 814.90, *www.admin.ch/ch/f/rs/c814_90.html.*
[35] Unlike French law for instance, Swiss law does not recognise the '*accouchement sous X*', ie allowing a mother to give birth anonymously.

THE UNITED STATES

UNCONVENTIONAL RELATIONS: DEVELOPMENTS IN FAMILY LAW IN THE UNITED STATES OF AMERICA IN 2001

Lynn D Wardle[*]

I INTRODUCTION

This chapter reports on significant developments in Family Law in the United States of America in the year 2001.[1] To understand the significance of these developments, two characteristics of American family laws and the American legal system must be noted. First, there is no such thing as THE family law of America. Constitutional government in the United States is organized on the principle of federalism; some subjects (mostly relating to the economy, commerce, foreign relations, national defense, and the fundamental Bill of Rights) are regulated by the national government, and other areas of human behavior (mostly relating to local conduct) are regulated by the states.[2] The regulation of family relations has long been said to fall 'within the virtually exclusive province of the States'.[3] Second, actual developments in the law of family relations must be distinguished from various kinds of proposals for family law reform. Paying too much attention to the hype and commentary can distort the form and confuse the perception of actual family law developments. This report does not describe the many theories, reform proposals, commentary, criticism, and movements published or promoted by academics, professionals, or popular media, nor does it cover bills and resolutions introduced in legislative bodies but not enacted, nor does it include state trial court decisions which individually have only minor precedential effect. This chapter reports only significant legislative enactments, appellate court decisions, and other generally applicable, legally operative rules or doctrines of family law that were decided, enacted, or became operative in the United States of America in 2001.

[*]   Professor of Law, J Reuben Clark Law School, Brigham Young University, Provo, UT 84602 USA. The research assistance of William J Perkins is gratefully acknowledged.

[1]   There are other more comprehensive reviews of family law developments in 2001, some of them for specific states. See, eg Linda D Elrod and Robert G Spector, 'A Review of the Year in Family Law: State Courts React to Troxel', 35 Fam LQ 577 (2002); 'Family Law in the Fifty States 2000–2001: Cases Digests', 35 Fam LQ 637 (2002); David Kader, et al, 'The Arizona Supreme Court: Its 2000–2001 Decisions', 34 Ariz St LJ 369 (2002); Joseph W McKnight, 'Family Law: Husband and Wife', 55 SMU L Rev 1035 (2002); see further Cassandra L Marshall, 'Family Law Case Update', Res Gestae (Ind St Bar Assn), July/Aug 2002 at 37.

[2]   US Constitution, amend X.

[3]   *Sosna v Iowa*, 419 US 393, 404 (1975); see also *Lehman v Lycoming County Children's Services Agency*, 458 US 502 (1982); *Moore v Sims*, 442 US 415 (1979); *Barber v Barber*, 62 US (21 How) 582 (1859).

The subjects covered by this report are organized in six categories of legal issues which cover two main categories of family relations: spousal (and quasi-spousal) relations and parent-child (and quasi-parent-child relations) during three chronological periods: creation of relations, ongoing relations, and dissolution/termination and post-dissolution relations.[4]

The theme of the developments in family law in the United States can be called 'unconventional relationships' because many of the developments concerned claims for family relationships status in law (marriage, parentage, etc.) for unconventional relationships that traditionally have not been deemed family relationships, if not prohibited, or legally ignored.

II   CREATION OF AND RELATIONS PRIOR TO MARRIAGE AND QUASI-MARRIAGE

A   Premarital agreements

In recent years, the use of ante-nuptial agreements has become more common, and litigation over their enforcement and interpretation has also become more common. 2001 saw a continuation of the long-established judicial trend in favor of upholding premarital agreements so long as the parties enter into them freely, with reasonable information about what they are doing (or waiver of that information), without fraud, and (perhaps) if the agreement is not unconscionable. For example, in *In re Estate of Ingmand*,[5] the Iowa Court of Appeals upheld a premarital agreement and explained: 'As a general rule, prenuptial agreements are favored and should be liberally construed to give effect to the parties' intent ... The person challenging the agreement must prove its terms are unfair or the person's waiver of rights was not knowing and voluntary.'[6] The facts in this case were troubling because of the ambush tactics. Frances and Eugene were both retired:

> '... both widowed, [and] had known each other for some time prior to their ... marriage. When Frances entered the marriage she owned a residence in Red Oak, Iowa, and had approximately $295,000 in other assets. Eugene owned a condominium in Sun City, Arizona, and had approximately $515,000 in other assets. Eugene was familiar with Frances' financial condition, as he had given her financial advice and assisted her with financial management after the death of her first husband. In contrast, Frances was not familiar with Eugene's finances or assets, other than the fact he was "comfortably well off".
>
>   [Just four days before their marriage,] Eugene went to the office of a Sun City attorney, William Don Carlos, and requested that Don Carlos prepare a prenuptial agreement. The next day, telling Frances that they were going to procure their

---

[4]   Thus, the six categories are: (1) Creation of and Relations Prior to Marriage and Quasi-Marriage, (2) Creation of and Relations Prior to Parenthood or Quasi-Parenthood, (3) Relations Between Spouses During Ongoing Marriage or Quasi-Marriage, (4) Relations Between Parent–Child During Ongoing Family or Quasi-Family Relationship, (5) Dissolution of Marital or Quasi-Marital Relationship and Post-Dissolution Relations, and (6) Termination of Parental or Quasi-Parental Relationship and Post-Dissolution Parent–Child Relations.

[5]   2001 WL 855406 (Iowa App, 2001).

[6]   Slip op at *2.

marriage license, he drove her to Don Carlos' office. Frances was not aware of the prenuptial agreement, or of Eugene's desire to have the couple sign such a document, until she was presented with it at Don Carlos' office. Eugene then made it clear to Frances that signing the prenuptial agreement was a precondition of their marriage.

Don Carlos informed Frances that he represented Eugene only, and informed her of the advisability of retaining independent counsel ... Feeling uncomfortable and embarrassed at the prospect of people finding out Eugene was conditioning their marriage on the prenuptial agreement, [Frances] signed the agreement in Don Carlos' office. While she could have obtained a copy of the agreement, she did not as she "didn't truly want to get into it any more".

The agreement reserved to each spouse his or her own separate property, income and debt, whether premarital or after-acquired, and waived the other spouse's rights and obligations in the same. It also required each spouse to bear his or her own expenses during the marriage, with some limited exceptions ...'[7]

Frances and Eugene were married in May 1986, and apparently stayed together for over a dozen years. When Eugene died, Frances challenged the prenuptial agreement. The Court of Appeals affirmed the trial court's judgment upholding the agreement. While condemning Eugene's 'surprise pressure tactics' of 'trick[ing] Frances into going to [his lawyer's] office just days before their marriage, and then condition[ing] the marriage on her signature', still her decision to sign rather than take the offer to seek independent counsel and study carefully the agreement 'did not negate the knowing and voluntary nature of the execution'. Likewise, while a prenuptial agreement may be invalidated if it is unfair, the court declared that a 'prenuptial agreement [like this one, does] little more than preserve to each party their independent financial status preceding the marriage and therefore cannot be deemed unfair to either [party]'.[8]

Likewise, in *Bowen v Bowen*,[9] a couple had executed an extensive prenuptial agreement before their 1985 marriage providing that any property each acquired during the marriage would remain separate property. The husband acquired during the marriage property that he had titled in both parties' names, with right of survivorship. When the wife filed for divorce seven years later, the South Carolina family court ruled that the property was non-marital, but proceeded to declare that the wife owned half of the properties. On appeal, the South Carolina Court of Appeals affirmed the ruling that the property was non-marital, but vacated the family court determination of the parties' respective interests holding that once the property was determined to be non-marital, the family court lost jurisdiction to determine interests in it. The wife then filed a declaratory action in the family court claiming that placing her name as joint or co-owner constituted a gift to her of one-half interest in the properties, and the trial court agreed because the ante-nuptial agreement did not prevent the husband from making a gift of his separate property to the wife. On appeal, the South Carolina Court of Appeals affirmed on different analysis. Because the premarital agreement eliminated mutual support obligations, the presumption of a gift to the spouse was not

---

[7]   Slip op at *1.

[8]   Slip op at *2.

[9]   547 S.E.2d 877 (SC Ct App 2001). The South Carolina Supreme Court affirmed this decision in 2003 *Bowen v Bowen*, 2003 WL 112451 (SC 13 January 2003) (No 25574).

effective, nor was the presumption of a resulting trust operative for the benefit of the husband. The plain language of the premarital agreement controlled, which made all property acquired by either spouse the property of that spouse, and since the wife had acquired a one-half interest by title from her husband, that was her separate property. The *Bowen* decision shows that a premarital agreement may override an otherwise applicable presumption of a gift between spouses as well as the presumption of a resulting trust when property paid for by one person is taken in the name of another person without consideration.

In *Rubino v Rubino*,[10] Donna and Michael signed a premarital agreement in which they agreed to divide equally most of the property acquired during marriage, and Donna waived all interest in the separate property of her husband or in alimony. When Michael filed for divorce two months after the marriage, Donna countered seeking and obtaining a temporary award of $5,000 as part of equitable distribution of property under the equitable distributions statute (which she had waived under the premarital agreement). The Supreme Court of Rhode Island held that, even though the wife had violated the agreement by accepting a partial equitable distribution, the agreement was still enforceable, and the division of property would be governed by the more-generous-to-the-wife premarital agreement than under the ordinary equitable distribution statute principles. The court approvingly noted and accepted the wife's argument that 'under Rhode Island law, ante-nuptial agreements are enforceable and must be upheld under all but extreme circumstances …'.[11]

A California case provides a good reminder that premarital agreements must conform to basic contract requirements including the Statute of Frauds. In *In re Marriage of Shaban*,[12] the California Court of Appeals affirmed the trial court's rejection of a man's assertion that a one-page Arabic document was an ante-nuptial agreement. The parties had been married in Egypt in 1974, and were divorced in California in 1998, after living in the USA for 17 years. The husband claimed that the short document the parties had signed (actually the wife's father had signed as her representative), meant that the parties had agreed that their financial relations would be governed by Islamic Law. But the text of the document contained no substantive provisions; only identified the parties and their property and declared:

> 'The above legal marriage has been concluded in accordance with his Almighty God's Holy Book and the Rules of his Prophet to whom all God's prayers and blessings be, by legal offer and acceptance from the two contracting parties.
>
> The foregoing was concluded after the two parties had taken cognizance of the legal implications …'[13]

The California courts held that this language failed to express any essential terms of a contract, was much too vague to incorporate the Islamic law conditions the husband claimed, that admissibility of parole evidence to explain the meaning of this language was barred by the Statute of Frauds, and that the document did not

---

[10]   547 S.E.2d 877 (SC Ct App 2001).

[11]   765 A.2d at 1224.

[12]   105 Cal Rptr 2d 863 (Ct App 2001), modified on denial of rehearing (9 May 2001), review denied (11 July 2001).

[13]   Ibid at 865.

amount to an enforceable ante-nuptial agreement. Therefore, division of property under the California community property rules was affirmed.

Related to the ante-nuptial agreement is the 'palimony' agreement between non-marital cohabitants. In *Della Zoppa v Della Zoppa*,[14] a California trial court had ruled that an oral agreement between an unmarried couple, that the wealthy man would share his acquisitions with the younger woman, was unenforceable because the agreement included her duty to bear children, and was meretricious. She moved in with the man, quit using birth control, became pregnant, and the couple married and had three children before divorcing. The appellate court reversed, holding that while meretricious agreements are not enforceable, that term refers to prostitution-like agreements and this involved an attempt to create a family which was not 'of or relating to a prostitute'.[15]

These decisions show that the rule favoring enforcement of premarital agreements benefits and burdens both sexes. In *Ingmand*, the premarital agreement was enforced against the wife, in *Bowen*, *Rubino*, *Shaban*, and *Della Zoppa* the agreement was enforced against the man. In the typical ante-nuptial agreement enforcement dispute scenario, the husband is the party with greater assets at the time of marriage. If the marriage has lasted a long time, the wife is parting objecting to enforcement of the agreement terms that seemed fair when made but after 10 or 20 years no longer seem adequate. But if the marriage is of short duration, the husband is the party objecting to enforcement of the agreement provisions giving a generous settlement to the wife that seemed reasonable when contemplating a long marriage, but which, after only six months seem like an exorbitant windfall. To address the 'margins' of greatest dissatisfaction with enforcement of ante-nuptial contracts, perhaps parties drafting prenuptial agreements should consider including duration provisions, requiring the marriage to last a minimum period (for example, two years) before the agreement provisions become enforceable, and providing a sunset clause providing that the provisions expire and are not enforceable without renewal after a maximum period (for example, 15 years).

B   Revitalizing marriage

The growing grass roots movement to revitalize marriage and to emphasize the social and personal importance of making marriages work received a boost by two developments in 2001.[16] First, a third state, Arkansas, enacted a 'covenant marriage' law.[17] The five distinguishing characteristics of covenant marriage are:

(1)   it provides an optional set of terms to govern the marriage which parties seeking a marriage licence may choose;

---

[14]   103 Cal Rptr 901 (Cal App 2001).

[15]   Ibid at 905; ibid at 908.

[16]   For a description of the marriage revitalization movement, see generally Lynn D Wardle, 'Divorce Reform at the Turn of the Millennium: Certainties and Possibilities', 33 Fam LQ 783 (1999).

[17]   Ark Code Ann. § § 9-11-801 to -811 (2002).

(2)   the parties who select covenant marriage must undergo premarital counselling;

(3)   they must complete an affidavit or declaration clearly establishing their voluntary selection of covenant marriage;

(4)   they agree to seek counselling to resolve marital difficulties before filing to dissolve the marriage; and

(5)   they agree that they may only dissolve the marriage upon 'fault' grounds or upon separation for a significant period of time (two years in Arkansas).[18]

Secondly, President Bush pushed through tax relief legislation that reduced the 'marriage penalty' in the federal income tax laws.[19] The Bush administration also announced that it intended to encourage and strengthen marriage as a means to fight or prevent poverty (and early in 2002 announced that it was committing $300 million in welfare funds to marriage promotion programs).[20]

C   Same-sex marriage or domestic partnership

The movement to legalize same-sex marriage or marriage-like domestic partnership continues to push for law reform to give same-sex relationships the same status and benefits as marriage. In *Brause v State*,[21] the Alaska Supreme Court affirmed the dismissal of the suit by a gay couple seeking legalization of same-sex marriage under the state constitution that had resulted earlier in a state trial court interlocutory decision ruling that the denial of same-sex marriage violated the privacy and equality provisions of the Alaska Constitution. The legislature had reacted to the ruling by proposing, and state voters had overwhelmingly ratified, an amendment to the state constitution specifically providing that 'marriage may exist only between one man and one woman' to be valid or recognized in Alaska.[22] In 2001, the state supreme court affirmed that the adoption of that amendment rendered the claim for same-sex marriage moot, and the plaintiffs lacked standing to challenge another statute for denying marital benefits for which they had not shown they were otherwise qualified.[23]

However, an intermediate state appellate court in Kansas showed that Americans certainly are not uniformly in favor of strengthening traditional marriage or opposed to novel kinds of relationships. In *In re Estate of Gardiner*,[24] the court ruled in an estate contest between the son and the 'widow' of a deceased wealthy man that a marriage between an old man and a younger male-to-female

---

[18]   See generally Kimberly Miller, 'Survey of Legislation, Title 9, Family Law', 24 U Ark Little Rock L Rev 483 (2002).

[19]   Benjamin A Jablow, 'Sunset and the Economic Growth and Tax Relief Reconciliation Act of 2001', 75 Fla BJ 47 (December 2001).

[20]   See generally David Orgon Coolidge and William C Duncan, 'Reaffirming Marriage: A Presidential Priority', 24 Harv JL and Pub Pol'y 623 (2001); see also Robin Toner, 'Welfare Chief is Hoping to Promote Marriage', *New York Times*, 19 February 2002, at A1 (Bush administration proposes to use one hundred million dollars of welfare money to promote marriage).

[21]   21 P.3d 357 (Alaska 2001).

[22]   Alaska Constitution, Art 1, § 25 (2002).

[23]   21 P.3d at 358.

[24]   22 P.3d 1086 (Kan App 2001).

transsexual was a valid marriage. The case turned on whether the transsexual was a male or female at the time of the putative marriage. A Kansas trial court, applying a traditional sex-determined-at-birth test, ruled that the 'wife' was not a female and the marriage was not valid. However, in 2001, the intermediate court of appeals rejected the genetic test, adopted an eight-part conceptual test for determining gender, reversed the lower court, concluded that the transsexual was a female, and ruled that the marriage was valid. (However, the following year the Kansas Supreme Court reversed the intermediate court of appeals and held that the legislature intended the traditional understanding be given to 'opposite sex' in the marriage law).[25]

Likewise, while same-sex couples may not marry in New Jersey, a New Jersey court held in *In re An Application for a Change of Name By: Jill Iris Bacharach*,[26] that they can adopt each other's name. In this case, one lesbian partner wanted to change her name to that of her lesbian partner. The trial judge denied the application on the ground that it would present the false appearance that New Jersey permits same-sex marriage. The appellate division reversed holding that if the name change was not prompted by criminal or fraudulent motives, the court ought not to deny the application to change her name unless the proposed new name is ridiculous, obscene or racist. While New Jersey does not allow same-sex marriages, the appellate court explained that the marriage prohibition is not violated by and does not preclude changing one's name to that of one's same-sex partner.

On the other hand, in *In re Maloney*,[27] the Ohio court of appeals affirmed a trial court denial of a 50-year-old male's petition to change his name to Susan. The man had recently ended his marriage of 22 years and was considering transsexual surgery. The court noted that the name change would cause confusion if the petitioner later chose not to go through with the surgery. (Surprisingly, the opinion does not mention whether, during his 22-year marriage, he had any children, or the impact of the new change upon interested others.) The following year, however, the Ohio Supreme Court summarily reversed this decision.[28]

III   CREATION OF AND RELATIONS PRIOR TO PARENTHOOD OR QUASI-PARENTHOOD

A   Gay-couple adoptions

In 2001, one federal court upheld a law prohibiting adoptions by h̶ᵉ and a state intermediate court of appeals ruled that the step-ṛ provisions of the state adoption laws could not be interpreᵗ same-sex partner of a legal parent to adopt that parent's child trend toward allowing gay couple adoptions was set back.

---

[25] *In re Estate of Gardiner*, 42 P.3d 120 (Kan 2002).

[26] 780 A.2d 579 (NJ Super 2001).

[27] 2001 WL 908535 (Ohio App, 13 August 2001).

[28] *In re Maloney*, 774 N.E.2d 239 (Ohio, 2002).

In *Lofton v Kearney*,[29] a gay couple who were foster parents challenged Fla Stat Ann § 63.042(3), which prohibits homosexuals from adopting. The federal district court upheld the statute. The plaintiff's privacy-related constitutional claims were rejected because foster parents and legal guardians do not possess any fundamental right to familial privacy, intimate association and family integrity, nor is there any fundamental constitutional right to adopt, be adopted, or apply for adoption. The court also ruled that homosexuals are not a suspect class, and the disputed statute serves a legitimate government purpose by promoting the best interest of the children.

In *Sharon S v Superior Court*,[30] a biological mother appealed denial of her motion to dismiss the adoption petition filed by her former lesbian partner. The California Court of Appeals held that the state adoption statutes did not permit a former partner to adopt the child of the biological mother. Therefore, the biological mother's motion to dismiss her former partner's adoption petition was granted.

But the movement to allow gay couples to adopt continued anyway in 2001. Various trial courts continued to permit the adoption of a child by the same-sex partner of the biological parent of the child,[31] and both of the noted cases have been appealed.

B   Children born out of marriage

The largest number of cases concerning parentage-recognition issues involved children born out of wedlock. While there were many different issues raised, the significance of phenomenon of children born out of wedlock cannot be denied. In 2000, it was reported that over 33% of all children born in the United States – 1,347,000 children – were born out of wedlock.[32]

The Supreme Court of the United States got involved in the issue. In *Nguyen v INS*,[33] the court upheld an immigration law that required a child born out of wedlock to a citizen father and alien mother to obtain a court order of paternity, or legitimation, or a written acknowledgement of paternity by the citizen father, before turning 18 to claim US citizenship, even though children of citizen mothers alien fathers are automatically entitled to claim US citizenship. The court (by vote) held that the different requirements imposed on children of citizen ea citizen mothers were substantially related to the real differences conveyd women regarding reliable proof of both the relationship (it is e mother of a child than the father) and the establishment of a ializing relationship by which citizenship values are reconfirmed and was the logical extension of the

---

29   157 F.Supp
30   113 Cal Rptr 2
31   See, eg, *In re Har*
32   Centers for Disease
      at 2; ibid at 9, Table D.
33   121 S.Ct 2053 (2001).
34   Ibid at 2060–2063.

al Statistics Reports, 12 February 2002

decision three years earlier in *Miller v Albright*,[35] and the most interesting facets of the decision are the surprisingly close vote (surprising given the strong, recent precedents for the ruling), and, given the heavy lobbying by feminist scholars to invalidate the law, the fact that both women justices voted in the dissent.

Callendar v Skiles,[36] involved the paternity claim of a man who had sex with a married woman while she was separated from her husband; she became pregnant, then reconciled with her husband who accepted the child when it was born. Blood tests showed that Callendar, the extramarital paramour, was the biological father, and he filed a paternity suit. The Iowa trial court held that under Iowa law Callendar lacked standing to challenge the presumed paternity of the husband, Mr Skiles. In 1999, the Iowa Supreme Court agreed that the statutes excluded Callendar, but ruled that the statutes were unconstitutional because they violated the due process rights and equal protection interests of unwed biological fathers.[37] On remand the Iowa trial court ruled that Callendar was the biological and legal father of the child (then four years old), terminated the parental rights of Mr Skiles (who had raised the child along with the children of the marriage), granted Callendar immediate visitation rights, and ruled that the child should be told that Callendar was her father. Mr and Mrs Skiles appealed, but the Iowa Supreme Court affirmed, except that it delayed the disclosure of paternity to the child until after she started kindergarten. Having radically altered the nature and character of the marital family, it is not a little ironic that the state supreme court tried mightily to emphasize its deference to the autonomy of the family unit, and to characterize the impact of the extremely disruptive judicial rulings as really 'in the best interests' of the child.

Likewise, in *RN v JM*,[38] husband and wife were married in 1992 and are still married. For a few months in 1996 and 1997, the wife was involved in an adulterous affair with RN while she still had sexual relations also with her husband. After the affair ended, the wife gave birth to a child on 17 August 1997, and the child has lived with the wife and husband since birth. RN wanted to establish a relationship with the child, but the wife would not allow him to see her except briefly on two occasions. When the child was about eight months old, RN filed a petition for paternity and testing. The husband and wife opposed, and the trial court held that RN lacked standing to assert paternity. The married couple relied upon the presumption that a child born to a married woman is the child of her husband, and argued that the paternity statute only applied to children born out of wedlock. RN argued that the presumption of paternity was rebuttable. The Supreme Court of Arkansas held, on the basis of statutory construction and under precedents, that the presumption of legitimacy was rebuttable, that the plain language of the statute allowed putative fathers standing to claim paternity, and that putative fathers were defined in other parts of the Arkansas Code simply as men not presumed or determined to be the father but who claim to be the biological father. (The court simply noted this dispositive definition with utterly no consideration or analysis.) The court also reversed the trial court finding that

---

[35]   523 US 420 (1998).
[36]   623 N.W.2d 852 (Iowa 2001).
[37]   *Callendar v Skiles*, 591 N.W.2d 182 (Iowa 1999).
[38]   61 S.W.3d 149 (Ark 2001).

RN was estopped from claiming paternity by waiting nearly nine months; the appellate court did not think the husband had shown misleading conduct by RN or reliance upon RN's failure to claim paternity.

On the other hand, the Texas Supreme Court ruled that an uncontested judicial determination that one man is the father of a child prevents another man from later asserting a paternity claim regarding the same child. In *Texas Dept of Protective and Regulatory Services v Sherry*,[39] Sheila gave birth to a child on 7 January 1992, while she was living with Charlie Cannon. Sheila listed Cannon as the father on the child's birth certificate. Because Sheila had been receiving welfare, the state brought a suit to establish paternity in order to impose child support and seek reimbursement from the father. Cannon agreed to be declared the biological father and filed a statement of paternity. The court declared that Cannon was the father and entered a voluntary child-support order against him. Cannon continued to live with and support the child until Cannon died in January 1995. About nine months later, Sheila and the child (then almost four years old) began living with Charles Sherry. They lived together (except for four months when Sheila was in a drug rehabilitation program and the state took custody of the child and placed her with a neighbor) until Sheila died of a drug overdose in June 1998. The state took the child into protective custody, but the next day, Sherry filed a paternity action and sought to be declared the child's biological sole managing conservator. The trial court held that the former adjudication precluded his paternity claim. The intermediate court of appeals reversed, holding that Sherry had a constitutional right to assert his paternity, but the state supreme court reversed, holding that 'Family Code § 160.007(a)(1) bars a paternity suit "if final judgment has been rendered by a court of competent jurisdiction: (1) adjudicating a named individual to be the biological father of the child"'.[40] Since Sherry's constitutional claims were not raised in the trial court, the supreme court declined to consider them.

Several courts also have protected the presumption of paternity of a husband. In *Fernandez v McKenney*,[41] an intermediate appellate court in Florida held that the presumption that a child born to a married woman is the child of her husband may only be rebutted by 'a clear and compelling reason why the children's best interests would be served by overcoming the presumption'.[42] The divorced mother and her lover had deceived her husband both before and after the divorce into thinking that the two children were the husband's. When the adulterous lover later sought paternity, the lower court granted summary judgment for him, but the appellate court reversed and remanded because the record did not meet the high standard required to overcome the presumption of husband's paternity.[43] Likewise, in *Douglass ex rel Louthian v Boyce*,[44] the South Carolina Supreme Court declared: 'Absent a paternity action, Child remains the presumed legitimate

---

[39]   46 S.W.3d 857 (Tex 2001).

[40]   Ibid at 860.

[41]   776 So.2d 1118 (Fla App, 2001).

[42]   Ibid at 1119.

[43]   But see *Stitham v Henderson*, 768 A.2d 598 (Me 2001).

[44]   542 S.E.2d 715 (SC 2001).

child of [his mother's husband].'[45] The child was suing the lawyers who represented his mother in her divorce for malpractice in failing to name the putative father a party. The lower courts dismissed the claim as did the South Carolina Supreme Court.

In *In re Kiana A*,[46] the intermediate California Court of Appeals also affirmed a Juvenile Court ruling that established paternity on the basis of a presumption and held that the presumption would be enforced, even if there were scientific evidence that another man was the biological father of the child. Kiana A's mother was living with Kevin W when she became pregnant with Kiana A. Initially she told Kevin that he was the father, but five months later when she left Kevin to live with Mario A, she told Kevin that Mario was the real father. For the next 12 years, she made conflicting statements about who was the father. During that time, Kevin was a part of Kiana's life as a father figure, while Mario was never seen. When the mother was arrested, the state took 12-year-old Kiana and her step-sibling into custody alleging general neglect (the mother allegedly was a drug addict, sold drugs, let people use her house for sex, abusively disciplined the children, and a man with whom she lived had allegedly molested Kiana). Kiana then had called Kevin her daddy, asked him to come get her and indicated she wanted to live with him. She and her mother had lived with Kevin for four years, Kiana had stayed with him for other periods, and he had consistently been a part of her life. Upon discovery of Kevin's concealed criminal history, the court had ordered Kiana to be placed in foster care.

Mario had been living with Kiana's mother when Kiana was born, had agreed to have his name put on her birth certificate, had married Kiana's mother two years later, but Mario had been continuously incarcerated for 12 years, since shortly after Kiana's birth. He was soon to be released from prison and wanted to become the father to Kiana. Both Kevin and Mario filed petitions to be declared the presumptive father of Kiana. The juvenile court denied Kevin W's request for genetic testing, found both Kevin W and Mario A were Kiana A's presumed father 'but concluded Kevin W's presumption prevailed over Mario A's because Kiana A had acknowledged Kevin W as her father and Kevin W had received Kiana A into his home'.[47]

On appeal the court of appeals acknowledged that in some circumstances the biological father may be barred from asserting paternity when statutes effectuating public policy favoring family stability so provide. However, 'the resolution of substantive due process attacks upon the ... presumption depends on the circumstances prevailing in each particular case'.[48] In this case two rebuttable statutory presumptions were involved; Mario was the presumed father as a man who married a child's mother after the child's birth and whose name appears with his consent on the child's birth certificate, while Kevin was the presumed father as a man who received a child into his home and acknowledged the child as his natural child. In the case of conflicting presumptions, the California statute directs the court to give priority to the one supported by 'the weightier considerations of

---

[45] Ibid at 717.
[46] 113 Cal.Rptr.2d 669 (Cal App 2001).
[47] Ibid at 674.
[48] Ibid at 675.

policy and logic ...'.[49] The appellate court agreed with the juvenile court that Kevin was entitled to priority because he had been functioning the most like a father. Even if Mario were to establish that he was the biological father, his presumption of paternity would be rebutted in these circumstances. 'The courts have repeatedly held, in applying paternity presumptions, that the extant father–child relationship is to be preserved at the cost of biological ties'. [50]

In *In re Matter of the Adoption of AFM*,[51] the Alaska Supreme Court upheld the application of a statute dispensing with the necessity of consent to adoption from a father whose sexual assault of the mother resulted in the conception of the child being adopted. In this case, following her divorce from David in Alaska, Laura moved to Washington where she had a relationship with Bruce, became pregnant, and ended the relationship. After the child was born, Bruce filed a paternity action, was adjudicated father of the child, and ordered to pay child support, which he did until losing his job. Laura returned to Alaska, remarried David, and David filed to adopt the child arguing that Bruce's consent was not necessary because, *inter alia*, the conception resulted from sexual assault. Bruce responded that such claim was precluded since the Washington court had made 'express finding, during the prior paternity action, that Farley had not sexually assaulted Laura'.[52] The record showed that Laura had raised the issue, been cross-examined about it, and the commissioner had expressly concluded that 'We don't have rape here.'[53] Nonetheless, the Supreme Court of Alaska simply held that the issue of sexual assault had not been 'actually litigated', and badly denied preclusion. The court recounted in great detail Laura's and Farley's account of their tumultuous relationship, and the weak legal analysis in the opinion is probably explained by the court's strong sympathy for the truly compelling story Laura told. Nonetheless, this decision, and the statute it enforces, shows that biological parentage plus a genuine desire to parent and provision of financial support of a child is not sufficient to guarantee that a non-marital biological father will have parental rights. Sometimes countervailing policies outweigh the claims of biological parentage.

In *In re Paternity of Cheryl*,[54] the Massachusetts Supreme Judicial Court ruled that a man who declined blood testing and stipulated that he was the father of a child born to an unmarried woman may not move to set aside a judgment of paternity five years later after genetic tests established that he was not the child's biological father. The trial court had ruled that he could seek relief from a judgment under the 'no longer equitable' exception, but the top court reversed noting that he had visited the child, the mother testified that the child had bonded to him, that his delay in seeking tests had been substantial, the need for finality in paternity judgments, and the potential devastating effects on the child of overturning the paternity order. The gender tilt of this decision, like several others, is notable.

---

[49]   Ibid citing §7612.
[50]   Ibid at 677, citing *Michelle W v Ronald W* 703 P.2d 88 (Cal 1985).
[51]   15 P.3d 258 (Alaska 2001).
[52]   Ibid at 262.
[53]   Ibid at 268.
[54]   746 N.E.2d 488 (Mass 2001).

Finally, a panel of the Ninth Circuit Court of Appeals ruled that an incarcerated felon had a fundamental right to procreate by artificial insemination in *Gerber v Hickman*.[55] Mr Gerber was imprisoned for 100 years to life, plus 11 years. He desired to send sperm to an artificial insemination laboratory so that his wife and he could have a child together. California law prohibits conjugal visits for prisoners sentenced to life or greater punishment, and prison officers denied his request to facilitate artificial insemination. When Mr Gerber filed suit, the federal district court upheld the restriction. But the Ninth Circuit panel reversed, holding: 'that the right to procreate survives incarceration' and includes the right to engage in artificial insemination.[56] The appellate court also determined that there were not legitimate penological justifications for restricting the use of artificial insemination. The dissent, however, suggested:

> 'This is a seminal case in more ways than one. Contrary to all precedent, the majority today holds that a prison inmate – in this instance, an inmate serving a life sentence – has a constitutional right to mail his semen from prison so that his wife can be artificially inseminated. With the utmost respect, the majority's reading of the Constitution is as unprecedented as it is ill-conceived.'[57]

(On rehearing en banc, the following year, the Ninth Circuit agreed with the dissent and held that there is no constitutional right for a prisoner incarcerated for life to engage in artificial insemination).[58]

While the decisions deal with different issues and seem to go in different directions, perhaps the most important phenomenon these cases show is that non-marital parentage is not uncommon and that paternity claims by biological non-marital fathers are increasing but are not always successful. Also, claims by same-sex non-biological parents are increasing. The courts seem to be split concerning whether and when to recognize such claims, reflecting to some extent the differences in the language of the different states' paternity, parentage and adoption statutes, and – sadly for the rule of law – the personal policy preferences of the judges.

C   Abortion and 'male abortion' issues

With the conclusion of the (Democratic Party) Clinton presidency and the inauguration of (Republican) George W Bush as President, in January 2001, the policy of the federal executive branch of government regarding abortion and other prenatal life issues changed significantly. In January, 2001, President Bush issued an executive order to stop taxpayer funding of groups that promote or perform abortions, and the new Secretary of Health and Human Services, Tommy Thompson, announced that the Bush administration would re-evaluate the recent FDA's decision to allow use of the controversial abortion drug RU 486.[59]

---

[55]   264 F.3d 882 (9th Cir 2001), vacated and remanded 291 F.3d 617 (9th Cir 2002).
[56]   Ibid at 884.
[57]   Ibid at 893.
[58]   *Gerber v Hickman*, 291 F.3d 617 (9th Cir 2002).
[59]   Associated Press, *Bush Administration Won't Fund Stem Cell Research,* January 2001 www.prolifeinfo.org/news083.html.

In August 2001, the President announced that he would limit federal funding of stem cell research using stem cells taken from human embryos to 60 existing stem cell lines.[60] The latter decision in particular immediately provoked a lot of criticism and debate about where and how to draw appropriate lines restricting medical research using human embryos or pre-embryos and about human cloning.

The issue of 'male abortion' was raised in *Wallis v Smith*.[61] In that case, it was alleged that Peter began having sexual relations with Kellie upon the express stipulation and condition that she use birth control pills; Peter made clear his desire not to father a child and Kellie agreed to use birth control pills to avoid conception. However, Kellie secretly changed her mind, and quit taking birth control pills without telling Peter. Kellie became pregnant and gave birth to a child. Under state law, Peter would be liable for child support of the child. Peter sued Kellie in a New Mexico state court asserting male abortion claims of breach of contract, contraceptive fraud, conversion, and prima facie tort, and seeking 'compensatory damages for the "economic injury" of supporting a normal, healthy child ...'.[62] The trial court dismissed his claims, and the intermediate appellate court affirmed. The court read the Uniform Parentage Act, adopted in New Mexico, to impose 'a form of strict liability for child support, without regard to which parent bears the greater responsibility for the child's being'.[63] It would violate the public policy making both parents equally responsible for the costs of child-rearing to allow the man to shift his burden onto the woman, even if she practiced fraud and deceit to conceive the child. 'The contract analogy fails because children, the persons for whose benefit child support guidelines are enacted, have the same needs regardless of whether their conception violated a promise between the parents ... Nor will we recognize a cause of action that trivializes one's personal responsibility in sexual relationships.'[64] Thus, relying heavily upon public policy, the court concluded that 'the actions asserted here cannot be used to recoup the financial obligations of raising a child'.[65]

IV   RELATIONS BETWEEN SPOUSES DURING ONGOING MARRIAGE OR QUASI-MARRIAGE

The expansion of marital benefits to non-marital couples, domestic violence laws, and protection of fidelity in marriage were among the leading issues of marital rights and benefits decided in 2001.

---

[60]   BBC News, Bush's stem cell decision: Full text (10 August 2001) *news.bbc.co.uk/hi/english/sci/tech/newsid_i483000/1483579.stm.*

[61]   22 P.3d 682 (NM Ct App 2001).

[62]   Ibid at 683.

[63]   Ibid at 684.

[64]   Ibid at 685.

[65]   Ibid at 686.

A Domestic violence

The imposition of greater penalties for assault upon family members than for assault upon unrelated individuals was upheld by the Idaho Supreme Court in *State v Hart*.[66] Rejecting the equal protection claim of the defendant who had beaten and bruised his wife while drunk, the court explained:

> 'The domestic relationship is a unique relationship. Even when the parties no longer share the relationship the law may impose obligations, such as alimony, child support, or child custody arrangements, which require the parties to continue to interact and to do so on a highly emotional level. Because of the nature of the relationship there is an increased opportunity for violence to occur and continue. The decision of the legislature to extend additional protection to household members is rationally related to the state's interest in preventing violence between those involved in some type of domestic relationship.'[67]

Likewise, the Uniform Interstate Enforcement of Domestic Violence Protection Orders Act,[68] proposed by the National Conference of Commissioners on Uniform State Laws in 2000, was adopted by the first three states (California, Montana and Texas) in 2001. It is intended to provide interstate recognition of orders that generally are only enforced in the states that rendered them.

B Protection of marital fidelity

A husband whose wife had an affair with a co-worker pastor at their church may not recover for intentional infliction of emotional distress, held an Oregon Court of Appeals in *Rosenthal v Erven*.[69] The wife worked at the church she and her family (husband and two children) attended. When the wife and the plaintiff sought marital counselling from the church, the defendant, a pastor employed at the same church, began a sexual relationship with the wife. On learning of the affair, the plaintiff pleaded with the defendant to discourage his wife from continuing the relationship, but the relationship continued for months afterward until the wife learned she was pregnant with the defendant's child and filed for divorce (but the defendant reconciled with his wife). The trial court entered summary judgment for the defendant and the appellate court affirmed. Recovery for intentional infliction of emotional distress can be had only if the defendant engaged in conduct that is an 'extraordinary transgression of the bounds of socially tolerable conduct'.[70] The appellate court feebly opined that adultery is 'unfortunate but not uncommon behavior', and that 'the circumstances here are far from extraordinary. When a marital relationship breaks down, a common cause – or effect – is an extramarital relationship by one or both marital partners. For better or worse, society tolerates extramarital relationships. That is not to say that society condones them, but it is clear from the treatment of such relationships in

---

66   25 P.3d 850 (Idaho 2001).
67   Ibid at 854.
68   9 Uniform Laws Annot, Pt IB (Supp 2002) at 28.
69   17 P.3d 558 (Or Ct App 2001).
70   Ibid at 560.

the entertainment, art, and news media, for example, that society at least tolerates them.'[71] Overlooking the fact that the 'workplace' where the defendant and plaintiff's wife worked was a church, and that the defendant was a pastor there with whom plaintiff pleaded for help,[72] the court found no aggravating factor in the circumstances. The fact that Oregon abolished the torts of criminal conversation and alienation of affections in 1975 best explains the poorly-reasoned decision.

C   Domestic partnership benefits

Irizarry v Board of Education[73] involved a challenge to a Chicago Board of Education policy that extended health benefits from married couples only to same-sex domestic partners, but not to heterosexual domestic partners. Milagros Irizarry, who had lived with the same man out of marriage for over two decades and had two children, challenged the exclusion of heterosexual couples. The Seventh Circuit affirmed a district court judgment dismissing the claim. The school board preference for marriage of heterosexual couples was not irrational because of 'the evidence that on average married couples live longer, are healthier, earn more, have lower rates of substance abuse and mental illness, are less likely to commit suicide, and report higher levels of happiness – that marriage civilizes young males, confers economies of scale and of joint consumption, minimizes sexually transmitted disease, and provides a stable and nourishing framework for child rearing ...'.[74] Moreover, the policy is justified economically because heterosexual non-marital cohabitants 'are much less likely than married couples to pool financial resources, more likely to assume that each partner is responsible for supporting himself or herself financially, more likely to spend free time separately, and less likely to agree on the future of the relationship'.[75] While there was only a 'loose fit' between the purpose of the policy and the 'same-sex' (as opposed to homosexual) means of discrimination,[76] and while 'only nine [Chicago public school] employees out of some 45,000 had signed up for domestic-partner benefits' within the first 18 months after the new policy was implemented,[77] the court declined to second-guess the school officials, and upheld the policy because it was rational.

In *Levin v Yeshiva University*,[78] the New York Court of Appeals held that a lesbian couple stated a valid claim for relief that the Jewish university's housing policy, that gave preference to married couples seeking to live in university housing but not same-sex couples, violated the New York City Civil Rights law

---

[71]   Ibid.

[72]   The trial court found no fiduciary relationship existed between the parties, which is relevant but hardly disposes of the outrageousness of the behavior in the context of a church-based relationship.

[73]   251 F.3d 604 (7th Cir 2001).

[74]   Ibid at 607.

[75]   Ibid at 608.

[76]   Ibid at 610.

[77]   Ibid at 607.

[78]   730 N.Y.S.2d 15 (2001).

prohibiting disparate impact discrimination on the basis of sexual orientation. The court agreed with the lower courts that the plaintiffs' claim of illegal discrimination on the basis of marital status failed to state a claim for relief under either state or city civil rights law. Rather woodenly, the court found that married couples and lesbian and other cohabiting couples are essentially indistinguishable in terms of the purposes of university housing.[79]

V RELATIONS BETWEEN PARENT–CHILD DURING ONGOING FAMILY OR QUASI-FAMILY RELATIONSHIP

A Domestic violence

Many of the cases arising in the context of ongoing parent–child relations involve juvenile court determinations of juvenile delinquency (criminal behavior by a minor) and child abuse, neglect or dependency. Juvenile court cases will not be reviewed in this chapter, but it is worth noting that removal of children from their parents and termination of parental rights often involve cases of another form of domestic violence, namely child abuse.

A civil protective order to prevent 'granny-bashing' was involved in *Turner v Lewis*.[80] In that case, the paternal grandmother had custody of her son's child; the parents of the ten-year-old had never married. After an incident in which the visiting mother repeatedly struck the grandmother, she sought and obtained an emergency protective order by one judge, but another judge refused to extend it finding that the paternal grandmother was not related by blood or marriage to the mother of the child who had struck her, so the domestic violence law did not cover violence inflicted by her grandchild's mother. The Massachusetts Supreme Judicial Court vacated and remanded, holding that since the paternal grandmother was related by blood to the child and the child was related by blood to the mother, the mother and paternal grandmother were related by blood through the child. This strained interpretation was consistent with the purpose of the act to prevent violence among those with a family connection, so the court found that the paternal grandmother was a member of the class of persons for whom the statute was created and was entitled to the protective order.

B Parental immunity

Parental immunity was involved in two interesting state high court decisions. In *Bushy v Northern Assurance Co. of America*,[81] parents lost two daughters in a car accident that occurred while their oldest daughter was driving her grandfather's car. The parents sued the estate of the oldest daughter (the driver) for wrongful death of the other daughter. The insurance company argued that the claim was barred by the parent–child immunity doctrine. The trial and Special Court of

---

[79]   730 N.Y.S.2d at 20–22.
[80]   749 N.E.2d 122 (Mass 2001).
[81]   766 A.2d 598 (Md 2001).

Appeals agreed, but the Maryland Court of Appeals held otherwise, and while refusing to abrogate entirely the parent–child immunity doctrine, held that parent–child immunity did not bar the parents' claim against the estate of the older daughter, because with both daughters deceased the parent–child relationship would not be impaired, there was no increased risk of fraud and collusion, and there was no risk that the award would exceed the available coverage.

Likewise, the Florida Supreme Court held that parent–child immunity did not bar a young man from suing his adoptive father for repeated sexual abuse in *Herzfeld v Herzfeld*.[82] The trial court held that parental immunity barred the claims, but the district court of appeals reversed, and the Florida Supreme Court agreed that the immunity doctrine did not apply because the policies underlying the doctrine were insufficient to extend the doctrine to bar plaintiff's intentional sexual tort claims. Familial discord or dysfunction obviously existed if the alleged parental sexual abuse occurred. Therefore, the purpose of the preservation of family harmony did not justify immunity to alleged sexual abuse of the plaintiff by the defendant. Since the parental immunity doctrine was judicially created, the court had the authority to modify it.

C Grandparent visitation

In *State Dep't of Social and Rehab Serv v Paillet*,[83] an unmarried male was adjudicated the father of a child born out of wedlock to a woman. A short time later he died and his parents sought visitation under the Kansas Grandparent Visitation statute. The trial court found that visitation would be in the best interests of the child and awarded them visitation one weekend per month. The intermediate appellate court affirmed. The Kansas Supreme Court reversed, ruling that the mother had a constitutional right to determine who may visit her children and there was no finding that showed the mother was not a fit parent nor unable to act in the best interest of the child. Citing the US Supreme Court decision in *Troxel*,[84] the Kansas Supreme Court held that the Kansas Grandparent Visitation statute was unconstitutional as applied in this case. Other state courts also found in 2001 that their Grandparent Visitation statutes were unconstitutional under *Troxel*.[85]

On the other hand, in *State ex rel Brandon L v Moats*,[86] the West Virginia Supreme Court held that its grandparent visitation statute was not unconstitutional. A child's paternal grandparents had supervised visitation with their divorced son and his child for over two years. After the child's mother remarried and her new husband adopted the child, she informed the grandparents that their visitation with the child was terminated. When the grandparents filed for grandparent visitation, the mother sought a writ of prohibition to prevent the hearing on grounds that the Grandparent Visitation statute was unconstitutional. The statute requires that

---

[82]   781 So. 2d 1070 (Fl 2001).

[83]   16 P.3d 962 (Kan 2001).

[84]   *Troxel v Granville*, 530 US 57 (2000).

[85]   See, eg *Punsly v Ho*, 105 Cal Rptr 2d 129 (Ct App 2001); *Belair v Drew*, 776 So.2d 1105 (Fla Dist Ct App 2001); *Langman v Langman*, 757 N.E.2d 505 (Ill App 2001).

[86]   551 S.E.2d 674 (W Va 2001).

grandparents demonstrate that visitation is in the best interest of the child and will not interfere with the parent–child relationship. The state supreme court concluded that the law avoids those constitutional concerns that had troubled the US Supreme Court in *Troxel* and upheld the statute. Other courts have likewise upheld other states' grandparent visitation statutes in 2001.[87] While there is no more precision in the state post-*Troxel* grandparent visitation cases than there was in the Supreme Court decision in *Troxel*, it is clear that a mere 'best interests of the child' standard for awarding grandparent visitation, that does not give a presumption in favor of the exercise of parental discretion, probably will not survive judicial scrutiny.

VI DISSOLUTION OF MARITAL OR QUASI-MARITAL RELATIONSHIP AND POST-DISSOLUTION RELATIONS

A ERISA

The Supreme Court of the United States emphasized the supremacy of federal retirement benefits law over conflicting state family law in *Egelhoff v Egelhoff*.[88] At issue was a Washington statute that automatically revoked upon divorce an employee's designation of a former spouse as beneficiary of an employee benefit plan. A man was divorced and in the decree was awarded his pension, but he failed to change the beneficiary designation before he died intestate two months later. His children from a prior marriage sued arguing that the benefits should go to them under the state statute that treated the ex-wife as predeceasing the husband, and the state courts agreed. The US Supreme Court reversed holding that the state law directly conflicted with and was pre-empted by the federal law – ERISA. The majority opinion (per Thomas) noted:

> '[R]espondents emphasize that the Washington statute involves both family law and probate law, areas of traditional state regulation. There is indeed a presumption against pre-emption in areas of traditional state regulation such as family law. See, eg *Hisquierdo v Hisquierdo*, 439 US 572, 581(1979). But that presumption can be overcome where, as here, Congress has made clear its desire for pre-emption. Accordingly, we have not hesitated to find state family law pre-empted when it conflicts with ERISA or relates to ERISA plans. See, eg *Boggs v Boggs*, 520 US 833 (1997) (holding that ERISA pre-empts a state community property law permitting the testamentary transfer of an interest in a spouse's pension plan benefits).'[89]

B Protection against violence

Violence between hostile ex-lovers and ex-spouses continues to receive attention. In a Vermont case, *Benson v Muscari*,[90] the imposition of a 1,000-foot buffer

---

[87] See, eg *Lilley v Lilley*, 43 S.W.3d 703 (Tex Ct App 2001); see also *Scott v Scott*, 19 P.3d 273 (Okla 2001) (distinguishing modification of visitation order).

[88] 532 US 141 (2001).

[89] Ibid at 151–152.

[90] 769 A.2d 1291 (Vt 2001).

zone, ordering a man to stay away from a woman with whom he had had a long non-marital sexual relationship, but whom he had severely beaten after finding her with another man, and ordering him to stay away from her child also for five years, was upheld. However, the restriction against the restaurateur possessing any dangerous weapons was vague and needed to be clarified by the trial court.

When the genders are reversed, courts often take a more tolerant approach. For example, in *Jeffers v Jeffers*,[91] an Ohio appellate court reversed in part the contempt order entered against an ex-wife. Upon divorce, the husband had obtained a protective order preventing any harassment by the wife of her ex-husband or his new wife. On the night of his retirement party, the ex-wife tried to 'crash' his retirement party at the Moose lodge, but never made any contact with him or his new wife because the lodge officials and party hosts turned her away (despite her 20-minute persistence). The court found that since no direct contact had been made she could not have 'harassed' her ex-husband, evading the question whether harassment can occur vicariously, by acts and comments made in the next room and conveyed to the ex-husband by others reporting her disruptive behavior.

The possibility of recovering damages for domestic violence was affirmed by the Wyoming Supreme Court in *McChulloch v Drake*.[92] The parties had endured a turbulent three-and-one-half-year marriage. The wife claimed that during the marriage the husband had repeatedly physically and sexually abused her, and shortly after filing for divorce she filed a tort claim for intentional infliction of emotional distress. The divorce and tort claims were consolidated and, while rejecting most of the tort claims, the trial judge 'found that the wife did prove a tort occurred in September of 1997 when the husband briefly held a pillow over her face and concluded that, although she did not currently suffer a disability, there was some proof she suffered emotional distress as a result of the incident. Accordingly, the trial court awarded damages of $4,250 and $750 in punitive damages …'.[93] Over the husband's objection that both no-fault divorce and spousal immunity principles barred such a claim, the Wyoming Supreme Court held that a cause of action for intentional infliction of emotional distress that occurred during marriage will lie, but only if the conduct was 'extreme and outrageous' and exceeded 'all possible bounds of decency.'[94] It was an error to join the tort claim (a jury claim) with the divorce claim (a non-jury claim). The statute of limitations for sexual tort claims was four years.

C Palimony for terminated heterosexual and homosexual partnerships

As noted earlier, courts apply similar principles to 'palimony' claims based on oral contracts as they do to claims upon marriage dissolution based on written premarital contracts.[95] However, some courts are reaching further and further to protect economic sharing by non-marital cohabitants. For example, in *Cochran v*

---

[91] 2001 WL 118530 (Ohio Ct App 13 February 2001).
[92] 24 P.3d 1162 (Wyo 2001).
[93] Ibid at 1166.
[94] Ibid at 1169.
[95] See *Della Zoppa* case review, *supra* note 14 and accompanying text.

Cochran,[96] a California appellate court held that an allegation that the parties had shared a stable, long-term relationship living together from two to four days per week was sufficient to state a valid palimony claim.[97] The defendant was the famous OJ Simpson murder trial lawyer, Johnnie L Cochran, Jr, who began a relationship with the plaintiff while he was still married to another woman. The relationship allegedly lasted 17 years, produced a child they both were raising, she took his last name, he held himself out as her husband, and provided her with maintenance, cars, clothes, money and a home, where he stayed two to four nights per week. After she learned of his infidelity, they signed a property settlement agreement and she alleged that he later orally promised to provide for her "'financially, emotionally and legally" for the rest of her life' if she would maintain their home, and care for him and their son as before.[98] Mr Cochran argued that the alleged palimony agreement was invalid because the parties never cohabited permanently. The court reviewed precedents and held that a 'less than full-time' arrangement can constitute cohabitation for purposes of palimony claims.

In *Northrop v Northrop*,[99] the North Dakota Supreme Court ruled that property accumulated during seven years of premarital cohabitation was marital property for purposes of property division following the dissolution of the couple's one and one-half year marriage. The parties had five children and purchased a house before marrying. The lower court divided the property on the basis of the short marriage, but the state supreme court reversed and remanded, noting: 'When parties live together and then marry it is appropriate for the court to consider all of the their time together in dividing the marital property.'[100]

On the other hand, an intermediate appellate court in North Carolina in *Glaspy v Glaspy*,[101] held that real property acquired during cohabitation prior to marriage with the intention that it be shared and titled in both names (as unmarried persons) was not transmuted into marital property upon marriage, even though a home had been purchased with the intent that it would become the marital residence. The trial court had ruled that it was marital property, imposed a constructive trust, and ordered the wife to convey her interest to the husband, who had furnished the bulk of the payments toward purchase. The appellate court reversed holding to the state's established rule that property acquired before marriage, even while cohabiting, is separate property and not transmuted into marital property upon marriage, and holding that there was insufficient evidence to support imposition of a constructive trust.

In *Vasquez v Hawthorne*,[102] the Washington Supreme Court indicated that same-sex partners may be able to recover palimony under Washington's meretricious relationship doctrine. Vasquez claimed that he and Schwerzler had been same-sex partners for 28 years. After Schwerzler died, Vasquez filed a claim

---

[96]   106 Cal Rptr 2d 899 (Ct App 2001).

[97]   Ibid at 906.

[98]   Ibid at 903.

[99]   622 N.W.2d 219 (ND 2001).

[100]   Ibid at 222, quoting *Kautzman v Kautzman*, 585 N.W.2d 561, ¶13 (ND 1998) quoting *Nelson v Nelson*, 584 N.W.2d 527, ¶7 (ND 1998).

[101]   545 S.E.2d 782 (NC Ct App 2001).

[102]   33 P.3d 735 (Wash 2001).

against the estate seeking an equitable share of the property. When it was denied by the personal representative, Vasquez filed suit claiming that he and Schwerzler had a meretricious relationship which, under Washington law, provides a claim to share in the property acquired by the partner. The estate argued that Vasquez was not a meretricious partner of Schwerzler's but only a handyman. The trial court granted summary judgment for Vasquez, but the intermediate court of appeals reversed on the ground that a relationship cannot be 'meretricious' unless the parties could marry and since same-sex couples cannot marry same-sex couples cannot have a meretricious relationship. The state supreme court reversed, vacated and remanded, finding the record inadequate to support either the trial court summary judgment or the court of appeals ruling on the question of law. Without deciding the legal issue, the court indicated that same-sex couples can recover under the meretricious relationship doctrine because '[e]quitable claims are not dependent on the "legality" of the relationship between the parties, nor are they limited by the gender or sexual orientation of the parties ... [E]quitable claims must be analyzed under the specific facts presented in each case'.[103] However, one concurring judge noted the significant distinction between the case at bar and the previous meretricious marriage cases – the fact that the parties were of the same sex – and criticized the majority for 'avoid[ing] any meaningful discussion of this issue ...'[104] He opined that same-sex couples cannot claim under the meretricious relationship doctrine because ability to marry has been a required factor and because to rule otherwise would defeat the purpose of the doctrine in several ways.

VII TERMINATION OF PARENTAL OR QUASI-PARENTAL RELATIONSHIP AND POST-DISSOLUTION PARENT–CHILD RELATIONS

A   Disposition of cryo-preserved pre-embryos

In *JB v MB*,[105] the New Jersey Supreme Court held that a divorced woman's desire to destroy frozen pre-embryos outweighed the ex-husband's wish to donate them to an infertile couple. During marriage, when the couple learned that the wife could not naturally conceive but might bear children through IVF, they had 11 IVF pre-embryos created, four were implanted (resulting in a pregnancy and birth) and seven were cryo-preserved. When the wife filed for divorce, she sought to have these frozen pre-embryos discarded. The husband wished to have them donated for implantation for infertile couples. The parties disputed whether they had agreed to such a donation. Since the husband was still able to procreate, the trial and intermediate appellate court ruled that the wife's interest in destroying the pre-embryos was paramount. The state supreme court agreed. It began by stating that the agreement of the parties would control. The IVF clinic agreement that the parties signed provided that in the event of divorce, the frozen

---

[103]   Ibid at 737–738.
[104]   Ibid at 739, Sanders, J, concurring.
[105]   783 A.2d 707 (NJ 2001).

pre-embryos would be donated to the clinic unless a court ordered otherwise. That exception gave the court the opportunity to decline to follow the parties' agreement despite its solemn insistence that it preferred contractual resolution of such issues. It adopted a policy preferring non-procreation over procreation.[106] Granting the wife's wish not to procreate would not extinguish the fertile husband's right to procreate, but the wife's 'fundamental right not to procreate is irrevocably extinguished if a surrogate mother bears [wife's] child. We will not force [wife] to become a biological parent against her will.'[107] It adopted as the state rule 'to enforce agreements entered into at the time in vitro fertilization is begun, subject to the right of either party to change his or her mind about disposition up to the point of use or destruction of any stored preembryos'.[108] The opinion was excessively long with little redeeming persuasive effect.

B Former partners of parents

In *TB v LRM*, 786 A.2d 913 (Pa 2001), the Pennsylvania Supreme Court ruled that a former lesbian partner had standing to seek custody and visitation of a child conceived through artificial insemination by her former partner and raised by both women for nearly three years. The mother and her lesbian partner allegedly decided that the former would have a child for the couple. The mother was artificially inseminated and bore a child, while supported by the lesbian partner. They lived together and both acted as parents and raised the child for approximately three years. After the lesbian partner left the biological mother for another woman, the ex-partner sued for joint legal custody, partial custody and visitation rights. The lower state courts held that the unrelated ex-partner had standing *in loco parentis* to seek custody and visitation, and the Pennsylvania Supreme Court agreed. Although the legislature has not recognized the parental rights of former non-marital partners of biological parents, the common law doctrine of *in loco parentis* has not been repealed and in appropriate cases it may cover former partners. An unrelated adult stands *in loco parentis* if he or she has assumed and discharged parental responsibilities.[109] Even if the former partner may not adopt, that does not prevent her from obtaining custody and visitation. While a mere caretaker does not stand *in loco parentis*, the fact-finder determined that the ex-partner was more than a mere caretaker. The court distinguished *Troxel v Granville*,[110] in which the US Supreme Court invalidated a Washington grandparent visitation statute, because the issue before the Pennsylvania Supreme Court was only whether the ex-partner had standing, not the merits. Two dissenters argued that the majority had ignored the custody and visitation statutes, and that the common law *in loco parentis* doctrine historically had been limited to persons with legal-family ties, such as blood relatives or step-parents of the child.

---

[106] Ibid at 717.
[107] Ibid.
[108] Ibid at 719.
[109] Ibid at 916–917.
[110] 530 US 57 (2000).

Similarly, in *Hollon v Hollon*,[111] after separating from her husband, the wife had a female friend move in with her to share expenses and childcare and sleep with her. The husband alleged that the wife was having a homosexual relationship, and sought custody of his young son, who had been living with the wife. The trial court awarded custody to father, placing great weight on the alleged homosexual relationship. On appeal, the Mississippi Supreme Court reversed, with a plurality finding that the trial court had placed too much weight on the 'moral fitness' custody factor and had not adequately considered all other factors. A majority found that most of the custody factors weighed in the wife's favor. Seven justices (three dissenting, four concurring in a separate opinion) disagreed with the dicta about too much emphasis being placed on the 'moral fitness' factor; the concurring plurality justices noting that because the ex-wife had terminated her room-sharing arrangement with her female friend she should keep custody, while the dissenters noted her suborning perjury and lack of credibility in indicating they would give custody to the father.[112]

In *State ex rel DRM v Wood*,[113] Kelly and Tracy lived as lesbian partners for three years, during which time they decided that Kelly would be artificially inseminated and Tracy would adopt the child. The parties separated after Kelly was pregnant but before either of them realized it. Tracy agreed in writing still to support and adopt the child. After the child was born, Kelly restricted Tracy's contact with the child, and Tracy stopped making support payments. Kelly sought state welfare and the state filed suit against Tracy for child support. Kelly also sued Tracy for enforcement of the support agreement she had signed. The trial court ruled against both claims and the intermediate appellate court affirmed, holding that since Tracy was neither a biological or adoptive parent, the Uniform Parentage Act did not provide any basis for a support obligation, that under the UPA a child did not have to have two parents, denied that the UPA violated equal protection (because an unrelated male boyfriend would be treated the same way as Tracy), held that there was no statutory basis for an independent duty of support apart from the UPA, and ruled that creation of a new cause of action for such a support duty was unjustified. Neither the state nor Kelly could rely either on contract estoppel theory to force Tracy to make support payments as Kelly had frustrated any attempts by the domestic partner to see or adopt the child.

C Challenging paternity upon or after divorce

In *State ex rel West v Floyd*,[114] the wife had an affair during marriage and became pregnant. She thought her adulterous lover was the father. Her husband found out and filed for divorce, and they stipulated that he was not the father of the unborn child and had no visitation or support obligation. She married her paramour, gave birth, and they later divorced. Later, blood tests excluded the paramour-second husband as the father of the child. The state petitioned to set aside the divorce

---

[111]   784 So. 2d 943 (Miss 2001).

[112]   Ibid at 952 (Wallers concurring in separate written opinion joined by Banks, Smith and Cobb); ibid (McRae dissenting joined by Mills and Easley).

[113]   34 P.3d 887 (Wash App 2001).

[114]   2001 WL 356274 (Tenn Ct App, 11 April 2001).

decree and to impose a child support obligation on the first husband, who objected, and the Chancellor denied the motion to set aside the judgment citing the untruthfulness of the mother. The court of appeals reversed, holding that a private agreement incorporated into a divorce agreement that relieves a parent of child support duty is void against public policy.

VIII CONCLUSION

Most of the cases reviewed above have been selected because they indicate where 'new' doctrines are developing. They identify the 'fringes' or 'borders' of contemporary family law. Fortunately, the great bulk of family law in America is not yet on the fringes, and these cases ought not to be seen as representing the majority of family law cases or doctrine in the United States. Nevertheless, to some extent these cases may be seen as a harbinger of family law in the future.

American family court developments in 2001 show that the traditional 'bright lines' defining and protecting family relations are fast disappearing. The levelling desire to treat equally all relations of intimacy is erasing the boundaries of the family and making family law much less predictable and reliable. The trend is far from uniform but it seems to be growing. In particular, issues concerning paternity of children born out of wedlock are many and the decisions are inconsistent. In a quest for fairness and equivalence for parties to informal relations of intimacy, the values of predictability, certainty, and finality in the best interests of children seem to have been lost. While judges are not responsible for the irresponsible, unstable, tragic and sordid situations that parties bring into court, they are responsible for protecting the rule of law which protects families and family relations much better in the long run than discretionary judgments reflecting subjective notions of dubious equivalence of informal relations.

YUGOSLAVIA

MAINTENANCE DUTIES OF PARENTS TOWARDS CHILDREN

*Olga Cvejic Jancic**

I INTRODUCTION

The maintenance duty between parents and children is regulated by the Marriage and Family Relations Act of Serbia (1980) and the Family Act of Montenegro (1989).

Parents are obliged to maintain their minor children,[1] whether legitimate or illegitimate. Parents contribute to the maintenance of children according to their capabilities, so that the contribution of both parents need not be the same if their resource capabilities are not the same. Exceptionally, the maintenance of children may also be prolonged after majority (which is acquired at 18) up to the end of schooling, provided that the child is continuing his schooling, but at the latest up to the age of 26. Parental rights, which as a rule expire when the child attains majority, are not extended alongside the duty to maintain.

The question of the maintenance of minor children (whether legitimate or illegitimate) does not arise if the parents live in a family union with their children, because the needs related to the maintenance of the child are satisfied by spontaneous spending within the framework of the family household. Only if the parents separate or divorce occurs, will the question of a contribution to the maintenance of the child by the parent with whom the child is not living arise.

In that event, parents may agree on the maintenance of children and, if they cannot reach agreement, the court is always competent to decide.[2]

II RULES OF PROCEDURE IN PROCEEDINGS FOR MAINTENANCE OF MINOR CHILDREN

If there is no agreement between parents on the maintenance of children, the court will decide on maintenance in a special procedure, or in a procedure for divorce or for marriage annulment. The agreement of parents on maintenance can also be reached and presented in judicial proceedings, and it is even favoured in several provisions, but the court is not obliged to accept the parents' arrangement if it

---

*   Head of Civil Law Department, Faculty of Law, University of Novi Sad.

[1]   This is also in relation to children who have attained majority over whom the parents' duty has been extended.

[2]   There is only one exception. In the case of termination of adoption *non plena*, the guardianship authority takes the decision on maintenance of the adopted person or adopter after termination of adoption (Art 179 of the Marriage and Family Relations Act).

establishes that it is not in accordance with the provisions of the Act on maintenance determination. The court may decide on maintenance which is different from that agreed, if the interests of the child require this.

The court is authorised to adjudicate ex officio on the maintenance of children in marital, paternal or maternal proceedings, regardless of whether the action has been commenced by parents.

If the court, in the proceedings for maintenance of children, establishes that parents have neither individually nor together the resources to ensure the maintenance of a minor child, it is obliged to advise the guardianship authority, which may, in the name of the minor child, extend the suit for maintenance to the relatives who are by statute obliged to maintain him or her (brothers, sisters, grandfathers, grandmothers). These persons may not object to the extension of the action.

The extension may be demanded by the parents or the child's guardian.

If it is established in this further procedure that the other relatives are also not able to provide for maintenance of the child, the guardianship authority must take steps to obtain maintenance in accordance with the social security regulations.

Our law provides for the establishment of so-called alimony funds, for the purpose of a statutory maintenance arrangement, through a pooling of resources, intended for social security, but this provision of family law does not make establishment of these funds compulsory. The importance of this fund has not diminished but its effectiveness has been limited by the general economic crisis in our country from which the family is not exempt. Establishment of alimony funds would represent an important step towards society's acceptance of the burdens of biological reproduction, and the resources could be provided not only by the budget, but also by sponsorship of large companies, by lotteries and in other ways. This would be subject to seeking reimbursement of the amount paid from those liable in law to support the child. The funds would effectively bear the costs of maintenance in a small number of cases, only when maintenance could not be provided by parents and other relatives, where maintenance would be covered by the resources intended for social security. The proposal of the working group for the drafting of the new Family Act is that the idea of establishing alimony funds is to be supported.

The court may ex officio make provisional measures for maintenance of children in all judicial proceedings where maintenance of minor children is to be determined. However, this provisional measure is granted in practice only on the explicit request of the parent with whom the child lives.

III DETERMINATION OF THE EXTENT OF MAINTENANCE CONTRIBUTION

The essential criteria on which the level of maintenance contributions are based are the creditor's needs and the debtor's capabilities. The court is obliged, starting from these criteria, to determine the total amount of resources required for maintenance. The court should, in this process, take account of the circumstances of each case, and especially the following: the resources of the claimant, the degree of his or her work capacity, possibilities for employment, state of health of the person asking for maintenance, the child's age, needs for vocational training, and any other circumstances that might be relevant for adjudication.

The needs of individual persons are different and depend on a range of factors. Only some of them are cited in the Act. The needs of a pre-school age child and those of a child engaged in education, vocational training, and so on, are essentially different.

The capabilities of the person liable to maintain will be taken into account in the process of determination of the extent of the maintenance contribution, as this is also in the final instance a limiting factor. In the evaluation of his capabilities the court should primarily take into account all permanent monthly and other income, his actual capabilities of earning a salary (eg supplementary work), his own needs, and any duty to maintain which he has towards other persons.

If a case is about the maintenance of minor children, the court particularly takes into account the work and contribution of the parent to whom a child is entrusted for custody and upbringing, and which he is investing through everyday guardianship, care and raising of the child.

Maintenance is principally expressed in terms of money. Very rarely maintenance is fixed in some other way (eg allocation of part of the assets for use, allowances in naturam, etc). This will be the case only when a maintenance debtor and creditor agree on a different form of maintenance provision, or when the debtor is not able to provide maintenance in money, but can provide it in naturam or in some other way.

Until 1993 the maintenance contribution was determined by a set figure. However, inflation in this country, which began after the break-up of the federal state, had led to a drastic devaluation, and during 1992 and 1993 reached such levels that the contribution set by a court award was very quickly eroded.[3] In fact, during a single day, money was losing so much value, that the amount could differ depending on whether you received your salary in the morning, or at the end of working day; therefore it could become important for you to get your salary a day earlier or later. That which could be bought in the morning for certain amount of money, by the afternoon was already devalued by over 50%. Henceforth, statutory provisions governing maintenance contributions were amended in March 1993 and percentages of the payer's salary were introduced in order to improve to some extent the claimant's position.

It was foreseen by the amended provisions that the maintenance contribution could not be less than 15% of the payer's permanent monthly income (ie of the salary or pension), nor more than 50%. The court in each case evaluates the claimant's needs and the payer's capabilities and, on the basis of that, within the lower and higher percentage limits, determines the percentage for maintenance in concreto.

However, these percentages are applied only if the payer is employed or is a pension beneficiary or has any other fixed monthly income. If this is not the case, ie if the person in question has no fixed monthly income (eg attorneys-at-law, doctors with a private practice, architects with private projects, farmers, craftsmen

---

[3]   As an example, an award of the Municipal Court of Para cited in (P 231/93 of 14 September 1993) of costs in divorce proceedings amounted to former 24,637,500,000 dinars, which was by then worth almost nothing.

and other private sector professionals) then, as a basis for maintenance contributions, the percentage is the amount of the guaranteed wage[4] in the Republic for the preceding month.

In this case the court is not bound by the lower limit of 15%, nor by the higher limit of 50% of the amount of the guaranteed, ie the lowest, wage in the Republic for the preceding month. The guaranteed wage serves only as a basis from which the percentage is determined and, if the capabilities of the payer enable it, the maintenance contribution can be fixed at 100% or more than 100% of the guaranteed wage in the Republic for the preceding month.

In our judicial practice, maintenance contributions determined in percentages are not readily applied if the payer has no permanent monthly income, ie where the percentage should be determined on the basis of the guaranteed wage, since in that case the monthly maintenance contribution would be very small. The courts then resort to a determination expressed in a fixed pecuniary amount,[5] and not in percentages of guaranteed salary, for in those cases neither the higher nor lower percentage can be ascertained.

However, in the year 2001 the provisions concerning the maintenance contribution were amended[6] and now the maintenance contribution cannot be less than 7% of the payer's monthly income or minimal wage, nor more than 22%. Where the payer is a pension beneficiary, or has any other permanent monthly income, these percentages are the same as in the amended Act of 1993 (15%–50%).

According to the Family Act of Montenegro, the maintenance contribution is also determined by the percentage of salary, ie the income of the payer, but the percentage is not set by the Act. Rather the court determines this in accordance with specific rules.

Another problem has appeared in judicial practice. This is where the payer has several maintenance duties towards different claimants, so that the limit of 50% of his salary or pension can be exceeded by the discharge of his duties towards them. For example, in a decision of the Supreme Court of Serbia, awards of the court of first instance and of the court of second instance were annulled, by which the payer was obliged to maintain his former spouse to the extent of 30% of his pension, which together with an earlier award of 40% of his pension for maintenance of his parents, made up 70% and exceeded the maximum 50% of his income, which could be available for fixed maintenance.[7] The Supreme Court of Serbia has decided in such cases that the plaintiff should extend the suit to the persons who, on the basis of a legally binding award, already established a maintenance right from the same payer. This is in order to establish all relevant facts, and particularly the payer's capabilities and the needs of all maintained

---

[4] The guaranteed wage is the minimum monthly wage which an employed person can receive. No wage must be lower than the guaranteed wage.

[5] Eg, an award of the Supreme Court of Serbia, Rev br 3165/95 of 19 July 1995 and an award of the Supreme Court of Serbia Gzz-105/96 of 15 October 1996.

[6] Official Herald of the Republic of Serbia No 29/2001.

[7] After the Enforcement Procedure Act (*Official Gazette of SFR Yugoslavia*, No 28/2000) debt enforcement on the salary or pension, where the debt is concerned with maintenance, can be executed up to the limit of one half of the salary or pension (Art 87).

persons, in order that the payer would be obliged by a single assessment to pay maintenance towards all maintained persons.[8]

This position of the Supreme Court of Serbia is not correct and will lead to unnecessary litigation and will require the earlier claimant to participate unnecessarily in fresh judicial proceedings. The payer's protection, ie a guarantee that 50% of his salary or pension will be reserved for his own needs and will be exempted from debt enforcement, is provided by the Enforcement Procedure Act (EPA). In accordance with Art 115 of the EPA in the aforesaid case, there is a proportional decrease of the claims of all claimants for statutory maintenance against him. The court will make a new enforcement award by which it will modify the earlier award and will determine the amount which will in the future be paid to the individual claimants. The new enforcement award will also be made known to the former payer, who has a right to appeal against it.

By these provisions the EPA has fully eliminated the need for bringing new proceedings against former maintenance payers, as their maintenance percentage will be decreased in enforcement proceedings by the new award of the enforcement court. The aforesaid award of the Supreme Court of Serbia is therefore absolutely incorrect.

IV   THE GUARDIANSHIP AUTHORITY'S ROLE IN THE REALISATION OF THE MAINTENANCE CLAIM

The Act in certain respects provides regulations to enable a minor to receive a maintenance claim more easily.

(1)   First, for the sake of the fuller protection of minor children, the Act authorises the guardianship authority, in the name of a minor child, to initiate and pursue a maintenance action, ie litigation for a maintenance increase against a parent, if the parent to whom the child is entrusted for custodianship and upbringing does not pursue the claim without good reason (Art 312/1 of the Marriage and Family Relations Act).

This happens where the parent with whom the child lives does not ask for maintenance or a maintenance increase from the other parent by reason of ignorance or lack of action, even though the conditions required by the Act are met. Consequently the child's position deteriorates below the standard of living the child could expect if that parent adequately contributed to his maintenance.

It is emphasised in the Act that the guardianship authority may intervene for the child's protection only if the parent for unjustified reasons does not pursue this right in the name of child. In addition to ignorance and lack of action, an unjustified reason would also include fear of violence of the other parent because of the initiation of maintenance proceedings. In the case of a propensity for violent behaviour on the part of the other parent, it is much better that the parent does not participate in the proceedings before the court, ie that the guardianship authority represents child in the proceedings.

---

[8]   Award of the Supreme Court of Serbia, Rev br 5387/94 of 9 November 1994.

If, on the other hand, the parent has justifiable reasons for not claiming maintenance from the other parent, the guardianship authority must respect them.

(2) If there is a legally binding and enforceable maintenance award, and the payer does not comply with it, the guardianship authority may seek to enforce it for the benefit of the child (Art 312/2 of the Marriage and Family Relations Act). This amounts to very important judicial assistance of the guardianship authority in the realisation of the child's maintenance right neglected by the unscrupulous and negligent parent. Where the parent with whom the child lives most often, for unjustified, subjective reasons does not claim maintenance from the other parent, this authorisation of the guardianship authority represents a significant measure for the social and legal protection of minor children.

(3) The guardianship authority also has other duties with the aim of a more efficient realisation of the maintenance duty between parents and children. Henceforth, it is obliged:

   (a) to keep a register of maintained children and parents and maintenance payers;

   (b) to undertake measures to facilitate agreement on child maintenance out of court;

   (c) to undertake measures to facilitate parental agreement on maintenance contributions out of court to take account of the modified needs of the child and the parents' capabilities.

(4) Furthermore, the guardianship authority can undertake measures to provide the child with provisional maintenance in accordance with regulations until the parent starts to fulfil his duty, where that parent, who is obliged to pay maintenance, does not discharge his duty regularly. This provision represents an attempt to transfer partly the reproduction burden to society for the sake of children and family protection, but unfortunately it can be said that it has no wider application in practice. The guardianship authority lacks sufficient resources even for the execution of its other activities, so this otherwise very good idea has not as yet produced results.

(5) Finally, in maintenance proceedings the guardianship authority is obliged at the court's request to collect all data relevant to maintenance decision-making. This data is related first to the payer's resources, and to the claimant's needs. In this respect, the guardianship authority's assistance can be very valuable, particularly if the payer hides the real facts, or fails to provide maintenance.

V   OTHER RULES FOR THE REALISATION OF THE STATUTORY RIGHT TO MAINTENANCE

For the purpose of protection of the payer, the Act also foresees another measure: that is the duty of the employer, where the payer is employed, to furnish data on the existence of the duty, in a case where his employment is terminated with that employer, to the new employer where he has obtained employment, if this data is available to him.

The new employer is obliged to advise on the change of employment, and to provide details of the parent to whom another parent pays, on the basis of a court award of maintenance for the child, so that the giving and receiving of the maintenance may continue without obstacles.

If the former employer (where the payer's employment has terminated) does not know where the debtor has obtained employment, he is obliged to advise the court immediately of that fact, and the court will advise the claimant who should, within a certain period, furnish the court with the data on the new employment of the payer. If the claimant does not know where the payer has obtained employment, the court will suspend enforcement.

This protection measure is directed to the prevention of evasion of the statutory maintenance duty through very frequent changes of employment, and where the claimant has been unable to enforce his or her input to maintenance where the payer's financial position has been obscured by changes of employment.

VI CONCLUSION

The maintenance duty between parents and children is regulated by the Marriage and Family Relations Act of Serbia (1980) and the Family Act of Montenegro (1989).

Parents are obliged to maintain their children until their majority (the age of 18) and, after that, the maintenance duty is extended if children continue their schooling. In that case, the duty lasts until children finish their schooling, but it cannot last after children reach the age of 26.

Up to the year 1993, the amount of money for maintenance was fixed. But legal norms governing maintenance were changed in 1993 (because of increasing inflation) and in 2001. Now, it depends on the parents' salary or the minimal wage, and it cannot be less than 7% nor greater than 22% of the salary. In cases where the payer has no salary, but is a pension beneficiary or has other fixed monthly income, the maintenance contribution cannot be less than 15% nor more than 50% of the pension or other fixed monthly income.

In practice, the biggest problem is to prove the amount of the salary of the obliged person. Another problem occurs when the payer fails to pay voluntarily. In accordance with our law the courts and minor children are assisted in this respect by the guardianship authority which has a significant role in the area of parents' statutory duty to maintain their children.

ZAMBIA

INHERITANCE CONFLICTS OVER THE MATRIMONIAL HOME: SAFEGUARDING THE FAMILY AGAINST HOMELESSNESS

Chuma Himonga[*]

I INTRODUCTION

The Intestate Succession Act of 1989[1] was aimed at reforming the customary law of succession.[2] Among the most important of the provisions of this Act is s 9, which provides for the devolution of the house of a man or woman who dies intestate. The deceased's surviving spouse, or spouses, and children are entitled to the house (if any) as tenants in common. In most cases, the house is the matrimonial home and only asset of real value in the estate. The devolution of the house to the deceased's immediate family, therefore, ensures that the family has an important and valuable asset and, most importantly, that it is secured against homelessness.

The problem of homelessness in Zambia, as in most other African countries, has to be seen in the wider context of the ravages of famine, poverty and HIV/AIDS, and the absence of state support systems for the poor. In this context, the death of the head of the family or the family member who owns the matrimonial home threatens the surviving spouse, or spouses, and minor children or dependants of the deceased with homelessness, unless the house devolves upon them. Section 9 is, therefore, critical to the material security of the deceased's immediate family, especially minor children. Furthermore, the unity of ownership and possession that characterises a tenancy in common ideally ensures that all members of the family or the tenants in common are equally protected in this regard. Yet the implementation of s 9 is fraught with difficulties. The tenancy in common has in some cases proved to be a source of conflicts among the beneficiaries. These conflicts are new to the scene of family disputes, as the Intestate Succession Act has only been in existence since 1989. The courts have therefore not as yet conclusively found a solution for these problems in their interpretation of the relevant law.

The aim of this article is to discuss the meaning of s 9 and to explore the solutions to the conflict of interests among the beneficiaries to the house. The paper will argue that the approach taken recently by the High Court in *Kamwi*

---

[*]   Professor of Law, University of Cape Town, Department of Private Law.
[1]   Chapter 59 of Laws of Zambia.

[2]   For a detailed discussion of the changes brought about by the Act, see Himonga, *Family and Succession Laws in Zambia: Developments since Independence* (Musnter Lit Verlag, 1995) 139 ff.

v Masiye[3] to resolve these conflicts is a development of the law in the right direction, in so far as it ensures the retention of the deceased's house within his or her family, thereby safeguarding the family or part of it against homelessness. Such an approach is, in our view, responsive to the needs of the ordinary Zambian in the current social and economic conditions. In the first two sections, the article will consider the idea of the tenancy in common in intestate succession, and secondly, the kinds of conflicts that it engenders. The third part will consider the legal solutions that are open to co-owners with conflicting interests and analyse their suitability to Zambian circumstances. The last part of the paper will discuss *Kamwi v Masiye.*

II   TENANCIES IN COMMON IN INTESTATE SUCCESSION

A tenancy in common is connected to intestate succession by the Intestate Succession Act. Section 9 of this Act provides that:

'(1) Notwithstanding section five[[4]] where the estate includes a house the surviving spouse or child or both, shall be entitled to that house provided that:

(a) where there is more than one surviving spouse or child or both they shall hold the house as *tenants in common*; [emphasis supplied] and

(b) the surviving spouse shall have a life interest in that house which shall determine upon that spouse's remarriage.

(2) Where the estate includes more than one house the surviving spouse or child or both shall determine which of the houses shall devolve upon them and the remainder shall form part of the estate.'

It seems clear from the wording of this section that the deceased's children and the surviving spouse or spouses have a tenancy in common, but the surviving spouse's interests in the property as tenant in common last only as long as she or he is unmarried. Upon remarriage, she or he automatically ceases to be a tenant in common, and her or his interest in the common property terminates, while the other co-owners continue to be tenants in common. As long as the surviving spouse remains unmarried, she or he enjoys a life interest in the common property and all the rights of a co-owner.

It would also appear that, even though the surviving spouse's interest in the common property (as a tenant in common) is real property, she or he cannot, on that basis alone, force the other co-owners to dissolve the tenancy in common, in order to enable her or him to share the property before her or his remarriage or death. A demand to dissolve the tenancy in common in these circumstances would not only undermine the interests of the children (the other co-owners) whose ownership is not limited in the same way as that of the spouse, but it would also seem to be contrary to the tenor of the provision as a whole. The only way the surviving spouse or any other beneficiary can have a separate individual share of

---

[3]   1999/HP/492.

[4]   Section 5 of the Act specifies the heirs to the intestate estate and provides for the general scheme of the distribution of the estate.

the estate is by the partition of the property or by sale in lieu of partition and the distribution of the proceeds of sale. These methods of individualising ownership of the common property are discussed later in the article.

A tenancy in common in immovable property was abolished in England in 1925.[5] This is, however, not the position in Zambia, because the reception of English law in this country is up to 17 August 1911.[6] The English law on tenancies in common in force in England on this date is therefore part of Zambian law.

A tenancy in common creates a unity of possession by which the co-owners possess the property in undivided shares. The tenants have a right to the undivided occupation of the property, and neither of them can claim any part of the common property as their own separate property, except by partition.[7] Although a tenancy in common resembles a joint tenancy in matters of unity of possession, it differs from it in so far as the nature of the title is concerned. While a joint tenancy creates an identical interest among the joint tenants in the whole property, and the interest of each tenant is the same in extent, nature, and duration,[8] a tenancy in common does not require unity of title, interest or time.[9] Thus, tenants in common may be entitled to the property in unequal shares and for estates which are of unequal duration. Furthermore, different limitations may be placed upon the different shares. Another important difference between a joint tenancy and tenancy in common is that while the former entitles the tenants to a right of survivorship, the separation of interests of the tenants in common excludes the right of survivorship.[10]

A tenancy in common is terminated by the union of the various interests in the same person, as a result of a testamentary disposition or acquisition inter vivios.[11]

The use of the concept of a tenancy in s 9 of the Intestate Succession Act ensures that all the members of the deceased's immediate family, that is, the children and spouse or spouses (in the case of a deceased person who was married to more than one wife) have an undivided right to his or her house in the estate. This means that none of them has a right to exclude the other beneficiaries from the house. Consequently, all members of the deceased's family are entitled to the material security provided by the house or matrimonial home, as the case may be.

III CONFLICTING INTERESTS AMONG TENANTS IN COMMON

The problem that has arisen in Zambia in connection with tenancies in common in intestate succession is that the beneficiaries to the estate under section 9 are not always willing or able to enjoy the possession of the house, or to live under the

---

5   See V Hailsham, *Halsbury's Law of England* (London, Butterworths & Co Publishers, 2nd edn, 1937) vol 27, 752 ff.

6   See English Law (Extent of Application) Act (chapter 11 of the *Laws of Zambia*).

7   See Earl of Halsbury, *The Laws of England* (London, Butterworths & Co Publishers, 1912) vol 21, 206–209.

8   Ibid at 202.

9   Ibid at 206.

10   Ibid at 209.

11   Hailsham, op cit, note 5 above, 760.

same roof as a family unit. Consequently, the tenancy in common creates a practical problem arising from the ownership and enjoyment of the house by all the parties. Conflicts of this kind commonly arise between the children of the deceased spouse with a person other than the surviving spouse(s). [12]

Occasionally, similar conflicts arise between surviving co-wives, and may be fuelled by customary practices that impinge on the operation of the statutory succession in practice. In one such case, [13] the deceased husband owned a farm. He had been married to three wives, all of whom lived in the farmhouse (in separate rooms) that constituted their matrimonial home. He was survived by all three wives and 17 children. Soon after the funeral, an arrangement was made by the deceased's extended family for his nephew to 'inherit' [14] the two junior wives of the deceased, according to customary law. [15] The senior wife of the deceased refused to be 'inherited' for personal reasons (a widow is entitled to do this under customary law). The conflict of interest among the surviving widows, with regard to the matrimonial home, arose from the fact that the 'inherited' widows, their minor children and their new 'husband' wanted to continue to live in the matrimonial home to the exclusion of the senior widow, who also wanted to remain in the matrimonial home. The 'inherited' widows (and their husband) have invoked what seems to be current practice under customary law, that a widow who refuses to be inherited must leave the matrimonial home (this was not the case under traditional law).

In this particular case, it might be argued that in accordance with s 9, the interests of the junior widows in the common property terminated upon their marriage to the deceased's customary law heir. This issue raises important questions about state intervention in matters of personal law in African cultural contexts, and the protection of individual rights in these contexts. But a discussion of these questions is beyond the scope of this article. The case has been cited only to show the nature of conflicts that s 9 of the Intestate Succession Act engenders, in addition to conflicts between the surviving spouse and the children of the deceased.

IV   RESOLVING THE CONFLICTS

The English law applicable to Zambia [16] presents four possible solutions to the conflicting interests of tenants in common that may be adopted by the courts to solve the s 9 conflicts. These are partition, sale in lieu of partition, payment of rent for occupation, and a consensual 'buy-out'.

---

[12]   See C Himonga, 'Protecting the Minor Child's Inheritance Rights', in *The International Survey of Family Law (2001 Edition)*, ed A Bainham (Family Law, 2001), 457 ff.

[13]   This is an ongoing case, which we are observing. The husband died in 2000, but the case has not gone to court as yet.

[14]   This is a customary practice whereby the widow or widows are married to the relative of the deceased, without contracting a new marriage with him. The deceased's relative steps into the shoes of the deceased as husband and provider of his household, although the children born to the marriage are the children of the heir and the widow.

[15]   For a discussion of the influence of customary succession law on the operation of the Intestate Succession Act, see Himonga, op cit, note 2 above.

[16]   See note 6 above.

A Partition[17]

This refers to the division of the common property and the allocation of the divided parts to the co-owners. Partition puts an end to community of ownership between some or all of the co-owners. If partial co-ownership is retained, the persons between whom the community of ownership continues must agree to this arrangement. The partition may be the result of an agreement by all the owners, or of the order of court upon application by one of the parties. It is also necessary to point out that the partition of the common property need not be in equal parts; it can be made to suit the convenience of the property and co-owners, provided that the owners who take a larger share compensate those who take a smaller share in money or other property.

Thus it is possible to partition the house of the deceased among all of his or her beneficiaries under s 9. It is also possible to divide the house in such a way that groups of beneficiaries can reside with each other as they like. The deceased's house may, therefore, be divided to give one section of it to the deceased's children with another person and the other section to the surviving spouse (and his or her children). Similarly the house may be divided to give different parts of it to the 'warring' widows. The new groups of owners would then hold their respective shares as tenants in common. If there is no agreement among the beneficiaries to partition, the property may nevertheless be partitioned by a court order upon application by any co-owner.

However, partition is only feasible and appropriate where the property subject to the tenancy in common is large. It would make little or no sense at all to divide a small house into a great number of parts. As few people in Zambia own large houses, the house or matrimonial home of an average deceased person would be too small for partition. This is coupled with the usually large number of the deceased's family (especially children) entitled to the house as tenants in common. Moreover, the legal and surveying costs of a partition may be completely out of proportion to the value of the property to be allotted to individual owners.

B Sale in lieu of partition[18]

The sale of the common property is the next possible solution to the problem of conflicting interests among the common owners. Any co-owner, including a tenant for life, may apply to the court for the sale of the property in lieu of partition and a distribution of the proceeds thereof. Upon such application, the court must order a sale unless it sees good reason to the contrary. The burden of showing good reason rests upon any party who opposes the sale. But such burden will be discharged by proving, among other things, that:

(a) great hardship would be inflicted on one of the parties, especially when the court considers that the party requesting a sale is actuated by vindictive motives; and

---

[17] See Earl of Halsbury, op cit, note 7 above, 810–834.
[18] Ibid, 834–846.

(b)   the property has temporarily much depreciated in value.

But good reason to the contrary will not be established by merely showing, *inter alia*, the dissent of other interested parties to the sale.

However, the court retains the discretion, despite the dissent, to order a sale and distribution of the proceeds if it appears to the court that it would be more beneficial to the interested parties to order a sale than a partition. In determining whether it would be more beneficial to order a sale, the court must take into account the following factors:

(a)   the nature of the property to which the action relates;
(b)   the absence or disability of some of the parties;
(c)   the number of parties interested in the sale; and
(d)   any other circumstances.

Furthermore, as a general rule, when determining whether sale is more beneficial than a partition, the court must consider only the pecuniary results and have regard to the interests of all the parties as a whole.

The disadvantage of sale as a method of resolving the s 9 conflicts is that it disposes of the house, which is usually the only asset of value the deceased has left to his family, to the detriment of the whole family. This problem is aggravated by the fact that the shared proceeds of the sale will, in most cases, never be enough to enable the individual family members to buy a house to live in. The minor children of the deceased are the most vulnerable in this regard, as they are faced with the possibility of a future on the street.

C   Rent for occupation[19]

A party in exclusive occupation of the common property may be charged a reasonable rent for its occupation, while an allowance is made for costs incurred by him or her in repairs to the property. Obviously, this method does not resolve a conflict among the owners about the ownership of the house; it merely postpones it. It should also be noted that in the Zambian context, it is unlikely that most owners will opt to receive rent instead of occupation, because of the difficulties of finding alternative houses to live in and the likely inadequacy of the amount received as rent to rent another house. Again the minor children of the deceased are the most vulnerable (if they happen to be among the group that is forced out of the home and receiving rent). This problem was alluded to by the High Court in *Estate of Lungu and others v Lungu.*[20]

The High Court in that case decided that renting the house and sharing the rental among all the beneficiaries was the solution to the conflict between the deceased's children from his previous marriage on the one hand, and the widow and her children on the other, regarding the occupation of the house inherited in terms of s 9. It held that, since the parties could not live together in harmony as a family, and in view of their indication that they were not interested

---

[19]   Ibid.
[20]   1997 HP/1695.

in selling the property, the best solution was for each party to vacate the house, so that the administrator of the estate could rent the house and share the proceeds or rentals between the parties. While noting the need to resolve the conflict between the parties, the court alluded to the fact that the order might not serve the interests of the minor children, who also had to vacate the house. In so far however as this method allows the retention of the house in the family, it is a much better solution than the sale of the house.

D Consensual 'buy-out'[21]

It is possible for co-owners to undertake to buy shares in the common property of the parties wishing to sell the property. However, the parties wanting to sell must accept the undertaking of the other co-owners to purchase. If the undertaking is accepted, the court may order a valuation of the shares in a manner that it thinks fit. This method is preferable to the sale of the property to strangers, because it ensures that the house remains within the family, to the benefit, at least, of some family members.

The problem, however, is that it may not be possible for the parties concerned to obtain the requisite consent for the 'buy-out'. And with the acrimonious nature of some cases of inheritance disputes, the likelihood of not securing this consent is not far-fetched. This brings us to the point at which we would support an approach whereby the court forces a 'buy-out' on unwilling parties, if necessary, in order to ensure the retention of the matrimonial home for the benefit of the needy members of the deceased's family, as the case may be. It is also with this idea of protecting the members of the deceased's family in mind that we laud the decision of the High Court in *Kamwi v Masiye*, in which the court ordered a 'buy out', in order to secure the house for the benefit of the minor children of the deceased. Apart from the actual protection from homelessness the court order gave to the vulnerable members of the family, the decision provides a lead to the courts to seek more dynamic ways of dealing with family property conflicts in a society where poverty and the lack of state social welfare services deny the people the basic requirements of life. In situations where poverty and homelessness are rampant, the resolution of family property disputes cannot consist merely of disengaging the parties from the immediate conflict, but there must be a search for ways of securing the long-term survival and interests of the family members. The decision in *Kamwi* is therefore worth highlighting as a development of the intestate law of succession in Zambia in the right direction.

V *KAMWI v MASIYE*[22]

The circumstances of the case were that the deceased was survived by a widow and six children from his previous marriage. He had no children with the widow. The children had lived with their father and the widow in the matrimonial home.

---

[21]   Earl of Halsbury, op cit, note 7 above, 845.
[22]   1999/HP/492.

After the deceased's death, his ex-wife moved into the matrimonial home, in order to live with her (apparently) minor children. The widow was forced to move out of the matrimonial home, because the deceased's ex-wife, supported by the administrator of the estate (the deceased's sister), made her continued stay in the home unbearable. Consequently, she applied to the High Court for the order to sell the house, and to share the proceeds of sale among the beneficiaries of the estate.

Having found as a matter of fact that the applicant was the surviving spouse of the deceased, Silomba J held that she was entitled to the matrimonial home as a tenant in common. However, he refused the application for sale. Instead, he made an order to have the interest of the widow in the house extinguished by a cash payment to her for her share in the estate. The court reasoned that selling the house would deprive the children of a future home and make them homeless.

With regard to the extinction of the interest in common by sale, the court held that 'under a tenancy in common, unlike a joint tenancy, a tenant wishing to sell his or her interest in the property held in common with others is at liberty to do so'. It held further that the applicant would sell her share to the children and thereby extinguish her interest in the house without affecting the entitlement of the six children as sole owners. The court also indicated the formula to be used to compute the value of the widow's entitlement for this purpose. In the first place, the house would be valued. Secondly, the children and the widow would be deemed to hold the valued house as tenants in common in 'equal shares'. And thirdly, the value of the house would be divided by seven, and the resulting figure paid to the widow as her share of the common property. The court explained that although the phrase 'in equal shares' is not included in the Intestate Succession Act, 'it is a very popular phrase in conveyancing when the extent of interests commonly held in a property are not specified'.

Thus, by adopting the 'buy-out' method, the court was able to preserve the tenancy in common in respect of the matrimonial home in favour of a section of the deceased's family, and to safeguard the minor children against homelessness.

However, the shortcomings of this approach seem obvious. First, it can only ensure the retention of the house for some, but not for all members of the deceased's family, even where the members whose interest is extinguished would have liked to retain the house. Secondly, the approach may jeopardise the entitlement of the co-owner(s) whose interest has been extinguished as a beneficiary to the estate, in the event of the remaining tenants in common not being able to pay him or her for his or her share.

The response to the first shortcoming is that it may be better, for example, to have only ten members of the deceased's family on the street, without shelter, than to have all 20 of them in this situation, especially when the latter include minor children. With regard to the second point, it may be observed that the inability of the remaining co-owners to pay the 'out-going' co-owner is, presumably, among the circumstances that the court would take into account in deciding whether to order a 'buy-out' or not. If it does not make a 'buy-out' order, it may use the rent for occupation method as a temporary measure to give the beneficiaries in serious need of accommodation the right to stay in the house, while giving the co-owners time to find the resources necessary for the 'buy-out'. Furthermore, the co-owner who has not been paid for his extinguished interest is not completely without remedy. He or she may still have recourse to execution of judgment, and, if necessary, to attachment of the property of the co-owners to satisfy his or her claim.

It should also be noted that the approach of the court in the case under consideration is not restricted to cases involving the interests of minors. It can equally be adopted to ensure the retention of the house by, for example, the widow or co-wife, where it would be more beneficial for her to buy out the other co-wife than to sell the house.

VI CONCLUSION

This article has highlighted the problems connected with tenancies in common in intestate succession law, when the tenants in common have conflicting interests with regard to the ownership or possession of the inherited house. The remedies available range from partition to the sale of the house to strangers, outside the deceased's family. While partition is the ideal solution, it is not feasible or advantageous to tenants in common whose houses are small, and most tenants in common in Zambia would fall into this category. On the other hand, the sale of the house results in the complete loss of the only asset that may offer the deceased's family long-term material security. Due to poverty and other factors, homelessness is a common problem for many families in Zambia. It would, therefore, appear that the approach taken by the High Court in *Kamwi v Masiye* is not only apposite, but also to be encouraged as a solution to the threat of homelessness that faces many families after the death of a parent or spouse.